# WOOD:
# MATERIALS AND PROCESSES
Revised

# FROM WOOD TO PRODUCT
# THROUGH PROCESSES

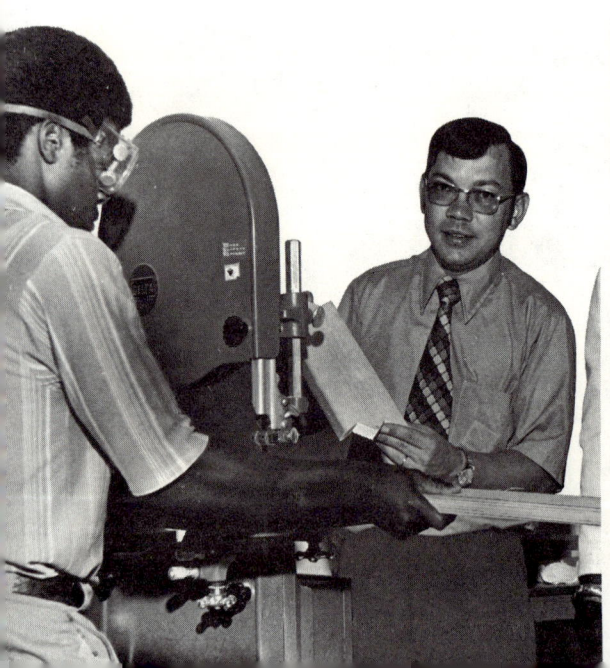

# WOOD:
# MATERIALS AND PROCESSES
### Revised

**JOHN L. FEIRER**
Head, Industrial Education Department
Western Michigan University
Kalamazoo, Michigan

**GLENCOE PUBLISHING COMPANY**
BENNETT & McKNIGHT DIVISION

Copyright © 1980 by John Feirer

Previous copyright in 1975

Published by Glencoe Publishing Company, a division of Macmillan, Inc.

Send all inquiries to:
Glencoe Publishing Company
15319 Chatsworth Street
Mission Hills, California 91345

Printed in the United States of America

**ISBN 0-02-666240-X (Student Text)**
ISBN 0-02-666250-7 (Teacher's Guide)
ISBN 0-02-666220-5 (Student Guide)

(Previously ISBN 0-87002-307-1)

4  5  6  7   89  88  87  86

## COLOR ILLUSTRATION LIST

Early American to Western Spanish and Traditional
    furniture, 16A
Contemporary furniture, 16B
Traditional influence on Contemporary furniture, 16C
French Provincial furniture, 16D
Bent hardboard chairs, 336A
Use of plastic furnishings, 336B and 336C
Acrylic plastics, 336D

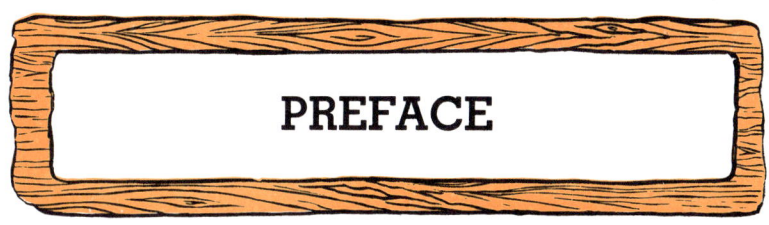

# PREFACE

Woodworking has always been one of the most popular of all industrial education activities. In spite of the many new materials and courses added in recent years, woodworking has increased rather than decreased in popular favor. The reasons are plain, for wood is one of man's most abundant materials and one of the easiest for students to work with. Products made of wood have general usefulness, and the tools and machines especially suited to school workshops are readily available.

This book covers the many changes that have taken place in wood products and processes in the last few years. Major features of this text include:

● An introduction to the two basic systems of measurement, customary (English) and metric, is given. Both measurements are shown in the text material. The projects are shown with customary dimensions. A handy conversion chart will enable students to add the metric measurements as needed.

● Since good design is so important to wood products, this unit has been given much prominence.

● Because career education is a responsibility of all teachers, a large unit on occupations in woodwork has been included.

● Wood, along with many of the common plastics, is a soft material. Since plastics are widely used in both manufacture of furniture and in construction of homes, a unit on plastics has been included. Students can use the standard hand and machine tools to work these plastics.

● Units are devoted to these important subject areas: antiquing; manufacturing, including the mass-production process; construction, with emphasis on home building; patternmaking and model making; trees and our environment, with attention given to pollution problems; and research and experimentation, including simple experiments students can conduct.

The book has been divided into four major parts. In each of these there are many illustrations, and new technical material is discussed.

**Sections I–X** give instruction on how to do the fundamental processes in hand woodworking, with particular stress on student participation in laboratory activities. The units have been written in informal style and have been well illustrated, using the visual approach. They are complete as to information about tools, materials, and the ways to use them. The units have been organized in the approximate order in which they will be needed to make larger projects. Tools, materials, and processes have been carefully evaluated to include only those which are considered important and significant as based on recent research. The student is given an opportunity to preview the contents in each section and to check his understanding. Throughout the text in these units, the metric system of measurement is used, in addition to the customary system, for reinforcement.

**Section XI** describes the use of fundamental machine tools in woodworking. Each tool has been completely treated without any unnecessary quantity of detail. This is done so that the instructor may conveniently determine what machines are desirable and in what order the students should be allowed to use them. Small woodworking machines have been used to illustrate instruction since these are best for most school and home workshops.

**Section XII** deals with the four major industrial areas in which wood is the basic building material, namely, *upholstering, manufacturing, construction,* and *patternmaking and model making.* These four units give students an overview of the importance of woodworking in our total economic system.

**Section XIII** deals with related information about woods and wood products. Emphasis has been given to ecology and how wood is important both in preventing, and sometimes causing, pollution. One unit covers the use of research and science in woodworking.

As with any other book, many individuals and concerns have cooperated generously. Their help is acknowledged in the list that follows.

# ACKNOWLEDGMENTS

Adjustable Clamp Company
American Forest Products Industries
American Hardboard Association
American Hardwood Company
American of Martinsville
American Plywood Association
American Screw Company
American Walnut Association
Amerock Corporation
Andersen Corporation
Appalachian Hardwood Manufacturers, Incorporated
Associated General Contractors of America, The
Athens Table Company
E. C. Atkins Manufacturing Company
Baker Furniture Company
Bassett Furniture Industries
Baumritter Corporation
Behr-Manning Company
Berry Brothers, Incorporated
Blue River Hand Prints
Brandt Cabinet Works, Incorporated, The
British Columbia Industrial Design Committee
Broyhill Furniture Factories
Buck Brothers Company
Buss Machine Works, Incorporated
Carborundum Company
Caterpillar Tractor Company
Chrysler Corporation
Cincinnati Tool Company, The
Clausing Corporation
Cumberland Furniture Corporation
Dansk Designs, Incorporated
Davis Furniture Industries
DeVilbiss Company, The
De Walt Power Tools
Directional Industries, Incorporated
Henry Disston & Sons, Incorporated
Dowl-It Company
Drake Corporation
Drexel Enterprises
Dunbar Furniture Corporation of Indiana
Dunning Industries, Incorporated
Dupont Corporation
E. I. duPont de Nemours Company, Incorporated
Dux Incorporated
Era Industries
Fine Hardwoods Association
Foley Manufacturing Company
Ford Motor Company
Forest Products Laboratory
Formica Corporation
General Builders Contractors Association
General Electric Corporation
General Motors Corporation
Georgia-Pacific Corporation
Allan Gould Designs
Gulf Oil Company
Imperial of Morristown, Incorporated
International Paper Company
Arvids Iraids Multi-Purpose Spring Clamp
Jam Handy Organization, The
John Mascheroni
Keller Company
Knob Creek of Morgonton
Lane Company, Incorporated
Lear Jet Corporation
Lockheed Corporation
Madison Glass Specialties Company
Masonite Corporation
McEnglevan Company

### Acknowledgments

Herman Miller Furniture Company
Howard Miller Clock Company
Millers Falls Company
Mobile Home Manufacturers Association
National Aeronautics and Space Administration
National Company
Nordson Corporation
North Brothers Manufacturing Company
No-Sag Spring Company
Ohio Blow Pipe Corporation
Panelyte Division, St. Regis Paper Company
Frank Paxton Lumber Company
Peter Pepper Products, Incorporated
Philippine Mahogany Association
Porter-Cable Machine Company
Powermatic Machine Company
Prestige Furniture Corporation
Redman Industries, Incorporated
Reynolds Metals Company
Rockwell Manufacturing Company
Rohm and Haas Corporation
Rubber Manufacturer's Association, The
Russell Electric Company
Samador Furniture Manufacturing Company
Sherwin-Williams Company, The

Simpson Magazine
Skil Corporation
Sprague and Carleton Furniture Company
Stanley Tools Division, The Stanley Works
Sunbeam Corporation
Tell City Chair Company
Tempo Products Company
Thayer Goggia, Incorporated
Toolmark Company
U.S. Forest Service
U.S. Department of Labor
United States Plywood Corporation
Victorian Furniture Corporation
Victorian Galleries
VSM Corporation
Watco-Dennis Corporation
Wesley Pusey
Western Electric
Western Pine Association
Western Woods Products Association
Weyerhaeuser Corporation
Consider H. Willett, Incorporated
*Woman's Day*
Wood Tape, Incorporated
Workrite Products Company
X-Acto Crescent Products, Incorporated

# TABLE OF CONTENTS

*Table of Contents*

# FROM WOOD TO PRODUCT THROUGH PROCESSES

**When you** see a wood project such as the desk shown in Figure A, you may feel an immense appreciation for the fine workmanship, the finish, and the beautiful lines of the piece. However, you may say to yourself, "But that is too complicated for me to build." Yet *the essential elements of this desk are as fundamental as the little trays in Figure B.* Each resulted from choosing a piece of wood and applying to it certain basic processes to shape, form, assemble, and finish it. Naturally, the desk contains many more pieces of wood and involves much more time and effort, but really it has only a few more basic processes.

If you want to build attractive projects, you must first start with good raw material. A fine piece of furniture or a good project cannot be made from poor wood.

Wood is the most fundamental of all materials used by man. This raw material, used to make the finished product, is supplied in its natural form. Also, many other manufactured articles, whether they are of metal, plastic, or other substances, are first made of wood in the factory. For example, automobiles, refrigerators, aircraft, and even the telephone were first made from wood in the designing rooms of factories.

## WHAT YOU CAN DO WITH WOOD

Wood is a very interesting material. It is made of fibers (grain). Cutting is easier *with* the grain than across it. Wood itself is only the raw material. From the same piece of wood you could build a beautiful tray with a very fine finish or a platform

**A.** An example of what an advanced high school student can make in woodworking. The rails and finesse of the legs are beautiful. The choice of woods and the design are excellent, not only for the building of the project but for final appearance as well.

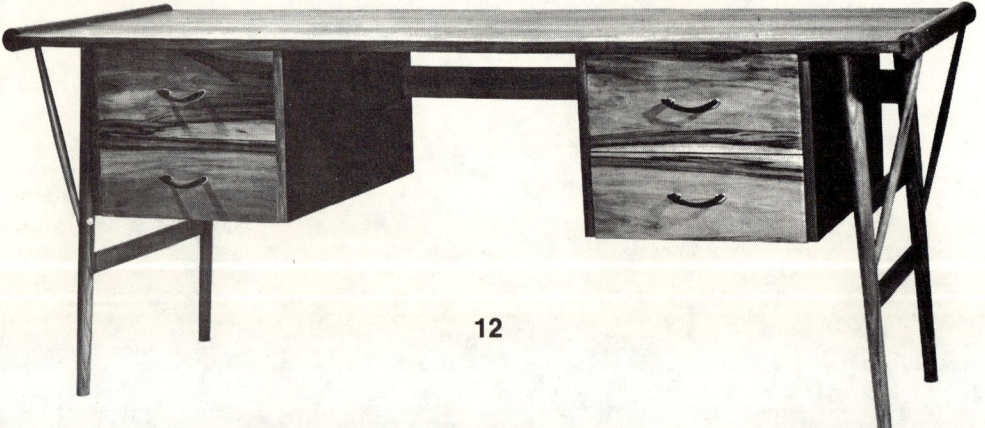

for your garbage can! The only difference in the products is the difference in the basic processes applied to the wood. These fundamentals are described in this book.

## THREE BASIC ELEMENTS IN CONSTRUCTION

Building an attractive project depends on the following three elements: the kind of wood you select, the design of the project, and how well you perform the basic processes. If you learn to do these basic processes correctly, you can apply them to any product with good results. In this and other books you can find many projects, some very simple and others that take more time. Regardless of size or difficulty, each one includes these same three elements.

If you are a beginner in wood, you must select your project wisely and learn to do the processes accurately and correctly. Once the skills are learned, greater enjoyment and success will be yours.

## WHY TAKE WOODWORKING?

Woodworking is much more than making a few small pieces of furniture that you can take home. Here are some of the other things that you should accomplish in your course:

● *Develop an interest in a career.* The wood industry is vital to the growth of our country. It has made possible the record-breaking building boom of homes, offices, and other commercial buildings. Well over two million people have found careers in woodworking. The four major industrial areas are upholstering, manufacturing, construction, and pattern-making. Figure C. All of these will be described in this book. Forester, carpenter, and cabinetmaker are only a few of

the many career possibilities open to those interested. Figure D.

● *Develop an appreciation for wood as a resource.* The whole furniture industry is dependent on wood as a raw material. Wood is and always will be essential to everyday living. You are probably sitting on a wooden chair and writing with a wooden pencil. You wouldn't have this book if it weren't for the wood used to make the paper. In this course you will study the sources of wood, the changes that take place in it from raw material to finished product, and how wood products such as homes, furniture, sports equipment, and other items are produced.

● *Develop basic hand and machine skills.* Learning to work with tools and machines can be very valuable to you if you should decide on an occupation in woodworking. Figure E. However, even if you don't earn a living in some area of woodworking, you will still find the skills very useful as a "do-it-yourselfer." You

**B.** In contrast to the desk, these simple serving trays are typical of what you might attempt as a first project. They involve many of the same processes needed to do all kinds of woodworking.

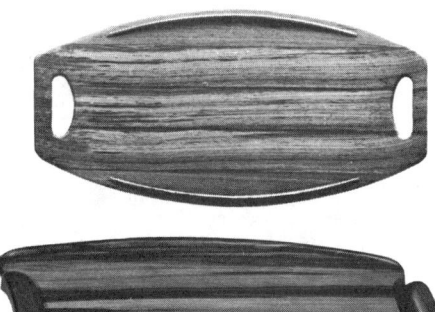

Upholstering

Patternmaking

Manufacturing

**c.** Four industrial areas of woodworking you will find described in this book.

may find making things of wood so fascinating that you will choose it as your hobby.

● *Develop good safety habits*. Using hand and machine tools safely and skillfully is a most important part of your work. More accidents happen in the wood shop than in any other area of industrial arts. Learn to perform each task carefully so that you will not contribute to the number of accidents.

● *Learn about good design*. You should learn to recognize good design in wood products. Figure F. After you learn the difference between good and bad design, you will never again find poor

Construction

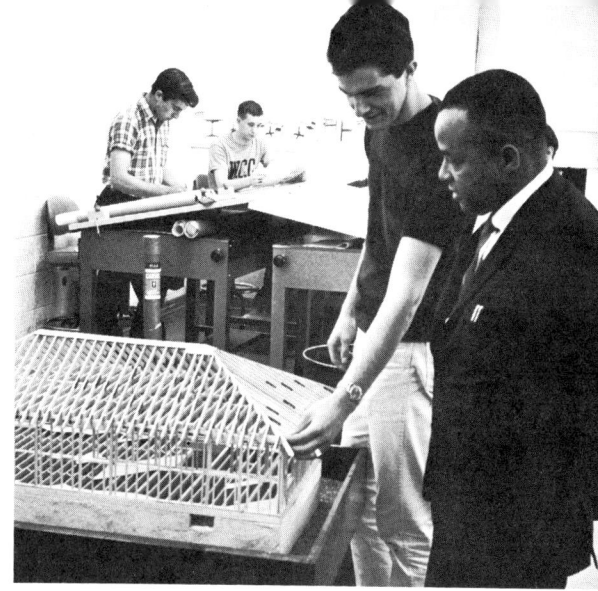

**D.** An apprentice patternmaker in a foundry has the opportunity to learn a highly skilled and well-paid woodworking occupation.

**E.** Drafting teachers must have knowledge and skills in woodworking. This teacher's students will learn much about house plans as he guides them in making a detailed model.

**F.** This beautiful teak table illustrates good design in furniture making. Even the small projects that you make should be attractive.

**G.** When you visit a furniture store, you should be able to recognize good woods, fine design, and excellent finish. This knowledge will help you obtain proper value for your money.

**H.** These young people are enjoying the satisfaction that comes with making something themselves. The wooden house number signs were not only fun to make but they will also be useful.

design attractive. You may also want to try your hand at designing a wood product, using your own ideas.

● *Learn to judge the quality of wood products.* A home and furniture are two of the largest expenses you will ever have. Figure G. Before you buy wood products, you should understand good design and construction and be able to judge if the product is good quality.

● *Enjoy the satisfaction of planning and building a product with your own hands.* Figure H. A real sense of accomplishment results from creating a wood product that is both attractive and well made. In completing the product you will learn to solve problems about materials and processes.

The room above is a pleasant adaptation of simplified Early American to Western Spanish styling, which produces a very functional room. The room below with its rich tones of brown and red is an adaptation of Traditional design which combines the best features of styling from the 18th and early 19th centuries. The furniture is handsome mahogany with a dark finish and attractive brass trim.

This Contemporary den is planned to fill the practical needs of today. Though the design concept of the furniture pieces is straightforward Contemporary, there is still an ingenious addition of some of the more Traditional characteristics.

The white painted furniture in this room shows the influence of Traditional design on Contemporary living quarters.

Note the differences in style between the furniture in these two bedrooms. Above you see Mediterranean furniture with geometric shapes represented in the heavy hardware and furniture lines. Below is French Provincial. The cabinets show the graceful curves typical of this style.

16D

# SECTION I
## Getting Started in Woodworking

**What you must know and be able to do in
Units 1–8:**

1. How to select a project: the size and kinds of wood; difficulties in using certain woods; design and finish.

2. Design qualities: how to design a product; what to look for in good design.

3. The basic measuring systems: customary and metric; how they differ; how both are used in construction and manufacturing.

4. The difference between pictorial and working drawings: what the terms mean; how to read, use, and understand working drawings.

5. The importance of a bill of materials: size and number of pieces; description and amount of lumber; choosing lumber according to the grade, quality, finish, and how it is dried.

6. Efficiency: planning and carrying out the steps needed for building with wood.

7. Care of the shop: how to keep the shop running well; how to be neat, orderly, and safe; what to do if an accident occurs.

8. Information on careers: opportunities in woodworking; how to obtain education and training.

You won't be able to start building a project during your first days in the woodshop. Instead, you'll be learning some very interesting things that will help you plan the project, decide on the materials to use, learn how to go about using these materials, and discover how to get the most from the woodshop experiences. In the school laboratory, it is important to become acquainted with the working conditions first.

# CHOOSING A PROJECT

**Since the project** is the end result of all of your efforts, it is very important that you spend some time choosing a good one. There are many things to consider: what you need; the size of the project; the kind and cost of the wood; the finish; and the design.

## DO YOU HAVE A NEED AND USE FOR THE PROJECT?

The most important thing to decide is whether you have a use for the article. Too many of the items made in school and home workshops find their way into storage rooms, attics, or basements. There are so many practical things that can be made of wood that it is foolish to wast your time and effort on something useless.

**1-1.** This student-built chair would be a rather ambitious project for a first experience in woodworking.

Before deciding, ask yourself what you need for your house, yard, for sports, or for some other activity in which you are interested. Figure 1-1. This should give you a good clue to the type of project you will find most satisfying.

For ideas consult the project section of INDUSTRIAL ARTS WOODWORKING by Feirer. Your school may have copies.

## CAN YOU BUILD IT?

The next thing to think about is the size of the project and how difficult it will be to build. Beginners usually want to make something too complicated. While you need not fear making any project, you must have the time and experience for it. Figure 1-2. If you choose too big a project at first, you face so many problems that you may lose interest, become discouraged, and never finish the project. So begin by making small articles that take only a few tools and processes until you have some experience and know how long it takes. The size of the project shouldn't be the measure of its appeal.

## IS THE KIND AND COST OF THE WOOD SATISFACTORY?

The kind of wood to use and how much you want to spend are both important decisions to make. Figure 1-3. The wood you choose will affect the cost of the project. One made of oak or walnut will cost twice as much as the same one made from fir, spruce, poplar, or red gum.

Differences in the working qualities of woods make the right choice important also. For the beginner, especially, it is much easier to work with softwoods like poplar, pine, or bass. It takes a good deal more skill to work on a hardwood like birch, for example, than on a softwood, because hardwoods tend to resist tools.

## WHAT KIND OF FINISH WILL YOU APPLY?

The color and kind of finish you want to apply must be decided early. If you use an opaque finish such as enamel or paint, it is just as well to choose an inexpensive wood like pine, basswood, or poplar. Figure 1-4. If you plan to have a transparent finish, it will be especially important to decide on the color and kind of finish before you begin in case you want to bleach the wood. All woods can be bleached to give them a light appearance, but generally speaking, we think of oak or maple as lighter than walnut, mahogany, or cherry. The kind of finish you apply should bring out the best qualities in the wood.

**1-3.** This Early American mirror is a fine example of clean simple lines, natural lacquer finish, and top craftsmanship. It is made of cherry.

**1-4.** This large project is relatively simple to make. Since it was made of pine, an enamel finish was applied. Would you use enamel over walnut veneer? Why not?

**1-2.** Even though these bookends are simple to make, they will test your skill. They require accurate cutting on the jig saw.

A.

## HAVE YOU CONSIDERED THE DESIGN OF THE PROJECT?

Regardless of the size or the kind of article you choose, the style or design should fit your needs and the kind of home in which you live. Too frequently small projects such as bookends, tables, and similar pieces are made with no regard for the room where they will be used. A project like a small table can be varied between Traditional and Modern styles to fit your tastes. Figure 1-5.

## WHERE CAN YOU FIND GOOD PROJECT DESIGNS?

After you have decided what you want to make, including the right size, shape, and design, Figure 1-6, you need a working drawing or sketch. There are many places to look for ideas. In this and other woodworking books there are plans for various projects for your room, your

**1-5.** Three small tables of similar size but very different designs: A. Traditional; B. Early American; C. Modern or Contemporary.

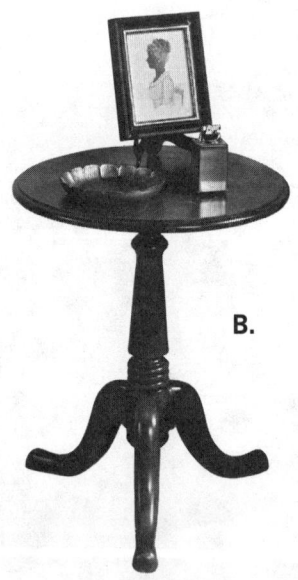

B.

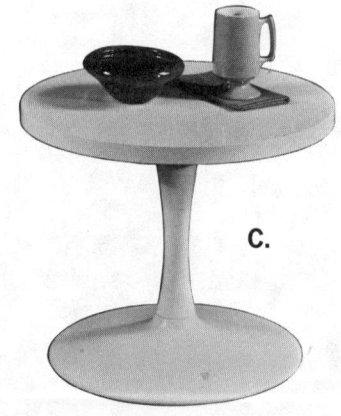

C.

**1-6.** Two magazine racks for a similar purpose. One is designed for a narrow wall space; the other is better for a wide space.

home, for sports, and for other activities. For additional ideas you can turn to magazines. You may have seen an article you like in a store, or you may want to design and make a finished drawing of one of your own ideas. It is better to wait, however, until you have had a little experience with available drawings before trying your own.

When all questions have been answered and exactly the right project selected, you are ready for the fascinating job of building it. From now on you will need lots of patience and attention to detail, but the results will be well worthwhile.

## CAN YOU ANSWER THESE QUESTIONS ON SELECTING THE PROJECT?

1. Name the most important thing to consider when you are selecting a project.
2. Why isn't it a good idea to start with a large project?
3. Do all woods work about the same? Explain your answer.
4. If oak is chosen for the project, a paste filler may be selected for finishing. Give other examples of how the wood chosen determines the kind of finish that is to be applied.
5. Give several sources for good projects.

# DESIGN

**2-1a.** Do you think this salad bowl is well designed?

**Every day** you see and use things that have been designed. Your home, the furniture in it, cars and parts of cars, appliances, and even lead pencils and bars of soap have been developed from a design on paper. Some of these are pleasing in design; some are not. Figure 2-1.

## WHAT IS DESIGN?

*A design is the outline, shape, or plan* of something. There is no one who will agree completely with everyone else as to what is good or bad design. Everyone looks at things in a slightly different way and sees in them things he likes or dislikes. Here, for example, are designs of some modern chairs. Figure 2-2. Not

**2-1b.** Compare the design of these two table lamps. Which do you prefer?

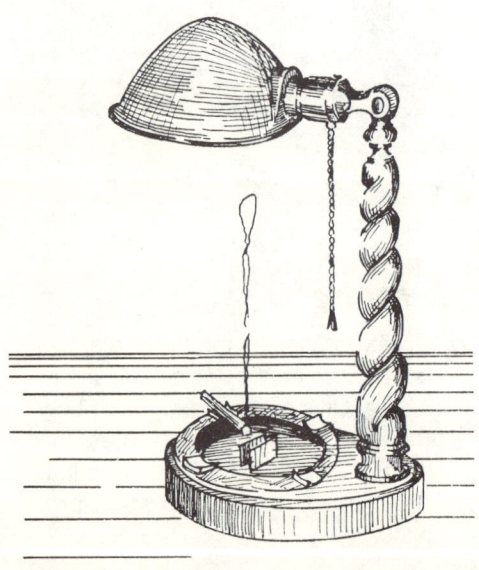

**2-2.** These chairs look different from those most of us are used to seeing, but they are very comfortable. If you could try them, you'd know why they are well designed.

everyone will agree that they are *attractive.* They are, however, *well designed.*

The three keys to good design are function, appearance, and solid construction. *Function* answers the question: What is the purpose of the product? A lamp, for example, should give the kind of light that is correct for a specific purpose. A lamp for reading would be much different from a night light. Figure 2-3. The purpose or function of a clock is to tell time. If the clock design is poor, it is difficult to read. Figure 2-4. *Appearance,* of course, refers to how the object

**2-3.** Which lamp design do you think would be best for reading?

**2-4a.** Compare these clock faces and choose the easiest and most difficult ones to read.

looks. Are the materials and shapes combined to form an object that is pleasing to the eye? Many combinations are often suitable. A reading lamp might be made of metal or wood, with a shade that is straight or tapered, and in any furniture style. *Sound construction* means that the product is well built of the correct material so that it will last a long time with a minimum of maintenance. Design defects may be due to the wrong kind of wood or to poor construction.

As far as design goes, woodworking projects can be divided into three groups:

● *Trinkets or gadgets which are made to satisfy your own interests and desires.* You may make a "dachshund-dog" tie rack or a "bowling-pin" pinup lamp for yourself or for someone in your family. Figure 2-5. You may use your own idea completely in designing it. Oftentimes it will be something you may like for a few years and then discard or redesign and make over. Such projects are fun to de-

**2-4b.** To read time accurately to the minute, which clock would be best?

sign and make even though the design may not be the best. You can learn and improve each time you make something.

● *Practical objects that must be some standard size if they are to be any good at all.* For instance, a basketball backboard must be 4 x 6 feet (1.2 x 1.8 m). A high hurdle must be a certain size also.

Although not always ornamental, these projects are well designed because they serve a certain purpose. Figure 2-6. *If you were to make them a different size, they would be poorly designed.*

● *Artistically designed objects including furniture, accessories for the home, and the home itself.* In furniture there

**2-5a.** These are some designs that might be used to make salt and pepper shakers.

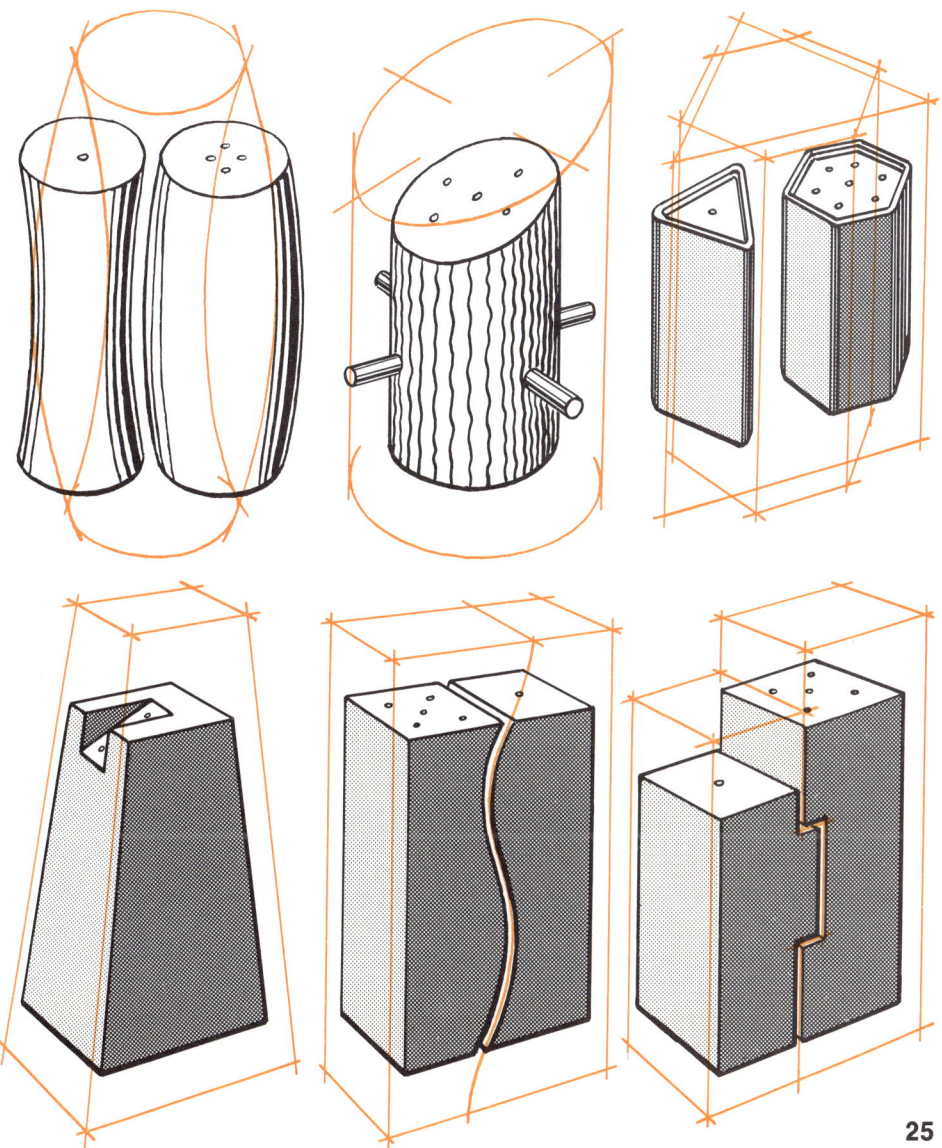

are many different designs and styles. You should become well acquainted with the best designs of today. *One of the great mistakes made in the home and school workshop in building furniture is making something with no design or style.* Figure 2-7. You shouldn't waste your time building furniture that is out-of-date, like the "moderne" of 1930, or the plain, "production-line" kind of furniture often seen in public buildings. You might say, "Yes, but I see some of these things in furniture stores." It is true that

**2-5b.** A salt and pepper set like this can be made for someone in your family.

| No. of Pieces | Part Name | Thick-ness | Width | Length | Material |
|---|---|---|---|---|---|
| | STOCK: Birch, Mahogany, or Maple Important: All dimensions listed below are FINISHED size. | | | | |
| 2 | Shakers | 2″ | 2″ | 3½″ | Birch, Mahogany, or Maple |
| 1 | Plug | 1″ | 1″ | 4″ | Hardwood |
| 2 | Corks | ¾″ D. | | | |

**2-5c.** Bill of materials for the salt and pepper set in 2-5b.

**2-5d.** Drawings for the salt and pepper set in 2-5b.

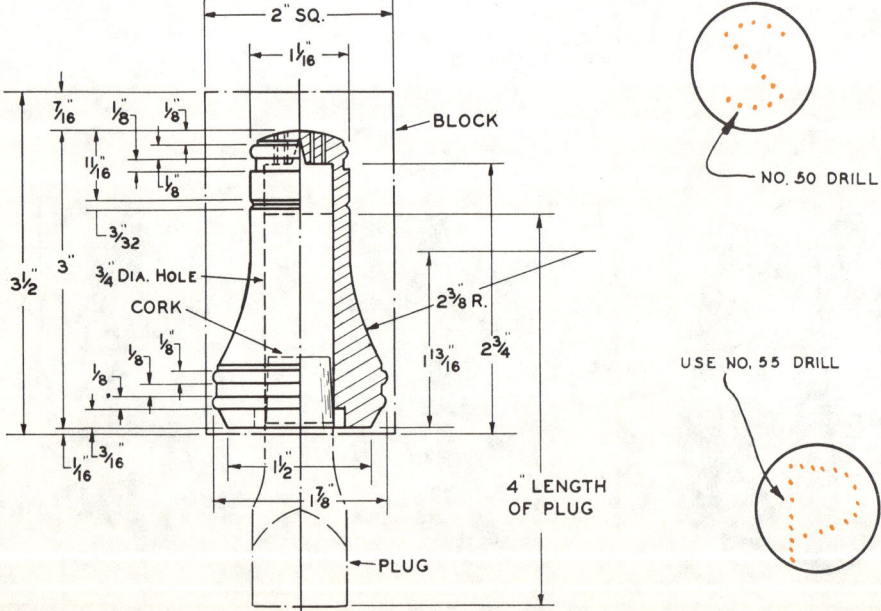

NO. 50 DRILL

USE NO. 55 DRILL

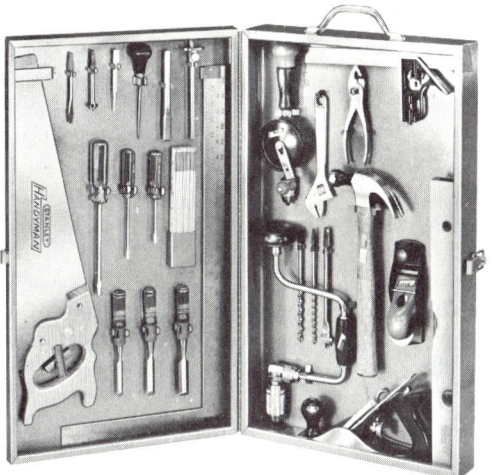

**2-6.** A well-designed tool chest must hold all tools securely.

**2-7.** Even a small accessory can be well designed.

a certain percentage of the furniture made today is what we call "commercial" or "unstyled" furniture. This is the cheapest and poorest kind. You might as well buy it already made.

### WHAT MAKES UP DESIGN?

• A *line* is a path moving through space. A line carefully drawn according to a plan makes for a good design. The basic lines are straight and curved. Straight lines suggest rigidity, precision, dignity, and strength. Slightly curved lines represent lightness, gracefulness, and softness. Curved lines which change directions rapidly show activity and forcefulness. Jagged or zigzag lines tend to show nervousness or excitement. Lines can be vertical, horizontal, or at an angle. Figure 2-8.

• *Shape* is a series of lines going in different directions, outlining an area. Some common shapes are square, rectangular, circular, and oval. Figure 2-9 (Page 29).

**2-8a.** Common kinds of lines.

. . **DIGNITY**        **REPOSE**            **ACTION**                    **STABILITY**

**2-8b.** Lines offer an emotional association.

**2-8c.** Straight vertical lines show stability and strength.

**2-8d.** Slightly curved lines of graceful design are shown on the front of this chest. What effect is created by the other curved lines?

**2-8e.** Circular lines represent activity.

**2-8f.** Zigzag lines show excitement.

**2-9a.** Common shapes.

**2-9b.** Most of the common shapes appear in this room. Can you point them out?

29

**2-10.** Simple geometric forms, rectangular solids, cubes, and a sphere, are employed to produce this striking modern bedroom set.

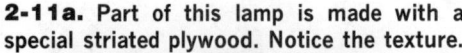

**2-11a.** Part of this lamp is made with a special striated plywood. Notice the texture.

● *Mass* is the solid form created by variations and combinations of the four basic shapes. The sphere, cone, cube, and cylinder are common solid forms, all having three dimensions, usually called depth, width, and height. Figure 2-10.

● *Texture,* or *surface quality,* adds to the surface design. Each different kind of wood has a texture. Wood is given additional texture by many processes. For example, the plywood used for the lamp in Figure 2-11 has a grooved surface. Another kind of plywood has the surface sandblasted to bring the grain into high relief. All natural woods have textures of their own. Finishes are used to bring them out and protect them. Figure 2-12.

● *Value* refers to the amount of lightness or darkness. The values used in design impart a feeling to the observer. Figure 2-13. If the contrast between the

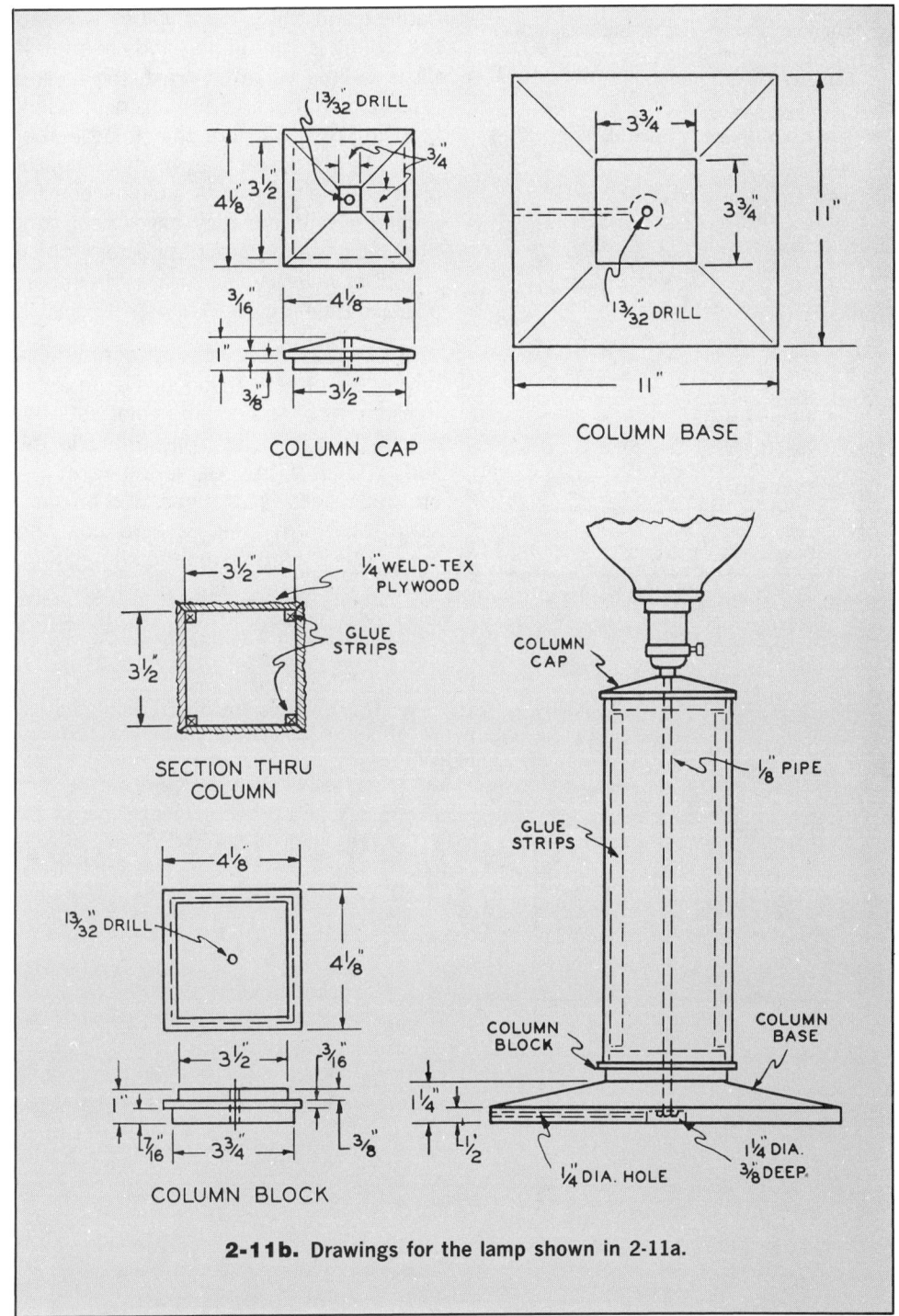

**2-11b.** Drawings for the lamp shown in 2-11a.

| Important: All dimensions listed below are FINISHED size. | | | | |
|---|---|---|---|---|
| No. of Pieces | Part Name | Thickness | Width | Length | Wood |
| 1 | Column Cap | 1″ | 4⅛″ | 4⅛″ | Oak |
| 1 | Column Base | 1¼″ | 11″ | 11″ | Oak |
| 4 | Column Sides | ¼″ | 4″ | 11″ | Oak Weldtex Plywood |
| 1 | Corner Block | 1″ | 4⅛″ | 4⅛″ | Oak |
| 4 | Corner Glue Strips | ⅜″ | ⅜″ | 10¼″ | White Pine |
| 1 | No. 8 IES Shade | | | | |
| 1 | 2¼ inch Shade Holder | | | | |
| 1 | 3 way Switch | | | | |
| 1 | 3 way Bulb | | | | |
| 1 | ⅛ inch Pipe, 13⅝ inches long, and Nut | | | | |
| 1 | Lamp Cord 6 ft. long | | | | |
| 1 | 14 inch Lamp Shade | | | | |

**2-11c.** Bill of materials for the lamp shown in 2-11a.

darkest and the lightest values is great, the feeling is stimulating and cheerful. If there is little value contrast, the feeling is more dignified and perhaps depressed. In planning a design, the mood established by the value plan must be appropriate to the subject. A circus scene for a child's bedroom may have great contrast, while the scene in a doctor's office should have less value contrast to impart a relaxed feeling.

● *Color* is generally recognized as having an effect on mood. Figure 2-14. In planning a design, the color sets the mood, so it must be appropriate to the subject matter. In general, the warm colors (reds, yellows, oranges, and browns) stand out from their backgrounds and are positive, aggressive, and stimulating. The cool colors (greens, blues, and violets) tend to recede more into the back-

**2-12.** Many kinds of surface quality, or texture, are found in this Traditional room. Cloth, wire mesh, cane, and ceramics are only a few of the materials with different surface qualities.

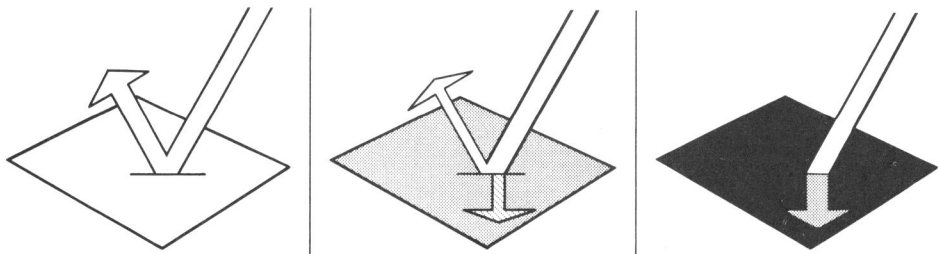

**2-13a.** Reflection and absorption of light by white, gray, and black surfaces.

ground. White reflects light, whereas black absorbs light. Some specific colors, or hues, and the feeling they each impart are listed below:

*Red*—Greatest power of attraction; most popular; exciting; dangerous; courageous; passionate.

*Yellow*—Least popular; bright; sunny; lively. *Darker greenish yellows*—Sickly; cowardly; treacherous.

*Blue*—Tranquil; serene; hopeful; sincere.

*Purple*—Stately; pompous; rich; royal.

*Green*—Restful; faithful; fresh; youthful.

*White*—Delicate; airy; pure; truthful; Symbolic of truce.

*Black*—Depressing; solemn; evil; Symbolic of death.

*Primary* colors are the three colors from which all other colors are derived. Unmixed, they have the highest strength and intensity possible. The three primary colors are red, yellow, and blue.

**2-13b.** The value contrast of these designs is great.

**2-13c.** There is much less value contrast in this design.

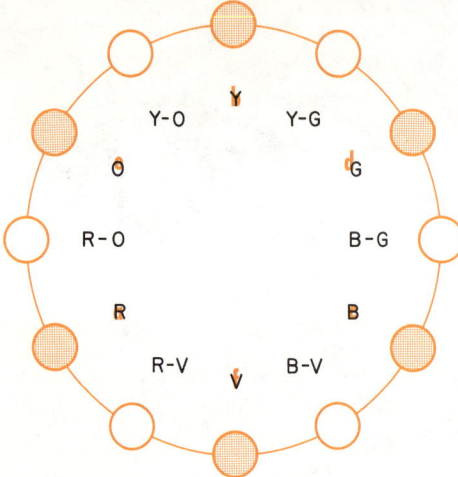

| Y | YELLOW | V | VIOLET |
| Y-G | YELLOW-GREEN | R-V | RED-VIOLET |
| G | GREEN | R | RED |
| B-G | BLUE–GREEN | R-O | RED-ORANGE |
| B | BLUE | O | ORANGE |
| B-V | BLUE-VIOLET | Y-O | YELLOW-ORANGE |

**2-14.** Color wheel.

*Secondary* colors are produced by mixing two primary colors:

> Red and yellow—orange.
> Yellow and blue—green.
> Blue and red—violet.

*Tertiary*, or intermediate, colors are a mixture of one primary and one secondary color:

> Red and violet—red violet.
> Red and orange—red orange.
> Blue and violet—blue violet.
> Blue and green—blue green.
> Yellow and orange—yellow orange.
> Yellow and green—yellow green.

*Neutrals* are black and white and the many grays produced by mixing black and white in different amounts.

## WHAT MAKES AN ATTRACTIVE PRODUCT?

In designing anything there are certain principles that should be followed.

**2-15a.** There is no doubt that these bedside tables and lamps show formal balance.

This is especially true in good furniture design. Some of these principles include:

● *Balance.* Exactly what it sounds like, balance makes things look stable. People are balanced. They have an arm on both sides, two eyes, and other body parts in balance. Generally, lopsided or unstable things are not pleasing to the eye.

There are two kinds of balance, formal and informal. Formal balance is present when both sides of an object are exactly equal. People are examples of formal balance. The lamps in Figure 2-15 show *formal* balance. *Informal* balance gives the impression of stability and balance by the "grouping" of the parts. For instance, two *small* boys on one side of the teeter totter and one *large* boy on the other is an example of informal balance. Figure 2-16 shows informal balance by the clever placement of the lamp, flower arrangement, and picture in one illustration and the desk design in the other.

**2-15b.** These balance scales illustrate formal and informal balance. The one on the left has units of equal size and shape. The scale on the right is balanced by units of different size but of the same weight.

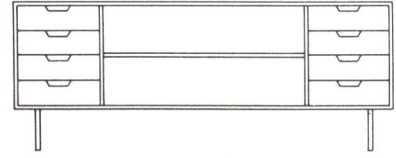

**2-15c.** A desk front that illustrates formal balance.

**2-16a.** Informal balance takes more thought and experience to create.

35

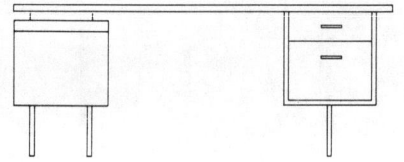

**2-16b.** A desk front that illustrates informal balance.

● *Proportion.* A well-proportioned piece is any object that looks good in relation to everything else in life. A dachshund dog doesn't look well proportioned because his legs are so short. We think a clown is funny if he has a great big nose and tremendous feet.

In designing many wood projects, we use a rectangular shape instead of a square one simply because it looks better proportioned to us. Proportion in design is achieved when the object is not too fat, tall, thin, or square, but is just right to our eyes and for the use we have for it. Figure 2-17. This is why large chairs should not have spindly legs. Babe Ruth was often referred to as "piano-legged" because his legs seemed too thin for his powerful body.

● *Harmony or unity.* When the parts, colors, shapes, and textures of an object seem to get along well together, we say the object has harmony or unity. Figure 2-18. Today, *many different materials are used in furniture,* but they are blended together to be pleasing. A good example of the *lack of harmony* is putting rough-welded legs on a smooth, dainty, table top. A piece of furniture with modern

**2-17a.** This lighted display case and chairside chest illustrate a 5-to-8 proportion between the height and width.

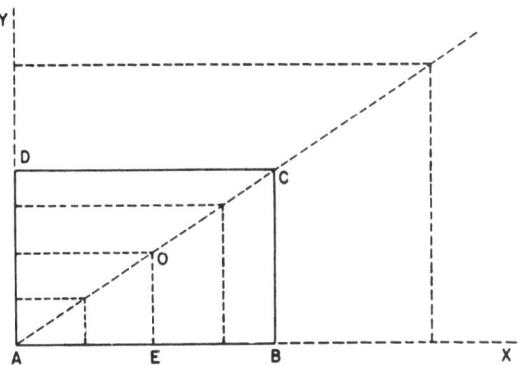

**2-17b.** A way of enlarging a 5-by-8 proportion to whatever size you want for a tray, pin-up board, or picture frame. Make AB eight units long and BC five units long. Then along the line AX lay off any length you want, for example, AE. The distance for width, then, would be EO.

**2-17c.** These turned candleholders are in good proportion.

lines would not be used with Chippendale "ball-and-claw" legs.

● *Emphasis.* An accent, or special point of interest, is often used for emphasis. Oftentimes in furniture this will be a beautiful piece of hardware on a cabinet or desk, the fine finish itself, or an interesting grain in the wood of a door or drawer. Figure 2-19.

In deciding whether something is well designed, you should ask yourself the following questions:

**2-18.** This modern desk is made of metal, wood, and plastic laminates. Don't they go well together?

**2-19.** Can you identify the point of emphasis in these unusual clock faces?

• Does the piece serve the purpose for which it is intended? Figure 2-20.

• Does it perform its job efficiently? For example, if it is a chair, is it comfortable to sit in? Figure 2-21.

• Is it within your ability to construct and maintain? Figure 2-22.

• Is it pleasing to the eye? Figure 2-23.

• Does it satisfy you and the other people you want it to satisfy?

**2-20.** A TV table must be sturdy in use, yet fold up to be compact.

**2-21.** Do you think this chair, designed and built by a student, would be comfortable?

**2-22.** Perhaps a simple cutting board would be a good beginning project.

38

## DESIGNING A WOODWORKING PROJECT

After you have had some experience and know what you can do with tools and machines, you may get a chance to design a project of your own. This is an interesting thing to do. It gives you an opportunity to be creative, which is not easy, but very fascinating.

To design and make a project in wood, follow these steps:

1. *Get the idea for the project you would like to build.* Maybe you have something in mind that you've always wanted to make. If not, magazines and books with projects in them are good sources of ideas. Another way to get ideas is to visit different stores selling furniture, hobby supplies, or sporting goods. You might like to build:

● Toys, models, games, puzzles, and other hobby equipment. Figure 2-24.

● Shelters for birds and pets.

● Things for your room or home such as lamps, bookends, shoe racks, and tie racks. Figures 2-25, 2-26, and 2-27.

**2-23.** Do you think these products are equal in design quality?

**2-25.** These desk accessories would be useful projects to make.

**2-24.** A model truck made of wood.

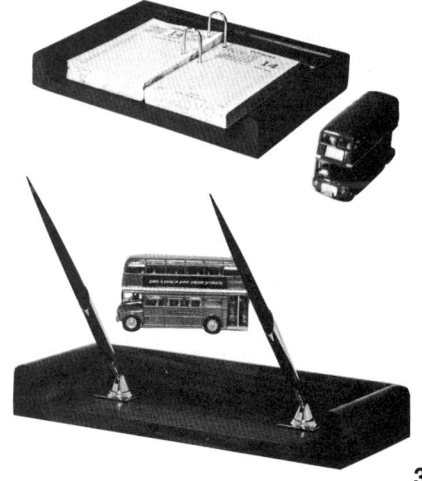

● Kitchen items such as cutting boards, salt and pepper shakers, and shelves. Figure 2-28.

● Sports equipment like boats and skis. Figure 2-29.

● Furniture including chairs, tables, chests, and desks. Figure 2-30.

2. *After you've decided what to make, ask yourself, "What is the purpose of the object?"* For example, if it's a book rack or book trough, it is supposed to hold books conveniently. How large are the books? What must be the depth of the shelf? If there is to be more than one shelf, what should the distance between

the shelves be? If the project is a magazine rack, it must be able to hold magazines efficiently. Figure 2-31 (Page 44). It is surprising to find so many commercial objects that look nice but don't do the job properly. For instance, one fancy shoe rack on the market was designed with the distance from the wall to the rung that holds the heels of the shoes too short. The shoes won't stay on it. If you design a shoe rack, remember that it must be different for men's and women's shoes.

If you are designing a piece of furniture, there are certain standards, especially of height, that must be observed. See Figure 2-32.

3. *Decide on the style or design of furniture.* It should blend with your room or home. If, for example, your room is furnished in Early American, then the

**2-26a.** A beautiful lamp you could turn on the wood lathe.

**2-26b.** Bill of materials for the lamp shown in 2-26a.

| STOCK: White Oak<br>Important: All dimensions listed below are CUTOUT size. | | | | |
|---|---|---|---|---|
| No.<br>of<br>Pieces | Part Name | Thick-<br>ness | Width | Length |
| 4 | Column Stock | 1¾″ | 5¼″ | 15″ |
| 4 | Column Stock | ¾″ | 2¾″ | 15″ |
| 1 | Base | ¾″ | 7¼″ | 7¼″ |
| 1 | Cap | ¾″ | 4½″ | 4½″ |
| 1 | Harp Support | 2″ | 2″ | 3½″ |
| 2 | Plugs | ¾″ | 2″ | 2″ |
| 1 | ⅛″ Std. Pipe | | | 19″ |
| 1 | ⅛″ Pipe Hex Nut | | | |
| 1 | Push Thru Brass Socket | | | |
| 1 | 9″ or 10″ Harp to suit shade | | | |
| 1 | Brass Finial | | | |
| 1 | Felt Pad 7″ dia. | | | |
| 4 | No. 8 x 1¼″ F. H. Wood Screws | | | |
| 1 | Lamp Cord of length to suit | | | |
| 1 | Lamp Shade to suit | | | |
| 1 | Male Plug | | | |

lamp or wall shelf should follow this style. Furniture designs have evolved over the years, and designers of one period have often borrowed ideas and designs from another period. The six most popular designs of furniture today are Traditional, Early American or Colonial, French Provincial, Italian Provincial, Spanish or Mediterranean, and Modern or Contemporary.

The *Traditional* design came from the best features of the eighteenth-century designers of England. This period is also sometimes known as the Golden Age of English furniture. The Big four of the eighteenth century designers were

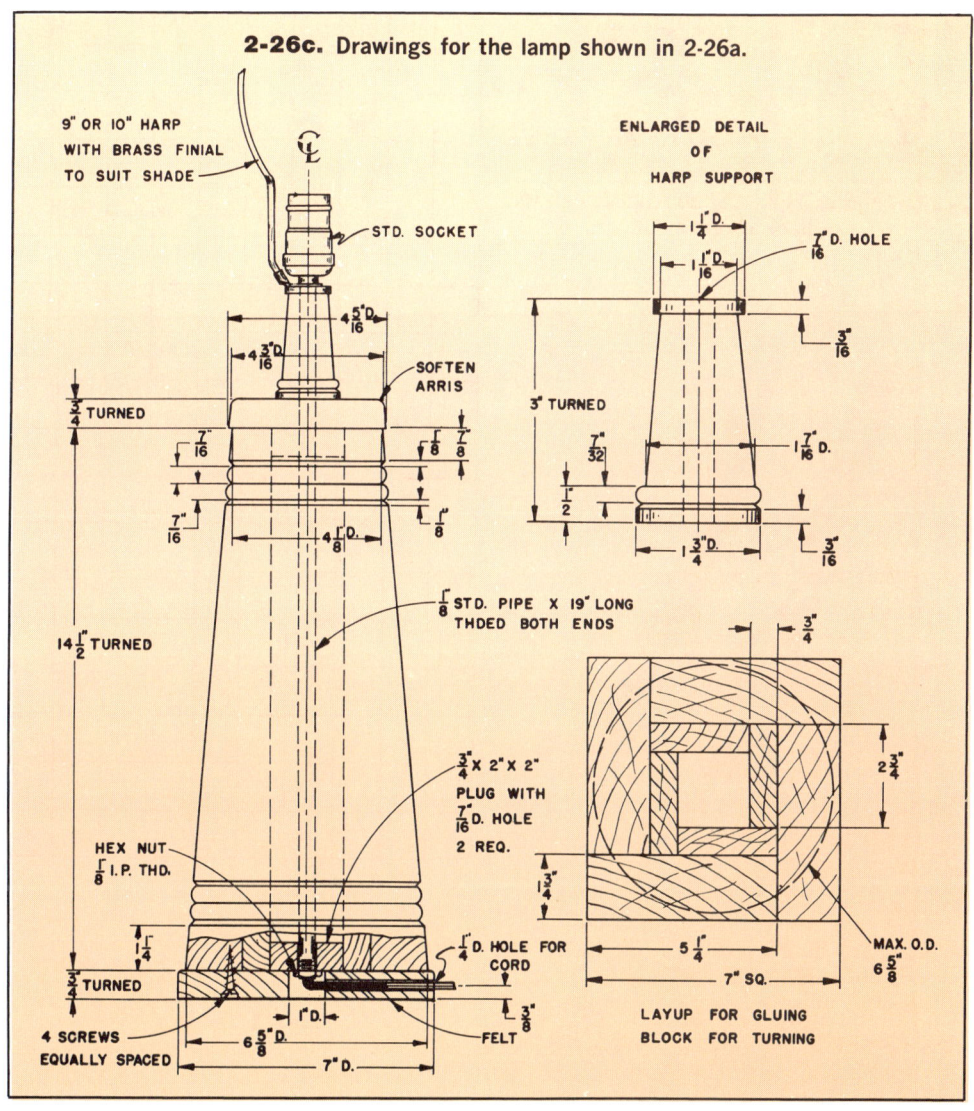

**2-26c.** Drawings for the lamp shown in 2-26a.

**2-27.** An interesting and unusual design for book shelves.

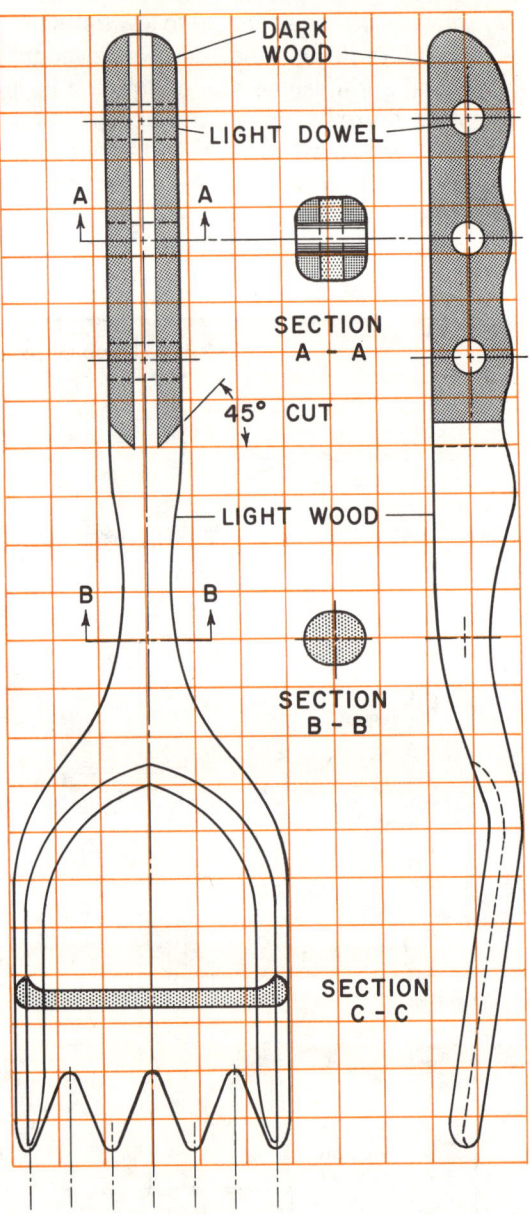

DARK WOOD

LIGHT DOWEL

A   A

SECTION A-A

45° CUT

LIGHT WOOD

B   B

SECTION B-B

SECTION C-C

6 EQUAL SPACES
ROUGH STOCK SIZE – 1 x 3 x 12
FINISHED SIZE – $\frac{7}{8}$ x $2\frac{15}{16}$ x $11\frac{5}{8}$

**2-28b.** Drawings for the salad set shown in 2-28a.

**2-28a.** A wooden salad set made by cutting and carving.

**2-28c.** Bill of materials for the salad set shown in 2-28a.

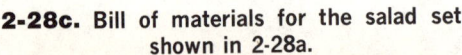

1 piece light-colored hardwood, 3″ x $\frac{7}{8}$″ x 24″
1 piece dark-colored hardwood, 4″ x $\frac{1}{4}$″ x $4\frac{1}{2}$″
8″ of $\frac{3}{8}$″ dowel.

DRILL SCREW HOLES 18 mm FROM EDGES.
COUNTERBORE 13 mm DEEP.
USE 70 mm SCREWS.

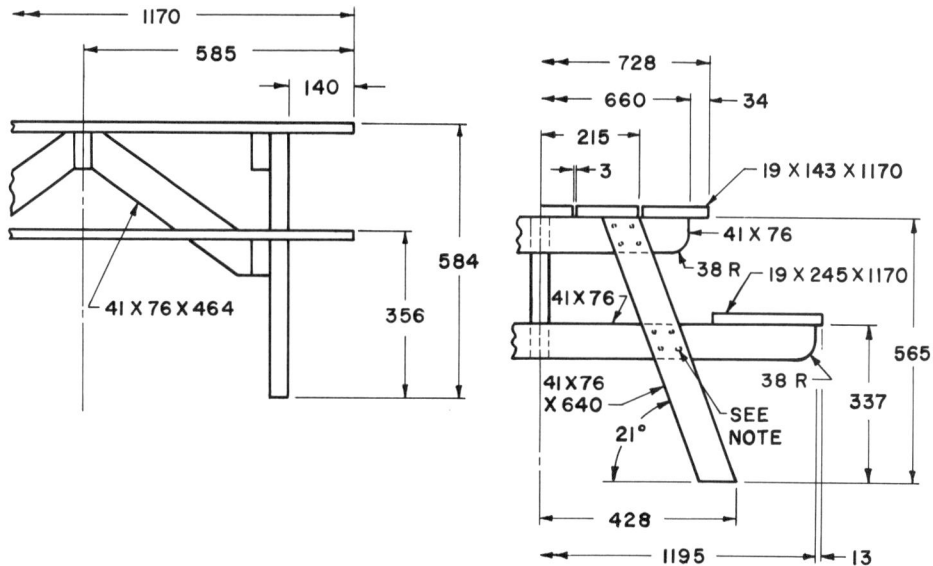

**2-29a.** A metric drawing of a picnic table. This is an example of recreation equipment you can make.

**2-29b.** A customary drawing of the same picnic table.

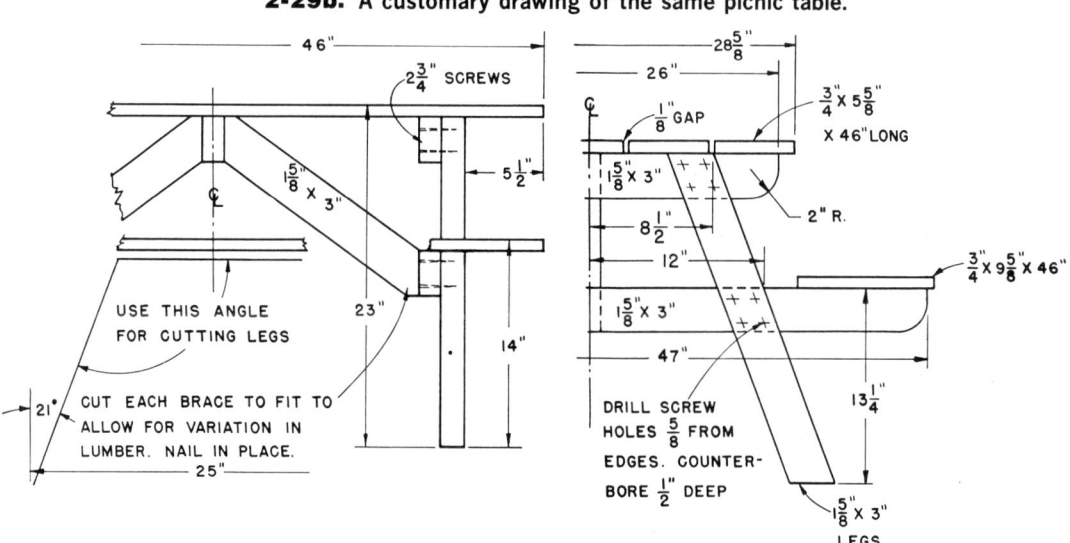

STOCK: Pine, Redwood, Cypress, Spruce
or Cedar
Important: All dimensions listed below are
FINISHED size.

| No. of Pieces | Part Name | Thick-ness | Width | Length |
|---|---|---|---|---|
| *4 | Legs | $1\frac{5}{8}''$ | $3''$ | $25''$ |
| *3 | Cross Ties | $1\frac{5}{8}''$ | $3''$ | $26''$ |
| *2 | Seat Ties | $1\frac{5}{8}''$ | $3''$ | $47''$ |
| *2 | Braces | $1\frac{5}{8}''$ | $3''$ | $18''$ |
| 5 | Top Boards | $\frac{3}{4}''$ | $5\frac{5}{8}''$ | $46''$ |
| 2 | Bench Seats | $\frac{3}{4}''$ | $9\frac{5}{8}''$ | $46''$ |
| 32 | $2\frac{3}{4}''$-14 F. H. Wood Screws $2\frac{3}{4}''$ | | | |
| 42 | $1\frac{1}{4}''$-14 F. H. Wood Screws $1\frac{1}{4}''$ | | | |
| | * May be ripped from standard 2 x 4's or other 2'' stock. | | | |

**2-29c.** Bill of materials for the picnic table shown in 2-29a.

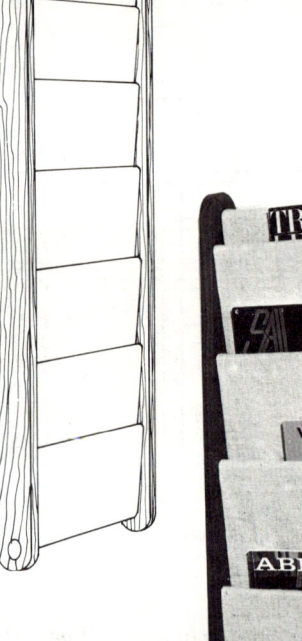

**2-30.** A student-designed table and desk. Would you be satisfied with the design and construction?

**2-31.** The same design for a magazine rack can be made wider when necessary.

| Item | Height | Depth-Width | Length |
|------|--------|-------------|--------|
| **Tables** | | | |
| Coffee or Cocktail | 14″ to 18″ (356 to 457 mm) | 18″ to 24″ (457 to 610 mm) | 36″ to 60″ (914 to 1524 mm) |
| Card | 29″ (737 mm) | 30″ (762 mm) | 30″ (762 mm) |
| Game | 30″ (762 mm) | 30″ (762 mm) | 30″ (762 mm) |
| Writing | 30″ (762 mm) | 24″ (610 mm) | 36″ to 40″ (914 to 1016 mm) |
| Kitchen | 30″ (762 mm) | 30″ (762 mm) | 42″ (1067 mm) |
| End | 27″ (686 mm) | 15″ (381 mm) | 24″ (610 mm) |
| Dining | 29″ to 32″ (737 to 813 mm) | 42″ (1067 mm) | 42″ to 70″ (1067 to 1778 mm) |
| **Chairs** | | | |
| Desk | 16½″ (419 mm) | 15″ to 18″ (381 to 457 mm) | 15″ to 18″ (381 to 457 mm) |
| Dining | 16″ to 18″ (406 to 457 mm) | 15″ to 18″ (381 to 457 mm) | 15″ to 18″ (381 to 457 mm) |

| Item | Height | Depth-Width | Length |
|------|--------|-------------|--------|
| **Cabinets** | | | |
| Sectional | 30″ (762 mm) | 12″ to 14″ (305 to 356 mm) | Any |
| China Storage | 54″ to 60″ (1372 to 1524 mm) | 20″ to 22″ (508 to 559 mm) | Any |
| Kitchen | 36″ (914 mm) | 12″ to 24″ (305 to 610 mm) | Any |
| **Chests** | 32″ to 54″ (813 to 1372 mm) | 24″ (610 mm) | Any |
| **Bookcases** | 32″ to 82″ (813 to 2083 mm) | 18″ (457 mm) | Any |
| **Desks** | 30″ (762 mm) | 24″ to 30″ (610 to 762 mm) | 40″ to 60″ (1016 to 1524 mm) |

**2-32.** Standard sizes of furniture.

**2-33a.** Traditional.

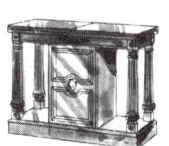

Thomas Chippendale, Thomas Sheraton, George Hepplewhite, and the Adams brothers. Figure 2-33.

Thomas Chippendale, the first and most famous of these designers, was a leading London cabinetmaker from 1750 to 1775. The Adams brothers, who were both designers and architects, were greatly influenced by the classic art of Italy. George Hepplewhite was a skilled designer and craftsman who developed furniture styles of delicate design. Thomas Sheraton, a very creative designer and cabinetmaker, produced furniture with a subtle gracefulness. While contemporary adaptations of the work of these men are still popular, a more typical traditional piece is a combination of all of these designs.

**2-33b.** Eighteenth-century style is still a favorite with many people.

Duncan Phyfe was the most influential American designer of the Traditional period. Many of the original designs of his work are still very popular. Figure 2-34.

The *Early American* or *Colonial* style is a development of the kind of furniture used in this country just before and after the Revolutionary War. Figure 2-35.

*French Provincial* is an adaptation of the furniture that was popular during the reign of Louis XV and XVI. Figure 2-36. *Italian Provincial* is a style adapted from craftsmen of the Italian provinces of the eighteenth and nineteenth centuries. Figure 2-37. *Spanish* or *Mediterranean* reflects the artistry of the Moorish and

**2-34.** The lyre-back chair illustrates one of the best known Duncan Phyfe designs.

**2-35a.** Early American.

**2-35b.** An antiqued pine hutch in Early American style.

**2-36a.** French Provincial.

**2-36b.** A French Provincial bedroom set.

**2-37.** Italian Provincial furniture features straight lines with tapered legs.

**2-38b.** Heavy sculptured designs are typical of Mediterranean styling.

**2-38a.** Mediterranean.

Spanish cultures. Figure 2-38. Modern design is best characterized by clean, beautifully contoured work with emphasis on simplicity. *Modern* or *Contemporary* furniture tends to be less ornate and omits unnecessary hardware. Much of its beauty lies in the clean lines and use of beautiful woods. Figure 2-39.

4. *Now make a sketch of what you would like to build to see how it will look.* Suppose you decide to make a wall rack or cabinet. Figure 2-40. Here are several sketches of possible designs. Figure 2-41. Let's suppose you decide on sketch A.

5. *Make a working drawing of the project.* Figure 2-42. This will be necessary to determine the exact size of each part and how it is to be made.

6. *Make a model.* It is sometimes difficult to imagine what the finished article will look like with only sketches and drawings. It is helpful to see the three-dimensional appearance of the item by making a small model. This can be made of balsa wood or some other light mate-

**2-39.** Tables and china cabinet in Modern design.

**2-40.** Some wall racks and shelves in Early American design.

A.

B.

C.

D.

**2-41.** All of these sketches are good examples of Early American design. Any one would make a well-designed project.

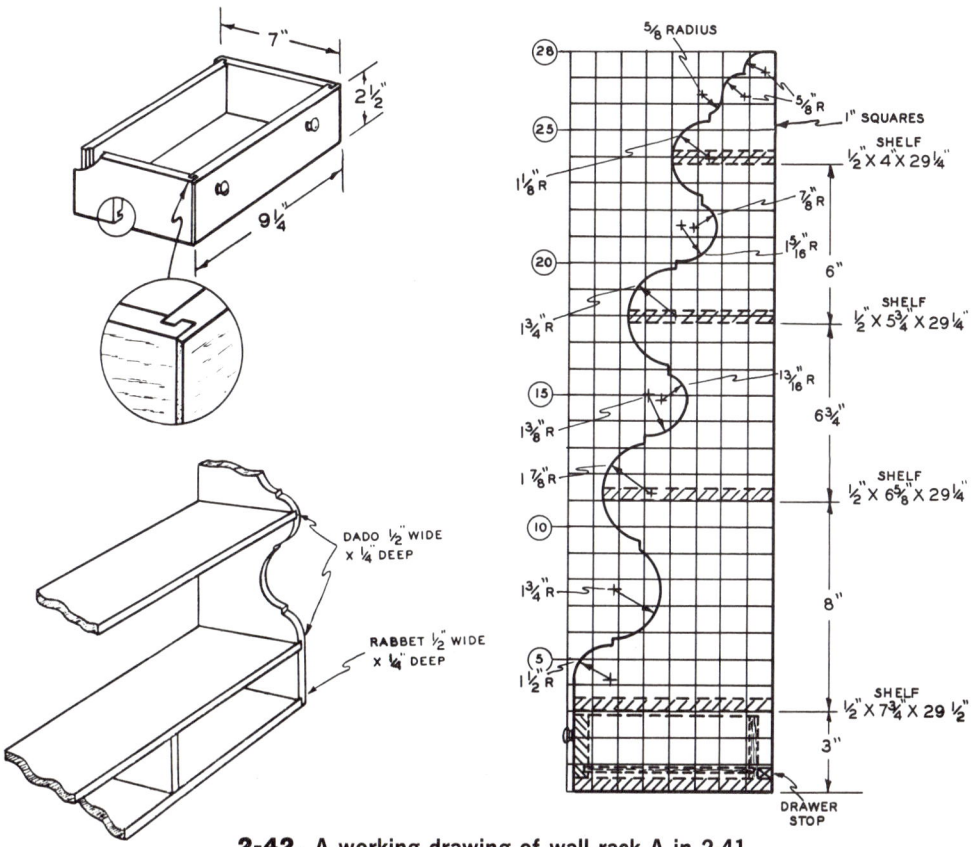

**2-42.** A working drawing of wall rack A in 2-41.

**2-43.** Bill of materials for the wall rack.

| No. of Pieces | Part Name | Thickness | Width | Length | Wood |
|---|---|---|---|---|---|
| | **Important: All dimensions listed above, except for length of dowel, etc., FINISHED size.** | | | | |

| No. of Pieces | Part Name | Thickness | Width | Length | Wood |
|---|---|---|---|---|---|
| 2 | Ends | $1/2''$ | $7\frac{3}{4}''$ | $28''$ | Knotty Pine |
| 1 | Shelf | $1/2''$ | $4''$ | $29\frac{1}{4}''$ | Knotty Pine |
| 1 | Shelf | $1/2''$ | $5\frac{3}{4}''$ | $29\frac{1}{4}''$ | Knotty Pine |
| 1 | Shelf | $1/2''$ | $6\frac{5}{8}''$ | $29\frac{1}{4}''$ | Knotty Pine |
| 2 | Shelves | $1/2''$ | $7\frac{3}{4}''$ | $29\frac{1}{4}''$ | Knotty Pine |
| 2 | Drawer Separators | $1/2''$ | $2\frac{1}{2}''$ | $7\frac{3}{4}''$ | Knotty Pine |
| 3 | Drawer Fronts | $1/2''$ | $2\frac{1}{2}''$ | $9\frac{1}{4}''$ | Knotty Pine |
| 6 | Drawer Sides | $3/8''$ | $2\frac{1}{2}''$ | $7''$ | Clear Pine |
| 3 | Drawer Backs | $3/8''$ | $2\frac{1}{2}''$ | $8\frac{7}{8}''$ | Clear Pine |
| 3 | Drawer Bottoms | $1/4''$ | $6\frac{1}{4}''$ | $8\frac{3}{4}''$ | Fir Plywood |
| 6 | Drawer Stops | $1/2''$ | $1/2''$ | $1''$ | |
| 1 | Hardwood Dowel | $1/4''$ | | $36''$ | |
| 6 | Hardwood Knobs | $3/4''$ | | | |

rial that cuts easily with a knife. The model does not have all the small details but will give the general appearance.

7. *Now make a bill of materials.* Here you need to keep in mind the sizes and kinds of woods and plywoods and the kinds of fasteners to be used. Figure 2-43.

8. *You are now ready to plan the building of the project.* You must decide in what order each job will be performed. Figure 2-44. Usually this will include *making a layout, cutting out the pieces and parts, shaping the parts, making the joints, fitting and assembling, and finishing.*

9. *The next step is to decide on what tools and machines you will need.* Your future experiences in woodworking will help you decide on how to use the equipment. For example, the jig saw is the ideal tool for cutting out the ends of the wall rack. Figure 2-44b.

10. *Now the building can be done.* This is the time to display your crafts-

manship by doing a fine job on each part.

11. *Last, you should judge your work.* Is the project useful, good in appearance, economical? Was it completed in a reasonable length of time? Did you learn by making it? "Yes" answers indicate a successful project.

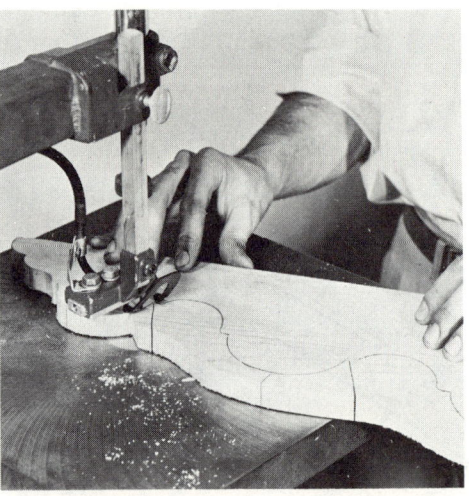

**2-44b.** Cutting out an end on the jig saw.

**2-44a.** Plan of procedure for the wall rack.

1. Lay out pattern of the ends on paper and trace on wood. Cut out on a jig saw.
2. Cut the dadoes for the shelves and the rabbet for the bottom board.
3. Saw the shelves and bottom board.
4. Dowel and glue the shelves and bottom in place. Before the glue sets be sure the entire structure is square.
5. Make drawer separators; install dowels and glue in place.
6. Cut the drawer fronts and fit into each opening. Then complete the drawers, using the joints suggested in the detailed drawing—or make a simple rabbet joint to fasten the sides and front, and a dado joint to fasten the sides and back. Glue drawer stops in place so the drawer fronts will be flush.
7. Sand edges to give a worn appearance.
8. Apply an antique pine finish, and add knobs.

**2-44c.** The finished project. Isn't it a beauty?

## CAN YOU ANSWER THESE QUESTIONS ON DESIGN?

1. Describe the meaning of design.
2. Name three keys to good design.
3. How can products be grouped as far as design is concerned?
4. Name four kinds of lines.
5. What is mass?
6. How can color be added to wood products?
7. Name the two kinds of balance.
8. Is a square in good proportion? Explain your answer.
9. What is emphasis?
10. Describe some of the kinds of things that you can build.
11. What are the most popular furniture styles?
12. What is the value of making a model of the project you wish to build?
13. Tell what a bill of materials is.

## Section I UNIT 3.

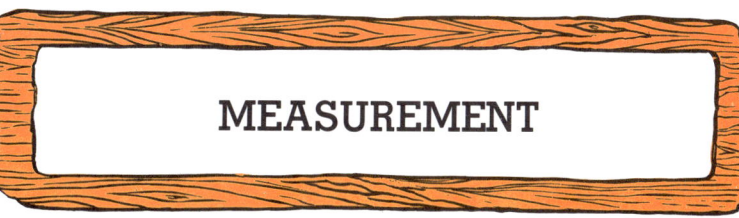

# MEASUREMENT

**Noah was indeed** a great carpenter. He built his wooden ark, 300 cubits long, 50 cubits wide, and 30 cubits high, to hold many people and animals. Figure 3-1. Even by today's standards, this is a very large wood ship. A cubit is roughly 18 inches. This means that Noah's ark was 450 feet from stem to stern. Noah built his ark according to instruction but without the aid of a yardstick. The lack of a yardstick, however, was not a serious drawback since it had not yet been invented. Actually the cubit of Noah's time was the length of a man's forearm, or the distance from the tip of the elbow to the end of the middle finger. This was indeed a handy measuring stick. It was always available and could not be lost. The cubit, however, was not a positively fixed dimension, not a *standard*, since its length varied from man to man.

Although we no longer use the cubit as a unit of measure, many of our present-day standards originated about the same way. Figure 3-2. A one-foot rule started as the length of a man's foot and since some people had bigger feet than others, the foot varied in length. Even when Columbus built his three vessels,

**3-1.** Noah built his ark to standards based on the human body.

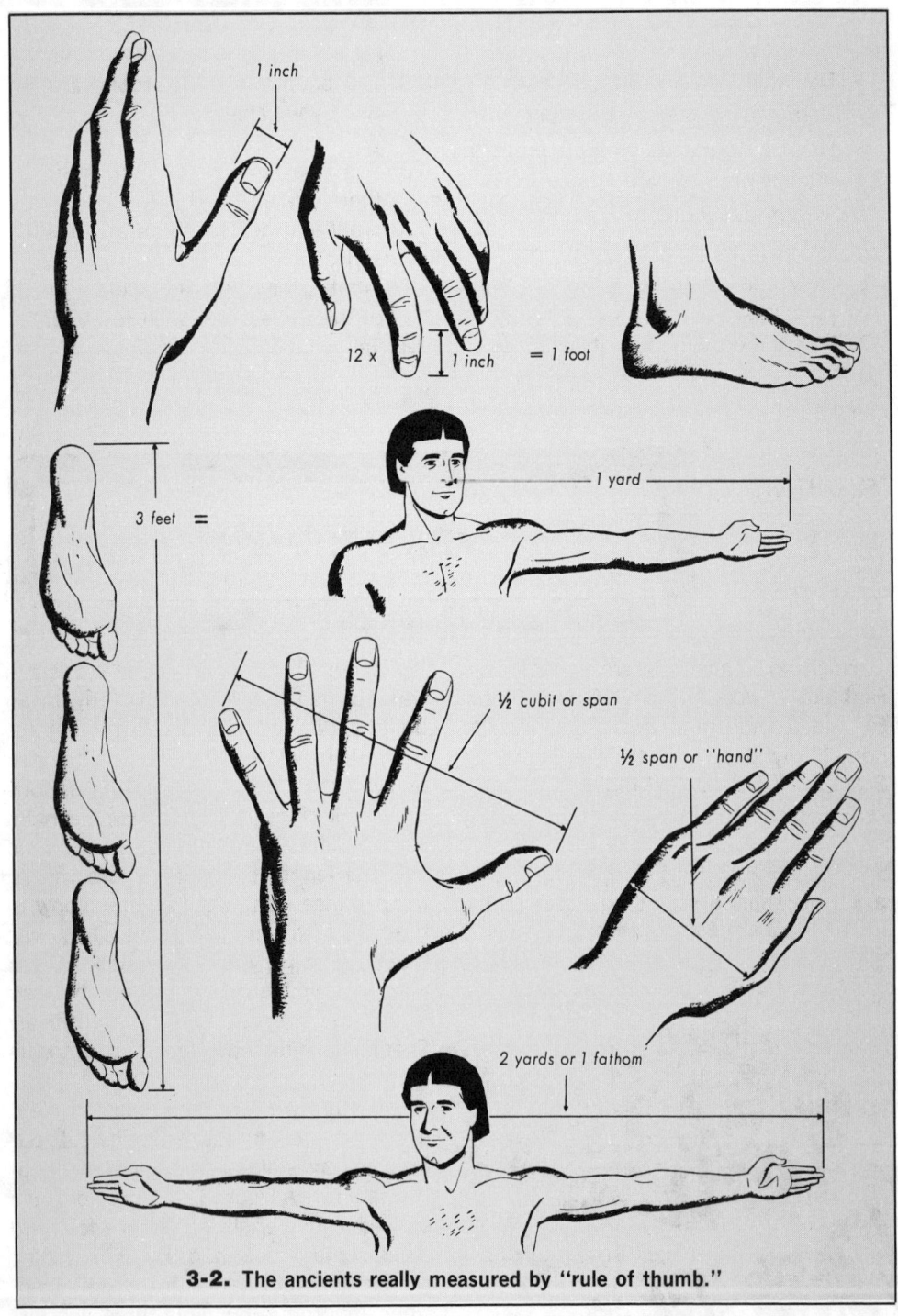

**3-2.** The ancients really measured by "rule of thumb."

1 inch

12 x  1 inch  = 1 foot

3 feet =

1 yard

½ cubit or span

½ span or "hand"

2 yards or 1 fathom

the Nina, Pinta, and Santa Maria, the same standards of measurement were accepted. In contrast to Noah's ark, the Santa Maria was only 117 feet long and the other two were about 50 feet each. For thousands of years, people used the human body as a means of measuring.

In the thirteenth century, King Edward of England took a tremendous step forward by ordering a permanent measuring stick made out of iron to serve as a master yardstick for the entire kingdom. This master yardstick was called "the iron." Surprisingly enough, this metal yardstick was very close in length to the one we have today. Even more important was King Edward's realization that a consistent standard was necessary and that the yardstick should be made of the strongest and toughest material available at that time. He also decreed that the foot measure should be one-third the length of the yard and that the inch should be one-thirty-sixth.

Over the years, the system of measurement based on inches and pounds developed into what is known as the customary (English, Imperial, or inch-pound) system. The United States has over 80 units of weights and measures from pounds to tons and inches to miles.

In 1793, at the time Napoleon was rising to power, the French government adopted an entirely new system of standards. Called the *metric* system, it was based on what they called the *metre*. Note the spelling. "Metre" is the official spelling even though "meter" is commonly used. The metre was supposed to be $\frac{1}{10,000,000}$ of the distance from the North Pole to the equator when measured on a line running along the surface of the earth through Paris. When the

metre was thus determined, the metric system was set up in decimal ratio. All units are in multiples of 10. There are 10 decimetres in a metre, 100 centimetres in a metre, 1,000 millimetres in a metre. In the other direction, there are 10 metres in a dekametre, 100 metres in a hectometre, and 1,000 metres in a kilometre. Figure 3-3.

For years, most of the European countries used the metric system while Great Britain, its colonies, and the United States continued to use the customary. Figure 3-4. In 1872, a meeting in France, which was attended by 26 countries including the United States, resulted in an international treaty since referred to as the metric convention. The treaty was signed by 17 countries including the United States. This treaty established well-defined metric standards for length and mass as well as the International Bureau of Weights and Measures. However, it was not until 1960 that the current SI Metric System was developed. SI means System International and it consists of seven base units and many derived units. Figure 3-5 (Page 58). Today the United States is moving toward the use of the metric measurement system. All others, including Great Britain, Canada, and Australia, already have adopted the metric system.

For everyday use, only three metric measurements are important, namely, the *metre* for length, the *kilogram* for weight, and the *litre* for volume. These units are fairly easy to remember: the *metre* is a little longer than the yard (39.37 inches); the *kilogram* is a little more than twice the pound (2.2 pounds), and the *litre* is a little more (about 6 percent) than the quart. Figure 3-6 (Page 58). For everyday use, only three prefixes are needed. They are kilo (1000 times the standard unit), centi ($\frac{1}{100}$ times the standard unit), and milli ($\frac{1}{1000}$ times the standard unit).

## ACCURACY IN MEASUREMENT

The smallest division on a customary woodworking rule is $\frac{1}{16}$ inch, and the smallest division on a metric rule is 1 millimetre or approximately $\frac{1}{25}$ of an inch. Figure 3-7. Remember that one millimetre is smaller than $\frac{1}{16}$ inch but larger than $\frac{1}{32}$ inch (one of the divisions found on a metal scale). Figure 3-8.

Therefore for most work, you can measure to the nearest millimetre. For example, 1 inch equals exactly 25.4 mm, and 2 inches equals exactly 50.8 mm. You can mark these as 25 mm and 51 mm for most woodworking. However, for accurate work as in making patterns or models, it is just as easy to estimate distances between the division marks on the metric rule as on the customary rule when fine divisions are required. Therefore you can also mark off 1 inch as 25.5 mm. Figure 3-9. This will be particularly true when you use a 25 mm chisel

**3-3.** Comparison of the metric and customary units of length measurement.

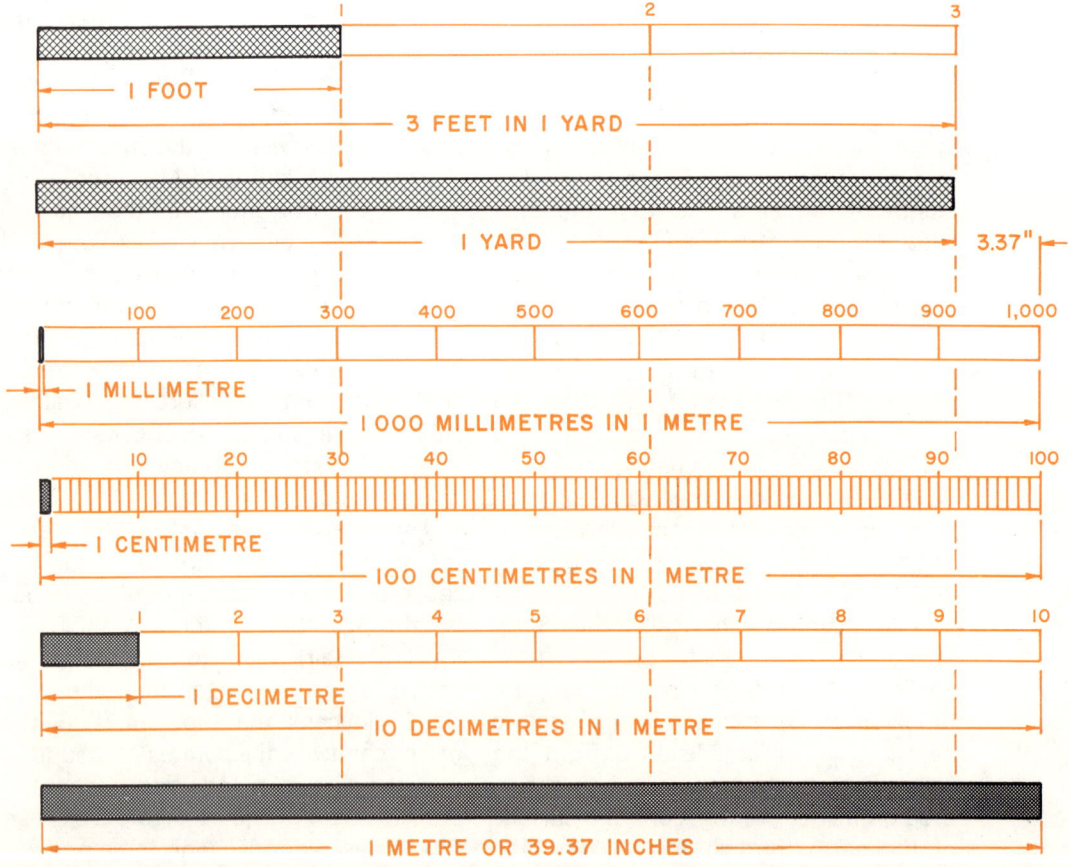

to cut a dado, for example. The chisel will actually measure 25.4 mm, so for a good fit the second part of the joint should be finished to 25.5 mm.

Since the United States is moving to the SI Metric System, it is important for you to be able to read a rule in both the customary and metric systems. You must also be able to convert liquid measures for finishing materials from pints and quarts to litres and to change weights of materials from pounds to kilograms.

## READING A CUSTOMARY RULE

The most common customary rules are either a foot or a yard long. Each of these rules is divided into major inch divisions and each inch is divided into either eighths or sixteenths as the smallest measurement. Let's look at a rule and find $\frac{1}{16}$ inch. Notice that the longest line between 0 and 1 inch is the $\frac{1}{2}$ inch mark. The next longest line is the $\frac{1}{4}$ inch mark. The next longest is $\frac{1}{8}$ inch and the shortest is $\frac{1}{16}$ inch. Therefore, four-sixteenths

**3-4.** Common conversions: customary to metric; metric to customary.

| LENGTH | |
|---|---|
| CUSTOMARY TO METRIC | METRIC TO CUSTOMARY |
| 1 inch = 25.40 millimetres·mm<br>1 inch = 2.540 centimetres·cm<br>1 foot = 30.480 centimetres·cm<br>1 foot = 0.3048 metre·m<br>1 yard = 91.440 centimetres·cm<br>1 yard = 0.9144 metre·m | 1 millimetre = 0.03937 inch<br>1 centimetre = 0.3937 inch<br>1 metre = 39.37 inches<br>1 metre = 3.2808 feet<br>1 metre = 1.0936 yards |
| **AREA** | |
| CUSTOMARY TO METRIC | METRIC TO CUSTOMARY |
| 1 sq. inch = 645.16 sq. millimetres·mm$^2$<br>1 sq. inch = 6.4516 sq. centimetres·cm$^2$<br>1 sq. foot = 929.03 sq. centimetres·cm$^2$<br>1 sq. foot = 0.0929 sq. metres·m$^2$<br>1 sq. yard = 0.826 sq. metre·m$^2$ | 1 sq. millimetre = 0.00155 sq. inch<br>1 sq. centimetre = 0.1550 sq. inch<br>1 sq. metre = 10.7640 sq. feet<br>1 sq. metre = 1.196 sq. yards |
| **MASS (WEIGHT)** | |
| CUSTOMARY TO METRIC | METRIC TO CUSTOMARY |
| 1 ounce (dry) = 28.35 grams·g<br>1 pound = 0.4536 kilogram·kg | 1 gram = 0.03527 ounce<br>1 kilogram = 2.2046 pounds |
| **VOLUME (CAPACITY)** | |
| CUSTOMARY TO METRIC | METRIC TO CUSTOMARY |
| 1 pint (liq.) = 0.473 litre = 0.473 cm$^3$<br>1 quart (liq.) = 0.9463 litre = 0.9463 dm$^{3**}$<br>1 gallon (liq.) = 3.7853 litres = 3.7853 dm$^{3**}$ | 1 litre = 1000 cm$^{3*}$ = 0.5283 pint (liq.)<br>1 litre = 1 dm$^{3**}$ = 1.0567 quarts (liq.)<br>1 litre = 1 dm$^{3**}$ = 0.26417 gallon (liq.) |

\* cubic centimetre
\*\* cubic decimetre

| Quantity | Unit | Symbol |
|---|---|---|
| Length | metre | m |
| Mass | kilogram | kg |
| Time | second | s |
| Electric current | ampere | A |
| Temperature* | degree Celsius | °C |
| Luminous intensity | candela | cd |
| Amount of substance | mole | mol |

\* For scientific work the kelvin scale (symbol K) is used.

**3-5.** The base units for the International System of Units (SI). All other units are derived from these. For example, the litre, a derived unit, is one cubic decimetre, or 1000 cubic centimetres (cm³).

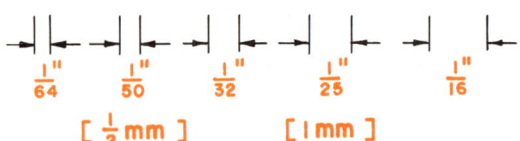

A MILLIMETRE IS ABOUT HALF WAY BETWEEN $\frac{1}{32}$" AND $\frac{1}{16}$".

ENLARGED 5 TIMES ACTUAL SIZE.

**3-8.** How ¹⁄₁₆ inch and 1 millimetre compare in size.

**3-6.** The three common units that you will use in all industrial work.

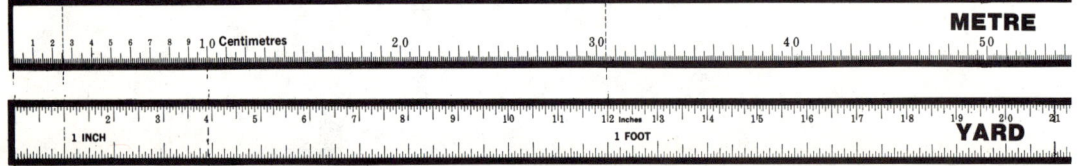

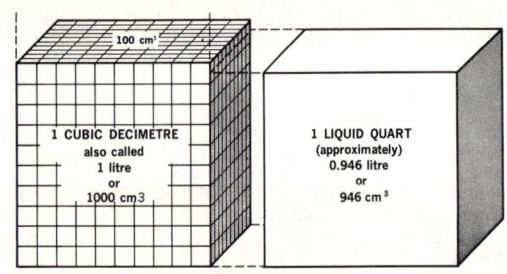

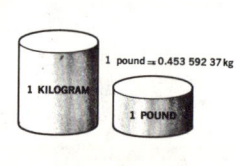

**3-7.** Comparison between the metric rule and the customary rule.

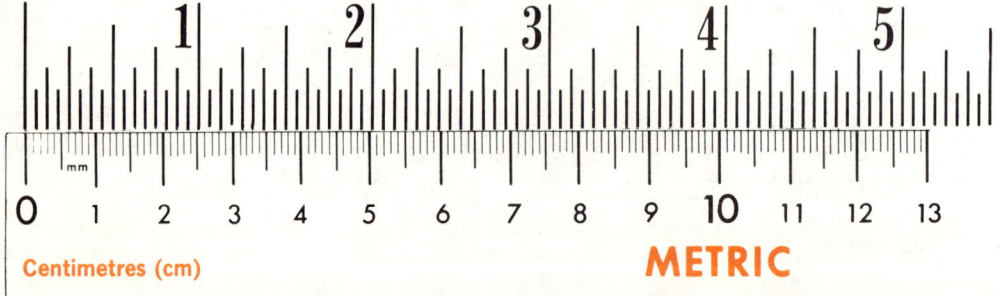

($^{4}/_{16}$) inch equals two-eighths ($^{2}/_{8}$) inch, or one-quarter ($^{1}/_{4}$) inch. Figure 3-10.

## READING A METRIC RULE

A metric rule is usually available in metre, half-metre, or 300-millimetre lengths. Figure 3-11. Remember that a metre is divided into 100 centimetres and 1000 millimetres. Generally the rule is marked with the centimetre divisions 1, 2, 3, 4, etc., and with 10 divisions between centimetre to equal millimetres.

**3-9.** Conversion table for woodwork.

| Customary (English) | Metric | | | | |
|---|---|---|---|---|---|
| | Actual | Accurate Woodworkers' Language | Tool Sizes | Lumber Sizes | |
| | | | | Thickness | Width |
| $^{1}/_{32}$ in | 0.8 mm | 1 mm bare | | | |
| $^{1}/_{16}$ in | 1.6 mm | 1.5 mm | | | |
| $^{1}/_{8}$ in | 3.2 mm | 3 mm full | 3 mm | | |
| $^{3}/_{16}$ in | 4.8 mm | 5 mm bare | 5 mm | | |
| $^{1}/_{4}$ in | 6.4 mm | 6.5 mm | 6 mm | | |
| $^{5}/_{16}$ in | 7.9 mm | 8 mm bare | 8 mm | | |
| $^{3}/_{8}$ in | 9.5 mm | 9.5 mm | 10 mm | | |
| $^{7}/_{16}$ in | 11.1 mm | 11 mm full | 11 mm | | |
| $^{1}/_{2}$ in | 12.7 mm | 12.5 mm full | 13 mm | | |
| $^{9}/_{16}$ in | 14.3 mm | 14.5 mm bare | 14 mm | | |
| $^{5}/_{8}$ in | 15.9 mm | 16 mm bare | 16 mm | 16 mm | |
| $^{11}/_{16}$ in | 17.5 mm | 17.5 mm | 17 mm | | |
| $^{3}/_{4}$ in | 19.1 mm | 19 mm full | 19 mm | 19 mm | |
| $^{13}/_{16}$ in | 20.6 mm | 20.5 mm | 21 mm | | |
| $^{7}/_{8}$ in | 22.2 mm | 22 mm full | 22 mm | 22 mm | |
| $^{15}/_{16}$ in | 23.8 mm | 24 mm bare | 24 mm | | |
| 1 in | 25.4 mm | 25.5 mm | 25 mm | 25 mm | |
| 1$^{1}/_{4}$ in | 31.8 mm | 32 mm bare | 32 mm | 32 mm | |
| 1$^{3}/_{8}$ in | 34.9 mm | 35 mm bare | 36 mm | 36 mm | |
| 1$^{1}/_{2}$ in | 38.1 mm | 38 mm full | 38 mm | 38 mm (or 40 mm) | |
| 1$^{3}/_{4}$ in | 44.5 mm | 44.5 mm | 44 mm | 44 mm | |
| 2 in | 50.8 mm | 51 mm bare | 50 mm | 50 mm | |
| 2$^{1}/_{2}$ in | 63.5 mm | 63.5 mm | 64 mm | 63 mm | |
| 3 in | 76.2 mm | 76 mm full | | 75 mm | 75 mm |
| 4 in | 101.6 mm | 101.5 mm | | 100 mm | 100 mm |
| 5 in | 127.0 mm | 127 mm | | | 125 mm |
| 6 in | 152.4 mm | 152.5 mm | | | 150 mm |
| 7 in | 177.8 mm | 178 mm bare | | | 225 mm |
| 8 in | 203.2 mm | 203 mm full | | | 200 mm |
| 9 in | 228.6 mm | 228.5 mm | | | 275 mm |
| 10 in | 254.0 mm | 254 mm | | | 250 mm |
| 11 in | 279.4 mm | 279.5 mm | | | |
| 12 in | 304.8 mm | 305 mm bare | | | 300 mm |
| 18 in | 457.2 mm | 457 mm full | 460 mm | | |
| 24 in | 609.6 mm | 609.5 mm | | | |
| 36 in | 914.4 mm | 914.5 mm | | Panel Stock Sizes | |
| 48 in (4 ft) | 1219.2 mm | 1220 mm or 1.22 m | | 1220 mm or 1.22 m width | |
| 96 in (8 ft) | 2438.4 mm | 2440 mm or 2.44 m | | 2440 mm or 2.44 m width | |

Figure 3-12. However, a rule with the numbered lines marked in millimetres, such as 10, 20, 30, 40, is easier to use. Remember that in the metric system, accurate measurements are always given in centimetres, millimetres, or metres. The decimetre is seldom used.

## BUILDING MATERIALS

Lumber sizes are usually given in inches for thickness and width, and length is given in feet. House plans show over-all sizes and room sizes in feet; detail sizes are often in inches. In the British metric system, only two dimensions are used for all measurement, namely, the metre for large measurements and the millimetre for small measurements. Therefore thickness and width of lumber are shown in millimetres and length in metres. For architectural plans, the millimetre is the standard unit of measurement. Many homes and buildings are currently designed on a modular size of 300 millimetres. This is very close to the present customary dimension of 12 inches. The metre is used as the unit of measure for plot plans.

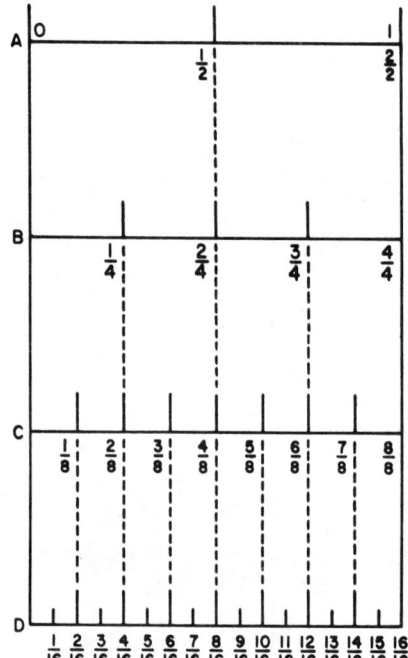

**3-10.** How an inch is divided.

**3-11a.** A *metre* stick.

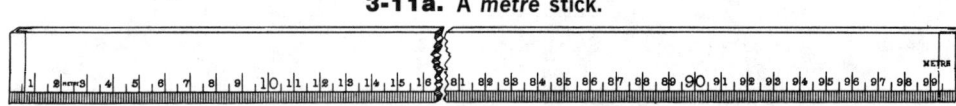

**3-11b.** A 300-millimetre rule.

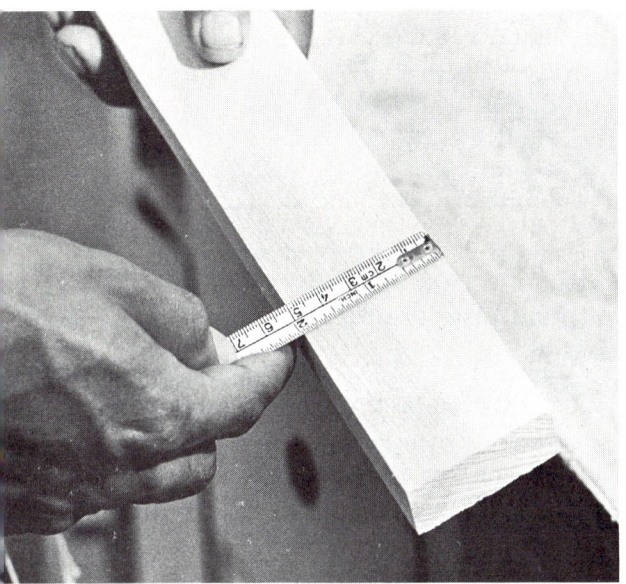

**3-12a.** Using a steel tape that measures in inches and millimetres.

**English**

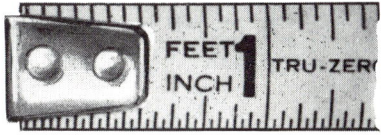

**Metric Centimetre**

**Metric Millimetre**

**Metric (Centimetre)—English**

**3-12b.** Four forms of rule graduations available on steel tapes.

## CAN YOU ANSWER THESE QUESTIONS ON MEASUREMENT?

1. How long is a cubit?
2. How did Noah's ark compare in size with Columbus's three ships?
3. Describe the two major systems of measurement.
4. What are the three major measurements used in the metric system and how do they compare to the customary units?
5. How does a millimetre compare to $\frac{1}{16}$ inch? Is it larger or smaller?
6. What other industrial countries use the customary system of measurement?
7. In the term "SI metric," what does "SI" stand for?
8. Is the metre a common metric unit? The millimetre? The decimetre?

# READING THE DRAWING OR SKETCH

**A drawing** or sketch is the map you follow in making the project. It will tell you the exact size of the article, the number and sizes of the pieces, the design of each part, the way in which the project fits together, and every other detail of construction and finish. Without it you would be lost, especially if you are just beginning to learn woodworking.

It is extremely important to understand your drawing *before beginning to build the project.* In industry, everything to be produced is first drawn in the drafting room. Figure 4-1. You should study the drawing carefully to keep from making mistakes.

There are many kinds of drawings. Pictorial and working (view) drawings are two types which are commonly used in woodworking.

## PICTORIAL DRAWINGS

A pictorial, or picture drawing is the kind you know best. It shows the project the way it looks in use. Figure 4-2. The most common kinds of pictorial drawings are isometric (equal angle), cabinet, and perspective. Figures 4-3 and 4-4. All three are one-view drawings (the total object is shown in one view). An *isometric* drawing has parallel lines drawn at angles of 120 degrees to each other. A *cabinet* drawing

**4-1.** You must be able to read drawings and prints even though you may not as yet have learned how to do drafting.

DADO JOINT
DOWEL JOINT
CROSS PIECE
3/8" DIA. HOLES
1 1/8" DEEP
SECTION THRU
LEG
1/2" R.
15 1/4
9 PIECES 3/4" x 1 3/4" x 34"
1/4" SPACE BETWEEN EACH
34"
17 3/4"
16"
2" No. 10 F.H.
SCREWS
15 1/2"
CROSS PIECE 3/4" x 2" x 24 1/2"
RAIL
3/4" x 2" x 15 1/2"
19 1/2"
25 1/2"

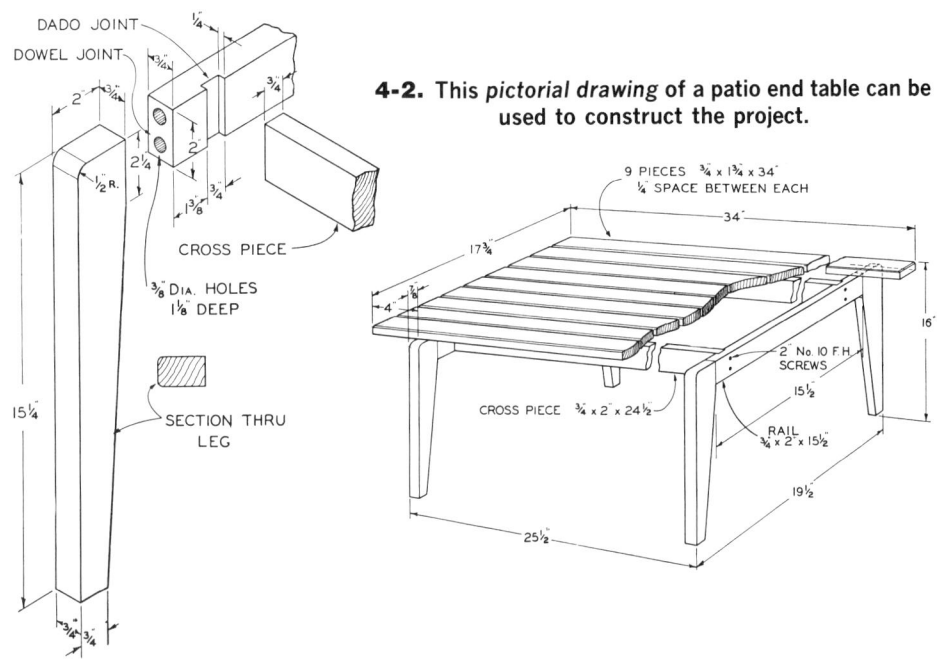

**4-2.** This *pictorial drawing* of a patio end table can be used to construct the project.

**4-3.** An *isometric* drawing of a make-up shelf.

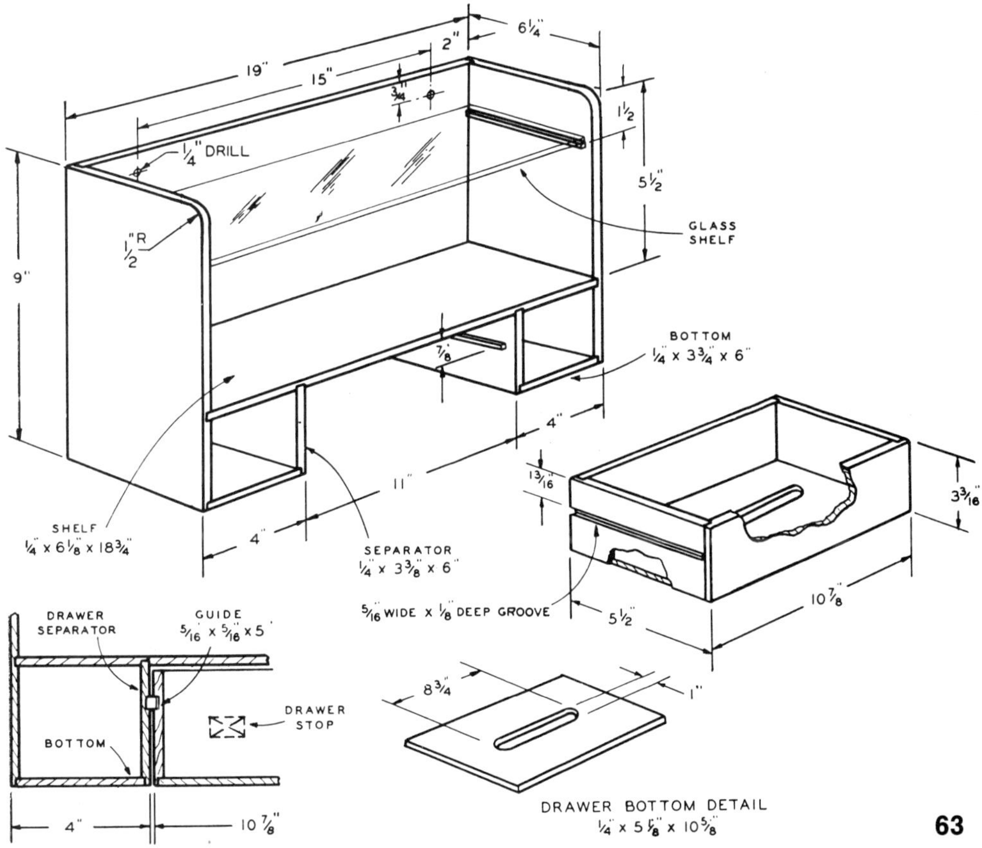

19"
15"
2"
6 1/4"
1/4" DRILL
1 1/2
5 1/2"
GLASS
SHELF
1/2"R
9"
BOTTOM
1/4" x 3 3/4" x 6"
4"
11"
4"
13/16
3 3/16"
SHELF
1/4" x 6 1/8" x 18 3/4"
SEPARATOR
1/4" x 3 3/8" x 6"
5/16" WIDE x 1/8" DEEP GROOVE
5 1/2"
10 7/8"
DRAWER
SEPARATOR
GUIDE
5/16" x 5/16" x 5"
DRAWER
STOP
BOTTOM
4"
10 7/8"
8 3/4"
1"
DRAWER BOTTOM DETAIL
1/4" x 5 5/8" x 10 5/8"

has the front of the object drawn just like the front of a three-view drawing but with the sides drawn at an angle of 30 to 45 degrees. The *perspective* drawing looks like a photo with either one or two vanishing points. The perspective with one vanishing point looks a great deal like a

**4-4.** A *cabinet* drawing of a small project.

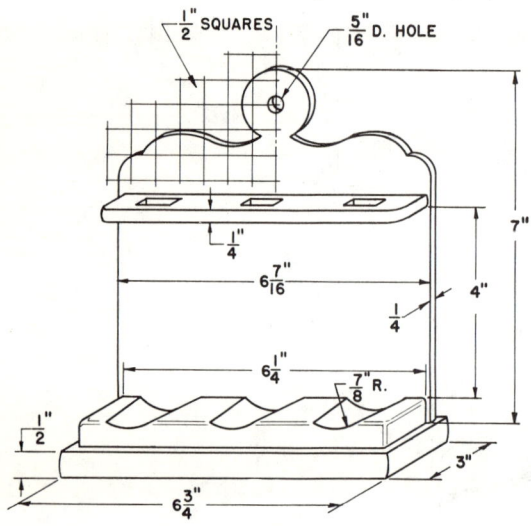

cabinet drawing, and the perspective with two vanishing points looks a great deal like an isometric drawing.

## WORKING, OR VIEW, DRAWINGS

Working drawings, which are used for construction, have one, two, three, or more *views* showing the article many different ways. Most projects require two or three views. In the three-view drawing, the lower left-hand view shows the way the project looks from the *front*, the view above that shows how the project looks from the *top*, and the view to the right is the *right side or end view* of the project. Figure 4-5. These views give the correct dimensions of each piece. The dimensions are placed on the views to be read from the bottom or right side. If only two views are included, either the front and top or front and side views are shown. Figure 4-6.

## VARIATIONS

Drawings for woodwork do not follow the rigid rules you may have learned for

**4-5.** A typical *three-view* drawing of a box. This is the type of drawing most commonly used for construction.

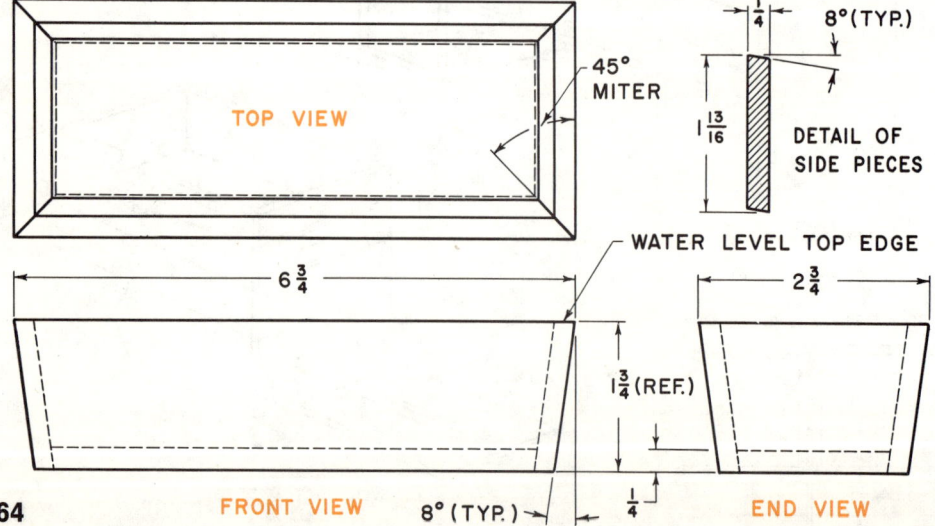

machine drawings. Figure 4-7. A drawing for a project will often be partly a view drawing and partly a pictorial drawing. Sometimes when view drawings are used, the views are not placed correctly; that is, the right side or end view isn't always to the right of the front view. You will also find that many isometric or perspective drawings are made as exploded (taken apart) drawings. Figure 4-8. The exploded view clearly shows the dimension of each part and how the parts go together.

## MEANING OF LINES

In a drawing or sketch, different kinds of lines are used, each showing a certain thing. A wrong line on a drawing is a much worse mistake than a wrong direc-

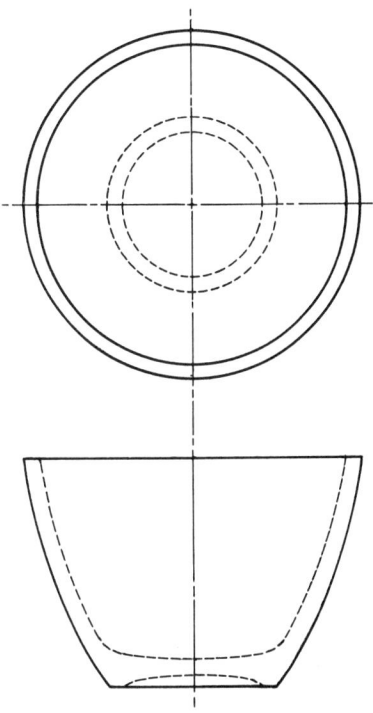

**4-6.** Many projects such as this turned bowl require only two views.

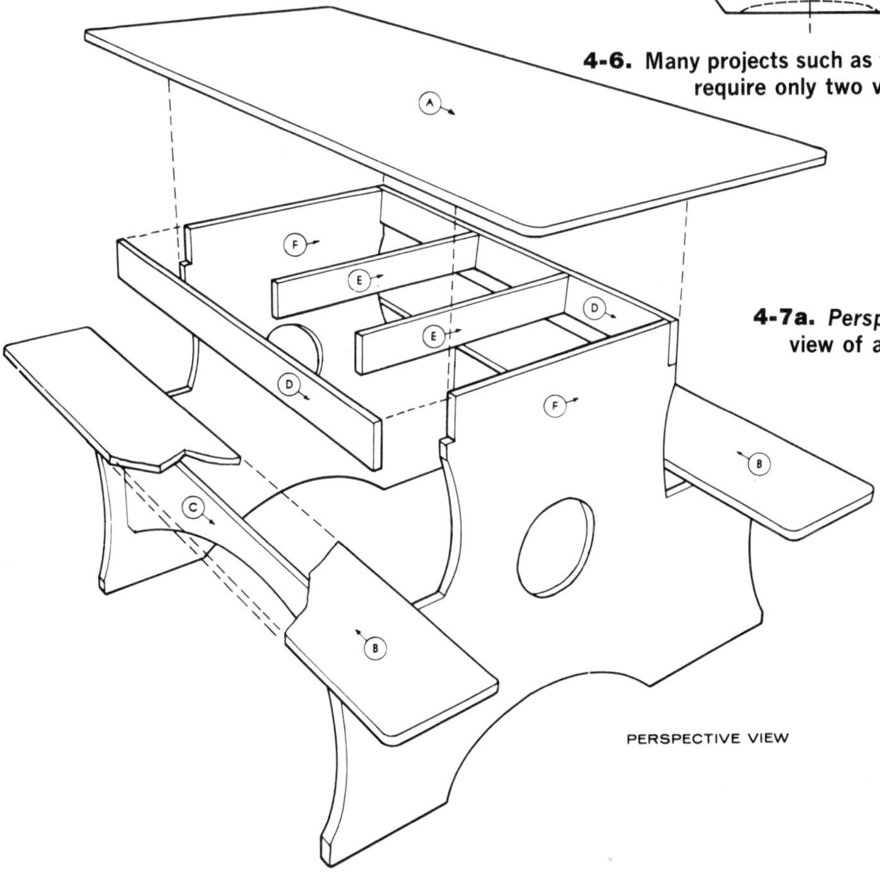

**4-7a.** *Perspective exploded view of a patio table.*

PERSPECTIVE VIEW

**65**

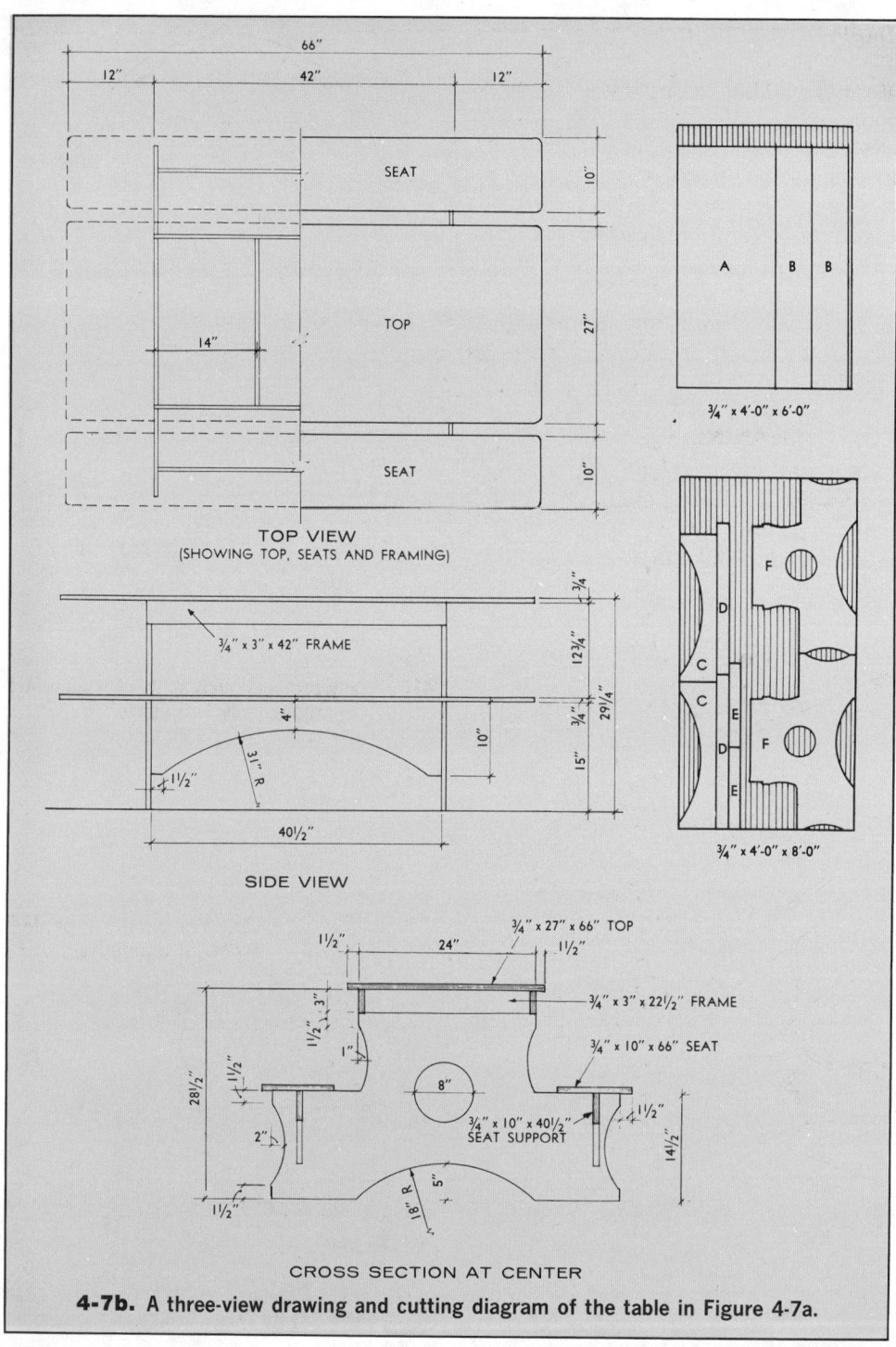

**4-7b.** A three-view drawing and cutting diagram of the table in Figure 4-7a.

tion for construction; however, any mistake on the drawing can give you a great deal of trouble in construction. Figure 4-9 shows the drawing of a table. These lines indicate the following:

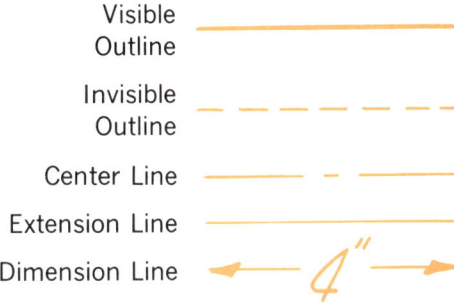

Visible Outline

Invisible Outline

Center Line

Extension Line

Dimension Line

*Visible outline:* The major outline of the article.

*Invisible outline:* Indicates the outline that cannot be seen from the surface.

*Center line:* Shows the center or divides the drawing into equal, or symmetrical, parts.

*Extension line:* Extends out from the outline; provides two lines between which measurements or dimensions can be shown.

*Dimension line:* Usually has arrowheads at each end and is broken in the center. These lines run between the extension lines and give the measurements or dimensions.

## SCALE OF THE DRAWING

When large projects must be drawn, it is necessary to reduce the size of the drawing so that all of it can be put on one page. In this case, the drawing is made to scale. Frequently, for example, a customary drawing is made half size

**4-8.** A fireplace log holder which shows how a combination of drawings can be used. The top drawing is an *exploded isometric.* The lower two are *view* drawings.

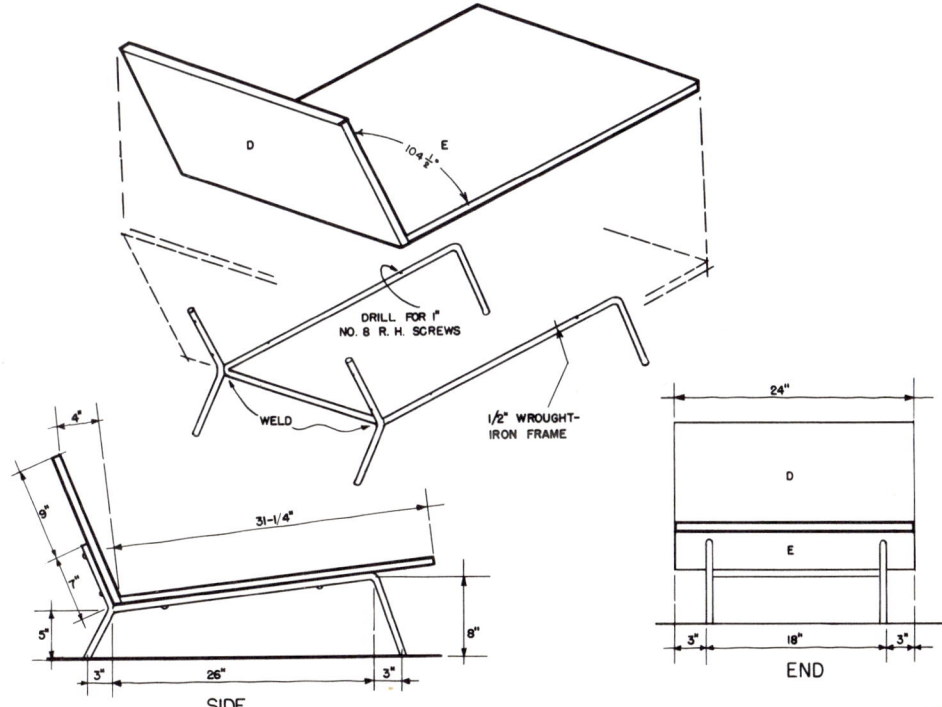

(6″ = 1′) and the scale is so stated. If even larger projects must be drawn, a scale such as ¼ inch to the foot (¼″ = 1′0″) may be followed, as in house plans.

On metric drawings, the common scales for reducing the size are 1:2 (half size), 1:5 (one-fifth size), 1:10 (one-tenth size), and 1:20 (one-twentieth size). In building drawings, a scale of 1:50 or 1:100 is often used. Note that all metric measurement is based on units

**4-9.** Two-view metric drawing of a table. Note the different lines in this drawing and then refer to the meaning of these lines as described on page 67.

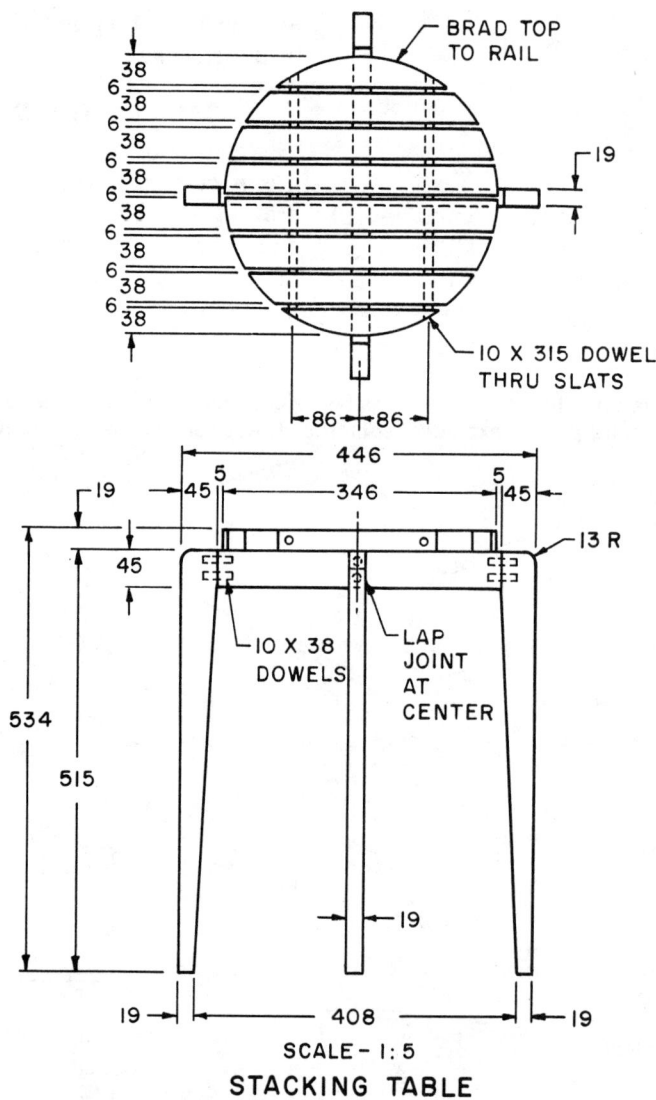

BRAD TOP TO RAIL

10 X 315 DOWELS THRU SLATS

10 X 38 DOWELS

LAP JOINT AT CENTER

13 R

SCALE - 1:5

STACKING TABLE

ALL DIMENSIONS IN mm

68

of 10 and that the scales must therefore be in the same proportions.

## READING DRAWINGS

In reading a drawing, it is important to read all dimensions. When you make out the bill of materials, you must be sure to read these dimensions correctly. Then, after the materials are purchased and you are ready to begin, equal care must be taken in transferring these measurements to the pieces of wood. Even if the drawing is made full size, never attempt to measure the drawing itself. Always use the dimensions stated, since the paper on which the drawing is printed may have shrunk. More mistakes are made through carelessness in reading the drawings and in transferring these measurements to the wood than in any other point in construction.

There are several ways to make drawings so they can be read either in metric or customary measurement:

● *Dual dimensioning.* In this method the customary measurement is placed first, with the metric measurement in parentheses directly behind or below it. Figure 4-10. For example, if the dimension is two inches long, it would read 2

**4-10.** This dual-dimensioned drawing makes it possible to build the product in either customary or metric measurement.

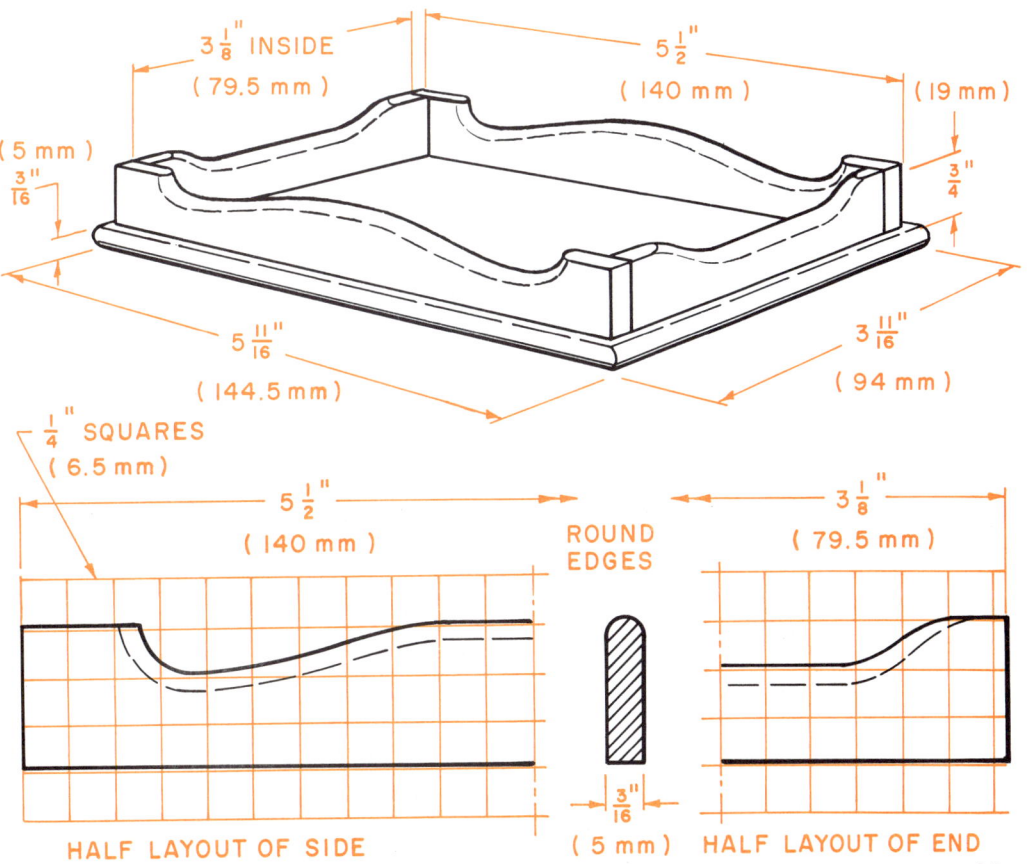

inches (51 mm). Since both dimensions must be shown for each measurement, the drawing looks more complicated than it actually is. This is one of the main disadvantages.

• *Metric dimensioning with customary read-out chart.* Here all dimensions on the drawing are shown in metric, and a small chart is added to each drawing giving the equivalent sizes in the customary measurement. Figure 4-11. For example, if the metric size is 12.7 mm, the chart would show that this equals ½ inch.

• *Dimensioning with identification letters.* All dimensions are shown by letters— A, B, C, D, etc.—along with a chart which shows both the metric and customary equivalents of these letters. For example, G would be shown as 2 inches in the customary and 51 mm in the metric column. Figure 4-12.

None of these methods, however, solves the basic problem of designing in metrics. Since the change from customary to metric is only a mathematical change, all metric sizes are very odd, such as 25.4 mm and 12.7 mm. If the original dimension is 1 inch, then the exact metric equivalent is 25.4 mm, or about 25.5 mm. If the drawing is to be truly metric, the product *should be designed in metric,* using the more common full numbers like 5, 10, 15, 20, and 25 mm.

**70**   **4-11a.** This bench can be made using the drawing in 4-11b.

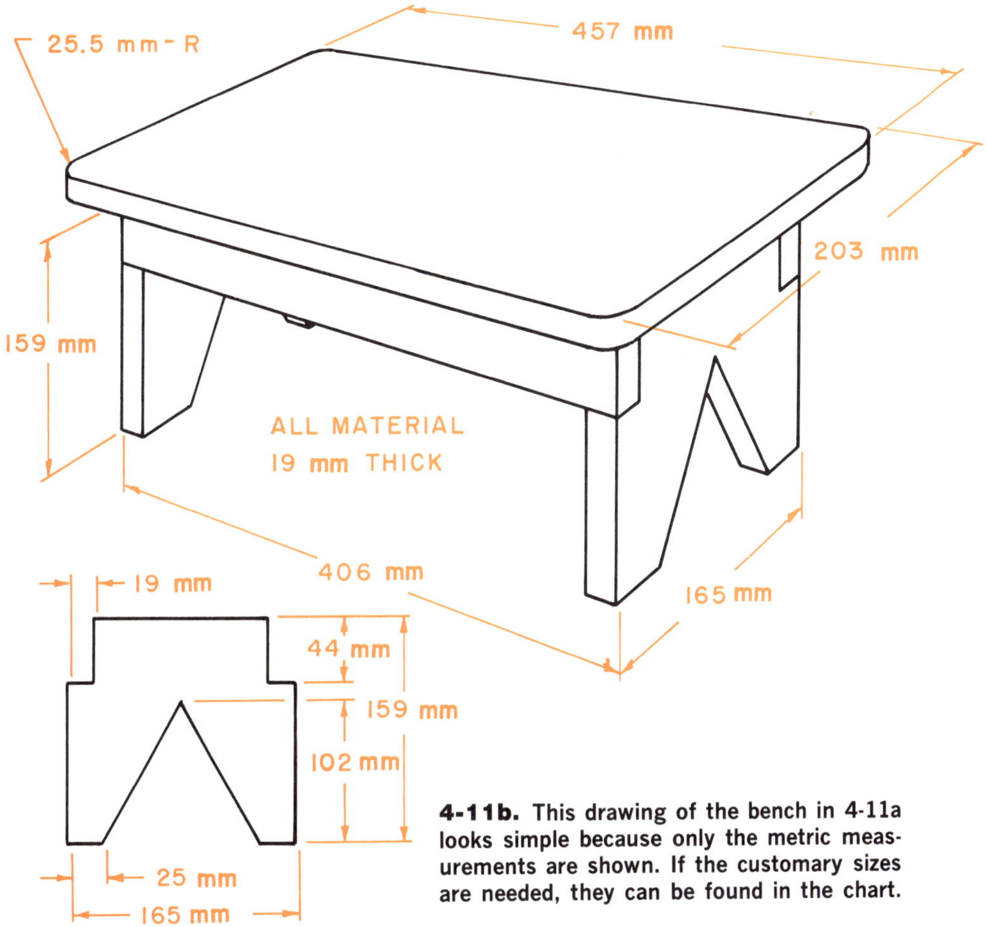

25.5 mm - R

457 mm

203 mm

159 mm

ALL MATERIAL
19 mm THICK

165 mm

19 mm

406 mm

44 mm

159 mm

102 mm

25 mm

165 mm

**4-11b.** This drawing of the bench in 4-11a looks simple because only the metric measurements are shown. If the customary sizes are needed, they can be found in the chart.

| Metric in mm | Customary in inches | Metric in mm | Customary in inches |
|---|---|---|---|
| 19 | 3/4 | 159 | 6¼ |
| 25 | 15/16 | 165 | 6½ |
| 25.5 | 1 | 203 | 8 |
| 44 | 1¾ | 406 | 16 |
| 102 | 4 | 457 | 18 |

**4-12a.** A planter that can be made using the metric or customary dimensions provided in 4-12b.

71

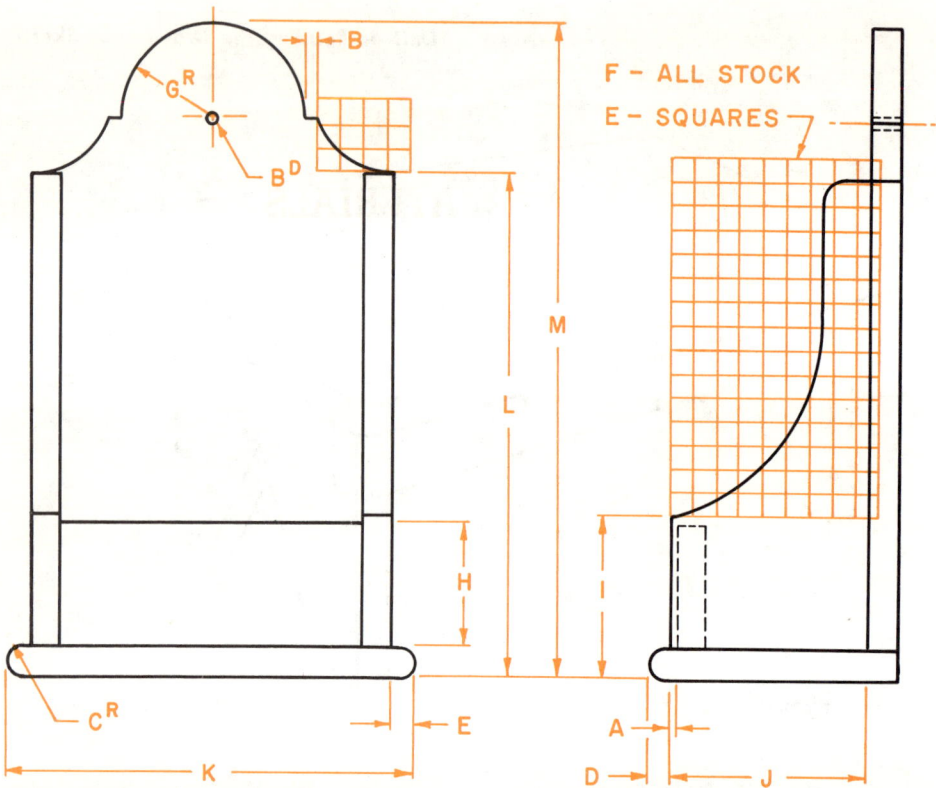

F — ALL STOCK

E — SQUARES

**4-12b.** Only capital letters are used to indicate dimensions on this drawing of the planter in 4-12a. The customary or metric sizes are found on the chart.

| Letter | Customary in inches | Metric in mm |
|--------|---------------------|--------------|
| A | $\frac{1}{8}$ | 3 |
| B | $\frac{1}{4}$ | 6.5 |
| C | $\frac{5}{16}$ | 8 |
| D | $\frac{3}{8}$ | 9.5 |
| E | $\frac{1}{2}$ | 12.5 |
| F | $\frac{5}{8}$ | 16 |
| G | 2 | 51 |
| H | $2\frac{5}{8}$ | 68 |
| I | $2\frac{3}{4}$ | 70 |
| J | $4\frac{1}{4}$ | 108 |
| K | $8\frac{7}{8}$ | 225 |
| L | $10\frac{1}{2}$ | 267 |
| M | $13\frac{5}{8}$ | 346 |

## CAN YOU ANSWER THESE QUESTIONS ON READING THE DRAWING OR SKETCH?

1. Why must you be able to understand your drawing?
2. Name the kind of drawing that is similar to a photograph.
3. Does a working drawing always have three views?
4. How are invisible parts shown on a drawing?
5. If the drawing is full size, can you trace it to make the layout?
6. Describe the three common methods of dimensioning for drawings that must be read in metric or customary measurements.

## Section
## I
## UNIT 5.

# MATERIALS

**You are** now ready to make a list of the materials you will need for your project. Figure 5-1. This list includes exactly what and how much is needed of lumber, hardware, finishing supplies, and similar items.

## FINISHED BILL OF MATERIALS

Use a form similar to the one in Figure 5-2. From information on the working drawing, write out a complete description of each different item. For each piece of lumber, include the number needed, the size, a description, and the kind of wood.

**5-1.** Regardless of the size of your first project, you will need to plan the list of materials very carefully.

Information about the size of each piece is given with thickness, width, and length indicated in that order. Thickness and width are always shown in inches (or mm), and length is indicated in inches or feet (mm or m in metric). For small pieces, the length is shown in inches (or mm). In listing these items, the width is always measured *across* the grain and the length *with* the grain. Therefore you may have some pieces that are wider than they are long. If you need

**5-2.** This bill of materials and the stock-cutting list are for a beverage cart.

| | FINISHED BILL OF MATERIALS | | | | |
|---|---|---|---|---|---|
| No. of Pieces | Size | | | Description | Kind of Wood |
| | T | W | L | | |
| 2 | $1\frac{5}{8}$ | $3\frac{5}{8}$ | 32 | Frame Sides | Pine |
| 2 | $1\frac{5}{8}$ | $3\frac{5}{8}$ | $18\frac{1}{4}$ | Frame Ends | Pine |
| 2 | $\frac{3}{4}$ | 6 | 24 | Front Legs | Pine |
| 2 | $\frac{3}{4}$ | 3 | 24 | Back Legs | Pine |
| 2 | $\frac{3}{4}$ | 6 | 36 | Exterior Sides | Pine |
| 2 | $\frac{3}{4}$ | 6 | 24 | Exterior Ends | Pine |
| 2 | $\frac{3}{4}$ | 2 | 17 | Handles | Pine |
| 1 | $\frac{3}{4}$ | $22\frac{1}{2}$ | $34\frac{1}{2}$ | Top | Fir Plywood |
| 4 | $\frac{3}{4}$ | 8 | 8 | Wheels | Fir Plywood |
| | (Two thicknesses must be nailed together for wheels) | | | | |
| 1 | $1\frac{1}{4}$ dia. | | $30\frac{1}{2}$ | Axle | Birch dowel |
| 2 | $\frac{1}{4}$ dia. | | $3\frac{1}{4}$ | Axle Pin | Birch dowel |

| STOCK-CUTTING LIST | | | | | | | |
|---|---|---|---|---|---|---|---|
| No. of Pieces | Size | | | Description | Bd. Ft. or Sq. Ft. | Cost per Bd. Ft. or Sq. Ft. | Total Cost |
| | T | W | L | | | | |
| 2 | $1\frac{3}{4}$ | $3\frac{3}{4}$ | $32\frac{1}{2}$ | Frame Sides | | | |
| 2 | $1\frac{3}{4}$ | $3\frac{3}{4}$ | $18\frac{3}{4}$ | Frame Ends | 6* | | |
| 2 | $\frac{7}{8}$ | $6\frac{1}{4}$ | $24\frac{1}{2}$ | Front Legs | | | |
| 2 | $\frac{7}{8}$ | $3\frac{1}{4}$ | $24\frac{1}{2}$ | Back Legs | | | |
| 2 | $\frac{7}{8}$ | $6\frac{1}{4}$ | $36\frac{1}{2}$ | Exterior Sides | $9\frac{1}{4}$* | | |
| 2 | $\frac{7}{8}$ | $6\frac{1}{4}$ | $24\frac{1}{2}$ | Exterior Ends | | | |
| 2 | $\frac{7}{8}$ | $2\frac{1}{4}$ | $17\frac{1}{2}$ | Handles | | | |
| 1 | $\frac{3}{4}$ | $22\frac{3}{4}$ | 35 | Top | | | |
| 4 | $\frac{3}{4}$ | $8\frac{1}{4}$ | $8\frac{1}{4}$ | Wheels | $7\frac{1}{2}$* | | |
| 1 | $1\frac{1}{4}$ dia. | | 31 | Axle | | | |
| 2 | $\frac{1}{4}$ dia. | | $3\frac{1}{2}$ | Axle Pins | | | |

Other items: nails, paint.
* Approximately.

different kinds of wood, organize the list with pieces to be made of one kind of wood listed together. In some cases, the dimensions given on the drawing will not include enough material for the joints, so you must add the length as needed.

## MAKING A STOCK-CUTTING LIST

The finished bill of materials must now be changed into what may be called a stock-cutting list. Figure 5-2. In this list you must add to the thickness, width, and length of the stock to allow for cutting, planing, chiseling, and other operations. Usually $\frac{1}{16}$ to $\frac{1}{8}$ inch (1.5 to 3 mm) is added to the thickness, $\frac{1}{4}$ inch (6.5 mm) to the width, and about $\frac{1}{2}$ inch (12.5 mm) to the length.

## DETERMINING BOARD FEET OF LUMBER

After you have made a stock-cutting list, figure the number of board feet in each piece or group of identical pieces.

In the customary system of measurement, a board foot of lumber is a piece 1 inch thick, 12 inches wide, and 12 inches long. Figure 5-3. Stock less than 1 inch thick is figured as 1 inch. Stock more than 1 inch is figured by actual measurement. For example, a piece of stock $\frac{1}{4}$ inch x 6 inches x 4 feet would contain 2 board feet of lumber.

The formula used to find board feet is:

$$Bd.\ Ft. = \frac{T \times W \times L(\text{all in inches})}{144}$$

Board feet equals thickness in inches times width in inches times length in inches divided by 144.

Another formula that can be used is:

$$Bd.\ Ft. = \frac{T(\text{inches}) \times W(\text{inches}) \times L(\text{feet})}{12}$$

In countries using the metric system, board lumber is figured and sold per *square metre* (about 11 square feet) face measure at specific thicknesses. For example, there would be one price for 12 mm thickness and another for 19 mm. Lumber is sold in bulk lots by the *cubic metre*. This is a very large unit in contrast to a board foot, which is only 0.00236 cubic metres. Strips are sold per *lineal metre*.

## FIGURING THE LUMBER ORDER

After making out the stock-cutting list and figuring the board feet you need, it is a good idea to decide on the number of pieces of standard size lumber required. Group together all of the pieces made from the same thickness of lumber. Then make an imaginary layout of these pieces on larger standard pieces of stock, as in Figure 5-4.

Softwood lumber in the customary system comes in standard widths from

**5-3.** Note the terms included in these drawings. Each piece is one board foot of lumber. The length of the board is always given *with* the grain, and the width of the board is given *across* the grain. The *arrises* are the sharp edges where two surfaces meet.

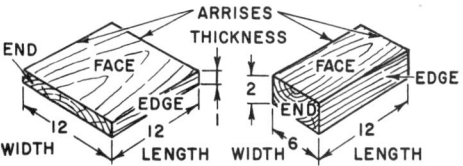

**5-4.** The cutting diagram for the wood bin shows how you can use a minimum of materials by making an efficient layout.

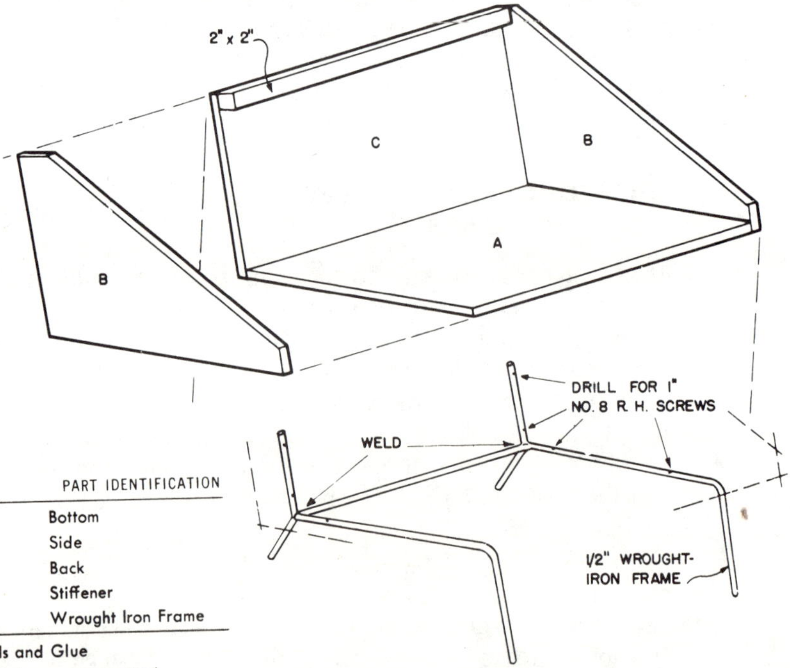

2" x 2"

C

B

A

B

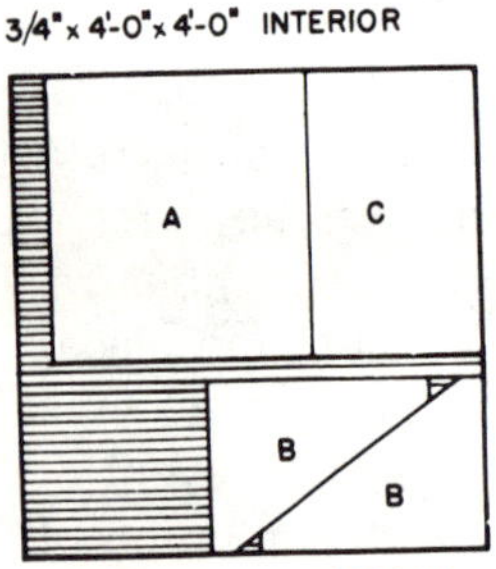

3/4" x 4'-0" x 4'-0" INTERIOR

A

C

B

B

CUTTING DIAGRAM

DRILL FOR 1"
NO. 8 R. H. SCREWS

WELD

1/2" WROUGHT-
IRON FRAME

| NO. REQ'D | SIZE | PART IDENTIFICATION |
|---|---|---|
| 1 | 26¼"x28½" | Bottom |
| 2 | 18"x27" | Side |
| 1 | 18"x28½" | Back |
| 2½ Lin. Ft. | 2"x2" | Stiffener |
| 1 Only | ½" Diameter | Wrought Iron Frame |

Miscellaneous—6d Finish Nails and Glue
1" No. 8 R. H. Screws as required

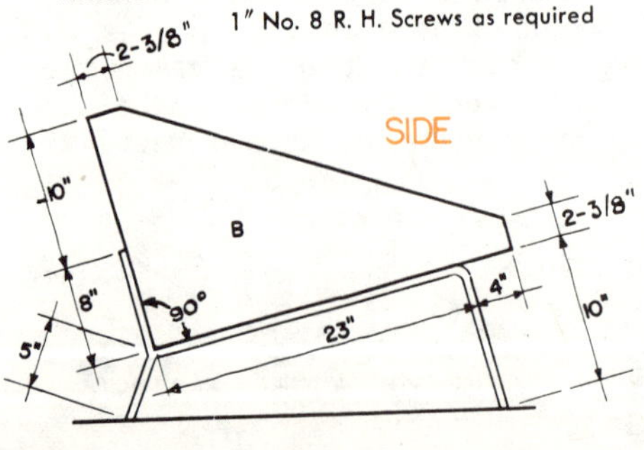

2-3/8"

10"

B

2-3/8"

8"

90°

4"

5"

23"

10"

SIDE

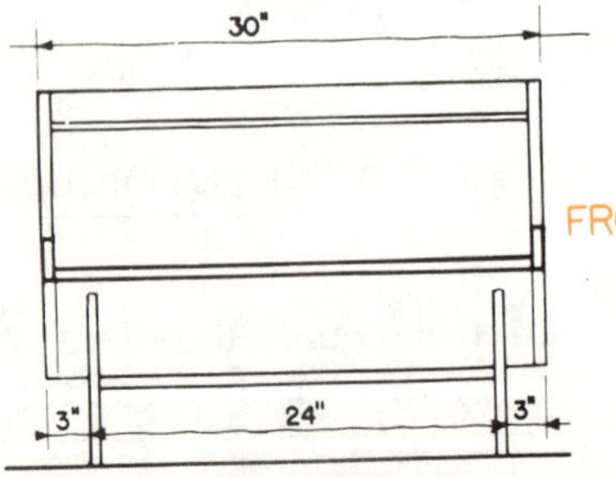

30"

FRONT

3"

24"

3"

2 to 12 inches, increasing by 2-inch intervals, and in standard lengths from 6 to 20 feet, increasing at intervals of 2 feet. The basic metric sizes of lumber are very similar, as shown in Figure 5-5. Hardwood lumber comes in standard thicknesses, but because of its high cost, it is cut in whatever widths and lengths are most economical and convenient. If you are selecting lumber from a rack, use short pieces first and cut the lumber as economically as possible. Never waste lumber.

Once you know the number of pieces of standard size lumber needed, you can make a lumber order that could be used to obtain the material from a lumber yard. In addition, you will need a list of other supplies. Figure 5-6.

## DETERMINING COST OF LUMBER

When you buy lumber, the price is quoted as so much per board foot, per hundred board feet, or per thousand board feet (M). Figure 5-7. To find the cost of each item on the rough bill of materials, multiply the number of board feet in each piece or group of identical pieces by the cost per board foot. When the cost of hardware items and finishing materials is listed, all items can be added up to find the total cost of materials. *Plywood, particle board,* and *hardboard* are sold as so much per square foot and molding and special pieces as so much per linear foot. Prices vary according to quality.

**5-5.** Basic British metric sizes of softwood. The common sizes used in schools are from 16 to 75 mm (⅝ to 3 inches) in thickness and 75 to 225 mm (3 to 9 inches) in width. Lengths begin at 1.8 m (6 feet) to 6.3 m (20 feet), increasing by 300 mm or 0.3 m (1 foot).

| Thickness in mm | Width in mm | | | | | | | | |
|---|---|---|---|---|---|---|---|---|---|
| | 75 | 100 | 125 | 150 | 175 | 200 | 225 | 250 | 300 |
| 16 | x | x | x | x | | | | | |
| 19 | x | x | x | x | | | | | |
| 22 | x | x | x | x | | | | | |
| 25 | x | x | x | x | x | x | x | x | x |
| 32 | x | x | x | x | x | x | x | x | x |
| 36 | x | x | x | x | | | | | |
| 38 | x | x | x | x | x | x | x | | |
| 40 | x | x | x | x | x | x | x | | |
| 44 | x | x | x | x | x | x | x | x | x |
| 50 | x | x | x | x | x | x | x | x | x |
| 63 | | x | x | x | x | x | | | |
| 75 | | x | x | x | x | x | x | x | x |
| 100 | | x | | | x | | | x | x |
| 150 | | | | x | | x | | | x |
| 200 | | | | | | x | | | |
| 250 | | | | | | | | x | |
| 300 | | | | | | | | | x |

## LUMBER ORDER

Instead of figuring bd. ft. and cost for each individual item in the materials bill, determine the size of boards from which the *Cutout Size* pieces can be cut. Figure bd. ft. and cost of these boards.

| No. of Pieces | T | W | L | Kind of Wood | No. of Bd. ft. | Cost Per Bd. ft. | Total Cost | Instr's O.K. |
|---|---|---|---|---|---|---|---|---|
| | | | | | | | | |
| | | | | | | | | |
| | | | | | | | | |
| | | | | | | | | |
| | | | | | | | | |
| | | | | | | | | |
| | | | | | | | | |
| | | | | | | | | |
| | | | | | | | | |

Total Cost _____

**5-6.** You can make up blank forms like these when you need to make a materials bill or to order lumber and other supplies. (Do not write in this book.)

## OTHER SUPPLY COSTS

(Metal, Plastic, Hardware, Finishing Materials, etc.)

| Item | Quan. | Size | Unit Cost | Total Cost | Instr's O.K. |
|---|---|---|---|---|---|
| | | | | | |
| | | | | | |
| | | | | | |
| | | | | | |
| | | | | | |
| | | | | | |
| | | | | | |
| | | | | | |

**COST SUMMARY**

Lumber Cost _____

Supply Cost _____

Total Cost _____

Less Allow. _____

Amount Due _____

Date Paid _____

## LUMBER DEFECTS

In selecting lumber, check for these common defects:

● A *knot* is the base of a branch that forms a mass of woody fiber running at an angle to the grain.

● A *check* is a lengthwise separation of the wood, like a small crack or split. Figure 5-8. It often appears at the end of a board. *Honeycombing* is an area of checks which are not visible at the surface.

● A *split* is a lengthwise break or a big crack in the board.

● *Decay* is rotting of wood.

● A *stain* is a discoloration of the wood surface.

Sometimes defects such as knots add interest. For example, knotty pine is used for interior paneling.

## POINTS TO CONSIDER WHEN BUYING WOOD PRODUCTS

When selecting wood for a project, you should know something about the different kinds of wood available.

### Lumber

Remember the following when you are ready to select lumber:

● *Rough or dressed.* You can purchase lumber rough (specified "Rough") or dressed (specified S2S or S4S, surfaced on two sides or surfaced on four sides). Rough lumber comes just as it was cut at the sawmill. Dressed (surfaced) lumber has been put through a planer. Of course, dressed lumber costs a little more than rough lumber, but it is worth the extra cost if you don't have a planer in the shop. When you buy dressed lumber, the actual dimensions will be less than the size indicated. For example, 1-inch hardwood will be about $\frac{13}{16}$ inch thick, and standard construction dry,

**5-7.** Lumber is sold in many standard sizes.

which is 2 x 4 inches, will actually measure $1\frac{1}{2}$ x $3\frac{1}{2}$ inches. Figure 5-9.

● *Green or dry lumber.* When the tree is first cut down, the wood may contain as much as 30 to 300 percent moisture. *Softwood* lumber is cut into logs and placed in the open air to dry. Lumber made this way is called air-dried lumber (AD). If this lumber is sold with a moisture content of more than 19 percent, it is called *green* lumber. If the lumber has a moisture content of 19 percent or less, it is classified as *dry* lumber. Most *hardwoods* are dried in special drying rooms

**5-8.** A check in a piece of lumber.

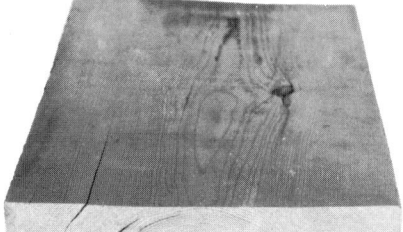

## YOUR GUIDE IN SELECTING LUMBER AND PLYWOOD

### LUMBER

| Surface | Grade | | Method of Drying | Method of Cutting |
|---|---|---|---|---|
| | Softwood | Hardwood | | |
| Rgh. or Rough—as it comes from the saw mill.<br><br>S2S—surfaced on two sides.<br><br>S4S—surfaced all four sides. | 1. Yard Lumber<br>*Select*—Good appearance and finishing quality.<br>Grade A—Clear.<br>Grade B—High Quality.<br>Grade C—For best paint finishes.<br>Grade D—Lowest select. | FAS—Firsts and seconds. Highest Grade.<br><br>No. 1 Common and Select. Some Defects.<br><br>No. 2 Common. For small cuttings. | AD—Air dried.<br><br>KD—Kiln dried. | Plain Sawed or Flat Grained<br>Quarter Sawed or Edge Grained |

| | Standard Sizes of Softwood | | | Standard Thickness of Hardwoods | |
|---|---|---|---|---|---|
| *Common*—General utility. Not of finishing quality.<br>Construction or No. 1—Best Grade.<br>Standard or No. 2—Good Grade.<br>Utility or No. 3—Fair Grade.<br>Economy or No. 4—Poor.<br>No. 5—Lowest. | Nominal or Stock Size | Actual Size | | Rough | S2S |
| | | Green | Dry | | |
| 2. Shop Lumber—For manufacturing purposes. Equal to Grade B Select or better of Yard Lumber.<br>No. 1—Average 8″ wide.<br>No. 2—Average 7″ wide.<br><br>3. Structural Lumber. | 1″ | $25/32$″ | $3/4$″ | $3/8$″ | $3/16$″ |
| | 2″ | $1 9/16$″ | $1\frac{1}{2}$″ | $1/2$″ | $5/16$″ |
| | 3″ | $2 9/16$″ | $2\frac{1}{2}$″ | $5/8$″ | $7/16$″ |
| | 4″ | $3 9/16$″ | $3\frac{1}{2}$″ | $3/4$″ | $9/16$″ |
| | 5″ | $4 5/8$″ | $4\frac{1}{2}$″ | 1″ | $13/16$″ |
| | 6″ | $5 5/8$″ | $5\frac{1}{2}$″ | $1\frac{1}{4}$″ | $1 1/16$″ |
| | 7″ | $6 5/8$″ | $6\frac{1}{2}$″ | | |
| | 8″ | $7\frac{1}{2}$″ | $7\frac{1}{4}$″ | | |
| | 9″ | $8\frac{1}{2}$″ | $8\frac{1}{4}$″ | | |
| | 10″ | $9\frac{1}{2}$″ | $9\frac{1}{4}$″ | | |

### PLYWOODS

| Hardwoods | | Construction and Industrial (Softwoods) | |
|---|---|---|---|
| Grade | Uses | Grade | Uses |
| Premium Grade | Best quality for very high-grade natural finish. Too expensive except for best cabinet work or paneling. | A-A | Best grade for all uses where both sides will show. Exterior or interior. |
| Good Grade (1) | For good natural finish. Excellent for cabinets, built-ins, paneling and furniture. | A-B | An alternate for A-A grade for high-quality uses where only one side will show. Exterior or interior. The back side is less important. |
| Sound Grade (2) | For simple natural finishes and high-grade painted surfaces. | A-D | A good all-purpose "good-one-side" panel for lesser quality interior work. |
| Utility Grade (3) | Not used for project work. | | |
| Reject Grade (4) | Not used for project work. | B-D | Utility grade. Used for backing, cabinet sides, etc. |

| | |
|---|---|
| Widths from 24″ to 48″ in 6″ multiples.<br>Lengths from 36″ to 96″.<br>Veneer-core panels in plies of 3, 5, 7 and 9 are available as follows:<br> 3 ply—$1/8$″, $3/16$″, $1/4$″; 5 ply—$5/16$″, $3/8$″, $1/2$″;<br> 5 and 7 ply—$5/8$″; 7 and 9 ply—$3/4$″.<br>There are three types: Type I is fully waterproof, Type II is water resistant, and Type III is dry bond. | Many other grades for special uses in home construction are available in thicknesses of $1/2$″, $3/8$″, $5/8$″, and $3/4$″; both exterior and interior; 1″ is also available in exterior grades. Common widths 3′4″, or 4′; common length is 8′. Be sure to specify exterior grade for outside work (including boats) and interior grade for interior construction. |

**5-9.** Lumber and plywood chart.

called kilns (often pronounced "kills"). Hardwood lumber used for furniture and interiors is *kiln dried* (KD) to about 6 to 12 percent moisture. This is the only kind to buy for furniture and other fine projects.

● *Grade of lumber—softwoods.*

It is important to specify the grade of lumber you want. The grading of softwoods (pine, fir, redwood, etc.) is a little different from the grading of hardwood. Softwood is classified first according to use: yard lumber, factory (or shop) lumber, and structural lumber.

*Yard lumber* is cut for a wide variety of uses, is handled by all lumber yards, and is divided into two main classes: select and common.

The select grade is lumber of good appearance that will take different finishes such as stain, paint, and enamel. It is the kind that you would choose for projects. Select lumber is available in four grades as follows:

Grade A: Practically clear and suitable for natural finishes.

Grade B: High quality, generally clear, and also suitable for natural finishes.

Grade C: Quality suitable for a good paint finish.

Grade D: Lowest select grade; can be painted.

Common lumber is the type suitable for rough carpentry. It is not of finishing quality. It is graded Nos. 1, 2, 3, 4, and 5. Only Nos. 1, 2, and 3 are suitable for good, rough construction.

Factory (or shop) lumber is lumber that is to be cut up for manufacturing purposes. It is usually handled only by lumber yards that do millwork or sell to manufacturing concerns and school shops. It is the grade that you would order for projects in place of one of the select grades listed above. There are two

grades of shop lumber, Nos. 1 and 2. Both compare in quality to B select or better of yard lumber and differ only in the average width of the pieces. No. 1 averages 8 inches wide and No. 2 averages 7 inches wide.

Structural lumber grading is based upon the strength of the pieces and is not of particular concern to the average woodworker.

● *Grade of lumber—hardwoods.*

The *top grade* is indicated by FAS, meaning firsts and seconds. This is not perfect lumber, but it will produce about 90 percent clear stand cuttings. The *next grade* is called No. 1 common and select. It contains more knots and defects. The *poorest grade* is No. 2 common, which contains many defects and is suitable for small cuttings.

● *Method of cutting.* Most lumber is cut in such a way that the annular rings form an angle of less than 45 degrees with the surfaces of the piece. This is called *plain sawed* (when it is hardwood) or *flat grained* (when it is softwood).

When lumber is cut with the annular rings making an angle of more than 45 degrees with the surface of the piece, it is called *quarter sawed* or edge grained or vertical grained. Quarter-sawed lumber usually costs more. It is more expensive to cut it this way and it is considered more beautiful.

## Plywood

The use of plywood is so common that you should become acquainted with typical differences. Plywood is either veneer core or lumber core. In *veneer-core* plywood, from three to nine layers of thin veneer make up the "panel." *Lumber-core* plywood has a thick middle layer of solid wood. This is commonly chosen for fine furniture. Figure 5-10.

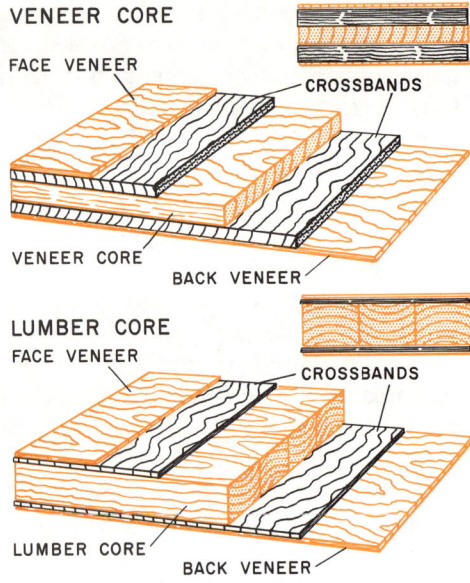

VENEER CORE

FACE VENEER

CROSSBANDS

VENEER CORE

BACK VENEER

LUMBER CORE

FACE VENEER

CROSSBANDS

LUMBER CORE

BACK VENEER

**5-10.** Here you see the difference between veneer-core plywood and lumber-core plywood. Most plywood used for interior and exterior buildings is veneer-core.

**5-11.** Plywood is an excellent material for many kinds of projects. The wide widths and smooth surfaces make rapid construction possible.

The grade of plywood depends on the quality of its two faces. The exact grading of soft and hard plywoods is shown on page 80. When you go to the lumber yard, you can usually get the grade of plywood you want by indicating "good two sides" (G2S) for the most expensive grade or "good one side" (G1S), which is only good on one side. Specify whether it is for interior or exterior use. Figure 5-11.

## Hardboard

Hardboard is a man-made wood board produced by "exploding" wood chips into wood fibers and then forming them into panels under heat and pressure. There are two types: standard, or untreated, and tempered, or treated. In the tempering, the board is dipped in drying oils and baked. On some hardboard one face is smooth and the other is rough and looks like screening. Other hardboard has two smooth surfaces. Tempered hardboard can be purchased with evenly spaced holes drilled all over the surface. Figure 5-12. This is used for hanger boards for tools, displays, and many other purposes. The standard sizes of hardboard are 4 x 6 feet ($\frac{1}{8}$ inch thick) and 2 x 12 feet ($\frac{1}{4}$ inch thick).

## Particle Board

Particle board is a type of composition board made from wood chips held together by adhesives. Small pieces of wood are bonded together under heat and pressure with an adhesive or other binder. This material is something like hardboard except that it is thicker and whole chips are used in making it. Shavings from lumber planing mills are an abundant and cheap source of chips, flakes, shavings, and splinters that go into the production of particle board. Particle board is available in common thicknesses of $\frac{3}{8}$, $\frac{1}{2}$, and $\frac{3}{4}$ inch and in sheet size of 4 x 8 feet. Both particle board and hardboard can be worked with regular woodworking tools and machines. Figure 5-13.

## CHOOSING LUMBER FOR PROJECTS

The choice of woods for projects is determined by three factors: adaptability to the project, price, and appearance (beauty).

### Elementary Projects

The wood should be easy to work with hand tools, and the grain should not become ragged when hand planed. The wood should not be expensive. Woods recommended include:

Basswood—soft and easy to work; easy to glue; sands smoothly; holds its shape well; will not twist or warp if properly seasoned. The texture is fine and even. Basswood is light in weight, and strong enough for most projects. Simple finishes are suggested. Strong stains should be avoided, as basswood is porous and does not stain evenly.

Poplar—not too difficult to handle, but harder than any of the others listed under this heading, so tools should be sharp. Poplar will take good furniture

finishes if the technique is correct. It tends to be slightly fuzzy when sanded.

Willow—the best wood for elementary work. It is easy to work, glue, and finish. If care is used in the finishing process, willow is a very handsome wood. It can be stained to resemble walnut, but is pleasing in its natural colors. There is a wide color range in willow, so pieces should be sorted for color harmony. A filler may be used for the best work, but isn't necessary as a rule.

Western soft pines—Sugar pine and Ponderosa pine do not take a finish as well as some of the other woods, but they are easy to work and are an excellent choice for many simple projects.

**5-13.** Cutting a groove in particle board, using a router.

**5-12.** Perforated hardboard. This is an excellent material for sliding doors, display boards, and other similar uses.

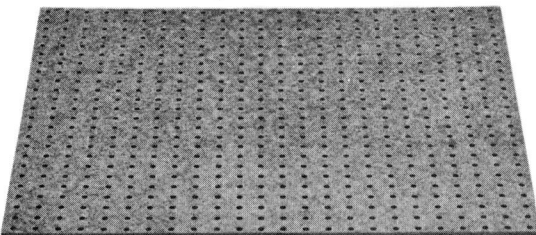

## Intermediate Projects

The wood should be relatively easy to work with hand tools and simple power tools. It should be reasonable in price. The wood should take a handsome finish. A few of the woods recommended are:

Poplar, Willow, and Western soft pines—described above.

Northern Soft Elm—a wood of prominent grain; the figure is less conspicuous than ash. Light in color, this elm is a good wood for contemporary designs in blond finishes. The coloring is generally even, with an occasional mineral spot or streak. It is not always available, so do not specify this wood unless you are sure you can get it.

Philippine Mahogany—reasonable in price; not too hard to handle; adaptable to almost anything you would choose to build.

## Advanced Projects

Woods listed here are recommended for their decorative and finishing quali-ties and their great worth as cabinet woods:

The Genuine Mahoganies—includes Honduras (American) Mahogany and African Mahogany; high-quality cabinet woods but quite expensive.

Philippine Mahogany—as described above.

Black Walnut—the most valuable cabinet wood which grows in the United States.

Cherry—suitable for the finest work; hard and durable.

Ash, White—A fine, firm-textured furniture wood.

Hard Maple—buy "Selected White" hard maple. *Important:* "Selected White" is not a grade but refers only to the color.

Oak—soft textured oak is excellent for many projects.

Aromatic Red Cedar—difficult to work with hand tools. It has a strong grain pattern and high color range from almost white to dark reddish brown.

## CAN YOU ANSWER THESE QUESTIONS ON MATERIALS?

1. Describe a bill of materials.
2. How is the width of stock measured?
3. Is the longest measurement of a piece of stock always the length? Explain.
4. How many board feet of lumber are there in a piece $1\frac{1}{2}$ inches thick, 8 inches wide, and 10 feet long?
5. If lumber costs $200.00 per M, what is the cost of five board feet?
6. How is plywood sold?
7. How is hardwood lumber cut?
8. What does "S2S" mean?
9. How would you describe the best grade of walnut? Pine?
10. Describe the two methods of drying lumber.
11. Name two good woods for beginning projects.

# PLANNING YOUR WORK

**Before you** begin to work with tools, it is wise to plan carefully the steps you will follow in making the project. This is just good sense and protects you from making unnecessary mistakes. This is done in industry. Like good business, you should "plan your work; then work your plan."

## PLANNING AN INDIVIDUAL PROJECT

The idea in planning a project is to think through exactly (1) what materials you need, (2) what tools and equipment are necessary, and (3) what steps you will follow and in what order they will be done to complete the project in the best way possible.

If you fail to plan your work, you may, for example, begin to sand parts of the project before all of the cutting tool operations are completed. This could dull some of your tools. You might also waste lumber by forgetting to make the proper allowance for the joints needed. Many such mistakes can creep into your work.

## METHOD OF PROCEDURE

In planning your job, you should first decide on the order in which the parts are to be made; then list all of the things you will need to do to complete each particular part.

For example, suppose you are making a sewing box as shown in Figures 6-1 and 6-2. You first decide on all of the materials needed. Figure 6-3. Then you decide

what tools and equipment will be needed and think through all of the steps in cutting, shaping, fitting, and finishing the project. In written form, this might be as follows:

### Sewing Box

### Tools and Equipment:

Crosscut saw, ripsaw, backsaw, plane, chisel, coping saw, twist drill, hand drill, jigsaw, rasp, sandpaper, try square, sliding T bevel, ruler, pencil.

### Procedure:

1. Cut all pieces to size.

**6-1.** This attractive sewing box might be a good beginning project. Note the various parts of the project as you read through the plan of procedure.

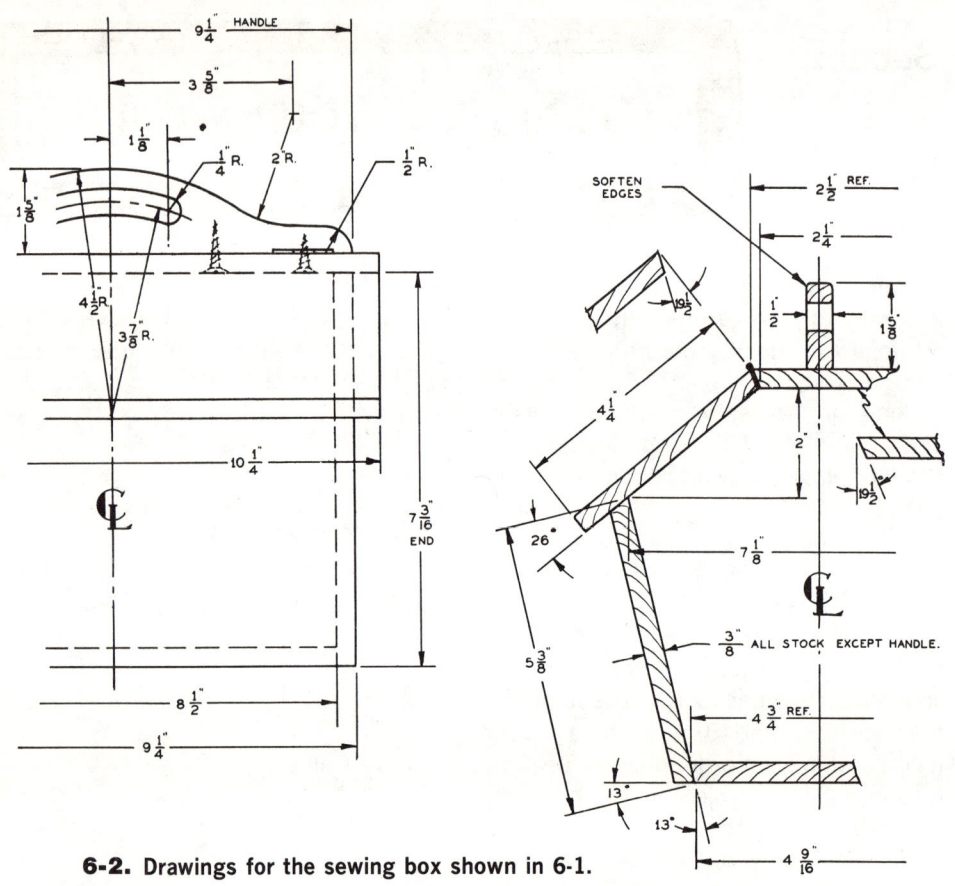

**6-2.** Drawings for the sewing box shown in 6-1.

**6-3.** Bill of materials for the sewing box.
Important: All dimensions listed below are *finished* size.

| No. of Pieces | Thickness | Width | Length | Description | Kind of Wood |
|---|---|---|---|---|---|
| 1 | $\frac{1}{2}''$ | $1\frac{5}{8}''$ | $9\frac{1}{4}''$ | Handle | Pine |
| 2 | $\frac{3}{8}''$ | $5\frac{3}{8}''$ | $9\frac{1}{4}''$ | Sides | Pine |
| 2 | $\frac{3}{8}''$ | $7\frac{1}{8}''$ | $7\frac{3}{16}''$ | Ends | Pine |
| 1 | $\frac{3}{8}''$ | $2\frac{1}{2}''$ | $10\frac{1}{4}''$ | Top | Pine |
| 2 | $\frac{3}{8}''$ | $4\frac{1}{4}''$ | $10\frac{1}{4}''$ | Lids | Pine |
| 1 | $\frac{3}{8}''$ | $4\frac{3}{4}''$ | $8\frac{1}{2}''$ | Bottom | Pine |
| 4 | | | | 1'' Brass Butt Hinges | |
| 2 | | | | No. 6 x $\frac{3}{4}''$ F.H. Wood Screws | |
| 2 | | | | No. 6 x $1\frac{1}{4}''$ F.H. Wood Screws | |
| 2 | | | | No. 18 x 1'' Wire Brads | |

**6-4.** A book holder that can be mass-produced.

2. Cut bevel on both edges of bottom piece. Cut the same angle on bottom edge of side pieces.

3. Cut bevel on one edge of each lid and both edges of top piece.

4. Cut angle on top edge of each side piece.

5. Cut side angles on end pieces. Cut top angles on end pieces.

6. Lay out handle. Cut outside contour. Bore $\frac{1}{2}$-inch hole in each end of handle opening and cut out interior on jigsaw. File and sand smooth all curved surfaces. Soften all edges.

7. Drill and countersink screw shank holes in top. Drill anchor holes in handle.

8. Cut gains in top piece and lids for hinges. Drill screw holes.

9. Sand all pieces.

10. Assemble ends, bottom, and sides with glue and wire brads.

11. Install hinges and attach handle to top with No. 6 flathead wood screws.

12. Attach top assembly to box with glue and wire brads.

13. Fill all nail holes and finish sand entire project.

14. Apply antique pine finish.

This written plan, though not always absolutely necessary, is an excellent idea. You should at least carefully think through each step you will take before you begin to work. In this way you avoid a great deal of trouble. Remember again: "Plan your work; then work your plan."

## PLANNING A MASS-PRODUCTION PRODUCT

If a product is to be mass-produced, planning will be very different from planning an individual project. Many workers will be involved and a large number of the product will be manufactured. This calls for extra planning of duties and supplies. The book holder shown is just one item that could be mass-produced. Figures 6-4 and 6-5. Plans for this book holder include:

• A bill of materials for one product. This can be multiplied by the number to be produced to determine the materials needed. Figure 6-6.

• A procedure sheet for each part of the product, including the tools, machines, jigs, and fixtures needed. Figure 6-7.

• A simple job description for each of the workers needed to produce the product. Figure 6-8.

If your class is to be organized for mass production, you should study Unit 69 "Manufacturing," before beginning this activity.

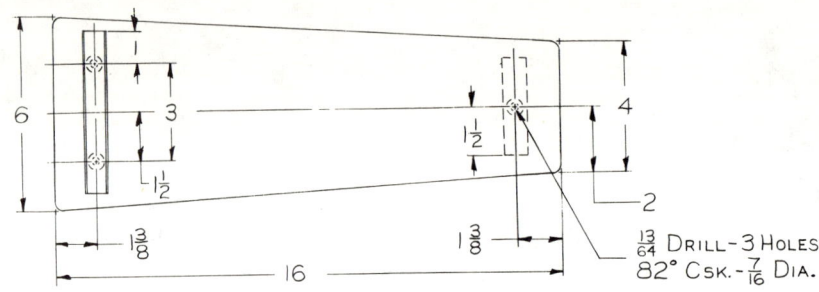

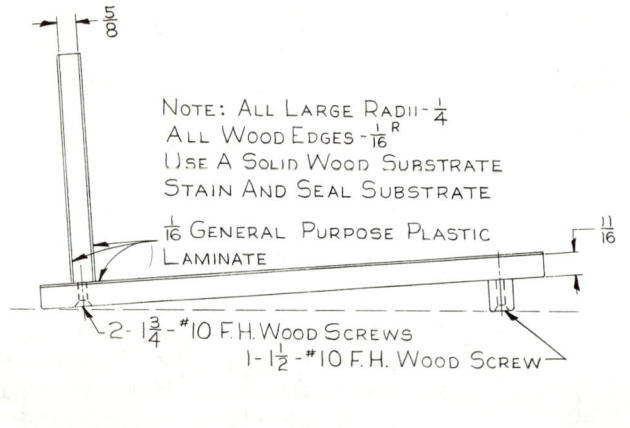

NOTE: ALL LARGE RADII - ¼
ALL WOOD EDGES - 1/16 R
USE A SOLID WOOD SUBSTRATE
STAIN AND SEAL SUBSTRATE
1/16 GENERAL PURPOSE PLASTIC
LAMINATE

2 - 1¾ - #10 F.H. WOOD SCREWS
1 - 1½ - #10 F.H. WOOD SCREW

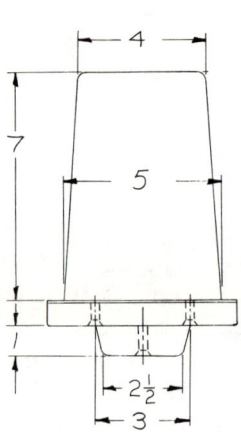

**6-5.** Drawings for the book holder.

1 piece $^{11}/_{16}$″ x 6″ x 16″ Base—White pine, fir, poplar or other suitable solid wood.

1 piece 6¼″ x 16¼″ Base Laminate—$^{1}/_{16}$″ General Purpose Plastic Laminate.

2 pieces 5¼″ x 7¼″ Upright Laminate—$^{1}/_{16}$″ General Purpose Plastic Laminate.

1 piece ⅝″ x 5″ x 7″ Upright wood—Same as is used for base.

1 piece ⅝″ x 1″ x 3″ Foot—Same wood as is used for base.

2—1¾″ — # 10 F. H. Steel Wood Screws.

1—1½″ — # 10 F. H. Steel Wood Screws.

Contact Adhesive.

**6-6.** Bill of materials for the book holder.

**6-7.** Procedures for the book holder.

| A. Base | | | B. Upright | | |
|---|---|---|---|---|---|
| Operation | Tools | Jigs | Operation | Tools | Jigs |
| Rough cut wood to $6\frac{1}{4}''$ x $16\frac{1}{2}''$ | C. Saw or Radial Arm Saw | | Rough cut wood to 15'' x $5\frac{1}{4}''$ | C. Saw or Radial Arm Saw | |
| Joint surface | Jointer | | Joint surface | Jointer | |
| Plane to $\frac{11}{16}''$ thickness | Planer | | Plane to $\frac{5}{8}''$ thickness | Planer | |
| Joint one edge | Jointer | | Joint one edge | Jointer | |
| Square one end | C. Saw or Radial Arm Saw, Planer blade | | Square one end | C. Saw or Radial Arm Saw, Planer blade | |
| Cut to 16'' length | C. Saw or Radial Arm Saw, Planer blade | | Cut to 7'' length | C. Saw or Radial Arm Saw, Planer blade | |
| Cut tapered sides | Circular Saw | Taper fixture | Cut a second 7'' length | C. Saw or Radial Arm Saw, Planer blade | |
| Joint tapered sides | Jointer | | Cut tapered edges | Circular Saw | Taper fixture |
| Rough cut laminate | Circular saw-carbide blade | | Joint tapered edges | Jointer | |
| Apply contact cement to substrate and laminate | Brush, spreader or roller | | Rough cut laminate | Circular Saw Carbide blade | |
| Adhere laminate to base | Hand Roller | | Apply contact cement to both sides of substrate and laminate pieces | Brush, spreader, or roller | |
| Trim edges of laminate | Router, laminate trimmer | | Adhere laminate to both sides of upright | J-Roller | |
| Round corners of base | Disc Sander | Sanding jig | Trim edges of laminate | Router, laminate trimmer, or file | |
| Hand sand edges of base and bottom surface | 150 grit abrasive paper and block | | Round corners of base | Disc Sander or Belt Sander | Sanding jig |
| Drill holes for upright | Drill Press | Drill jig | Hand sand edges of upright | 150 grit abrasive paper and block | |
| Stain and seal edges and bottom of substrate to match or compliment laminate surface | Penetrating finish | | Drill anchor holes in upright | Drill Press | Drill jig |
| | | | Stain and seal edges of substrate to match or compliment laminate surface | Penetrating finish | |

**Table continued on page 90**

**6-7.** Procedures for the book holder. (Continued)

| C. Foot | | | D. Assembly | | |
|---|---|---|---|---|---|
| Operation | Tools | Jigs | Operation | Tools | Jigs |
| Joint one edge of a 1¼" wide strip | Jointer | | Assemble base to upright with 2 1¾" #10 wood screws | Screw driver | Assembly fixture |
| Rip to 1¹/₁₆" wide | Circular Saw | | Assemble foot to base 1 1½" #10 wood screw | Screw driver | Assembly fixture |
| Joint to 1" wide | Jointer | | Polish surface with a soft cloth | | |
| Cut angle on each piece | Circular Saw with miter gauge | Stop block | | | |
| Sand, bevel, and curve | Disc sander or belt sander | | | | |
| Drill hole | Drill press | Drill jig | | | |
| Hand sand all surfaces and edges | 150 grit abrasive paper | | | | |
| Finish with the same stain and sealer used on edges of base and upright | Penetrating finish | | | | |

**6-8.** Job descriptions of the workers needed to mass-produce the book holder.

*Supervisor*—Coordinate all parts of production and make adjustments to keep production going.

*Time Keeper*—Keep accurate records of the time involved to produce each piece of the final assembly.

*Inspectors*—Inspect each piece as it is produced for accuracy, finish, etc. Must be able to read measuring devices.

*Runners*—Convey materials from one work station to another work station.

*Circular Saw Operator*—Set up and operate circular saw.

*Jointer Operator*—Operate and adjust jointer.

*Glue Man*—Spread contact cement evenly and correctly.

*Laminate Assembler*—Line up materials and adhere them to each other.

*Laminate Trimmer*—Operate a router or a laminate trimmer.

*Disc Sander Operator*—Sand edges and curves accurately.

*Hand Sanders*—Sand a part so it is smooth and scratch free.

*Drill Press Operator*—Use a drill jig and drill holes accurately as well as setting up the drill press.

*Planer Operator*—Adjust and operate the planer.

*Finishers*—Apply finish to edges evenly without finish getting on laminate surface.

*Assemblers*—Drive screws straight and use an assembly fixture.

*Polisher*—Wipe off assembled piece so it is ready for distribution.

*Radial Arm Saw Operator*—Set up radial saw and cross cut pieces to length.

*Belt Sander Operator*—Sand edges and curves accurately.

## CAN YOU ANSWER THESE QUESTIONS ON PLANNING YOUR WORK?

1. What is a good motto to adopt in starting a project?
2. List the important parts of a plan sheet.
3. Answer these questions about the sewing box:
   a. What kind of wood is used?
   b. How many different thicknesses of wood are needed?
   c. How many parts make up the box?
4. What kind of a drawing is Fig. 6-2?
5. How does planning for mass production differ from planning a project for your own use?

## Section I

## UNIT 7.

# SAFETY

**The woodshop** is filled with fascinating tools and machines that make it possible to produce wonderful things made of wood. Figure 7-1. All it takes is a willingness to start right and always do your best. Once you get started in woodworking, you will find that a great deal of satisfaction and pleasure can be had. Woodworking can become a source of interest and enjoyment for many years to come.

To make your experiences with woodworking good ones, you will need to learn something about caring for the shop and proper work habits.

Tools are designed to help with the work, and machines are built for certain jobs. Figure 7-2. When tools and machines are treated with proper respect and used and cared for as they deserve to be, they give better service and add greatly to the enjoyment of shopwork. If you use tools exactly as they should be used and keep them sharp and in their proper places, they will be easy to handle. Figure 7-3. When you are qualified, use the machines as they are meant to be used, keep them in good shape, and they too will increase your ability to do woodworking.

Horseplay, running, and playing practical jokes are dangerous activities in the shop. You will find that you resent those who mistreat the shop, the tools, or the machines.

### START RIGHT; WORK RIGHT

First, think of the place in which you work as *your* laboratory. Each one of you has an equal responsibility to care for it and to see that the tools and machines are used correctly. If *you* don't, the others won't either, and the shop will become anything but a place for work.

The procedures you learn in the shop should be carried out accurately and cor-

**7-1.** Many useful products can be made of wood. Whenever tools and machines are used, however, there is always the chance of an accident.

rectly. The best way to get your project done and to develop the ability to do things well in woodworking is to try to do everything the correct way. When you come into the shop, treat it as your own.

When you are taught to do a mechanical job properly, don't try to do it differently *just this once.* It's learning the hard

**7-2.** Every tool is designed to do a specific job. Make sure you learn to use tools correctly and safely.

way if you let a piece of wood kick back from a circular saw and strike you in the stomach. It's no joke to see a fellow student lose several fingers because he has tried to plane a piece that was too small on a jointer. In the shop we learn by doing, and that means by doing correctly.

## ACT THE PART

For everything that you do, whether it's ice skating, playing football, or working, correct clothes should be worn. In the shop, all extra clothing, such as coats, sweaters, and jackets, should be removed. Make sure your tie is tucked into your shirt. Roll up your sleeves and put on a shop apron. Figure 7-4. The shop apron will protect your clothes from dust, paint, and dirt. Following these suggestions will help prevent accidents, since nothing is more likely to cause trouble than a loose tie or sleeves hanging over a machine.

92

If your hair is long, make sure that it doesn't fall loosely where it can catch in some revolving machine. Also, wear approved eye protection for safety at all times while in a shop or laboratory, except in safe areas designated by your instructor. Figure 7-5.

## DOING YOUR SHARE

Keeping up a shop requires cooperative effort. Everyone must do his part in maintaining a safe and well-kept shop. Figure 7-6. Here are some of the things you can do:

• Pick up small pieces of wood on the floor and throw them in the waste box. Some student may turn his ankle on them.

• Keep the aisles clear by placing projects in their proper places.

• Keep your tools properly arranged on your bench. Don't allow sharp-pointed tools to stick out.

• Keep oil wiped up from the floor. Oil may cause a bad fall.

• Don't walk up behind a student when he is working on a machine. He may be startled and make a sudden move. If someone is using a machine, wait until he is finished. Accidents usually happen at this time.

• Be ready and willing to sign a safety pledge card. Your instructor has you do this to protect you, himself, and your fellow students.

• Know the fire regulations in your laboratory. The laboratory is one of the places most likely to have a blaze. This is because there is a great fire hazard due to wood dust and finishing materials. Dust in the air can cause an explosion, especially if it is ignited by a spark from a loose wire on a piece of electrical equipment. The finishing room is a particularly dangerous place. The solvents used in applying finishes form a vapor in the air that ignites easily and can cause an explosion.

## IT CAN HAPPEN HERE

This is a true story. Two boys were turning a large table top on a lathe. They had come to the shop to work extra time. One boy stood by the lathe as the other

**7-3.** Here is the correct way to keep your tools. Never pile them one on top of another. The results you achieve in woodworking depend largely on the way in which you take care of your tools. An additional reward will be found in your health and safety.

7-4. This boy is dressed properly for work in the woodshop. He is wearing a shop apron; his sleeves are rolled up; his tie is tucked in; his hair is not too long; and he has no loose articles dangling from his clothing. However, he must also wear eye protection for most work.

7-5. For most work, approved safety glasses, goggles, or a shield must be worn.

7-6. This laboratory has a good exhaust system that will aid in keeping it clean and safe.

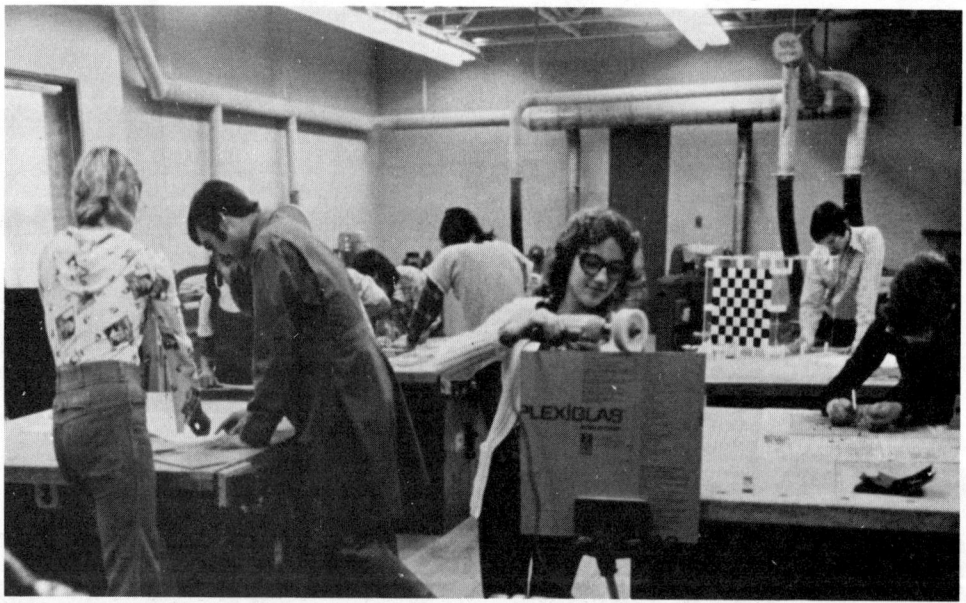

turned on the master switch. By mistake the lathe was set at high speed. The lathe started with terrific force. The table top flew off, struck, and killed the boy standing there. This actually happened and it could happen in your shop. Not many accidents occur in school shops, but each year some students are victims. *Every one of these accidents can be prevented.* They all occur because someone does something he is not supposed to do. You can do your part to prevent this by:

• Carefully watching your instructor's demonstrations on how to use each tool and machine. Figure 7-7.

• Getting your teacher's permission before using a power machine. Figure 7-8. You may not be ready to use power machinery, so don't try it until you are. The machines may look harmless, but they are far from it.

### AN OUNCE OF PREVENTION

Even when you are working correctly with tools and machines, small accidents happen. The most common are slight cuts and bruises, a sliver in the finger, minor burns, and getting something in the eye. None of these may be serious, but they all *can* be. A sliver, for example, can cause blood poisoning. Your eyes can be permanently damaged if they are not treated immediately. Get immediate first aid from a nurse or doctor unless the injury is very minor.

Some minor injuries can be treated with simple first aid procedures. Allow a slight cut to bleed freely for a short time and then bandage it properly. Remove slivers immediately with a clean knife or tweezers and then sterilize the wound.

**7-7.** Always follow good safety practices that your instructor has demonstrated.

**7-8.** Your instructor will want to check your use of all machines to make sure you know how to operate them correctly.

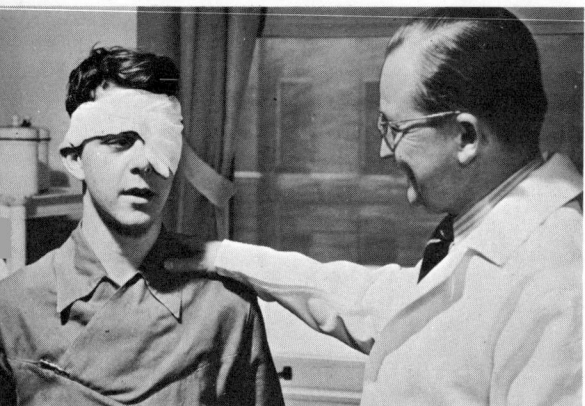

**7-9.** Eye injuries are a serious matter. See a doctor or nurse immediately to take care of this type of injury.

**7-10.** If you have an opportunity to work on a building construction job, you must know and follow good safety practices. Do you see any way in which safety practices could be improved here?

For a slight burn, apply baking soda and water or carbolated petroleum jelly. A more serious burn should be treated immediately by a doctor. If you get something in your eye, hold your handkerchief over it lightly, without rubbing, to let your eye water. If this doesn't remove the trouble, have a doctor or nurse take it out. Figure 7-9. Don't let another student remove a particle from your eye.

## IS IT WORTH IT?

In the laboratory or on the job, you will be handling many different kinds of materials including lumber, nails, screws, and unfinished projects. You should learn to handle them correctly. Figure 7-10.

When carrying lumber, be careful not to pinch your fingers. Always make sure that the lumber is kept in a neat pile; poorly stacked lumber is dangerous.

Screws and nails are fine for fastening work together, but they don't digest; so don't carry them around in your mouth! There is also danger of infection when you do this. When storing your project, do it neatly and never place it high on a locker or window ledge where it can fall off and hurt someone. If you have a large finished project or a machine that should be moved, lift it correctly. There is danger of rupture from improper lifting.

## IT'S THE LITTLE THINGS THAT COUNT

Many of the tools in the woodshop have sharp cutting edges that are used for marking, shaping, and cutting stock. These tools can cause accidents. Some rules to follow are:

• Never carry pointed tools in your pockets. Figure 7-11.

• Always grind off a mushroom (flattened) head.

96

**7-11.** Here are some things that should NOT be done. This careless woodworker is not looking where he is going. He is also carrying sharp-pointed tools incorrectly and has his arms too full.

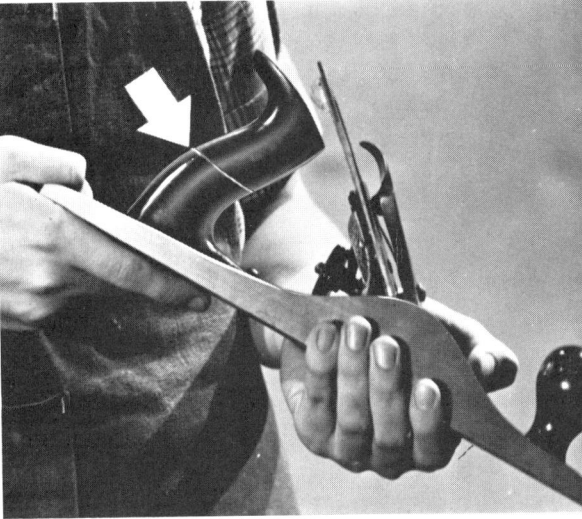

**7-12.** Check your tools to see that the handles are in good condition. Cracked or rough handles on saws, chisels, planes, and gouges can cause blisters which may become infected. Also, it is irritating to work with a tool that has a rough handle, and you can't do a good job with it.

● Always cut and chisel *away from* yourself.

● Never use tools with loose handles. Figure 7-12.

● Always carry cutting tools with the sharp edge down.

● Use tools for the proper purpose. Figure 7-13.

The best way to work with hand tools and machines is to follow the instructions given in the units that follow. Always remember that the correct way is the safe way.

## CAN YOU QUALIFY?

Before you are allowed to drive a car, you must be a certain age, have instructions, and be able to pass certain tests. This is to protect you and others. The

**7-13.** Here is a picture you should study, for it shows good practices, especially protection of the eyes. You have only two eyes and money can't buy a new pair.

97

same things apply to your laboratory. You can't expect to use power machinery until you are old enough to use it safely, until you have been given proper instruc- tions, and until you have shown your ability by passing a performance test. In this book you will find suggestions for using each machine.

## CAN YOU ANSWER THESE QUESTIONS ON SAFETY?

1. Who is responsible for taking care of the tools and machines?
2. Why is the right attitude important before beginning to work?
3. Describe the proper clothes for the woodshop.
4. Why can long hair be dangerous?
5. List five things you can do to keep the shop in order.
6. Can you tell what causes most acci- dents?
7. How would you treat a slight burn?
8. If you get something in your eye in the shop, should you ask a fellow student to remove it? Explain your answer.
9. List three rules to follow when using sharp cutting tools.

## Section I

## UNIT 8.

# CAREERS IN WOODWORKING

**Wood is** one of our most important natural resources. It is one of the few materials that can renew itself. Despite the fact that many products are now produced of metal, plastic, and other materials, wood continues to be a most important resource in our industrial soci- ety. Figure 8-1.

By the year 2000, in order to meet the demand, enough wood must be produced each year to build a highway 1 foot thick, 24 feet wide, and long enough to reach the moon 230,000 miles away. With the increasing use of wood come many ca- reer opportunities for you. Wood and wood products are responsible for the employment of over one million people. Indirectly, over two million people in the

United States alone depend on products of the American forests for a living. Over 20,000 concerns produce lumber and lumber products, making up the fifth largest manufacturing industry.

## OPPORTUNITIES IN INDUSTRY

Many career opportunities are avail- able to anyone who is interested in wood. Jobs can be found at all stages in the manufacture of lumber and lumber products.

Many work in and around the forests and sawmills where logs are converted into rough lumber. Others are employed in the grading and seasoning of lumber. Considerable numbers are also needed in order to move lumber from forest to mill and mill to factory.

In processing plants, people are needed to convert lumber into plywood, hardboard, particle board, and other manufactured products. Furniture and housing industries provide thousands of job opportunities. Workers in these and other industries use woodworking machines. The planer, jointer, circular saw, tenoner, and dovetailer are a few. Assembling and finishing operations supply jobs for many. The sash-and-door and box-making industries, for example, have jobs of this type. Maintenance work is also important. Millwrights are needed to keep woodworking machines in good condition. Saw filing is just one of their responsibilities.

## CAREER LEVELS

Throughout the wood industry, three major career levels are open to you. They are (1) craftsperson, (2) technician, and (3) professional. As you read about these three levels, think about which jobs appeal to you the most.

### Craftspeople

Craftspeople have the knowledge and skill needed to build with wood—houses and furniture, for example. About 27 percent of the 10,000,000 workers employed as craftspeople and forepersons work in the construction trades. There is a need for about 46,000 new craftspeople each year due to the rapid rise in construction activity. Construction crafts

**8-1.** Even a jet aircraft must be built of wood to a full-size mock-up to check out problems of production before it is built of metal. Technicians and skilled model makers are needed for this kind of wood construction.

**8-2.** Carpenters make up the largest group in the building construction industry.

**8-3.** You too can learn to be a carpenter. With a skilled trade you can always find a good job wherever you may want to live.

include such skilled workers as carpenters, bricklayers, electricians, and plumbers. Are you familiar with any of the skilled occupations that follow?

*Carpenters* comprise the largest, single group of craftspeople in the building trades. There are over 830,000 currently employed. Figure 8-2. Even though much of our housing is factory-built, there is still a great need for skilled carpenters. You can learn to be a carpenter by becoming a carpenter's helper, learning the trade informally by working with experienced carpenters. Still another method is to prepare in a trade vocational school. A small number of people complete a four-year apprenticeship in the trade. Figure 8-3. The carpenter must have a knowledge of commercial and home construction and be able to read architectural drawings. Carpenters are usually divided into two groups: the rough carpenter who does the basic framing and the finish carpenter who does the exterior and interior trim.

The *cabinetmaker* is a highly skilled woodworker. He or she may work as a finish carpenter. A cabinetmaker may also be involved in building kitchen cabinets, making furniture, or in remodeling. Figure 8-4.

The *millwright* takes care of the machinery in a plant and does repair work, resharpening of tools, and similar jobs. She or he must have a thorough knowledge of the construction and operation of all woodworking machines and be able to make machine setups. Figure 8-5.

*Patternmakers* make wood or metal patterns of the shapes needed for production. They must know and understand foundry work, how patterns are made, and how to use special tools.

*Model makers* build models for manufacturing and construction for such

**100**

products as airplanes and buildings. Figure 8-6.

**Technicians**

A technician works on a team with professional personnel and skilled craftspeople, converting theories and ideas to products and processes. Technicians hold many important jobs in manufacturing, building construction, and the lumber industry. Figure 8-7.

The technician is a graduate of a one- or two-year technical institute or community junior college. Two-year technical programs are available in many fields related to woodworking, including forestry, building construction, model building, and manufacturing. Certain jobs, such as a real estate broker, can also be secured with technical training. Drafters are technicians. There are many opportunities to work in architectural drafting, furniture production, manufacturing, and other areas. About one-third of a million drafters are now employed and about 16,000 new ones are needed each year. Figure 8-8.

**Professionals**

The professional has a college degree in some area such as forestry, engineering, architecture, industrial technology, or industrial education. There are many professional opportunities available if you can secure a college degree and, in some cases, take graduate work. Figure 8-9. Professional positions in woodworking are of all types. Are you familiar with the positions described here?

*Foresters* work for private owners of timber land and forest product industries as well as for the federal government. There are about 22,000 foresters now employed and there is a need for about 1,000 each year. Figure 8-10.

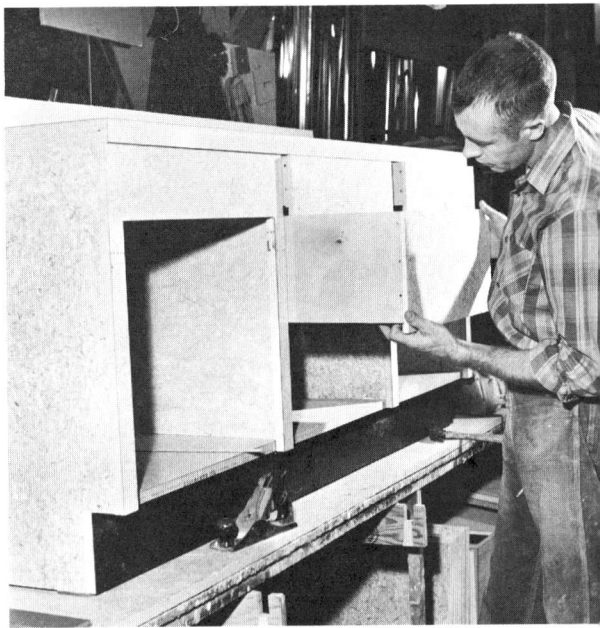

**8-4.** A cabinetmaker must be able to use all types of hand and machine tools.

**8-5.** The two men on the left are millwrights working in a lumber mill. They must be able to work with metal and wood machines.

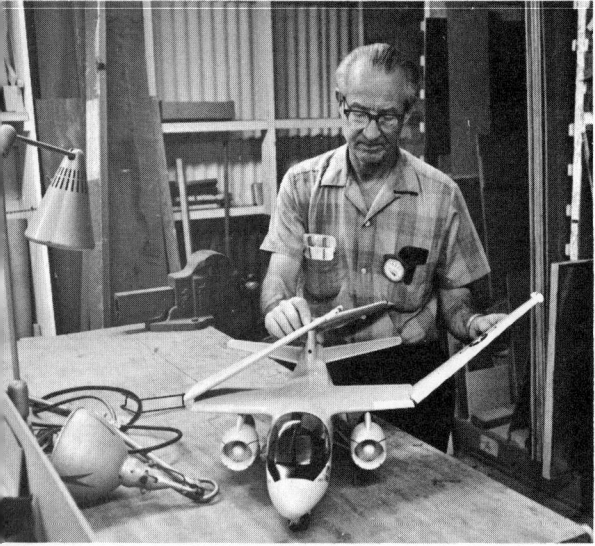

**8-6.** Model builders have the satisfaction of seeing a new product in three dimensions even before it is put into production.

**8-8.** Drafters must be able to make and read prints of all types.

*Architects* plan and design buildings and other structures. They work with other professionals such as engineers, urban planners, and landscape architects in designing buildings that are a part of major developments. There are

**8-7.** Many technicians who understand woodworking are needed. In manufacturing, they use their knowledge of woodworking to build patterns.

about 34,000 registered architects with a need for about 1,000 new ones each year. Architecture is a very demanding profession, for the architect must be an artist, an engineer, and a business manager all in one.

*Interior designers and decorators* do creative work to enhance the attractiveness of homes and other buildings. Designers and decorators plan the functional arrangement of interior space and coordinate the selection of fabrics, draperies, and other materials to provide for a pleasant setting. There are about 15,000 people employed in interior designing and decorating.

*Industrial education teachers* are included in a group of approximately 100,000 industrial arts, vocational, and technical teachers. At least one-third of these teach woodworking and building construction either full or part time. There will be a need for about 20,000

**8-9.** Most large wood industries and many governmental agencies employ research workers who study the utilization of wood.

**8-10.** Foresters should enjoy working both indoors and outdoors as they watch living things grow.

new industrial education teachers a year. If you like to work with young people and are creative, you may want to consider becoming an industrial education teacher.

## SELECTING AND PREPARING FOR A CAREER

In considering a career in woodworking, you should realize a few facts. Many of these jobs require that you work in noisy and somewhat dusty surroundings. For some jobs you will be exposed to the elements. There is also danger of accidents, including cuts to the hands and fingers. Figure 8-11.

All opportunities in the crafts offer great satisfaction to you as well as a

**8-11.** Carpenters and others in the building trades often work on top of buildings and on scaffolding. There is always danger of accidents.

**103**

chance to construct and build. An expert in any of the craft occupations will not only earn a good living but will also be doing a rewarding job. There are many opportunities for advancement. The carpenter, for example, can become a contractor. The patternmaker can become a foreperson or supervisor.

Before you decide on a career as a craftsperson, you should think about these questions:

• Do you have a knack for understanding tools and materials?

• Do you have the patience to complete a job?

• Do you work well with your hands?

• Is your math work satisfactory?

• Do you feel that you could be happy working in one of the skilled trades?

• Do you have enough initiative and interest to train for a job as a skilled crafts worker?

• Do you think you'd be a success if you decided to enter a craft?

If the answers to these questions are yes, you may want to consider taking some additional courses in carpentry, building construction, or patternmaking. You could also become an apprentice in one of these areas.

Do you want to become a technician? If so, you must be willing to spend at least two years in a technical institute or community junior college. You will spend about half your time in classroom studies and the other half in laboratory and shop work. Not all schools offer two-year programs in fields relating to wood and the construction industry. However, there are opportunities to get this kind of program. You should check with your counselor, who will have an index to technical education opportunities.

In order to become a professional person, you must be ready to take a four-year college degree program and sometimes a one- or two-year internship beyond this. This, for example, is the route an architect must follow. To succeed in professional schools, you will need to have a good background in mathematics and science and an above-average ability in written and spoken English. Each type of professional opportunity demands a different kind of personality and preparation. The forester should be interested in working outdoors. The architect must have creative talent, skill in math and science, an understanding of people, and be able to draw so he or she can communicate ideas and designs. If you want to become an industrial education teacher, you must be interested in working with tools and machines as well as people.

More specific information about careers can be found in the *Occupational Outlook Handbook* and in the *Dictionary of Occupational Titles*.

## CAN YOU ANSWER THESE QUESTIONS ON CAREERS IN WOODWORK?

1. How many people indirectly earn a living from products of the American forest?

2. Describe the three career levels.

3. What is the largest skilled trade area in woodwork?

4. List three professional occupations in which an understanding of woodworking is important.

5. What are some of the points to consider in selecting a woodworking trade?

# SECTION II
## Getting Out the Rough Stock

**What you must know and be able to do in Units 9 and 10:**

9. Identification and use of measuring and marking tools: kinds of rules; other layout and measuring tools; marking tools; holding devices; how to measure and mark for cutting.

10. Identification and use of saws: set, point, and size; ripsaw and crosscut saws; how to saw correctly.

*Measuring, marking, and cutting are the important things to learn now because you are ready to get out the rough stock for your project. The actual work with wood and shop tools is about to begin. Everything you have done so far has been in preparation for this. Some instructors prefer to let students choose their lumber from a shop lumber pile. Others may have already cut the lumber to rough-cut size to help the class get started and to save time.*

*Measuring, marking, and cutting skills will be repeated in any kind of woodworking you do for the rest of your life, so learn them well. Through practice these skills will become automatic.*

# MEASURING AND MARKING OUT ROUGH STOCK

**After you** have the lumber for your project, you will measure and mark out the amount of stock needed for each piece shown in the rough bill of materials or the drawing. Figure 9-1. You need several measuring tools. These tools may seem very simple, but accuracy is impossible unless you take enough time and care to use them properly.

## RULES FOR MEASURING SHORT LENGTHS

Rules are available with three forms of graduation, namely: *customary* (English),

**9-1a.** Measuring accurately is important in all woodwork. Here a customary measurement is taken.

*metric,* or a *metric-customary* combination. The best rule for measuring small pieces and marking short distances is the *bench rule.* In the customary form, this is a wooden rule 1, 2, or 3 feet long with a brass cap at both ends to protect it. Figures 9-2 and 9-3. The metric bench rule is available in lengths of 300 millimetres or 30 centimetres (about 1 foot), ½ meter, and 1 meter. All metric rules are divided into millimetres, with every tenth millimetre numbered 1, 2, 3, etc., to show centimetres, or 10, 20, 30, etc., to show millimetres. The metric-customary rule is usually divided into inches and fractions of an inch on the top half of the rule and in millimetres and centimetres on the bottom half. Figure 9-4. The *fold-*

**9-1b.** Accurate measurements must also be taken when using the metric system.

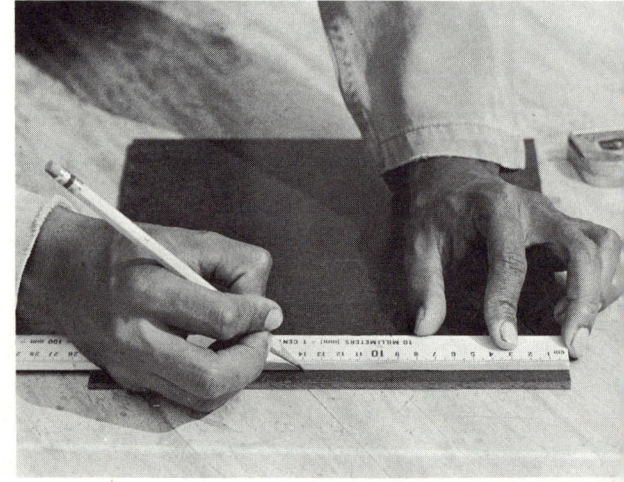

*ing rule* is simply a rule that can be folded. The 3-foot rule is called a *yardstick,* and the similar metric rule is called a *metre stick.* A small wood *caliper* can be used to measure round stock conveniently. Figure 9-5.

## RULES FOR MEASURING LONG LENGTHS

The *zigzag rule* for long measurements (Figure 9-6) is about 8 inches

(203 mm) long when folded and can be extended to its full length of 6 to 8 feet (2 to 3 m). Most carpenters keep this rule handy at all times.

Another rule for measuring long dimensions is the *steel tape.* Figure 9-7. A small catch at its end slips over the end of a board, making it easier to pull out the tape. The steel tape has a length of 6 to 12 feet (2 to 4 m).

## SQUARES

The *try square* has a metal blade and a handle usually of metal. The blade is marked in eighths of an inch on one side and sometimes in millimetres on the other. Figure 9-8. The try square is used for many purposes. The most common are laying out a line square with an edge,

**9-2.** The customary bench rule is 12, 24, or 36 inches long. Sometimes a 3-foot (36-inch) rule is called a yardstick. The rule is graduated in sixteenths of an inch on one side and eighths of an inch on the other. The illustration shows these graduations and larger ones for comparison.

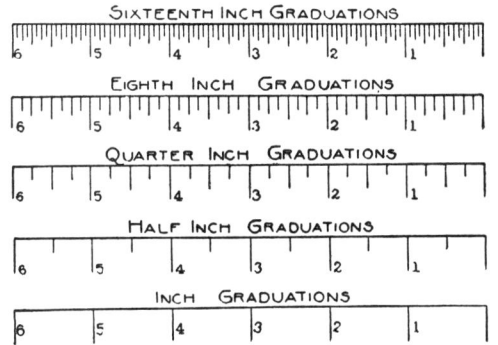

**9-5.** This wooden caliper is marked in millimetres only.

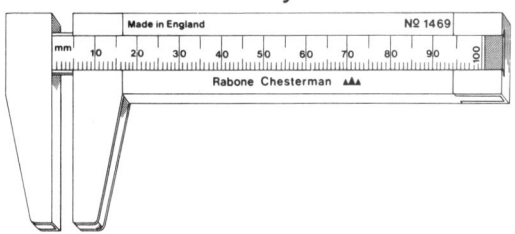

**9-3a.** One-foot bench rule.

**9-3b.** Two-foot bench rule.

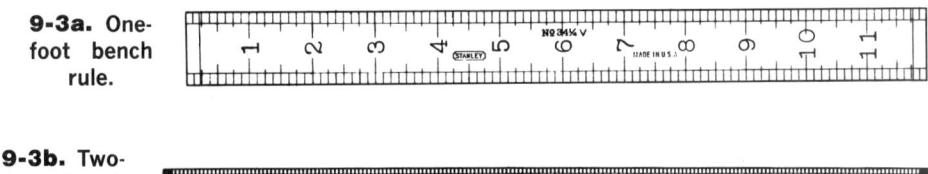

**9-4.** The top half of this rule is marked in inches and the bottom half in millimetres. It is easy to see that 1 inch is about 25 mm and 2 inches is about 50 mm.

checking the squareness of two surfaces, and testing 90-degree angles. Figure 9-9. *Never use this tool for hammering or pounding* because this makes it inaccurate.

The *carpenter's square* (framing square) is used in general building work. Figure 9-10.

The *combination square* is very useful for measuring and marking. Figure 9-11. It is called a combination tool because it is a try square, a miter square, a level, a plumb, a depth gage, and a scriber. The combination blade has a groove cut

**9-6a.** This 6-foot zigzag extension rule is useful, mostly to carpenters, in measuring long lengths.

**9-7b.** This steel tape has metric-customary marking for easy reading in either system.

**9-7c.** Using a steel tape to locate a point.

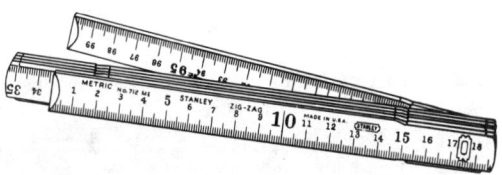

**9-6b.** This zigzag rule is divided into millimetres, centimetres, and decimetres. Every tenth millimetre is shown with a figure 1, 2, 3, etc. These numbers represent centimetres. Every tenth centimetre is shown with an enlarged 10, representing 10 centimetres or 1 decimetre.

**9-7a.** This push-pull steel tape rule is particularly adaptable as a shop rule. It will take inside and outside measurements accurately.

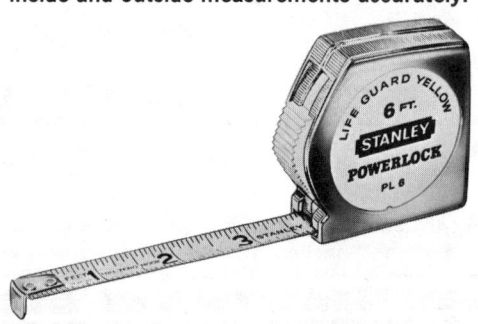

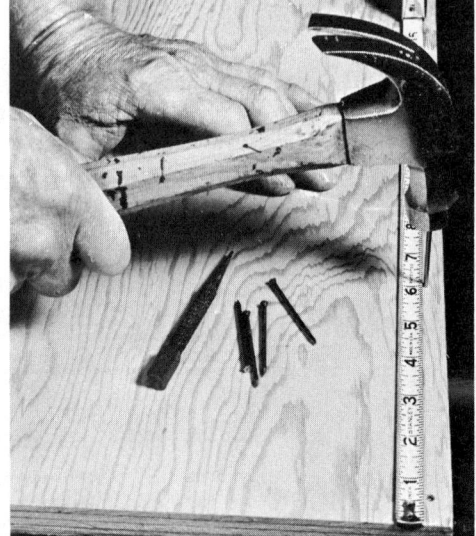

**9-8.** Try square.

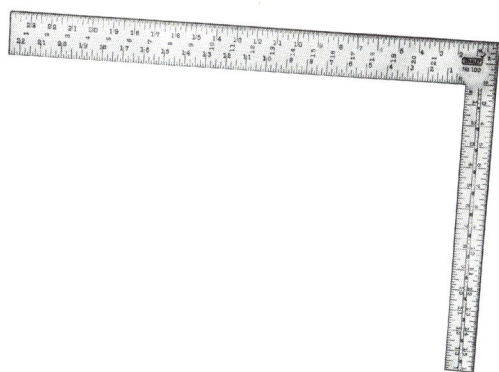

**9-9.** A 6-inch (150 mm) try square with a metal blade and handle. This tool is accurately machined so that the handle and the blade will be at right angles to each other. Therefore never use the tool as a pounding device. The lower picture shows a try and miter square with one edge of the handle shaped at an angle of 45 degrees. For many layout jobs this kind of try square is better and more convenient to use.

**9-10.** Carpenter's framing square. Of all the carpenter's tools, none is more nearly indispensable than this steel square. It has a table stamped on the body for figuring rafters. Other squares also contain tables for figuring board measurements.

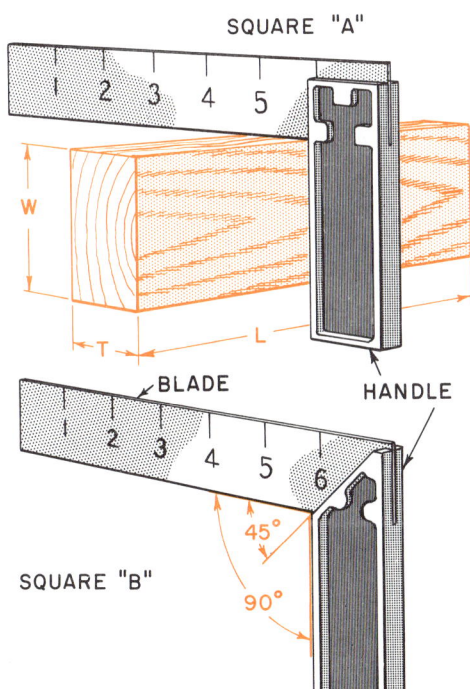

SQUARE "A"

W

T    L

BLADE    HANDLE

45°

90°

SQUARE "B"

L – LENGTH
T – THICKNESS
W – WIDTH

**9-11a.** A combination square is a valuable tool for measuring and marking.

**9-11b.** Combination square and pencil used as a marking gage.

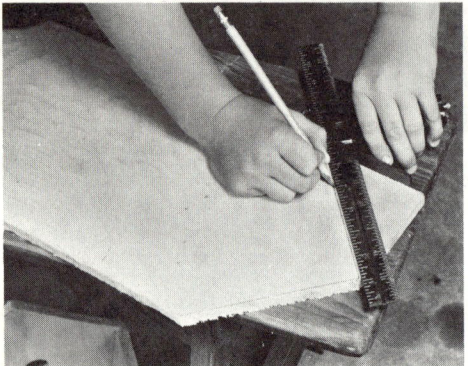

**9-11c.** Laying out a 45-degree angle with a combination square.

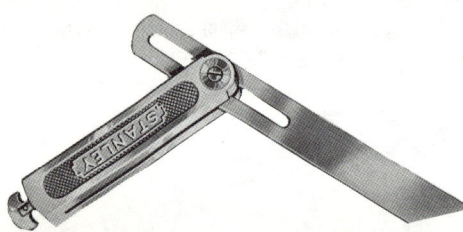

**9-12.** This tool is called a sliding T bevel. It gets its name from the fact that it can be adjusted to any angle desired. The blade slides back and forth in the handle and can be locked in position with a little thumb screw.

**9-13.** A method of setting the sliding T bevel by using a steel square. This shows the bevel set at an angle of 45 degrees.

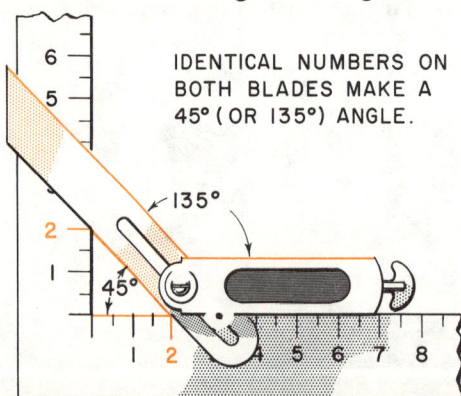

IDENTICAL NUMBERS ON BOTH BLADES MAKE A 45° (OR 135°) ANGLE.

along its length. The head slides along and can be tightened at any position.

The *sliding T bevel* is for laying out all angles other than 90 degrees. Figure 9-12. It has an adjustable blade in a handle. To lay out a 45-degree angle, for instance, the adjustable T bevel can be set with the framing square as shown in Figure 9-13. To set the tool to such angles as 30 and 60 degrees, the bevel can be checked with the triangles used in drawing. It can also be set by laying out a right triangle with the hypotenuse (the side opposite the 90-degree angle) two units long and one side one unit long. Figure 9-14. For other angles, the sliding T bevel can best be set with a protractor as shown in Figure 9-15.

## MARKING TOOLS

An ordinary *lead pencil* is the most common marking tool. Its mark can be seen easily on both rough and finished lumber, the mark is easy to remove, and the pencil does not scratch or mar the wood surface. Use a pencil with a rather hard lead for laying out fine, accurate lines. Keep the pencil sharpened in the shape of a chisel so the point can be held

**9-14.** Using a triangle to set a sliding T bevel. By drawing a right triangle with the hypotenuse two units long and one leg one unit long, you have a triangle with 30- and 60-degree angles.

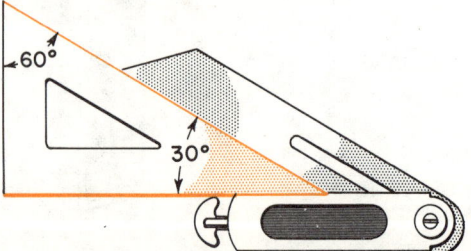

directly against the edge of the rule or square.

A *knife* is a good tool for very accurate marking. Figure 9-16. Be careful, however, to use it only when you know that the mark will disappear as the wood is cut, formed, or shaped.

A *sloyd knife* (Figure 9-17) is used for marking. This is a very handy tool because it can be used for such jobs as trimming a fine edge, slicing a piece of thin veneer, and whittling a small peg.

The *scratch awl*—a thin metal-pointed tool with a wooden handle—is good for marking and punching the location of holes to be drilled or bored. Figure 9-18.

## HOLDING DEVICES

For good work you must have a solid workbench with a sturdy bench vise. Figure 9-19. The *bench vise* holds work to be cut, formed, or shaped. Figure 9-20. Line the metal jaws with wood inserts to protect the pieces to be clamped. The movable jaw of the vise has a small, sliding section called a vise dog. This, with a metal stop, can be placed in holes across the top of the bench for holding long, flat pieces of stock when planing, cutting, forming, or shaping. Figure 9-21.

When handling large pieces for layout, sawing, and assembling, one or two wood sawhorses are needed. They should be about 20 inches (508 mm) high; the best kind to have is one like that shown in Figure 9-22, which is open down the center.

## MEASURING STOCK

● *Measuring thickness*. The lumber should be checked for thickness, width, and length. Measure the thickness of the lumber by holding the rule over the edge. The thickness is found by reading the

125° — READ AS
55°

**9-15a.** Setting a sliding T bevel by using a protractor. Any angle can be quickly and accurately established.

**9-15b.** Using a sliding T bevel to mark out a wood joint.

**9-16a.** The layout and cutting knife. This type has a blade that slides into the handle.

two lines on the rule that just enclose the stock. Figure 9-23.

● *Measuring width.* Measure the width by holding the left end of the rule (or the inch mark) on one edge of the stock. Slide your thumb from right to left along the rule until the width is shown. Figure 9-24.

**9-17.** The sloyd knife is excellent for layout work and also for many odd jobs such as cutting, trimming, and whittling. This tool was so named because it was used in the old "sloyd" (Swedish) system of teaching.

**9-18.** The scratch awl is another layout tool that is very handy. It is used to lay out the positions for drilling and boring holes.

**9-16b.** A sharp knife will cut an accurate layout line.

**9-19.** A sturdy woodworking bench is a requirement for doing good work.

● *Measuring short lengths.* Select the end of the stock from which the measurement is to be taken. Check its squareness by holding a try square against the truest edge. Make sure that the end is not split or checked. If it is, the end of the wood should be squared off and cut and the measurement taken from the sawed end. If a short length of stock is needed, hold the rule on edge and mark the length with a pencil or knife. Figure 9-25.

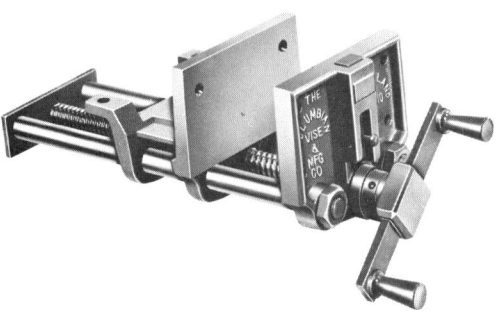

**9-20.** A woodworking vise with wood-lined jaws should be attached to the left front side of the bench.

**9-22.** This kind of sawhorse is most practical for layout and cutting. Because it is open down the center, the sawing can be done with the blade free to move down the center of the opening.

**9-21.** The proper method of locking stock on a bench top for doing planing, cutting, forming, and shaping. As you can see, the vise dog is in a raised position so that the wood can be clamped between it and the metal stop at the other end which cannot be seen in this picture. The metal stop fits into one of the holes drilled along the top of the bench.

**9-23.** Measuring the thickness of stock with a bench rule. One end of the rule is held directly over one arris of the wood, and the thumb is slid along until the thickness of the stock is indicated.

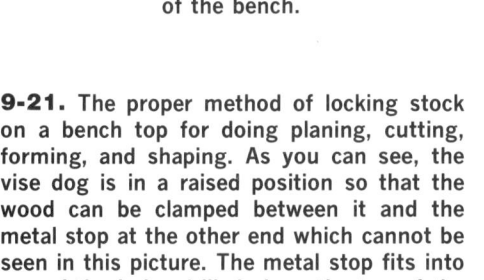

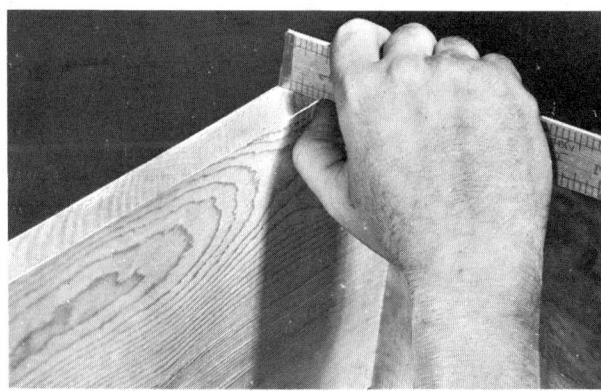

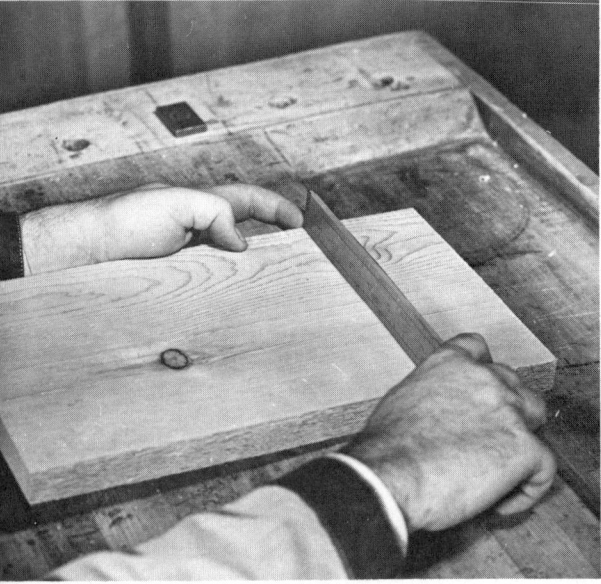

**9-24.** Measuring the width of stock. The rule is held on edge for more accurate measurement. The left end of the rule is held even with the left side of the board with the forefinger of the left hand. The thumb is slid along the rule until the correct width is indicated.

**9-25.** For measuring short lengths, the end of the rule is placed directly over the end of the stock, with the rule on edge. Then the correct length of stock needed is marked with a pencil.

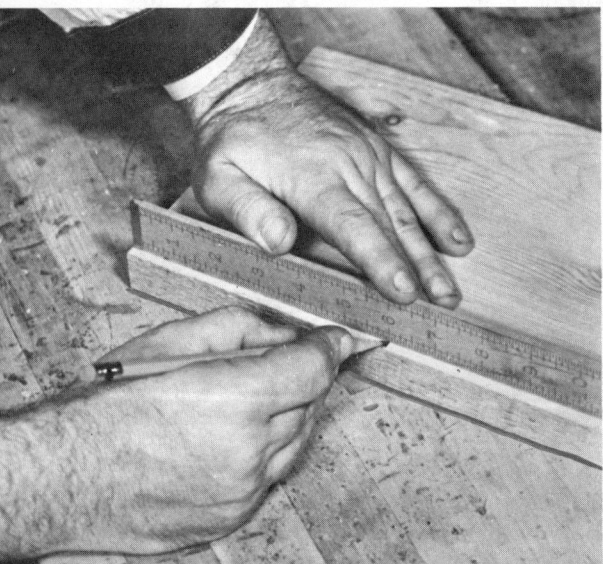

● *Measuring long lengths.* For measuring long stock use a zigzag rule or a steel tape. This will eliminate measuring errors that come from moving a short rule several times. Figure 9-26. Make a small mark at the point to be squared.

## MARKING STOCK FOR CUTTING TO LENGTH

● *Marking lengths on narrow lumber.* If rather narrow lumber must be marked for cutting, hold the handle of the try square firmly against the truest edge of the stock. Square off a line. Figures 9-27 and 9-28.

**9-26.** Using a steel tape to measure long lengths. This procedure is more accurate than using a short rule. With a short rule there is always the possibility of mistakes. A steel tape is especially convenient because the metal hook on the end can be dropped over the end of the stock and the tape drawn out easily to length.

● *Marking lengths on wide lumber.* Use a framing square on wide stock. The framing square is uniform in thickness. Therefore the blade should be tipped slightly and then held firmly against the truest edge while the mark is made across the stock. Figure 9-29. To be sure of trueness, square a line across the edges with the face line. This can be done with a try square as shown in Figure 9-30.

● *Marking duplicate parts.* If a group of pieces must be measured and marked out to equal lengths, place them side by side. Make sure that the ends are lined up by holding a try square over the ends. Then move the try square to correct length to mark the pieces. Figure 9-31.

## MEASURING AND MARKING STOCK FOR CUTTING TO WIDTH

Decide on the width of stock you need. Hold the rule at right angles to the truest edge of the stock and measure the correct width. Figure 9-32. This can also be done with a try square or combination square (Figure 9-11b). Do this at several points along the stock. Then hold a

**9-28.** Marking across the face of stock with a knife. Notice that the try square is held firmly against one edge of the stock and the knife is drawn toward you. Always *turn the knife in slightly* toward the blade of the try square.

**9-27.** Using a pencil to mark across the face of stock. Make sure it is sharpened to a point so it will make a thin, accurate line on the wood surface.

**9-29.** On wide stock the framing square is used to mark the line. The blade is tipped slightly and is held firmly against the edge of the stock as the knife marks across the face of the work.

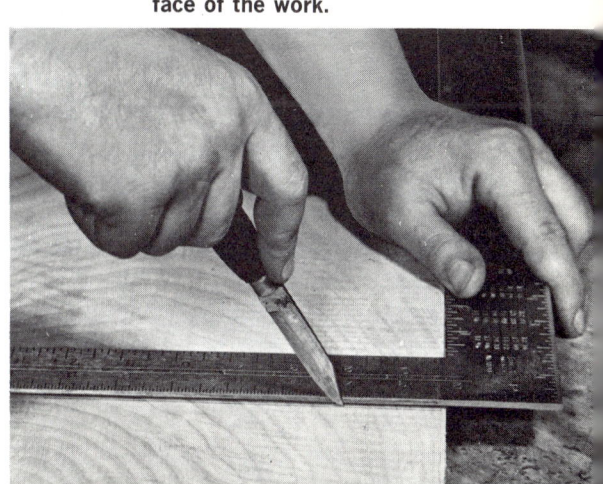

9-30. Squaring the lines across the edge of stock. It is a good idea to mark a line on the edge as shown. This will help you make the saw cut more accurate.

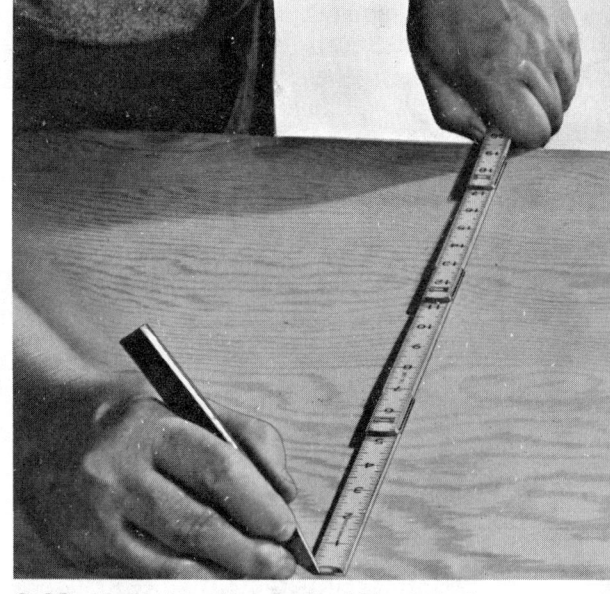

9-32. Measuring the correct width of stock with a zigzag rule. On narrow widths, a try square is the marking tool. Place your left thumb on the correct width and hold this firmly against one edge of the stock while you mark the width with a sharp pencil.

9-31. Frequently, several pieces of the same length are needed. It is easier and more convenient to mark them at the same time as shown here. Hold the try square over the ends to align them before marking the correct length.

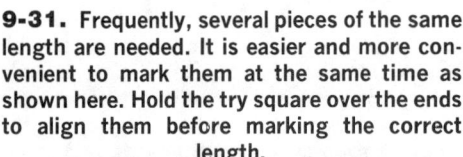

9-33. After several points have been indicated, a straightedge is held over these points and a knife or pencil used to mark the correct width. In doing this be careful that the straightedge doesn't slip.

straightedge over these points and connect them. Figure 9-33.

A framing square may be used to measure the width of stock needed. Another method for marking the width of rough stock is to hold a rule to the correct width between the thumb and forefinger. Then guide it along the truest edge of the stock with a pencil held against the end of the rule. Figure 9-34.

## DIVIDING A BOARD INTO EQUAL PARTS

To divide a board into two or more equal parts, hold a rule at an angle across the face of the stock until the inch marks evenly divide the space. Figure 9-35. The board must be true along both sides for this to work.

**9-34.** Laying out the width of stock. Hold the rule in one hand. Hold the pencil in your other hand against the end of the rule and slide both along at the same time.

**9-35.** The proper method of dividing a board into several equal parts. This piece is $3\frac{5}{8}$ inches wide and is divided into four parts. The end of the rule is held over one edge of the board and the rule shifted at an angle until the 4-inch mark is over the other edge. Then by placing a mark at the 1-, 2-, and 3-inch marks, the board is divided equally into four parts. This same idea can be used with a metric rule.

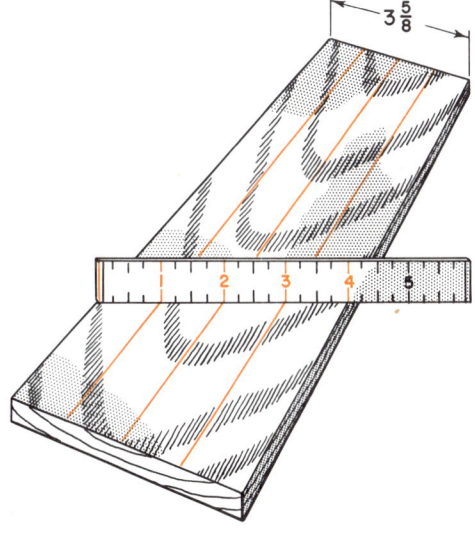

## CAN YOU ANSWER THESE QUESTIONS ON MEASURING AND MARKING OUT ROUGH STOCK?

1. Name two rules used for measuring short distances.
2. The carpenter usually employs what square?
3. Give the parts of a try square. List three uses.
4. When is a framing square used in the woodshop?
5. The sliding T bevel can be used in a way that no other layout tool can. What is this use?
6. Why is the lead pencil the most commonly used tool for marking on wood?
7. What kind of knife is best for marking wood before making a fine cut?
8. The scratch awl is a marking tool but is also used for what other job?
9. How many sixteenths in $1\frac{1}{4}$ inches?
10. Why is the bench vise frequently lined with wood inserts?
11. To secure the most accurate measurement, should the rule be held flat or on edge?
12. For measuring long lengths, why is it better practice to measure with a zigzag rule or steel tape than with a bench rule?
13. Why do you square a line across a board with a try square or framing square rather than with a rule?
14. Describe the method of dividing a board into equal parts.

## Section II

## UNIT 10.

# CUTTING OUT ROUGH STOCK

**For cutting** stock into unfinished pieces you will need either a ripsaw or crosscut saw and sometimes both. Figure 10-1. If a circular saw is available, much time can be saved. (See Unit 58.)

### SAWS

The saw used for cutting across grain is the crosscut and the one for cutting with the grain is the ripsaw.

The teeth of the *crosscut saw* are shaped like little knife blades. Figure 10-2. They are bent alternately to right and left. This is called the "set" of the saw. When you use a crosscut saw with the proper set, the outside edges of the teeth cut the small fibers on either side and the center of the saw removes these fibers to form the saw *kerf* (the slit or notch made in cutting). Figure 10-3. The teeth are bent in this way to make them wider than the saw itself; this keeps the saw from buckling or scraping. Figure 10-4.

Crosscut saws come in many different lengths, but the easiest size to handle is one about 20 to 26 inches (508 to 660 mm) long. If you are cutting rather wet, green wood, use a saw with about five or six points to the inch (25 mm).

**10-1a.** A high-quality handsaw. It is always wise practice to buy a good grade. With proper maintenance, it will give years of service.

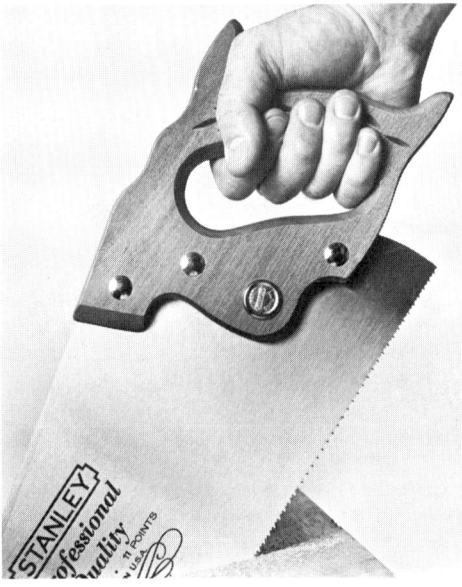

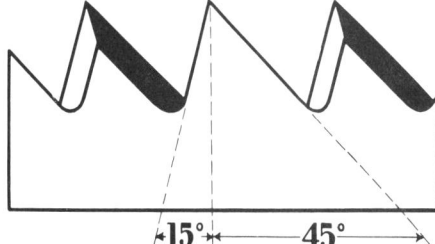

**10-2.** An enlarged view of a crosscut saw blade section, showing the knifelike shape of the teeth. Looking at the blade from the top, the teeth are bent alternately to the left and right.

**10-1b.** A correctly designed saw handle plays an important part in the way the saw performs. An easy grip makes the push-pull action easier.

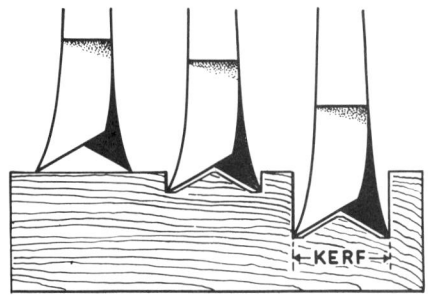

**10-3.** Here you see how the teeth of the saw blade form a kerf that is wider than the blade.

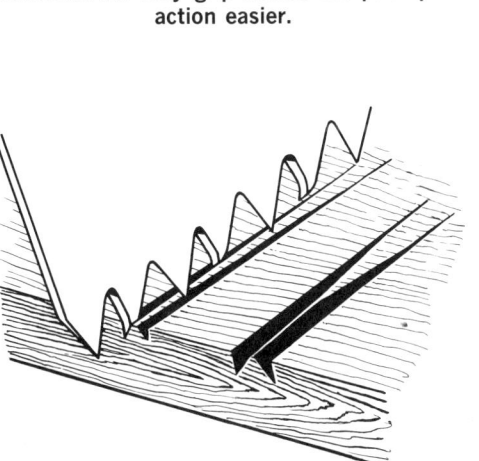

**10-4.** An example of how a crosscut saw performs its cutting operation. The beginning cut makes two grooves if drawn lightly over the surface.

Note the difference between points and teeth. Figure 10-5. There is always one more point to the inch than there are teeth, as you can see in Figure 10-5. For hard, dry wood, a finer saw with perhaps seven, eight, or nine points to the inch is best.

The *ripsaw* is used to cut with the grain. Figure 10-6. It has chisel-like teeth that form the saw kerf by cutting the ends of the fibers. Figures 10-7 and 10-8. A ripsaw used for ordinary woodworking ought to be 24 to 26 inches (609 to 660 mm) long with 5½ points per inch (25 mm).

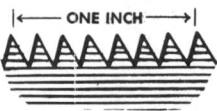

**10-5.** Here you see the difference between points and teeth on the saw. There is always one more point to the inch than there are teeth. The fewer the number of points *to the inch,* the rougher the cut.

**10-6.** Ripsaw teeth cut like vertical chisels. First, on one side of the set, small pieces of the wood are cut loose across the grain and pushed out. Then, on the other side, the following tooth plows out a similar bit of material.

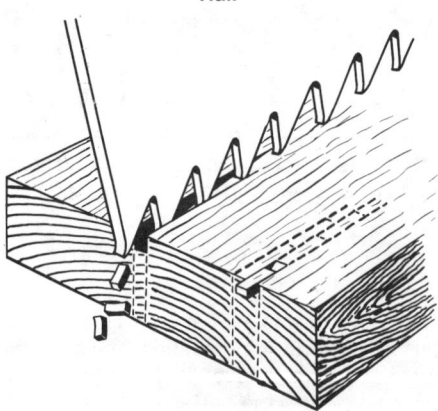

Saws cut better and stay sharper longer when properly cared for. Figure 10-9.

## SAWING LONG STOCK TO LENGTH

*Laying out the cutting line.* If the stock must be cut from stock 8 to 16 feet (2.44 to 4.88 m) long, the board should be laid across two sawhorses. Mark the cutting line and place this point beyond the top of one of the sawhorses. Figure 10-10.

● *Beginning the cut.* Place your left knee over the board to hold it. Then grasp the handle of the saw with the forefinger straight out on one side of the handle and the thumb and other fingers clamped tightly around the handle opening. Put your left thumb against the

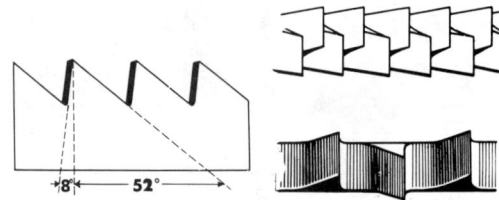

**10-7.** Ripsaw teeth are designed to cut with the grain. When you look at the edge of a ripsaw, the teeth appear as a series of chisel edges. Note that the teeth are filed straight across.

**10-8.** This shows the chisel-like action of ripsaw teeth.

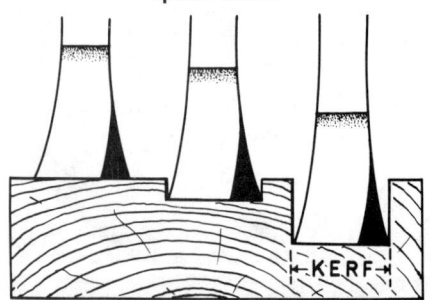

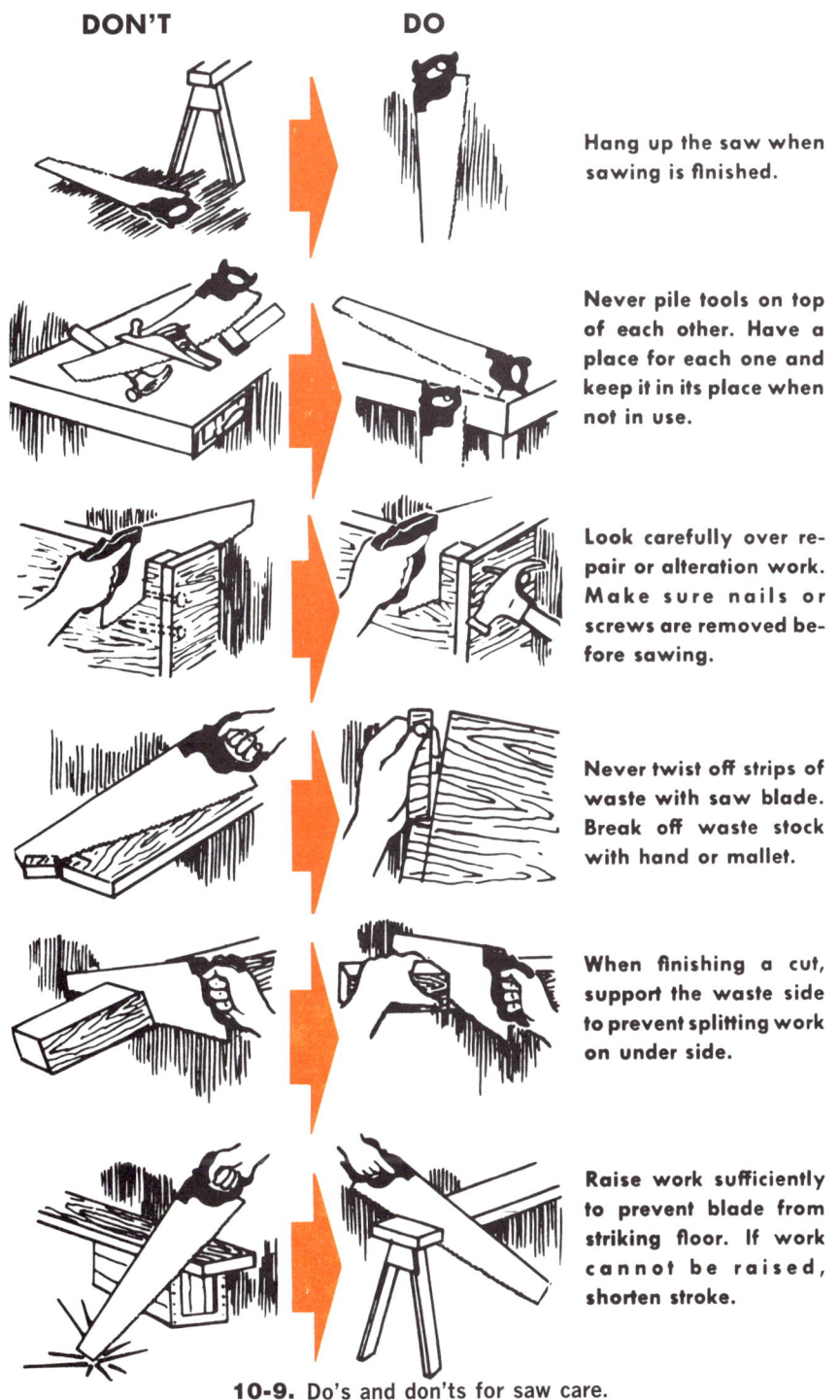

**DON'T**      **DO**

Hang up the saw when sawing is finished.

Never pile tools on top of each other. Have a place for each one and keep it in its place when not in use.

Look carefully over re-pair or alteration work. Make sure nails or screws are removed before sawing.

Never twist off strips of waste with saw blade. Break off waste stock with hand or mallet.

When finishing a cut, support the waste side to prevent splitting work on under side.

Raise work sufficiently to prevent blade from striking floor. If work cannot be raised, shorten stroke.

**10-9.** Do's and don'ts for saw care.

smooth surface of the blade to guide the saw in starting. Figure 10-11. Start the saw near the handle and draw up on it to begin the kerf. Hold the saw at an angle of about 45 degrees to the stock. Figure 10-12. Make sure the cut is started just outside the measuring line, to keep the kerf in the waste stock.

● *Precautions to take in beginning the cut.* If you try to begin the cut on the downward stroke, you may find that the saw jumps out of place to cut your hand or nick the wood. Therefore draw up on the saw once or twice before you begin the cutting. When cutting, establish a steady, even movement. Do not force the saw. If it is sharpened properly, its own weight is enough to make it cut correctly.

● *Making the cut.* Make sure that you are cutting square with the surface of the board. If you are a beginner, you should hold a try square against the side of the

saw blade to check it. Figure 10-13. As you saw, watch the line and not the saw itself. Blow the sawdust away from the line so you can see it. If the saw starts to go wrong, twist the handle slightly to get it back on the line. When you have cut almost through the board, hold the end of the board to be cut off while you make the last few cuts. This will keep the board from splitting off before the saw kerf is complete. Figure 10-14.

## CUTTING SHORT PIECES OF STOCK TO LENGTH

If you are working with short lengths of stock, you will be cutting them to length with the work held in a vise. Figure 10-15. Place the stock in the vise in a flat position with the cutting line sticking out just a little bit from the left side of the vise. Hold and start the saw in the same way as previously described. You will do a good job if you follow these directions.

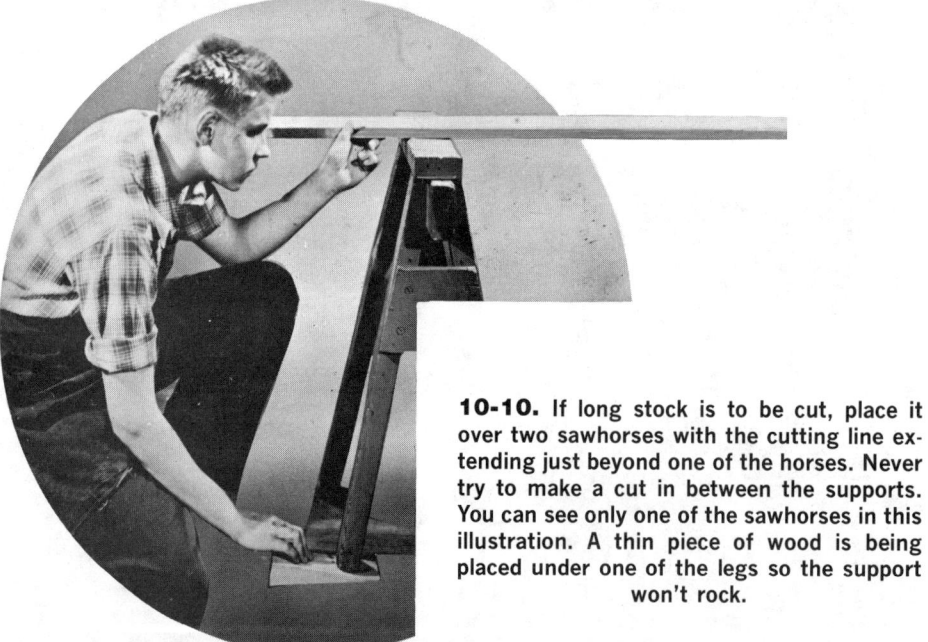

**10-10.** If long stock is to be cut, place it over two sawhorses with the cutting line extending just beyond one of the horses. Never try to make a cut in between the supports. You can see only one of the sawhorses in this illustration. A thin piece of wood is being placed under one of the legs so the support won't rock.

## CUTTING LONG PIECES OF STOCK TO WIDTH

Sometimes lumber is too wide and must be cut to width. For cutting along the grain of the wood you will use a ripsaw. Short stock is easily handled, but if the stock is long, place it over two sawhorses. Because the teeth are different from the crosscut, the saw should be held at an angle of about 60 degrees. Figure 10-16. As you cut a long piece of stock to width, the saw kerf may close in behind the saw and cause binding. Figure 10-17. Placing a little wedge at the beginning of the saw kerf will help keep it open. Move the wedge along as you proceed.

## CUTTING SHORT PIECES OF STOCK TO WIDTH

If a short length is to be ripped, place it in the vise as in Figure 10-18. The sawing should not be done too far away from the side of the vise, because this causes too much vibration. Begin with the board near the top of the vise and move it up a little at a time as you continue your work.

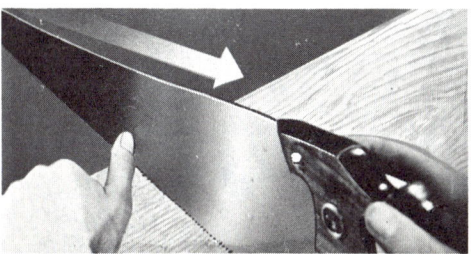

**10-11.** Starting a cut. The thumb of one hand is held against the smooth surface of the blade to guide the saw as it is drawn toward you. Draw the saw toward you slowly and carefully for several strokes where cut is being made. A slight groove will be formed. After the cut is started, take long easy strokes using light pressure on the push stroke. To start a cut when ripping, make short forward thrusts.

**10-13.** A way to keep the saw cut square with the face of the board. The operator places the handle of the try square firmly on the face of the wood and then slides it along until the blade of the try square comes in contact with the blade of the saw, to check it for squareness.

**10-12.** Hold the crosscut saw at an angle of about 45 degrees to the stock.

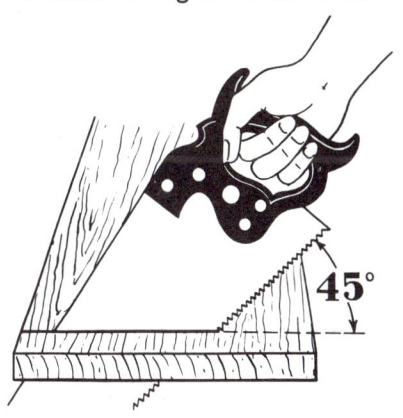

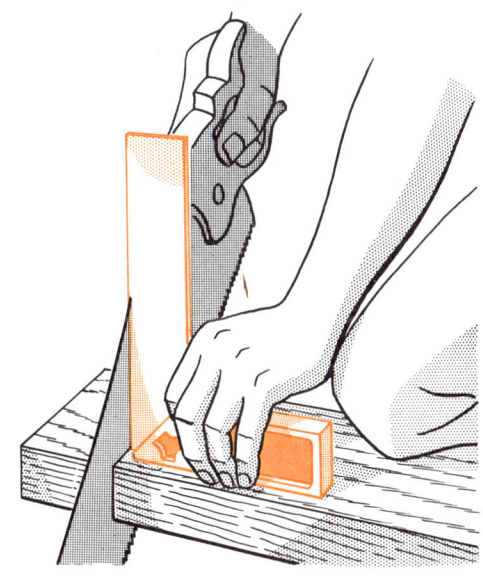

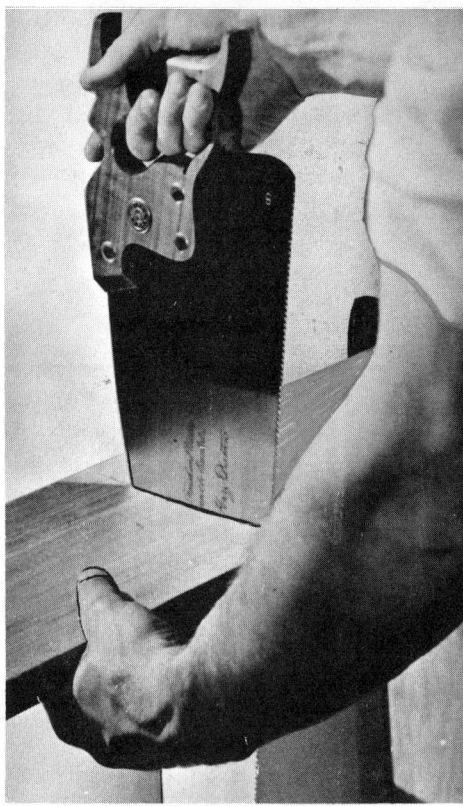

**10-14.** Taking the last few cuts in sawing off a board. Notice that you should hold the stock to be cut off in one hand while sawing with the other. In this way, the wood will not crack off before the saw kerf is completed.

**10-15.** Cutting stock to length with the work clamped in a vise.

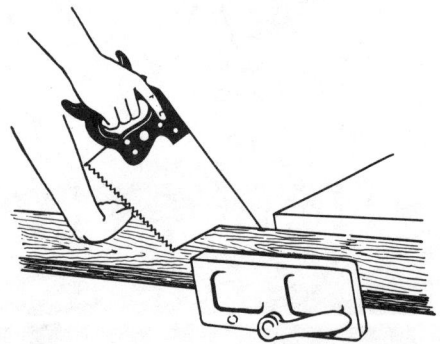

## CUTTING PLYWOOD

Place the plywood with the finished face up. Use a saw having about ten points per inch. Support the panel firmly so that it won't sag. You can reduce splitting out of the underside by putting a length of scrap lumber under the saw line. Use a sharp saw and hold it at a low angle, about 30 degrees, to do the cutting. Figure 10-19.

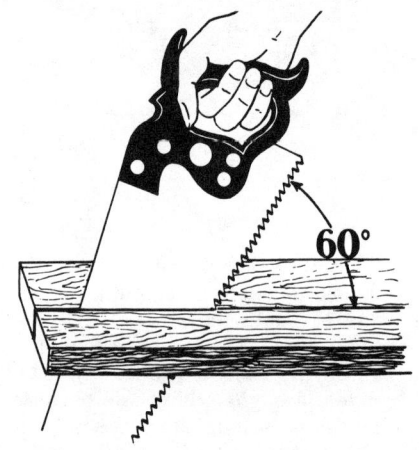

**10-16.** Hold a ripsaw at an angle of about 60 degrees when cutting to width.

**10-17.** Ripping a board with the work held over sawhorses. As the saw progresses, place a little wedge at the beginning of the saw kerf to hold it open. You may have to move it along as you work.

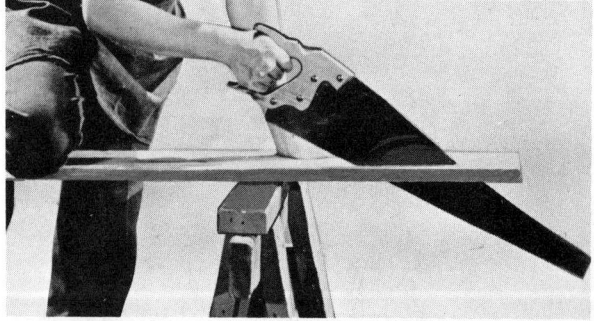

**10-18.** Ripping with the work held in a vise. Notice that the saw is held at an angle of about 60 degrees to the work. Always do the sawing close to the vise jaws, so that the board will not vibrate. It is preferable to rip on a saw-horse but for cutting short pieces of stock, work can sometimes be done more conveniently in a bench vise. Make sure that the saw does not strike any other tools on the bench or cut the bench.

**10-19.** When hand sawing plywood, place the wood with the finished face up, using a sharp saw having ten to fifteen points to the inch. Make sure the panel does not sag during the cutting. Hold the saw at a low angle.

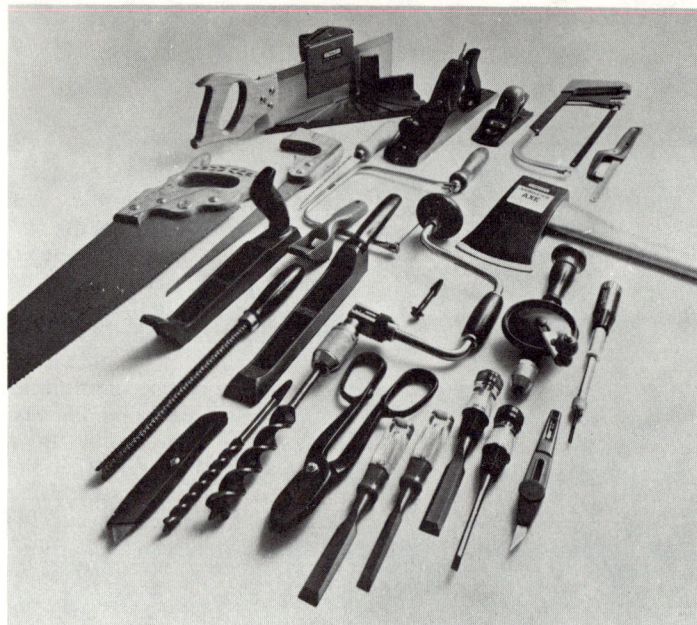

These are all edge-
cutting tools.

## CAN YOU ANSWER THESE QUESTIONS ON CUTTING OUT ROUGH STOCK?

1. There are two kinds of handsaws. Name them and tell what the parts of a handsaw are.

2. Why must a saw have the proper set in order to cut correctly?

3. Why is a saw with five points to the inch best for cutting wet, green wood?

4. What does a ripsaw tooth resemble?

5. If you could have only one saw for your shop, which one would you choose?

6. Why shouldn't the cutting line on a long board be placed between the sawhorses?

7. At what angle to the stock should you hold the crosscut saw?

8. To start a cut, should you push down or draw up on the saw? Why?

9. Which should you watch, the action of the saw or the cutting line?

10. What is a saw kerf?

11. Why does the crosscut saw have knifelike teeth?

12. When a saw binds or sticks, what is the most likely cause? How do you prevent it?

13. Tell how you can prevent the board from splitting off just before the saw cut is completed.

14. How is plywood handled in sawing? What support may be required under the sawline? Why?

# SECTION III
# Completing the Squaring Operations

**What you must know and be able to do in Units 11–17:**

11. Everything about a plane: its parts; the kinds and how they differ; why we keep the iron sharp; how to put a plane together so it is ready to use.

12. The first surface: how to identify and remove warp or wind; locking the board in place; how to plane the surface true and smooth and how to check it.

13. Working to width and thickness: which edge to choose first; what plane to choose; holding the stock; using a marking gage; how to hold the plane correctly; how to do planing; planing the stock to thickness and width.

14. Learning to cut end grain: why it is more difficult to cut; cutting with the block plane; how to plane end grain; how to check.

15. Making a very fine saw cut: how to use the backsaw, the dovetail saw, and the bench hook; how to do crosscutting and ripping with a backsaw.

16. Gluing up stock: how wood is prepared for gluing; how to select glue and clamps; different ways of joining wood with glue; how to do the gluing.

17. Correct procedure for squaring up stock: the three different methods that can be followed.

*When lumber is delivered to the shop, it is usually dressed (surfaced), which means it has been run through a planer. These planed surfaces must be planed a little by hand because every piece used must be true, smooth, and square on at least two surfaces.*

*When stock is too small in thickness or width, pieces can be glued up to form larger pieces before any squaring up is done.*

# ASSEMBLING AND ADJUSTING A PLANE

**After the** pieces are sawed, they are rough and need to be planed smooth. For most of your work you will begin with stock that has been surfaced on two sides (S2S) at the mill. However, if you look closely at the surfaces, you will see small mill or knife marks (waves) made by the rotating cutter of the planer, or surfacer. Figure 11-1. These must be removed before using the stock in any project. Enough hand planing must be done to remove these mill marks completely. If you do not hand plane the surface, these marks will show up after you have applied a finish.

## KINDS OF BENCH PLANES

There are three common types of bench (hand) planes, all very similar. The big difference is in their lengths. Figure 11-2. The *jack plane* is from 11½ to 15 inches (292 to 381 mm) long. This tool is for all types of general planing. The

**11-1.** Exaggerated mill or knife marks that are made by the planer, or surfacer. These must be removed by hand planing.

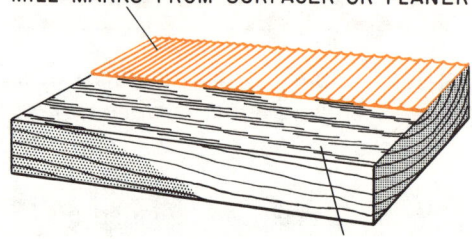

MILL MARKS FROM SURFACER OR PLANER

SMOOTH HAND PLANED SURFACE

**11-2.** Three types of hand planes: A. This is a jack plane, which has a bed commonly 14 or 15 inches (355 or 380 mm) long. It can be used to true the edges of boards and for general planing. B. This is a smooth plane which can be purchased in lengths from 8 to 9 inches (203 to 228 mm). It is good for smoothing and finishing work for which a light plane is preferred. C. This is the fore or jointer plane. It is the type used to obtain a true surface on long edges in preparation for gluing up stock.

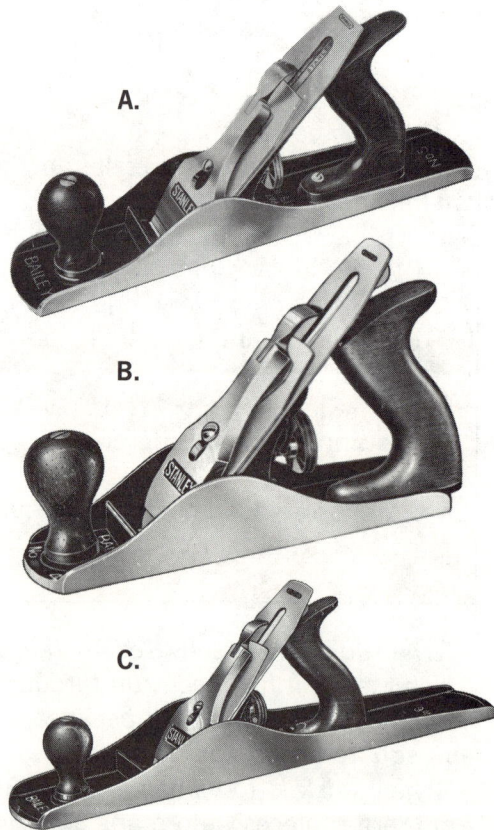

A.

B.

C.

smooth *plane* is the same, except that it ranges from 7 to 9 inches (178 to 228 mm) in length. The *fore* and *jointer* planes are much longer, from 18 to 24 inches (457 to 609 mm). These are especially useful for planing long edges straight, as in fitting large doors. They are used frequently when making joints for (jointing) long pieces of stock before gluing them up.

## PARTS OF A PLANE

The plane is perhaps the most complicated hand woodworking tool you will use. It takes more care, attention, and adjustment than any other tool. Figure 11-3 shows major parts of a plane.

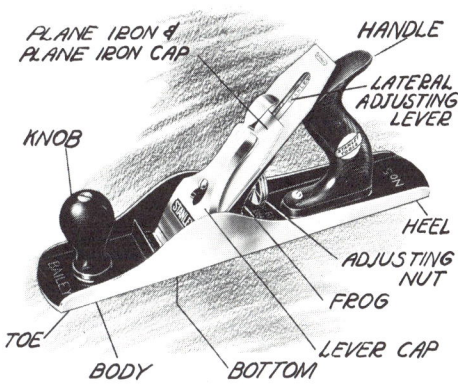

**11-3a.** Study the parts of this plane, as you will need to know them when learning to use it.

**11-3b.** Exploded view of a plane, showing its parts.

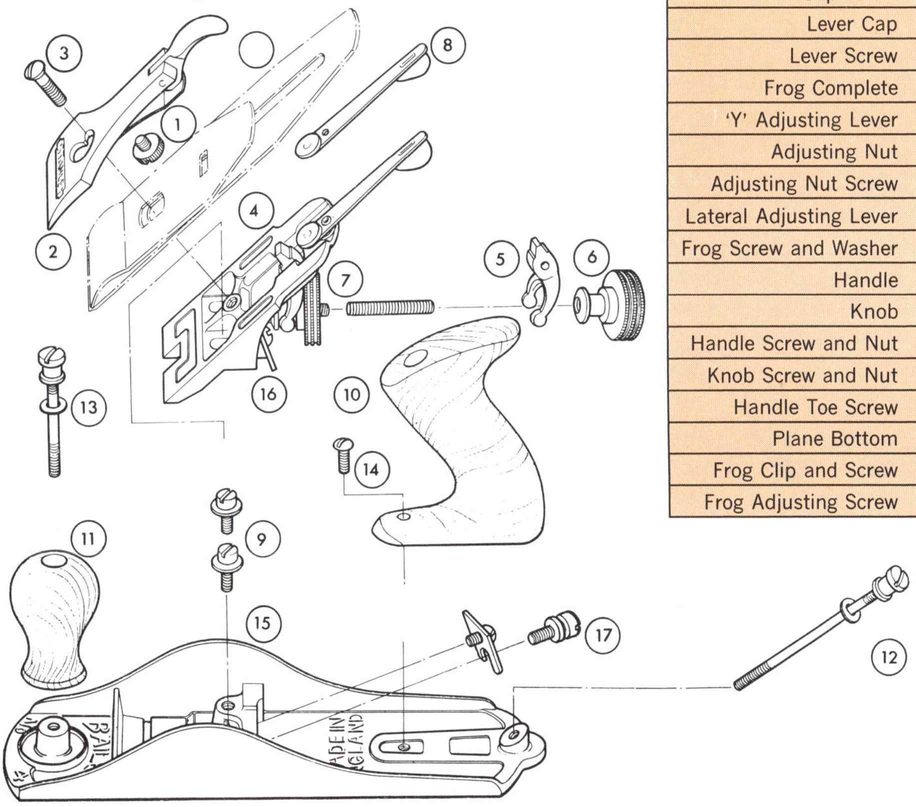

|  | Key No. |
|---|---|
| Cap Screw | 1 |
| Lever Cap | 2 |
| Lever Screw | 3 |
| Frog Complete | 4 |
| 'Y' Adjusting Lever | 5 |
| Adjusting Nut | 6 |
| Adjusting Nut Screw | 7 |
| Lateral Adjusting Lever | 8 |
| Frog Screw and Washer | 9 |
| Handle | 10 |
| Knob | 11 |
| Handle Screw and Nut | 12 |
| Knob Screw and Nut | 13 |
| Handle Toe Screw | 14 |
| Plane Bottom | 15 |
| Frog Clip and Screw | 16 |
| Frog Adjusting Screw | 17 |

The body of the plane is made of cast steel. The *base,* or *bottom* as it is sometimes called, is either smooth or ribbed (corrugated). There is no difference between these two planes, except that some woodworkers feel that the plane with the ribbed base works a little better.

Right behind the opening in the plane is a *frog* that provides the support for the plane iron. This frog contains two adjustments. An *adjusting nut* (brass knurled nut) adjusts the depth of cut, regulating the thickness of the shavings. A long slender lever, called the *lateral adjusting lever,* provides for the sidewise adjustment of the cutter.

The *double plane iron* consists of the plane iron itself, sometimes called the cutter, and the plane iron cap. The cutter width varies with the size of the plane. The most common sizes are $1\frac{3}{4}$, 2, and $2\frac{3}{8}$ inches (45, 50, and 60 mm). The plane iron fits over the frog and is held firmly with a *lever cap.*

**11-4. One method of checking a plane for sharpness. The blade will cut paper when it is sharp.**

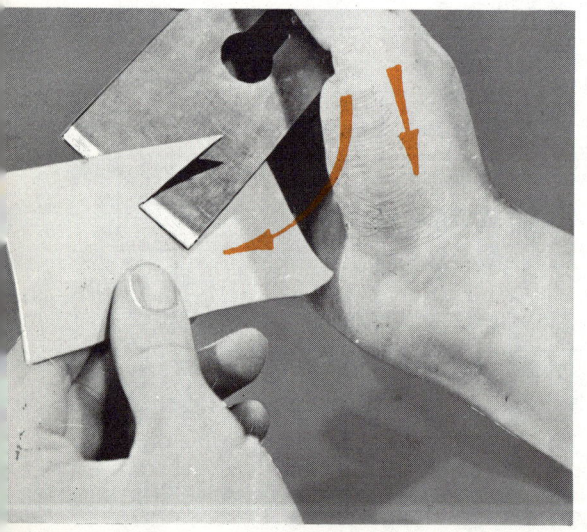

## TESTING A PLANE IRON FOR SHARPNESS

Check the plane iron, or cutter, to be sure it is sharp. One way to do this is to sight along the edge. A sharp blade will not reflect any light. Another method is to cut a piece of paper with it. Figure 11-4. It can also be tested on your thumbnail. Let the cutting edge rest on your nail and then push it lightly. If the blade tends to cling to the nail, it is sharp; but if it slides easily it needs sharpening, or whetting. You should never use a dull plane iron. Sharpen it before you assemble the plane. (See the unit on sharpening hand tools.)

## ASSEMBLING THE DOUBLE PLANE IRON

Hold the iron in your left hand, with the bevel (slanted edge) away from you. Place the plane iron cap at right angles to the plane iron and drop the setscrew into the plane iron through the large opening. With the plane iron cap still at right angles, slide it back and away from the cutting edge. Turn the plane iron cap parallel to the plane iron. Slip it up until it is about $\frac{1}{16}$ inch (2 mm) away from the cutting edge for finish work. Figure 11-5. Make sure that you do not injure the cutting edge of the plane iron by shoving the cap too far forward. Tighten the setscrew firmly.

The plane iron cap serves two purposes. It helps to stiffen and strengthen the plane iron and serves as a chip breaker. Figure 11-6.

## INSERTING THE PLANE IRON IN THE PLANE

Insert the double plane iron in the plane with the bevel side down. There are several things that you must watch when doing this. Figure 11-7. First, don't hit the

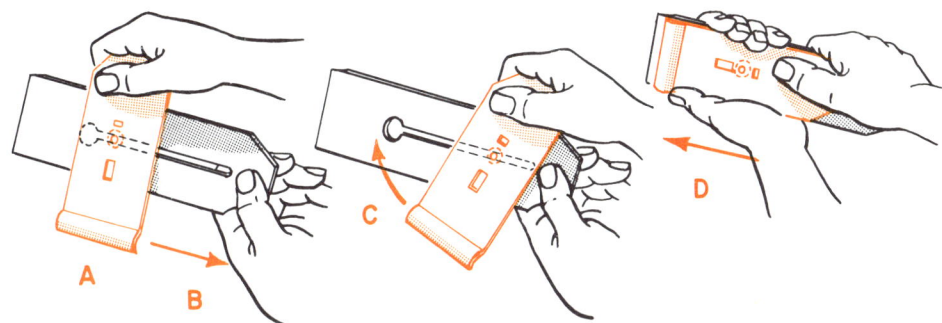

**11-5.** The correct method for assembling a double plane iron: A. Hold the plane iron in one hand, with the bevel side down and away from you. Place the plane iron cap at right angles to it and drop the setscrew through the large opening. B. Slide the plane iron cap back as far as it will go and then, C, turn it so it is parallel to the plane iron. D. Move the plane iron cap to within about 1/16 inch of the cutting edge. Then tighten the setscrew with a screwdriver or the lever cap.

cutting edge on the body of the plane as you insert it over the frog. Second, make sure that the slot in the plane iron cap fits over the little Y adjustment. Third, check to see that the roller on the lateral adjustment slips into the slot of the plane iron.

Next, pull the little thumb-adjusting cam on the lever cap up at right angles. Figure 11-8. Then slip the lever cap over the lever cap screw on the frog. Push the thumb-adjusting cam down to fasten the plane iron securely in the plane. If you find it must be forced, you probably need to unscrew the lever cap screw just a little bit or tighten it a little if it is too loose.

## ADJUSTING THE PLANE

The plane should be adjusted before beginning the cutting and again several times while the planing is done. To make the first adjustment, turn the plane upside down with the bottom about eye level. Turn the brass knurled nut until the plane iron appears just beyond the bottom of the plane. Then, with the lateral adjustment lever, move the blade to one

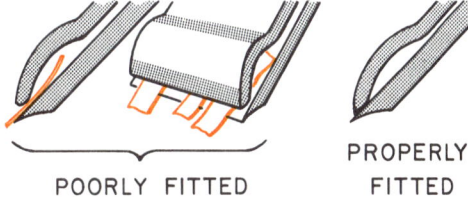

POORLY FITTED  PROPERLY FITTED

**11-6.** The plane iron cap must be properly fitted to the plane iron so that chips of wood do not get between the two parts.

**11-7.** Inserting the plane iron in the plane. Be extremely careful in doing this to keep the cutting edge from becoming nicked.

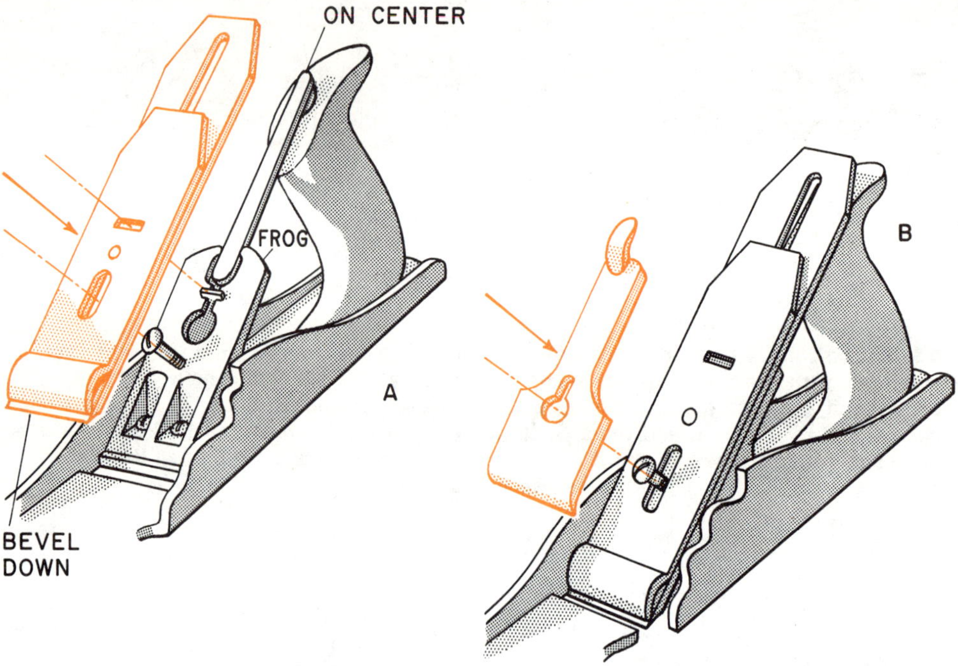

ON CENTER

FROG

BEVEL
DOWN

A

B

USE ONLY THUMB
PRESSURE

C

**11-8.** Steps in installing a double plane iron in the plane: A. The iron is assembled and placed over the frog. B. The iron is in place and the cap is inserted. C. The plane iron cap holds the other plane iron in place.

side or the other until it is parallel to the bottom. Figures 11-9 and 11-10.

The experienced woodworker then tries the plane on a piece of scrap stock to see how it cuts, adjusting it to the chip he wants. For rough planing and when much stock is to be removed, set the plane deeper. When you are truing up a surface and making it smooth, a light cut that forms a feathery shaving is best.

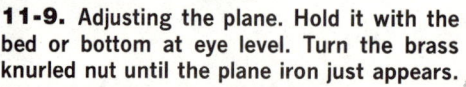
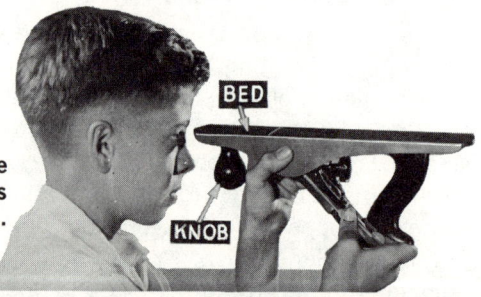

BED

KNOB

**11-9.** Adjusting the plane. Hold it with the bed or bottom at eye level. Turn the brass knurled nut until the plane iron just appears.

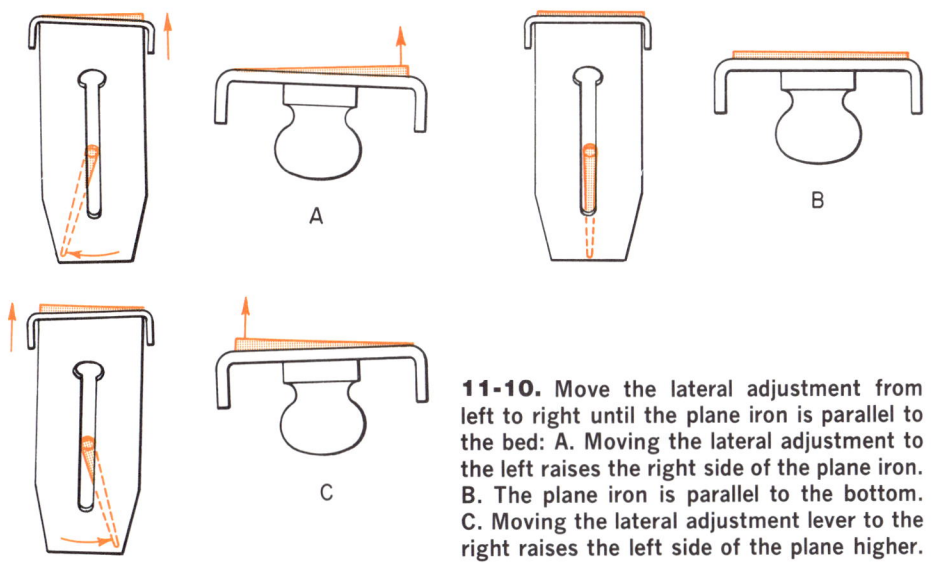

**11-10.** Move the lateral adjustment from left to right until the plane iron is parallel to the bed: A. Moving the lateral adjustment to the left raises the right side of the plane iron. B. The plane iron is parallel to the bottom. C. Moving the lateral adjustment lever to the right raises the left side of the plane higher.

## CAN YOU ANSWER THESE QUESTIONS ON ASSEMBLING AND ADJUSTING A PLANE?

1. Name the important parts of a plane. Why is it necessary to know these parts?
2. Name the three common types of bench planes. What is the major use of each?
3. Why do you suppose the jack plane is best for the school shop?
4. Tell three ways of testing the sharpness of the plane iron.
5. To do finish planing, how far should the cap be set from the cutting edge?
6. What is the purpose of the plane iron cap?
7. Describe in detail the steps to follow in fastening a plane iron in a plane.
8. Tell how to make the depth adjustment on a plane.

# PLANING A SURFACE

**The first** surface you choose to plane should be the best flat surface of the piece. It should be free of flaws and should be the side with the most interesting grain, because it will show.

## INSPECTING A SURFACE FOR WARP

*Warp* is any variation from a true, or plane, surface. It includes crook, cup, bow, wind (twist), or any combination of these. *Crook* is a deviation edgewise from a straight line drawn from end to end. *Bow* is a deviation flatwise from a straight line drawn from end to end of a piece. *Cup* is a curve across the grain or width of a piece. A beginner can check if the board is cupped with a straightedge or the blade of a try or framing square. Figure 12-1.

*Wind*, or *twist*, in a board indicates that the board is twisted throughout its length. One way to check this is to lay the board on a level surface to see if it rocks on two corners. Another method is to place two parallel pieces of wood across the grain, one on each end of the board. Then sight along the top of the first parallel. If you can see one end of the second parallel, you know that the board has a wind. Figure 12-2. With a pencil, mark the high points of the board if it is warped or has a wind; more stock must be removed at these points.

## FASTENING A BOARD IN THE VISE

The board should be locked in the vise lengthwise, with the grain running toward the ends where pressure is applied. Locking a board cross-grain tends to warp it. If the wood is rough, you may need to take a few cuts with the plane before the direction of the grain shows.

Lock the board between the dog of the vise and the bench stop, or lay the board on top of the bench with one end sup-

**12-1.** Checking the material to see if it is cupped.

**12-2.** Sticks placed across the ends of the board will show wind or twist.

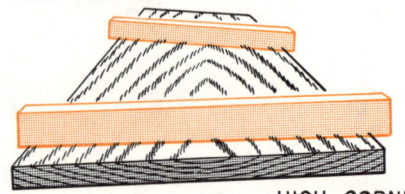

HIGH CORNER

HIGH CORNER

THE STICKS DO NOT LIE LEVEL

ported against the bench stop. Figures 12-3 and 12-4.

## PLANING THE SURFACE TRUE AND SMOOTH

Always plane with the grain. If you plane against it, you will roughen the surface. Figure 12-5.

Grasp the knob of the plane in your left hand and the handle in your right hand. Figure 12-6. Stand just back of the work with your left foot forward. In this way you can swing your body back and forth as you plane and at the same time use a forward motion with your arms.

Place the toe or front of the plane on the board. Apply pressure to the knob at the start of the stroke. As the whole base comes in contact with the wood, apply even pressure to the knob and handle. Then, as the plane begins to leave the surface, apply more pressure to the handle. Figure 12-7. In this way you won't cut a convex (dome-shaped) curve in the board.

Lift the plane off the board on the return stroke. Don't drag the plane back to the starting position. This would dull the blade. Sometimes the plane will cut more easily if you take a shearing cut rather than a straight cut.

Work across the board gradually. If you have marked any high points, these will take more planing than other areas.

## REMOVING WIND FROM A BOARD

Wind in a board requires taking a partial cut at either the beginning or end of the board.

To remove wind at the beginning of the board, take a partial cut there, beginning the stroke as before. Then as you plane along the board as far as you think necessary, slowly lift the handle to finish the cut.

To take the wind out of the end of the board, start the partial cut at some point in the center of the board. Begin with the handle held away from the surface and gradually lower it as you begin the forward motion.

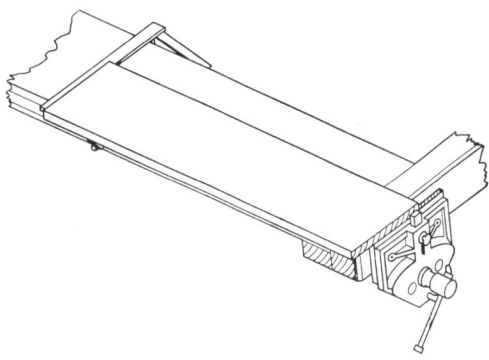

**12-4.** Note how the stock is held between the dog of the vise and a bench stop.

**12-5.** The arrow indicates the direction in which the stock should be planed.

DIRECTION TO PLANE

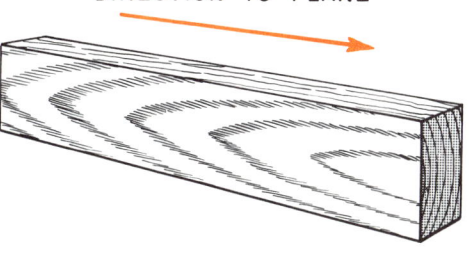

**12-3.** A bench or board stop.

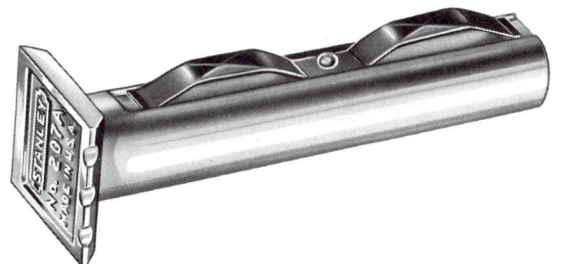

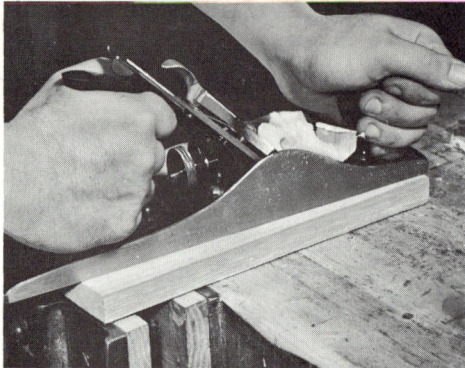

**12-6.** Planing the face of a board. Note that the work is locked securely between the bench stop and the dog of the vise. You can tell when the plane is cutting properly by the kind of shaving formed. The shaving should be uniform in thickness and width. The thickness of the shaving depends on the setting of the plane. For rough cutting, a heavy shaving should be taken. For finish work, shavings should be light and silky. Always plane with the grain of the wood.

**12-8.** Checking a board. Hold the board at about eye level and place a straightedge across it. If any light shows through, you know that it is a low spot. Mark the *high spot* on the board with a pencil and then plane lightly over this area.

## CHECKING THE SURFACE

After the surface begins to get smooth, check it with a straightedge to see if it is true. Light will show through where there are low spots on the board. The straightedge will touch the high points. Figures 12-8 and 12-9. It is a good idea to check the total width and length every few inches and diagonally across

**12-7.** Proper method for applying pressure when planing. More pressure is applied to the knob at the start of the stroke and to the handle at the end of the stroke so that you don't cut a convex surface.

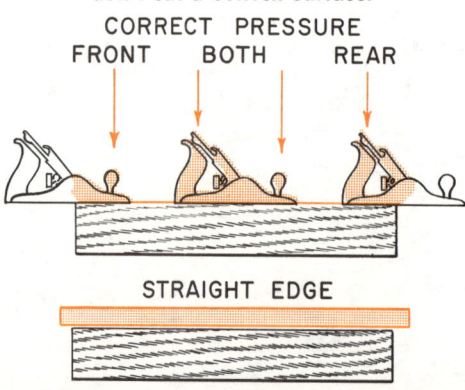

CORRECT PRESSURE
FRONT    BOTH    REAR

STRAIGHT EDGE

NO LIGHT SHOWS UNDER STRAIGHT EDGE

**12-9.** Check several places across the width of the board for high and low spots.

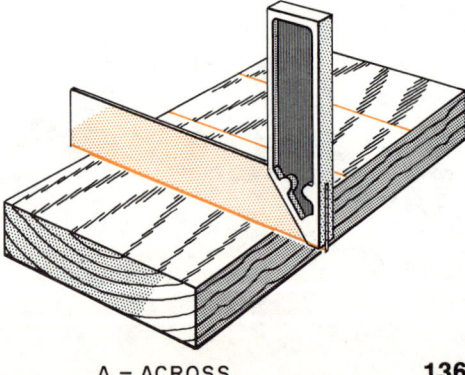

A – ACROSS

**136**

the corners, using a pencil to mark the high points. Figures 12-10 and 12-11. Sometimes one plane stroke will remove these. Figure 12-12.

The first surface which has been planed true and smooth is called the *face surface* or *face side*. This is the side you use as a start in squaring up stock. Squaring up stock will be explained in Unit 17.

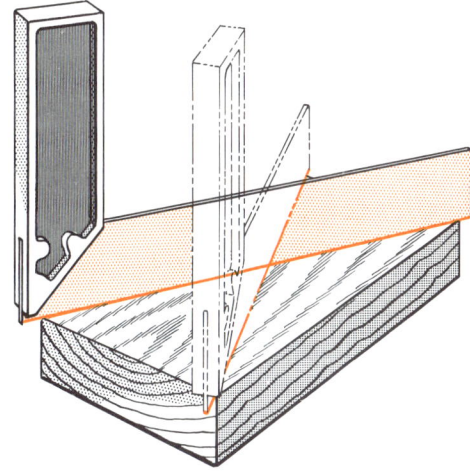

C–ACROSS CORNERS
**12-11.** Checking across the corners.

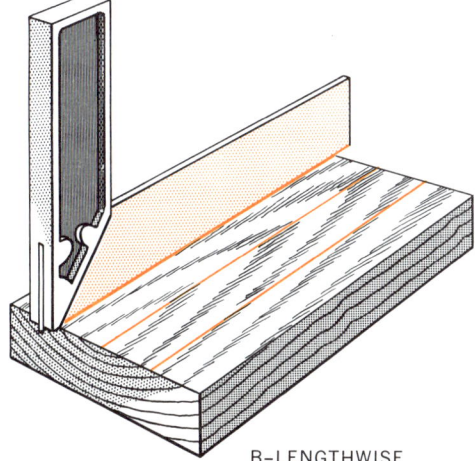

B–LENGTHWISE
**12-10.** Check with a straightedge from one end to the other. Make sure that the surface is straight and true.

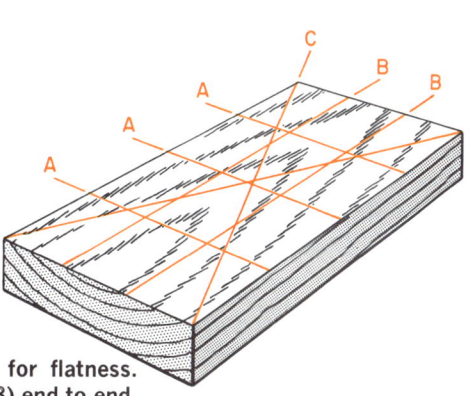

**12-12.** Checking the surface for flatness. Check from (A) edge to edge, (B) end to end, and finally (C) across the corners.

## CAN YOU ANSWER THESE QUESTIONS ON PLANING A SURFACE?

1. Which surface of the board is the first to be planed?
2. Can you see if a board is warped?
3. What are the two ways of checking wind in a board?
4. What is likely to happen if the plane is dragged rather than lifted back to the starting position?
5. Tell how you would go about removing wind from a board.
6. What is the surface that is planed first called?

# Section III
## UNIT 13.

**Most project** pieces must be planed to width and thickness to make the surfaces smooth and true and to bring the stock down to the finished size. In planing to thickness and width, all measurements should be taken from the face surface or side, which you planed in the last unit. This surface should be marked with the number "1," or another small mark, near the first edge to be planed.

### SELECTING AND CHECKING THE FACE, OR JOINT, EDGE

Select the edge that is truest and best to plane first. This is called the face, or joint, edge. With the try square held against the face surface, test the edge at several points along the stock for squareness. Also check with a straightedge along the length. Mark with a pencil the high points where you must do most of the planing.

### SELECTING THE PROPER PLANE

For short pieces, the jack plane is very satisfactory. In planing an edge, how-

ever, especially a long one, it is better to use a plane with a long base such as the fore or jointer plane. As you can see in Figure 13-1, the jointer plane tends to straighten the edge, whereas the shorter plane will follow any curve that may be in the edge.

### FASTENING THE WORK IN THE VISE

Lock the stock in the vise with the edge above the surface. Figure 13-2. If the stock is long, one end should be supported by the vise and the other held in place with a hand screw as shown in Figure 13-3. Sometimes the work is held against a V block on the top of the bench. Figure 13-4.

### HOLDING THE PLANE

Adjust the plane to take a very fine cut. In planing an edge you may hold the handle of the plane the same way as for

**13-1.** This shows the reason for using a plane with a long bed to plane the edge of long stock. The longer plane tends to straighten out any irregularities, whereas the shorter plane tends to follow curves.

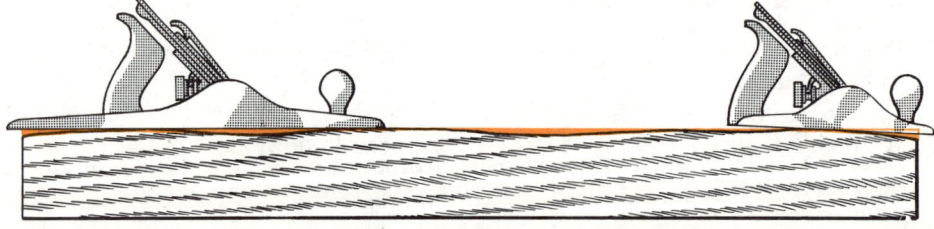

surface planing. Figure 13-5. To use a second method, you can place your thumb around the back of the knob with your other fingers curled under the bottom of the plane. In this way you can use your fingers along the face side to guide the plane and keep it at a right angle to the face. Figure 13-4.

### PLANING THE FACE EDGE

Plane with the grain. First remove any high spots that you have marked. Then take long, continuous strokes to remove a thin chip all along the edge. Be sure to apply pressure on the knob in starting the stroke and on the handle when finishing it. Figure 13-6. The idea in planing this first edge is not to remove stock but

to get the edge square with the face surface and straight along its entire length. Check with the try square and straight edge as shown in Figures 13-7 and 13-8. Mark this edge with two light pencil lines to show that it is the face, or joint, edge.

### SETTING THE MARKING GAGE

To bring the stock down to the correct width and thickness, you will need a marking gage. Figure 13-9.

As you can see, the marking gage has a scale along one surface. This scale is usually not correct. In sharpening the small spur to wedge shape by filing, the starting point of the scale becomes inaccurate. You will need to keep this in mind as you set the gage.

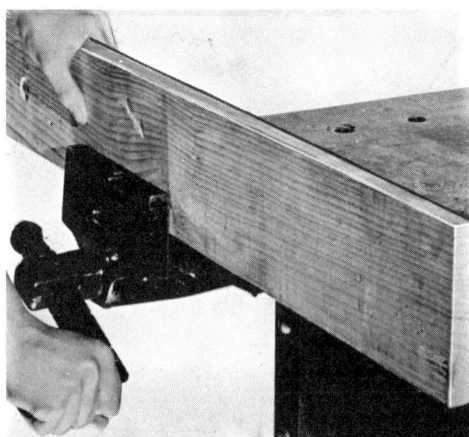

**13-2.** Locking stock in a vise. Make sure that the stock is held firmly in the vise jaws so that there will be no movement when using the plane.

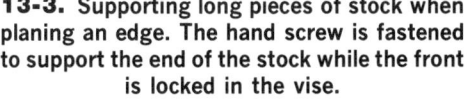

**13-3.** Supporting long pieces of stock when planing an edge. The hand screw is fastened to support the end of the stock while the front is locked in the vise.

First set the head of the scale to the correct distance as shown on the beam and then lightly turn the thumbscrew. Hold the marking gage upside down in one hand and use the rule to check the distance from the head to the point of

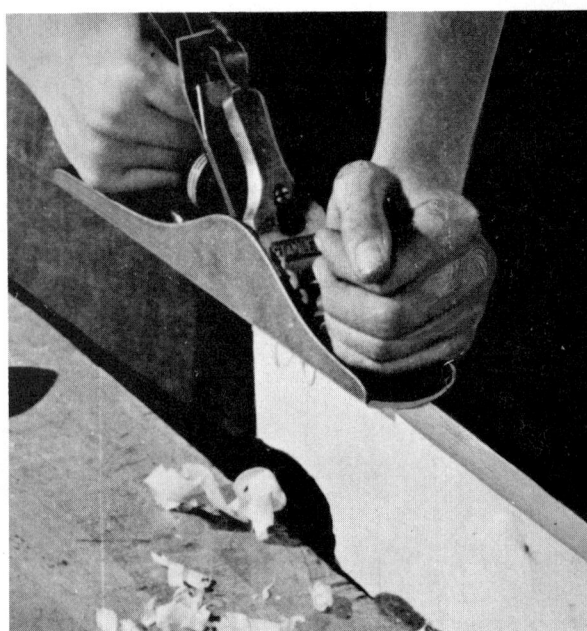

**13-6.** Starting the cutting stroke in planing an edge. Pressure is applied to the knob.

**13-4.** Holding stock against a V block to do edge planing. This is especially satisfactory for planing long stock or when a vise is not available. Note how the thumb is held around the back of the knob and the fingers are curled under the bottom of the plane to guide it.

**13-5.** Planing the edge of a board by holding the knob firmly in one hand. When using this method, you must be extremely careful not to rock the plane.

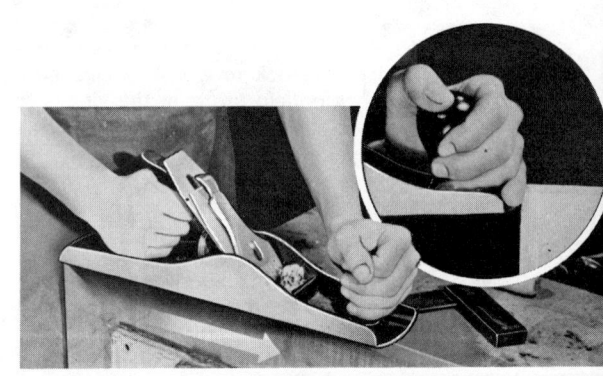

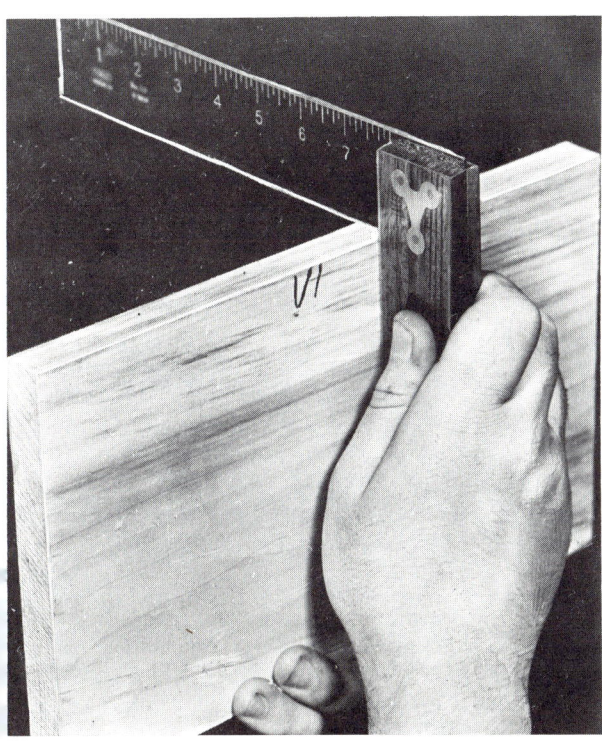

**13-7.** Checking the joint edge by holding the handle of a try square against the face side or surface. Move the try square to make certain that the edge is square along its total length.

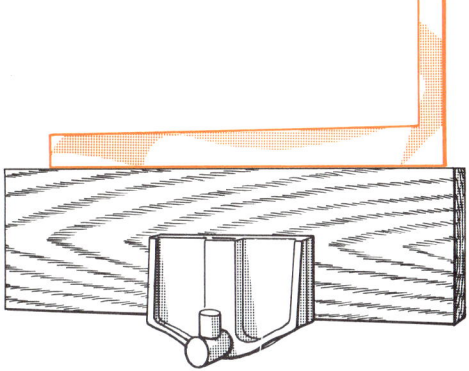

**13-8.** Checking an edge for straightness. This is especially important on long stock. The edge must be square with the face surface and not form a convex or concave curve. Hold the straightedge against the planed edge and sight at eye level to see if any light shows through.

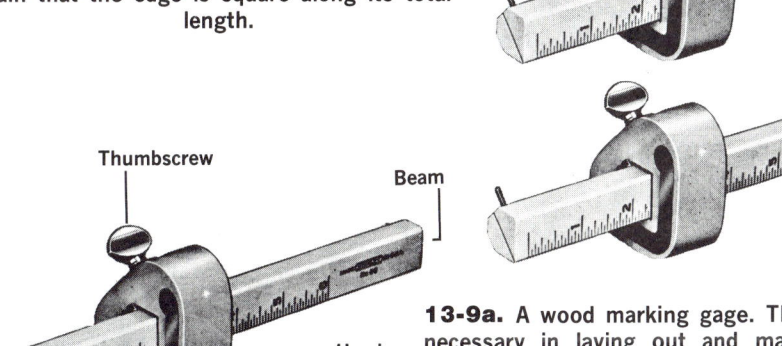

Thumbscrew

Beam

Head

Spur

**13-9a.** A wood marking gage. This tool is necessary in laying out and marking the thickness and width of stock.

**13-9b.** A metal marking gage.

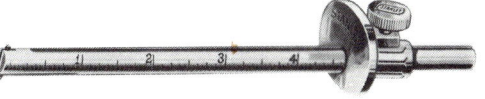

141

the spur. Figure 13-10. If the measurement is wrong, tap the head a bit one way or the other to correct it for the measurement you want, then tighten the thumbscrew. Always recheck the measurement before using the marking gage.

## MARKING THE STOCK
## TO WIDTH

Check the drawing for the width of stock needed and then set the marking gage to this width. Hold the stock to be marked with the face surface up and the face, or joint, edge to your right. Place the head of the marking gage firmly against this joint edge. Then tip the marking gage forward with a slight twist of your wrist until the spur just touches the surface of the wood. Beginning at the end toward you, push the marking gage forward, applying pressure as shown in Figure 13-11. The spur will make a fine layout line that marks the correct width of stock.

Sometimes, when widths too wide for the gage must be marked, it will be necessary to mark the width at several points. Hold a straightedge along these points, marking a fine line with a knife. You can also use a pencil and a combination square. Figure 13-12.

## PLANING THE SECOND EDGE

If there is much stock to be removed, the board should be ripped to within $\frac{1}{8}$ to $\frac{3}{16}$ inch (3 to 5 mm) of the layout line.

Lock the stock in the vise as described above and begin to plane the second edge. As the plane approaches the layout line, use the try square frequently to check the edge for squareness with the face surface and a straightedge to check the length. Take special care at the layout line to take light, even shavings that are the total width and length of the edge.

The last cut you take should just split the dent made by the marking gage.

## MARKING THE STOCK
## TO THICKNESS

Check the thickness of the stock and then set the marking gage to this measurement. Hold the head of the marking gage against the face surface. Mark a line on both edges to indicate the proper thickness.

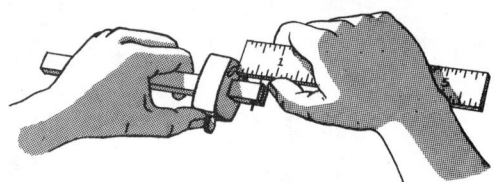

**13-10.** Setting a marking gage. Note that the gage is held upside down in one hand and a rule held in the other hand to check the distance from the point or spur to the head of the marking gage.

**13-11.** Using a marking gage. Notice that the marking gage is tilted slightly and that the worker is pushing it away from himself. In doing the marking, pressure should be applied to hold the head of the gage firmly against the edge while forward pressure is applied.

## PLANING TO THICKNESS

Check the lines that show thickness to see if there are any spots that are higher than the rest of the board. These need extra planing. Lock the stock between the dog of the vise and the bench stop and plane these areas first. Then begin to plane the total length of the stock on the second surface, working from one side to the other to bring it down to proper thickness. Planing to thickness is the same as planing the first surface, except that you must constantly check the two lines showing thickness. You should be able to hold the handle of the try square against this second surface and find that the edges are square, as they were with the face surface.

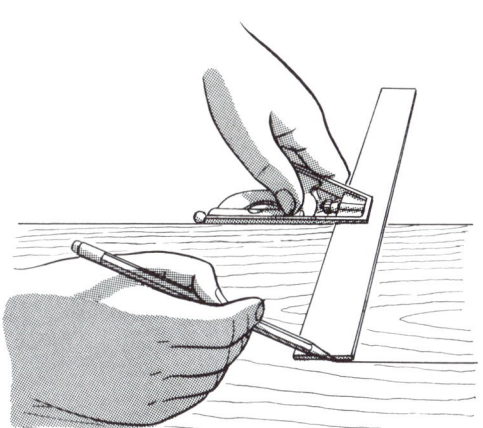

**13-12.** Using a combination square and pencil to mark for correct width. The carpenter uses this method.

## CAN YOU ANSWER THESE QUESTIONS ON PLANING STOCK TO WIDTH AND THICKNESS?

1. When is a fore or jointer plane used?
2. The first planing should be done on which edge?
3. How can a piece of long stock be supported for planing along one edge?
4. Describe the two ways of holding the knob of the plane in planing an edge.
5. What should be accomplished by planing this first edge? Should a large amount of stock be removed? Explain.
6. Describe a marking gage and name its parts.
7. Should you depend on the marking gage scale for setting the tool to width? Why?
8. Should the mark made by the marking gage be heavy and deep?
9. Suppose that considerable stock must be removed to bring the stock to width. Can you tell how this should be done?
10. Should you completely remove the marking gage line when you plane the second edge?
11. A piece of stock that has been squared to thickness and width has certain characteristics. What are these?

143

# PLANING END GRAIN

**Planing end grain** is harder than planing the face or edge with the grain. In planing the end, you actually cut off the tips of the wood fibers. This takes a very sharp plane iron.

## THE BLOCK PLANE

When the stock to be planed can be locked in a vise, a jack plane is used. For other jobs, use the block plane. The block plane can also be used for planing with the grain, especially in model work. The block plane is much smaller than the others you have used so far. Figure 14-1. It has a single plane iron which is placed in the plane with the *beveled side up*. The plane iron also rests in the plane at a much lower angle than the iron in a regular plane. This makes it easier to cut end grain. Figure 14-2.

Some block planes have a lateral adjustment. Others do not. As you can see, the planes in Figure 14-1 do have this adjustment.

## ADJUSTING THE BLOCK PLANE

The block plane is adjusted the same way as other planes, except when there is no lateral adjusting lever. To make a lateral adjustment, loosen the plane iron cap and sight along the bottom of the plane. Then with your fingers, press the plane iron to the right or left until it is parallel to the bottom of the plane. Tighten the lever cap screw. The depth adjustment is made the same way as on other types of planes.

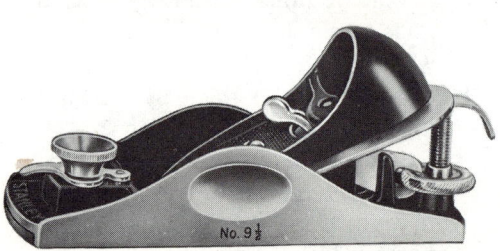

**14-1a.** Here is a block plane that can be used for planing end grain and for doing small forming and shaping work.

**14-1b.** Parts of a block plane.

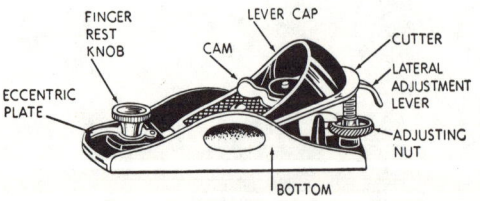

## USING THE BLOCK PLANE

Make sure that the plane iron is very sharp. The iron cap should be set very close to the cutting edge, not over $\frac{1}{32}$ inch (1 mm). Lock the stock firmly in the vise with the end showing a little.

Hold the block plane in one hand with the thumb on one side, the forefinger over the finger rest, and the other fingers on the other side. Take pains to hold the block plane square with the work. Figure 14-3.

You will find that it takes effort and experience to cut end grain properly. It is best to take a shallow cut to keep the plane from jumping. When planing end grain, it is not possible to go completely across the end; this will split out the wood. Therefore one of the following methods should be followed:

● Plane about halfway across the stock; then lift the handle of the plane slowly. Figure 14-4. Begin at the other end and do the same thing. Figure 14-5.

**14-2.** The cutter of a block plane rests at a much lower angle than on other types of planes, which makes it ideal for planing across grain.

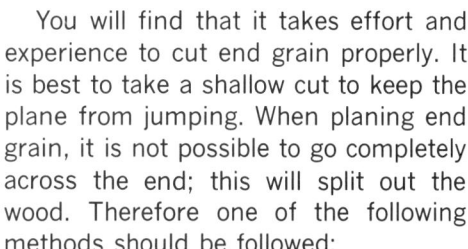

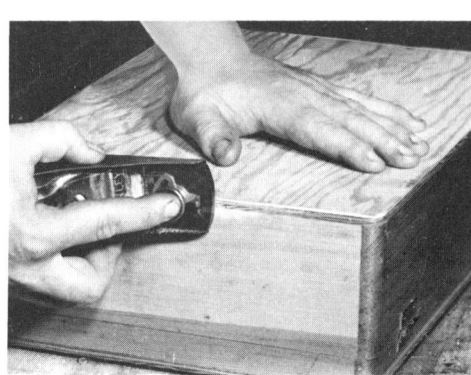

**14-3.** Planing end grain with a block plane. Note how the plane is held. Because of its size, the block plane is most convenient when work cannot be locked in the vise.

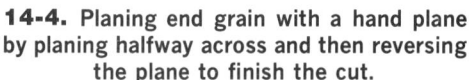

**14-4.** Planing end grain with a hand plane by planing halfway across and then reversing the plane to finish the cut.

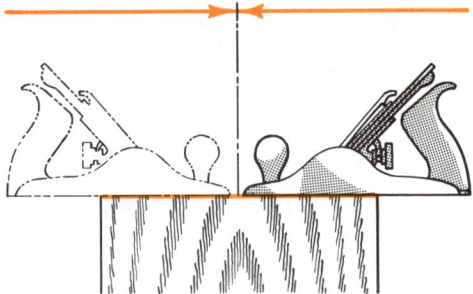

**14-5.** Planing end grain halfway across the stock.

Check the end for squareness with the working face and working edge. Figure 14-6.

● Plane a short bevel on the waste edge of the stock and then begin from the other side to plane all the way across. Figure 14-7.

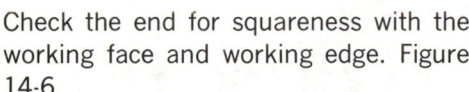

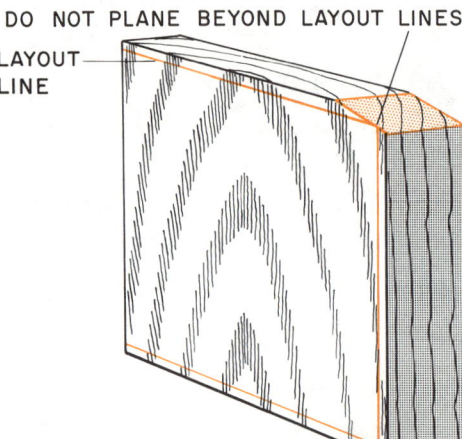

DO NOT PLANE BEYOND LAYOUT LINES

LAYOUT LINE

**14-7.** A second method for planing end grain. Note that a bevel is cut. This tends to prevent the wood from splitting out, and you can, therefore, plane completely across the end.

**14-6a.** Testing the end from the face surface. Move the try square back and forth.

**14-6b.** Checking the end from the edge. Hold the try square against the joint edge to make sure that the end is square both ways.

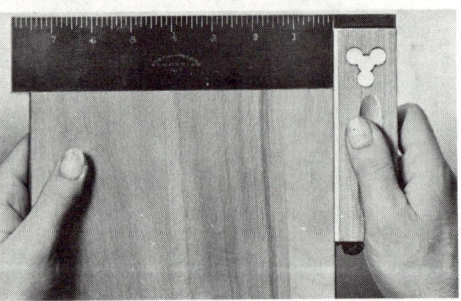

**14-8.** A third method for planing end grain. A scrap piece of the same thickness is placed against the edge of the piece to be planed. With this method you are actually extending the end grain.

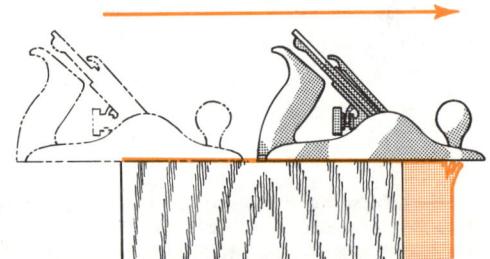

146

• Get a piece of scrap stock exactly the same thickness as the piece you are working. Lock it in the vise just ahead of the piece you are planing. In this way you have actually extended the end grain. Then you can plane all of the way across the end grain without fear of splitting out the piece. Figure 14-8.

Whichever method is used, check the end grain from both the working face and working edge frequently to make sure that it is square.

### CAN YOU ANSWER THESE QUESTIONS ON PLANING END GRAIN?

1. What is there about end grain that makes it difficult to plane?
2. How is a block plane different from other planes?
3. When would you choose a block plane to plane with the grain?
4. Describe the three ways of planing end grain.

## Section III
## UNIT 15.

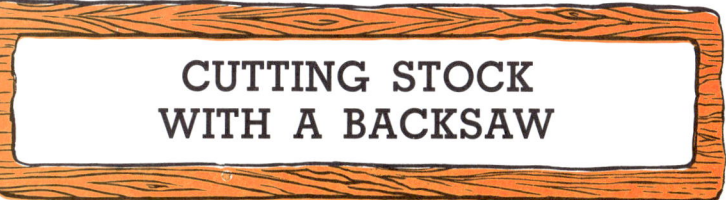

# CUTTING STOCK WITH A BACKSAW

**To make** a very fine saw cut, as in squaring up stock or in making joints, you will use a backsaw or a dovetail saw.

### THE BACKSAW AND DOVETAIL SAWS

The *backsaw* has a very thin blade with fine teeth. Figure 15-1. It can make a very accurate cut. This saw is used to cut both across grain and with the grain. It gets its name from the fact that an extra band of metal must be put across the back to make it stiff. The *dovetail* saw is very similar to the backsaw except that it has a narrower blade and finer teeth. Figure 15-2a. It cuts a true, smooth, and narrow kerf. Figure 15-2b.

### THE BENCH HOOK

A helper that you will need with the backsaw is the bench hook. Figure 15-3. This is a piece of wood with a hook or

stop on opposite surfaces of each end, which is shorter than the width of the board itself. When in use, the wide stop goes over the edge of the bench and the piece to be sawed is held against the shorter stop. This hook protects the top

**15-1.** A backsaw. In hand woodworking, this is one of the most frequently used tools whenever an accurate cut is required. Because the blade is relatively thin, it is strengthened on the back with a metal strip, from which it gets its name. It comes in lengths from 10 inches (254 mm) to the most common length of 14 inches (356 mm).

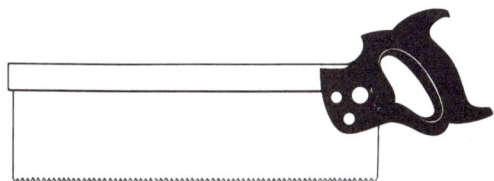

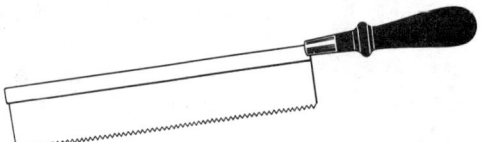

**15-2a.** A dovetail saw. This is very similar to the backsaw except that it is smaller and has a thinner blade. It is used for extremely accurate work. The common length is 10 inches (254 mm).

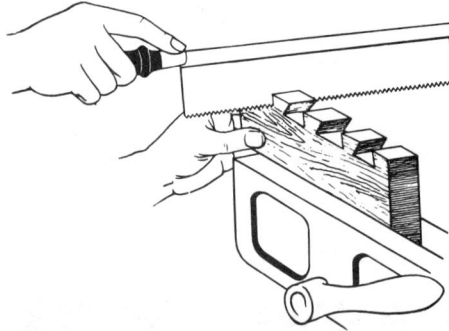

**15-2b.** Dovetail saws are designed for cutting dovetails, tenoning, and other types of precision work such as ship-model building, toy making, and patternmaking.

**15-3.** The bench hook, which is simply a piece of wood with wood cleats on both ends, is used to protect the top of the bench when sawing, cutting, and doing other forming operations.

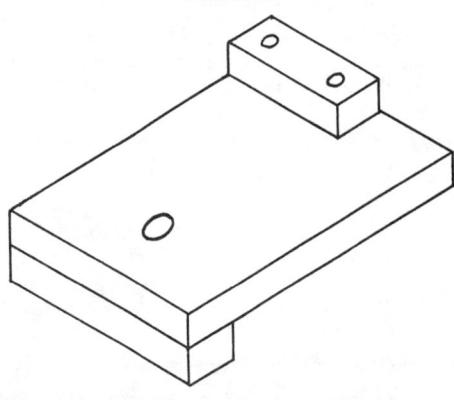

of the bench from damage by the back-saw.

## LAYING OUT THE CUT-OFF LINE

Accurately lay out the location of the cut to be made, using a try square and pencil. For very accurate layout, mark a line with a knife. If the stock is to be cut to length, lay out a line across the face side of the board and across both edges. If no planing is to be done, the cut should

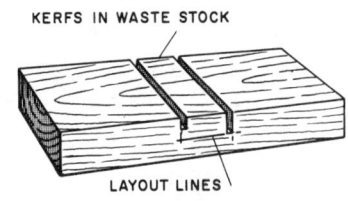

KERFS IN WASTE STOCK

LAYOUT LINES

**15-4.** Always make sure that the saw kerf is in the waste part of the stock.

**15-5.** Starting a cut with a backsaw. The stock is held firmly against the bench hook and the handle of the saw is held high until the first two or three strokes are taken.

be taken just inside or outside the layout line, *with the saw kerf in the waste stock.* Figure 15-4. However, if the edge is to be planed or chiseled, allow about $\frac{1}{16}$ inch (1.5 mm).

## CROSSCUTTING

Place the bench hook over the edge of the bench. Hold your work with one hand firmly against the stop as shown in Figure 15-5. Use the thumb of your left hand to guide the blade of the saw. Hold the saw in a slanting position across the work and draw it back once or twice to start the saw kerf. As the cut begins, gradually lower the saw until it is parallel to the wood. Figure 15-6.

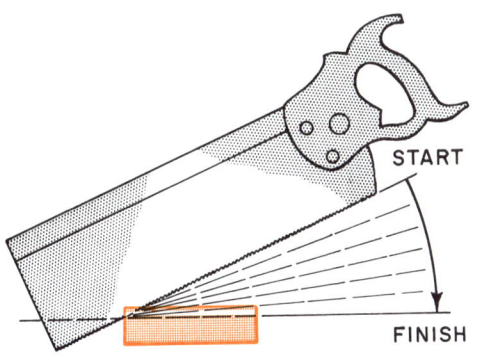

START

FINISH

**15-6.** After the saw kerf is started, the handle is lowered slowly until it is parallel with the top of the bench.

**15-7.** Continuing the cut with the backsaw.

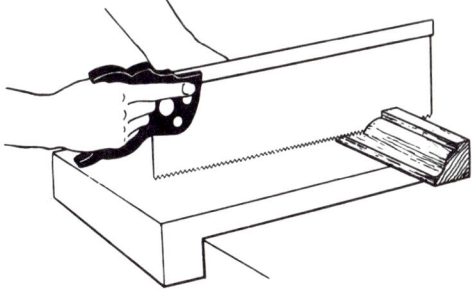

Make sure that you are holding the saw at right angles to the face of the work. Be careful to take light, easy cuts as the saw goes through the opposite side of the wood. Figure 15-7. If you aren't careful, the wood will splinter.

## RIPPING

The backsaw is also used for cutting with the grain of stock, especially in making joints and in doing other fine cabinetwork. Lock the stock in a vise, with the end to be cut showing slightly above the vise jaws. Begin the cut the same way you did in crosscutting; continue to lower the handle until it is cutting the total width of the wood. Figure 15-8. In cutting with the grain, be very careful not to allow the saw to creep in at an angle, as this will make a crooked cut.

There are many uses for the backsaw in making all types of joints, as you will see later.

**15-8.** Ripping with the backsaw. The proper method of cutting with the grain to form a tenon for a mortise-and-tenon joint.

## CAN YOU ANSWER THESE QUESTIONS ON CUTTING STOCK WITH A BACKSAW?

1. How did the backsaw get its name?
2. In what ways does the dovetail saw differ from the backsaw?
3. What is a bench hook and how is it used?
4. Can the backsaw crosscut and rip?
5. When using the backsaw, some stock must remain for planing. How much?
6. Which saw resembles the backsaw the most—the crosscut or the ripsaw?
7. Why must care be taken when sawing with the grain?

# Section III

# UNIT 16.

# GLUING UP STOCK TO FORM LARGER SURFACES

**When you** begin to make large projects, one of the first problems is gluing up several pieces of stock to form a larger piece. Sometimes this means gluing stock edge to edge for making such projects as a cutting board or a table top. At other times, you will need to glue stock face to face to form a thicker piece for making a turned bowl or perhaps the legs of a table or stool. Later you will need to clamp and glue up stock when you assemble your project.

The term *adhesive* is used to describe substances that will hold other materials together. Common adhesives include glues, cements, pastes, and mucilage. The term *gluing* is used to mean assembling parts with any type of adhesive. Figure 16-1.

The fact that two pieces of wood can be held together with an adhesive is due to *adhesion.* This is the force that causes certain molecules of different materials to attract each other. This force, for example, makes it possible to glue wood together or for paint or enamel to stick

to wood. Glue holds pieces of wood together because the molecules of glue adhere to the wood and also to other molecules of glue.

## KINDS OF ADHESIVES

There are eight common adhesives that may be used in the school shop.

**16-1.** Good wood gluing of this table means that the joints will last almost forever and are stronger than the wood itself.

Figure 16-2. These come under many trade names. A description of the glue will tell you which type it is. Learn about these basic glues so you can use them properly.

● *Animal or hide glue* is made from hoofs, hides, bones, and other animal refuse. It is refined, purified, and then made into sticks or ground into powder. There are many grades, depending on the quality and kind of wood for which the glue is meant.

Animal glue makes a stronger-than-wood joint, but it is not waterproof. If it is used dry, you need a glue pot or double boiler to prepare it. It has long been used as an all-purpose furniture glue. It also comes in liquid form which doesn't need to be heated or mixed.

Stick or powder glue must first be soaked in cold water for 6 to 12 hours. Although there are strict manufacturer's specifications as to the amounts of glue and water, a satisfactory mixture can be made by soaking the glue in just enough water to cover. The glue will absorb this water. When the heating is done, a small amount of water can be added as needed. After animal glue is soaked, place it in the top of a double boiler or a regular glue pot, and heat it to steam temperature. The glue will dry out too much if heated directly over a flame. Animal glue is ready to use when it runs off the brush in a light stream.

Before applying hot animal glue, the wood must be brought to a temperature of about 80 to 90 degrees. This type of glue must be applied rapidly, as it sets very quickly after cooling. Cold liquid animal glue eliminates tedious preparation and the necessity for speed and critical temperature control.

● *Casein glue,* made from milk curd, is available in powdered form. It is mixed with cold water to the consistency of cream and applied cold to the wood. It is easy to mix and makes a stronger-than-wood joint. It is not completely waterproof. Some types stain oak, mahogany, and other acid woods and must be bleached off. It is excellent for all indoor and outdoor gluing with the exception of articles which require complete waterproofing.

Do not mix more than you need at one time, since it loses its strength in a few hours after mixing. To mix, pour the powder in a container and add a small amount of water, stirring until it becomes a heavy paste. Add more water until the mixture is about the consistency of thick cream. Allow the glue to set (takes about fifteen minutes) before applying it with a stick or brush.

● *Urea-resin adhesive* is made from urea resin and formaldehyde. It comes in powder form and is mixed with water to the thickness of cream. It does not stain woods, is waterproof, and dries to a light color. It is used the same way as casein glue, but the manufacturer's directions must always be followed for mixing and drying. It is very good for cabinetwork and for bonding plywood. Figure 16-3 (Page 154).

● *Resorcinol* is made by mixing liquid resin with a powder catalyst. It comes in a can divided into two compartments and should be mixed only as needed, according to the manufacturer's directions. It does not require much pressure. It will fill gaps and can be used for gluing poorly fitted joints. It provides complete protection from both fresh and salt water and is therefore ideal for outdoor sports equipment.

● *Liquid resin (polyvinyl) glue,* white in color, is excellent for furniture making and repair. It is always ready for use, is

| Type | Description | Recommended Use | |
|---|---|---|---|
| HIDE GLUE | Comes in flakes to be heated in water or in prepared form as liquid hide glue. Very strong, tough, light color. | Excellent for furniture and cabinetwork. Gives strength even to joints that do not fit very well. | |
| CASEIN | From milk curd. Comes in powdered form. Must be mixed with water. | For inside and woodwork. Almost waterproof. Good for oily woods. Inexpensive. Good for heavy wood gluing. | |
| UREA-RESIN ADHESIVE | Comes as powder to be mixed with water and used within 4 hours. Light colored. Very strong if joint fits well. | Good for general wood gluing. First choice for work that must stand some exposure to dampness, since it is almost waterproof. | |
| RESORCINOL (WATERPROOF) | Comes as powder plus liquid; must be mixed each time used. Dark colored, very strong, completely waterproof. | This is the glue to use with exterior type plywood for work to be exposed to extreme dampness. | |
| LIQUID RESIN (WHITE) POLYVINYL GLUE | Comes ready to use at any temperature. Clean working, quick setting. Strong enough for most work, though not quite as tough as hide glue. | Good for indoor furniture and cabinetwork. First choice for small jobs where right clamping or good fit may be difficult. | |
| CONTACT CEMENT | Comes in a can as a light tan liquid. | Excellent for bonding veneer plastic laminates, leather, plastics, metal foil, or canvas to wood. | |
| EPOXY CEMENT | Comes in two tubes, or cans, that must be mixed in exact proportions. | Excellent for attaching hardware and metal fittings to wood. Good for extremely difficult gluing jobs. Will fill large holes. | |
| HOT-MELT GLUES | Cream colored polyethylene based adhesive in stick form. | Quick bonding adhesive; best for small areas. | |

**16-2.** Chart of wood adhesives.

nonstaining, economical, and odorless. It cannot be exposed to weather and is not as strong or lasting as liquid hide glue, which is best for fine furniture. Figure 16-4.

● *Contact cement* is a ready-mixed, rubber-type, bonding agent. It bonds practically all materials to themselves or in combination without need for clamps, nails, or pressure. It is an ideal material for bonding veneer or plastic laminates to plywood.

● *Epoxy cement* is a two-part adhesive that sticks to practically anything. It can be used on wood, plastics, leather, metal, ceramics, and other materials to produce a strong waterproof joint. Epoxy cements come in two containers because, unlike ordinary glues, they do not contain an evaporative solvent. They consist of a special resin and a chemical hardener that are mixed together at the time of use. This cement produces super-strength joints without clamping.

| Care in Using | Correct Use |
|---|---|
| Not waterproof; do not use for outdoor furniture or anything exposed to weather or dampness. | Apply glue in warm room to both surfaces and let it become tacky before joining. Clamp 3 hours. |
| Some types require bleaching. Will deteriorate when exposed to mold. | Mix with water to creamy consistency. For oily woods, sponge surfaces with dilute caustic soda one hour before gluing. Apply with brush. Clamp and allow to dry for three hours at 70 degrees. |
| Needs well-fitted joints, tight clamping, and room temperature 70° or warmer. | Make sure joint fits tightly. Mix glue and apply thin coat. Allow 16 hours drying time. Dries in seconds with electronic gluer. |
| Expense, trouble to mix, and dark color make it unsuitable to jobs where waterproof glue is not required. | Use within 8 hours after mixing. Work at temperature above 70°. Apply thin coat to both surfaces. Allow 16 hours drying time. |
| Not sufficiently resistant to moisture for outdoor furniture or outdoor storage units. | Use at any temperature but preferably above 60°. Spread on both surfaces, clamp at once. Sets in $1\frac{1}{2}$ hours. |
| Adheres immediately on contact. Parts can't be shifted once contact is made. Position accurately. Temperature for working must be 70° F. or above. | Stir cement. Apply two coats to both surfaces. Brush on a liberal coat. Let dry for 30 minutes. Apply second coat. Allow to dry for not less than 30 minutes. Test for dryness by pressing wrapping paper to surface. If paper doesn't stick, the surfaces are dry and ready for bonding. |
| Epoxies harden quickly. Mix only what can be used in half hour. Use at temperatures above 60 degrees. Keep epoxy compounds separate. Don't reverse caps. | Mix small amounts. Clean and roughen the surfaces. Remove oil, dirt, and other loose matter. Apply to surfaces with putty knife. Clean tools immediately. Press parts together. |
| Glue hardens quickly. Work fast before glue cools. | Apply small amounts. Don't spread. Press surfaces together for 20 seconds. |

• *Hot-melt glues* are adhesives supplied in either stick or chunk form for use with an electric glue gun. For occasional gluing, a small electric glue gun is used. A stick of the hot-melt glue fits into the gun itself. Figure 16-5. In industry, however, a large hot-melt unit consists of an electric glue pot that uses chunks of glue. A glue gun is attached by a flexible hose, much like a spray unit. Figure 16-6.

In industry a wide variety of adhesives are used for gluing all kinds of materials, including paper, plastics, wood, and metal. The small glue gun uses a stick of thermoplastic polyethylene adhesive. To use the glue gun, make sure that the flow-control valve in the gun tip is closed. Figure 16-7. Insert the hot-melt glue stick in the gun and plug in the cord. Allow about three minutes for the gun to heat. Clean the surface to be glued. Then soften the end of another glue stick on the hot tip of the gun and insert the stick into the gun. It will fuse with the stick already in the gun. Open the flow valve by tapping the valve pin against any hard surface. Feed the glue onto the work by pressing the glue stick with your thumb. Then press the glued pieces together for 20 seconds. In just one minute the glue will develop 90 percent of its full bonding strength.

## TEN HINTS FOR SUCCESSFUL GLUING

- Make sure the surfaces are clean and dry.
- Make well fitting joints. Figure 16-8.

**16-3.** With a high-frequency electronic gluer, urea-resin adhesive dries in a matter of seconds. This type of equipment is used in industry to speed up production.

**16-5.** A small electric glue gun that uses a stick of adhesive.

**16-4.** White liquid resin glue from a squeeze bottle provides a good way to apply an adhesive.

**16-6.** Applying glue with an industrial-type, hot-melt gun.

- Choose the correct glue.
- Mix the glue to proper thickness.
- Mark the pieces to be glued for correct assembly.
- Have the proper clamps ready.
- Apply the glue to both surfaces of the joint. Figure 16-9.
- Clamp parts together properly.
- Remove extra glue from joints before it dries.

- Allow the assembly to dry completely.

## KINDS OF CLAMPS

*The cabinet, or bar, clamp* is used for gluing up large surfaces edge to edge and for clamping parts together when assem-

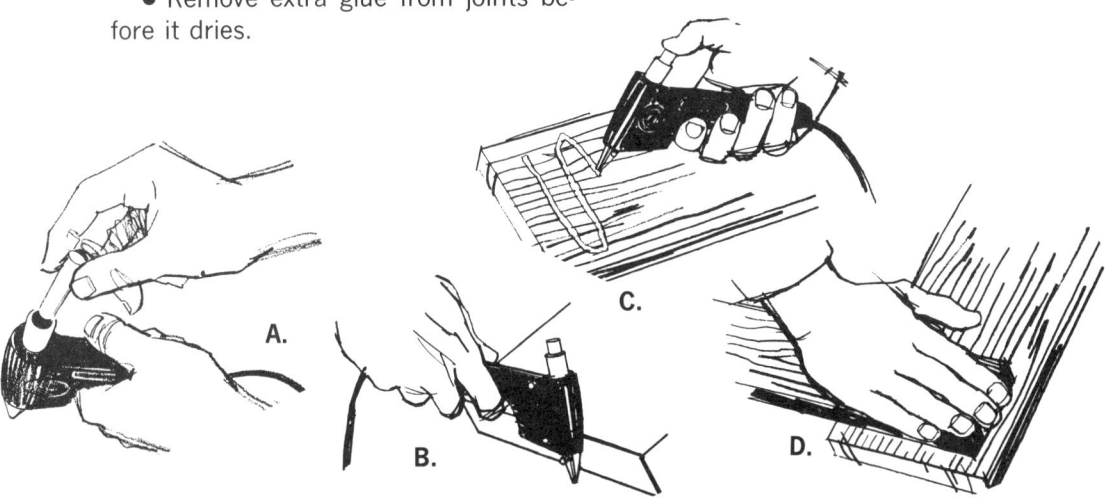

**16-7.** Using a small electric glue gun: A. Insert glue stick in gun; B. Open flow control valve by tapping nozzle; C. To feed glue, press glue stick with thumb; D. Press glued surfaces together for 20 seconds.

**16-8.** Make sure that the parts fit properly. Test the fit of the joint before applying glue.

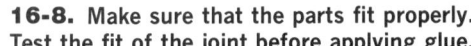

**16-9.** Chair rungs and similar joints can be reglued even when it is not possible to pull them apart. Drill a small hole into the joint and inject glue with an oil can. A hypodermic needle is also excellent for this.

155

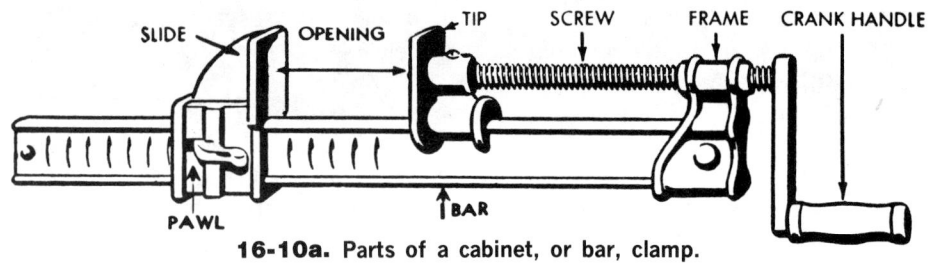

SLIDE    OPENING    TIP    SCREW    FRAME    CRANK HANDLE

PAWL    ↑BAR

**16-10a.** Parts of a cabinet, or bar, clamp.

**16-10b.** Cabinet clamps can be used for general-purpose work. They are particularly useful in all wide clamping for furniture construction.

**16-11.** Bar clamps are made with single or double pipes, as shown here.

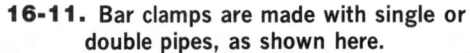

bling projects. Figure 16-10. It is made in lengths from 2 to 10 feet (0.61 to 3 m) and in several styles. One end is adjusted to length by friction or by a pawl while the other is moved in and out by a screw. Figure 16-11. When using a cabinet clamp, the screw is turned out completely; then the pawl or friction end is moved in until the clamp is slightly wider than the total width of the stock to be clamped. When using cabinet clamps on finished stock, the surface of the wood should be protected. Place small pieces of scrap stock between the clamp jaws and the wood.

• *Hand screws* are wooden parallel clamps about 6 to 20 inches (152 to 508 mm) long which open from 4 to 20 inches (102 to 508 mm). Figure 16-12. When using hand screws, the center screw is held in the left hand and the outside screw in the right hand. The clamp can then be opened and closed by twisting the handles in opposite directions. Figure 16-13. The hand screw is for gluing stock face to face or for clamping together any work that is within the range of the clamp jaws.

• *The C clamp* comes in many sizes. It is used to assemble and clamp parts. Figure 16-14.

• *Speed (instant-acting) clamps* are very convenient because they can be instantly adjusted for quick assembly. Figure 16-15.

● *Spring clamps* are quick and easy to use. Some types have pivoting jaws made of stainless steel with double rows of serrated teeth along the pressure edge. These toothed jaws take hold of the surface of parts so that miter joints and other odd shapes can be held together. Figure 16-16.

### MAKING AND GLUING UP AN EDGE JOINT

Choose and cut the stock. Select *rough* stock that will form the larger surface. If it is wider than 8 to 10 inches (203 to 254 mm), it is usually ripped into narrower strips. In this way the total surface will not warp so much when the pieces are glued together. After the pieces have

been cut, arrange them in their correct order. Remember these three points:

● Make sure that the grain of all pieces runs in the same direction so that after you have glued up the pieces, it will not be difficult to plane.

**16-12b.** Correct and incorrect ways of clamping with hand screws. On the left the clamps are not parallel and therefore will not apply pressure correctly.

**16-12a.** Hand screws are convenient clamping devices, since no other protective pieces are needed.

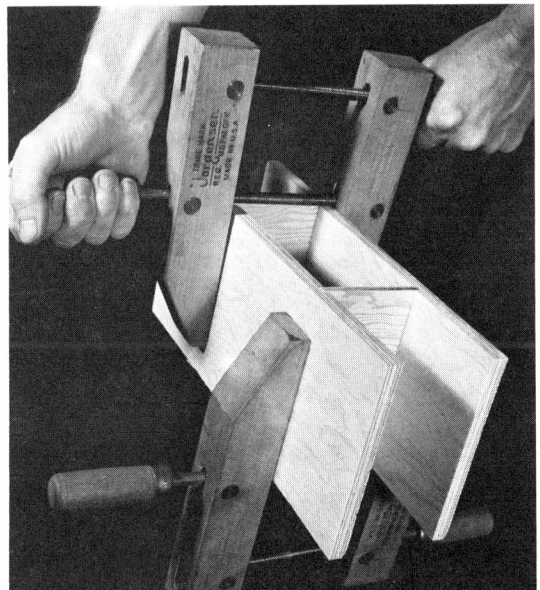

**16-13.** Hold the middle spindle and revolve the end spindle to open or close a hand screw.

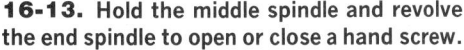
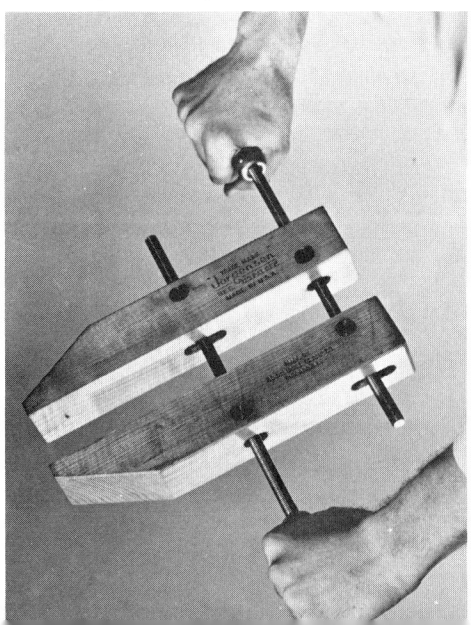

● Alternate the pieces so the annular rings face in opposite directions. Figure 16-17. This will help to prevent the surface from warping.

● Try to match the pieces to form the most interesting grain arrangement.

Now mark the adjoining face of each matching joint with matching numbers, "X's," or lines, in a place where the marks can be easily seen.

Plane face surface of each piece to remove wind or warpage. This will also help you to see the direction the grain runs. If you have any pieces running in opposite directions, reverse them and re-mark the ends. It will not be necessary to plane this surface accurately now because the assembled stock will have to be planed again.

Plane both edges until they are square with the face surface. Hold a straightedge against the face surfaces of all the pieces to make sure they do not bow. Figure 16-18. Tap the top piece with your finger to see that it does not rock. Finally, slide the top piece along the bottom one to see if it tends to have a suction action. Continue to plane one surface and the two edges of each piece and match each of the joints.

**16-14c.** With a C clamp, wood shims must be used so that the surface of the wood will not be damaged.

**16-14a.** The C clamp is used for clamping irregular or odd-shaped pieces and for many special jobs in the workshop.

**16-15.** Speed bar clamps such as this one are easily adjustable. This makes gluing a great deal easier.

**16-14b.** Parts of a C clamp.

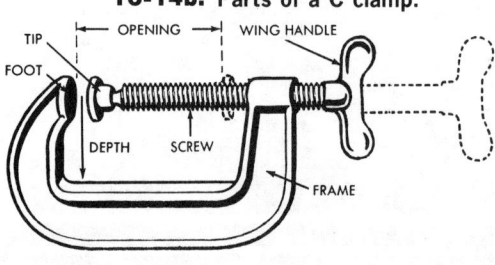

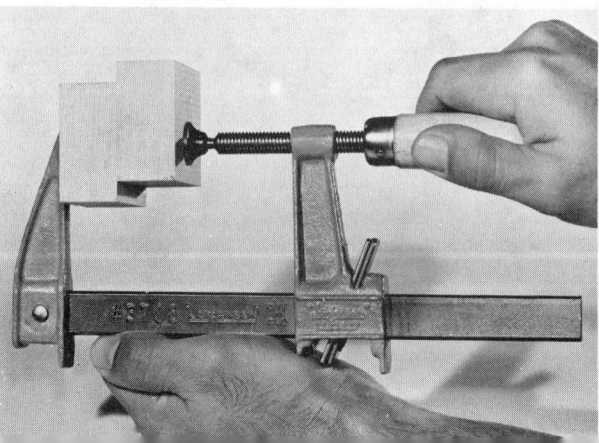

## Adding Dowels or Splines

When joints with additional strength are needed, dowels or splines can be added to each joint. Unit 28 gives detailed instructions for making an edge dowel joint. To make a spline joint, use the circular saw to cut a groove that is about one-third as wide and deep as the thickness of the stock. Figure 16-19. Then cut and fit splines into these grooves. Allow a small clearance at the bottom of each spline for glue.

## Making a Trial Assembly of the Stock

After all joints have been constructed, place the pieces in position again on the

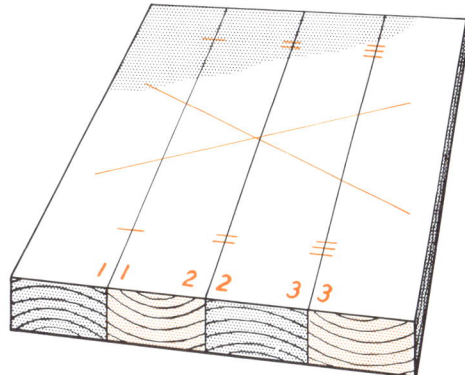

**16-17.** Note the proper method of arranging stock before it is glued together. Also mark the adjoining boards so that they will be easy to assemble.

**16-18.** Holding a straightedge against the face surfaces of stock to see if the surfaces are straight and do not bow.

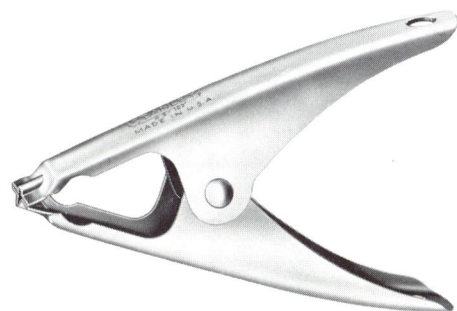

**16-16a.** A spring clamp is good for small work and delicate jobs. These come in assorted sizes. Some have rubber covered jaws to protect the work.

**16-16b.** Spring clamps with special jaws make it possible to clamp odd-shaped pieces.

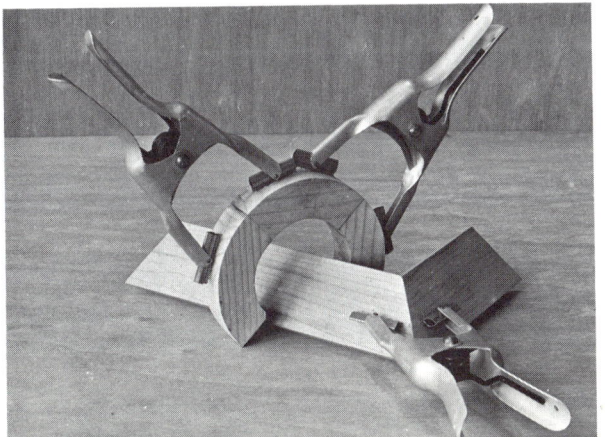

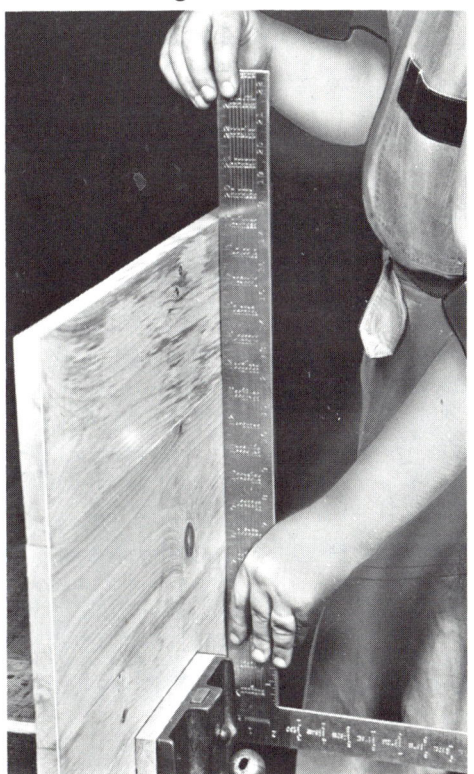

159

top of a bench. If the pieces are very long, place them over two sawhorses. If they are placed on top of a bench, use a jig to hold the bar clamps. Figure 16-20. Select three or more cabinet, or bar, clamps, depending on the length of the stock. There should be a clamp for about every 15 inches of stock. Carefully set all cabinet clamps to the proper openings, so they will be ready to clamp the stock as soon as the edges are glued. When gluing on a wood-top bench, cover the surface with wrapping paper to protect the surface.

## Gluing up the Stock

Hold the two matching edges together so they are flush. Apply (spread) the glue with a brush, stick, or roller. Figure 16-21. Make sure that both edges are completely covered. This is called *double spread*. When glue is applied to only one

**16-20.** A jig to hold the bar clamps. With a jig of this sort, the clamps will be held in correct position, making it a simple job to apply glue to the edges and to place the stock in between the clamps.

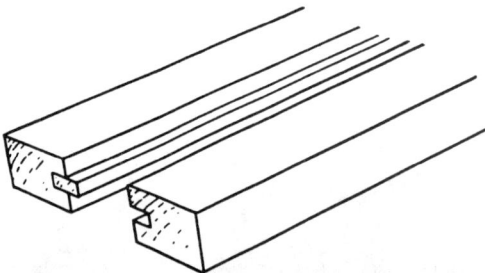

**16-19.** Enlarged view of spline-joint construction. This type strengthens the two adjoining pieces.

**16-21.** Two methods of spreading glue: A. Spreading cold glue with a roller after it is applied with a brush; B. Applying hot glue with a brush.

surface and the surfaces rubbed together, it is called *single spread.* Do not apply too much glue. It will squeeze out of the joint when it is put together and give you extra trouble in removing it later.

When all edges have been glued, rapidly lay the pieces on the lower clamps till all are in place. If possible, rub the two pieces together to work the glue into the pores. Tighten the outside clamps lightly; then place another clamp upside down on the stock at the mid-point and clamp this lightly.

Use a rubber mallet to tap the ends or the face surfaces to line them up. Check all the joints to make sure that the face surfaces are flush and the ends are in line. Strike the pieces with a mallet to bring them in place. Then tighten each clamp until it applies firm pressure. Don't squeeze the wood too tightly. If the joint is constructed badly, it will never draw into place. Place a wood cleat above and below the surface at each end and clamp these in place with hand screws or clamps. Figure 16-22. This will tend to keep the surface true and free from warpage. A piece of paper under the cleats will keep them from sticking. Be-

fore the glue begins to harden, wipe off the excess from the outside of the joint.

## MAKING AND GLUING UP STOCK FACE TO FACE

Select and cut out several pieces of stock that will make up the correct size when glued together. Arrange the pieces with the annular rings alternating in direction. Also make sure that the grain of the pieces runs in the same direction. Mark the ends and face surface so that you will know how the pieces should be arranged for gluing. Plane the face surface of the two outside pieces true and smooth. If more than two pieces are glued together, the center pieces must be planed to thickness.

Select several hand screws or C clamps and open them slightly wider than the stock to be clamped. Apply glue evenly and then clamp as shown in Figure 16-23. When you tighten the hand screw, you must take care that the jaws are parallel. In this way pressure will be even.

**16-23.** Gluing up stock face to face. Several different types of clamps are holding two pieces of work together. Cleats are fastened underneath the clamps to protect the surfaces of the wood.

**16-22.** Stock glued up and bar clamps holding the stock together. Note the cleat that has been fastened to one end of the stock.

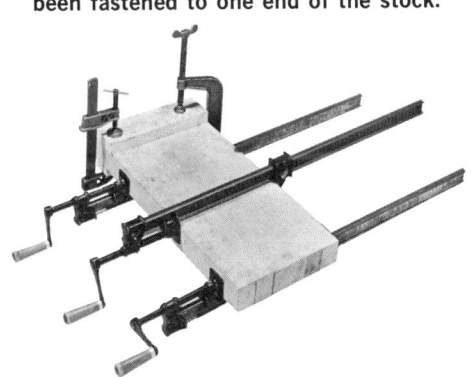

## REMOVING EXCESS GLUE AND SQUARING UP

Most glues should be allowed to dry overnight. When the assembly is dry, remove the clamps. Scrape off the excess glue with a chisel or hand scraper. Plane the *face surface* level again. Start by planing at an angle with a jointer plane. Then straight plane with the grain. Continue to square up the assembly by hand or machine.

### CAN YOU ANSWER THESE QUESTIONS ON GLUING UP STOCK TO FORM LARGER SURFACES?

1. Name eight kinds of glue and tell of what they are made.
2. Which glues are waterproof?
3. Which is best for a small repair job?
4. Tell what cabinet, or bar, clamps are needed for and how they are used.
5. Of what material are the clamps of hand screws made?
6. For what special kinds of gluing jobs can C clamps be helpful?
7. To glue up a large board, wide stock is ripped into narrow strips. Explain the reason for this and how it is done.
8. What three things must you consider when gluing up stock for edge joints?
9. Describe an edge joint.
10. How can this type of joint be made stronger?
11. A trial assembly is always made before gluing. What is accomplished by it?
12. About how much glue should be applied to the edges?
13. With what kind of mallet should wood surfaces be pounded?
14. How can you keep the surface true and free from warpage?
15. Why must the jaws of hand screws be parallel?

## Section III
## UNIT 17.

# SQUARING UP STOCK

**It is** usually necessary to plane several or all of the surfaces of the pieces for your project. Figure 17-1. In some cases, you will be planing only the edges of the stock and sawing the ends. In other cases, such as in making a cutout design, you may plane the face surface, one edge, and the other surface. In many instances in which parts are to be assembled, you will be planing the stock to thickness and width and perhaps finishing the ends by sawing with the backsaw and then sanding.

There are many times, however, when you will need to plane all six surfaces of the board. This is called squaring up the stock. If you apply the instructions given in the last six units, you should be able to do a good job. It should be remembered, though, that this job is very diffi-

**17-1.** The legs of this table are good examples of stock that must be planed on all sides.

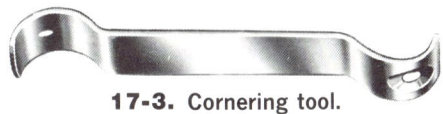

**17-2.** This is the recommended method for squaring up stock.

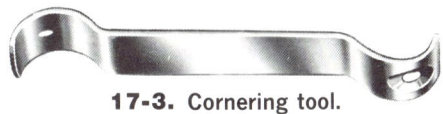

**17-3.** Cornering tool.

cult when done with a hand plane and you should not attempt to plane any more surfaces than are necessary to do the job properly. If machine tools are available, a planer and jointer can be used, following the same procedure as with a hand plane. There are several methods of squaring up stock.

### METHOD A

1. Plane the face surface or side (working face) with a hand plane or jointer.
2. Plane the working edge (same tools).
3. Plane the stock to thickness (second surface or side). Use hand plane or planer.
4. Plane the stock to width (second edge). Use a saw, hand plane, or jointer.
5. Plane one end (working end).
6. Cut stock to length.
7. Plane other end (second end).

### METHOD B

1. Plane the face surface (working surface).
2. Plane the working edge.
3. Plane one end square with the face surface and joint edge.
4. Plane stock to width.
5. Plane stock to thickness.
6. Cut off stock to length.
7. Plane other end.

### METHOD C (recommended)

1. Plane the face surface. Figure 17-2.
2. Plane the working edge.
3. Plane one end square with the face surface and joint edge.
4. Cut off stock to length and plane other end.
5. Plane stock to width.
6. Plane stock to thickness.

After squaring up stock, use a cornering tool to remove the sharp corners (arrises). Figure 17-3.

### CAN YOU ANSWER THESE QUESTIONS ON SQUARING UP STOCK?

1. Must all six surfaces of the board be planed?
2. Name the machine tools that are useful in squaring up stock.
3. There are three methods of squaring up stock. Describe them.
4. After squaring up stock, what tool is used for removing sharp corners?

# SECTION IV
## Making Pieces of Curved or Irregular Designs

**What you must know and be able to do in Units 18–20:**

18. How to transfer curves and irregular lines: using dividers, drawing circles, working with some geometric patterns like the octagon and hexagon, and drawing an ellipse.

19. Cutting many curved patterns with the coping saw and the compass saw; the proper way to cut with these saws.

20. Forming and trimming shapes to make them smooth and ready for assembly; using the spokeshave, drawknife, and file or rasp.

You would find woodworking rather dull if everything were made in flat, straight planes. Curves, geometric designs, and shapes in the forms of animals and objects are added. These lend beauty to your projects and interest to the building of them. There are many things which must have a curved or molded shape, such as archery bows, canoe paddles, and boat hulls. In this section you will begin your work with saws and other cutting tools especially suited to the making of irregular, molded, curved, and formed designs.

# LAYOUT AND TRANSFER OF CURVES AND DESIGNS

**When a project** contains pieces with irregular designs or curved shapes, these must be transferred to the wood from a drawing. Figure 18-1. If it is a geometric design, the layout can usually be made directly on the wood. However, if the design is irregular, you must first draw a full-size pattern on paper and then transfer it to the wood.

## DIVIDERS

Dividers or an ordinary pencil compass is used for laying out small circles. Figure 18-2. Dividers are more accurate and have other uses in layout work, such as dividing space equally, transferring measurements, and scribing arcs. Figures 18-3 and 18-4. To set the dividers, place one leg over the inch mark on the

**18-1.** The legs and base of this table must be enlarged to full size and transferred to the wood before they can be cut out and finished. The table is 18½ inches (470 mm) high and 14 inches (356 mm) round.

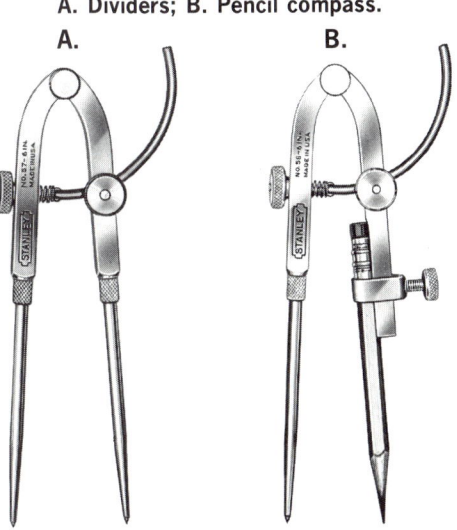

**18-2.** Two tools for drawing circles and arcs: A. Dividers; B. Pencil compass.

rule and then open the other leg to the width you want. Lock the thumbscrew. Some dividers have an additional spring nut that is used to make fine corrections in settings.

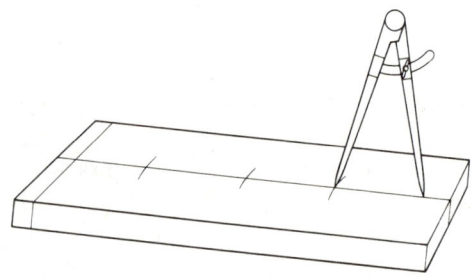

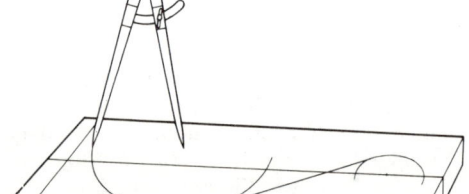

**18-3.** Dividers are used for marking out radius work and for stepping off measurements.

**18-4.** Set the dividers for the correct distance and then step off these equal distances.

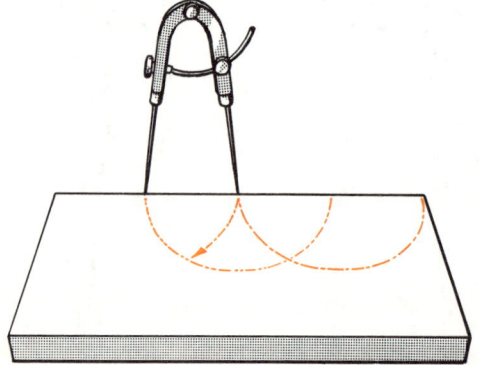

## DRAWING CIRCLES

Set the dividers to equal half the diameter of the circle. Place one leg over the center of the circle, tip the dividers at a slight angle, and, working from left to right, scribe the circle. Figure 18-5. When drawing circles on finished wood, place an eraser from the end of a pencil over the point that is to act as the center.

To lay out large circles, use a set of trammel points (Figure 18-6) or tie a piece of string to a pencil and use this as a compass.

**18-5.** Laying out a circle with dividers. The dividers are tipped slightly as they are swung around.

## LAYING OUT A ROUNDED CORNER

The corners on many projects are rounded. To lay out these corners, first check the drawing to get the radius of the arc. Then mark this distance from the corner on the side and end. Figure 18-7. With a try square held against edge and end, draw two lines that intersect (cross) the center of the arc. Set the dividers to the proper radius and draw the arc.

## LAYING OUT AN OCTAGON

An octagon has eight equal sides with all angles equal. Find the distance across the octagon from one side to the other and lay out a square this size. Next, set a dividers or compass to half the diagonal length across the square. Set the point of the compass at each corner of the square and strike an arc from one side of the square to the other. Do this from each of the four corners. Join the points where the arcs meet the sides of the square. Figure 18-8.

## LAYING OUT A HEXAGON

A hexagon has six equal sides with all angles equal. Find the length of one side. Set a compass or dividers to equal this measurement and draw a circle with this radius. Begin at any point on the circle; without changing the setting, draw a series of arcs, moving the point to the place where the preceding arc has intersected the circle. Figure 18-9. The last arc

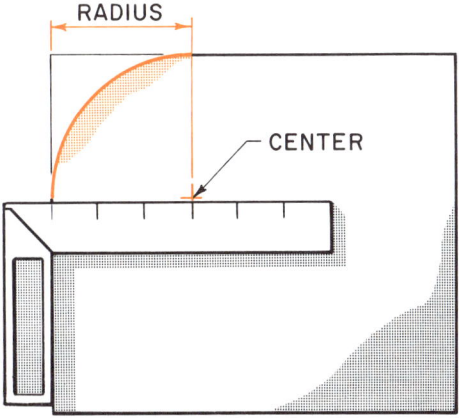

**18-7.** Locating the center for laying out a rounded corner.

**18-6.** Trammel points are used when laying out large circles. These points fit on a long, thin piece of metal or wood and can be adjusted to any length.

**18-8.** Layout of an octagon—an eight-sided figure.

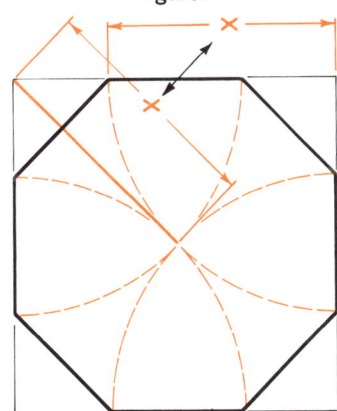

should intersect the circle at the first point made by the compass. Join these points with a straightedge.

## DRAWING AN ELLIPSE

An ellipse is a regular curve that has two different diameters. Lay out the two diameters at right angles to each other—namely, AB and CD as shown in Figure 18-10a. Set a dividers equal to half the longest diameter. Place the point of the dividers on point C and strike an arc to intersect the longest diameter at points X and Y. Place a thumbtack at these two points and another at one end of the shortest diameter. Tie a string around the three thumbtacks. Figure 18-10b. Remove the outside thumbtack and place a pencil inside the string. Hold the pencil at right angles to the paper and carefully draw the ellipse. Figure 18-10c.

## ENLARGING IRREGULAR DESIGNS

Projects found in a book or magazine are seldom drawn to full size. If the project contains irregular parts, it will be necessary to make an enlarged drawing. This is used as a pattern in making the layout on wood. Figure 18-11. Do this as follows:

1. Find out how much smaller the original drawing is than full size. Usually drawings in books or magazines are one-half or one-fourth full size.

2. If the original drawing is not already on squared paper, lay out squares over the print. *For example, if the pattern is one-fourth full size, draw* ¼-*inch (6.5 mm) squares.*

3. On a large piece of wrapping paper, carefully lay out 1-inch (25.5 mm) squares.

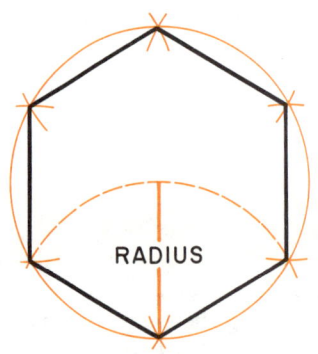

**18-9.** Layout of a hexagon—a six-sided figure.

**18-10.** How to make an ellipse: A. Laying out the two diameters at right angles to each other; B. Striking on arc to intersect two points, X and Y, on the long diameter; C. Drawing the ellipse. Note that the outside thumbtack has been removed and a pencil put in its place. Be sure the pencil is held at right angles to the wood in forming the ellipse.

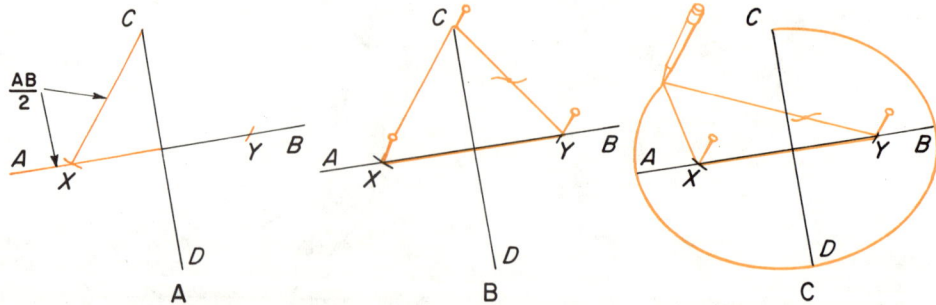

12
11
10
9
8
7
6
5
4
3
2
1

A B C D E F G H I J K L M N O P Q R

$\frac{1}{4}''$ SQUARES

$\frac{1}{2}''$ SQUARES

12
11
10
9
8
7
6
5
4
3
2
1

A B C D E F G H I J K L M N O P Q R

**18-11.** Enlarging an irregular design. Crosshatch paper is numbered the same, both in the original and the enlargement. This helps to locate the points needed to make an enlargement.

4. From the lower left-hand corner of both the original drawing and the layout paper, letter all horizontal lines A, B, C, etc., and all vertical lines 1, 2, 3, etc.

5. Using these letters and numbers, locate a position on the original drawing and transfer this point to the full-size pattern.

6. Repeat the procedure in step 5 until you have enough points on the full-size pattern to be able to complete the pattern accurately.

7. Sketch the full-size pattern. Use a ruler for straight lines. On curved sections, a piece of wire solder can be bent

**18-12.** Using a templet to make a layout. When several pieces of the same design are to be cut, it is much simpler to use a templet of thin wood or metal.

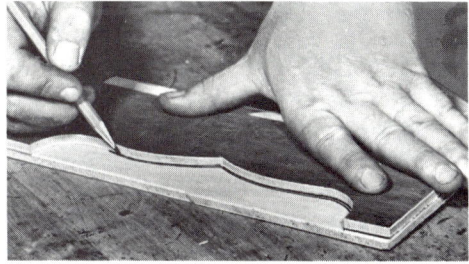

to serve as a guide in drawing these lines. Now examine your design. A little change here and there may smooth out the curves and make it look the way you want it to. (If the piece is symmetrical, the same on both sides, you need to lay out only half the design. Then fold the sheet of paper down the center and cut the full pattern.)

8. Place this paper pattern on your piece of stock and trace around it. You may need a little tape to hold it in place. Care is needed to do this. (If you are making many parts of the same design, make a templet or pattern, of thin wood or sheet metal from the paper design. Use this templet to make the layout. Figure 18-12.)

## CAN YOU ANSWER THESE QUESTIONS ON LAYING OUT AND TRANSFERRING CURVES AND DESIGNS?

1. Name three uses for a dividers.
2. How should a dividers be set to measurement?
3. What precautions should be taken when drawing a circle on a finished piece?
4. What are trammel points?
5. How many sides has an octagon? A hexagon?
6. How is an octagon drawn?
7. Define an ellipse. Describe the method of drawing one.
8. When is it necessary to enlarge an irregular design?
9. Why are most of the designs in books drawn on squared paper?
10. Is it always necessary to lay out the whole design? Why?
11. Describe a templet and how it is used.

Section

IV

UNIT 19.

# CUTTING OUT CURVES

**Many projects** have curves or irregular shapes that must be cut to form the design. To cut curves, the saw must have a thin blade. Figure 19-1. The two saws most commonly used are the coping and compass. This work can also be done on the jig or band saw. (See Machine Woodworking.)

### THE COPING SAW

The *coping saw* has a handle and a U-shaped frame into which a removable blade is fastened. One inexpensive type has a wire frame in which the blade is held tight by the spring of the frame itself. The one shown in Figure 19-2 is more practical for general woodworking because the blade is tightened by a screw in the handle. It is also better because the blade can be turned at any angle to the frame. Blades for the coping saw have ripsaw-like teeth and are made with several different numbers of points to the inch. For most work, choose a blade

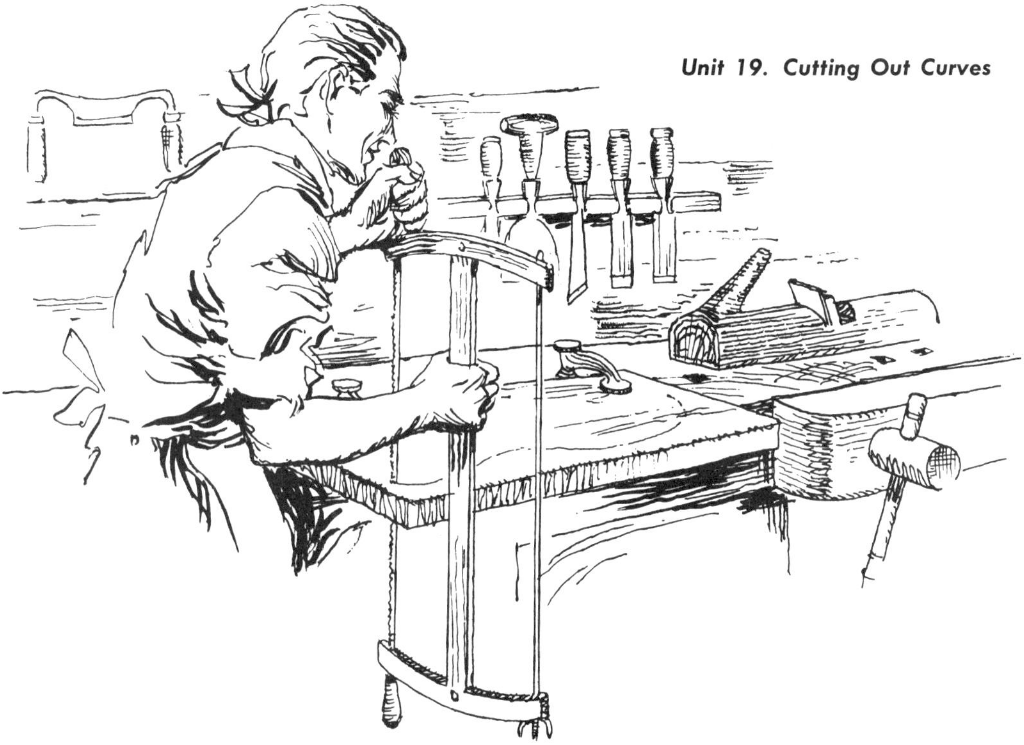

**19-1.** The cabinetmaker of years ago used a *turning* saw to cut out large curved parts. Now this kind of cutting is done with a compass saw by hand or with a band saw.

with sixteen points (fifteen teeth) to the inch.

### Cutting with the Work Supported on a Saw Bracket

Mount the blade in the frame with the teeth pointing toward the handle. If the opening to be cut is internal, drill a small hole in the waste material just large enough for the blade to pass through. Slip the blade through the hole and fasten it into the frame.

Hold the work to the bracket with your left hand. Figure 19-3. Grasp the handle of the coping saw in your right hand and move the saw up and down. The cutting action takes place on the downward stroke, with the pressure released as the saw is pushed upward. The saw must be worked freely, so there should be very little pressure. Hold the work firmly.

As you cut, it is better to move the work, keeping the saw blade inside the V cut of the bracket. If the cutting is hard, apply a little soap or wax to the blade. Keep the blade moving at a steady pace of about twenty to thirty strokes per minute. At sharp corners turn the handle

**19-2.** A coping saw. This type is tightened by screwing up the handle. The blade can also be adjusted at any angle to the frame.

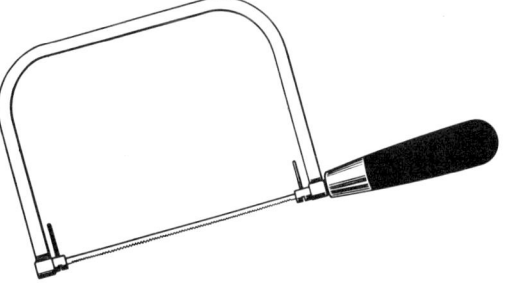

171

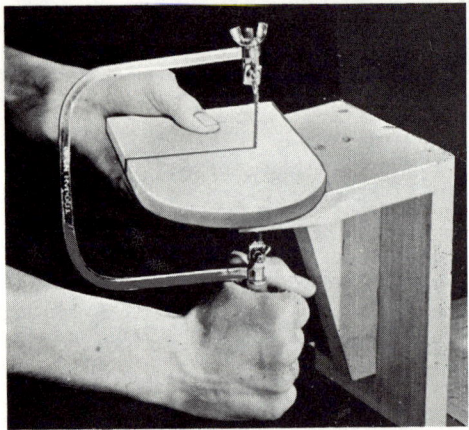

**19-3a.** Cutting work with the stock held over a saw bracket. When doing this type of sawing, the blade is put in the frame with the teeth pointing toward the handle. This method is especially satisfactory for cutting intricate designs.

slowly in the direction of the line and keep moving the saw up and down without applying any pressure to the blade. Begin cutting again as the blade is turned. Twisting or bending the blade at the corners usually breaks it.

## Cutting with the Work Held in a Vise

Put the blade in the frame with the teeth pointing away from the handle. Lock the work in the vise with the place to be cut near the top of the vise jaws. Begin the cutting in the waste stock. Keep your strokes even as you bring the blade to the cutting line. Make sure that the saw kerf is in the waste stock and that the blade is held straight up and down on the work at all times. While cutting, the saw can be supported with both hands as shown in Figure 19-4. If

**19-3b.** On all work, shift the position of the work to accommodate the saw most easily. Full, easy strokes, carefully guided through securely held work, will prevent excess blade breakage. For some types of wood, plywood in particular, cutting will be easier if the blade is drawn through beeswax at intervals during the cutting.

**19-4.** Cutting with a coping saw with the work held in a vise. In this type of work, the saw can be held in both hands, thus giving it more support for cutting heavy stock. The blade should be inserted with the teeth pointing away from the handle.

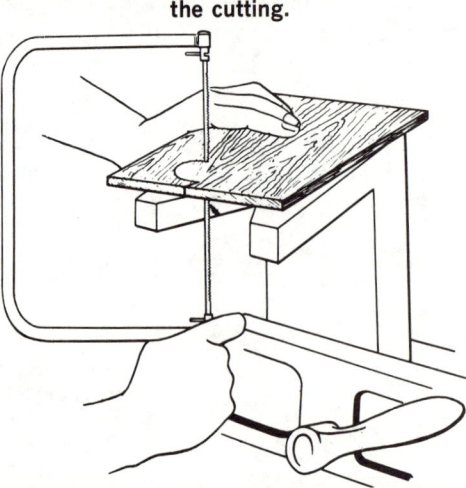

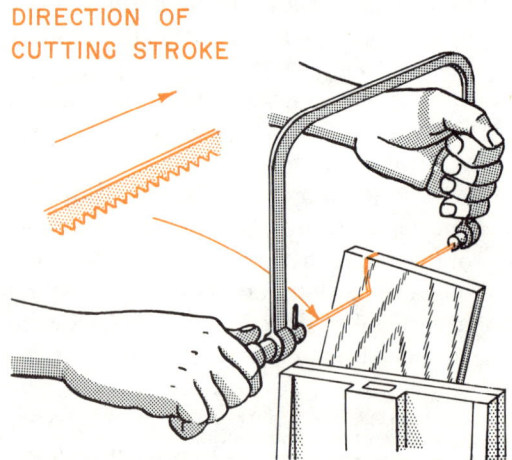

DIRECTION OF CUTTING STROKE

the stock is very light, you can support the work itself with your left hand to prevent vibration.

## THE COMPASS SAW

The *compass saw* looks like any other handsaw except that it is much smaller and has a thin, tapered blade. Usually a compass saw comes with several different-sized blades to fit into the handle. Figure 19-5. The narrow point at the end of the saw makes it possible to start the tool in a small opening and to cut small curves and circles. The saw is made in lengths from 10 to 18 inches (254 to 457 mm) with eight points to the inch. The average compass saw is 10 to 14 inches (254 to 355 mm) long.

A *keyhole saw* is very similar except that it is even smaller and is named for its most common use.

### Cutting with the Compass Saw

Bore a hole in the waste stock large enough for the saw point to enter. Figure 19-6. Insert the point of the saw in the first hole. Take several short, quick strokes to force more of the blade to pass through the stock. Figure 19-7. Cut a curve by slightly twisting the handle of the saw to follow the pattern. Figure 19-8.

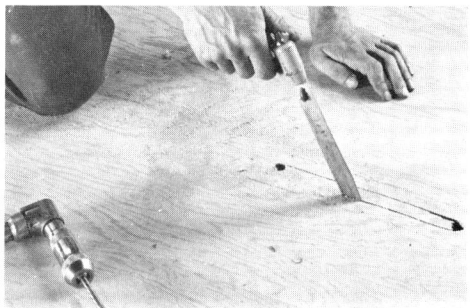

**19-6.** Using a compass saw for internal cutting. A hole is drilled in the stock to permit the saw blade to enter.

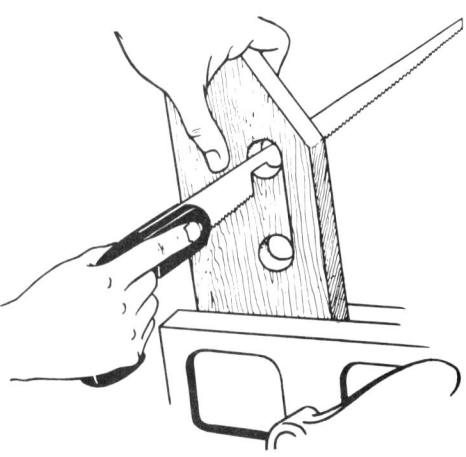

**19-7.** Cutting an internal opening in which two bored holes are part of the pattern.

**19-5.** Compass saw. This one has several interchangeable blades for different types of jobs. Compass and keyhole saws have small, highly tempered blades with specially filed teeth designed for cutting curves and circles. In addition to the several types available for woodworking, special compass saws have been designed for cutting jobs such as those encountered by plumbers and electricians.

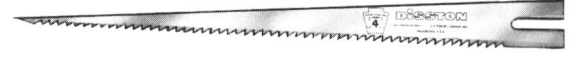

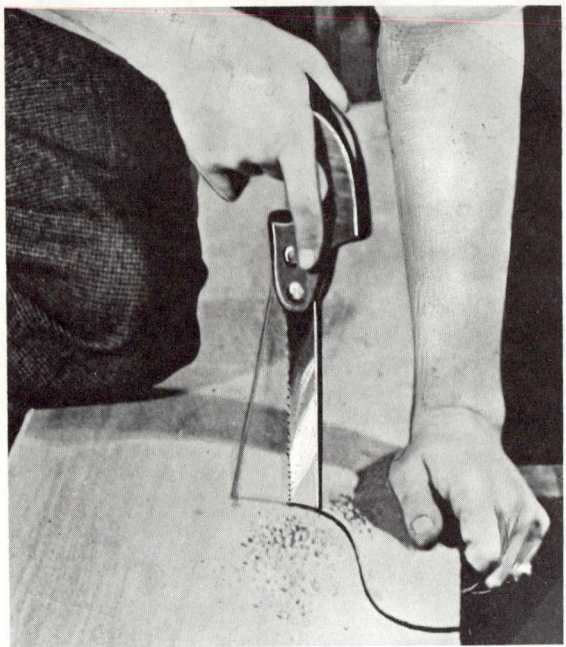

**19-8.** Before starting to cut with a compass saw, clearly mark the line to be cut and make certain that the work is securely supported. Hold the saw almost perpendicular to the work for best results. To get the saw to turn with the pattern, gently guide the saw by turning the handle in the direction of the cut. Forcing the blade too vigorously in the cut may cause it to bend, buckle, or break.

## CAN YOU ANSWER THESE QUESTIONS ON CUTTING OUT CURVES?

1. What machine tools will cut curves in wood? What hand tools?
2. Blades of a coping saw resemble what type of handsaw?
3. When work is cut on a saw bracket, should the teeth be pointed toward or away from the handle?
4. How can you prevent the saw from sticking?
5. About how many strokes per minute should be taken with the coping saw?
6. What are the most common causes of saw blade breakage?
7. Exactly where should the saw kerf be in regard to the layout lines?
8. Describe a compass saw and give its use.

# FORMING AND SMOOTHING CURVES

**After the** curve has been cut, the edge is rough. Some stock must be removed to smooth the edge and to bring it down to the finished line. Sometimes it is necessary to form or mold a curved surface. Figure 20-1. These jobs can be done with a cutting tool, such as a spokeshave or drawknife, or with a scraping tool, such as a file or rasp.

## THE SPOKESHAVE

A *spokeshave* has a frame with two handles which hold a small cutting blade. It is used to plane convex (dome-shaped) and concave (cup-shaped) edges. The depth of cut can be regulated with one or two small thumbscrews. The spokeshave was originally used for shaping the spokes of wheels but since has come to be a common tool for finishing the edges of curves and molding irregular shapes. Figure 20-2.

## Cutting with a Spokeshave

Place the piece in the vise with the edge to be smoothed near the surface of the vise. Hold the tool with both hands. You can either draw the spokeshave toward you or put your thumbs behind the frame and push it as you would a small plane. Figures 20-3 and 20-4. Place the cutting edge on the wood and apply even pressure. Work *with* the grain of the wood. Your experience in using a plane will tell you if the proper chip is being formed. If the blade is set too deep, the tool will chatter (vibrate and cut unevenly).

**20-1.** This coffee table has legs and rails that require forming.

**20-2a.** A spokeshave is used to cut concave and convex edges and for molding and forming work. This type has two narrow nuts on the top for adjusting the depth of the cutter. The cutter is held in place with a cap, which is fastened by a thumbscrew.

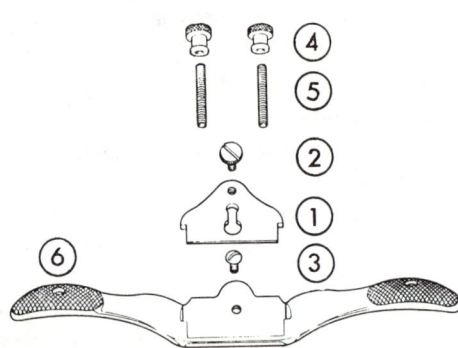

**20-2b.** Parts of a spokeshave: 1. Cap; 2. Thumbscrew; 3. Cap screw; 4. Adjusting nuts; 5. Adjusting screw; and 6. Body.

When concave curves are planed, the cutting is done from the top of the curve downward. Use the spokeshave as you would a small plane.

## THE DRAWKNIFE

The *drawknife* is a U-shaped tool. It has a blade 8 or 10 inches (203 or 254 mm) long with a handle at each end. Figure 20-5. This tool is very good for removing large amounts of stock rapidly and for doing molding work such as shaping a canoe paddle or building a model boat or airplane. Be very careful in using this tool, because the long, exposed blade can be dangerous.

### Cutting with the Drawknife

Clamp the work in a vise in such a way that the cutting will take place *with* the grain of the wood. Hold the tool in both hands, with the blade firmly against the wood and the bevel side down. Turn the blade at a slight angle to the work. Carefully draw it into the wood until a thin chip forms; then draw the knife steadily

**20-3.** Cutting with a spokeshave by drawing it toward you. The blade should be set just deep enough to form a thin shaving. If set too deep, the tool will chatter.

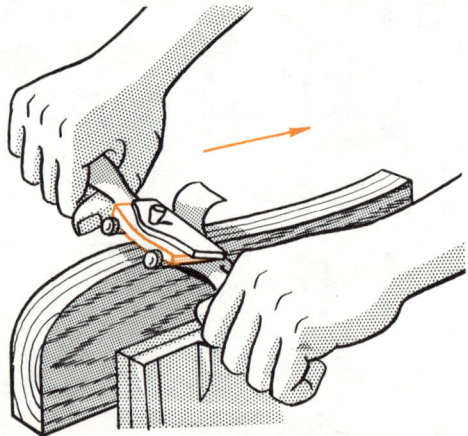

**20-4.** Cutting with a spokeshave by pushing it away from you. Even pressure must be applied to do the cutting.

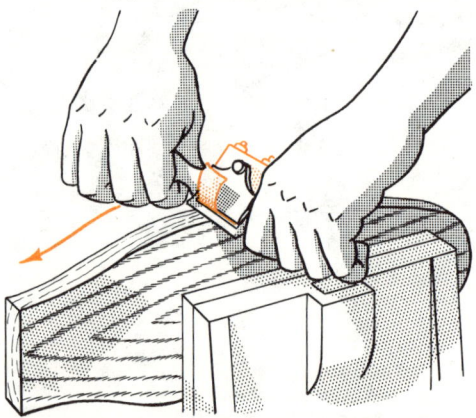

toward you. Figure 20-6. Do not try to take too deep a cut at one time, as this will split the wood.

## THE FILE AND RASP

The *file* and *rasp* are scraping tools. They should be used only as a last resort. Too often the inexperienced woodworker prefers to use one of these tools when a cutting tool would do a much better job.

There are a great many kinds of files, in many shapes and sizes. It would be impractical to describe even a few of them here. The two files used most often are half-round cabinet and flat files. Figure 20-7.

A *rasp* looks a lot like a file, except that the face is cut with individually shaped teeth. Figure 20-8. The rasp removes large amounts of stock quickly and leaves a rough surface; the file leaves a smoother finish. Always put a handle on the rasp and file when using them because the tang (the projecting point) can cause a bad injury. Figure 20-9.

### Smoothing with a File or Rasp

Clamp the work tightly in the vise. Hold the handle in your right hand and the end of the tool in your left. Apply pressure on the forward stroke, making a slight shearing cut across the edge of the work. Figure 20-10. Release the pressure on the return stroke. When you are using a half-round or rattail file for finishing a convex curve, twist the tool

**20-5.** A drawknife is especially useful when removing large amounts of stock rapidly.

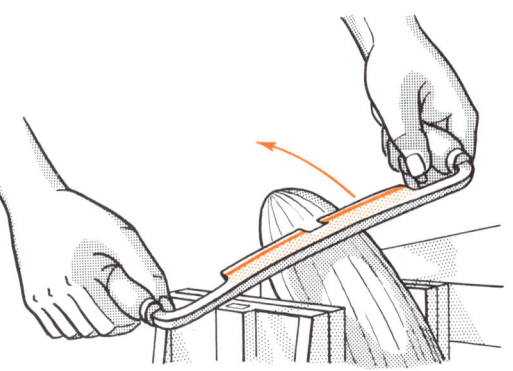

**20-6.** Using a drawknife to shape the hull of a model boat.

**20-7.** A cabinet file. Be sure that the handle is attached when using it for smoothing operations. Never use a file without a handle.

**20-8.** A rasp. Notice the individually shaped teeth. This tool is used when removing large amounts of stock, but it leaves quite a rough surface.

slowly as the forward stroke is made. Don't rock a file or rasp as this will round off the edge of the work. These tools should be cleaned often with a file card. Figure 20-11.

### THE SURFORM TOOL

This is a cutting tool with a hardened, tempered tool-steel cutting blade. Figure 20-12. These tough, sharp teeth are pre-set in a hardened, tempered blade. Figure 20-13. This tool never needs sharpening, setting, or adjusting. The tool can be used for cutting, shaping, shaving, smoothing, filing, rasping, and forming. The teeth are shaped so that they bite into the material and then allow the shavings to pass through the blade without clogging. The blade makes it easy to cut wood, plastics, and other soft materials. The tool is available in a variety of types. The replaceable blade fits into a file, block plane, or plane-type holder. Figure 20-14.

The surform tool is used like a rasp. To obtain best results, apply light pres-

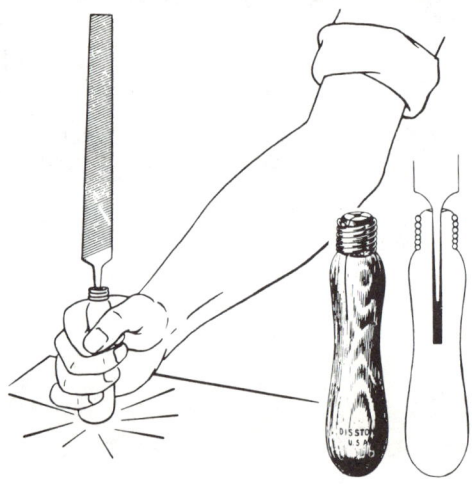

**20-9.** Always fit a handle on a file before using it.

**20-10.** Using a file to dress an internal curve. Make sure that you hold the file flat against the stock and that you do not rock it.

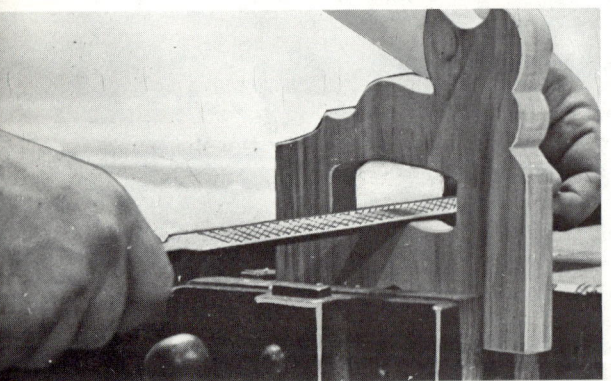

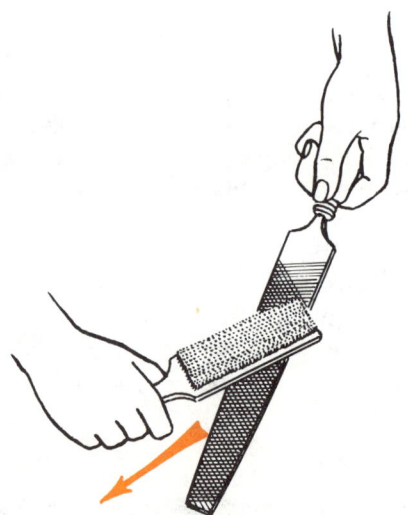

**20-11.** Keep the file clean by brushing it at regular intervals with a file card. Always follow the angle at which the teeth are cut.

**20-12.** A file type of surform tool.

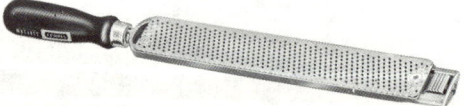

sure against the material. Figure 20-15. This will produce a smooth, flat surface. It is a good repair tool for smoothing an edge or end that is chipped or splintered. It is also good for shaping gun stocks, canoe paddles, wooden tool handles, and other odd shapes. A rotary-type unit is also available that fits into a drill press or portable drill for shaping an edge. Figure 20-16.

## SOLID-ROUTER DRILLS

There are other types of tools for forming curves. The solid-router drill is ideal for enlarging holes, making circles and scrolls, and doing other types of shaping operations. Figure 20-17.

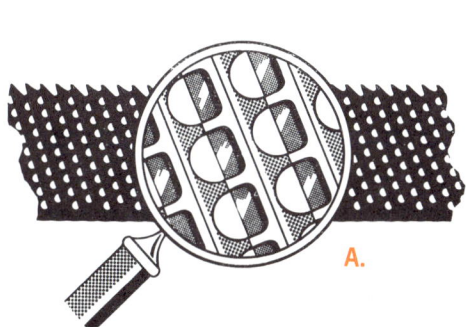
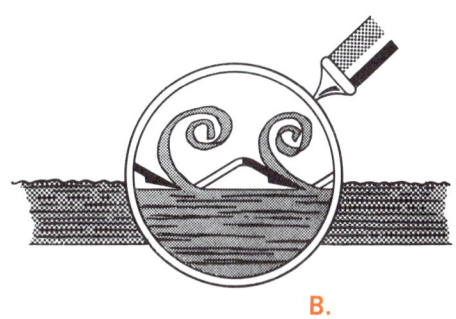

A.

B.

**20-13.** Notice the enlargement (A) of the surform tool. It consists of nearly 500 cutting teeth that are shaped in such a way as to bite into the material (B) and then allow the shavings to pass straight through.

**20-14.** Common types of surform tools: A. File; B. Plane; C. Block-plane; and D. File type.

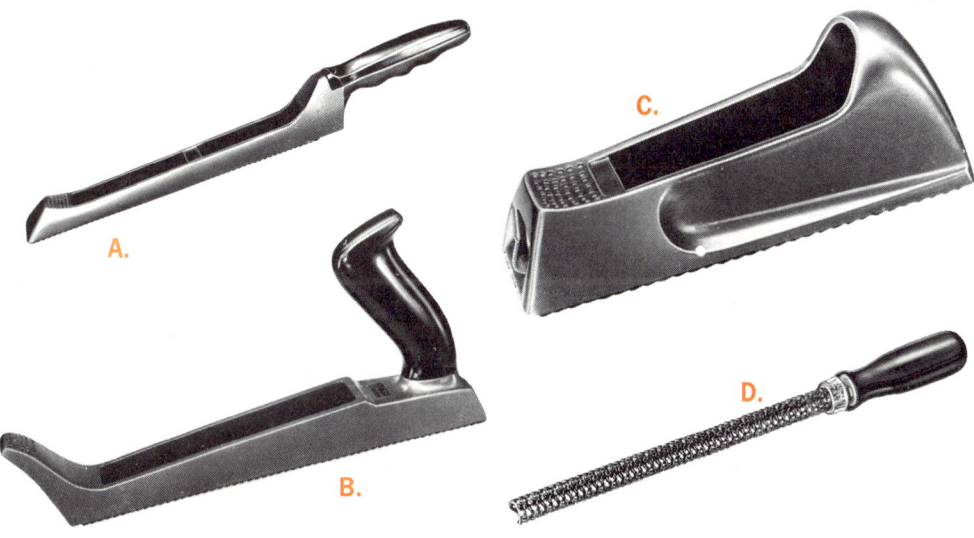

C.

A.

B.

D.

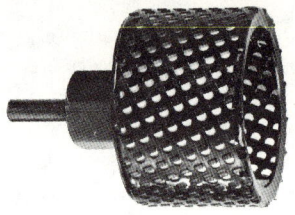

**20-16.** A rotary type of surform tool which can be used in a drill press or in a portable electric drill.

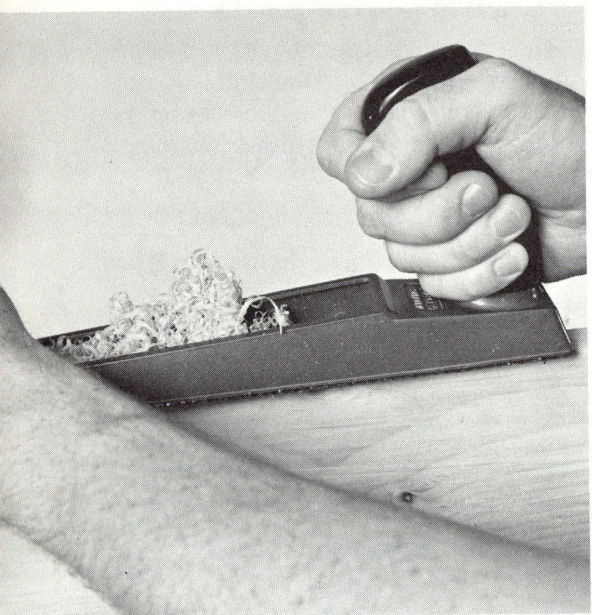

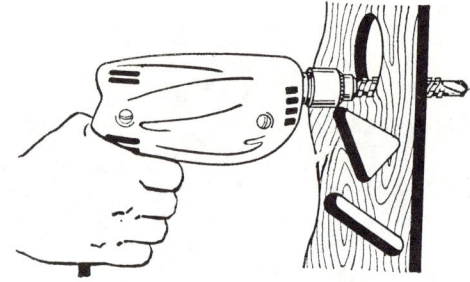

**20-15.** Using a plane type of surform tool for smoothing the edges of a door.

**20-17.** Note how the router-drill can be used to shape wood stock.

## CAN YOU ANSWER THESE QUESTIONS ON FORMING AND SMOOTHING CURVES?

1. In what ways is a spokeshave like a plane?
2. Where did the spokeshave get its name?
3. Can a spokeshave be both drawn and pushed?
4. To what job is the drawknife best suited?
5. To make the cut, how should the drawknife be held against the wood?

6. What is the difference between a file and a rasp?
7. Does a good woodworker use a file or rasp very often?
8. What safety practice should be observed when using a file or rasp?
9. Describe how a file or rasp is handled; also a surform tool.

# SECTION V
## Decorating, Shaping, and Bending Woods

**What you must know and be able to do in Units 21–25:**

21. How to make chamfer, bevel, and taper cuts: what they are used for and how they are different from other procedures.

22. Chiseling and gouging operations: kinds of chisels and gouges; chiseling with the grain, across grain, vertically and horizontally, and other uses; how to use a gouge.

23. Carving: kinds of wood; woods to use; correct tools; treating wood; and carving techniques.

24. Wood bending: equipment needed and how to heat and bend the wood over forms.

25. Laminating: what it is; advantages; industrial application; how to make a laminated project, including a serving tray; use of the hydraulic press.

*To make straight or curved cuts in wood, a great many different sharp-edged tools are needed. The plane, chisel, and gouge are three of the most useful ones that you will frequently use. A molded shape for a boat model could be cut, shaped, and formed from a single piece of stock. A large project, a boat for example, gets its shape when the wood is bent.*

# CHAMFER, BEVEL, AND TAPER

**Three angular** cuts made in much the same way but used for different purposes are the chamfer, bevel, and taper.

The *chamfer* is an angular cut only part way across the corner or edge, used mostly as a decoration on an edge or end. Figures 21-1 and 21-2. The *bevel* is an angle cut completely across the edge or end of a piece. This is done when one piece is set at an angle to another, such as the sides of a book trough. Figures 21-3 and 21-4. A *taper* is cut on the legs of tables and stools to make them appear more lightweight and graceful. Figures 21-5 and 21-6. On some projects the taper is cut on all four sides; on others only the two inside surfaces are cut.

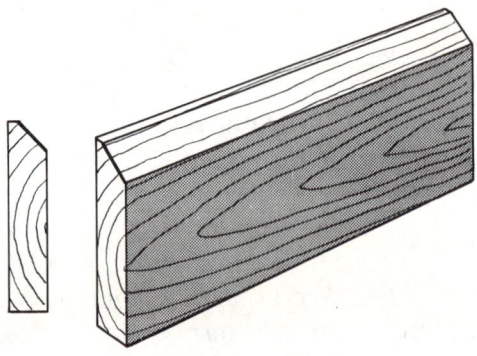

**21-2.** A chamfer.

**21-1.** The base of this lamp illustrates the use of a chamfer.

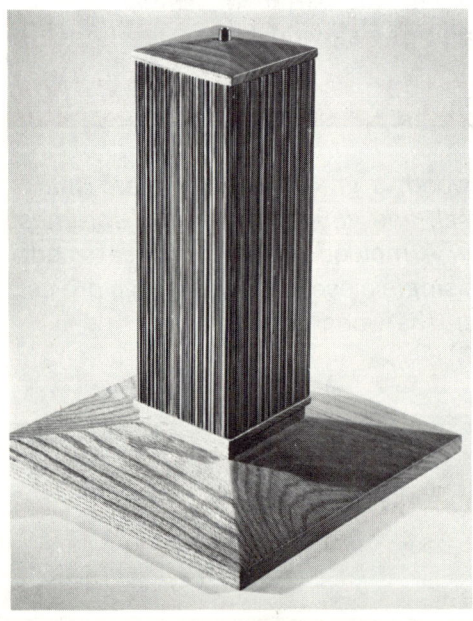

**21-3.** A bevel was cut to form the joint on the two pieces at the roof line of this bird house.

## MAKING A THROUGH CHAMFER

A through chamfer is one that extends the whole length of the board. To make one, first determine the amount of chamfer from the drawing. If this is not given, the usual practice is to cut a chamfer of about $\frac{3}{16}$ inch (5 mm) on stock 1 inch (25.5 mm) thick.

There are three methods for marking the chamfer. One is to hold a pencil between the fingers as a gage and run it along the face surface and edge or end as shown in Figure 21-7. Another way is to insert a pencil point in a marking gage and use the marking gage to lay out the line. Do not use a regular marking gage, however, as this would leave a rough edge on the chamfer. A third way is to use a combination square and pencil to mark the line.

Lock the stock in a vise. In some cases it may be easier to clamp the stock first in a hand screw as shown in Figure 21-8, and then to lock the handscrew in the vise. In this way the plane can be held level as the cutting is done.

Plane the corner with the grain along the total length of the stock. Remove the stock evenly so that the chamfer will come to the marked line on both sides at the same time. Use the fingers of your left hand to guide the plane and hold it at the proper angle. In taking the last cut,

**21-5.** The inside of each leg of these nested tables has a taper cut along its length.

**21-6.** A taper.

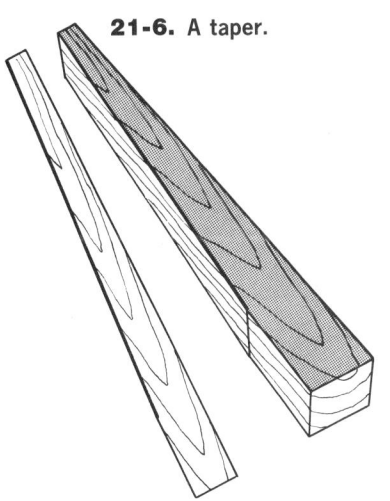

**21-4.** A bevel.

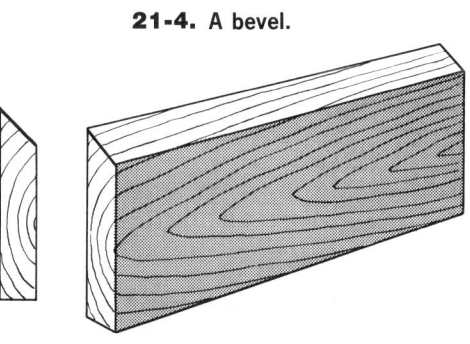

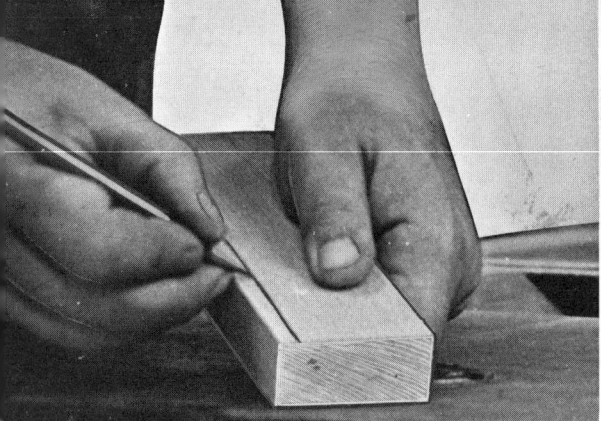

**21-7.** Marking a chamfer by using a pencil guided with your fingers held against the edge of the stock.

**21-8.** Planing a chamfer with the wood held in a hand screw. By this means you can cut the chamfer with the plane held in a level position.

form a chip that is the full width of the chamfer across the total length of the stock.

When cutting a chamfer on end grain, hold the plane or chisel at an angle to the surface and take a shearing cut across the edge. Figure 21-9. If this is not done, there is danger of splitting out the chamfer on the edge. Figure 21-10. To check the chamfer, set a sliding T bevel at an angle of 45 degrees and hold it against the chamfer edge. Figure 21-11.

## CUTTING A STOP CHAMFER

A stop chamfer is one that does not extend the whole length of the board. Mark the width and length of the stop chamfer with a pencil. Cut or pare with a chisel from one end of the chamfer to about half the length of the chamfer. Make thin cuts until you reach the layout line. Reverse the board and cut from the opposite end. You must be careful not to

**21-9a.** Cutting a chamfer on end grain, using a plane. A shearing cut is taken to prevent the edge of the stock from splitting out.

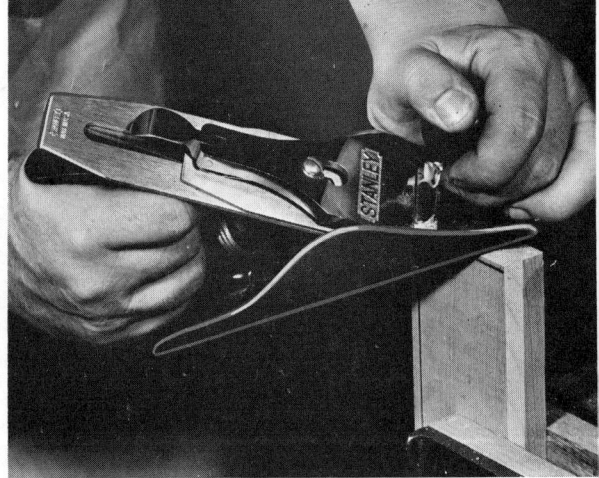

cut into the stock that is not chamfered. Figure 21-12.

## PLANING A BEVEL

Determine the angle at which the bevel is to be cut and, with a protractor, set a sliding T bevel to this angle. Hold the sliding T bevel against the face surface and mark the angle of the bevel on both ends of the stock. Figure 21-13. Begin to plane the bevel as you would plane an edge, except that the plane must be tipped at about the angle at which the bevel is to be cut. Check this angle frequently with a sliding T bevel. Continue to plane the edge until the bevel is formed.

## CUTTING A TAPER

Square up the legs on which the taper is to be cut. Lay the four legs side by side and mark the position at which the taper is to start. Then square a line around all four sides of each leg. A taper may be cut on only one side of a leg. Figure 21-14a. However, most designs call for tapers on two adjoining sides or all four sides of the legs.

If tapers are cut on two or four sides, the layout and cutting must be done in

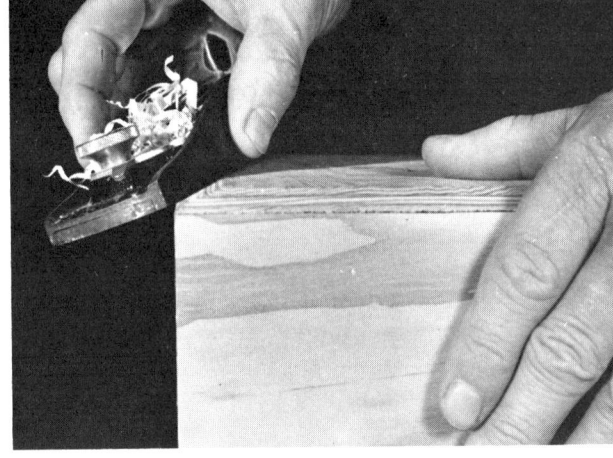

**21-10.** Using a block plane for cutting a chamfer on the edge of plywood.

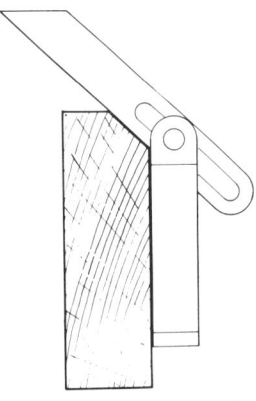

**21-11.** Checking a chamfer with a sliding T bevel set at 45 degrees.

**21-12.** Cutting a stop chamfer.

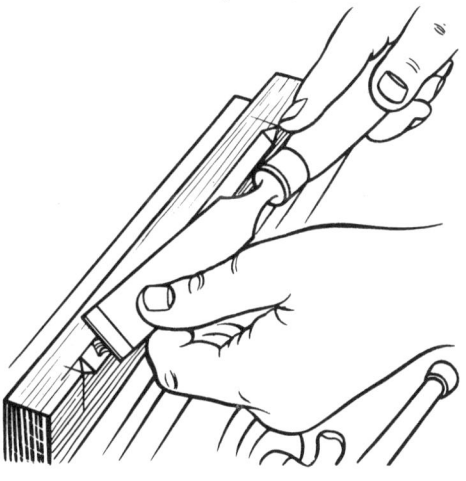

**21-9b.** Using a chisel to cut a chamfer on end grain.

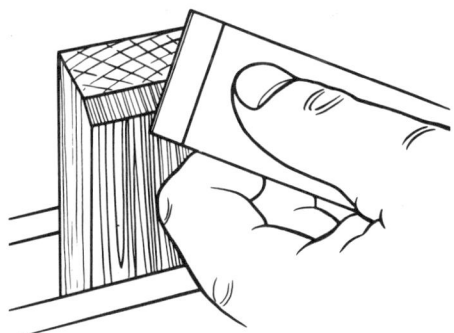

two steps. The example in Figure 21-14b shows the layout and cutting for tapers on two adjoining sides. Determine the amount of stock to be removed at the foot of the taper. Set a marking gage to this amount and mark a single line across the lower edge of the leg. Draw

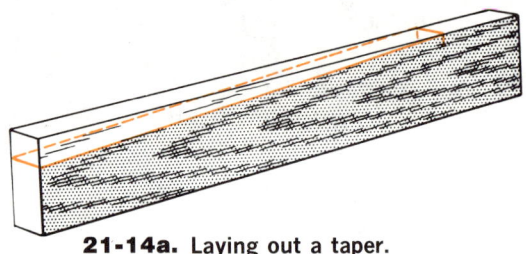

**21-14a.** Laying out a taper.

**21-13.** Using a sliding T bevel to lay out a bevel on one edge of a piece of stock. As the plane approaches the finish line, the sliding T bevel can be used in the same manner as a try square to check the bevel along the edge.

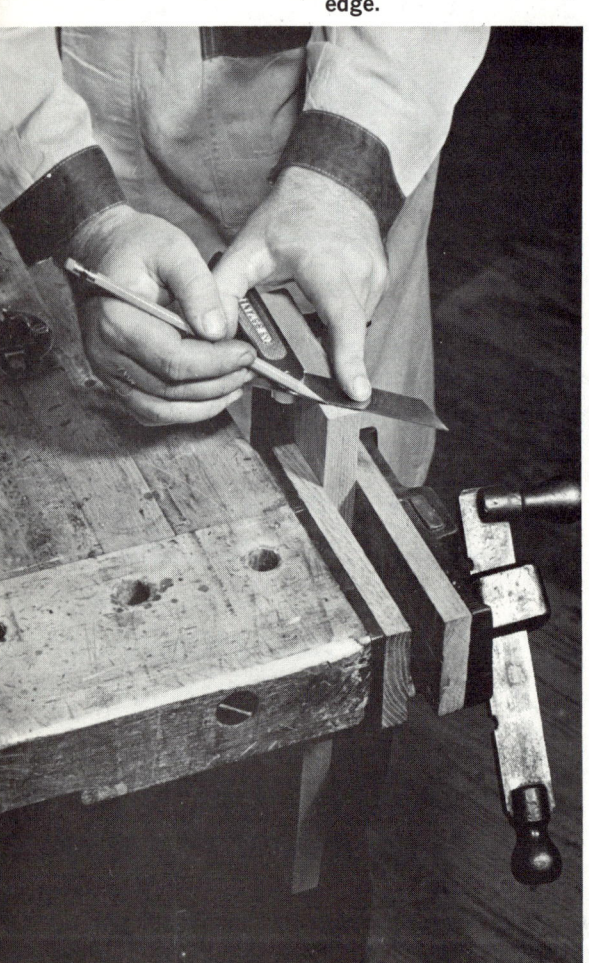

FIRST TAPER MARKED

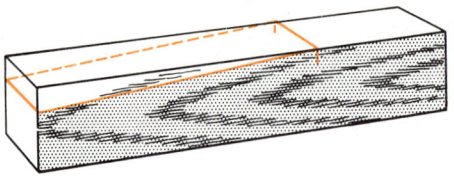

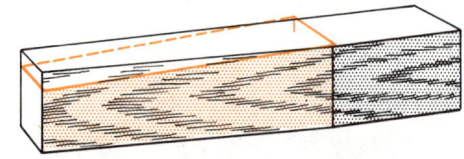

FIRST TAPER CUT, SECOND TAPER MARKED

**21-14b.** When the taper is to be cut on two adjoining surfaces, one side should be laid out and cut before the second layout is made.

**21-15.** Planing a taper. Hold the plane on the angle of the taper. Notice that longer and longer strokes are made until the total length of the taper is planed.

HOLD PLANE ON ANGLE OF TAPER
STROKES ARE PRO-
GRESSIVELY LONGER

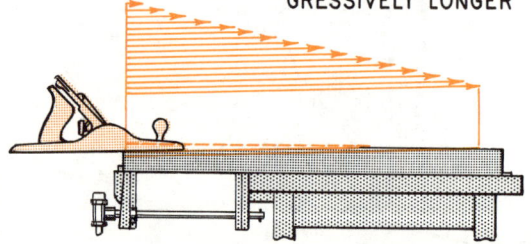

lines along opposite sides to show where the taper is to be cut. Cut the taper with a handsaw or, if one is available, a band or circular saw. Plane the tapered surface smooth and true. Figure 21-15. Now mark the taper across the bottom of the leg on the adjoining side. Draw lines along opposite sides. Cut and smooth the second taper. If tapers are cut on all four sides, mark and cut the first two opposite tapers and then mark and cut the second two opposite tapers.

## CAN YOU ANSWER THESE QUESTIONS ON THE CHAMFER, BEVEL, AND TAPER?

1. In what way is a chamfer different from a bevel?
2. Would you lay out a chamfer with a regular marking gage? Discuss two methods of laying out an ordinary chamfer.
3. What precautions must be taken in cutting a chamfer on end grain?
4. How can you hold the plane level and still cut a chamfer?
5. Describe a stop chamfer.
6. Why is a sliding T bevel necessary when making a bevel?
7. How should the planing strokes be taken when cutting a taper?

## Section V

## UNIT 22.

# SHAPING STOCK WITH A CHISEL OR GOUGE

**Many cutting** jobs cannot be done with a saw or plane. These can be done with either a chisel or a gouge.

To cut with a chisel or gouge, it is often necessary to pound the tool with a mallet that has a head of wood, hard rubber, or rawhide. Figure 22-1.

### SAFETY

Correct use of the chisel and gouge requires care and caution. Follow these guidelines when using these tools:

● Hold the workpiece so that it cannot move.

● Keep both hands behind the cutting edge and the chisel or gouge away from the body.

● Hold the tool correctly. The right hand should push with the handle while the left hand guides the blade. When using a mallet, the left hand should hold the handle, while the right hand taps the tool.

● Always hit the tool squarely on top of the handle.

● Never allow the edge to touch other tools. Avoid dropping the chisel or gouge on the floor or any other hard surface.

• Always be on the lookout for metal fasteners in the wood.

• Protect the handle by using a wood or plastic mallet. Never use a metal hammer.

• When finished, store the chisel or gouge safely in a tool rack.

## CHISELS

You will find many uses for a set of good chisels. Figure 22-2. The chisels you buy can be either of two types, the *socket* or the *tang* chisel. The handle of the socket chisel fits into a funnel-shaped socket at the top of the blade. Socket chisels have heavier blades and will take pounding better than tang chisels. The tang chisel has a straight shank formed at the end of the blade. This tang is force-fitted into a plastic handle. Figure 22-3. The tang chisel is designed for paring, shaping, and similar light chiseling. It has a thin blade. Figure 22-4.

There are several kinds of chisels, including:

• *Paring* chisels which have a light, thin blade about 2½ inches (63 mm) long.

• *Butt* chisels which have standard weight blades but are about 3 inches (76 mm) long. They are used on work where a longer chisel might be difficult to use.

• *Pocket* chisels which have heavier-weight blades about 4½ inches (114 mm) long.

• *Firmer* chisels that are all around chisels with heavier-weight blades about 6 inches (152 mm) long. They are used for both heavy and light work.

When grinding a chisel, make sure the proper angle and shape are obtained. The harder and tougher the material, the greater the angle of the cutting edge. Figure 22-5.

You will need at least six chisels with blades from ¼ to 1 inch (6 to 25 mm)

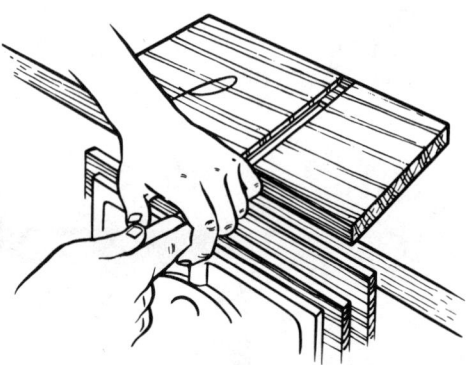

**22-2a.** Using a paring chisel to trim a dado on a wide board.

**22-2b.** Using a butt chisel for cutting a dovetail joint.

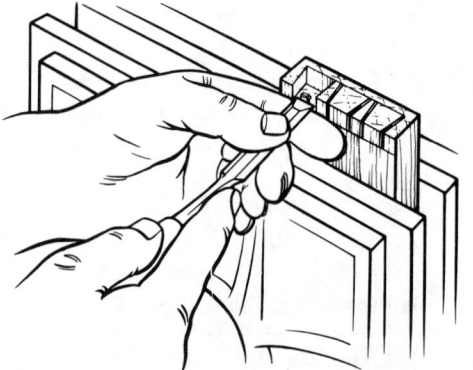

**22-1.** A mallet is used for pounding a chisel or gouge. The head should be wood, leather, or rubber.

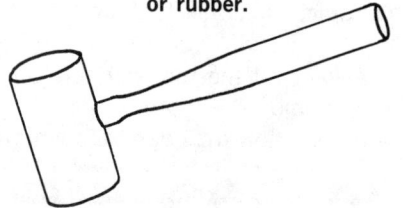

wide, increasing at ⅛-inch (3 mm) intervals.

## Cutting Horizontally with the Grain

Lock the work in a vise so the cutting can be done with the grain of the wood. Figure 22-6. Never attempt to cut against the grain, as the wood will split out.

For rough cutting, hold the chisel with the bevel side against the stock. Grasp the chisel handle in your right hand and the blade in your left. Figure 22-7. Use your right hand to apply pressure to the tool and your left hand to guide the cutting action.

The cutting action may be taken in two ways. The blade may be forced into the stock parallel to the wood, or a shear-ing cut can be made with the blade moving from right to left as it cuts. You will find that the straight cutting takes more pressure. Also, it is more convenient to hold the tool in your left hand and pound with the mallet held in your right hand.

When making light, paring cuts with the chisel, turn the tool around with the flat surface next to the wood. Hold the blade between your thumb and forefinger to guide it in taking these cuts.

## Cutting Horizontally Across the Grain

Lock the work in a vise or clamp it to the top of the bench. Rough cutting can be done with the bevel down or by paring with the flat side down. In cutting across the grain to make a rabbet, dado, or lap joint, work from one side to about halfway across the stock. Figure 22-8. Never go completely across the stock, as this will chip out the opposite side. Work from both sides to the finished line, leaving the center higher. Figure 22-9. Then with light paring cuts bring the center down to the line. Figure 22-10. To clean out the corners, hold the chisel in one hand with the flat side toward the shoulder and draw it across as you would a knife. Figure 22-11.

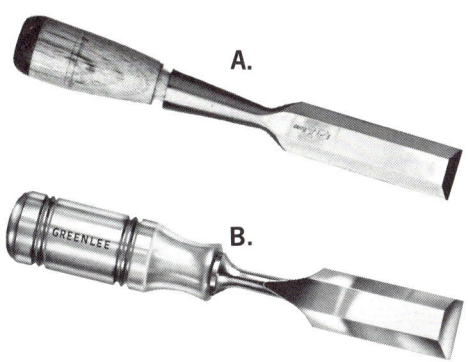

**22-3.** Types of chisels: A. A socket-type chisel is made in such a way that the handle fits into a socket of the blade; B. A tang-type chisel has the tang of the chisel itself running into the handle.

**22-5.** This shows correct and incorrect grinding edges for chisels. The angle of the chisel will depend on the kind of work to be done.

**22-4.** Parts of a chisel.

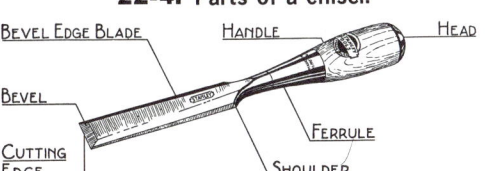

BEVEL EDGE BLADE    HANDLE    HEAD
BEVEL
CUTTING EDGE    FERRULE    SHOULDER

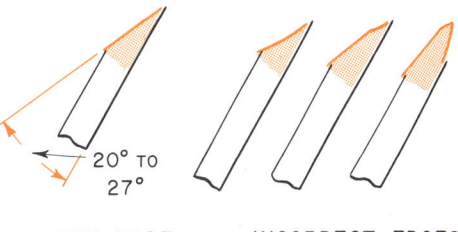

20° TO 27°

CORRECT EDGE        INCORRECT EDGES

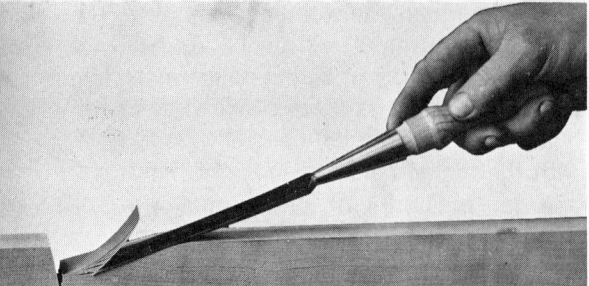

**22-6.** Cutting action of the chisel when cutting horizontally with the grain. Always cut with the grain, never against it, for this procedure.

**22-7.** Holding a chisel for doing heavy horizontal cutting with the grain. The blade of the chisel is held firmly in the left hand.

**22-8.** Roughing out a cut across grain. The chisel is held with the bevel side down and the mallet is used for driving. This illustrates the cutting of a lap joint.

## Cutting Convex Curves Horizontally

Remember when you lock the work in the vise that you will be cutting with the grain. Begin by taking straight cuts that tend to follow the convex (dome-shaped) curve. Figure 22-12. Remove most of the extra stock with these straight cuts until the curve is almost formed. Then hold the chisel with the flat side down and carefully cut the curve by applying forward pressure and raising the handle to follow the curve. Figure 22-13. Move the chisel sideways across the work, making a series of cuts close together.

## Cutting Vertically Across the Grain

Hold the stock over a bench hook, clamp it over a scrap piece of wood, or place it over a bench stop. Never do vertical chiseling directly on the top of a bench, as this would damage it.

Hold the chisel in a vertical position with the handle in your right hand and the blade guided between your left thumb and forefinger. Take a shearing cut, working from right to left. On wide stock, you can regulate the depth of the cut by holding the flat side of the chisel against the surface that has already been cut. Figure 22-14.

**22-9.** Proper method of cutting a lap joint from both sides, leaving the center high and then trimming the center down.

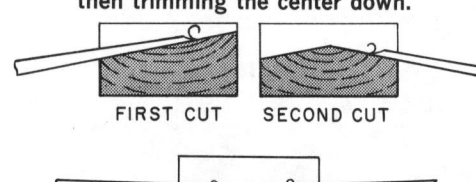

FIRST CUT    SECOND CUT

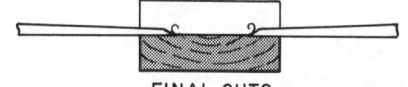

FINAL CUTS

## Cutting End Grain Vertically

Lay the work flat over a bench hook, or piece of scrap stock, and clamp it firmly in place. Begin at one corner of the stock to make the cut by tipping the handle to one side. Rotate the handle to get a shearing cut. Figure 22-15. Always start from the corner and work toward the center. Working the other way would split out the end grain.

## Cutting Concave Surfaces Vertically

Lock the work in a vise with the concave (cup-shaped) surface to be removed just above the end of the vise. Take straight cuts until most of the waste stock is removed. Work as always from the edge toward the end to avoid splitting out the stock. To form the concave curve, hold the chisel with the bevel side toward the stock. Apply forward pressure, at the same time moving the handle in an arc (curve). Figure 22-16.

## GOUGES

Gouges are chisels with curved blades. They are sharpened either with the bevel on the inside or the outside. Figure 22-17. Gouges vary in size from ¼ to 2 inches (6 to 51 mm).

**22-10a.** Horizontal cutting across grain for heavy cuts. Support the chisel with your left hand resting on the bench or vise. Cut with a slicing action.

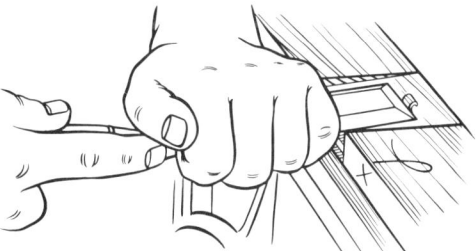

## Cutting with a Gouge

Gouges are used in the same general way as chisels. Outside bevel gouges are handled in the same way as a chisel is handled when the bevel side is down. An inside bevel gouge is used as a chisel, with the bevel turned up.

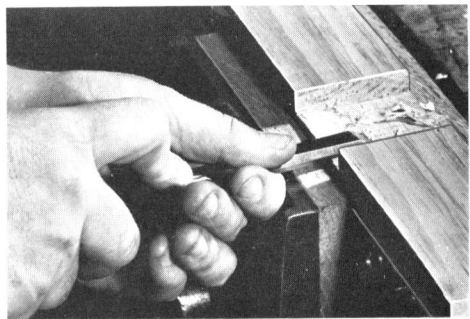

**22-10b.** Making light paring cuts across the grain. The blade of the chisel is held between the thumb and forefinger for accurate control. The chisel is held with the flat side down.

**22-11.** Cleaning out the corners of a lap joint by pulling the chisel across with the flat side held against the shoulder of the joint.

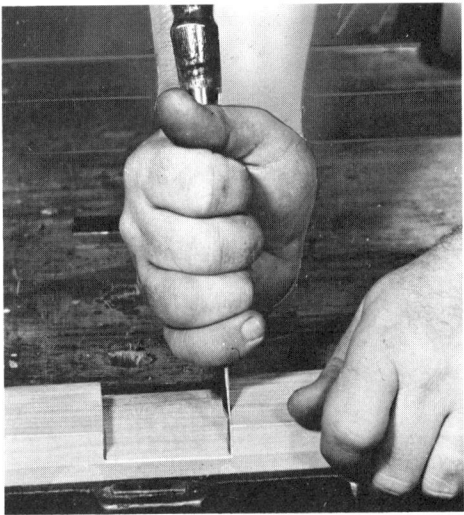

191

To do heavy gouging with an outside bevel gouge, hold the handle in your right hand and the blade in your left hand. Push the gouge forward and rock it slightly from side to side to make a shearing cut. Figure 22-18. For very heavy work, the gouge can be held in the left hand and the force applied with a mallet. If a large surface is to be gouged out, it is better to work across the grain. The reason for this is that the gouge is less likely to dig in than when cutting in the direction of the grain.

To do light gouging, hold the blade in your left hand as shown in Figure 22-19, and take a long, thin shaving. Force the tool into the wood lightly and then push on the handle to finish it.

Gouging is done to form recesses, to do veining and decorating work on the surface of wood, to shape such articles as boat hulls, and to imitate the appearance of age as on a treasure chest.

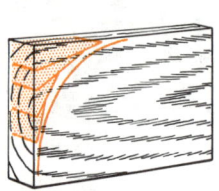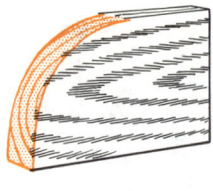

**22-12.** Cutting a convex curve. Note that several straight cuts can be taken to pre-form the curve to the approximate arc.

**22-13.** Finishing a convex curve. Forward pressure is applied and the handle is raised gradually to follow the proper curvature.

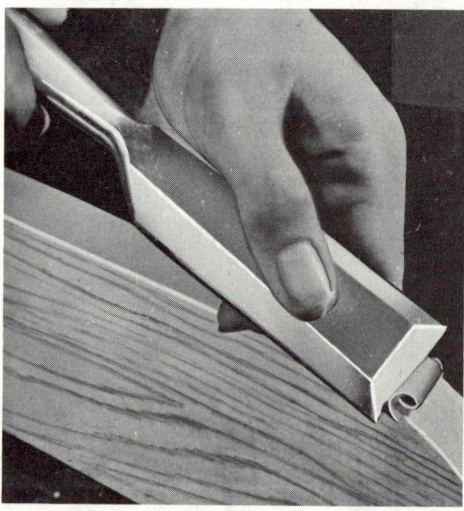

**22-14.** Cutting vertically across the grain: A. Notice how the left hand guides the chisel as the right hand applies pressure. The chisel should be tilted slightly to give a sliding action. B. Cut with the grain so that the waste wood will split away from the layout line.

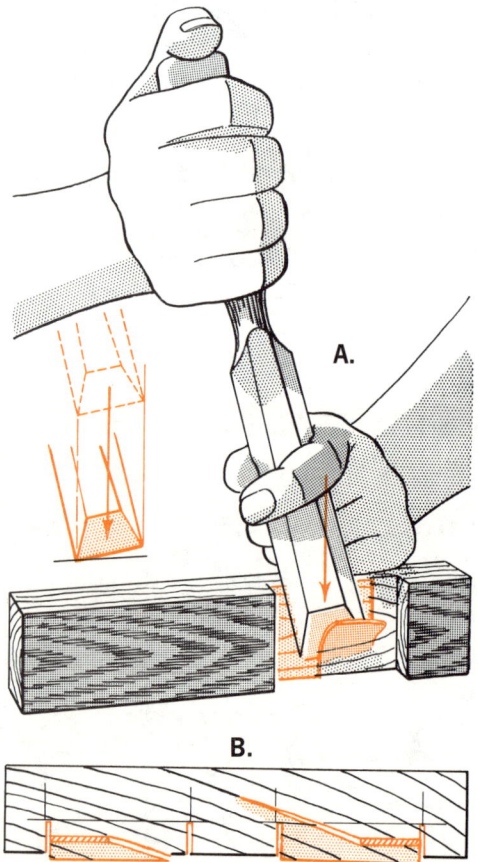

A.

B.

RIGHT     WRONG

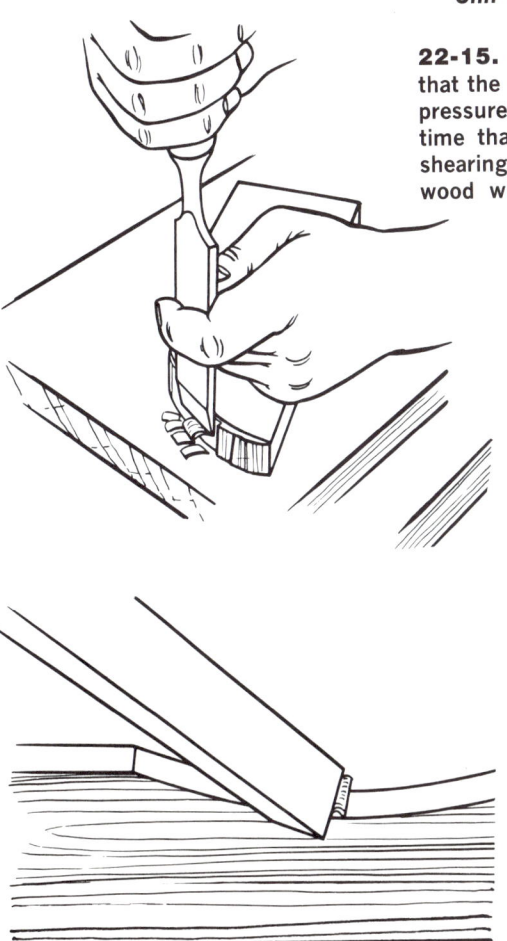

**22-15.** Cutting end grain vertically. Note that the stock is held over a bench hook and pressure applied to the handle at the same time that it is rotated slightly to obtain a shearing cut. The left hand should rest on the wood with the first finger controlling the chisel.

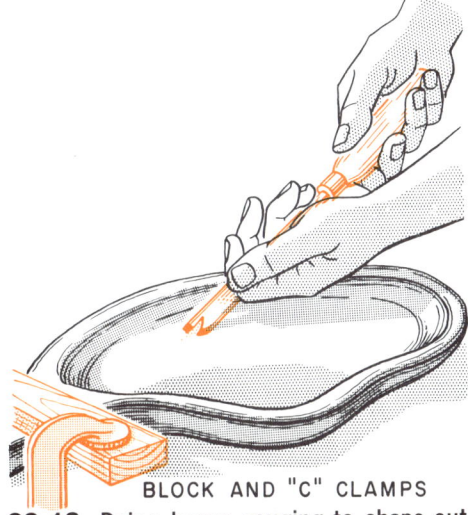

BLOCK AND "C" CLAMPS

**22-18.** Doing heavy gouging to shape out the inside of a tray. The left hand holds the blade firmly, while the right hand applies the pressure.

**22-16.** Cutting a concave curve. The chisel is held with the bevel side down and the cut is taken from the edge to the end grain. In this way the cut is made with the grain of the wood.

**22-19.** Doing light gouging with the gouge held between the thumb and other fingers for accurate, light work.

**22-17.** Types of gouges: A. Gouge with a bevel on the outside; B. Gouge with a bevel on the inside.

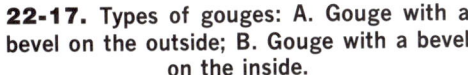

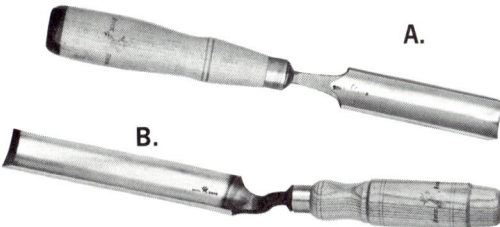

A.

B.

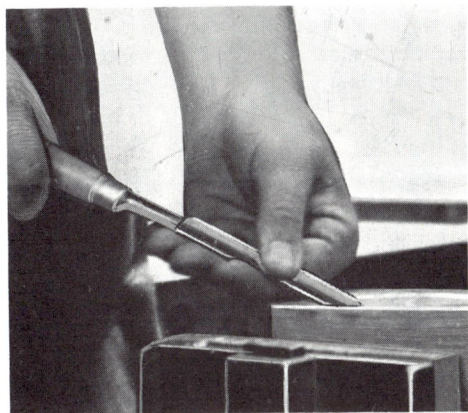

## CAN YOU ANSWER THESE QUESTIONS ON SHAPING STOCK WITH A CHISEL OR GOUGE?

1. Name the two types of chisels. What is a butt chisel?
2. Do you cut with the grain of the wood?
3. How should a chisel be held for making heavy cuts?
4. What are the two ways to do rough cutting with a chisel?
5. When making light paring cuts, how should the blade be held?
6. Give the procedure for cutting a rabbet, dado, or lap joint.
7. How can the corners be chiseled out?
8. Should vertical chiseling be done directly on the top of a bench?
9. In cutting convex curves, why are straight cuts made first?
10. What kind of chisel action is best for cutting end grain vertically?
11. Can a concave surface be cut with a chisel?
12. How does a gouge differ from a chisel?
13. How are gouges sharpened?
14. What kind of gouge is best for heavy gouge work?
15. To remove a great deal of stock with a gouge, is it better to work with or across the grain?
16. What is the purpose of gouging?

# Section V
# UNIT 23.

# WOOD CARVING

**Wood carving** is a most ancient art, examples of which can be seen in museums, churches, and public buildings all over the world. Figure 23-1. It is also one of the most interesting woodworking hobbies. Many artistic and attractive objects can be made with very simple tools.

## KINDS OF CARVING

There are several kinds of carving, which include the following:

● *Whittling* is a kind of freehand carving done with knives. Many interesting and useful projects can be made by using only the knife as a cutting tool. Figure 23-2.

● *Chip carving* is a method of forming a design by cutting shapes in the wood surface. It is used mostly for cutting geometric shapes such as triangles, squares, and curved variations of these. Chip carving can be done with carving tools or knives.

● In *chase carving*, a design is laid out and gouges are used on the surface with long, sweeping cuts. Figure 23-3. Carved free-form bowls and a variety of other items can be made in this manner.

● In *relief carving*, the background is cut away to form the surface design. This is one of the most difficult kinds of carving. The design stands out in three-dimensional form. If the carving is fairly shallow, it is called *low* relief. If the design has greater depth, it is known as *high* relief. In high relief the design is undercut so that it seems to stand away from the background. Figure 23-4.

● *Wood sculpture* or "carving in the round" is very interesting and perhaps the most difficult kind of wood carving. This method is used in forming a figure such as an animal, human replica, or caricature. The design is first traced on two sides of the wood. The outline can be jig-sawed on one face, then the block turned around a quarter turn and the side view cut out with the jig saw. From this point on, the work is completed with knives and gouges. Figure 23-5. Routing bits or carving burrs can be used on a drill press to do some of the rough shaping. Figure 23-6.

## WOODS FOR CARVING

Many kinds of woods can be used for carving. Some of the most desirable are described here.

*White pine* is a good choice for the beginner. The fibers are close together yet are easily cut clean, both with and across grain. Pine is relatively straight-grained and has a rather even structure that makes for few hard and soft spots.

Both *genuine mahogany* and *Philippine mahogany* are excellent woods for carving. Genuine mahogany has a deep brown color that gives it a rich appearance. It also has an interesting grain pattern. Philippine mahogany is also easy to work but has a less interesting grain.

**23-1.** Carving is an ancient art.

**Jumbo**

USE 1¼" THICK WOOD, PLACE ON BLOCK WITH GRAIN VERTICAL

BEGIN WHITTLING AT POINTS MARKED WITH ARROWS

BOTH SIDES WILL BE THE SAME.

NOTE, CURVE IN TAIL

¾" DEEP AT THIS POINT

FINISH BY PAINTING WITH A MIXTURE OF BLACK & WHITE. DO NOT VARNISH.

THREE BLACK TOE-NAILS ON EACH FOOT

**23-2.** This kind of whittling can be done with simple knives.

**23-3.** Chase carving is illustrated in these hand-carved trays of walnut.

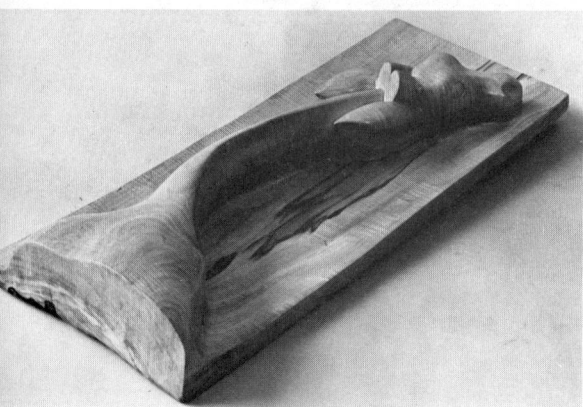

*Walnut* is somewhat more difficult to work but is, nevertheless, an excellent wood for carving. It is especially good for such projects as handles for sports equipment.

## Treating Wood for Carving and Wood Turning

One of the problems in making wood carvings and turning thin bowls on the lathe is that after the project is completed, it often will split, check, or warp as the wood dries out. This is especially true if the moisture content of the wood is higher than that of the room in which it is used. However, with a relatively simple chemical treatment, these defects can be prevented even when starting with green or only partially dry wood.

The first step is to rough shape the carving or rough turn the bowl to about

**23-4.** High relief carving on domestic buckwood. Carving is a wood activity in which you can use your creative ability.

**23-5.** The delicate, sculptured pieces on both sides illustrate fine craftsmanship and creative design ability.

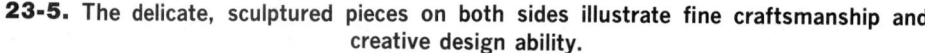

¹⁄₈ inch (3 mm) oversize. Then make a watertight container of plywood or line a wood box with thin plastic sheet. Place a 30-percent solution of polyethylene glycol-1000 in the tank. Soak the rough carving or bowl in the solution at room temperature for about three weeks. The water-soluble, wax-like chemical is absorbed by the wood, thus preventing checking, splitting, and warping. Allow the rough carving or bowl to air dry on shelves in a heated shop for several weeks. Now complete the carving or bowl to final size.

The only finish that works well on the treated wood contains polyurethane resin. Complete information on the use of this wood treatment can be obtained from the Forest Products Laboratory at Madison, Wisconsin.

## KINDS OF CARVING TOOLS

Gouges, knives, and carving tools are needed for wood carving. There are many special carving tools that can be purchased, but only a few are required for basic work. Figure 23-7. These include the following:

• A *skew,* or *flat chisel,* that is ground on both sides to a sharp edge. Figure 23-8A.

• A *parting* tool, which is V-shaped, used to cut triangular shapes in the wood. Figure 23-8B.

• A *veiner,* a very small gouge with a sharp V cutting edge. Figure 23-8C.

• *Gouges* and *fluters* which are ground on the outside, in sizes from ³⁄₈ to ⁵⁄₈ inch (10 to 16 mm) and with cutting edges of different radii. Some are quite flat—almost chisel shaped—while others are shaped like half an ellipse. Figure 23-8D.

• *Knives* for whittling. Figure 23-9.

A complete set of carving tools can be purchased as individual tools or as a set with a single handle into which various blades can be inserted.

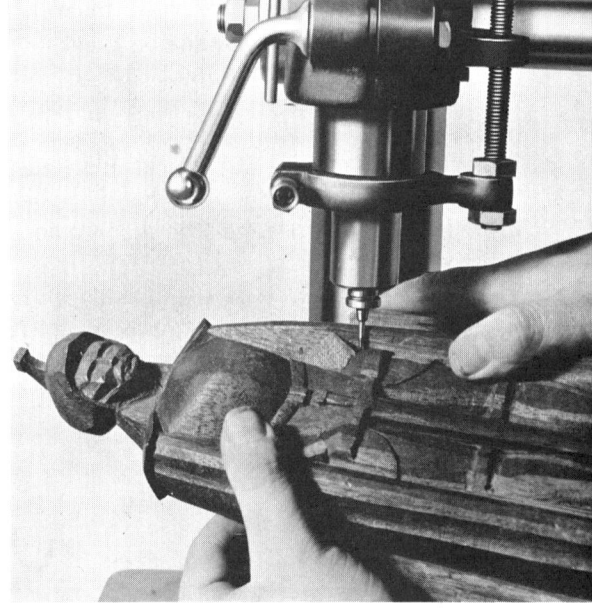

**23-6.** To do freehand carving on the drill press, use a high speed of at least 5,000 r.p.m.

**23-7.** A matched set of carving tools.

197

## GENERAL SUGGESTIONS FOR CARVING

● Always work out a pattern before starting the carving. Enlarge the pattern to the size you want. Then carefully transfer the design to the wood.

● Clamp the work securely. It is much better to work with the wood in a vise or clamped to the top of the bench. In this way both hands are free to do the carving. For some work, the tool is held in one hand and the end struck with a mallet. For other cutting, one hand applies the pressure while the other hand guides the tool.

● Keep your fingers and body away from the front cutting edge as much as possible. There is always danger that the tool will slip and cut you severely. Some-times, in whittling, it isn't always possible to keep your hands away from the front of the cutting edge. At these times, try to keep your fingers below so that if the knife slips it will not cut you.

● The first cut should always sever or cut apart the grain. After the outline has been drawn (in chip carving, for example), the design is outlined with a sharp V parting tool. Figure 23-10. After this is done, you can then work up to the cut by removing clean-cut chips.

● Try to cut with the grain as much as possible. Cutting with the grain is always easier and there is less chance that the tool will cut in and chip out a piece of your design. When cutting against the grain, roll the tool to the right and left to cut the fibers. This will help prevent tearing into the fibers and gouging out.

● When cutting the raised portion (on relief carving, for example), cut so that the base will be slightly wider than the upper part. Don't undercut until all of the carving is completed, as this will cause real trouble.

● Start with a relatively simple design, to practice the art of tool control.

● Remember that *sharp* cutting tools are best for all kinds of carving.

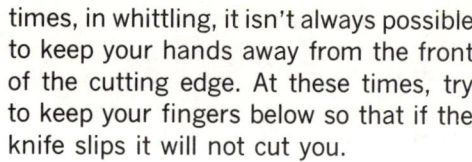

**23-8. Patterns of cutting edges of carving tools: A. Chisel; B. V parting tool; C. Veiner; D. Gouges and fluters.**

**23-9. A complete set of knives and other cutting tools for whittling.**

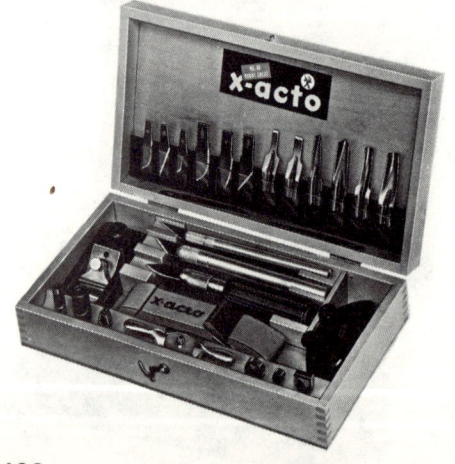

**23-10. A parting tool used to outline the design.**

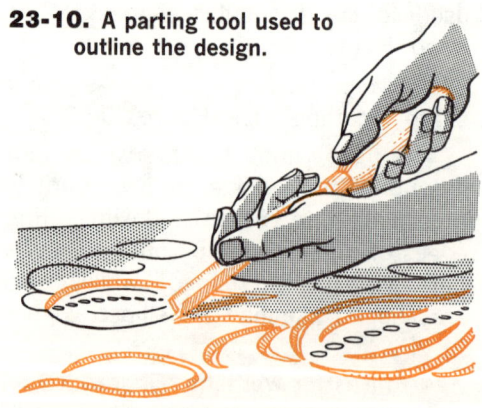

## CAN YOU ANSWER THESE QUESTIONS ON WOOD CARVING?

1. Describe low relief carving.
2. What kind of carving is done to produce an animal or other freestanding object?
3. Tell what kinds of wood are best for carving.
4. List the common cutting tools needed for wood carving.
5. Is the procedure for all carving the same? Describe.
6. Tell how to treat wood to prevent warping and checking.

## Section V
## UNIT 24.

# BENDING SOLID WOOD

**To make** sports equipment such as toboggans, skis, and surfboards, stock must be bent. Figure 24-1. Sometimes stock is bent to form a furniture part that must be curved such as the front of a drawer. There are many kinds of wood suitable for building these projects, but ash, hickory, birch, and oak are the best.

Wood can be bent more easily when it is steamed or made soft by soaking in hot water. This makes the wood cells more plastic so they can be stretched or compressed. Most of the bending is due to compression (squeezing the cells on the inside curve), and much less is due to the stretching of the cells (on the outside curve). As a matter of fact, the outside will stretch only 1 or 2 percent, but the inside will compress as much as 25 percent. When wood is properly moistened and heated, it will bend ten times more easily than dry wood.

### EQUIPMENT

The most popular method of bending wood is to soften it by steaming or boiling in hot water. A necessary piece of equipment is the heating tube. It is closed on the lower end and has a cover on the upper end. Figure 24-2. The lower end of this tube is placed directly above a gas flame. Water is poured into the tube and the end closed. The heat and moisture soften the wood, as explained later.

Another piece needed is the form for bending the wood. A form like the one

**24-1.** A toboggan is only one of the many pieces of sports equipment that require bending. Length can be made to suit your needs.

199

shown in Figure 24-3 can be used for the staves of a toboggan. Another form is satisfactory for bending the tips of water skis. Figure 24-4.

## HEATING THE WOOD

Fill the heating tube about half full of water. Light the gas flame and close the end of the tube with a tight cover. There should be a tiny hole in the cover to keep it from blowing off. Prepare the staves

at the same time. These should be cut to thickness and width and the edges chamfered or rounded off with a radius of $\frac{1}{8}$ inch (3 mm).

When the water in the tube is boiling, put in the wood pieces. Don't add too many at one time, as the water should completely surround the end of each one. Leave the wood in the tube for two to three hours.

Prepare the bending equipment while the wood is heating. You need the form for bending these pieces, several C clamps, and parallel handscrews. Also have ready a piece of thin sheet metal the same width as the staves and the length of the bend.

## BENDING THE WOOD

When the pieces have been heated, remove them from the tube and insert the heated end under the protecting bar

WATER IN HEATING TUBE

BURNER          TUBE STAND

**24-2.** This is the type of heating tube you will need for bending wood. An old hot water heater can also serve this purpose. A tube is fastened to the wall or on a stand at a slight angle and a burner placed under the lower end.

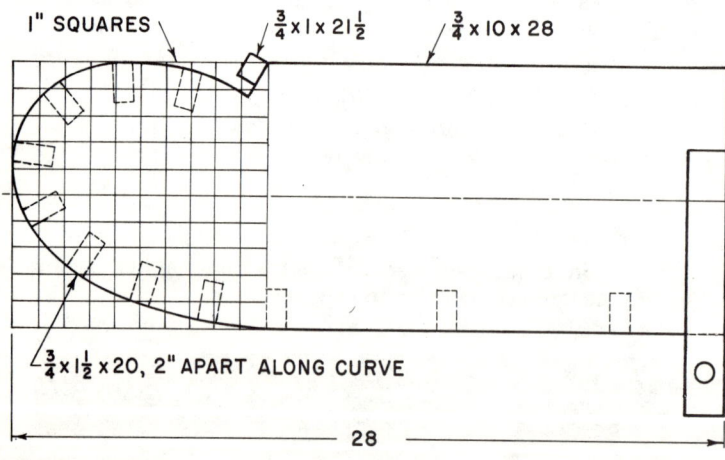

1" SQUARES          $\frac{3}{4}$ x 1 x 21$\frac{1}{2}$          $\frac{3}{4}$ x 10 x 28

$\frac{3}{4}$ x 1$\frac{1}{2}$ x 20, 2" APART ALONG CURVE

28

**24-3.** A form similar to this one is required to shape the front of toboggan staves or slats.

at the top of the form. Insert the thin sheet metal directly under it. Then begin to draw the stock around the form. Work slowly and clamp the staves at each cross support with a C clamp.

Do not try to pull the stave around the form too rapidly, as this will split out the wood. Continue to clamp the stave to the form, as shown in Figure 24-5. Allow each piece to dry for at least twenty-four hours before removing it from the form. You are now ready to sand, shape, and assemble the pieces.

## BENDING WITHOUT HEAT AND MOISTURE

Water skis can be made by bending flat stock to shape without steam or soaking. Make the skis of mahogany, spruce, or ash. A bending form is needed. Cut the stock to size and square it up. Saw one or more kerfs, 13 to 15 inches (330 to 381 mm) in length from

**24-6.** Cutting several saw kerfs from the end of stock as you would do in resawing lumber. This will make the tips of the skis easier to bend.

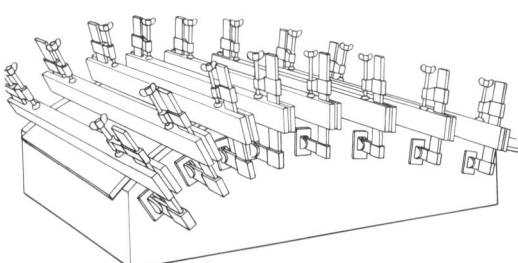

**24-4.** A form similar to this is needed to bend the tips of water skis. Each clamp must be tightened a little at a time.

**24-5.** Clamping a stave or slat to the form with C clamps. A piece of sheet metal is placed directly over the wood to protect it.

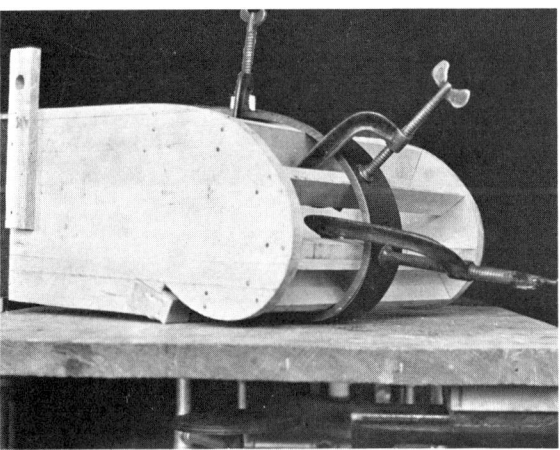

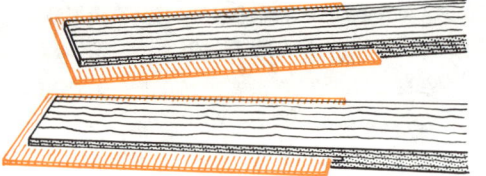

**24-7.** Waterproof adhesive has been applied and the veneer has been slipped into the saw kerfs.

one end. Figure 24-6. Then cut veneer the thickness of the kerf, slightly wider than the stock and as long as the saw kerf. Apply waterproof glue to both sides of the veneer and slip it into the kerf. Figure 24-7. Clamp the stock in the form and allow it to dry at least twelve hours. Then shape and complete the skis.

### CAN YOU ANSWER THESE QUESTIONS ON BENDING SOLID WOOD?

1. Toboggans, skis, and surfboards are most commonly made from what kinds of wood?
2. List the equipment needed for bending wood.
3. Wood is softened for bending in two ways. What are they and how is this done?
4. Can wood be bent rapidly? Why or why not?

## Section V

## UNIT 25.

# WOOD LAMINATION

**Simple lamination** is the process of building up the thickness or width of material by gluing several layers together, all with the grain running in approximately the same direction. Figure 25-1. However, in plywood lamination the layers of veneer are put together with the grain running at right angles to each other. Laminating is done commercially to produce a wide variety of structural pieces. Straight and bent parts for furniture, plywood panels, arches, and beams used in the construction of homes, schools, buildings, and churches are a few examples of lamination. Figures 25-2 and 25-3.

**25-1a.** This handsome wood, metal, and leather chair has structural parts made of solid laminated wood.

Wood laminations resist warpage, reduce the number of splits and checks, and produce a unit that is stronger than regular wood. A great advantage, also, is that shorter pieces of material can be used to make the whole.

The laminating process can be applied very effectively in the school shop to make small, formed projects such as salad servers and bent bookends. Figure 25-4.

## STEPS IN MAKING A LAMINATED WOOD PROJECT WITH SIMPLE EQUIPMENT

1. Determine the kind of project and design you will use.

2. If you are going to make a curved project like a salad server, make a full-size pattern of the curve on a piece of heavy paper.

3. Decide on the number of thicknesses needed. Usually the number is odd, such as three, five, or seven. Some furniture manufacturers use four layers of veneer for curved laminations. This makes it possible to use two good quality

veneers for face surfaces and two less expensive layers for the inside. Figure 25-5.

4. For the form, select a piece of hard maple or birch that is wide enough and long enough to enclose the veneer sandwich needed to make the project. (Molds, dies, and cauls are metal or wood forms or surfaces placed between presses or clamps to protect and shape the laminated assembly.) The form must be thick enough to allow for at least 1 inch (25.5 mm) of material on each side of the curve.

**25-2a.** This framework for a modern gymnasium is made of high-strength laminated wood beams, eliminating posts under the arch.

**25-1b.** The top of this table, designed and built by a student, is laminated with solid wood strips.

5. Transfer the full-size curve to the side of the form block, following the grain direction.

6. Carefully cut the curve on the band saw. Be especially careful to eliminate as many irregularities as possible. The two halves of the form or die should fit perfectly. Figure 25-6.

7. Sand very lightly with fine paper to remove saw marks if necessary.

8. Apply a thin coat of flexible material such as thin rubber to both sides of the form. This isn't absolutely necessary, but it helps in providing a better rough lamination. If rubber is used, it should

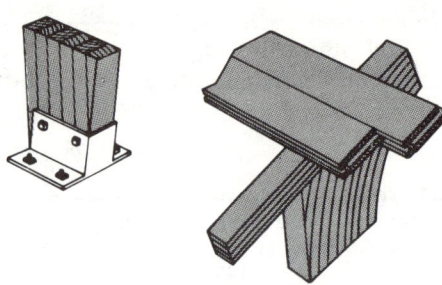

**25-2b.** These laminated beams are fastened to the pier foundations with metal brackets, and the beam structures are covered with a laminated deck.

**25-4a.** This laminated, fireplace, log holder can be made in the school shop.

**25-3.** In industry, laminated parts for furniture are made in huge quantities on a hot press such as you see here.

**25-4b.** These projects are typical of the laminated products that can be made in school shops.

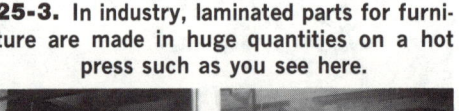

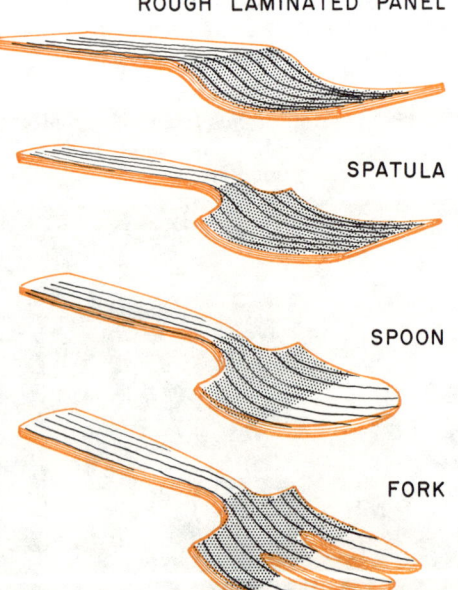

ROUGH LAMINATED PANEL

SPATULA

SPOON

FORK

be tacked onto the form and then the surface covered with wax.

9. Cut several pieces of veneer, $\frac{1}{32}$ to $\frac{1}{28}$ inch (1 mm) thick and large enough to make the project. One kind of material, such as mahogany or walnut, may be used, or the layers can be alternated with a lighter wood, such as birch or maple, for contrast.

10. Spread the glue on the veneer surfaces with a roller or notched glue spreader. Select a good quality casein glue or white resin glue. The glue must be spread evenly on both sides of each piece of veneer with, of course, the exception of the two outside pieces. The finished sides of these must be free of glue.

11. Place a piece of wax paper over one side of the form.

12. Stack the layers of veneer on the form.

13. Place another piece of wax paper over the last piece.

14. Place the other half of the form over the pieces, and clamp the two forms together with standard wood clamps. Figure 25-7.

15. Allow the sandwich to remain under pressure for at least twenty-four hours.

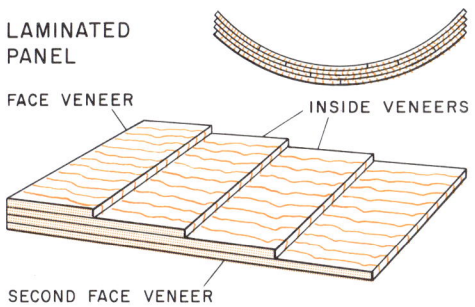

**25-5.** Four-ply laminated panel for curved furniture parts.

**25-6.** This is the kind of form needed to make the rough blank for a salad-server set.

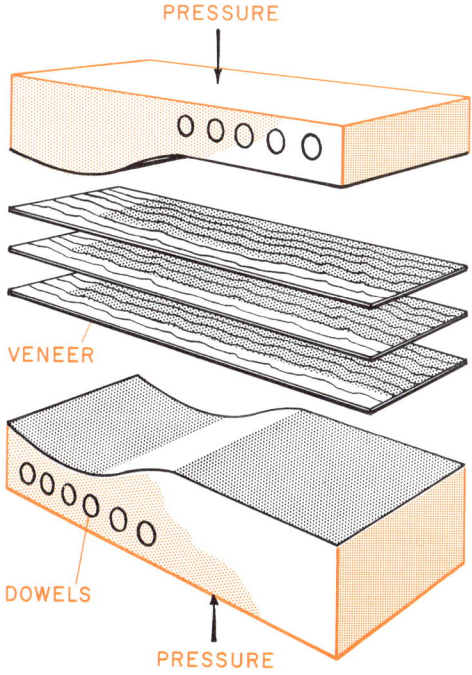

**25-7.** A simple lamination clamped over a form.

16. Remove the rough lamination from the form and pull off the wax paper.

17. Trace the outline of the project on the rough lamination.

18. Cut on a band or jig saw.

19. Sand and smooth the edges.

20. Apply penetrating finish to the object as soon as possible.

**Caution:** If the laminated project is to be used around food, use mineral oil as a sealer.

## MAKING A LAMINATED SERVING TRAY

### Bill of Materials

1 piece, 7 x 13 inches (178 x 330 mm), $\frac{1}{32}$-inch (1 mm) vertical grade plastic laminate or .050 postforming grade laminate; color, pattern, and surface finish is optional. 4 pieces, $6\frac{1}{2}$ x $12\frac{1}{2}$ inches (165 x 318 mm), approximately $\frac{1}{32}$-inch (1 mm) wood veneer; the bottom veneer should complement or match the color of laminate used on the surface. 2 pieces, $\frac{3}{16}$ x $\frac{3}{16}$ x 7 inches (5 x 5 x 178 mm), solid wood rails; choice of wood should complement or match the color of laminate used on the surface. Urea resin adhesive, paste wax, and clear wood finish.

### Plan of Procedure

1. Construct the two dies used to form the tray shape. Refer to the drawing for dimensions. The die should be one inch deeper than the height of the finished ends. Figure 25-8.

2. Cut the plastic laminate and wood veneer to correct size.

3. Glue up the plastic laminate and wood veneer.

  a. Use a urea resin adhesive, following manufacturer's directions for mixing and curing.

**25-8a.** Laminated serving tray.

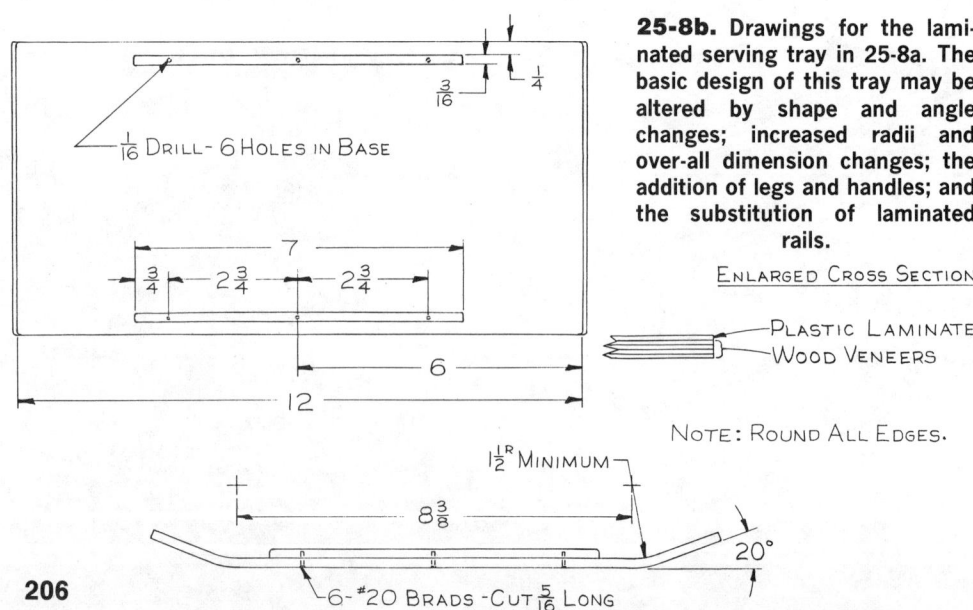

**25-8b.** Drawings for the laminated serving tray in 25-8a. The basic design of this tray may be altered by shape and angle changes; increased radii and over-all dimension changes; the addition of legs and handles; and the substitution of laminated rails.

ENLARGED CROSS SECTION

PLASTIC LAMINATE
WOOD VENEERS

NOTE: ROUND ALL EDGES.

$\frac{3}{16}$   $\frac{1}{4}$

$\frac{1}{16}$ DRILL- 6 HOLES IN BASE

7

$\frac{3}{4}$   $2\frac{3}{4}$   $2\frac{3}{4}$

6

12

$1\frac{1}{2}$R MINIMUM

$8\frac{3}{8}$

20°

6-#20 BRADS -CUT $\frac{5}{16}$ LONG

b. Some adhesive will squeeze out. To keep it from sticking to the laminate surface, wax the surface with a good grade of wax or apply masking tape to the surface and veneer.

c. Apply glue with a stiff bristle brush. Coat both sides of the center veneers, the back side of the bottom veneer, and the back of the plastic laminate.

d. Place waxed paper between the plastic laminate and bottom veneer and the surfaces of the dies to prevent the adhesive from sticking.

e. Clamp with a veneer press, jaw clamp, or bar clamp. Figure 25-9.

4. Lay out the shape of the finished tray on the plastic laminate assembly with a soft pencil.

5. Rough cut to shape with a band saw.

6. Sand on a belt or disc sander or with a hand file. If the finished shape is rectangular, edges may be jointed and circular sawed to make them parallel. For final smoothing, hand sand edges and bottom with 150 grit abrasive paper. Be sure to protect the laminate surface.

7. Cut the rails from solid wood.

8. Sand and finish with the same finish as the bottom veneer.

9. Drill holes in the base according to the dimensions on the drawing.

10. With a brad driver or hammer, install the rails on the base.

11. Apply finish to the wood veneer.

12. Attach felt pads to the bottom.

**25-9.** This type of veneer press can be constructed in the laboratory.

UPPER CAUL
WORK
BED FRAME

REMOVE ¾″ BOLT TO OPEN ONE SIDE OF FRAME

¾″ PIVOT BOLT

ROUND ENDS FOR CLEARANCE

BORE ¾″ DIA. FOR NO. 67 SCREW (or 9/16″ for No. 68 screw)

15, 18, or 24″ (depending on length of screw)

9½
9½
9½
4⅝
4⅝
4⅝
3⅝

COUNTER BORE 1″ DIA. FOR NO. 67 NUT (or ¾″ for No. 68 nut)

½ x 4″ CARRIAGE BOLTS

3⅝
37¾
45
3⅝

## USING THE HYDRAULIC PRESS
## FOR LAMINATING

A small hydraulic press with electrically heated and water-cooled steel platens is a very useful piece of equipment for laminating. Figure 25-10. This unit can apply even and uniform pressure up to 25 or more tons, depending on its size. The candelabra shown in Figure 25-11 is a typical product that can be made following these general instructions.

The amount of curvature of the laminated piece is optional. It should be designed with smooth, free-flowing lines. The design of the base should harmonize with the lines of the lamination. Figure 25-12. The sockets that hold the candles

**25-10.** A 25-ton hydraulic press.

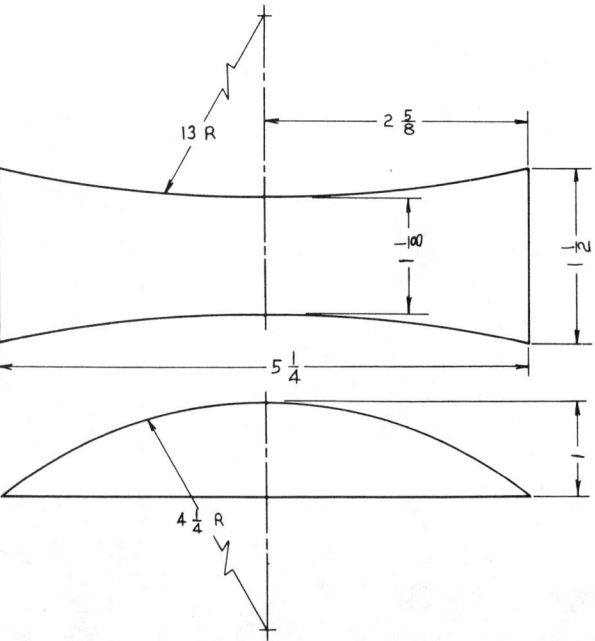

**25-11.** Candelabra.

**25-12.** Drawings for candelabra base.

have standard-size candle openings. Figure 25-13. Over-all size of the candelabra is also optional. However, the size of the parts should be established in terms of the over-all appearance. The base of the candelabra may be made of hard wood. The mold dies or cauls used to form the laminated arm of the candelabra should be made of aluminum to conduct heat. Figures 25-14, 25-15, and 25-16.

Cut three pieces of $\frac{1}{28}$-inch (1 mm) veneer to a rough dimension of 2

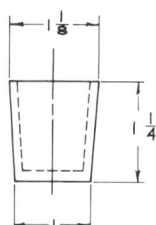

**25-13.** Drawings for candle socket.

**25-14.** Drawing of pattern for cauls.

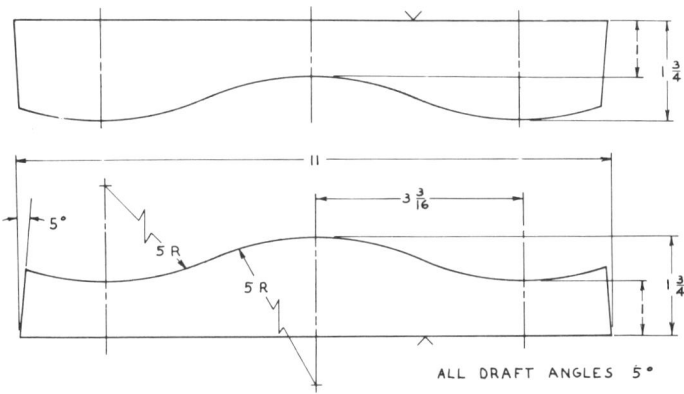

ALL DRAFT ANGLES 5°

**25-15.** Mahogany wood *patterns* are needed to pour the aluminum cauls in a foundry. See Unit 71.

**25-16.** Aluminum cauls. *Note the heatproof gloves* worn to prevent burns.

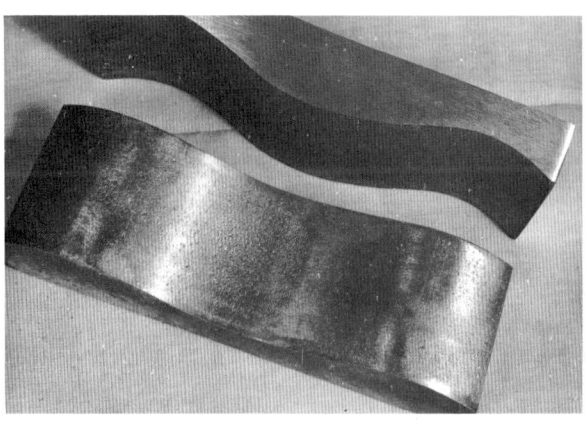
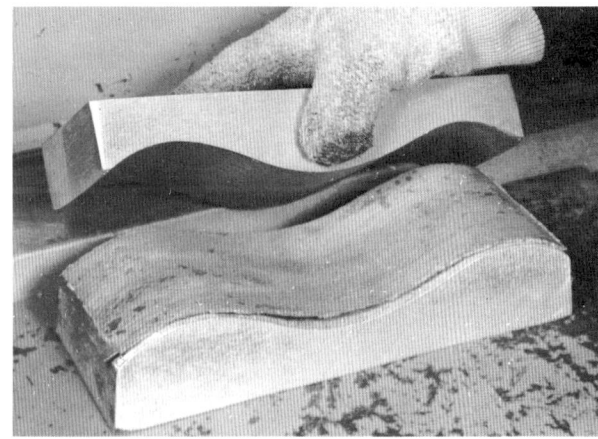

inches x 11 inches (51 x 279 mm). The two face pieces should be cut so the grain runs parallel to the longest dimension of the material. The crossband should be cut with the grain running across the width of the piece. Pre-heat the press to approximately 250 degrees F (121 degrees Celsius). *From this point on, the press will be hot. Use gloves to avoid burning your hands.*

Use an adhesive that is suitable for hot-press application. Mix the adhesive and the catalyst carefully, following the manufacturer's instructions. With a small brush, apply adhesive to the inside surface of the two outside pieces of veneer. It is not necessary to apply adhesive to the crossband. Place the crossband between the two face pieces of veneer. Separate the cauls and place the three pieces of veneer between the cauls. Close the cauls and place them in the press. The bulletins published by adhesive manufacturers tell the correct curing temperatures for their products. After the required curing time has elapsed, remove the laminated piece from the press.

The part can be cut to shape on a band saw or jig saw. Drill three holes in the laminated part for the candleholders. Also drill a hole through the center of the base. This may be done by laying out the locations and drilling the holes, or a jig may be used. Assemble and finish.

## CAN YOU ANSWER THESE QUESTIONS ON WOOD LAMINATION?

1. What is the difference between a laminated wood product and plywood?
2. Describe some of the uses for wood lamination.
3. Describe the steps used to make projects by wood lamination.
4. Describe the procedure for making a laminated serving tray.

# SECTION VI
# Cutting Holes

**What you must know and be able to do in Units 26 and 27:**

26. How to bore holes with the auger, expansion, and Foerstner bits held in a bit brace; how to bore holes in both horizontal and vertical positions; through boring to prevent breaking out the opposite side of the hole; use of the depth gage for regulating the depth of hole.

27. How to drill holes with a drill: kinds of drills; use of the automatic drill, hand drill, breast drill, and portable electric drill; regulation of the depth of the hole with a depth gage.

*The entire process of assembling the parts of a project is based on the use of nails, screws, and dowels. Boring and drilling round holes for these fasteners can be done with many different bits and drills, each of which is a fine cutting tool that must be handled carefully. When a hole is ¼ inch (6.5 mm) or larger in diameter and is cut with a bit, this is called boring. In drilling, a small hole is cut with a drill. Usually a woodshop has only one set of bits or drills, and particular care should be taken not to break them. Later in woodworking you will drill a square hole in the drill press with a mortising attachment.*

**Section VI**

**UNIT 26.**

# BORING HOLES

Cutting out a design, making a mortise-and-tenon joint, fitting dowel rods, and many other construction procedures call for knowing how to bore holes.

## BITS

For holes that are $\frac{1}{4}$ to $1\frac{1}{4}$ inches (6 to 32 mm), an *auger bit* is used. Figure 26-1. The size of the auger bit is stamped on the tang, always in a single number such as 4, 5, or 6, etc. Figure 26-2. This shows that it will bore a hole $\frac{4}{16}$, $\frac{5}{16}$, $\frac{6}{16}$, etc., inch (6, 8, 10, etc., mm) in diameter. Figure 26-3.

For holes larger than 1 inch, you need an *expansion* (expansive) *bit*. Figure 26-4. This tool can be adjusted with different cutters for diameters from $\frac{7}{8}$ to 3 inches (22 to 76 mm).

When you want to bore a hole part way into a thin board or when you want to enlarge an existing hole, a *Foerstner bit* is the tool to choose. Figure 26-5.

*Speed,* or *flat, bits* are also useful for boring holes, especially when using an electric drill. Figure 26-6.

## BORING WITH AN AUGER BIT

### Installing an Auger Bit in a Brace

The auger bit is held in a bit brace. Figure 26-7. To install the bit, hold the shell of the chuck in your left hand and turn the handle to the left until the jaw is open slightly larger than the shank of the bit. Figure 26-8. Then insert the bit and turn the handle to the right to fasten it in the brace. Most bit braces have a ratchet attachment. This makes it possible to drill in corners or other tight places.

### Horizontal Position

Be sure that the center of the hole is properly located; punch the center with a scratch awl. Figure 26-9. Place the stock in a vise so that the brace can be held in a horizontal position. Figure 26-10. Hold the head of the brace with your left hand cupped around it. Hold your body against the head for added pressure. Turn the handle with your right hand to start the hole. Figure 26-11

**26-1a.** A single twist auger bit with solid center.

**26-1b.** A double twist auger bit.

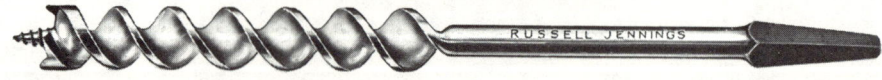

212

(Page 216). Be careful to keep the auger bit square to the work. It is easy to sight the top to see if it is square to the right and left. If another person is present, have him sight to make sure it is straight up and down.

Do not press too hard on the brace. The auger bit tends to feed itself into the wood. Figure 26-12. (Page 216) Continue to bore the hole until the point of the bit just comes through the opposite side. Then turn the wood over to com-

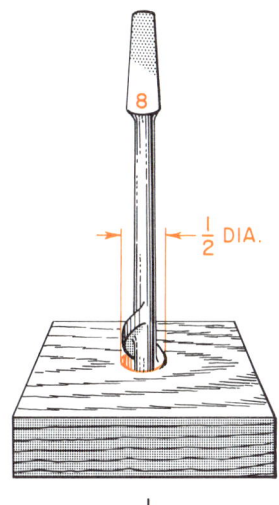

NO. 8 = $\frac{1}{2}$ DIA.

**26-2.** Check the size of the auger bit carefully. It is stamped on the tang.

**26-3a.** The number 8 on this auger bit indicates that it will bore a $\frac{1}{2}$-inch (13 mm) hole.

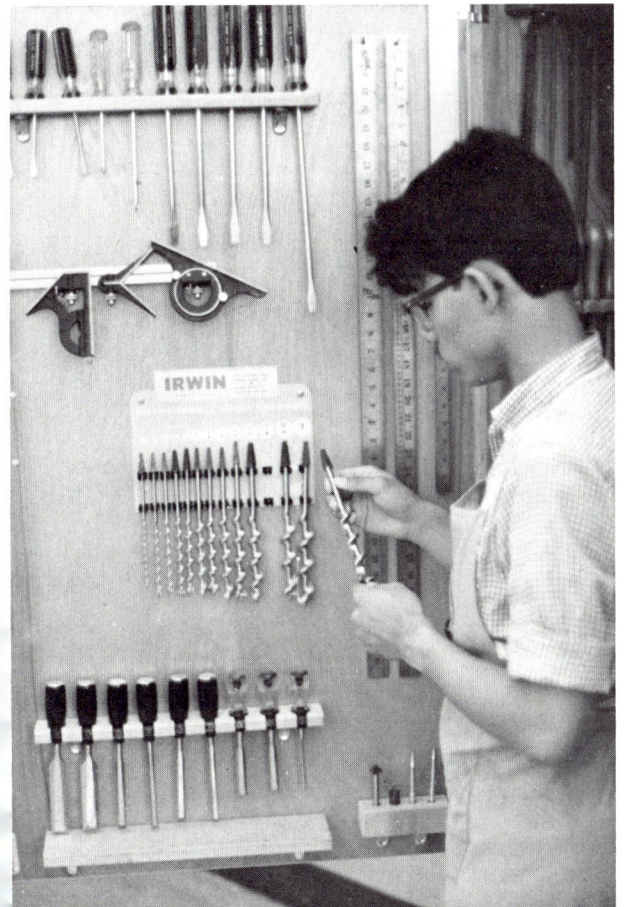

**26-3b.** Study this chart to see what number auger bit you will need to bore the correct size of hole.

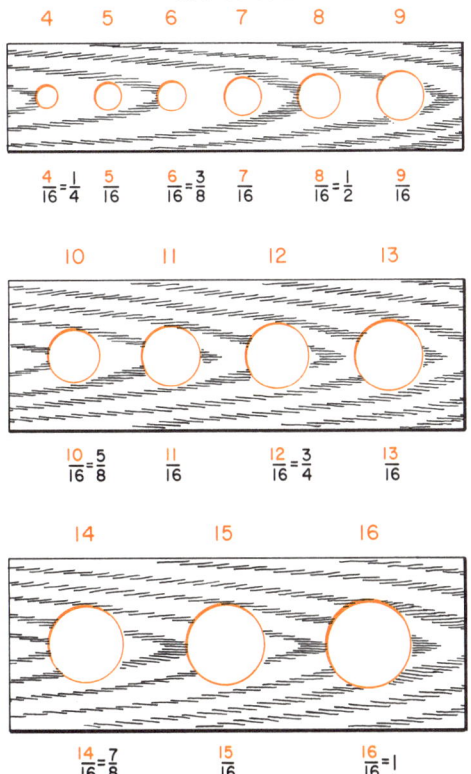

| 4 | 5 | 6 | 7 | 8 | 9 |
|---|---|---|---|---|---|
| $\frac{4}{16}=\frac{1}{4}$ | $\frac{5}{16}$ | $\frac{6}{16}=\frac{3}{8}$ | $\frac{7}{16}$ | $\frac{8}{16}=\frac{1}{2}$ | $\frac{9}{16}$ |

| 10 | 11 | 12 | 13 |
|---|---|---|---|
| $\frac{10}{16}=\frac{5}{8}$ | $\frac{11}{16}$ | $\frac{12}{16}=\frac{3}{4}$ | $\frac{13}{16}$ |

| 14 | 15 | 16 |
|---|---|---|
| $\frac{14}{16}=\frac{7}{8}$ | $\frac{15}{16}$ | $\frac{16}{16}=1$ |

THE SET CONTAINS 13 AUGER BITS.

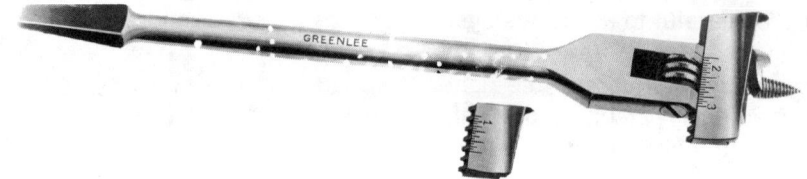

**26-4.** An expansion (expansive) bit. There are usually two cutters, a small one for holes of ⅞ to 2 inches (22 to 50 mm) in diameter and a larger one for holes 2 inches (50 mm) and more in diameter.

plete the hole. If this is not done, the hole will split out on the opposite side as the auger bit comes through. Another way to keep from splitting the wood is to put a piece of scrap wood in back of the piece you are boring. Then you can go all the way through from one side. Figure 26-13.

**Vertical Position**

Holes sometimes have to be bored with the auger bit held in a vertical position. Lay out and locate the position of the hole as before. Put one hand over the head of the brace and use the other hand

to turn the handle. Figure 26-14. Sometimes you will find it natural to rest your chin on the handle to steady it. To make sure that you are boring square with the surface, you can sight along the board or use a try square. Figure 26-15.

In some construction you will need to bore only part way through the stock. You

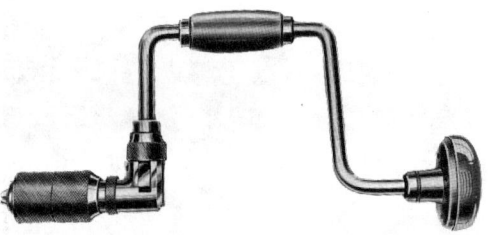

**26-7a.** The bit brace is used for holding auger bits, Foerstner bits, and other tools with rectangular-shaped shanks. Most braces have a ratchet arrangement, making it possible to bore in corners and otherwise inaccessible places.

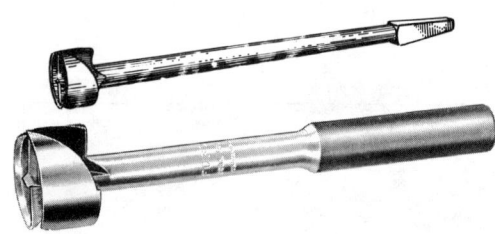

**26-5.** A Foerstner bit is used to enlarge existing holes or to cut a hole partway through thin stock. Both hand and machine types are shown.

**26-6.** A speed, or flat, bit is an excellent cutting tool to use, especially in a portable electric drill.

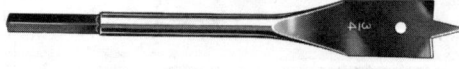

**26-7b.** Parts of a brace.

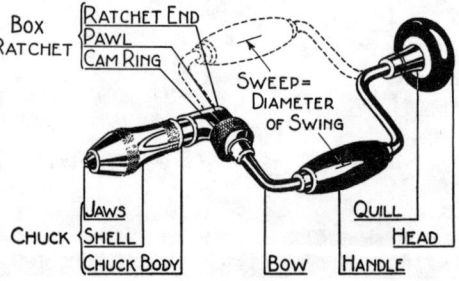

Box Ratchet — Ratchet End, Pawl, Cam Ring

Sweep = Diameter of Swing

Chuck — Jaws, Shell, Chuck Body

Bow — Quill, Head, Handle

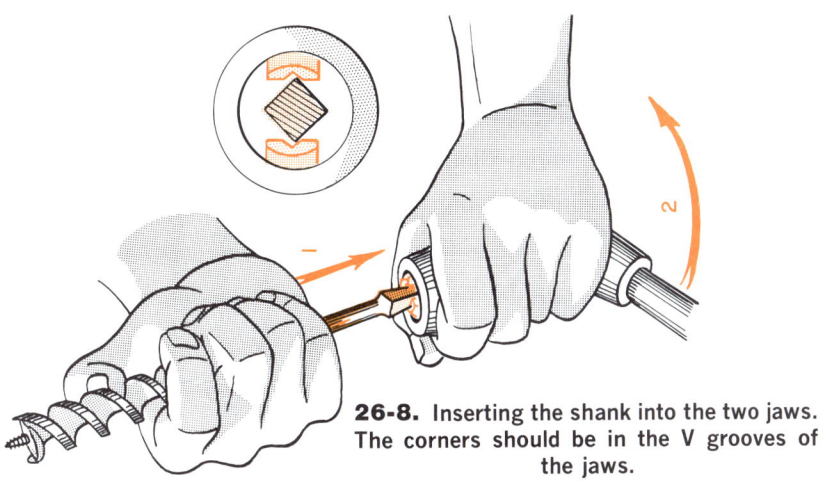

**26-8.** Inserting the shank into the two jaws. The corners should be in the V grooves of the jaws.

need a depth, or bit, gage. There are two commercial types that can be clamped on the auger bit to the proper depth. Figure 26-16. Another kind of depth gage can be made by boring through a piece of wood or dowel rod, exposing the auger bit to the correct depth.

## Angle Boring

To bore a hole at an angle, first adjust a sliding T bevel to the required angle. This is used as a guide. Start the auger bit as you would for straight boring until the screw feeds into the wood. Then tilt the bit so that it is parallel to the blade

**26-9.** Marking the center of the hole with the scratch awl.

**26-10.** The proper setup for a hole to be bored. The center has been accurately located. On thin stock a piece of scrap wood should be fastened to the back to support the wood while boring, as shown.

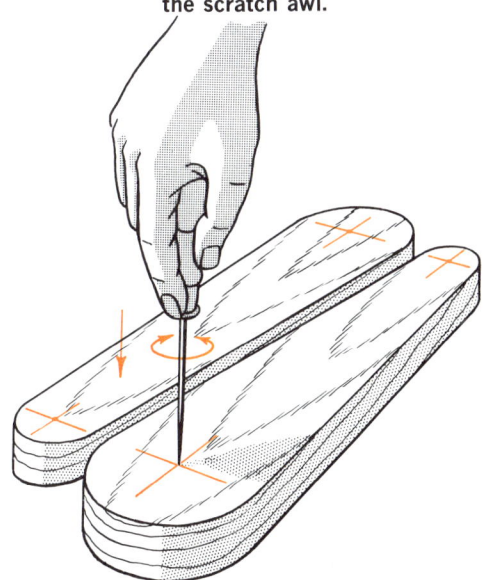

**26-11.** Horizontal boring with a bit and brace. Make sure that the auger bit is held at right angles to the stock.

**26-12.** A bit bores a hole as follows: (1) The screw point pulls the bit into the wood; (2) The spurs scribe the diameter of the hole in advance of the cutter; (3) The cutter lifts the chips, which then pass through the twist.

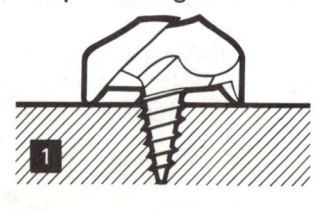

of the T bevel. If several holes must be bored at an angle, it is a good idea to use a simple wood jig. First, bore a hole at the correct angle through a piece of scrap stock. Slip this jig over the auger bit. Place the feed screw of the auger bit

**26-13.** The correct and incorrect methods of boring a hole: A. Use a piece of scrap wood; B. Stop when feed screw pricks through and bore from the other side; C. Never bore straight through without scrap wood.

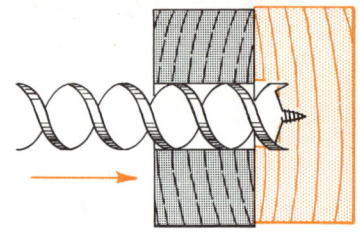

USE A PIECE OF SCRAP WOOD
**A. CORRECT**

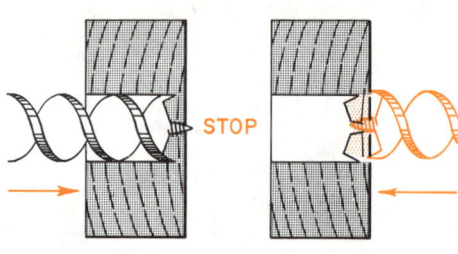

STOP - WHEN FEED SCREW    & BORE FROM
PRICKS THROUGH              OTHER SIDE

OR – BORE FROM BOTH SIDES
**B. CORRECT**

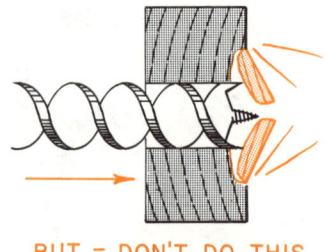

BUT – DON'T DO THIS
**C. INCORRECT**

on the center of the hole. Slip the jig against the wood and clamp it with a hand screw. This will guide the bit. Figure 26-17.

## BORING WITH AN EXPANSION BIT

Choose a cutter of the correct size and slip it in the bit. Adjust the cutter until

**26-14.** Boring holes with a bit and brace held in a vertical position. The hand is cupped over the head of the brace. Sometimes the chin is rested on the hand to steady the tool. Most boring in the shop will be done in a vertical position.

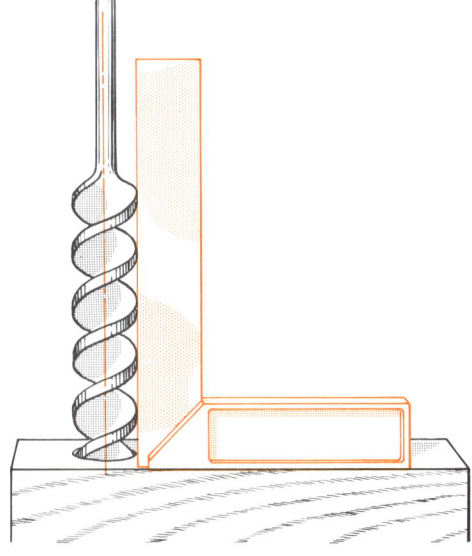

**26-15.** Checking to make sure the auger bit is square with the work.

**26-16a.** Solid-type bit, or depth, gage.

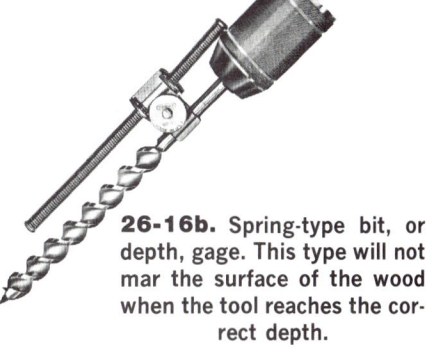

**26-16b.** Spring-type bit, or depth, gage. This type will not mar the surface of the wood when the tool reaches the correct depth.

the distance from the spur to feed screw equals the radius of the hole. Figure 26-18. Fasten the bit in a brace. Then make sure the work is held tightly. It's a good idea to put a piece of scrap stock behind the work. As you rotate the tool, use just enough pressure to make a cut.

Figure 26-19. After the feed screw shows through, reverse the stock and cut from the other side.

## BORING WITH A FOERSTNER BIT

Foerstner bits are numbered the same as auger bits. The sizes range from $\frac{1}{4}$ to 2 inches (6 to 51 mm). Locate the center of the hole. Draw a circle with a dividers the same size as the hole. Clamp the stock securely. Carefully guide the bit over the circle to start the boring. Figure 26-20.

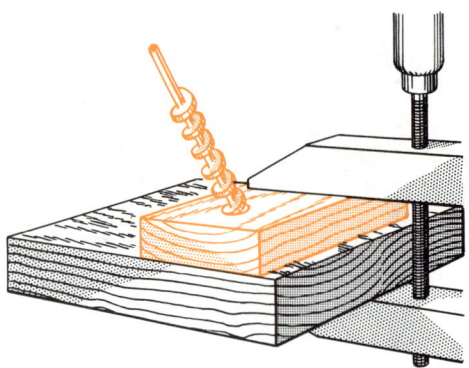

**26-17.** Using a small wood jig to bore a hole at an angle.

**26-18.** Notice that the expansion bit is set to 2½ inches (64 mm) in diameter.

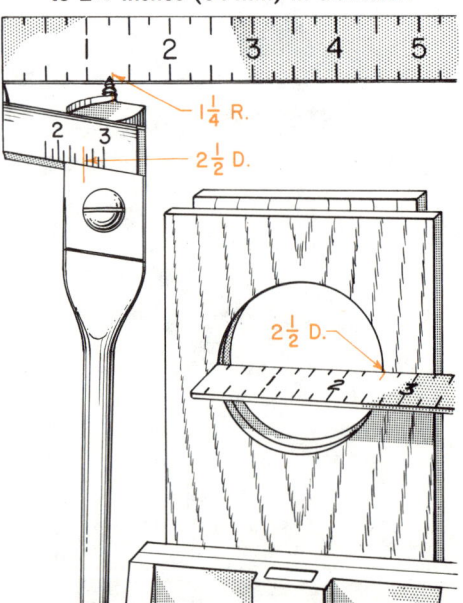

**26-19.** Using an expansion bit. Care should be taken as the bit begins to go through the opposite side to prevent it from splitting out. It's a good idea to cut a little over halfway through, reverse the stock, and cut through the other side.

**26-20.** Boring a hole that has a flat bottom.

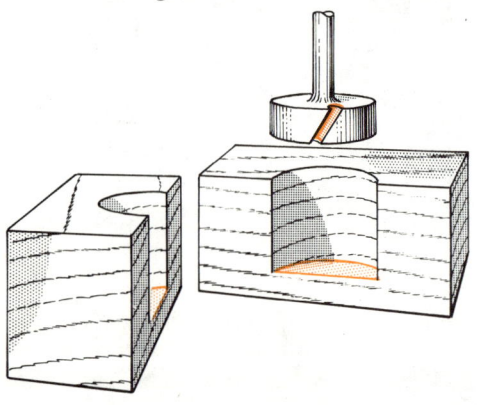

## CAN YOU ANSWER THESE QUESTIONS ON BORING HOLES?

1. What is an auger bit?
2. How is the size marked on the auger bit?
3. What is an expansion bit and how is it used?
4. The Foerstner bit has what primary use?
5. Name the parts of a brace.
6. Why do some braces have a ratchet attachment?
7. To bore holes in a vertical position, how can the tool be kept square with the work?
8. Should you bore the hole completely through the stock from one side? Explain.
9. Describe how the brace should be held when boring in a vertical position.
10. Describe a depth gage and tell how it is used.
11. How is a depth gage made?
12. Tell how to do angle boring.
13. How do you adjust an expansion bit to cut a 2½-inch (64 mm) hole?

**Section**
**VI**
**UNIT 27.**

# DRILLING HOLES

**Holes** ¼ inch (6 mm) or smaller must be drilled to assemble projects with nails and screws, to start an inside cut, and for many other purposes.

### DRILLS

A small set of *twist drills* ranging in size from ¹⁄₁₆ to ½ inch (1.5 to 13 mm) in intervals of ¹⁄₆₄ inch (0.4 mm) are used for drilling both metal and wood. Figure 27-1. If the drills are used only for wood, they can be made of carbon steel and the point ground at an angle of 80 degrees.

*Masonry drills* are tipped with a special ultra-hard metal, cemented carbide, for drilling concrete or masonry materials. Figure 27-2. These drills may be used on any portable electric drill or drill press. Normal speeds on the portable electric drill are satisfactory for drilling the usual

masonry material. Use lower speeds when drilling extremely hard or very abrasive materials.

The *bit stock drill* can be used in a brace. Figure 27-3.

### DRILLING DEVICES

#### Automatic Drill

An automatic drill with drill points is handy to have when many small holes must be drilled. Figure 27-4. The drill points are numbered from one to eight. Number 1 is ¹⁄₁₆ inch (1.5 mm), 2 is ⁵⁄₆₄ inch (2 mm), 3 is ³⁄₃₂ inch (2.5 mm), 4 is ⁷⁄₆₄ inch (3 mm), 5 is ⅛ inch (3 mm), 6 is ⁹⁄₆₄ inch (3.5 mm), 7 is ⁵⁄₃₂ inch (4 mm), and 8 is ¹¹⁄₆₄ inch (4 mm).

To use the automatic drill, first insert the drill in the chuck. Tighten the chuck.

**219**

**27-1a.** A straight shank twist drill can be used for drilling holes in both wood and metal. The size of the drill is stamped on the shank.

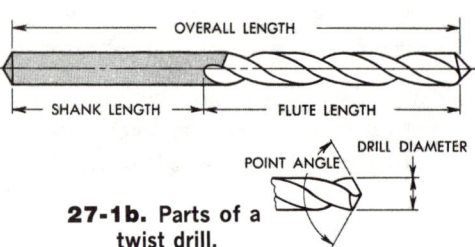

**27-1b.** Parts of a twist drill.

**27-2.** Masonry drill.

**27-3.** The bit-stock drill must be used in a brace because of the shank design.

**27-4.** The automatic drill is very efficient for drilling many small holes, such as in boat construction or for installing hardware.

**27-5.** Using an automatic drill to install a coat hanger.

Place the drill point where the hole is needed. Then simply push down a few times, allowing the handle to spring back after each stroke. This will give you a good, clean hole. Figure 27-5.

**Hand Drill**

The hand drill is used to hold twist drills for drilling holes. It has three jaws in the chuck for holding round shanks. Figure 27-6.

To operate select a twist drill of the correct size. Hold the shell of the chuck in your left hand. Pull the crank backward until the jaws are open slightly wider than the shank. Place the shank in the chuck and tighten the chuck by pushing the crank forward. Make sure the drill is in the chuck straight. Locate the position of the hole and mark it with a scratch awl. Hold the handle in your left

**27-6.** Hand drill.

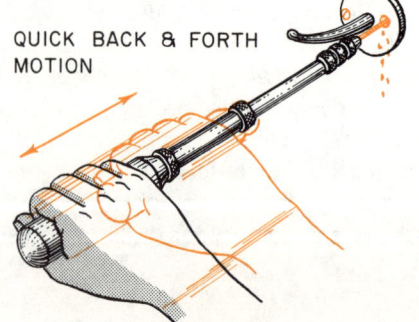

QUICK BACK & FORTH MOTION

hand and turn the crank with your right hand. Make sure the drill is square with the work. Figure 27-7.

Never bend the hand drill to one side or the other. Small drills will break. Continue to turn the handle until the hole is drilled. If holes of a certain depth are needed, make a depth gage from a piece of scrap wood or dowel rod. Figure 27-8.

## Breast Drill

A breast drill is very similar to a hand drill. It is, however, larger and made to hold drills up to $\frac{1}{2}$ inch (13 mm) in diameter. Figure 27-9.

The breast drill is designed so that pressure can be applied with your shoulder or breast to increase the amount of pressure when drilling in hard wood or with a larger sized drill. The crank gear

is larger than on a hand drill to increase the amount of torque (force that produces a rotation motion).

## Portable Electric Drill

The portable electric drill is an excellent all-around tool for drilling and boring holes. Drill size is shown by the largest twist drill it will hold. The most common sizes are $\frac{1}{4}$, $\frac{3}{8}$, and $\frac{1}{2}$ inch (6, 10, and 13 mm). Figure 27-10. Horsepower is also important. Light-duty, $\frac{1}{4}$-inch

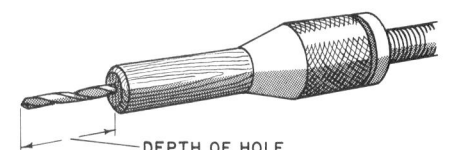
DEPTH OF HOLE

**27-8.** A depth gage made from a piece of dowel rod which covers a part of the drill. Cut the piece until the drill extends the correct amount.

**27-7.** Vertical drilling with a hand drill. The handle is grasped in one hand and the crank turned with the other. Be sure to hold the drill square with the work. Control the feed by the pressure you apply.

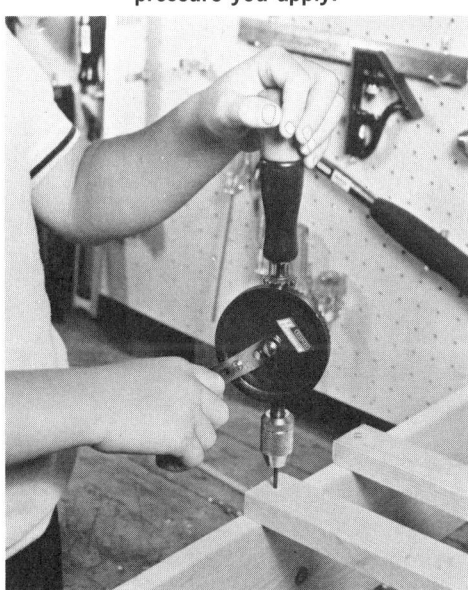

**27-9.** Breast drill.

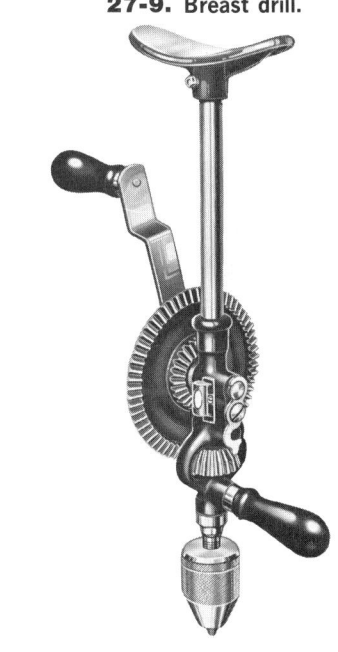

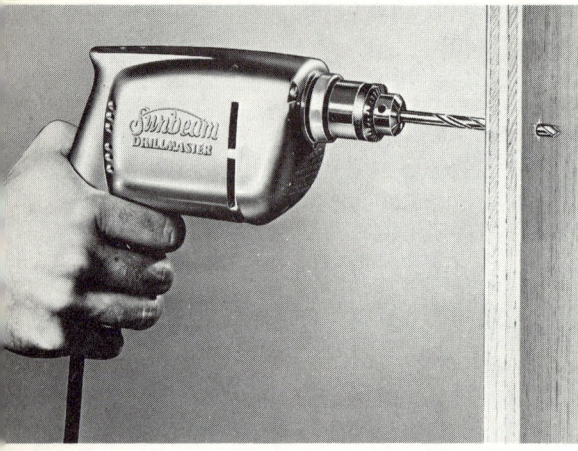

**27-10a.** A portable electric drill.

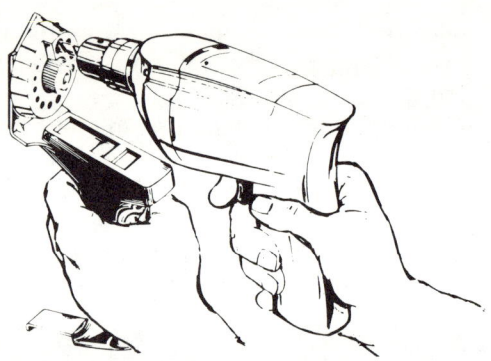

**27-10b.** A drill guide can be used with a portable electric drill. Mark the location of the hole. Rotate the dial to the correct drill size. The guide will hold the drill straight so that the hole is drilled accurately.

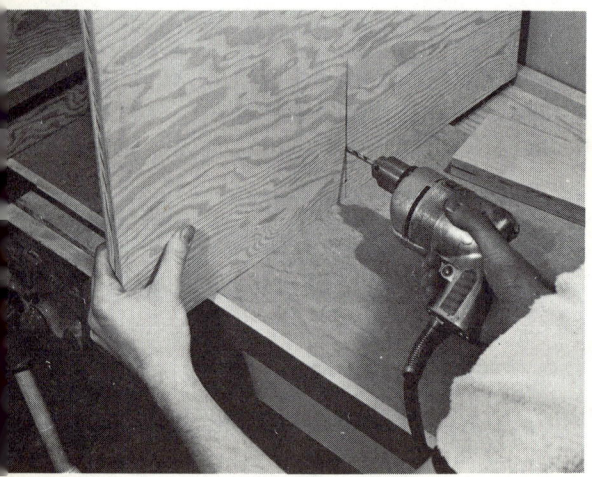

**27-11.** Using a portable electric drill for drilling screw holes.

(6 mm) electric drills may develop as little as $\frac{1}{8}$ horsepower (93 watts). A good $\frac{1}{2}$-inch (13 mm) electric drill should develop at least $\frac{2}{3}$ horsepower (497 watts).

Use the chuck wrench to open the jaws until the twist drill will slip in. Then tighten the drill firmly. Always remove the chuck wrench. Make sure that thin work is backed up with a piece of scrap stock. Grasp the control handle firmly and point the drill as you would a pistol. Use your left hand to control the feed as necessary. Make sure that the tool is straight. Always start with the power off. Place the point on the stock. Figure 27-11. Turn on the switch and guide the tool into the work.

## CAN YOU ANSWER THESE QUESTIONS ON DRILLING HOLES?

1. Name the kind of cutting tool used for drilling holes in wood.
2. Describe a hand drill.
3. Why can a breast drill be faster than a hand drill?
4. How is the hand drill held for drilling?
5. How is the size of a portable electric drill indicated?
6. What tool holds a drill so that holes can be drilled accurately?

# SECTION VII
# Making Joints

**What you must know and be able to do in Units 28–33:**

28. Butt, edge, and dowel joints and variations of the dowel, such as the edge, corner, and leg-and-rail dowel joints: what they are and how to make them, including layout, cut, fit, assembly, and fastening.

29. The rabbet joint and the steps in making this joint, including its assembly.

30. Constructing and assembling the dado joint and its variations, such as the rabbet, dado, and blind dado joints.

31. Kinds of lap joints and their uses; laying out, cutting, and assembling a cross-lap joint.

32. Use of the miter box, either commercial or homemade; cutting, assembling, and applications of the miter joint.

33. Kinds of mortise-and-tenon joints: layout, construction, and assembly.

*Would it surprise you to know that there are over a hundred different types of woodworking joints? Many are similar, of course, but each is used to join wood pieces together in a special way. All joints in woodworking are laid out, cut, fitted, and assembled. To do these things well, you must know how to use all of the common hand tools. You will not use more than one or two kinds of joints on any one project, but these ought to be chosen wisely, for each has a special purpose. When you make large articles, such as desks and tables, you will have the added problems of joinery in making drawers and doors.*

# BUTT, EDGE, AND DOWEL JOINTS

**Of the hundreds** of different joints used in woodworking, some of the simpler ones are the *butt, edge,* and *dowel.* You should always select the simplest joint that will be satisfactory for the kind of work to be done. For example, a dowel joint on a leg and rail is often just as satisfactory as a mortise-and-tenon joint, which would be more difficult to construct.

## BUTT JOINTS

The simplest joint to make is the butt, or plain, joint. Figure 28-1. In a butt joint, the end of one member is connected to the flat surface, edge, or end of the second member. This joint is fairly weak unless strengthened with a corner block, dowels, or some kind of metal fastener like screws or nails. Figure 28-2.

The ends of a butt joint must be square or at right angles to the side and edge. The two parts of the joint must fit flush against each other.

Before assembly, clean the surface and apply a coating of glue to the mating parts to give added strength to the joint. Position the pieces so that they will line up perfectly. Always install the fastener that will provide the greatest holding strength.

## EDGE JOINTS

In an edge joint the edges of two pieces are fastened together. This is also a simple joint to make. Figure 28-3. It is excellent for joining narrow boards to make wider widths for table tops and other large parts. Strengthening this joint with dowels or a spline is a good idea. See Unit 16.

## DOWEL JOINTS

Dowels are wooden or plastic pins placed in matching holes where the two pieces of a joint are attached. Figure 28-4. They add strength to the joint and

**28-1a.** This simple footstool is assembled with a butt joint.

**28-1b.** A butt joint like this one is used to join the ends and rails of the footstool.

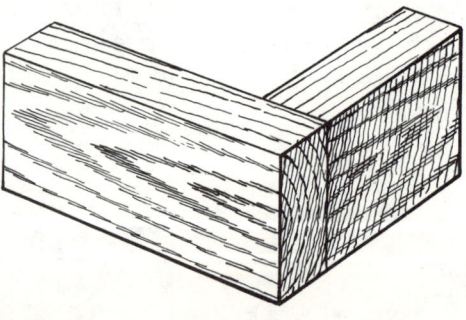

may be used on butt, edge, and miter joints. When dowels are added, the joint may be called a dowel joint. Often terms are used together to describe a joint accurately. An edge dowel joint, for example, is an edge joint made with dowels.

### Dowel Tools and Materials

*Dowel rod* is usually made of birch in diameters from $\frac{1}{8}$ to 1 inch (3 to 25 mm) in 3-foot (90 cm) lengths. Small dowel pins are made with spiral or straight grooves and pointed ends. The grooves allow the glue to flow more freely. A *dowel sharpener* points the ends of the dowels. *Dowel centers* are small metal pins used for spotting the location of holes on two parts of a joint. Figure 28-5.

### Making an Edge Dowel Joint

To make this joint, clamp the two pieces to be joined with the edges flush and face surfaces out. With a try square, mark across the edges of both pieces at

the several points where the dowels will be. Next, set a marking gage to half the thickness of the stock and mark the center locations of the dowel joints. Figure 28-6. Make sure that you mark these from the face side.

Decide on the size dowel you want to use and the depth to which the dowel will go. The diameter of the dowel should never be more than half the thickness of the stock. Usually the dowel should be no longer than 3 inches (76 mm); therefore, the holes will be drilled about $1\frac{5}{8}$ inch

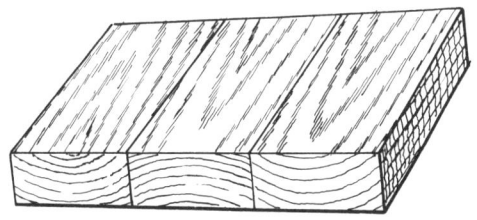

**28-3.** A plain edge joint.

**28-2.** A corner block is added to the thin plywood corner to give added strength.

**28-4.** The corners of this Early American sewing cabinet are fastened with dowels.

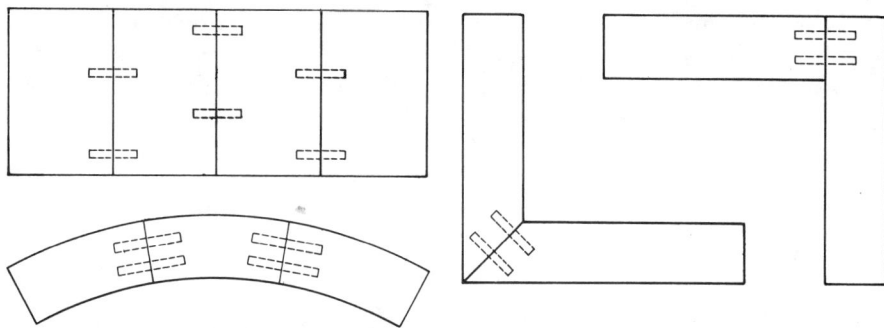

**28-5a.** Dowel joints are simple to construct.

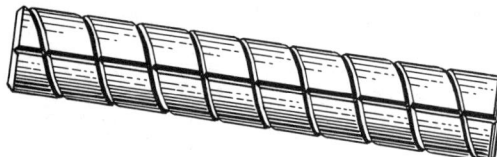

**28-5b.** Dowel pins usually have a spiral groove which helps the glue flow.

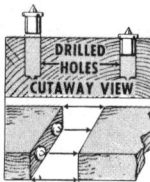

**28-5e.** The locations for the dowels are marked on the first piece and drilled. Then the dowel centers are put in place. When the two pieces are held together, the dowel centers show the hole locations on the second piece.

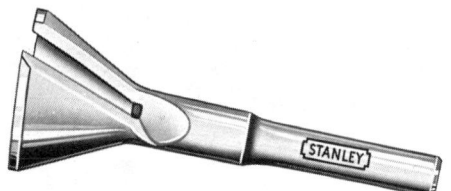

**28-5c.** A dowel sharpener. This is used to cut a slight bevel at the end of dowel rod.

**28-6.** Marking the position for an edge dowel joint. The pieces are fastened in a vise with the face surfaces outward. Then a marking gage is set to half the thickness of the stock and the center location is marked. The location for the three dowels has already been marked with a try square and pencil.

**28-5d.** Dowel centers are useful in locating adjoining holes.

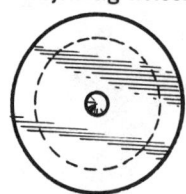

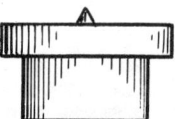

(41 mm) deep. This provides about $\frac{1}{8}$-inch (3 mm) clearance at the bottom on each side to help hold glue and prevent a dry dowel joint.

After the points have been located, make a small dent with a scratch awl. Select an auger bit the same size as the dowel rod. Carefully bore the hole to the proper depth, making sure that you are working square with the edge of the stock. Use a depth gage as a guide. A doweling jig should be used if one is available. Figures 28-7, 28-8, and 28-9. With this tool you will always be able to bore the holes square and in the right place. Figure 28-10.

After the holes are bored, saw off the dowel. Cut a slight bevel at each end to make the dowel pieces slip into the holes easily. When gluing, dip the dowels about halfway in glue and drive them into the holes on one edge. Figure 28-11. Then coat the other half and the edges and assemble. Figure 28-12.

## Making a Dowel Joint on a Frame

One way to strengthen a butt joint on a simple frame is to install two or more dowels at each corner. Do this in the following manner:

1. Square up pieces of stock that are to go into the frame and carefully saw and sand the ends.

2. Lay out the frame and mark the corners with corresponding numbers.

3. Indicate on the face surfaces the location and number of dowels. Figure 28-13.

4. Place the two pieces that are to form one of the corners in a vise. Have the butting end and the butting edge sticking out a little, with the face surfaces of the two pieces out and the end and edge flush.

5. Hold a try square against one of the face surfaces and mark lines across to show the location of the dowel rods. Figures 28-14 and 28-15.

6. After setting a marking gage to half the thickness of the stock, hold it against

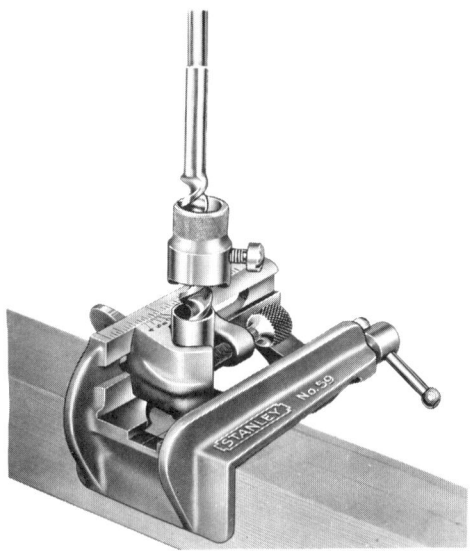

**28-7.** A doweling jig that will help locate the position of holes and guide the auger bit for boring. This jig comes with several metal guides in sizes of $\frac{3}{16}$, $\frac{1}{4}$, $\frac{5}{16}$, $\frac{3}{8}$, $\frac{7}{16}$, and $\frac{1}{2}$ inch (5, 6, 10, 11, and 13 mm).

**28-8.** A self-centering dowel drill guide. This holds the material like a vise. When the workpiece is clamped in the tool, the guide holes for the drill are automatically centered over the work. The jaws will clamp on work up to 2 inches (51 mm) in thickness. The guide accommodates five bit sizes.

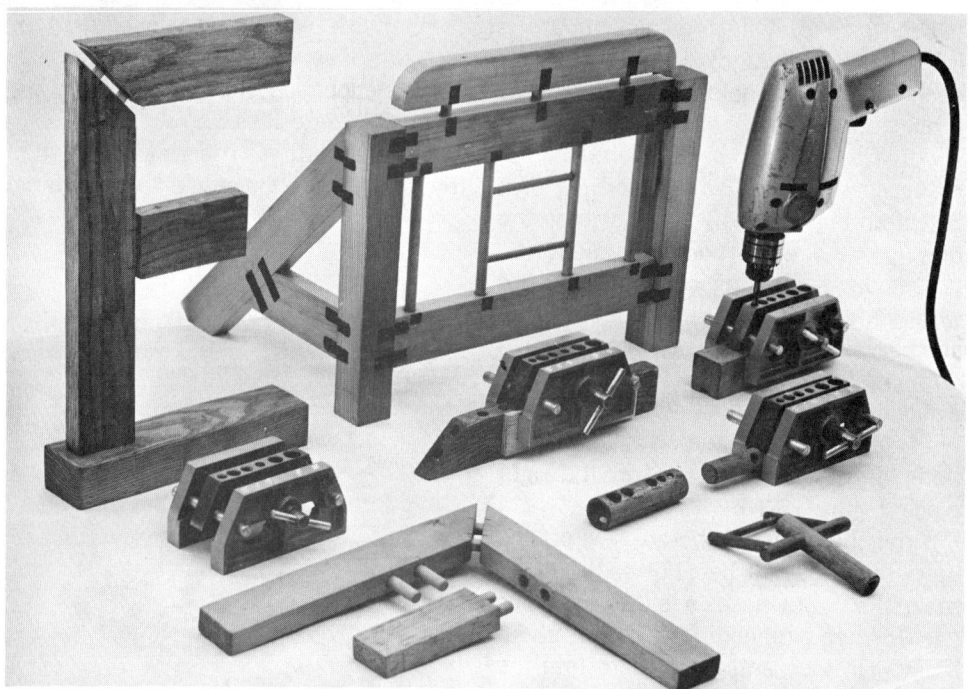

**28-9.** Some uses for the self-centering dowel jig.

the surface of each piece and mark the exact location.

7. Mark these points with a scratch awl and bore the holes as described above. Figure 28-16.

## Making a Dowel Joint on a Leg and Rail

For ease and speed a dowel joint is often made on a leg and rail instead of a mortise-and-tenon joint. Figure 28-17.

Square up the leg and rail as for any joint, making sure that the end of the rail is square. Next clamp the leg and rail in a vise with the butting end and the butting edge sticking out and the face surface of each turned out. Hold a try square against the face surface of the rail and mark the location of the dowels on the end of the rail and the edge of the leg.

**28-10.** Using a doweling jig. This jig has been clamped to the stock and the proper size guide fastened in it. An auger bit of the correct size is being used, and a depth gage is attached to control the depth of the hole.

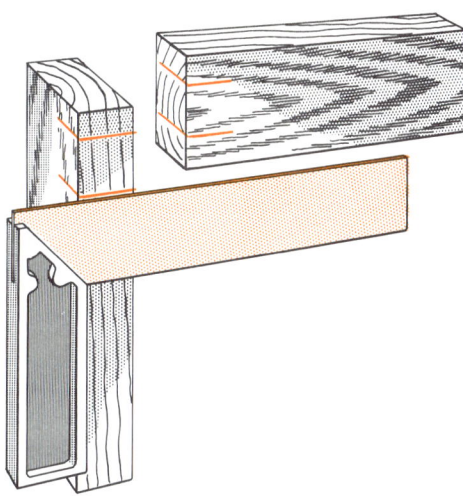

**28-11.** Gluing an edge dowel joint. The dowels have already been dipped halfway in the glue and driven into one edge. Glue is now applied to the two edges and to the other half of the dowels.

**28-14.** Squaring a line across the edge and end of both pieces.

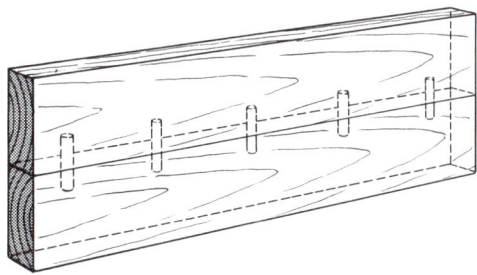

**28-12.** Edge dowel joint with the dowels installed.

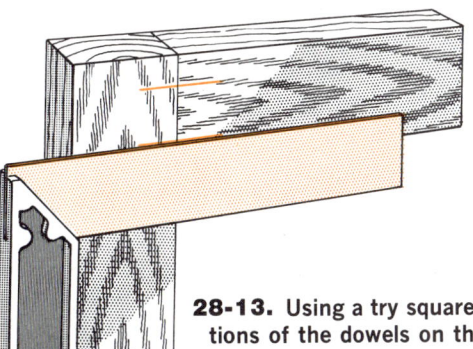

**28-13.** Using a try square to mark the locations of the dowels on the face surfaces.

**28-15.** Here the butting edge and end are held in a vise while a try square is used to lay out the position of the two dowels.

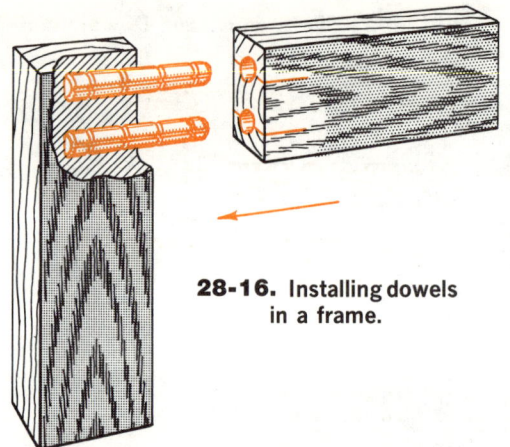

**28-16.** Installing dowels in a frame.

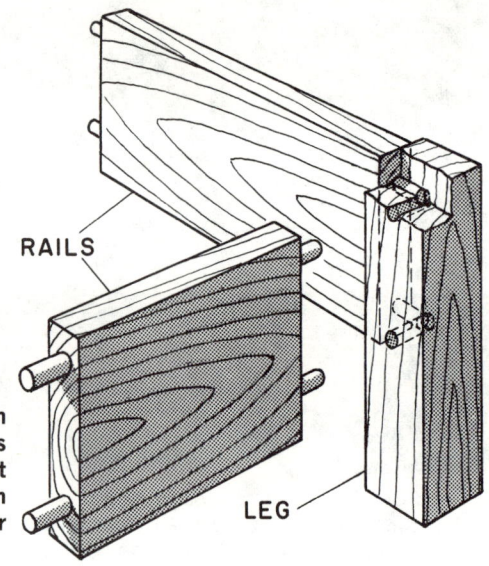

RAILS

LEG

**28-17.** Notice that the rails are thinner than the leg. The dowels are centered on the ends of the rails and on the legs. If the rails must be flush with the surface of the legs, then the dowel holes on the legs must be closer to the outside surface.

Next set a marking gage to half the thickness of the rail. From the face surface of the rail, mark the crossline that will show the location of the dowel joints. Then decide how far back you want the rail to be from the face surface of the leg.

Add this amount to the setting you already have on the marking gage. From the face surface of the leg, mark the crossline that will show the exact location of the dowel. Bore the holes, cut the dowels, glue, and assemble as before.

## CAN YOU ANSWER THESE QUESTIONS ON BUTT, EDGE, AND DOWEL JOINTS?

1. How can a butt joint be strengthened?
2. From what kinds of wood is dowel rod usually made?
3. Dowel joints are sometimes used as a substitute for another kind of joint. What is this joint and why is the dowel joint substituted?
4. Why are dowels used in making an edge joint?
5. State the rule for choosing the correct dowel diameter.
6. Should there be clearance at the bottom of a dowel hole? Why?
7. What is a doweling jig? Explain how it is used.
8. List the steps in making a dowel joint on a frame.
9. What would happen if the dowel holes of two joint pieces were not aligned perfectly?
10. How do you think a dowel joint on a leg or rail will compare with a mortise-and-tenon joint?

# Section VII
## UNIT 29.

### RABBET JOINT

Another simple joint to make is the rabbet joint. Figure 29-1. A slot is cut at the end or edge of the first piece into which the end or edge of the second piece fits. Figure 29-2. It is made with the end grain hidden from the front. This joint is commonly found in drawer construction, boxes, and cabinet frames. Figures 29-3 and 29-4. It is also popular for modern furniture since it provides great simplicity in both construction and appearance.

### LAYING OUT A RABBET JOINT

Make sure that the end on which the joint is to be made has been squared properly. Place the first board on the bench with the face surface down. Hold the second piece directly over the first, with the face surface of the second piece flush with the end grain of the first. Figure 29-5. This is called superimposing. You will frequently use this method in laying out many different kinds of joints.

With a sharp pencil or knife, mark the width of rabbet to be cut. Then remove the second piece. With a try square held on the joint edge, square a line across

**29-1.** These decorator shelves illustrate the use of the rabbet joint.

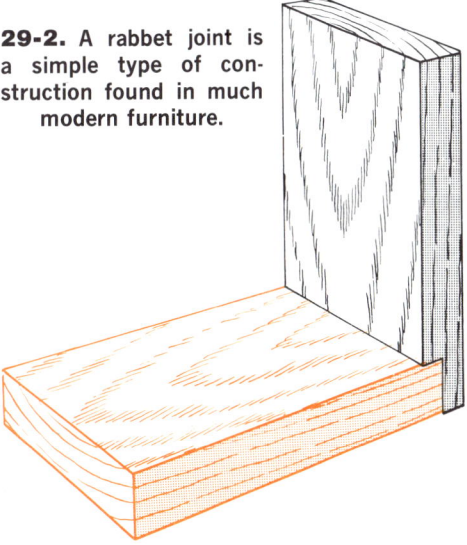

**29-2.** A rabbet joint is a simple type of construction found in much modern furniture.

the surface of the first piece. Then mark a line down each edge. From the face surface, mark the depth of the rabbet on the sides and end with a marking gage. In this type of joint the depth of the rabbet is cut one-half to two-thirds the thickness of the stock. Figure 29-6.

**29-3.** This cabinet has a rabbet cut around the back of the unit to install the back panel.

## CUTTING THE RABBET

In cutting the rabbet joint, the piece should be held firmly against a bench hook. For the beginner, it is better to clamp the stock directly to the bench top. Use a backsaw to make the cut. Make sure that the saw kerf is in the waste stock or inside the layout line. The beginner should clamp a square piece of scrap stock directly over the layout line. Then the backsaw can be held against this edge to make the saw cut. Figure 29-7. Cut the joint to the proper depth as indicated by the layout line.

The excess stock from the joint can either be sawed out or pared out with a chisel. If you decide to saw it out, lock the stock in a vise with the joint showing. With a backsaw, carefully saw out the excess stock. If you use a chisel, leave the stock clamped to the top of the

**29-4.** Note how the back of a cabinet or case fits into a rabbet joint.

bench. Pare out the excess stock as you have learned from the unit on cutting with a chisel. Regardless of which method you follow, you will need to use the chisel for trimming the joint and making it fit properly. Figure 29-8.

It is a good idea to mark this joint on both edges with corresponding numbers. If there are several to be made, they can be easily identified when the project is ready for assembly.

## ASSEMBLING THE JOINT

This type of joint is usually assembled with glue or with both glue and nails (or screws). Figure 29-9. If the joint is nailed, drive the nails in at a slight angle to help them fasten the joint more tightly. Figure 29-10. Screws should be long and thin, as they will have to go into end grain.

**29-7.** Making a shoulder cut on a rabbet joint. Notice that a piece of scrap stock is clamped over the layout line with hand screws; then the backsaw is held against the edge of the scrap stock. This prevents the saw from jumping out of the kerf and damaging the wood.

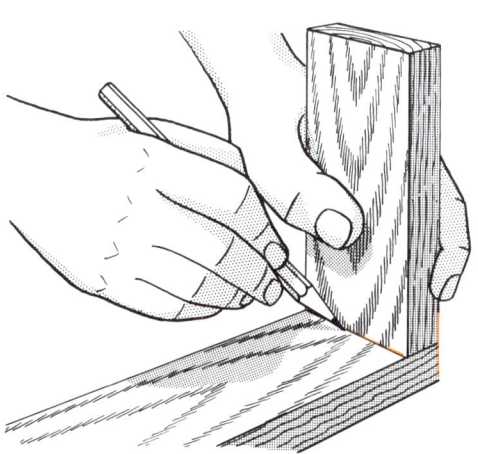

**29-5.** Marking the width of the rabbet.

**29-6.** The width of the rabbet must be equal to the thickness of the stock. The depth of the rabbet is usually one-half to two-thirds the thickness.

W – WIDTH OF RABBET

D – DEPTH OF RABBET

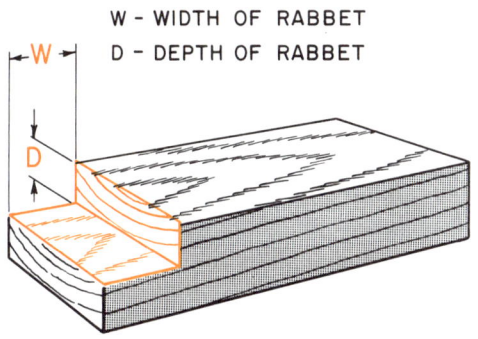

**29-8.** After the rabbet has been cut, it should be trimmed with a chisel. The blade of the chisel is held between thumb and forefinger to trim the excess stock.

**29-9.** Nailing a rabbet joint so that the front has no visible joint. Since the nails must be fastened in end grain, it is a good idea to drive them at a slight angle to give them more holding power.

**29-10.** Rabbet joints are neat, strong, and easy to make. You'll find them the ideal choice for drawers, chests, and cupboards.

## CAN YOU ANSWER THESE QUESTIONS ON A RABBET JOINT?

1. What is a rabbet?
2. How is the rabbet used?
3. Explain superimposing.
4. What tools should be used to mark a rabbet?
5. How can the pieces of several different rabbet joints be kept in order?
6. What kind of saw should be selected for cutting a rabbet?
7. When can a chisel be chosen for making a rabbet joint?
8. If you decide to assemble a rabbet joint with nails, how would you insert them?

# Section VII
# UNIT 30.

## DADO JOINT

**A dado is a groove** cut across the grain of wood. Figure 30-1. It differs from a rabbet joint in that the groove is not cut along the end of the stock. The dado joint is relatively easy to make and, when snugly fit, is quite strong. This joint is commonly found in bookracks, drawers, cabinet shelves, ladders, and steps. Figure 30-2.

### LAYING OUT A DADO JOINT

From the end of the board, measure in the correct distance to one side of the dado. Then square off a line across the surface of the piece at this point. Superimpose the other piece with one arris (edge) directly over the line. With a sharp knife or pencil, mark the correct width of the dado.

Remove the second piece and square off a line across the surface to show the proper width. Continue both lines down both edges. Figure 30-3. Then, with a marking gage, lay out the correct depth of the joint—one-half the thickness of the workpiece.

### CUTTING A DADO

Using a backsaw, follow the directions for cutting out a rabbet joint. Cut the dado to the proper depth at both layout lines. Make sure that the saw kerfs are

**30-1b.** Sometimes a dado is cut across two sides of table legs, and the corners of the shelf are cut off to complete a corner dado. This construction makes a very sturdy table shelf.

**30-1a.** A dado joint is commonly used if the crosspieces must support considerable weight, such as for shelves, stairsteps, or ladders.

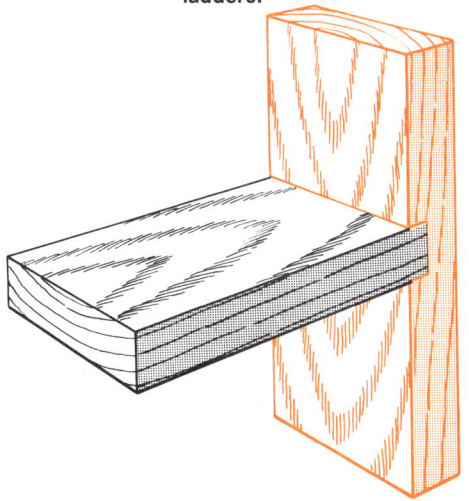

in the waste stock and not outside the layout line. Figure 30-4.

With a chisel, cut and trim the dado to the proper depth. A router plane may be used to trim out the waste stock. Figures 30-5 and 30-6.

If the dado is very wide, you may need to make several saw cuts to depth so that the waste stock can be easily trimmed out. With a combination square, check the dado to make sure that it is the same depth throughout. Figure 30-7. Check the

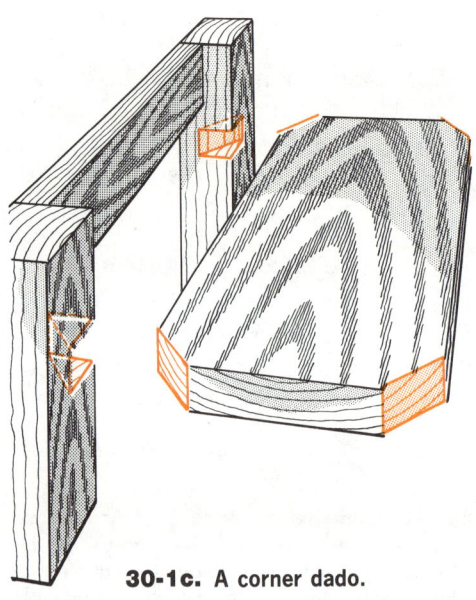

**30-1c.** A corner dado.

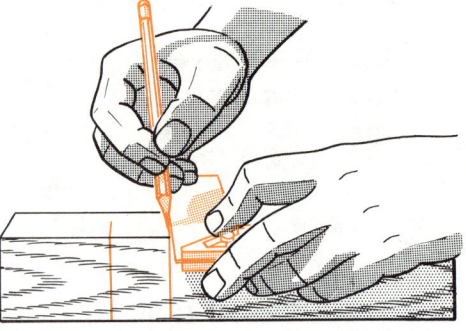

**30-3.** Making the layout for a dado joint. One line is laid out on the face surface and then, by superimposing, the width of the dado is marked. Finally the lines are drawn across the surface and down the edge of the stock.

**30-2.** This attractive wall shelf makes use of the dado joint.

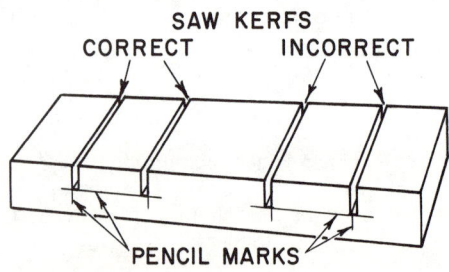

**30-4.** Make sure that the saw kerfs in the dado joint are inside the waste stock.

**30-5.** A router plane is equipped with blades of different widths. It is used for surfacing the bottom of a groove or other depression.

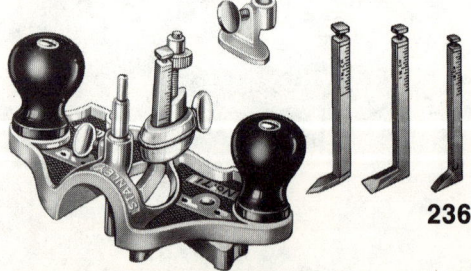

236

dado joint by inserting the piece in the joint. Figure 30-8.

You may have to trim the joint to make it a little wider. It may be easier, however, to plane the side of the second piece slightly to make it fit into the joint.

### ASSEMBLING THE JOINT

The dado joint is usually assembled either with glue alone or with glue and nails or screws in the same way as a rabbet joint. Figure 30-9.

### MAKING A RABBET-AND-DADO JOINT

A rabbet-and-dado joint is frequently used when additional strength and rigidity (stiffness) are needed. Figure 30-10. This joint is popular for drawer construction. The joint consists of a rabbet with a tongue. The tongue fits into the dado. To make this kind of joint, lay out and cut the rabbet first. Then lay out the position of the dado joint by superimposing the tongue of the rabbet. Mark the width of the dado. Make the dado as described earlier and fit the tongue of the rabbet into it.

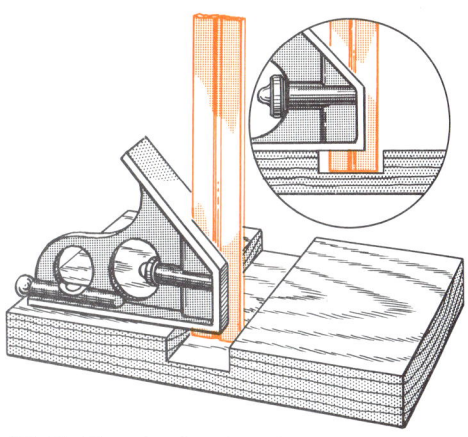

**30-7.** The depth of a dado joint can be checked by setting the blade of a combination square to correct depth.

**30-8.** Checking a dado joint. The second piece is inserted in the dado. If it is necessary to fit the joint, it is simpler to remove a little stock from the second piece rather than to cut the dado wider.

**30-6.** Using the router plane to trim out the bottom of a dado joint. A cutter that is the same width or slightly narrower than the width of the dado should be selected. The thumb screw is adjusted to the proper depth, and the cut is taken by holding the router plane firmly on the surface of the work and applying pressure with both hands. Don't attempt to cut the total depth with one setting.

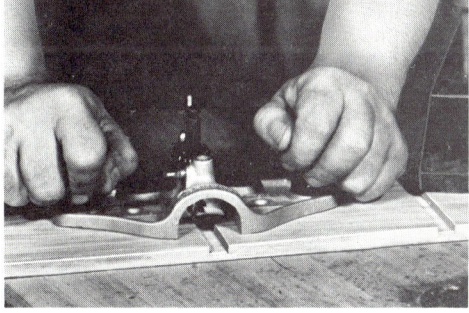

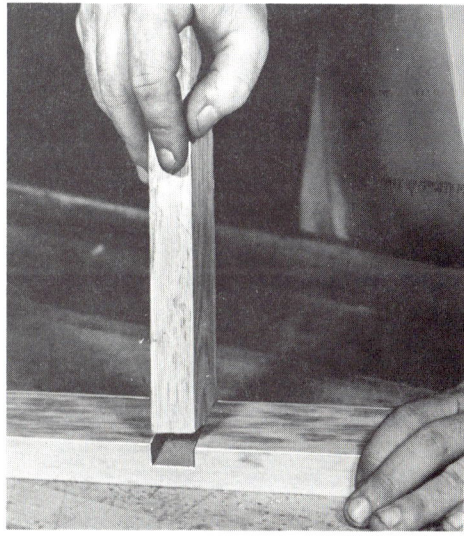

**30-9.** Assembling a shelf with dado joints.

**30-10.** A rabbet-and-dado joint gives added strength and rigidity. It is commonly used for the back corner of drawers.

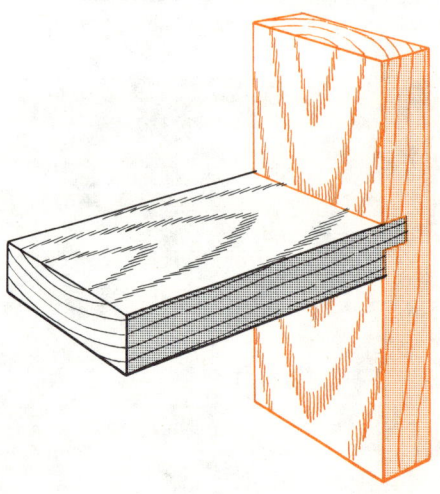

**30-11.** A blind dado joint has the same strength advantage as the dado joint and, in addition, does not show the joint. It is built into bookcases and other projects of this type when a neat appearance at the front of the shelves is desirable.

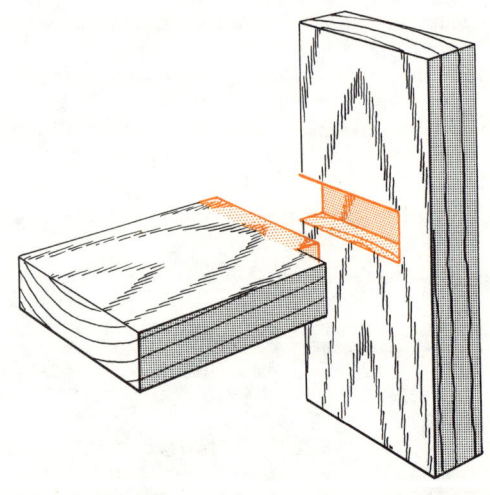

## MAKING A BLIND DADO JOINT

In a blind dado joint the dado is cut only part way across the board. Figure 30-11. The piece that fits into the dado is notched so that the joint doesn't show from the front. Lay out the width of the dado as described before. Mark the depth of the dado on the back edge only. Also lay out the length of the dado from the back edge to within $\frac{1}{2}$ to $\frac{3}{4}$ inch (12.5 to 19 mm) of the front edge. The dado can be cut by boring a series of holes in the waste stock and then trimming out with a chisel.

## CAN YOU ANSWER THESE QUESTIONS ON THE DADO JOINT?

1. What is a dado?
2. Point out the difference between a dado and a rabbet.
3. When cutting a dado, where should the saw kerf be formed?
4. Explain a router plane. What is it used for?
5. How could you make a depth gage to check a dado?
6. In fitting a dado joint, is it better to plane the side of the second piece or to cut a wider dado?
7. What advantage does a rabbet-and-dado joint have? Where is it frequently found?
8. Sketch a blind dado joint.
9. Why would a blind dado joint be found in more expensive furniture?

# Section VII
# UNIT 31.

# LAP JOINT

**There are many** different lap joints. Figure 31-1. The end lap is found in screen doors, chair seats, or any type of corner construction in which the surfaces of the two pieces must be flush. The middle lap is also found in screen-door construction, in making cabinets, and in framing a house. The cross-lap is widely used in furniture building whenever two pieces must cross and still be flush on the surface. The half-lap is used to make a longer piece of stock from two shorter pieces. Figure 31-2. The cross-lap is by far the most common. To make any of the other types, follow the same general directions as for the cross-lap.

## LAYING OUT THE CROSS-LAP JOINT

The cross-lap joint is usually made in the exact center of the two pieces that cross at a 90-degree angle. However, a cross-lap joint can be made at any angle. The two pieces must be exactly the same thickness and width. Lay the two pieces on the bench side by side, with the face surface of one (piece A) and the opposite surface of the other (piece B) upward.

Divide the length of each into two equal parts and lay out a center line across the two pieces. Measure the width of the stock and divide this measurement in half. Lay out a line this distance on each side of the center line. Figure 31-3.

Now check this measurement by superimposing piece B over piece A at right angles. Be sure to place it in the position that the joint will be when assembled. Figure 31-4. The layout line should just barely show beyond the edge of each piece.

Now continue the lines showing the width of the joint down the edge of each piece. Next, set a marking gage to half

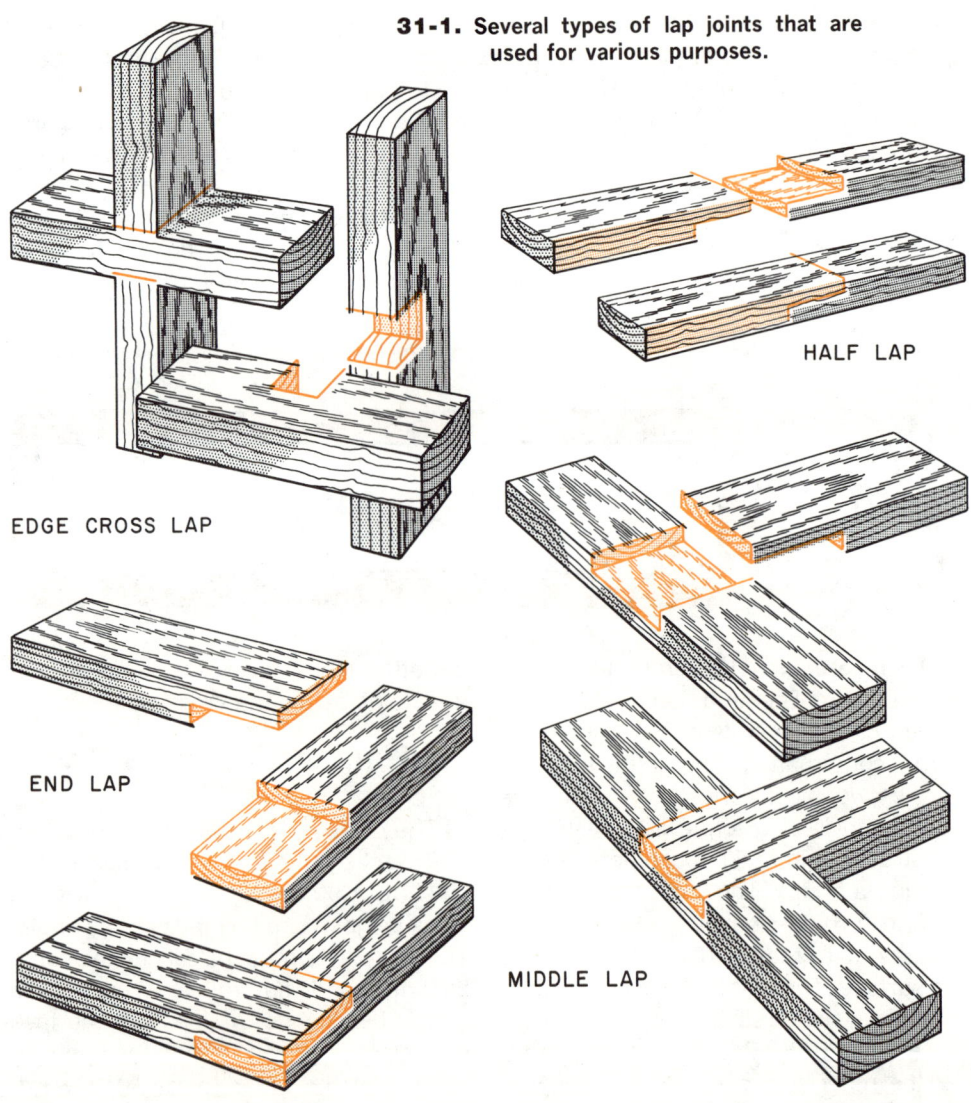

**31-1.** Several types of lap joints that are used for various purposes.

HALF LAP

EDGE CROSS LAP

END LAP

MIDDLE LAP

**31-2a.** This attractive serving tray is made by joining many pieces of stock with edge cross-lap joints. When this many joints must be cut, it is almost a necessity to use a circular saw.

**31-2b.** The cross stretchers (lower rails) on this end table have an edge lap joint cut at an angle.

**31-2c.** This chair, designed and built by a student, has several types of lap joints. The front rail and legs are joined with end-lap joints while the side rails and back legs have cross-lap joints.

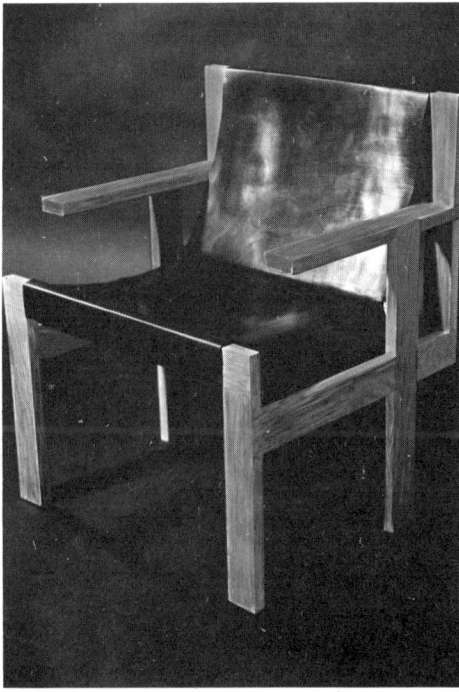

the thickness of the stock. From the face surface of each piece, mark along the edge on each side to show the depth of the joint. If you make this measurement from the face surface, the two pieces will be flush when the joint is made. This is because you will be cutting the joint from the face surface of one piece and the opposite surface of the other.

## CUTTING THE LAP JOINT

Hold the piece in a bench hook or clamp it to the top of the bench. Cut with a backsaw to the depth of the joint just inside each of the layout lines, as you did to make a dado joint. If the joint is wide, you should make several cuts in the waste stock. This helps to remove the waste and also acts as a guide when you chisel it out.

Next, use a chisel to remove the waste stock. Work from both sides of each piece, tapering up toward the center. If you try to chisel out across the stock from only one side, you may chip the opposite side.

After you have brought the joint down to the layout line on either edge, continue

**31-3.** Correct layout for a lap joint. Both pieces should be marked at the same time.

**31-4.** The layout has been made and the lap joint is checked. A try square keeps the pieces at right angles. The lines on the lower piece, which indicate the width of the lap joint, should be just visible.

**31-5.** Fitting a lap joint. The lap joints should fit together with a moderate amount of pressure. It is simpler to trim off a little from the edges of the stock than it is to make the joint wider.

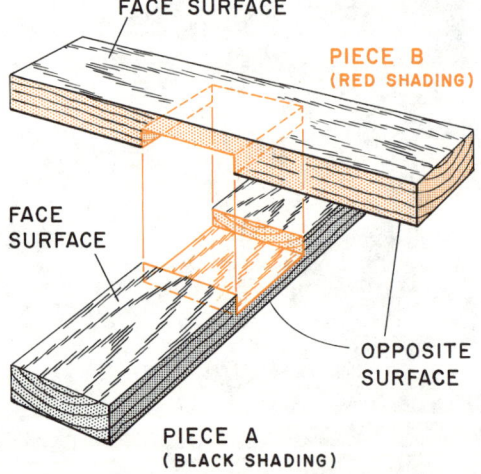

to pare (cut) the high point in the center of the joint. (See the unit on shaping stock with a chisel.)

Complete this on both pieces; then try to fit them together. Figure 31-5. The pieces should fit snugly. They should not be so loose that they fall apart or so tight that they must be forced together. If the fit is too tight, it is better to plane a little from the edge of one piece rather than to try to trim the shoulder.

## ASSEMBLING THE JOINT

When assembled, the surfaces of both pieces should fit flush with one another. Both glue and nails or screws are used. If the nails or screws are installed from the underside, they will not show and the joint will be very neat.

## CAN YOU ANSWER THESE QUESTIONS ON THE LAP JOINT?

1. Name several lap joints. What are the common uses of each?
2. Which type of lap joint is most common?
3. At what angle do the pieces of a lap joint usually cross?
4. How can you make sure that the two pieces will be flush when the joint is assembled?
5. Cutting a lap joint is similar to what other joint?
6. At what point in the fitting can you say that the two pieces fit together properly?

Section

VII

UNIT 32.

# MITER JOINT

**A miter joint** is used when the end grain should not show on the finished project. Figure 32-1. It is similar to the butt joint except that the jointing ends are cut at less than a right angle— usually 45 degrees. Figure 32-2. It is not a very strong joint and, therefore, is used mostly to make picture frames, casings, and decorative edges for furniture. Figure 32-3. It can be strengthened by adding dowels, a spline, or a key across the corner. Figure 32-4.

## MITER BOXES

The metal miter box and saw has a metal box in which a saw can be adjusted to any angle from 30 to 90 degrees. Figure 32-5. If one is not available, it is quite simple to make one of your own. This can be done by fastening two pieces of stock to a base. Then, with a sliding T bevel, lay out a 45-degree angle in both directions. Usually this and a 90-degree angle cut are all that is ever needed. Figure 32-6. (Page 246) Cutting a frame is the most common use for the miter joint, so this will be described.

## CUTTING A FRAME

If a metal miter box is available, swing the saw to the left and set it at 45 degrees. If a wood box is used, use the cut that is to the left as you face it. Place the edge of the frame in the box with the rabbet edge down and toward you. Hold

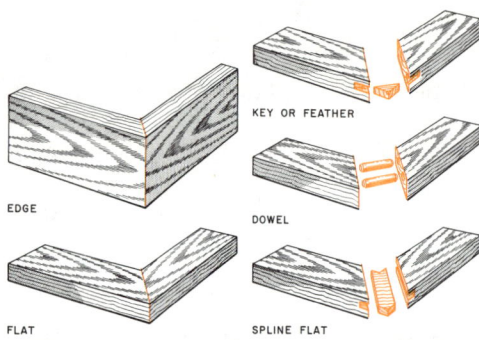

EDGE

KEY OR FEATHER

DOWEL

FLAT

SPLINE FLAT

**32-1.** The miter joint is weak by itself. It can be strengthened by adding dowels, a spline, or a key.

the stock firmly with the thumb of one hand against the side of the box. Figure 32-7. Then carefully bring the miter saw (or backsaw or fine crosscut saw if the box is homemade) down on the stock and cut the angle. Be especially careful not to let the stock slip when starting the cut. This could ruin the surface of the frame.

Next, determine the length of the glass or the picture. Add to this length twice the width of the frame, measured from the rabbet edge to the outside edge. Lay out this measurement along the outside edge of the stock. Figure 32-8. Then swing the miter-box saw to the right and set it at 45 degrees. Hold the stock firmly with one hand and cut the stock to length, using your other hand to operate the saw. If you find this awkward, clamp the stock to the box with a hand screw and then operate the saw with your favored hand. Repeat this for the second side and the ends.

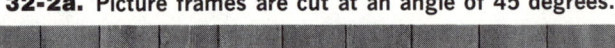

**32-2a.** Picture frames are cut at an angle of 45 degrees.

## ASSEMBLING THE
## MITER JOINT

Check the joint to make sure the corners fit properly. Figure 32-9. The miter joint is usually put together by gluing and nailing. Dowels, a spline, or a key may be added to strengthen the joint. To nail a miter joint, drive the nail part way into one piece. Lock the other piece in a vise in a vertical position. Hold the first piece over the vertical piece with its corner extending somewhat outside the edge of the vertical piece. Figure 32-10. As you nail the corners together, the top piece will tend to slip down until it fits squarely.

A miter and corner clamp is the ideal clamp for assembling frames. This clamp

**32-2b.** To cut a polygon miter which has an angle of more or less than 45 degrees to form a three-to-ten-sided object, the correct gage setting can be found as follows: Divide 180 by the number of sides and then subtract this amount from 90 degrees. A twelve-sided polygon miter would be cut at an angle of 75 degrees.

**32-3.** If a miter joint is used on a boxlike construction such as this cabinet, the joint must usually be reinforced with a spline or dowel.

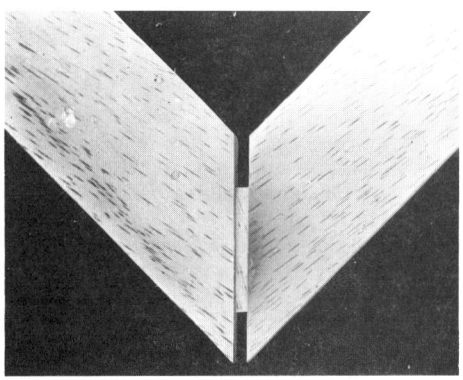

**32-4.** The miter joint is used for frames, contemporary furniture, and in places where end grain should not show. The corner can be strengthened by adding a spline as shown here.

**32-5.** A metal miter box. This box consists of a frame and a saw which can be adjusted to various angles.

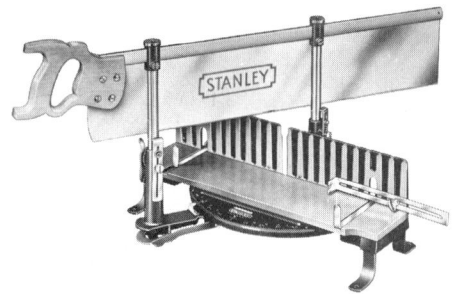

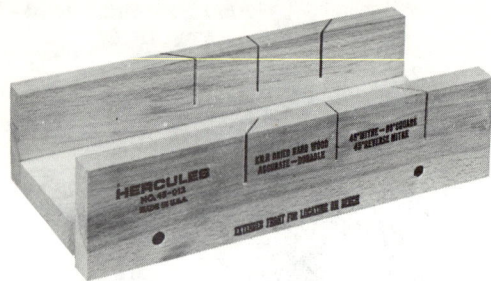

**32-6a.** A simple miter box that you could make for cutting 45-to-90-degree angles.

**32-6b.** Cutting a miter joint with a homemade miter box and backsaw. Be certain that the line to be cut is directly under the saw teeth. Hold the work tightly against the back of the box; start the cut with a careful backstroke.

**32-7.** In using a metal miter box, make sure the stock is held firmly against the back of the box so that it does not slip when the saw kerf is started.

allows you to fasten the corners with the two pieces held firmly in place. Figure 32-11. A wooden frame clamp can be made to use in assembling picture frames. Figure 32-12. There are also special spring clamps that will hold a miter corner together. Figure 32-13. Another method is to use a little-known trick. With

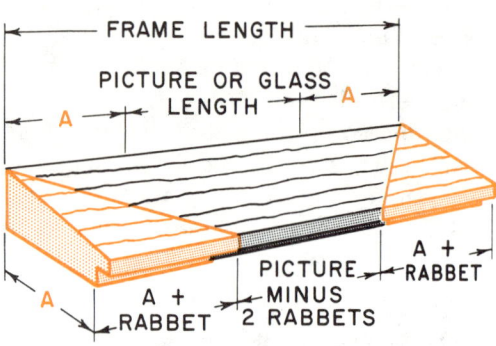

**32-8.** Laying out the proper measurement for cutting miter joints on a picture frame. The length as marked on the outside of the frame is equal to the length of the glass plus twice the width of the stock measured from the rabbet to the outside edge.

**32-9.** Checking a miter joint to make sure that it fits properly.

paper sandwiched between to permit easy removal, glue triangular blocks to the ends of each mitered piece. Let the glue set. Apply glue to the joint and pull together with C clamps. Remove the clamps after the glue has set and pry blocks away. Then sand the surface. Figure 32-14.

## MAKING PICTURE FRAMES WITH STANDARD WOOD MOLDINGS

Standard wood moldings can be used in one design or in a combination of

**32-10.** Nailing a miter joint. One piece is locked in a vise and the second piece held over it, with the corner extending slightly.

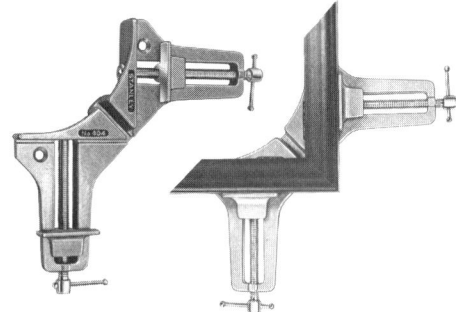

**32-11a.** This corner clamp holds the corners together as they are fastened.

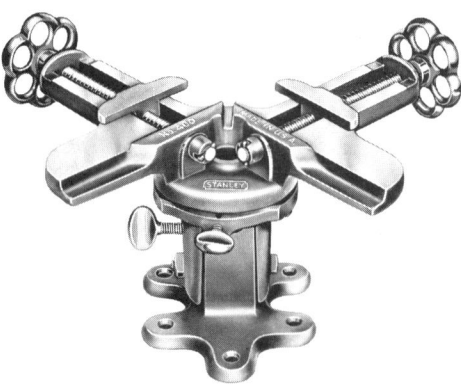

**32-11b.** A miter vise with tilting base. This vise can clamp moldings up to 4 inches (101.5 mm) wide and will join any frame larger than 3½ x 3½ inches (89 x 89 mm).

**32-12.** This adjustable frame clamp can be made. The major disadvantage is that it does not permit nailing the corners together when the frame is in the clamp.

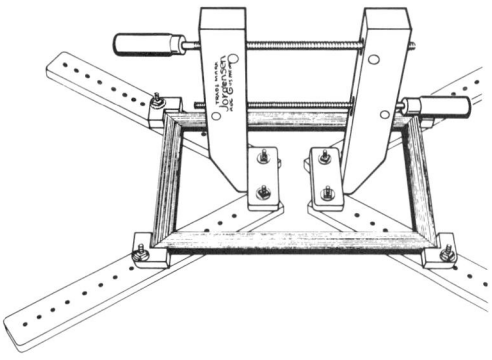

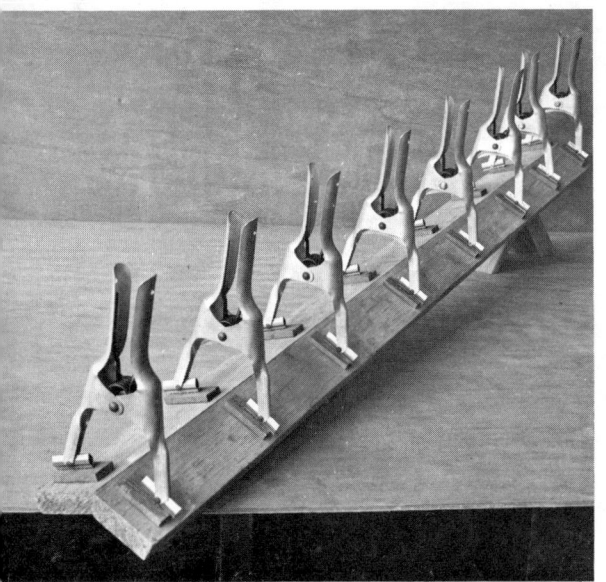

**32-13.** Spring clamps with special grooved teeth will hold a miter joint together after fastening.

**32-14.** This miter joint is held together by first gluing scrap stock to the exterior of each piece.

**32-15.** Wood molding can be used to make very stunning picture frames.

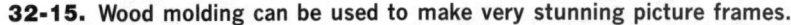

**32-16.** These moldings are typical of the more than 250 patterns and 400 sizes available for picture framing.

designs to frame pictures. Figure 32-15. Moldings are available in over 250 patterns and 400 sizes. Figure 32-16. The tools needed are the same as those available for making any kind of frame.

To make the frame, first select molding pattern and size. Purchase enough to make the frame. Produce the frame as follows: Glue up the molding strips that will make the complete frame and clamp them together until the glue is set. Figure 32-17. The extra piece that is glued onto the first piece will form the rabbet into

which the glass and picture fit. When dry, cut one end of each piece of molding at 45 degrees. Figure 32-18. Carefully measure the bottom edge of the picture and add $\frac{1}{8}$ inch (3 mm) to this measurement. Figure 32-19. Transfer this measurement to the moldings, starting from the edge of the miter at the point where the picture inserts into the frame. Mark and cut a 45-degree angle at the opposite end of the first cut. Measure the second piece from the first so that you will have two identical pieces.

**32-17.** Gluing up molding strips to make framing material. The smaller molding serves to form a rabbet edge into which the glass and picture will fit.

**32-18.** Cut one end of each of the pieces of molding at a 45-degree angle using a metal miter box.

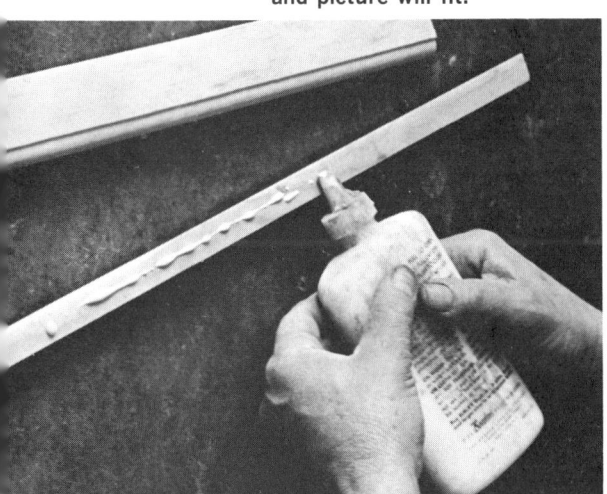

**32-19.** Measure the second cut along the picture rabbet. Add ⅛ inch (3 mm) for clearance for the glass and picture.

Measure the side edge of the picture and cut two pieces of molding to this length, making sure to add the extra $\frac{1}{8}$

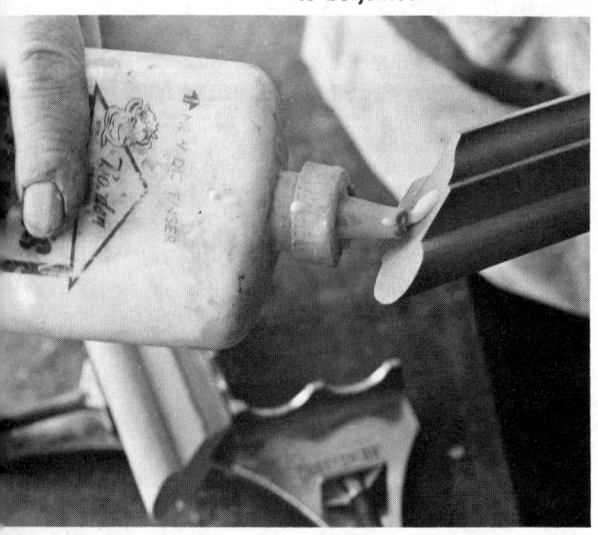

**32-20.** Apply polyvinyl glue to both surfaces to be joined.

inch. Assemble the frame one corner at a time. If you have four corner clamps, this can be done in one operation. Cover the ends of one side piece and one bottom piece with glue and insert them in a corner clamp. Figure 32-20. Align the miter joint carefully and then tighten the clamp. Figure 32-21. Drive two or more brads through the corner from each side. Figure 32-22. Allow the heads of the brads to protrude slightly. Now carefully drive the heads of the brads about $\frac{1}{16}$ inch (1.5 mm) below the surface of the frame with a nail set. Figure 32-23. Fill the nail holes with plastic wood. When necessary, use a flat corner plate at each corner of a large frame to give it added strength. Complete each of the other corners and then allow the glue to dry thoroughly. After the frame is dry, sand lightly. Figure 32-24. Many different types of finishes may be used on the frame, including paint, stain, natural finish, or glaze.

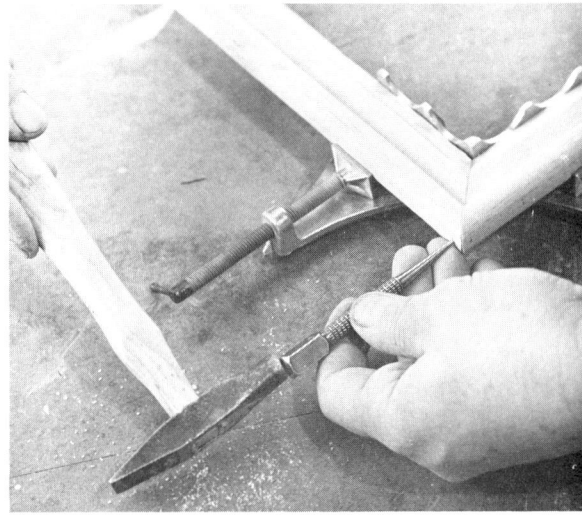

**32-23.** Use a nail set to drive the nail heads $\frac{1}{16}$ inch (1.5 mm) below the surface. Then fill the nail holes with plastic wood.

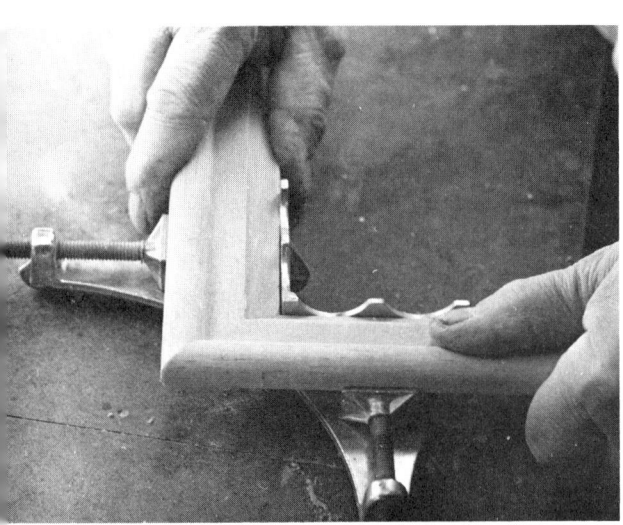

**32-21.** Clamp the corner tightly. Then wipe off the excess glue with a warm, damp rag.

**32-24.** Sand the frame lightly so that the miter joint matches perfectly.

**32-22.** All finishing nails are nailed from both edges. Allow the heads to protrude $\frac{1}{16}$ inch (1.5 mm) so that you do not mar the frame.

251

## CAN YOU ANSWER THESE QUESTIONS ON THE MITER JOINT?

1. What is the advantage of a miter joint? Disadvantage?
2. Name the common uses.
3. Describe a miter box.
4. Explain how to make a simple miter box.
5. At what angle is a miter joint made?
6. What kind of saw is best for cutting a miter joint?
7. Are there any precautions that should be observed in starting a miter cut?
8. In what two ways can a miter joint be strengthened?
9. What implements would you choose for holding a miter joint after it is glued?
10. Explain how to build a picture frame with standard wood moldings.

## Section VII
## UNIT 33.

# MORTISE-AND-TENON JOINT

**The mortise-and-tenon** joint is found in better furniture construction. Figure 33-1. There are many kinds of mortise-and-tenon joints. A few are shown in Figure 33-2. By far the most common is the blind mortise-and-tenon joint. As you will see, this is a rectangular projection on the end of a rail that fits into a rectangular hole in a second piece, usually a leg. Making a mortise-and-tenon joint by hand takes skill and should not be attempted if another type of joint will be just as satisfactory. Before beginning, note the names and measurements given in Figure 33-3. After the layout is complete, the joint can be cut with machines.

### MAKING THE PRELIMINARY LAYOUT

For most projects it will be necessary to make several mortise-and-tenon joints. For example, a simple table with four rails and legs takes eight. Before laying out the joints, hold the several pieces to be assembled in the position they will be when the project is finished. Place the face surface of the rails and the face surface and joint edge of the legs outward. Begin at one corner to mark No. 1 on the leg and No. 1 on the adjoining rail, No. 2 on the next, etc. Do this until you have marked with matching numbers the pieces that make up each mortise-and-tenon joint. In this way, you will be sure the pieces will fit together in the proper order when you are ready to assemble them.

### LAYING OUT THE TENONS

The size of the mortise-and-tenon joint is usually given on the drawing. These measurements should be followed carefully. However, if they are not given, the tenon is made half as wide as the total thickness of the piece and about $\frac{1}{2}$ to $\frac{3}{4}$

inch (12.5 to 19 mm) narrower than the total width.

From the ends, mark out the length of the tenon and square a line completely around the end of each piece. Do this on all pieces and then check to see that all

**33-1a.** Tables of all sizes and designs often use the mortise-and-tenon joint to fasten the rails to the legs. One example is this coffee table which has one drawer.

**33-1b.** This oval dining room table also uses the mortise-and-tenon joint.

of the rails are the same length from shoulder to shoulder. Next, set the marking gage to half the thickness of the stock to be removed and, working from the face side, mark a line across the end and down each edge.

Next, add to this measurement the thickness of the tenon and check the gage. Again mark a line across the end and down the sides. Subtract the width of the tenon from the total width of the stock. Divide this amount in half and set this measurement on a marking gage.

From the joint edge of the rail, mark a line across the end and down the side. Next, add to this measurement the width of the tenon and set the gage again. Repeat the mark across the end and down the side.

Now you have all of the necessary measurements on the tenon. Figure 33-4. If several tenons are to be marked, make sure that you do them at the same time to keep from making a mistake.

## LAYING OUT A MORTISE

With a pencil point on your marking gage, make all lines on all four legs at the same time. From the top end of each leg, lay out two lines on the inside surfaces (opposite the face side and joint edge) that indicate the total width of the rail.

Next, lay out two more lines on these surfaces to show the width of the tenon. Decide how far back the rail is to be set from the outside edge of the leg. Add to this measurement the thickness of the stock removed from one side of the tenon. Set the marking gage to this measurement. Now hold the marking gage against the face side and joint edge and mark a line between the lines that indicate the width of the tenon. Add to this measurement an amount equal to

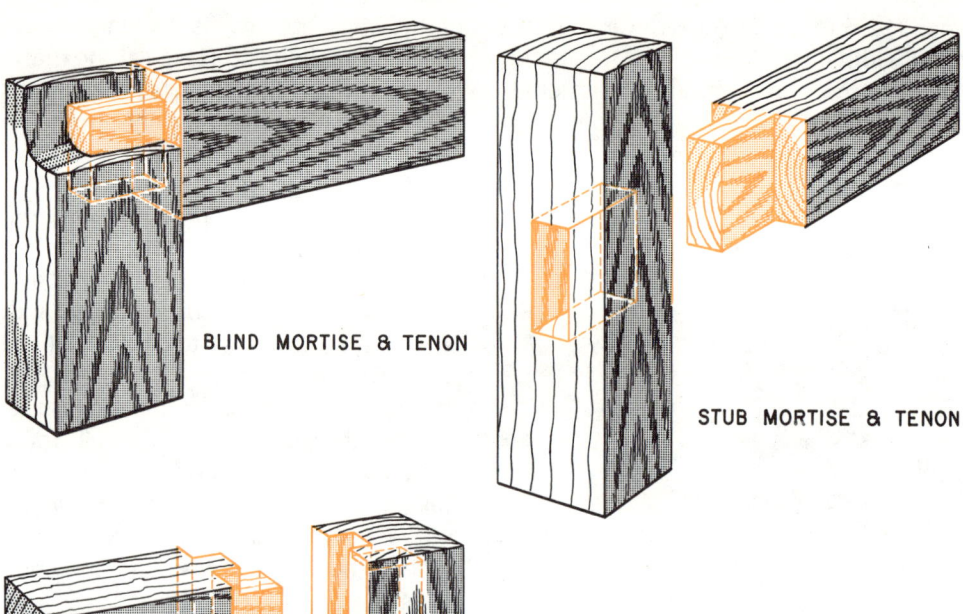

BLIND MORTISE & TENON

STUB MORTISE & TENON

HAUNCHED MORTISE & TENON

**33-2.** Common types of mortise-and-tenon joints.

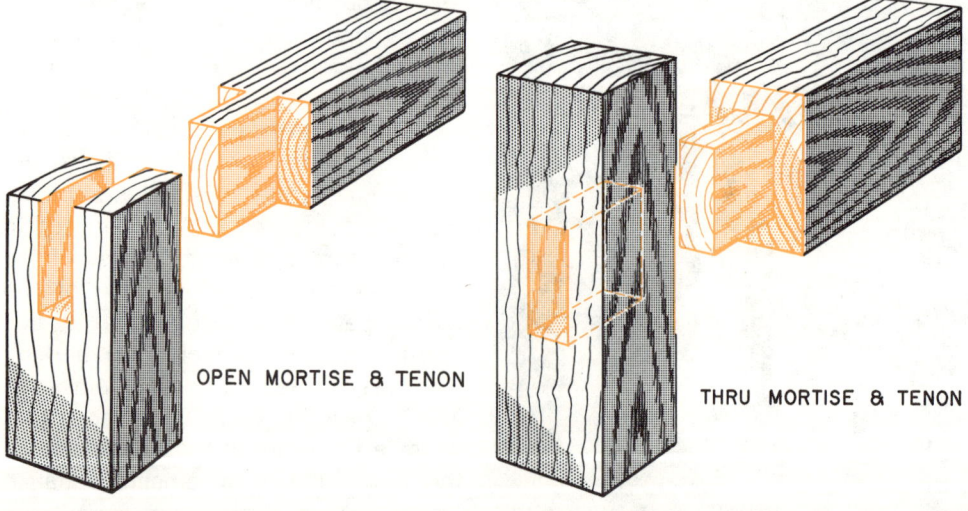

OPEN MORTISE & TENON

THRU MORTISE & TENON

the thickness of the tenon. Mark another line to complete the outline. This will be exactly the same as the thickness and width of the tenon. Figure 33-5. If an auger bit is to be used to remove the waste stock from the mortise, lay out a line down the center of the outline.

## CUTTING THE MORTISE

The most common way to remove most of the stock from the mortise opening is with an auger bit and brace. The auger bit should be the same diameter or slightly smaller than the width of the opening. Bore a series of holes to remove most of the stock from the mortise open-

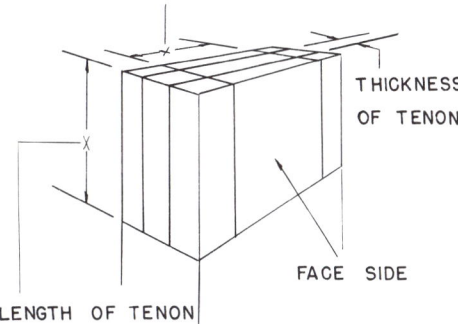

**33-4.** Proper layout for a tenon. These lines should be made accurately so the tenon will be the correct size and shape.

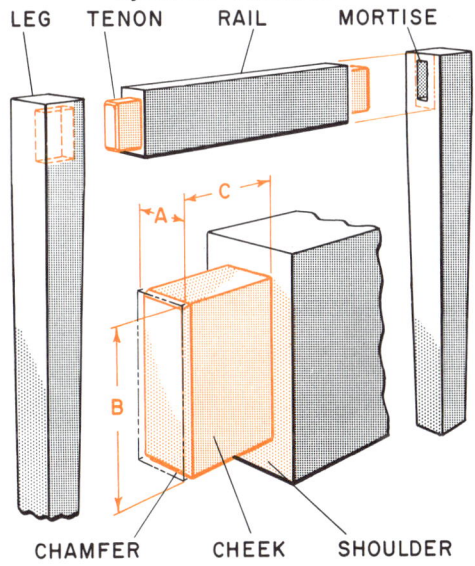

**33-3.** Study the parts of the mortise-and-tenon joint, as these will be referred to in its layout and construction.

A — THICKNESS OF TENON
B — WIDTH OF TENON
C — LENGTH OF TENON

**33-5.** The proper layout of a mortise. Only the part indicated by the shading is absolutely essential to the layout.

X — DISTANCE FROM EDGE OF LEG TO FACE SIDE OF RAIL

Y — THICKNESS OF RAIL

Z — WIDTH OF RAIL

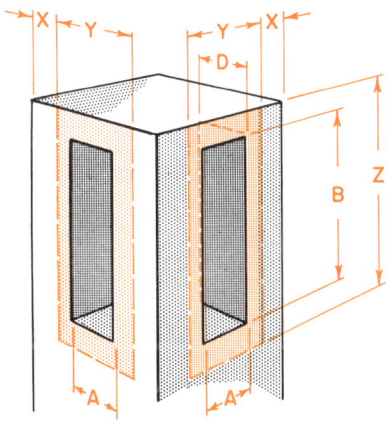

A — WIDTH OF MORTISE (TENON THICKNESS)
B — LENGTH OF MORTISE (TENON WIDTH)
C — LENGTH OF TENON
D — MORTISE DEPTH = $C + \frac{1}{8}$ (3mm)

255

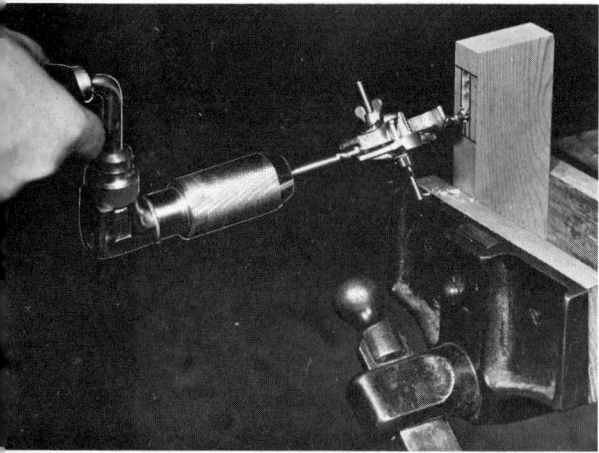

**33-6.** Boring out a mortise. Note that the bit selected has the same diameter as the thickness of the tenon or the width of the mortise. A depth gage controls the amount of stock removed.

**33-7.** Trimming out a mortise with a chisel. After the holes are drilled, it is necessary to trim out the sides and end of the mortise. To do this, hold the chisel with the flat side against the side of the mortise and take a shearing cut. It will be necessary to use a narrow chisel to trim out the ends.

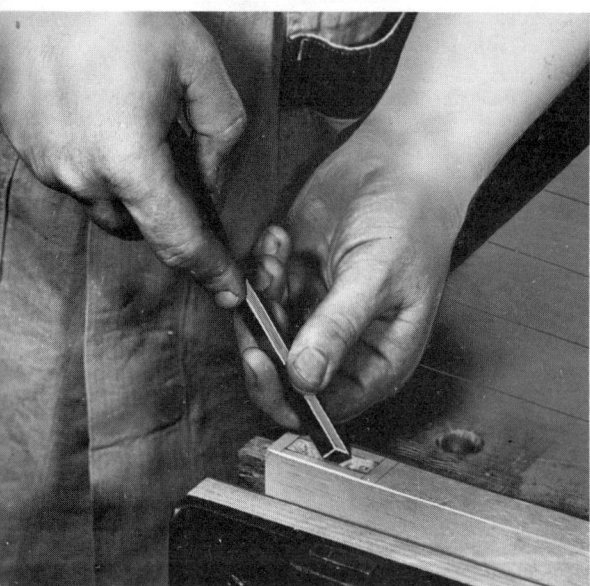

ing. Figure 33-6. Use a depth gage set to make the holes slightly deeper than the length of the tenon. With a chisel, pare out the side and ends of the opening to the layout line. Figure 33-7. To finish the ends, use a narrow chisel.

Some woodworkers prefer to remove all of the stock with a chisel. For this, use a heavy, thick mortise chisel that can stand quite a bit of pounding. The width of the blade should be exactly the width of the opening. Clamp the workpiece firmly to the bench. Figure 33-8. Begin to cut at the center of the mortise. Hold the chisel in a vertical position with the bevel side toward the end of the mortise. Cut out a V-shaped notch to the depth required. Then continue to remove the stock by driving the chisel down with a mallet. Draw down on the handle to remove the chips. Figure 33-9. Stop when you are within about $\frac{1}{8}$ inch (3 mm) of the end of the opening. Turn the chisel around with the flat side toward the end of the mortise and cut out the remainder of the stock. Figure 33-10.

**33-8.** Make sure the workpiece is clamped securely when cutting the mortise with a chisel.

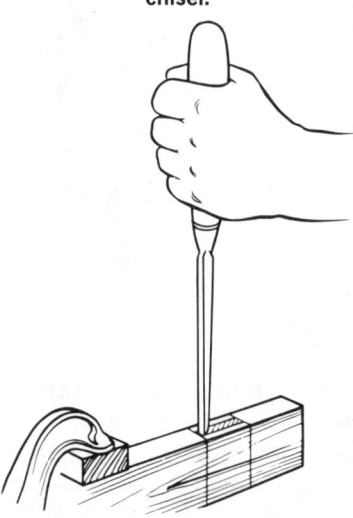

The mortise can also be cut on the drill press using a mortising attachment. See Unit 64.

## CUTTING THE TENON

Lock the stock in a vise with the marked tenon showing. Use a backsaw or fine crosscut saw to make four saw cuts in the waste stock that will shape the thickness and width of the tenon. Figure 33-11.

Next, remove the stock from the vise and clamp it on the top of the bench. Make the shoulder cuts to remove the waste stock which forms the thickness and the width of the tenon. *Be especially careful,* as it is essential that these saw marks be accurate for a tight-fitting tenon. The cutting of a tenon can be simplified by using a circular saw. See Unit 58. The tenon must then be trimmed with a chisel. Figure 33-12.

Cut a small chamfer around the end of the tenon to help it slip easily into the mortise opening. This must be very slight.

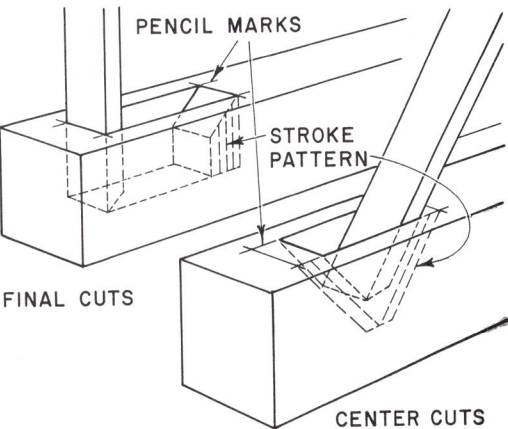

**33-10.** Proper method of cutting a mortise with a mortising chisel. The center cuts are taken with the chisel held with the bevel toward the outside. Other cuts are taken with the bevel turned in.

**33-9.** Cutting a mortise with a heavy chisel that will take considerable pounding. The chisel selected must be the same width as the mortise.

**33-11.** Cheek cuts completed. This shows the four cuts that will shape the thickness and width of the tenon. *Make the cuts in waste stock.*

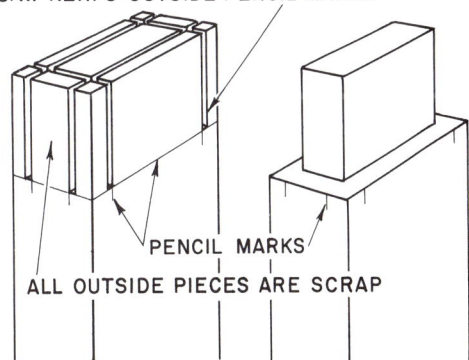

SAW KERFS OUTSIDE PENCIL MARKS

PENCIL MARKS

ALL OUTSIDE PIECES ARE SCRAP

**33-12.** After the shoulder cuts are made, the tenon is trimmed with a chisel to make it fit accurately into the mortise.

## ASSEMBLING THE MORTISE AND TENON

After the mortise-and-tenon joint has been cut, it will be necessary to do some fitting before the tenon will fit into the mortise properly. Use a chisel to pare off stock from the thickness and width of the tenon until you can force the tenon into the mortise with a moderate amount of pressure. Make sure that the shoulder of the tenon fits squarely against the face of the mortise.

This joint is usually glued. Gluing is discussed at length in another part of the book.

## CAN YOU ANSWER THESE QUESTIONS ON THE MORTISE-AND-TENON JOINT?

1. Is a mortise-and-tenon joint found on better-quality furniture? Why?
2. Which part is the mortise? The tenon?
3. Make a sketch showing the cheek and shoulder.
4. Name several types of mortise-and-tenon joints.
5. How many mortise-and-tenon joints could be found on a simple table?
6. What is the rule for the thickness of the tenon? What should the length of the tenon be?
7. Tell how to lay out a tenon.
8. Could a marking gage be used to lay out a mortise? Explain.
9. How do the width of the mortise and the thickness of the tenon compare?
10. Should the shoulder cuts be made first? Why?
11. Which of the two methods of cutting a mortise is the most common? What are these two methods?
12. How are mortise-and-tenon joints usually fastened for permanency?

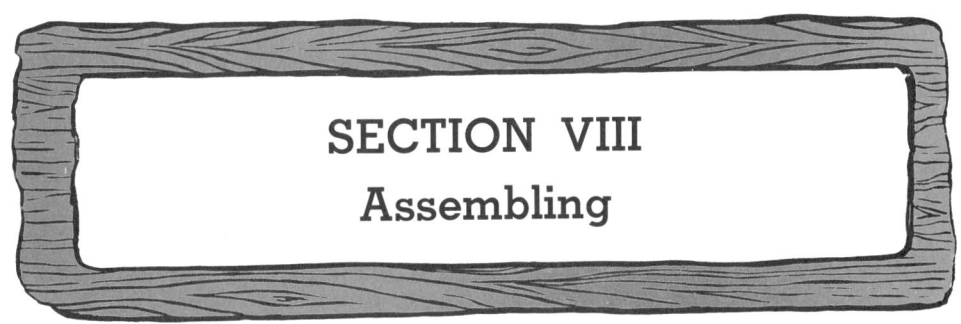

# SECTION VIII
## Assembling

(Continued on page 260)

259

44. Applying plastic laminates: kinds of materials; correct tools to use; proper adhesive; method of applying adhesive.

45. Adding beauty and utility to wood products with mosaic tile: kinds of tile; tools and materials; method of installing.

46. Working with acrylic plastics: kinds of plastics; cutting, forming, and assembling acrylic plastic materials.

*There are three common methods of permanently fastening pieces together: with nails, screws, or glue. Before assembly, be sure that each part of the project is scraped and sanded. Before finishing, you must go over the project to remove excess glue, fill in dents, and scrape and resand the surface. Hardware should be fitted, then removed.*

# BUILDING TABLES, DESKS, AND CABINETS

**To build** a table, desk, or cabinet several new steps must be added to those already covered in this book.

## STRENGTHENING CORNERS

Most tables, chairs, and simple desks are made with four legs joined by rails. The rail and leg are fastened together with dowel construction or mortise-and-tenon joints. To add strength to the adjoining parts, a corner block is cut and fastened in each corner. Figure 34-1. The block helps to hold the table square and gives added support at its weakest points. *Glue blocks* are small triangular blocks of wood placed along the edges of two adjoining pieces to strengthen them.

**34-1a.** Four corner blocks are needed to add strength and rigidity to this coffee table.

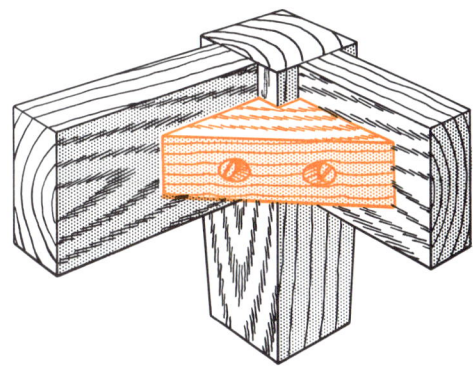

**34-1b.** A block used to strengthen corners of a table.

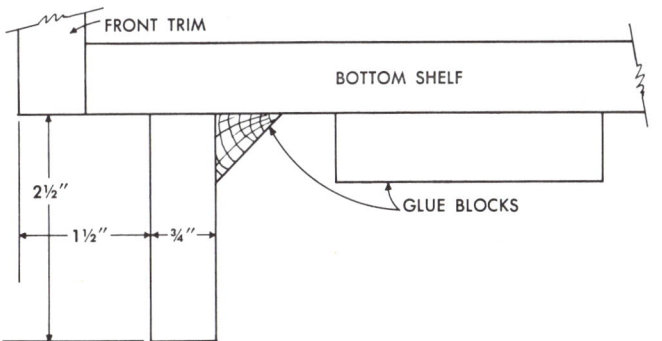

FRONT TRIM

BOTTOM SHELF

2½″

1½″   ¾″

GLUE BLOCKS

**34-1c.** Glue blocks used in cabinet construction.

## FASTENING TABLE TOPS

Figure 34-2 shows three common ways of attaching a table top to the rails.

## DRAWER CONSTRUCTION

There are three steps in installing a drawer in a table: cutting the rail to receive the drawer; making the drawer, and making the drawer guide. In desk and chest construction only the last two steps need to be done.

### Cutting the Rail

To cut the rail to receive the drawer, first decide on the exact size of the drawer. Then cut an opening that is $\frac{1}{16}$ inch (1.5 mm) wider and $\frac{1}{8}$ inch (3 mm) longer than the drawer front. Figure 34-3.

### Making the Drawer

The drawer may be made to fit flush with the opening, or it may be a lip drawer (fit over the frame). Figure 34-4.

**34-2a.** The tops of these bunching tables can be fastened using one of the methods shown in Figure 34-2b.

To make a lip drawer, a $\frac{3}{8}$-inch (9.5 mm) rabbet is cut around the inside edge of the drawer front. Then the lip drawer overlaps the frame.

The front is usually made of $\frac{3}{4}$-inch (19 mm) material. The grain and color usually match the material used in the project. The sides and back are made of

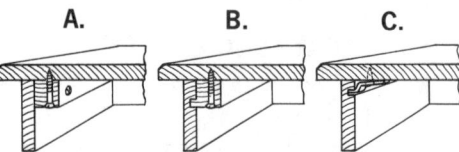

**34-2b.** Several ways of attaching a table top to the rails: A. Square cleat; B. Square cleat with rabbet and groove; C. Metal tabletop fastener.

**34-3.** Openings in the upper rail must be cut for the three drawers of this table.

½-inch (12.5 mm) stock such as pine, birch, or maple. The bottom is usually made of ¼-inch (6.5 mm) fir plywood or hardboard. Figure 34-5.

A common way of joining the front to the sides is with a rabbet joint. The rabbet is cut to a width of two-thirds the thickness of the sides. This will allow some clearance for the drawer. Other kinds of drawer joints can also be used.

The back is joined to the sides with a butt or dado joint. The back should be cut so that the drawer is slightly narrower at the back than at the front.

Cut a groove ¼ inch by ¼ inch (6.5 x 6.5 mm) about ½ inch (12.5 mm) above the bottom on the inside front and sides. Sometimes a groove is also cut across the back.

Cut the drawer bottom slightly smaller, about $\frac{1}{16}$ inch (1.5 mm), than the width between the grooves. This will allow for shrinkage and swelling.

Assemble the drawer. Glue and nail the sides to the front. Never put glue into the grooves for the bottom. Slip the bottom in place and then glue or nail the sides to the back.

## Making the Drawer Guide

The three most common drawer guides are the slide-block guide and runner (simple drawer guide), the side guide, and the center guide. Drawer guides sup-

A.  **34-4.** Two basic types of drawer fronts: A. Flush drawer; B. Lip drawer.  B.

port the drawer and keep it from slipping from one side to the other.

To make a slide-block guide and runner for a table drawer, cut a rabbet in a piece of wood. This piece will fit between the rails at the lower corner of the drawer. Figure 34-6.

Figure 34-7 shows a side guide with a groove in the side of the drawer and with the runner attached to the project itself. Another method is to attach a runner to the side of the drawer and then cut a groove in each side of the project. Figure 34-8.

The center guide is made by attaching a runner to the project. Then two extra pieces are attached to the bottom of the drawer to act as the guide. If desired, a groove can be cut in an extra piece that is fastened to the bottom as a guide.

For heavy drawers such as those for letter files, special ball-bearing guides should be fastened to each side of the drawer. If a drawer sticks, rub a little paraffin at the tight points. In best quality furniture, the dovetail joint is made to fasten the sides to the front and a rabbet-and-dado joint joins the back and sides. When there are several drawers, a dust panel is usually placed between drawers.

## CASE CONSTRUCTION

Any case, such as a bookcase or stereo cabinet, is a box turned on its side. Figure 34-9. The corners are joined with a rabbet, miter, or similar joint. A rabbet is usually cut around the back edge so that the back will fit into it. The back is usually made of plywood or hardboard.

**34-5.** A. Simple ways of fastening the sides to the front and back in drawer construction. B. Parts of a drawer.

A.

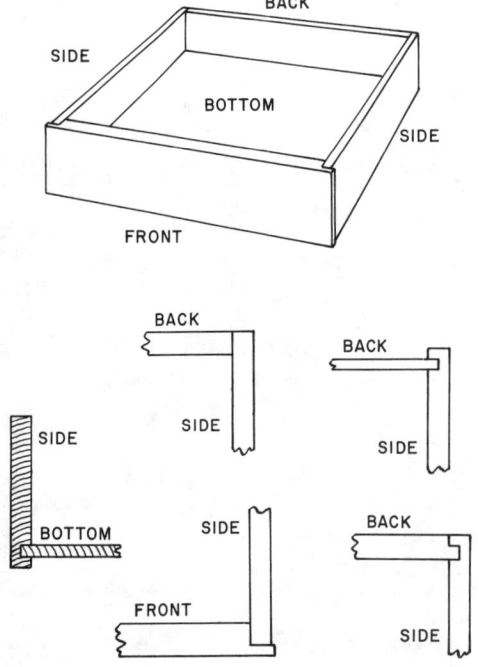

B.

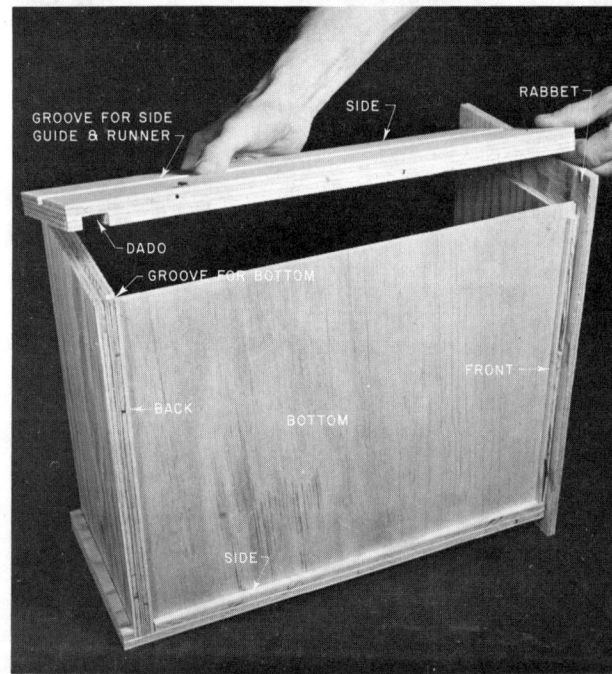

If the case has fixed shelves, these are usually installed with a dado joint. The most common way to provide for movable shelves is to use adjustable shelf brackets with snap-on clips. Figure 34-10. These can be obtained in any

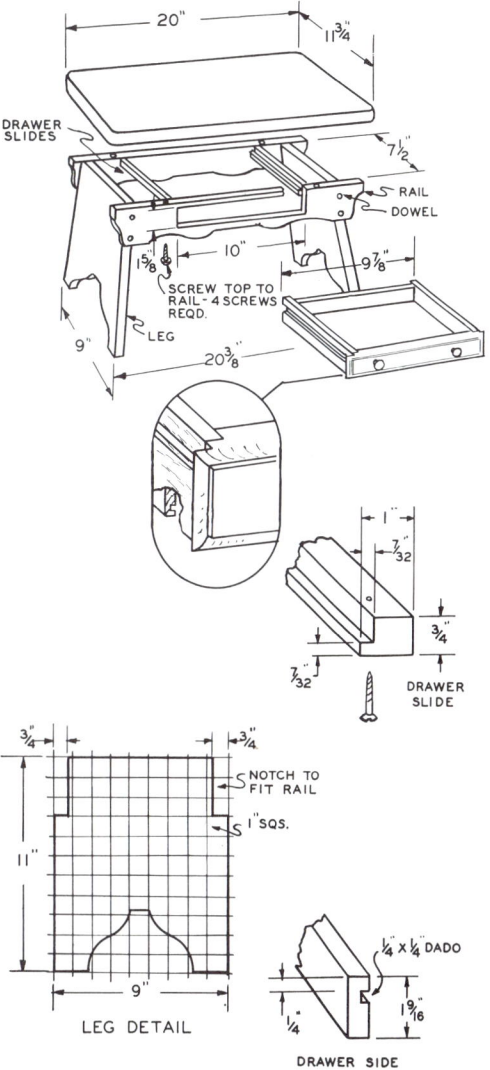

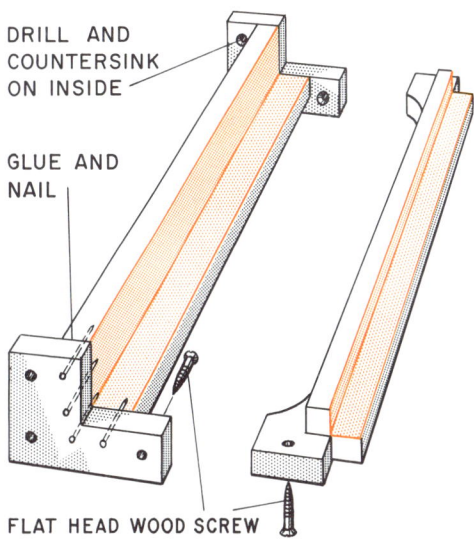

DRILL AND
COUNTERSINK
ON INSIDE

GLUE AND
NAIL

FLAT HEAD WOOD SCREW

**34-6.** A simple drawer guide. This type can be easily made and will work well when fitting a drawer between rails.

**34-7a.** This beautifully crafted foot stool has a small drawer installed in the rail.

LEG DETAIL

DRAWER SIDE

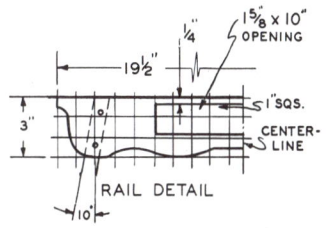

RAIL DETAIL

**34-7b.** A side guide and runner are used for a drawer fitted between the rails of the foot stool.

**34-7c.** Side guide and runner with a groove cut in the drawer and a strip fastened to the case.

**34-8.** Side guide and runner with the dado cut in the case and a strip attached to the drawer.

**34-9a.** A large case unit with drawers, doors, and open shelves.

**34-9b.** A miniature case only 16½ inches (419 mm) high with a mirror-lined interior for storing toiletries.

**34-9c.** A cedar chest which is a box with a cover.

**34-10a.** Movable shelves installed with adjustable shelf brackets.

**34-10b.** This display stand has adjustable glass shelves held in place by shelf brackets.

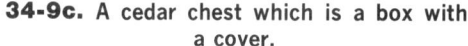

lengths. Two are needed for each side. The best way to use them is to cut a groove into which the shelf bracket fits. Then cut the shelves to the correct length. Another method is to drill holes in the sides of the case for metal or plastic shelf pins. Figure 34-11.

## USING COMMERCIAL LEGS

There are many kinds of commercial legs that can be purchased for use on all types of furniture projects. Figure 34-12. They come in many lengths, shapes, and kinds of materials. Legs are made of metal, wood, and plastic. They may be round tapered, round straight, square tapered, or square straight. The common lengths are 7, 13, 17, 22, and 29 inches (178, 330, 432, 559, and 737 mm). The shorter lengths are used for cabinets and chests. The longer lengths are used on tables and desks.

Some types of commercial legs are made as a one-piece unit that is fastened directly to the wood. Other types come with metal attaching brackets. These are made so that the legs can be fastened either in a straight up-and-down position or at a slight angle.

**34-11a.** These wall bookcase units each have two adjustable shelves.

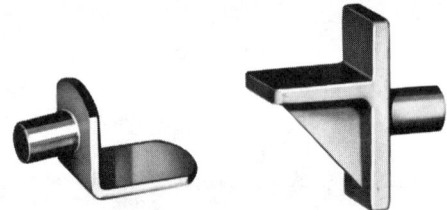

**34-11b.** Shelf-support pins of metal and plastic.

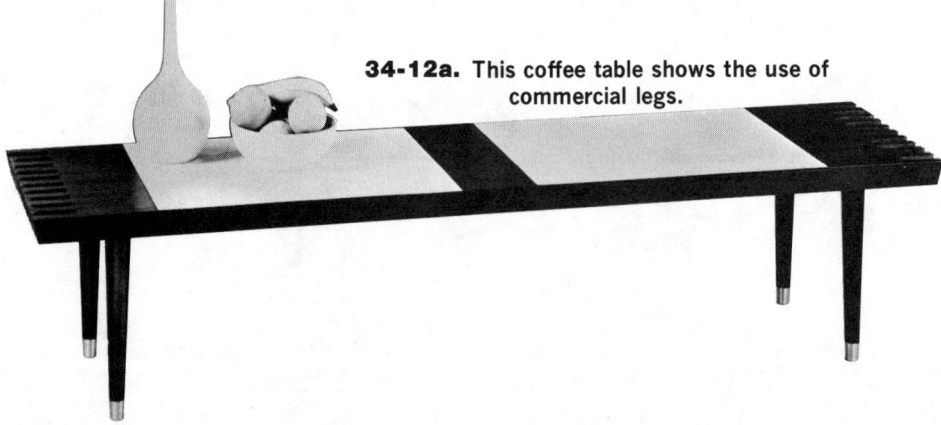

**34-12a.** This coffee table shows the use of commercial legs.

**34-12b.** A wood table with bent metal legs.

## CAN YOU ANSWER THESE QUESTIONS ON BUILDING TABLES, DESKS, AND CABINETS?

1. How can the corners of a table be strengthened?
2. What are three ways of fastening a table top to the base?
3. Describe a drawer guide. What purpose does it have?
4. Relate the three steps in installing a drawer in a table.
5. What things should you think about when choosing the wood for the front of the drawer?
6. How can a simple drawer guide be constructed?
7. What joints are found in a drawer?
8. Explain why the sides of the drawer are not parallel.
9. Tell how to use commercial legs for a table.

# Section VIII
## UNIT 35.

## PANELED DOOR OR FRAME

**Panel construction** is found in such things as chests, desks, and other pieces of cabinet furniture. Figure 35-1. It consists of a frame into which is fitted a piece, or panel, of plywood. It has the advantage over solid construction of less warpage, since only the frame can change in size, while the panel inside is free to expand or contract. The construction is the same whether the panels are made for parts of furniture or for doors.

### PARTS OF A DOOR

The upright parts of a door are called stiles and the cross parts are called rails. Figure 35-2. Door construction is similar to other panel construction in which the frame fits together with a haunched mortise-and-tenon joint. Window construction is also very similar, except that the open mortise-and-tenon joint is used.

### MAKING A PANELED DOOR

Lay out and cut the stock for the frame. Allow extra length to provide for making the joint. Square up the stock. Select the panel to be used to fill the frame. Check this thickness and then cut a groove along the joint edges of each piece into which the panel will fit. This groove should be as deep as it is wide. The simplest way of cutting it is to use the circular saw, although it can be done with a hand combination plane.

**35-1.** The doors on this birch dry sink are panel doors.

**35-2.** Parts of a door.

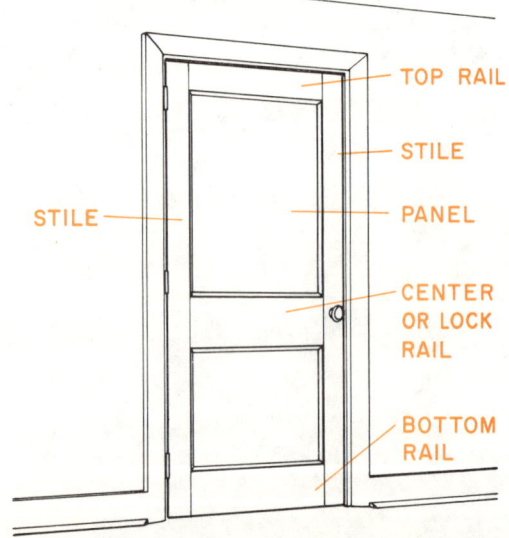

STILE

TOP RAIL

STILE

PANEL

CENTER OR LOCK RAIL

BOTTOM RAIL

270

The mortise should be far enough away from the ends of the stiles to keep it from breaking out under pressure. The mortise should be made the same width as the width of the groove, and the length should be about two-thirds the width of the rail. The tenon should be cut as thick as the width of the groove. The length of the tenon should equal the depth of the mortise plus the depth of the groove.

Cut a notch out of the tenon. The long part of the tenon should fit into the mortise opening and the short part should fit into the groove of the stile. Figure 35-3. Sometimes, in making a panel frame, no mortise is cut and only a stub tenon is made which fits into the groove in the stiles.

PANELED FRAME
WITH OPEN MORTISE & TENON JOINTS

**35-3.** Methods of joining the corners for panel construction.

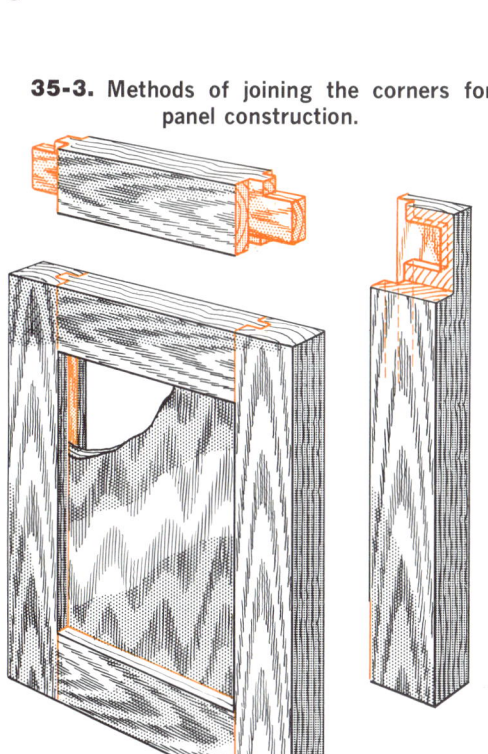

PANELED FRAME WITH
HAUNCHED MORTISE & TENON JOINTS

PANELED FRAME
WITH BUTT JOINT EFFECT, USING BLIND
MORTISE & TENON JOINTS

Fit the panel temporarily into the frame to check it. Take the frame apart and cover the edge of the panel with soap or wax to keep any glue from getting into the groove or edge of the panel. Apply glue and clamp the frame together.

## FITTING A PANEL DOOR

Check the opening for the door. Plane the edge of the stile which will fit against the frame and have the hinges straight and true. After the edge has been planed true, hold the door against the opening as close as possible to get a rough check on how well it fits. Make sure that each stile will be about the same width when the door is fitted.

Use a framing square to check the frame. If the frame is square, then square off a line on the upper rail. Cut and plane this end square with the edge that has been fitted. Continue to check and plane until the door fits properly, since the frame sometimes is a little "out of square."

Measure the height of the opening, and lay out and cut the bottom rail. If the frame is square, plane this end square with the first edge. Measure the width of the opening at the top and at the bottom. Sometimes the frame opening will not be exactly parallel from top to bottom. Lay out these measurements on the top and bottom rail and join these lines, using a straightedge, along the stile.

Cut and plane the edge until the door fits properly. The door must not be too snug since, after the hinges are installed, it must have some "play" to swing open. This edge should be planed at a slight bevel toward the back of the door. This gives the stile proper clearance when the door is opened and closed.

## CAN YOU ANSWER THESE QUESTIONS ON A PANELED DOOR OR FRAME?

1. Why are doors and frames made of panel construction?
2. Make a sketch of a door naming its parts.
3. What kind of joint is found most frequently in panel construction?
4. Should the panel be glued to the frame? Explain your answer.

# ASSEMBLING STOCK WITH NAILS

**The simplest** and easiest way to join two pieces of wood is with nails. You have probably done quite a bit of nailing. Yet, although it seems simple, much skill is needed to do it properly.

## TOOLS FOR NAILING

The most common tool is the *claw hammer*. Figure 36-1. The face of the head should be slightly curved to eliminate hammer marks. Figure 36-2. This lets you drive the nail flush with the wood surface without damaging the wood itself. Be sure the hammer face is free from dirt, glue, etc., so it won't slip and mar the wood or bend the nail.

A *nail set* is a short metal punch with a cup-shaped head used to drive the head of the nail below the surface of the wood. Figure 36-3.

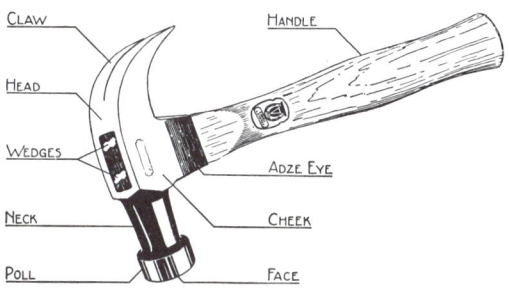

**36-1b.** Parts of a claw hammer.

**36-1a.** Claw hammers are available in many sizes with heads that weigh from 5 ounces to 20 ounces (142 to 567 g). A 13-ounce (368 g) hammer is good for average work.

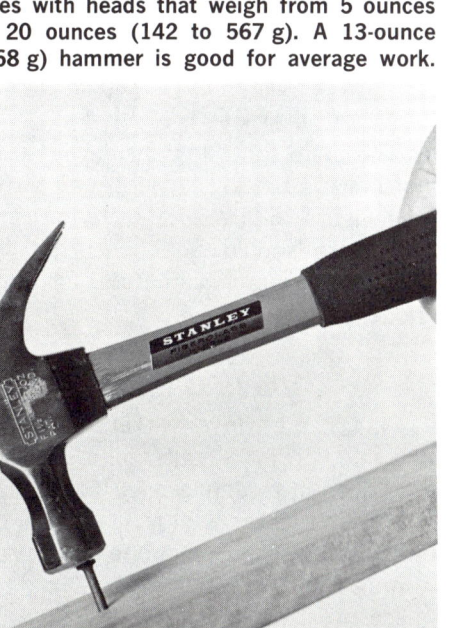

**36-2.** The head of the hammer is domed slightly to help keep the nail from bending if you don't strike it exactly square and to concentrate force at the contact point.

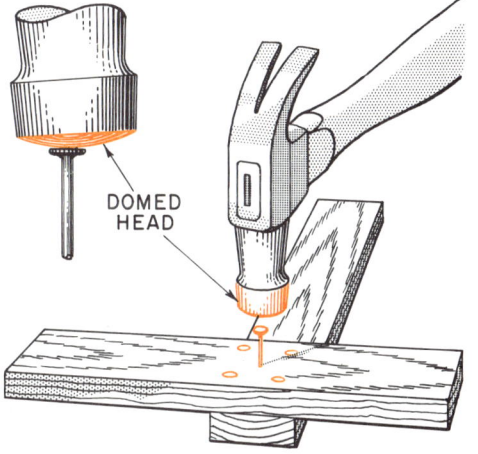

273

A *ripping bar* has a gooseneck with a nail slot on one end. The other end is chisel-shaped and carefully beveled. The tool is used for ripping down old buildings, removing machinery from crates, and similar jobs. Figure 36-4.

## KINDS OF NAILS

There are so many kinds of nails, brads, and tacks that it would be impossible to list them here. Nails are made of mild steel, copper, brass, and aluminum.

Mild steel nails are sometimes galvanized (coated) to protect them from rusting. There are four kinds that you will use the most: common, box, casing, and finishing. Figure 36-5.

The system of nail marking with "penny" or "d" is rather old fashioned. This term comes from one of two sources: either it was considered to be the weight per thousand or the cost per thousand. Regardless of its origin, it is still used.

Nails range in size from 2d, the smallest, to 60d, the largest. Figure 36-6. You will find that a 4d common nail has a larger diameter than a 4d finishing nail.

**36-3.** The nail set is used to drive the nail head below the surface of the wood. This hole is then filled with putty or similar material before the project is finished.

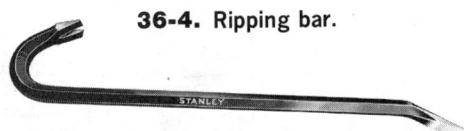

**36-4.** Ripping bar.

The larger sizes are called *spikes. Box nails* are mostly for construction of packing cases and other similar carpentry work. The *casing nail* has a small head. It is a rather heavy nail for more finished carpentry or for the assembly of projects on which the nail heads are to be recessed (below the surface). The *finishing nail,* the finest of all nails, is used for all fine cabinet and construction work. *Brads* are similar to finishing nails, but are marked a little differently. They are indicated by the length in inches ($\frac{1}{4}$ inch to 3 inches) (6 to 75 mm) and a gage number from 11 to 20. The higher the gage number, the smaller the diameter. They are sold in pound boxes. *Escutcheon nails* or pins are small brass nails with round heads. They are used to assemble small projects, especially if a decorative head is desirable. Figure 36-7. They come in lengths from $\frac{1}{4}$ inch to $1\frac{1}{4}$ inches (6.5 to 32 mm) and gage numbers of 20 to 16. Corrugated fasteners, shown in Figure 36-8, are used for holding joints and are particularly good for repair work.

## SELECTING NAILS

The main thing to consider in selecting nails is the proper kind and size of nail. Figure 36-9. You will learn that small diameters should be chosen for thin stock and large diameters for heavy stock.

## DRIVING NAILS

Nails can be driven either straight into the wood or, for a tighter joint, they may be driven at a slight angle. If two pieces are to be nailed together, as on the corner of a box, first drive one or two nails through the first piece. Then hold this piece over the other piece to drive the nails in place.

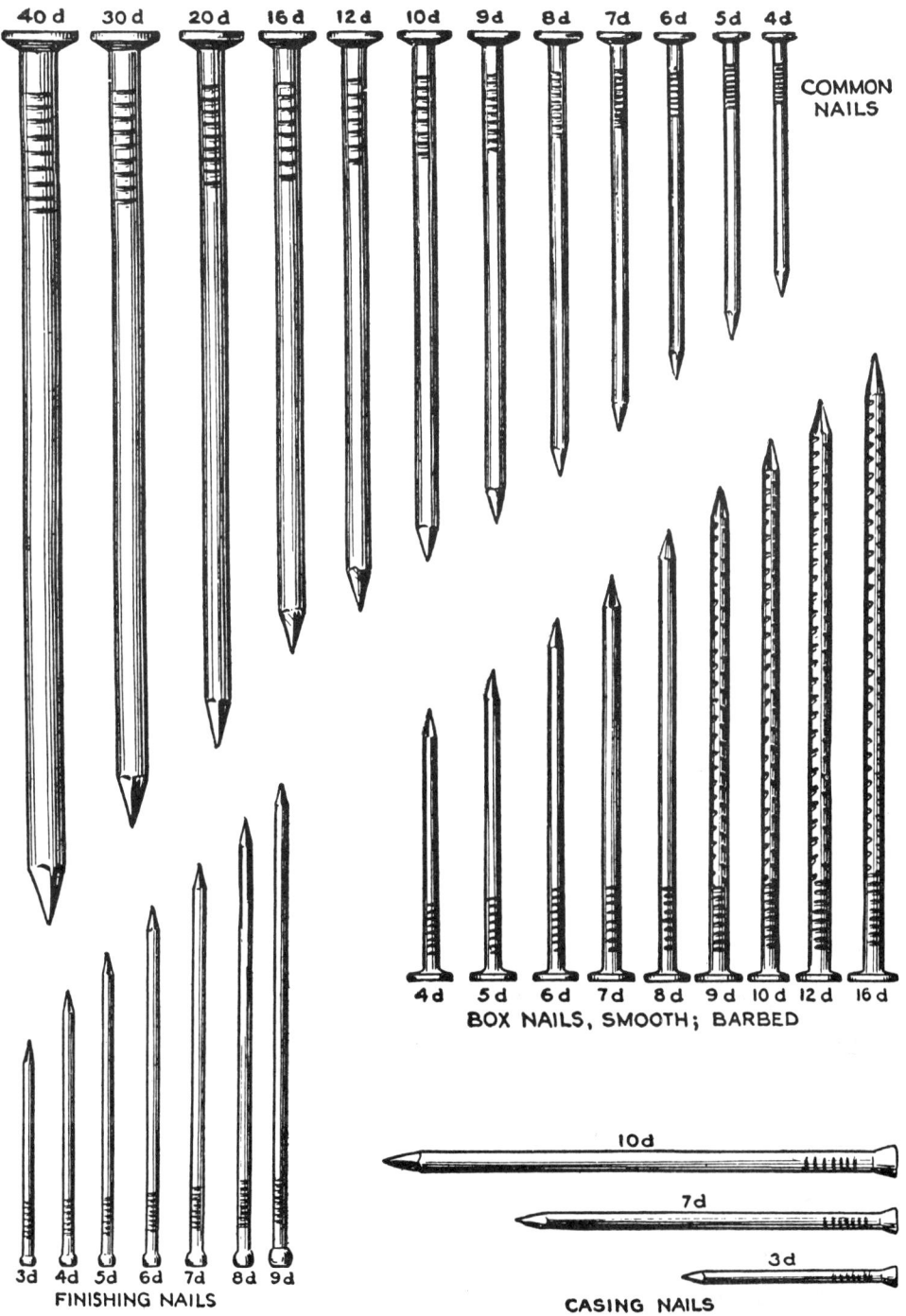

**36-5.** Common types of nails with which you should be acquainted.

## NAIL CHART

| Size | Length in Inches and Millimetres | American Steel Wire Gage Number | | |
|------|-----------------------------------|----------|-----------------|-----------|
| | | Common | Box and Casing | Finishing |
| 2d | 1 (25) | 15* | 15½ | 16½ |
| 3d | 1¼ (32) | 14 | 14½ | 15½ |
| 4d | 1½ (38) | 12½ | 14 | 15 |
| 5d | 1¾ (44) | 12½ | 14 | 15 |
| 6d | 2 (50) | 11½ | 12½ | 13 |
| 7d | 2¼ (56) | 11½ | 12½ | 13 |
| 8d | 2½ (64) | 10¼ | 11½ | 12½ |
| 9d | 2¾ (70) | 10¼ | 11½ | 12½ |
| 10d | 3 (75) | 9 | 10½ | 11½ |
| 12d | 3¼ (82) | 9 | 10½ | 11½ |
| 16d | 3½ (88) | 8 | 10 | 11 |
| 20d | 4 (101) | 6 | 9 | 10 |
| 30d | 4½ (114) | 5 | 9 | |
| 40d | 5 (127) | 4 | 8 | |

\*Note: The decimal equivalent of common gage numbers is:

| | | | | | |
|---|---|---|---|---|---|
| 15 = .072 | 13 = .092 | 11 = .121 | 9 = .148 | 7 = .177 | 5 = .207 |
| 14 = .080 | 12 = .106 | 10 = .135 | 8 = .162 | 6 = .192 | 4 = .225 |

**36-6.** A chart showing the comparative sizes of nails. Note, for example, that a 2d common nail is larger in diameter than a 2d finishing nail.

For any nailing to be done, hold the nail in one hand between thumb and forefinger and close to the point. To start the nail, grasp the hammer with the other hand near the hammer head. Figure 36-10. To hammer, hold the handle near its end. Use wrist as well as elbow and arm movement, depending on the size of the nail being driven. Tap the head of the nail with the hammer to get it started. Figure 36-11. Then remove your fingers from the nail as you continue to strike it with firm, even blows.

Watch the head of the nail and not the hammer. Try to drive the nail with a few well-placed blows rather than with many quick taps. If a nail begins to bend, it is better to remove it and start over with a new one.

When nailing two pieces together, choose the location for the nails wisely. Do not put several nails along the same grain as this will split the wood. A few well-placed nails in a staggered pattern will do a better job of holding than a larger number placed carelessly.

**36-7.** This chest is decorated with brass, using escutcheon nails to hold the metal in place.

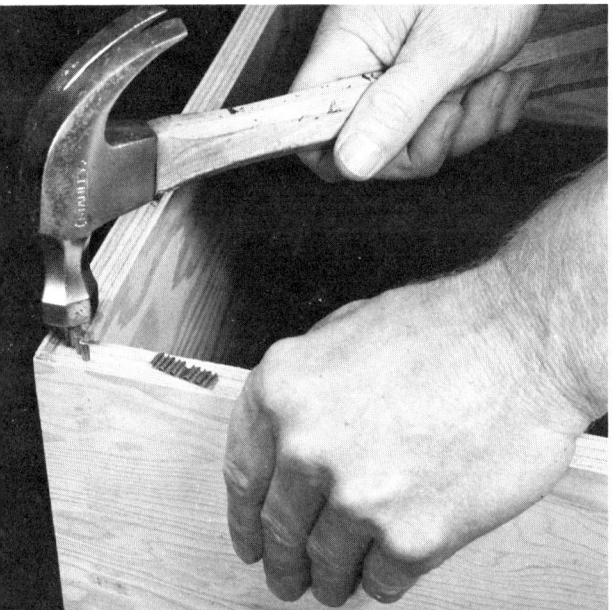

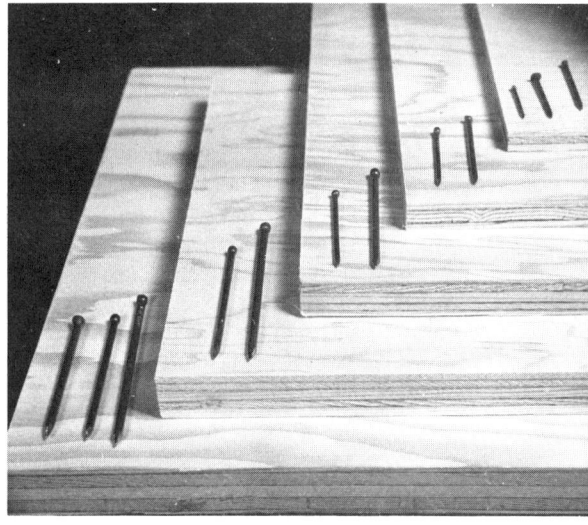

**36-9b.** Nail size is determined primarily by the thickness of the plywood used. Used with glue, all nails shown here will produce strong joints. The different nail sizes should be used as follows: ¾-inch (19 mm) plywood—6d finishing nails or 6d casing nails; ⅝-inch (16 mm) plywood—6d or 8d finishing nails; ½-inch (12.5 mm) plywood—4d or 6d finishing nails; ⅜-inch (9.5 mm) plywood—3d or 4d finishing nails; ¼-inch (6.5 mm) plywood—¾-inch (19 mm) or 1-inch (25.5 mm) brads, 3d finishing nails, or (for backs where there is no objection to heads showing) 1-inch (25.5 mm) blue lath nails. Substitute casing for finishing nails whenever you want a heavier nail.

**36-8.** Corrugated fasteners or "wiggle" nails are used in place of standard nails—for repair work and box-and-frame construction.

If you are using casing or finishing nails, do not drive the heads completely down to the surface. Complete the driving with a nail set. Hold the nail set in your left hand with the middle finger against the surface of the work and the

**36-9a.** Special nails: A. Common nails with annular or spiral threads—these nails are almost six times as strong for fastening as ordinary smooth-shank nails; B. Masonry nail of hardened steel which can be driven into concrete; C. Roofing nails; D. Flooring nail.

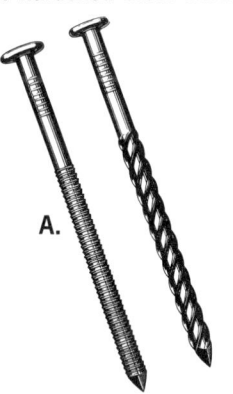
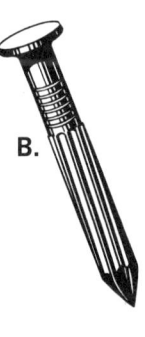
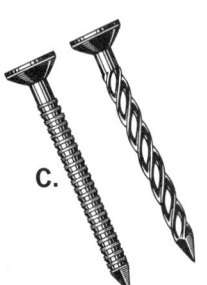
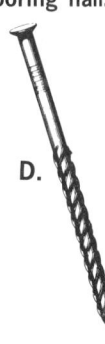

A.

B.

C.

D.

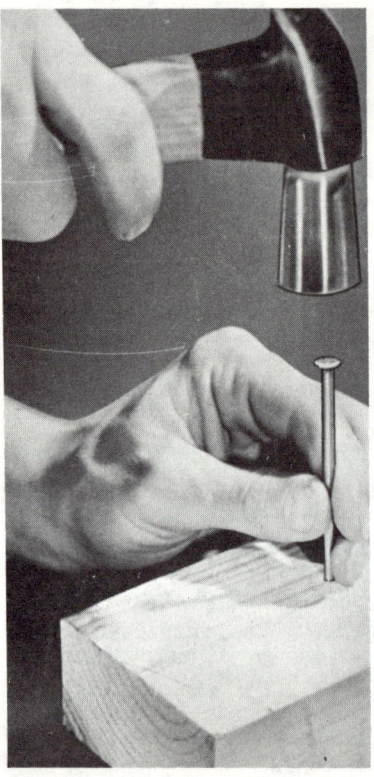

**36-10.** Starting a nail. The nail is held between the thumb and forefinger and the hammer grasped close to the head.

**36-11.** Use wrist movement for driving small nails, and elbow movement as well for driving large nails.

**36-12.** Using a nail set. The nail set is held between the thumb and forefinger and guided by the other fingers. This helps keep it from slipping off the nail head and marring the wood surface.

side of the nail. Then drive the nail in until it is about $\frac{1}{16}$ inch (1.5 mm) below the surface. Figure 36-12. To finish the job, the small hole can be covered with a wood filler.

If you are nailing *hardwood,* special steps must be taken. In the wood, drive holes that are slightly smaller than the diameter of the nail. Apply a little wax to the surface of the nail and drive it in.

Sometimes you will need to use nails that are longer than the total thickness of both pieces to be nailed together. In this case, the points of the nails should be driven completely through the pieces and then bent or clinched. Bend the nails over *with the grain* so they can be flattened easily. Figure 36-13.

Sometimes it will be necessary to nail the end of one piece of wood to the side of another. The nails are then driven into the wood at an angle from both sides. This is called "toenailing." Figure 36-14.

## REMOVING NAILS

Force the claw of the hammer under the head of the nail and pull on the handle. When the nail is drawn part way out, slip a piece of scrap wood under the hammer head before continuing to draw out the nail. Figure 36-15. This is a good way to protect the wood.

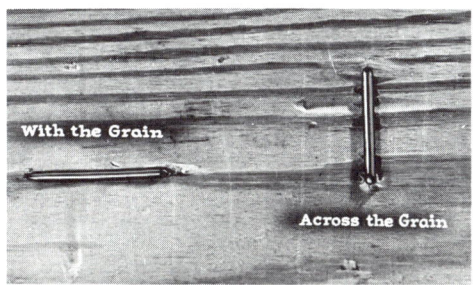

**36-13.** Clinching a nail. It is better to clinch a nail with the grain than across. The nail will sink into the wood more easily since it does not have to break the fibers.

**36-15.** Removing a nail. A piece of scrap wood is placed under the hammer head to provide leverage for drawing it out and to save the surface.

**36-14.** Toenailing. When it is necessary to nail the end of one piece to the side of another piece, the pieces should be toenailed together by driving the nails in at an angle on each side.

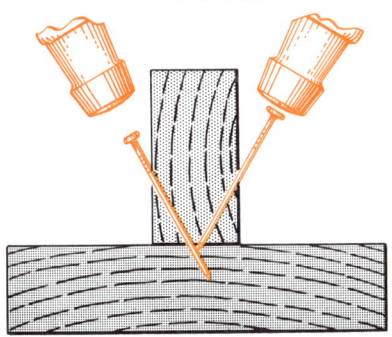

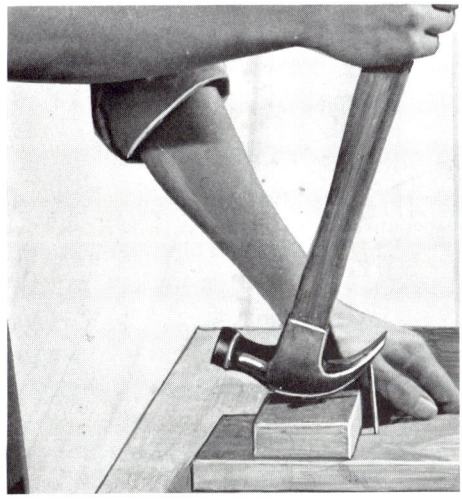

## CAN YOU ANSWER THESE QUESTIONS ON ASSEMBLING STOCK WITH NAILS?

1. Name the parts of a claw hammer.
2. Explain how to use a nail set.
3. Name and describe the four most common kinds of nails.
4. What does the word "penny" mean?
5. How large is a 7d finishing nail?
6. What are the larger sizes of common nails called?
7. How is a brad different from a finishing nail?
8. Tell how you would start a nail.
9. When you use a hammer, would you watch the head of the hammer or the nail?
10. How are finishing and casing nails set?
11. Hardwood is very difficult to nail. What would you do to overcome the difficulty?
12. Tell how to clinch a nail. Is this done with or across the grain?
13. Explain what toenailing is.

## Section VIII UNIT 37.

# ASSEMBLING WITH SCREWS

**Screws take more** time to assemble than nails, but they make a stronger bond. Also, the project can be taken apart. If screws are installed correctly, a few will do the work of several nails yet will hold much better. Figure 37-1.

### SCREWDRIVERS

There are three common types of screwdrivers. The *plain screwdriver* is used to install slotted-head screws. The size depends on the length and diameter of the blades. Figure 37-2. Make sure that the tip of the screwdriver is about the same width as the diameter of the screw head. If it is wider, it may mar the surface of the wood as it is set in place. Figure 37-3. The Phillips-head screwdriver is made for driving screws with recessed heads. Figure 37-4. The spiral-type screwdriver is usually sold in a set with three sizes of screwdriver bits and a No. 2 Phillips screwdriver bit. Figure 37-5.

*Offset screwdrivers* are used to install or remove screws located in tight places where a standard screwdriver can't be used. They are available for slotted or Phillips-head screws. Figure 37-6.

Notice in Figure 37-7 the proper method of grinding a screwdriver. This is very important. If a screwdriver is ground to a sharp edge, it tends to slip out of the slot. This would mar the surface of the wood or injure the head of the screw. A screw that has been set with a poor screwdriver usually has a ragged slot.

Screwdrivers are abused even by people who should know better. Here are some hints for using them:

● Select a screwdriver of length and tip fitted to the work. The tip should fit the slot snuggly and not be wider than the screw head.

● Use the longest screwdriver convenient for the work. More power can be applied to a long screwdriver than to a short one with less danger of it slipping out of the screw slot.

● Hold the handle firmly in the palm of the right hand with thumb and forefinger grasping the handle near the fer-

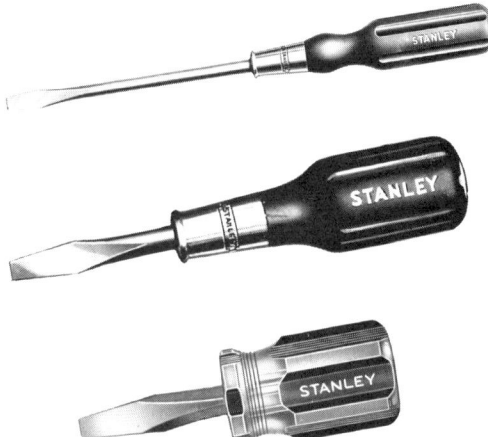

**37-2a.** Plain screwdrivers. Screwdrivers are available with blades in lengths from 1½ to 12 inches (38 to 305 mm) and in diameters from $\frac{7}{32}$ to $\frac{3}{8}$ inch (6 to 9.5 mm). The short type is called a stubby screwdriver.

**37-1.** Screws were used in assembling this bookcase. The holes for the screws were recessed and fancy wood plugs used to cover the heads.

**37-2b.** Parts of a screwdriver.

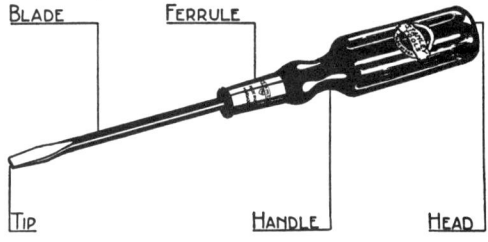

BLADE    FERRULE

TIP    HANDLE    HEAD

**37-3.** Selecting the proper size of screwdriver. Note the following: A. The screwdriver is too narrow with the result that it causes a burr on the head; B. The screwdriver is the correct width; C. The screwdriver is too wide. It would mar the wood surface.

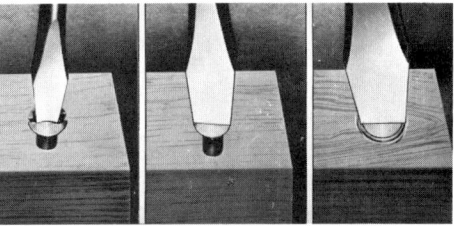

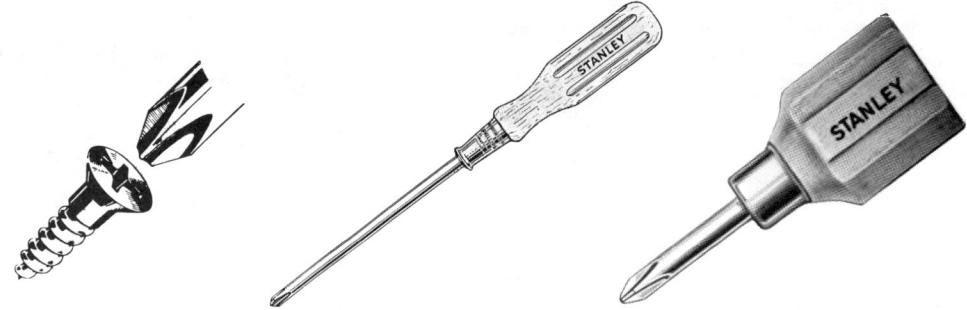

**37-4.** Phillips-head screwdriver. This is available in sizes from 1 to 4. Size number 1 is used for screws number 4 or smaller, number 2 for screws from 5 to 9 inclusive, number 3 for screws from 10 to 16 inclusive, and number 4 for screws number 18 or larger.

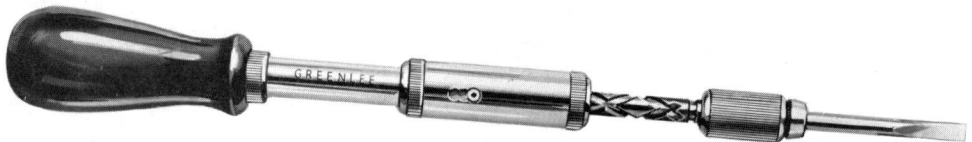

**37-5.** The spiral ratchet screwdriver is excellent for quick installation of screws.

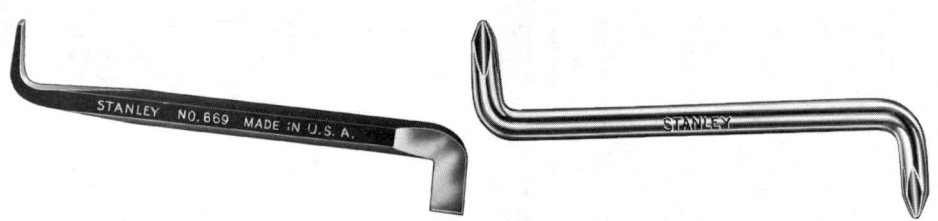

**37-6.** Offset screwdrivers.

**37-7a.** If the tip is rounded or beveled, the driver will raise out of the slot, spoiling the screw head. Regrind or file the screwdriver tip to make it as shown above on right.

**37-7b.** If the tip is too wide, it will scar the wood around the screw head. If the screwdriver is not held in line with the screw, it will slip out of the slot and mar both the screw and the work. The driver and screw should fit as shown on right.

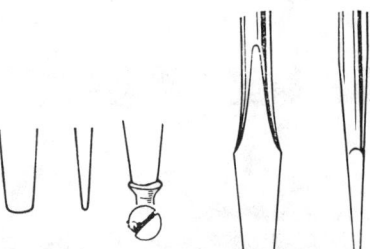
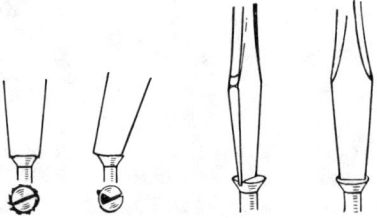

rule. Use the left hand to steady the tip and keep it pressed into the slot, while the grip of the right hand is on the handle for further turning.

• When driving brass screws into hardwood, use the same size steel screw to complete pilot holes. This reduces damage and the risk of shearing the head off brass screws.

• If a screw tends to bind, back off and enlarge the pilot hole or rub soap on the screw head.

• Heating the top of a screw head with a soldering iron will make it easier to screw out after it cools.

### SCREWS

There are several things you should know about the size and kind of screw to use. These are: the kind of head, the diameter or gage size, the length, the kind of metal, and the finish. As you see in Figure 37-8, screws are roundhead, flathead, ovalhead, and drive screw. Of course they come with either a slotted head or a Phillips head, and are almost any length from ¼ to 6 inches (6.5 to 152.5 mm). Figure 37-9. Most screws are made of mild steel, although it is possible to buy them in brass or aluminum. These

last two are used primarily for boat construction or wherever moisture would rust the other kind. Most flathead screws have a bright finish. Roundhead screws are usually finished in a dull blue. Sheet-metal screws are ideal for fastening thin metal to wood such as attaching metal legs to a plywood top. The sheet-metal screw has excellent holding power because, unlike wood screws, the threaded shank is the same diameter through its length. Figure 37-10.

Wood screw sizes are indicated by the American Screw Wire Gage with numbers from 0 to 24. The smallest number is 0, which has a diameter of .060. The diameter of each succeeding number is .013 larger. For example, a number 5 screw

**37-9.** The difference between slotted head (left) and recessed Phillips-head (right) screws.

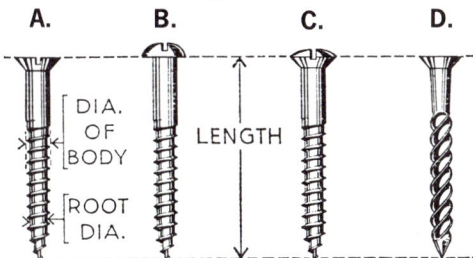

**37-8.** The four kinds of screws: A. Flathead; B. Roundhead; C. Ovalhead; D. Drive screw. The portion of each style screw included in the length measurement is shown in the diagram.

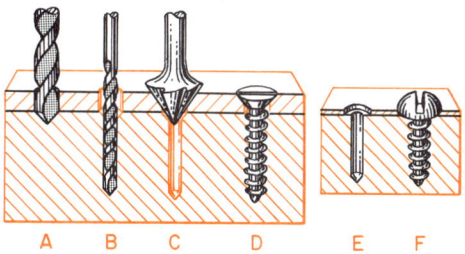

**37-10.** Installing a flathead sheet-metal screw: A. Drilling the clearance hole; B. Drilling the pilot or anchor hole; C. Countersinking; D. Screw installed; E. Hole for roundhead sheetmetal screw; F. Screw installed.

is .125 (.060 + .013 × 5), or ⅛ inch (3.5 mm) in diameter. A number 11 screw would be .203, or ¹³⁄₆₄ inch (5.5 mm) in diameter. You will notice that the shank clearance hole is always about this diameter. Figure 37-11.

Two screws can be the same length but have a different gage size. Figure

## BORING CHART FOR WOOD SCREWS
### Customary and Metric Sizes

| No. of Screw | Max. Head Dia. Inch | SHANK DIAMETER* | | | ROOT DIAMETER** | | | Thread per Inch | No. of Screw |
|---|---|---|---|---|---|---|---|---|---|
| | | Basic Dec. Size Inch | Nearest Drill Equivalent Inch | mm | Average Dec. Size Inch | Nearest Drill Equivalent Inch | mm | | |
| 0 | .119 | .060 | ¹⁄₁₆ | 1.5 | .040 | ³⁄₆₄ | 1.0 | 32 | 0 |
| 1 | .146 | .073 | ⁵⁄₆₄ | 2.0 | .046 | ³⁄₆₄ | 1.0 | 28 | 1 |
| 2 | .172 | .086 | ³⁄₃₂ | 2.5 | .054 | ¹⁄₁₆ | 1.5 | 26 | 2 |
| 3 | .199 | .099 | ⁷⁄₆₄ | 3.0 | .065 | ¹⁄₁₆ | 1.5 | 24 | 3 |
| 4 | .225 | .112 | ⁷⁄₆₄ | 3.0 | .075 | ⁵⁄₆₄ | 2.0 | 22 | 4 |
| 5 | .252 | .125 | ⅛ | 3.5 | .085 | ⁵⁄₆₄ | 2.0 | 20 | 5 |
| 6 | .279 | .138 | ⁹⁄₆₄ | 3.5 | .094 | ³⁄₃₂ | 2.5 | 18 | 6 |
| 7 | .305 | .151 | ⁵⁄₃₂ | 4.0 | .102 | ⁷⁄₆₄ | 2.5 | 16 | 7 |
| 8 | .332 | .164 | ⁵⁄₃₂ | 4.0 | .112 | ⁷⁄₆₄ | 2.5 | 15 | 8 |
| 9 | .358 | .177 | ¹¹⁄₆₄ | 4.5 | .122 | ⅛ | 3.0 | 14 | 9 |
| 10 | .385 | .190 | ³⁄₁₆ | 5.0 | .130 | ⅛ | 3.0 | 13 | 10 |
| 11 | .411 | .203 | ¹³⁄₆₄ | 5.5 | .139 | ⁹⁄₆₄ | 3.5 | 12 | 11 |
| 12 | .438 | .216 | ⁷⁄₃₂ | 5.5 | .148 | ⁹⁄₆₄ | 3.5 | 11 | 12 |
| 14 | .491 | .242 | ¼ | 6.5 | .165 | ⁵⁄₃₂ | 4.0 | 10 | 14 |
| 16 | .544 | .268 | ¹⁷⁄₆₄ | 7.0 | .184 | ³⁄₁₆ | 4.5 | 9 | 16 |
| 18 | .597 | .294 | ¹⁹⁄₆₄ | 7.5 | .204 | ¹³⁄₆₄ | 5.0 | 8 | 18 |
| 20 | .650 | .320 | ⁵⁄₁₆ | 8.0 | .223 | ⁷⁄₃₂ | 5.5 | 8 | 20 |
| 24 | .756 | .372 | ⅜ | 9.5 | .260 | ¼ | 6.0 | 7 | 24 |

*Shank clearance hole
**Pilot hole

**37-11.** Table showing the proper size bit or drill needed for the shank hole and the pilot hole for assembling stock with screws.

37-12. This means that they have different diameters. In most cases, the size of the screw is shown on the drawing. For example, No. 8 R.H. 1½ (38 mm) means that the screw is No. 8 gage size, roundhead, and 1½ inches (38 mm) long. If the size isn't shown, you should choose a screw that will go at least two-thirds of its length into the second piece. If the second piece is end grain, the screw should be even longer, since end grain does not hold well. Other screw devices are shown in Figure 37-13.

### DRILLING CLEARANCE HOLES

Select the kind and size of screw needed. Note in Figure 37-11 the two drill sizes required. The first one is for the shank clearance hole, drilled in the first piece. The second one is for the pilot hole, drilled in the second piece. Figure 37-14. The shank clearance hole should be the same size or slightly smaller than the shank of the screw. In this way the screw can be inserted in the first piece without forcing.

Drill the shank clearance hole in the first piece of stock. Then hold this piece

over the second and mark the location for the pilot hole with a scratch awl. If you are assembling softwood pieces, drill the pilot hole only about half the depth to which the screw will go. If you are drilling hardwood, make sure that it is drilled to the total depth of the screw.

### COUNTERSINKING FOR FLATHEAD SCREWS

Countersinking is a way of enlarging the top portion of a hole to a cone shape so that the head of a flathead screw will

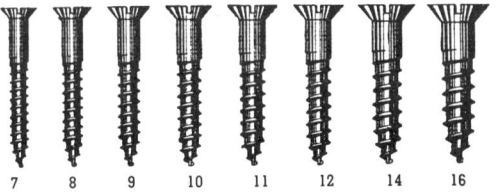

**37-12a.** Different gage sizes of 1¼-inch (32 mm) screws. Wood screws range in length from ¼ to 6 inches and in gage sizes from 0 to 24. Of course, each length is not made in all gages, as shown by the 1¼-inch (32 mm) screw.

**37-12b.** Flathead wood screws are useful when nails will not provide adequate holding power. Glue should also be used if possible. Sizes shown here are minimums; use longer screws when work permits. This list gives plywood thickness; length and diameter of the smallest screws recommended; and the size of hole to drill: ¾-inch (19 mm) plywood, 1½-inch (38 mm) No. 8 screw, ⁵⁄₃₂-inch (4 mm) hole; ⅝-inch (16 mm) plywood, 1¼-inch (32 mm) No. 8 screw, ⁵⁄₃₂-inch (4 mm) hole; ½-inch (12.5 mm) plywood, 1¼-inch (32 mm) No. 6 screw, ⁹⁄₆₄-inch (3 mm) hole; ⅜-inch (9.5 mm) plywood, 1-inch (25.5 mm) No. 6 screw, ⁹⁄₆₄-inch (3 mm) hole; ¼-inch (6.5 mm) plywood, ¾-inch (19 mm) No. 4 screw, ⁷⁄₆₄-inch (3 mm) hole.

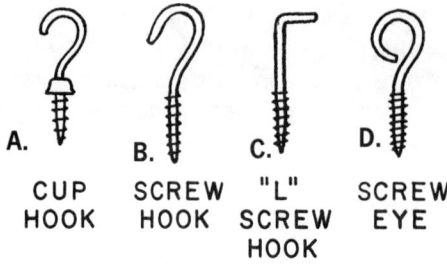

A. CUP HOOK  B. SCREW HOOK  C. "L" SCREW HOOK  D. SCREW EYE

**37-13.** Cup hooks (usually of brass) come in sizes from ½ to 1½ inches (13 to 38 mm). *Screw hooks* are made in lengths from 1¼ to 2½ inches (32 to 64 mm). "L" (square-bent) *screw hooks* come in lengths from 1 to 2¼ inches (25.5 to 57 mm). *Screw eyes* are made with either small or medium eyes in many sizes.

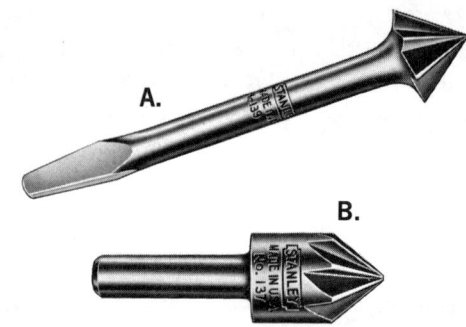

A.

B.

**37-15.** Two types of 82-degree counter-sinks: A. For use in a brace; B. For use in a drill press.

be flush with the surface of the wood. If flathead screws are installed, countersink the upper surface of the first piece to allow the head of the screw to be flush with the surface. Figure 37-15. Check the depth of the countersunk hole by turning the screw upside down and fitting it in the hole. Figure 37-16. A *screw-mate drill* and *countersink* can be used with flathead screws. Figure 37-17. A counterbore

will do all the operations performed by the screw-mate drill and countersink plus drill plug holes for wooden plugs. Figure 37-18.

**PLUGGING SCREW HOLES**

In most furniture construction screws are not supposed to show. Choose a drill or auger bit the same size as the head of the screw. Counterbore a hole in the first surface about ⅜ inch (9.5 mm)

**37-14.** Here the shank hole and pilot hole are properly drilled and the screw is installed.

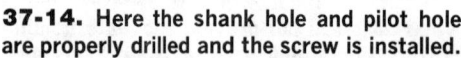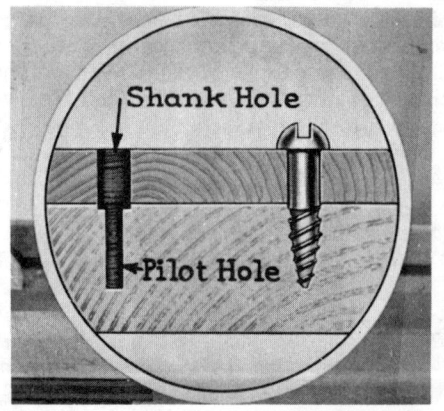

Shank Hole

Pilot Hole

**37-16.** Steps in installing a flathead screw: A. Drill the shank hole; B. Drill the pilot or anchor hole; C. Countersink; D. Check the amount of countersink with the screw head; E. Install the flathead screw.

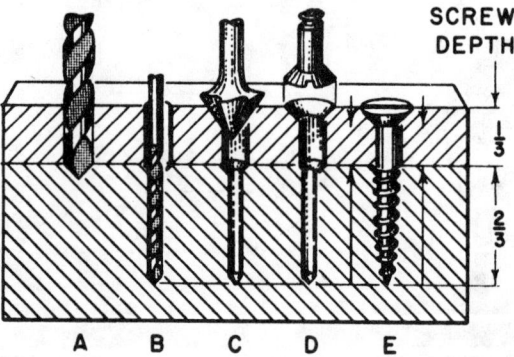

SCREW DEPTH

A B C D E

deep. The screw will then be below the surface of the wood. After the parts are assembled, this hole can be filled with plastic wood or surface putty. Figure 37-19. Or you can make a little screw plug with the tool shown in Figure 37-20. Furniture supply companies can supply fancy, decorated plugs. Figure 37-21.

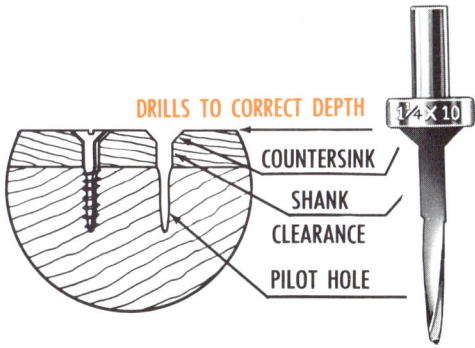

37-17. The screw-mate drill and countersink will do four things: (1) Drill to the correct depth; (2) Do the countersinking; (3) Make the correct shank clearance; and (4) Drill the correct pilot hole.

37-18. A screw-mate counterbore does five things at once, as shown in the illustration. A wood plug can be used to cover the screw head.

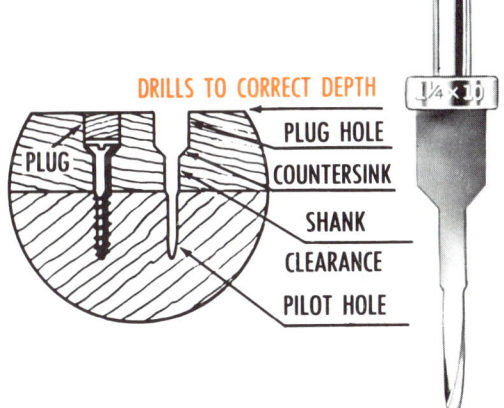

## DRIVING THE SCREW

To install a screw, hold the blade between your thumb and forefinger. Figure 37-22. Grasp the handle of the screwdriver in the palm of your hand. Let your thumb and forefinger point toward the shank. Start the screw and then move your left hand up just back of the point of the screwdriver. This will guide the tool and keep it from slipping off the head as the screw is set in place. Continue to turn the screw until it is firmly set, but don't strip the threads or shear off the screw from the wood. Be especially careful if the screws are small or made of brass. A screwdriver bit can be used in a brace for setting screws. Figure 37-23.

37-19. Apply filler so it is slightly higher than the plywood. Then sand level when dry.

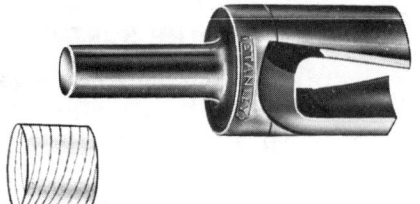

**37-20a.** A plug cutter. Available in different sizes for cutting wood plugs.

**37-20b.** If you do much furniture work where screws are countersunk or counterbored, it will pay to use a plug cutter. These tools permit cutting perfect plugs from the same stock of which the item is built. The plug cutters are made in sizes, 6, 8, 10, and 12 to match the commonly used screw sizes. The plugs are a snug fit in the counterbored holes.

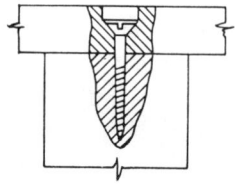

**37-21.** Three methods of covering the heads of screws: A. With plastic wood; B. With a plain wood plug; and C. With a fancy wood plug.

**37-20c.** Using a plug cutter. The plug should be cut from the same kind of wood that is used in the project.

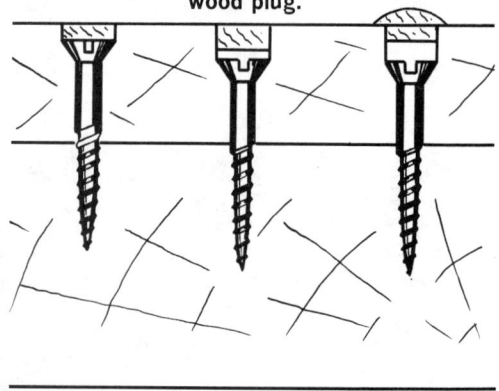

A.            B.            C.

**37-22a.** Starting a screw. Hold the screw and the tip of the screwdriver as shown.

**37-23a.** Screwdriver bits to use in a brace.

**37-22b.** After the screw is started, move your left hand back to support and guide the blade.

**37-23b.** Installing a wood screw with a bit and brace.

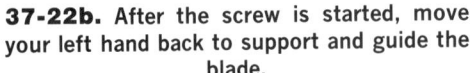

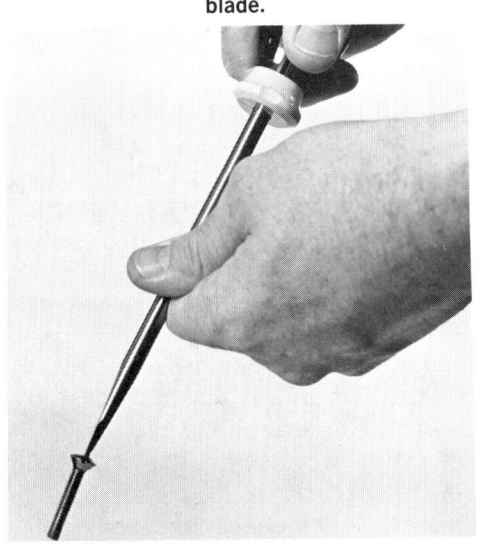

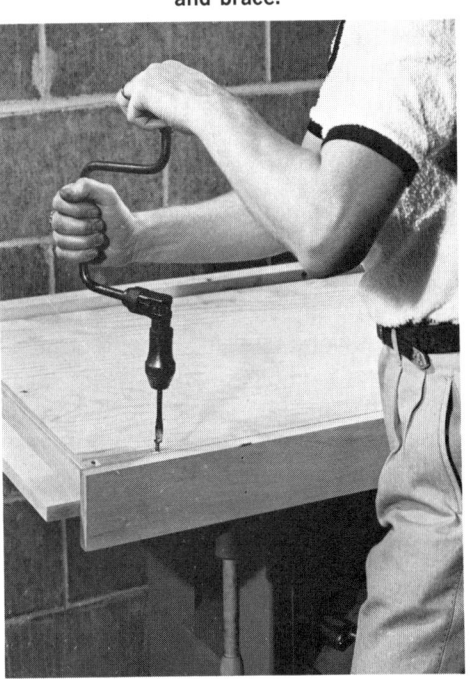

## CAN YOU ANSWER THESE QUESTIONS ON ASSEMBLING STOCK WITH SCREWS?

1. A screw has several advantages over a nail. Name them.
2. How do you know what size screwdriver to choose?
3. Describe the proper way of grinding a screwdriver.
4. What information must you have in order to secure the proper kind and size of screw for your work?
5. As the gage number increases, how is the diameter of the screw affected?
6. What is the general rule for selecting screw lengths?
7. Name two types of screws.
8. What is the shank clearance hole and what purpose does it serve?
9. Is the pilot hole drilled in softwood in the same way it is drilled in hardwood?
10. When is it necessary to countersink the hole?
11. How can you check the depth of the countersink hole?
12. What is the purpose of screw plugs?
13. Describe the proper method of holding a screwdriver when starting a screw.
14. Why is it important to set the screw with the correct size screwdriver?

## Section VIII
## UNIT 38.

# SCRAPING A SURFACE

**For a really** fine surface on open-grain wood such as oak, mahogany, and walnut, the wood can be scraped after the planing is done by using a hand or cabinet scraper. Figure 38-1. Scraping removes the small bumps left by the plane iron. Some woods, such as curly maple and cedar that can't be planed very well, can be scraped for a very smooth surface. It is very important that the hand scraper be sharp. See Unit 56. It is always necessary to sharpen the scraper before each use—and frequently during its use.

### USING A HAND SCRAPER
Clamp the stock firmly in a vise or on top of the bench. Using both hands, hold the hand scraper between the thumbs and forefingers, with the cutting edge toward the surface of the wood. Figure 38-2. Turn the blade at an angle of about 50 to 60 degrees to the wood surface. Apply firm pressure to the scraper blade and push or draw it across the surface. Be careful to keep the cutting edge flat against the wood so that the corners do not dig in or mar it. Always scrape with the grain. Sometimes the scraper is

turned a little and a shearing cut made across the surface. Experience will help you decide. If you are working on curly maple or other burly-type wood, keep changing the direction of the scraping action to match the grain direction.

## USING A CABINET SCRAPER

The cabinet scraper is simpler to use than the hand scraper. To adjust it, first loosen the adjusting thumbscrew and the clamp thumbscrews. Insert the blade from the bottom, with the bevel side towards the adjusting screw. Make sure the edge of the blade is even with the bottom. This can be done by standing the tool on a wood surface and pressing the blade lightly against the wood. Tighten the clamp thumbscrews. Bow the blade slightly by tightening the adjusting thumbscrew. Apply equal pressure with both hands as you push the scraper along the wood. Figure 38-3.

**38-1.** A. Hand scraper; B. Cabinet scraper.

**38-2.** Scraping a surface with a hand scraper. Note that the scraper is held in both hands and tipped at an angle to the wood surface.

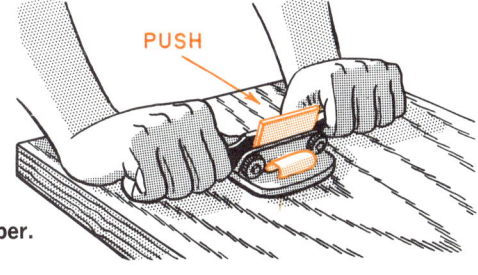

PUSH

**38-3.** Using a cabinet scraper.

SCRAPE WITH GRAIN

291

## CAN YOU ANSWER THESE QUESTIONS ON SCRAPING A SURFACE?

1. On what kinds of wood is scraping necessary to produce a smooth surface?
2. At what times should a scraper be sharpened?
3. The hand scraper is held at what angle to the surface of the wood?
4. How can you prevent the corners of the hand scraper from marring or digging into the wood?
5. Tell how the hand scraper should be used on burly woods.
6. Explain how to adjust a cabinet scraper.

# Section VIII
# UNIT 39.

# SANDING A SURFACE

**Sanding** is done to finish the wood surface, not to form or shape it. All planing, cutting, and forming should be completed before beginning to use sandpaper. Sanding is one of the last steps and should never be done in place of using cutting tools. Figure 39-1.

## KINDS OF SANDPAPER

There is really no such thing as "sand" paper, though the name is given to several types of abrasives. Abrasives are made in a wide range of grades from very coarse to very fine. They are produced by bonding (gluing) graded sizes of abrasive material to paper or cloth backing. The common types are the natural abrasives such as flint and garnet and the manufactured or man-made abrasives such as aluminum oxide and silicon carbide. Further identification follows:

● Flint, or quartz, which has a yellowish cast, is an inexpensive abrasive that is commonly used for the hand sanding of woods.

● Garnet, reddish brown in color, is harder, sharper, and better for most woods, especially hard woods. It is long lasting and fast cutting.

**39-1.** Sanding is an important step in completing any project.

• Aluminum oxide is a man-made abrasive that is either reddish brown or white in color. It is used for both hand and machine sanding.

• Silicon carbide is shiny black in color, almost diamond hard, and very sharp. It is used for sanding lacquers, shellac, and varnishes. It is also used for sanding between finishes and is made in wet or dry types.

Abrasive materials come in chunk form which must first be crushed into fine particles and sorted. These abrasive grains pass through screens of different sizes. For example, one screen may have

36 openings per inch, and the next screen may have 40 openings per inch. The grains that pass through the screen with 36 openings and not through the next are numbered 36. The higher the number, the smaller the grain and, therefore, the finer the sandpaper. Abrasive papers are sold in many forms including sheets, discs, and belts. Figure 39-2. The common material used in the wood shop is garnet paper, which comes in sheets measuring 9 x 11 inches (229 x 279 mm). The paper ranges from $2\frac{1}{2}$, which is very coarse, to 8/0, which is very fine. This is the old grit-size number system. The new system uses the mesh (symbol) number. For example, 30 is the same as $2\frac{1}{2}$. Figure 39-3.

**39-2.** Grades and types of sandpaper. Sheets of flint abrasive, 9 x 10 inches (229 x 254 mm), or sheets of garnet paper, 9 x 11 inches (229 x 279 mm), are often used for hand sanding. For the belt sander, narrow-roll abrasive or cloth or prepared belts can be selected. On disc sanders wide-roll abrasive cloth or paper is needed. For machine sanding, No. 1 abrasive paper or cloth is generally used. No. 0 abrasive paper and No. 3/0 abrasive cloth are used for smoothing woods.

## TEARING SANDPAPER

To make the sheet of sandpaper softer, draw it over the edge of the bench. A sheet measuring 9 x 11 inches (229 x 279 mm) is usually divided into four or six pieces. This depends on the work to be sanded and the size of the sanding block. To tear the sheet, fold it lengthwise with the abrasive surface toward the inside. Then hold one-half of the sheet over the bench and tear the paper along the folded line. You can also tear the piece by holding a straightedge or the cutting edge of a hacksaw blade over the folded line. Figure 39-4.

A sandpaper block is a good backing for most sanding. If the sheets are torn into six pieces, the block should be $1\frac{1}{2}$ inches (38 mm) thick, 3 inches (76 mm) wide, and 5 inches (127 mm) long.

A piece of foam rubber or felt can be glued to the base to give a better surface.

## SANDING A FLAT SURFACE

Fasten the piece between the vise dog and bench stop or hold it firmly against

| Coarseness | Flint (Common Sandpaper) | Garnet (Old Grit Numbers) | Garnet, Silicon Carbide and Aluminum Oxide (New Symbols Numbers) |
|---|---|---|---|
| Very Fine | Extra Fine | 8/0<br>7/0<br>6/0 | 280<br>240<br>220 |
| Fine | Fine | 5/0<br>4/0<br>3/0 | 180<br>150<br>120 |
| Medium | Medium | 2/0<br>0<br>½<br>1 | 100<br>80<br>50 |
| Coarse | Coarse | 1½<br>2 | 40<br>36 |
| Very Coarse | Extra Coarse | 2½ | 30 |

**39-3.** How common abrasives are graded.

**39-4.** Cutting standard sandpaper, 9 x 11 inches (229 x 279 mm), into smaller sizes can be done by tearing along a hacksaw blade nailed to a wood jig.

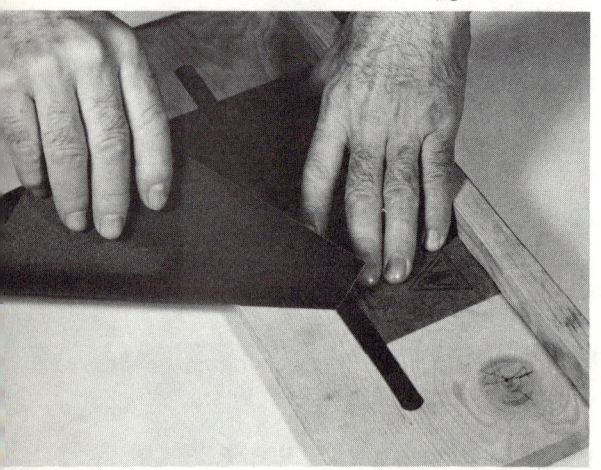

the surface of the bench. If the piece is held in the vise, grip the sanding block as shown in Figure 39-5. Apply even pressure to the block and sand the surface *with the grain* of the wood. Move the block back and forth and work slowly from one side to the other to get an even surface. Take special care to keep from sanding the edges too much.

After coarse paper has been used, substitute finer and finer grades. If the piece is held against the top of the bench, you can use the block with one hand. Figure 39-6.

### SANDING AN EDGE

Lock the work in a vise with the edge showing. Grasp the sanding block in both hands. Place your forefingers on each side of the edge to keep it square with the sides. Figure 39-7. It is just as important to sand an edge square as it is to plane it square. After the edge has been sanded, the arris (the sharp edge) should be rounded slightly by drawing the sandpaper over the edge.

### SANDING AN END

To sand an end, the same procedure as for sanding an edge is followed. However, the surface is sanded in only one direction rather than back and forth. This produces a smoother finish. Figure 39-8.

### SANDING CONVEX SURFACES

Convex surfaces can usually be sanded with a block in the same way as an edge is sanded. A convex surface such as a rounded end can be sanded more satisfactorily by holding the paper in your fingers or the palm of your hand. Figure 39-9.

**39-5.** Two kinds of sanding blocks. On the left is a commercial block with a foam-rubber base. The one on the right is homemade. It has a piece of leather tacked in place under the sandpaper.

**39-6.** Sanding a surface. The sanding block, held firmly against the surface, is moved back and forth.

**39-7.** Sanding an edge. The sanding block is grasped in both hands with the thumbs on top and the fingers curled underneath. This will keep the block square with the surface. If this is not done, there is danger of rounding the edge.

**39-8.** Sanding end grain. Sand in *one direction.* Notice the guide boards clamped over the end to keep the sanding square with the face surface.

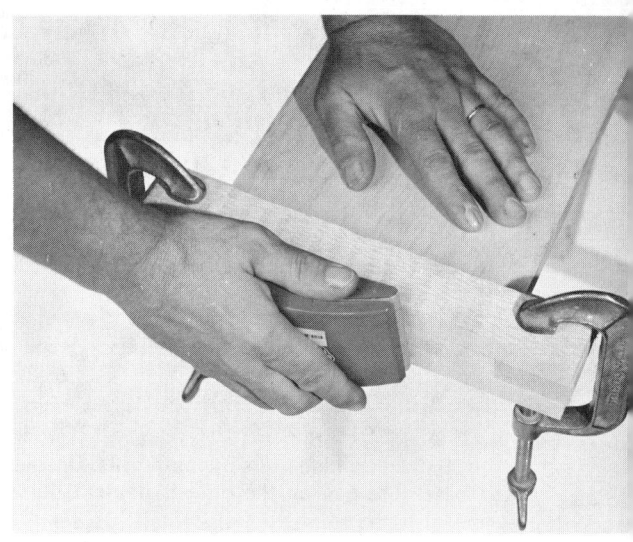

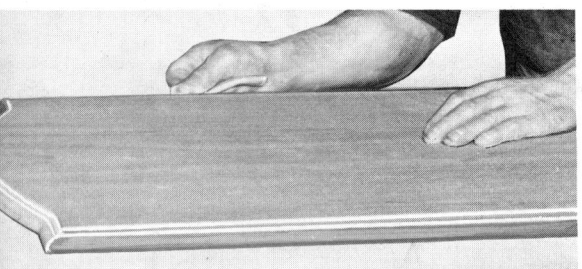

**39-9.** When sanding a molding by hand, the sandpaper is held in the fingers and guided along the edge.

**39-10.** Sanding a concave surface. Here the sandpaper is wrapped around a half-round file so that it will conform to the general curve of the surface.

**39-11.** Sanding a round spool with a piece of sandpaper.

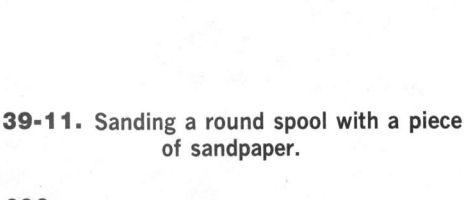

## SANDING CONCAVE OR OTHER INSIDE SURFACES

These surfaces are most easily sanded by wrapping the paper around a stick such as part of a broomstick or the handle of a tool. The half-round surface of a file also makes a good backing. Figure 39-10.

## SANDING CURVED SURFACES

Certain round pieces such as turned parts will require cross-grained sanding. Figure 39-11. It is usually best to use a fine abrasive material for this kind of work. One method of sanding is to pull the material back and forth in a "shoeshine fashion." Straight turned parts can be sanded with the grain.

## SANDING SMALL PIECES

The best method for sanding small pieces of wood is first to fasten a full

sheet of abrasive paper to a jig board. This can then be clamped to the top of the bench. Then hold the small pieces on the abrasive paper and move them back and forth. Figure 39-12.

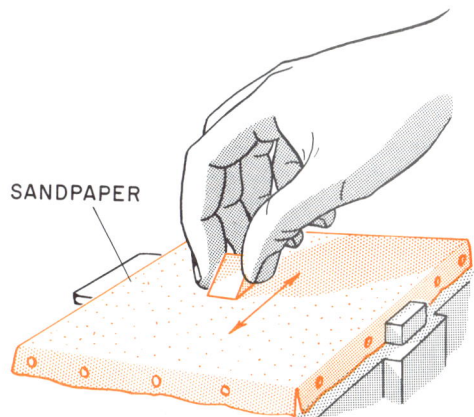

SANDPAPER

**39-12.** Sanding small pieces of a project.

### CAN YOU ANSWER THESE QUESTIONS ON SANDING A SURFACE?

1. Is sanding done for the purpose of forming or shaping wood?
2. At what point in building the project should the sanding be done?
3. Is there any sand on sandpaper? What are the abrasives used in sandpaper?
4. Which sandpaper is best for hardwood? For softwood?
5. How is sandpaper usually sold?
6. What number would you ask for when buying very coarse sandpaper? Very fine sandpaper?
7. What grades of sandpaper are commonly found in use in school shops?
8. How would you soften a sheet of sandpaper before using it? How would you tear it into smaller pieces?
9. How is a sanding block useful?
10. Is it correct to sand across grain? Why?
11. There is a very common error often made in sanding a flat surface. What is it?
12. How can you keep the edge square when sanding?
13. Describe how you would sand a convex surface.
14. How would you sand a concave surface?
15. When is the "shoeshine" method used?

# FITTING, ASSEMBLING, AND GLUING UP THE PARTS

**You are now ready** to assemble your project. How difficult this is, of course, depends on the kind of project and its size. For a small project such as a shelf, the problem of assembly is fairly simple. Figure 40-1. For an end table, bookcase, or a desk with drawers, assembly is much more complicated. Figure 40-2. However, certain things must be done regardless of the size of the project.

## COLLECTING THE PARTS

Get together all the parts that are to go into the finished project. If you were careful when you made them, your identification marks will still show. You will know how each part, joint, and piece fits to the next. This is very important. You

**40-1.** A small project such as this shelf is easy to assemble since it can be done in one operation.

will find yourself in a very unhappy position if, when you begin to glue, the joints don't fit or the parts don't match. This can easily happen unless you are careful.

## CHECKING ALL THE PARTS TO SEE THAT THEY ARE FINISHED

To be considered completed, the parts should be scraped and sanded. If there are duplicate parts, rails, or legs, check each one of them to make sure that they are all exactly the same in size and shape. If the project has joints, try each joint to see that it fits properly. Figure 40-3. Check whether it is clearly marked in a place that can be seen after glue is applied and after the joint is assembled. This checking is especially important. You will usually find some small correction to make before you can go ahead with the assembling. Parts that have been stored for some time may have swelled slightly; therefore the joints may not fit just right.

Your plan of procedure or the drawing shows whether the project is to be assembled with glue, screws, or nails. If screws or nails are used, carefully check to see that you have the correct type and number to complete your job. You should have a couple of extra screws or several more nails than necessary as you may spoil a few. If glue is to be used, decide whether it is to be animal glue, casein, or plastic resin glue. Be sure that you have enough glue ready to apply.

## MAKING PROTECTIVE PIECES

Before attempting to clamp the pieces together, cut some softwood pieces to place between the clamps and the project. Figure 40-4. It is a good idea to plane the surface of the pieces. These protective pieces are not needed if you use hand screws. It may be necessary to cut special shapes if the project is not square—for example, if you are clamping a table with legs that taper outward. Of course, you will know when this is necessary. Figure 40-5.

## ASSEMBLING THE PROJECT TEMPORARILY

Now use cabinet clamps and hand screws to clamp all parts together temporarily. This will give you an idea of how your pieces fit together and also you can see if any small corrections need to be made. Your problem is simple if you are assembling a project such as a bookcase or a hanging wall shelf made with parallel sides and crosspieces with dado or rabbet joints. All you need are flat pieces of scrap stock, cabinet clamps that fit

**40-2.** Assembling an end table, bookcase, or desk with drawers will require careful planning and must be done in several steps.

**40-3.** Checking the joints of this drawer construction to make sure that everything fits properly before gluing.

**40-4.** Using scrap pieces of wood to protect the surface during gluing.

across the project both on the front and back, and a pair of clamps for each shelf. Such projects as end tables, stools, and small desks usually have legs and rails with corners made with mortise-and-tenon joints or dowel joints. In either case, you will need clamps to go across the ends and cabinet clamps to go across the sides.

After the project is assembled with clamps, check with a square to make sure that the project is squared up. Figure 40-6. Also use a steel tape or rule to take measurements across the corners and up and down to see that the sides and ends are parallel and that the project is the same height throughout. Figure 40-7. By shifting a clamp or tapping a side or leg with a mallet, you can bring it into place.

This trial assembly will give you a chance to adjust all clamps to the correct width and get you ready for the final assembly.

**40-5a.** The legs and rails of this pine doughbox table will require special care in clamping since they are not square.

## ASSEMBLING WITH NAILS AND SCREWS

Follow the directions given in the unit on assembling stock with nails and screws. Figure 40-8.

## ASSEMBLING WITH GLUE

It is helpful if a special glue bench or gluing room is available. If not, place wrapping paper over the bench or floor where the gluing is to be done. If the project is to be glued, carefully remove the clamps from top to bottom. Lay the clamps on the bench in definite order so that you can pick them up easily. Place the scrap pieces of wood next to the clamps so that everything will be on hand as needed.

**40-7.** Checking the project for levelness.

**40-5b.** When clamping awkward angles, make protective blocks to fit.

**40-6.** Checking the project for squareness.

**40-8.** Assembling a desk with wood screws.

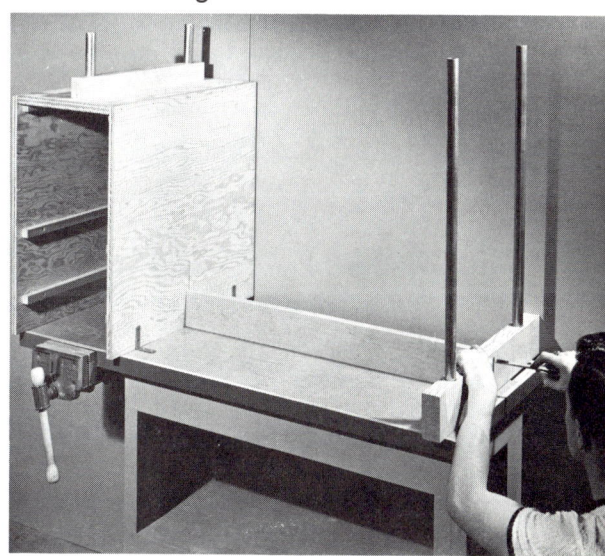

301

If the project can be assembled all at one time, such as a book shelf or hanging shelf, go ahead and do it that way. If the project is a desk, table, or stool, you may assemble and glue the end section one day and then assemble the rest later.

In addition to your project parts, clamps, scrap pieces, and glue, have a *rubber mallet* ready, a *rule* or tape measure, and a *square*. If *hot animal glue* is used, heat the wood parts before assembling. Work very rapidly, as the glue sets quickly. If *cold liquid glue* is used, you do not need to work quite so fast.

With a brush, bottle, stick, or glue gun, carefully apply the glue to both parts of

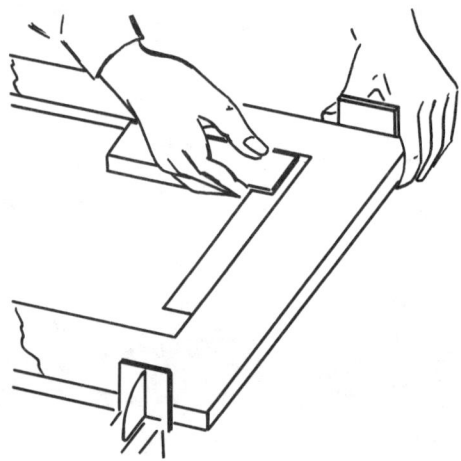

**40-10a.** Checking the assembly with a square.

**40-9a.** Applying glue to a project before clamping it.

**40-9b.** Applying glue to chair rungs with an electric glue gun.

**40-10b.** Checking across corners to make sure the measurement is equal in both directions.

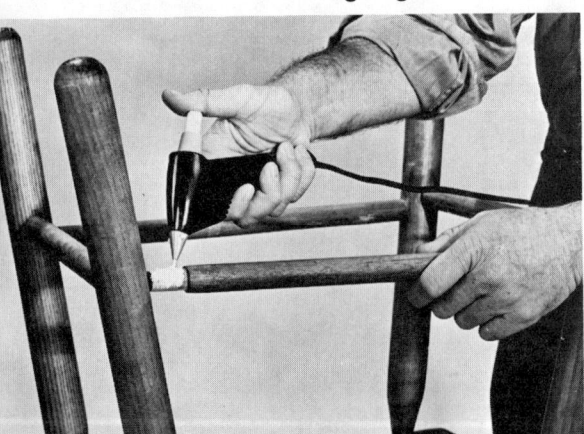

the joint. Figure 40-9. Do not use too much glue, since any excess is just a problem to remove later. Animal glue, especially, tends to dribble. As quickly as possible, fasten the joints.

Place the scrap pieces over the proper places and lightly screw up the clamps. Do this until all the clamps are in place. Then turn up all clamps, each a little at a time. Check often to see that the project is squared and that it measures the same distance wherever there are paral-

lels. Figure 40-10. You may need to use the rubber mallet to tap a joint in place or to change the position of a clamp.

As soon as the project is all clamped together, remove any excess glue with an old chisel or glue scraper. *Be careful not to mar the surface of the project.* Then put the project in a safe place where no one will bump it. Allow most work from twelve to twenty-four hours to dry. Carefully remove each of the clamps and the scrap pieces.

## CAN YOU ANSWER THESE QUESTIONS ON FITTING, ASSEMBLING, AND GLUING UP THE PARTS?

1. Why should identification marks be kept on all pieces before they are assembled?
2. What things must be completed before a part of a project can be considered ready for assembly?
3. Should joints be checked again just before assembly? Why?
4. What should be a guide for determining how a project should be assembled?
5. Name the three things commonly used for fastening parts together permanently.
6. Why are protective wood pieces unnecessary when hand screws are chosen for assembly?
7. Name several projects which would require specially shaped protective pieces.
8. Why is it necessary to make a trial assembly first?
9. Would you always assemble a project completely in one operation?
10. Describe the checks that should be made when the project is temporarily assembled.
11. How much glue would you apply?
12. How would you tap the parts into place and what kind of mallet should be used? How should excess glue be removed?
13. How long should a project be allowed to dry?

# PREPARING THE PROJECT FOR FINISHING

**After the project** is assembled, it is very important to go over it carefully to get it ready for finishing. This is an important step and one that is frequently neglected. Figure 41-1. As a result, a poor finish is attained.

## REMOVING EXCESS GLUE

First of all, remove all excess glue from around the joints and anywhere else you see it. Use a good, sharp chisel. On flat areas, the glue may be removed with a hand scraper. Be especially careful not to gouge the wood or cut off a sliver of stock. This can easily happen when removing glue around a mortise-and-tenon joint, for example. Carefully separate the glue from the wood surface. Figure 41-2. Make sure that every fleck of glue has been completely removed, as glue will not take stain.

If casein glue has been used, it may be necessary to apply a bleach to all glue spots. One bad thing about certain kinds of casein glue is that they darken the wood, especially open, porous types. There is one type of casein glue on the market that will not do this. However, if you think it necessary, bleach out these glue spots before staining. This can be done by mixing oxalic acid crystals in very hot water; then brush the solution on the areas and let them dry. These spots can then be sanded out. Commercial bleaching solutions are also very good.

## CHECKING HOLES AND CRACKS

Go over the entire project carefully to see if there are any holes, cracks, or

**41-1.** Whether the table you build is Modern or Early American, much of its beauty will be in the fine finish.

dents that need filling. There are several types of fillers that can be chosen. Plastic wood comes in neutral, mahogany, walnut, oak, and other colors. Figure 41-3. You can also purchase stick shellac in various colors. Figure 41-4. If necessary, you can make your own filler by mixing equal parts of wood sanding dust and powdered glue. Add water to make a paste. Wood dough, a synthetic wood, can also be used for filling holes and cracks. Knots should be filled, sanded, and then covered with knot sealer such as white shellac. If the project is to be painted, filling can be done with putty. Figure 41-5. A shallow dent in the wood can sometimes be raised by applying a moist cloth and then covering it with a warm iron. Figure 41-6. Make sure that the iron is not so hot that it burns the surface. Also keep the iron moving so that the wood isn't scorched.

## SCRAPING AND SANDING THE PROJECT

After all irregularities and holes have been filled, go carefully over the entire

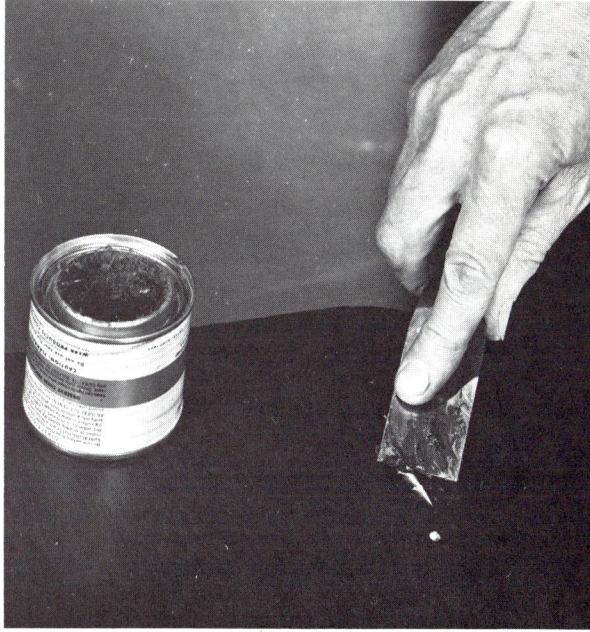

**41-3.** Filling a crack with plastic wood. A natural shade can be tinted with colors in oil. Remember that plastic wood shrinks when it dries, so fill the hole above the level of the wood.

**41-4.** Filling a crack with stick shellac, using a warm putty knife.

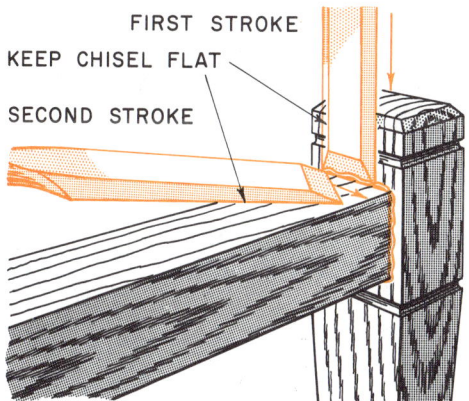

**41-2.** Removing glue around a joint with a sharp chisel. As much glue as possible should be wiped away when it is still wet. Hardened glue around the joints is difficult to remove.

FIRST STROKE
KEEP CHISEL FLAT
SECOND STROKE

**41-5a.** Drive all visible nails about ⅛ inch (3 mm) below the surface and fill, as you learned earlier. The filler should be applied so that it is slightly higher than the wood, then sanded level when dry. Another method of covering nails is with pegs. Pegs can be made by using small ¹⁄₃₂-inch (1 mm) stock of the same material as the project. Point the end in a pencil sharpener. Apply glue to the point and insert in the hole. Then cut off and sand smooth.

**41-5b.** Filling the tops of screw holes with putty. This can be done if the surface of the wood is to be painted.

**41-5c.** To fill end grain on plywood edges that are to be painted, several varieties of wood putty are available, either powdered (to be mixed with water) or prepared (ready for use). Plaster spackling also works well. Sand smooth when thoroughly dry and then finish.

project, scraping and sanding where necessary. When you sand, change to finer and finer paper, ending with No. 3/0 to 6/0 garnet paper. Figure 41-7. Before the final sanding, moisten the project slightly, allow it to dry, and then use a very fine sandpaper as a final finish. Wipe off any dust with a clean cloth. Now the project is ready for the finish.

**41-6.** Swelling a dent in wood with a damp cloth and a hot iron. Remember that too much wetting is not good, especially if you are working with plywood.

**306**

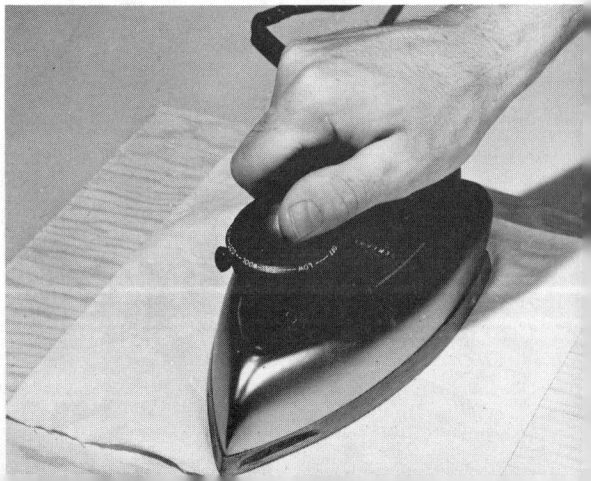

**41-7.** Give the project a final sanding with a fine abrasive paper. The corners should be *slightly* rounded.

**41-9.** Applying a commercial bleach with a synthetic rubber sponge. Caution: Remember always to wear rubber gloves to protect your hands when working with bleaches. When the bleach is dry, sponge off lightly with water.

## BLEACHING

Bleaching is done whenever a very light finish is to be applied to the wood surface. Chemicals that remove some of the wood color are used. For simple bleaching, a solution of oxalic acid crystals mixed in hot water can be applied to the surface with a rope brush or sponge. This should remain on the surface for ten or fifteen minutes. Then apply a solution made from 3 ounces (85 g) of sodium hyposulphate to 1 quart (0.9 litre) of water. In a few minutes apply a mild solution of borax mixed in water to neutralize the acid. NOTE: For most large projects, it is better to use a commercial bleach and always follow the directions very carefully. Figure 41-8. All bleaches remove the color from the wood by a process of oxidation. Figures 41-9 and 41-10.

**41-8.** There are several kinds of bleaches. Some require the application of two liquids—a bleach followed by a neutralizer. Others consist of two liquids that are mixed in equal parts at the time of use and applied as a single material. Use a glass or porcelain jar for mixing.

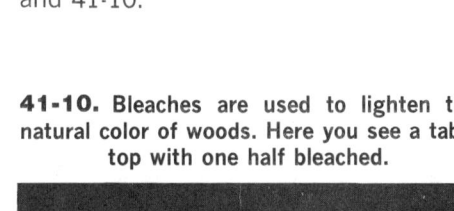

**41-10.** Bleaches are used to lighten the natural color of woods. Here you see a table top with one half bleached.

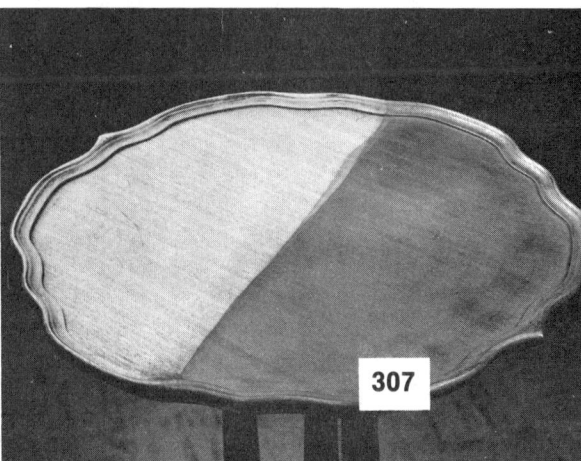

307

Section

VIII

UNIT 42.

# INSTALLING CABINET HARDWARE

**Hardware** is installed on many large projects such as chests, cabinets, and desks. Figure 42-1. This is usually in the form of hinges, locks, pulls, or knobs. A hacksaw with 32 teeth per inch should be used to cut metal bolts, screws, and hardware. Figure 42-2.

## KINDS OF CABINET HARDWARE

There are many different types of cabinet hinges. Figure 42-3. The butt hinge requires that a recess, or gain, be cut. In most cases, a gain is cut both in the door and in the frame on which the door is fastened. Sometimes a deeper gain is cut either in the frame or in the door so that the hinge is recessed in only one part of the two surfaces.

Figure 42-4 illustrates different types of drawer pulls and knobs suited to different furniture styles. The most common catches are friction, magnetic, elbow, and ball. Figures 42-5 and 42-6 (Page 312). The elbow catch holds one side of a double door closed when the other side is opened.

**42-1a.** Hardware is functional and adds a note of emphasis to a product.

## INSTALLING A BUTT HINGE

Select the proper size and kind of hinge for the door. The hinge size is indicated by its length. A 1-inch (25 mm) hinge is for a cabinet door for a desk, while a 3½-inch (89 mm) hinge is needed for a house door.

Fit the door into the opening. Place a thin piece of wood under the door, on the side away from the hinges, to hold the door in place. Measure from the top of the door to the upper location of the top

hinge and from the bottom to the lower point of the bottom hinge. The hinges should be located just inside the upper and lower rail. A mark is made on both the door and the frame.

Remove the door and place it on the floor or bench with the hinge edge upward. Hold the hinge over the edge of the door with one end flush with the mark. Draw another line to show the length of the hinge. Mark this length on the door frame also. Then, with a try square held against the face side of the door, square off these lines across the edge. Repeat on the door frame. Determine how far in the hinge will be from the face of the door. Set a marking gage to this measurement. Hold the marking gage against the face side of the door and mark a line between the two lines to show the position of the hinge. Repeat on the door

**42-1b.** Complete sets of matching hardware are available in many styles.

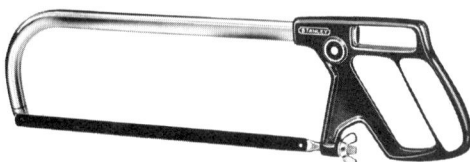

**42-2.** A hacksaw is necessary when hand-cutting any metal parts in the woodshop.

**42-3a.** Butt hinge.

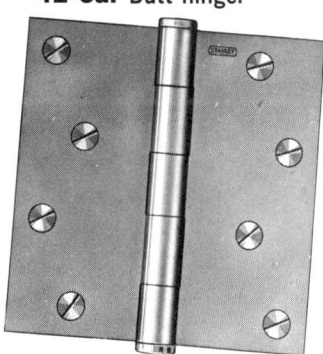

**42-3b.** Pivot hinge.

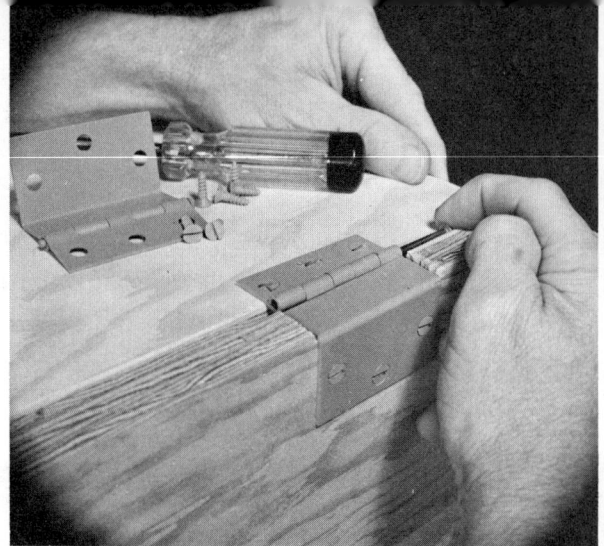

**42-3c.** Semiconcealed hinge.

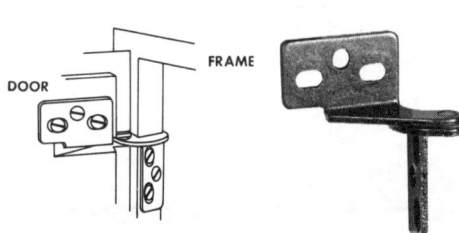

**42-3d.** Hidden hinge for lip doors.

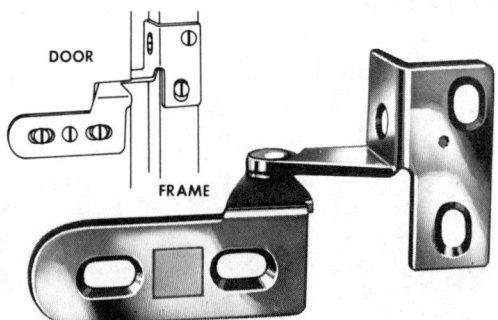

**42-3e.** Hidden hinge for flush overlay door.

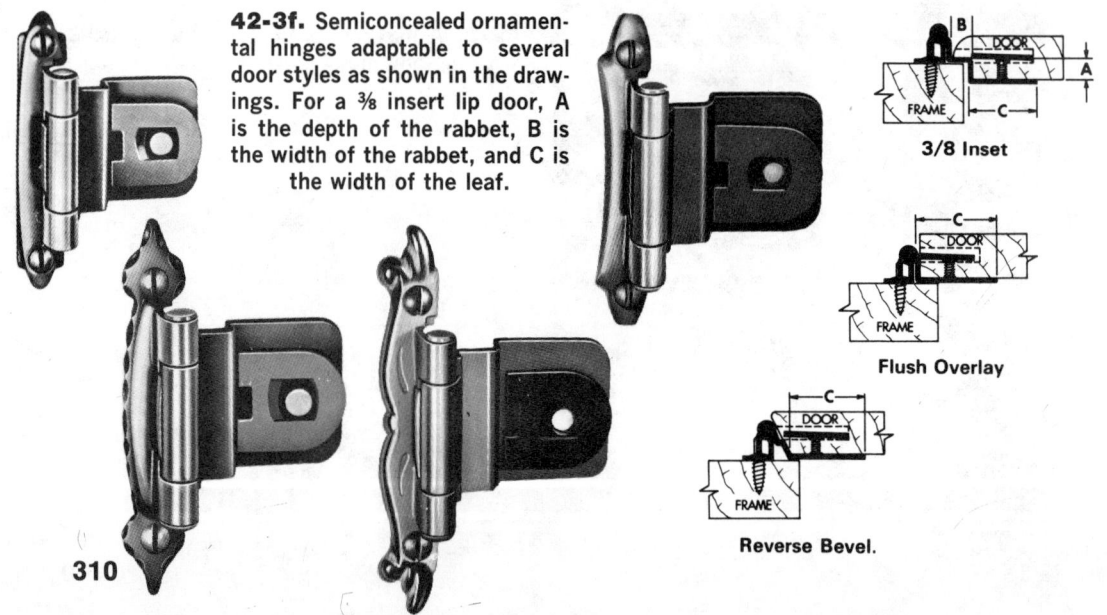

**42-3f.** Semiconcealed ornamental hinges adaptable to several door styles as shown in the drawings. For a ⅜ insert lip door, A is the depth of the rabbet, B is the width of the rabbet, and C is the width of the leaf.

3/8 Inset

Flush Overlay

Reverse Bevel.

frame. Then set a marking gage to the thickness of one leaf of the hinge. From the edge, mark a line indicating the depth to which the stock must be removed, both on the door and on the frame. This cut in the wood is called a gain.

With a chisel, outline the gain on the door as shown in Figure 42-7. Then make several V cuts in the stock to be removed.

Figure 42-8. Pare out the stock to the depth of the gain. Try the hinge in the recess to see whether it fits flush with the edge of the door.

Mark the location of the screw holes and drill the pilot holes as needed. Fasten half the hinge to the door section.

Cut out the gains in the frame of the door. Locate the position of the holes, drill, and insert one screw. Put the door

**42-4a** Choose knobs that fit the design of your article.

**42-4b.** Various types of pulls. Like knobs, these should match the design of your project.

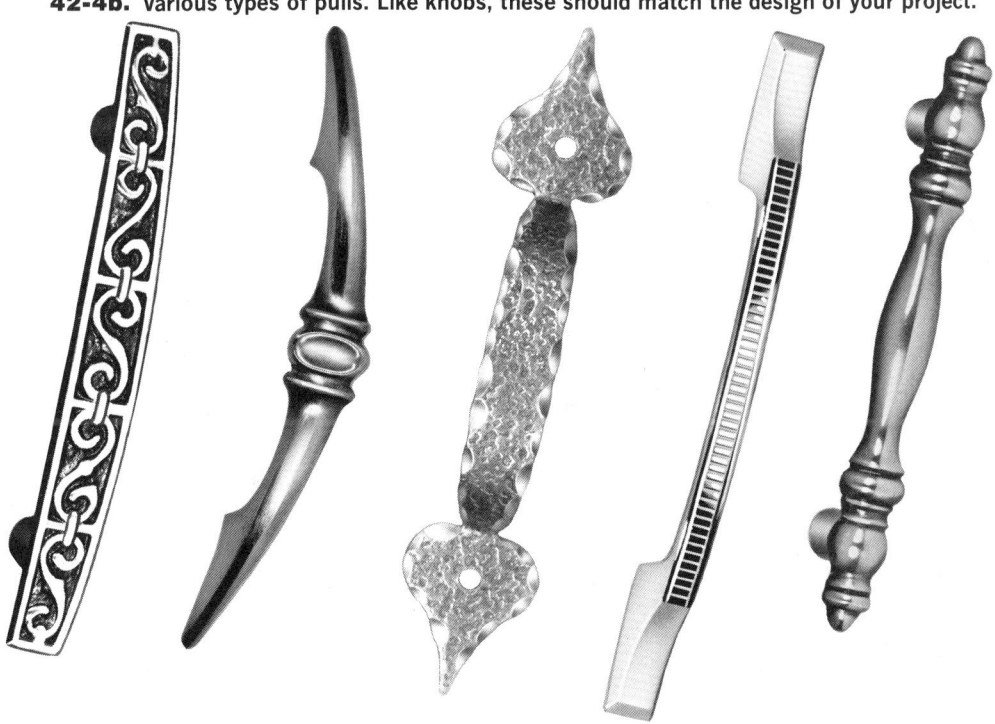

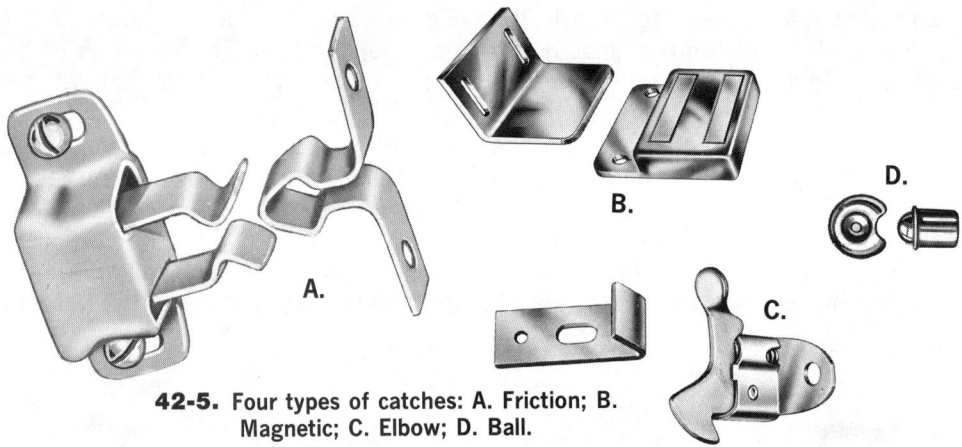

**42-5.** Four types of catches: A. Friction; B. Magnetic; C. Elbow; D. Ball.

in position and place the pins in the hinges. Try the door to see how it operates. It may be necessary to shift slightly the position of half the hinge. Sometimes it is necessary to cut the gain a little deeper or to raise it by putting a piece

**42-6.** Installing a touch-type catch. This allows the door to open by pushing lightly on the exterior.

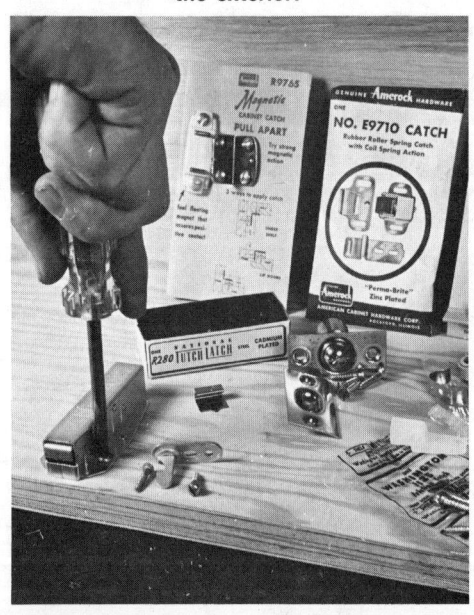

of paper under it. After any needed correction has been made, drill the other pilot holes and fasten the other half of each hinge securely.

## INSTALLING DRAWER KNOBS AND PULLS

Draw two parallel lines horizontally across the face of the door to locate the upper and lower edge of the knob. Then measure in from each end to the outside of the knob. Draw two vertical lines to complete the outline of the knob. Measure inward from this outline to locate the positions of the holes. Drill a hole the same size as the machine screws used to fasten the knob. Insert the machine screws from the back side of the drawer front and tighten the knob.

Pulls are installed in a similar way. Figure 42-9.

## USING REPAIR PLATES

Repair and mending plates come in many sizes and shapes. Figure 42-10. *Mending plates* are used to strengthen a butt or lap joint. The *flat-corner iron* is used to strengthen corners of frames such as a screen door or window. The

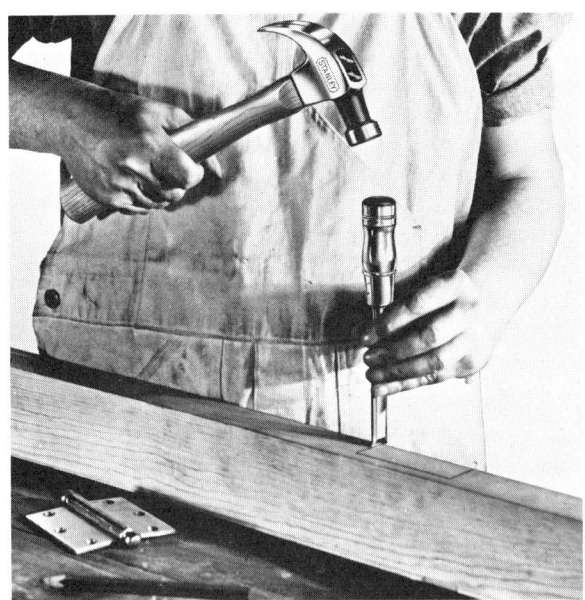

**42-7.** After the gain has been laid out on the edge of the door, it is outlined with a chisel.

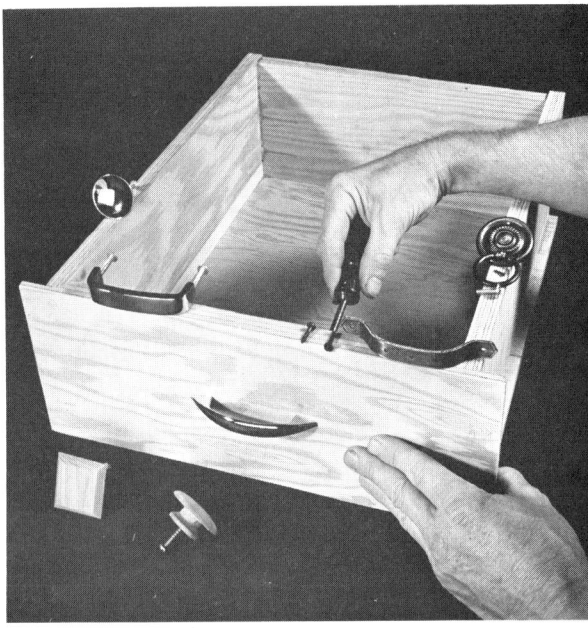

**42-9.** Attaching a handle to a drawer.

**42-8.** A. Chisel cuts in the stock to be removed to form the gain. B. The gain is cut and ready to have the hinge installed.

**42-10.** Four types of repair plates: Mending; Flat corner; Bent corner; and T plate.

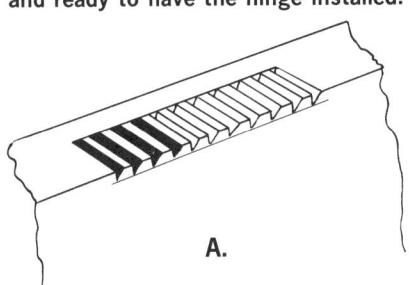

A.

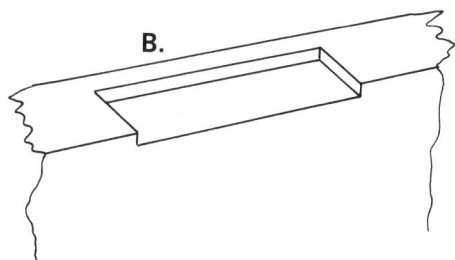

B.

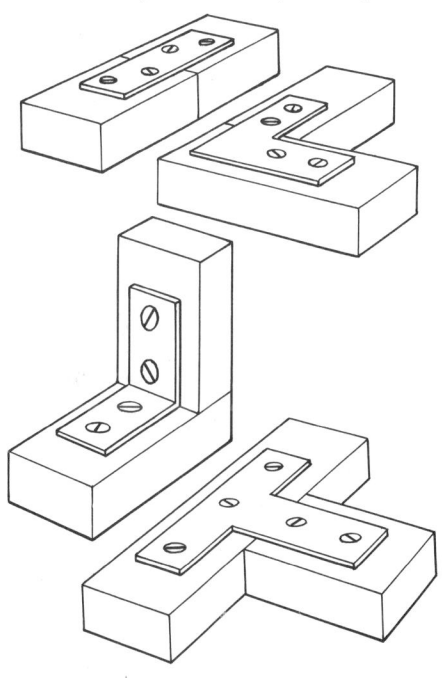

*bent-corner iron* can be applied to shelves and the inside corners of tables, chairs, and cabinets. It can also be used to hang cabinets and shelves. *T plates* are used to strengthen the center rail of a frame.

## REMOVING HARDWARE FOR FINISHING

Before applying a wood finish, remove any items such as knobs, hinges, locks, and catches that do not require the finish. Figure 42-11. You may also want to paint or enamel the metal hardware so that everything matches. Figure 42-12.

**42-11.** Removing the drawer knobs.

**42-12.** This hardware for a traditional piece of furniture has all been painted the same color.

## CAN YOU ANSWER THESE QUESTIONS ON INSTALLING CABINET HARDWARE?

1. Name some of the common types of hinges.
2. Define a gain.
3. What indicates the size of a hinge?
4. Sketch the position of hinges on a panel door.
5. Describe the method of laying out a gain.
6. A gain is trimmed out with what tool?
7. How can you test a hinge to make certain that it has been installed correctly?
8. What should you think about before selecting drawer knobs or pulls?
9. Why are hardware pieces removed for finishing?

## Section VIII
## UNIT 43.

# VENEERING SMALL PROJECTS

**If you wish to build** a small jewelry box or other small project of some exotic wood, such as rosewood or teak, or a fine American cabinet wood, such as walnut, oak, cherry, or birch, you can use hardwood plywood of the correct thickness. Figure 43-1. Although less expensive than the solid wood, this material is still very costly, and the construction is difficult since you must use miter joints to hide corners.

**43-1a.** This jewelry box was made of inexpensive softwood plywood and then covered with fine veneer. Note that one more edge must be covered. The plywood *core* is showing.

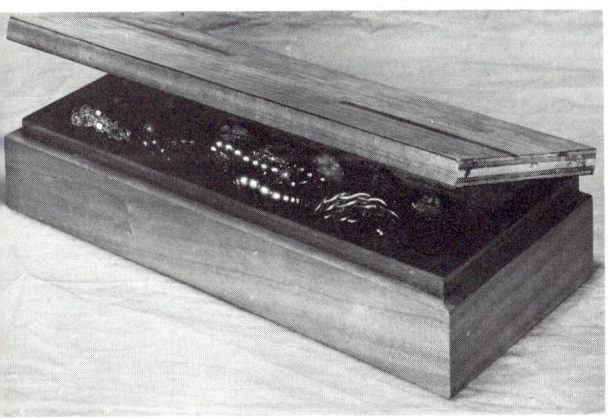

**43-1b.** A veneered box made of basswood and decorated with a metal casting.

## VENEER CUTS

In the furniture industry, veneered parts such as the tops of tables are made in the factory by building up the part to size, using core stock, cross bands, and veneers. Figure 43-2. Four different kinds of veneer cuts are used. Figure 43-3. Each method of cutting produces a different grain and figure pattern.

### Flat Sliced

This is the method of cutting veneer used most frequently. The half log, or flitch (section of a log), is mounted so that slicing is started at a tangent to the growth rings of the tree. Flat-sliced hardwood veneer is available in the largest volume and in more figure types than other cuts.

### Half Round

Half-round cuts normally display a broader and stronger grain pattern than flat sliced. This is true because the half log, or flitch, is caused to rotate against the veneer knife in such a way that the cut goes across the annual growth rings more gradually.

### Quartered

Unlike the flat-sliced and the half-round, which are cut from halved logs, quartered veneer is produced from log quarters. Quarter-cut flitches are sliced approximately at right angles to the growth rings to produce a straight, or so-called "pencil" stripe, grain pattern.

### Rotary

Rotary-cut hardwood is uncommon today. In practice the full log turns on a lathe against a knife, producing a continuous sheet of veneer. This method of cutting is used primarily for softwood plywood.

**43-1c.** Metric drawing for a veneered box.

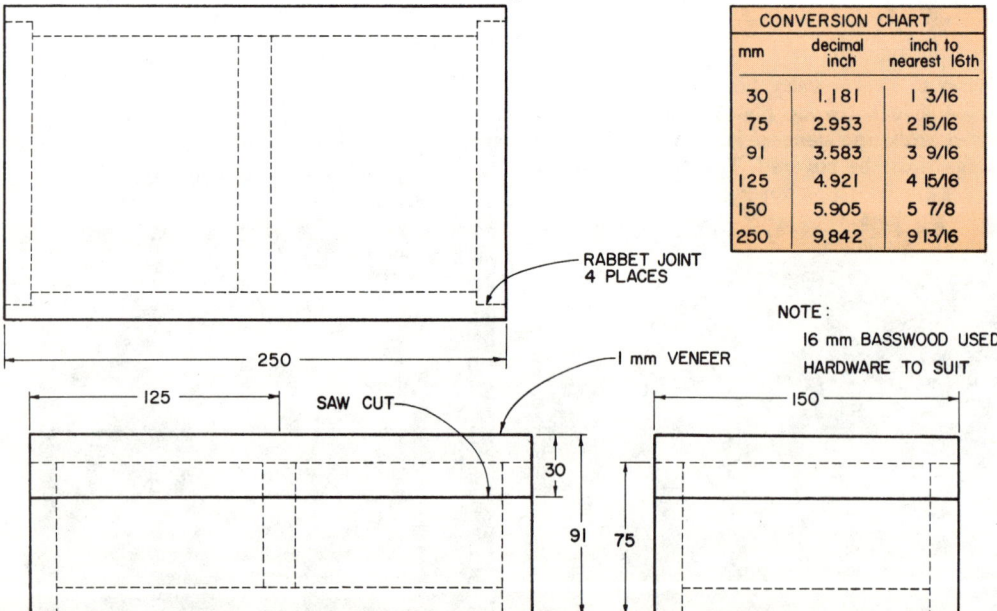

CONVERSION CHART

| mm | decimal inch | inch to nearest 16th |
|----|----|----|
| 30 | 1.181 | 1 3/16 |
| 75 | 2.953 | 2 15/16 |
| 91 | 3.583 | 3 9/16 |
| 125 | 4.921 | 4 15/16 |
| 150 | 5.905 | 5 7/8 |
| 250 | 9.842 | 9 13/16 |

RABBET JOINT 4 PLACES

NOTE:
16 mm BASSWOOD USED
HARDWARE TO SUIT

1 mm VENEER

250

125   SAW CUT

30

91   75

150

## VENEER MATCHING

In many furniture designs, face veneers have patterns made by some type of matching. To do this type of veneering, the pieces of veneer must be cut and glued edge to edge before they are applied to the core. Figure 43-4. This is rather complicated even when done with machines. However, for small projects such as jewelry boxes and chess boards the veneering can be done in a much simpler way. Figure 43-5. The project is built of some relatively inexpensive material such as softwood plywood, particle board, or inexpensive solid wood such as pine or poplar. Figure 43-6. Then it is covered with fine veneer. Simple joints such as butt or rabbet can be used since the entire exposed surface will be covered with veneer.

## VENEER THICKNESSES

Most veneers are cut $\frac{1}{28}$ inch (1 mm) thick. The normal flitch is about 12 to 14 inches (305 to 355 mm) wide and 16 feet (4.88 m) long. However, veneers are also available in standard sizes such as 18 x 24 inches (457 x 609 mm), 18 x 36 inches (457 x 914 mm), and 24 x 48 inches (609 x 1220 mm). These sizes are designed specifically for veneering small projects. Veneer edging is available in matching woods in widths of $\frac{1}{2}$ inch (12.5 mm), $\frac{5}{8}$ inch (16 mm), $\frac{3}{4}$ inch (19 mm), 1 inch (25.5 mm), and 2 inches (51 mm).

## VENEER EDGING

Veneer edging is available as follows:
• Plain edging that must be attached with adhesive.
• Edging with pressure-sensitive adhesive covered with paper. Figure 43-7. To glue this edging the cover paper is stripped away and the edging fastened in place.
• Edging coated with adhesive that must be heated with an electric iron to make it stick.

## TOOLS

A sharp *cutting tool* such as a carving knife, paper cutter, or heavy-duty shears

**43-2.** The top of this handsome table is built of lumber-core plywood with matching veneer.

**43-3.** Four common methods of cutting veneers.

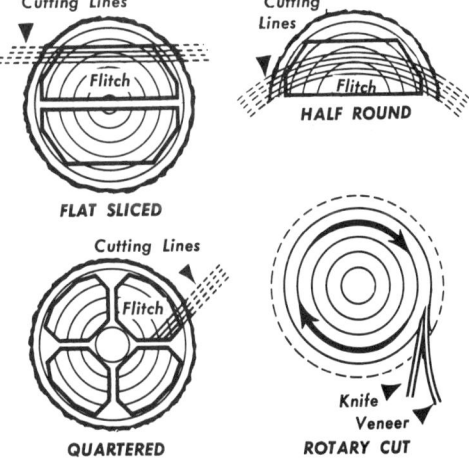

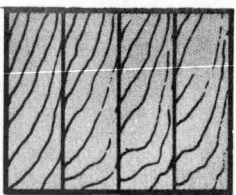

## SLIP MATCH

In slip matching, veneer sheets are joined side by side, repeating the flitch figure. All types of veneer may be used, but this type of matching is most common in quarter-sliced veneers.

## BOOK MATCH

All types of veneers are used. In book matching, every other sheet is turned over, just like the leaves of a book. Thus, the back of one veneer meets the front of the adjacent veneer, producing a matching joint design.

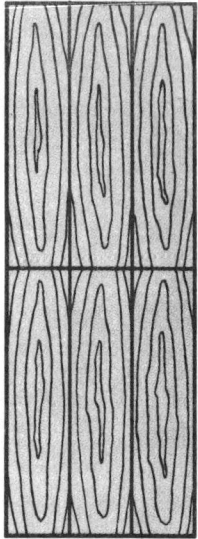

## VERTICAL BUTT AND HORIZONTAL BOOKLEAF MATCH

Panels can be matched vertically and horizontally when additional height or width is desired.

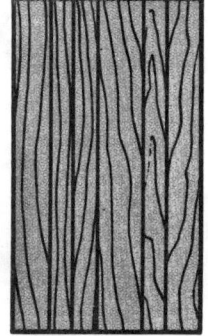

## RANDOM MATCH

Veneers are joined to create a casual, unmatched effect. Veneers from several logs may be used in a set of panels.

**43-4a.** Basic veneer matching effects.

---

**43-4b.** Special veneer matching effects.

DIAMOND

"V"

REVERSE DIAMOND

HERRINGBONE

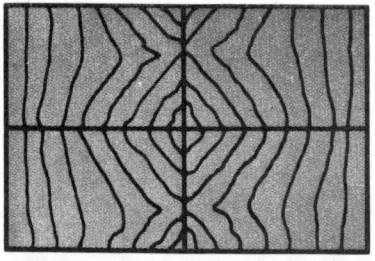

## FOUR-WAY CENTER AND BUTT

This match is ordinarily used with veneers cut from the butt, crotch, or stump of a tree, since this is the most effective way of revealing the beauty of their patterns. Occasionally flat-cut veneers are matched in this manner when panel length requirements exceed the length of available veneers.

can be used for cutting the veneer to size. Figure 43-8. A special *veneer saw* is excellent but not necessary. A *household iron* is needed for heating the veneer to set veneer adhesive.

## APPLYING VENEER WITH ADHESIVES

Two adhesives can be used to attach veneer, namely, *contact cement* and *ve-*

*neer adhesive*. With contact cement, there is an instant bond and the material cannot be moved once contact is made. Veneer adhesive is almost like contact cement, except that the permanent bond does not occur until heat is applied.

### Using Contact Cement

Cut sheets of veneer slightly larger, about $\frac{1}{4}$ inch (6.5 mm) on each side, for each major surface of the project. Coat the surface of the project and one surface of the veneer with contact cement, brushing thoroughly. Allow to dry about 30 minutes or until the gloss is gone. Hold the veneer over the surface and

**43-5.** This handsome chess set was built on a base of fir plywood with solid wood for the edging.

**43-6.** This cheese and cracker tray is made of softwood plywood covered with fine veneer. One edge is still to be completed.

**43-7.** Thin strips of real veneer edging are available coated with pressure-sensitive adhesive. Simply peel off the backing paper and apply the edging to the plywood edge according to the manufacturer's recommendations. This photograph shows one edge already covered with a strip of wood matching the plywood surface.

align it. Then lower it in place. *Remember that it cannot be moved once it touches the surface.* If a relatively large area is to be cemented, use strips of scrap plastic laminate or plastic. Lay them lightly across the cement-coated surface of the project with the smooth surface down and place the veneer on the scraps. Then remove one strip of scrap at a time and press the veneer to the surface. Roll the surface with a small roller. A block of softwood can also be placed over the veneer; strike the surface until the veneer is in complete contact with the surface. Trim excess material with a knife. Then sand lightly for a square edge. Make sure all sawdust is removed from the edge before applying contact cement for the edging.

## Using Veneer (Thermo-Set) Adhesive

The main advantage of using veneer adhesive instead of contact cement in

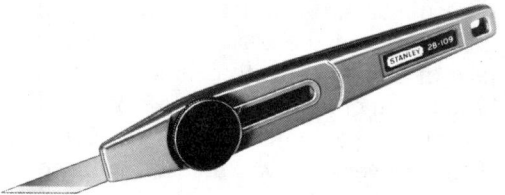

**43-8a.** A sharp cutting knife like this one can be used to cut thin veneer.

**43-8b.** Veneer can be cut with heavy-duty shears.

**43-9.** This plaque is made of small pieces of different colored veneers.

making small projects is that pieces can be cut and fitted for a design before adhesive is applied. Figure 43-9. Even after adhesive is applied to both surfaces, the design can be assembled on the second surface and moved around until heat is applied. Also, a design can be built up piece by piece since the veneer will not adhere until heat is applied.

To use veneer adhesive, apply the adhesive directly from the container by brushing it on both surfaces. It is white in the container. Allow it to dry to a clear gloss. Now place the veneer over the surface and align it properly. Apply heat with a regular household pressing iron set at a high heat. Once the iron has reached the proper heat, start at one corner, moving the iron slowly. This is important because heat must penetrate the veneer to liquify the two adhesive coatings, making them thermoplastic so they will fuse. As the veneer cools, the bond becomes permanent. While using the iron, it is good practice to cover the surface with a very smooth block of wood, since this will hold the veneer in contact while the cement dries. Trim any excess veneer at sharp right angles to the edge. Make sure that the edge is square, relatively smooth, and free of all sawdust.

If heat-adhesive edging is used, remove the paper liner and apply to the edge with hand pressure. Apply an iron to the tape until the heat penetrates the veneer, activating the adhesive. Follow directly behind the iron with a block of wood to hold the adhesive until it cools. Figure 43-10.

To prepare the product for finishing, use light sandpaper action with a wood block and 4/0 sandpaper. Sand off the excess edging and round it slightly. Finish sanding with 6/0 sandpaper. Figure 43-11.

**43-10.** Using a home electric iron set at a high heat to apply the veneer. Move the iron slowly, allowing the heat to penetrate through the wood and into the adhesive. After the heat has been applied the full length of the veneer tape, allow the veneer to set until cool to the touch.

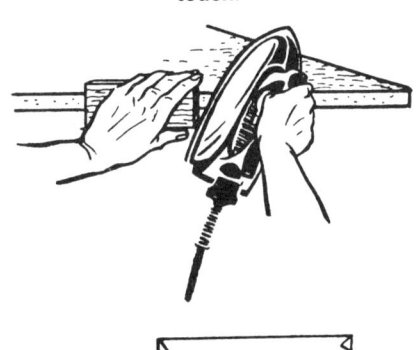

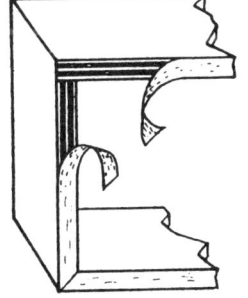

**43-11.** Sanding the edge of the veneer surface. The corner should be rounded slightly.

## CAN YOU ANSWER THESE QUESTIONS ON VENEERING SMALL PROJECTS?

1. Name the four different methods of cutting veneer.
2. What is the most common veneer thickness?
3. Describe the three kinds of veneer edging available.
4. What two types of adhesive can be used and tell how they differ.
5. Describe the process of covering a project using contact cement.
6. What is the advantage of using thermo-set adhesive?

# Section VIII

# UNIT 44.

# PLASTIC LAMINATES

**Furniture** manufacturers often cover the tops of tables, cabinets, and chests with an extremely hard material called plastic laminate. Most new homes feature this covering for the tops of kitchen cabinets and built-ins. Figure 44-1. For some furniture, plastic laminates imitate the wood grain appearance, matching natural wood. Plastic laminates are also made with patterns.

You may know this material by one of its trade names: Panelyte, Formica, or Texolite. Plastic laminate is what its name implies: a layer of materials, primarily kraft paper that has been impregnated with resin and a rayon surface paper covered with another kind of resin. The laminates are placed under high heat and pressure to produce a $\frac{1}{16}$-inch (1.5 mm) sheet of material that is very hard, but brittle. Such things as tea, coffee, ink, iodine, alcohol, and crayon wax have no effect on this surface. Soap and water can be used to clean it.

## WORKING WITH PLASTIC LAMINATES

Because plastic laminates are brittle, they must be well supported for doing any kind of cutting. Since a sheet is only $\frac{1}{16}$ inch (1.5 mm) thick, it cracks very easily. Plastic laminates are usually applied to plywood, solid wood, or hardboard. They can be cut with any of the standard woodworking tools. However, the carpenter or cabinetmaker usually prefers carbide-tipped tools, which are very hard and remain sharp longer than ordinary tools.

The following is an example of the use of this material in covering the top of a dressing table:

1. Place a piece of wrapping paper on a bench to make a pattern.

2. With a grease pencil, trace the size of plastic laminate needed by placing the table top over it. Figure 44-2. Allow about $\frac{1}{8}$ to $\frac{1}{4}$ inch (3 to 6.5 mm) oversize, since

**44-1a.** Plastic laminates are used on the cabinet faces and counter tops in this kitchen.

the material may chip slightly at the edges when sawed. This extra material is removed after the piece is fastened to the table top.

3. Attach the paper pattern to the *good side* of the plastic laminate with masking tape. Cut out the laminate with a compass saw and a hacksaw. Always cut with the good side up. Make sure that it is firmly supported to keep it from cracking. Figures 44-3 and 44-4. Then place the laminate on the bench with the good side down.

4. Make sure that the surface to be bonded is clean, dry, sound, and level. On an old surface, remove any varnish and sand the surface smooth.

5. Apply a coat of contact cement to both the table top and the back of the plastic laminate. Figures 44-5 and 44-6. This is the best adhesive for attaching the plastic laminate to the wood. It can be applied with a brush or metal spreader

**44-1b.** These attractive snack tables are covered with plastic laminates that are bright and colorful.

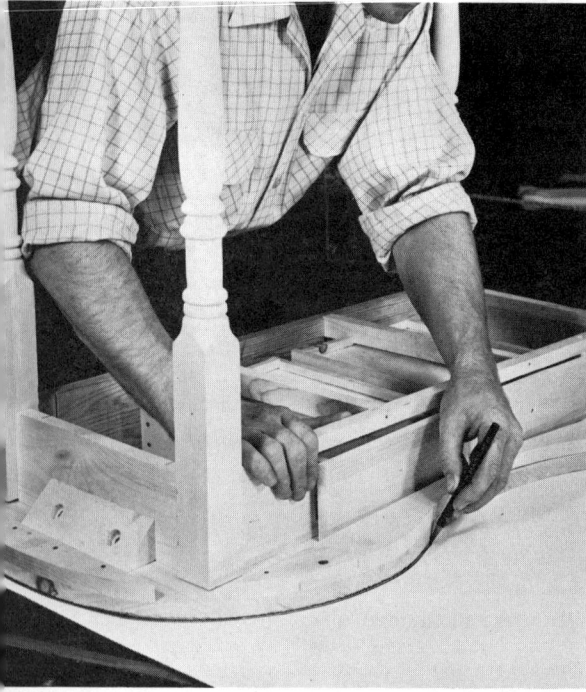

that has a serrated edge. Make sure that every square inch of both surfaces is completely and evenly covered with the cement. An adequately coated surface will have a glossy film when dry. Any dull spots after drying indicate that too little cement was used. These spots must have a second coat.

6. Allow both surfaces to dry at least 30 to 40 minutes. You can test for dryness by applying a small piece of wrapping paper lightly against the cemented surface. If no cement sticks to the paper, the cement is dry and ready for bonding.

7. Bond the two surfaces. This can be done any time within 3 hours after the

**44-4.** Cutting away a section of the waste material.

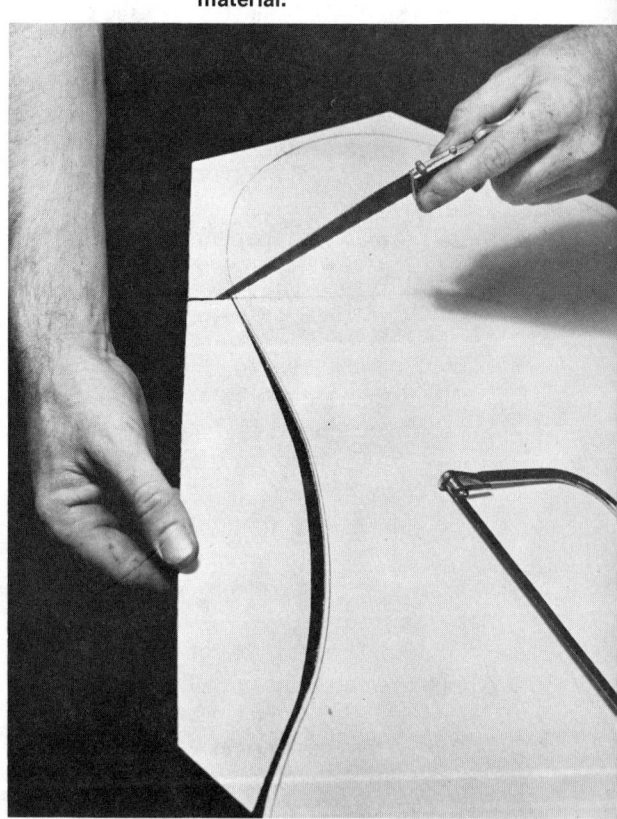

**44-2.** Tracing the shape of the table top on a paper pattern with a grease pencil. With a larger table or kitchen counter, the top can be removed.

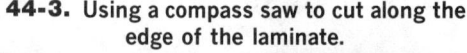

**44-3.** Using a compass saw to cut along the edge of the laminate.

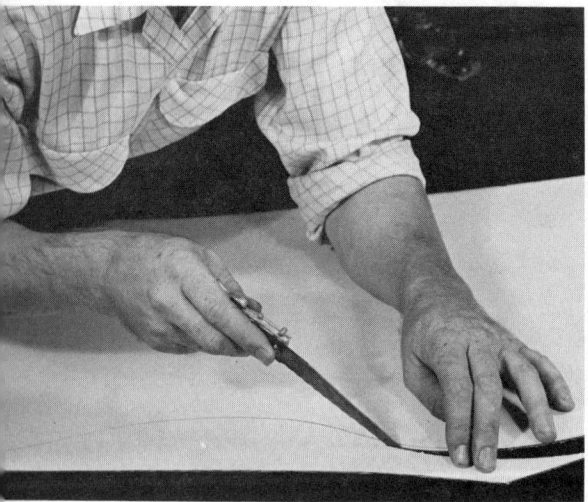

contact cement is applied, so don't rush. It is better to wait a little longer and be sure. Remember, there is a complete bond immediately when the two surfaces come in contact. Therefore no adjustment can be made. To avoid any mistake, use the following technique:

Place a piece of heavy wrapping paper lightly over the entire base surface. Figure 44-7. Now place the plastic laminate

**44-6.** Applying contact cement to the back of the laminate.

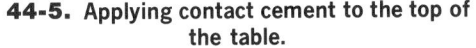

**44-5.** Applying contact cement to the top of the table.

**44-7.** Fastening the plastic laminate to the table top. Do not press down. Notice the wrapping paper that is placed between. This must be removed slowly after the material is positioned properly.

in position over the wrapping paper and align it carefully. Raise one side of the laminate slightly, and draw the paper away 2 or 3 inches (51 to 76 mm). Now check to see that the parts are still aligned and press down where the paper

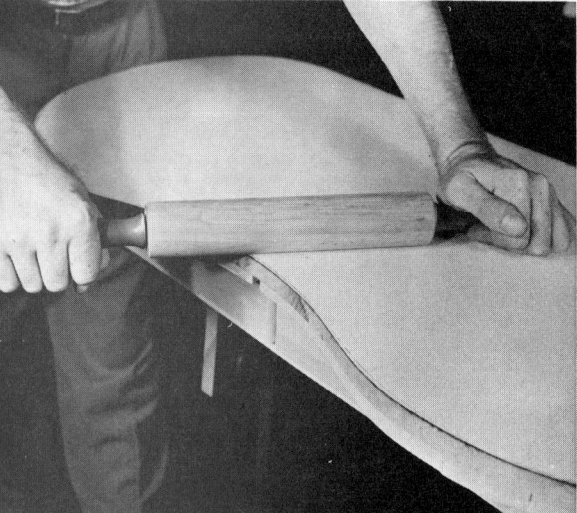

**44-8.** Using a rolling pin to flatten the surface.

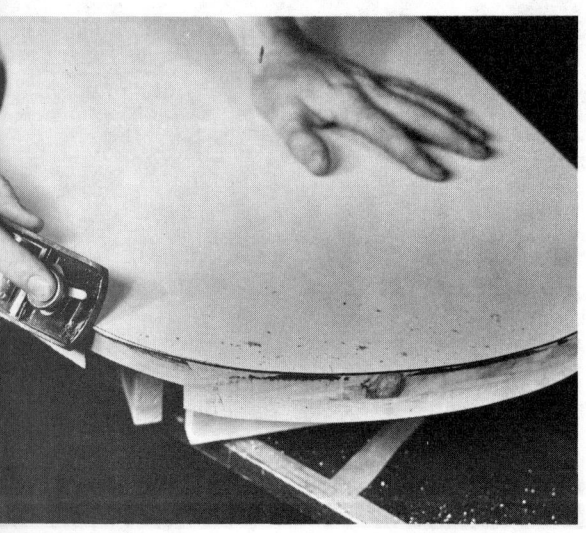

has been withdrawn. Then remove the paper completely.

8. Roll the entire surface with a rolling pin or other hand roller. Figure 44-8.

9. Trim the edge with a block plane and/or file. Figures 44-9 and 44-10. Hold the tool at an angle of about 20 to 25 degrees for bevel finishing.

10. Finish the edge of the table top. It can be covered with a metal or plastic laminate edge. Edge-banding material to match the plastic laminate is available. It can be easily bent around a curved surface. A more pleasing appearance can be obtained on the edge of a table top by adding a strip of wood to the underside for added thickness. Figure 44-11.

### MAKING A COFFEE TABLE (FIGURE 44-12)

1. Cut the particle board to exact size. Corners must be square. Using the circular saw or shaper, cut the groove in the edge of the board.

2. Cut the plastic laminate to 15¼ x 45¼ inches (387 x 1149 mm).

3. Adhere the plastic laminate to the particle board, using contact cement and following manufacturer's directions. Trim the laminate even with the substrate (base).

4. Where necessary cut and joint the long and short edge pieces to size. Cut 45-degree miter corners to fit around the particle board.

5. Glue the edge pieces to the particle board, using polyvinyl glue. Make sure excess glue is removed from the edge pieces and laminate.

6. Sand the edge pieces, stain if desired, and finish. Care should be taken

**44-9.** Trimming off the excess material with a block plane.

to protect the laminate surface when sanding.

7. Cut and joint the legs and rails to correct dimensions.

8. Lay out the dowel locations on all rails and drill dowel holes. Mortise-and-tenon joints may be substituted for dowel joints.

9. Lay out the location of dowel vertical centers on legs and by the use of dowel centers, mark the holes on the legs for the top rails. Measure the height of the bottom rail and mark with the dowel centers.

10. Drill dowel holes in the legs.

11. Lay out, drill, and countersink holes to fasten the rails to the table top.

12. Dry assemble the parts and make adjustments if necessary.

13. Sand all parts, rounding all exposed edges to a $\frac{1}{8}$-inch (3 mm) radius.

14. Assemble, using polyvinyl glue.

15. Remove excess glue, sand, stain, and finish to match top edging.

16. Assemble top to base with $2\frac{1}{2}$-inch (63.5 mm), No. 10 wood screws.

**44-10.** Beveling the edge of the plastic laminate with a file. Use light, regular strokes to keep the bevel even.

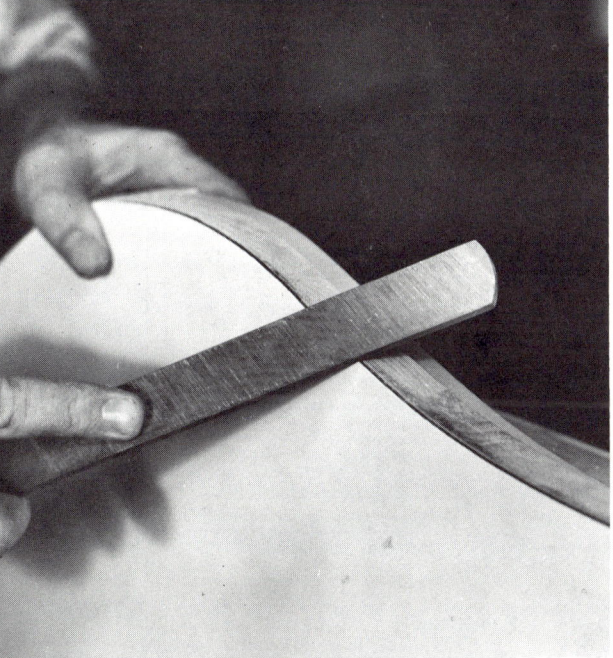

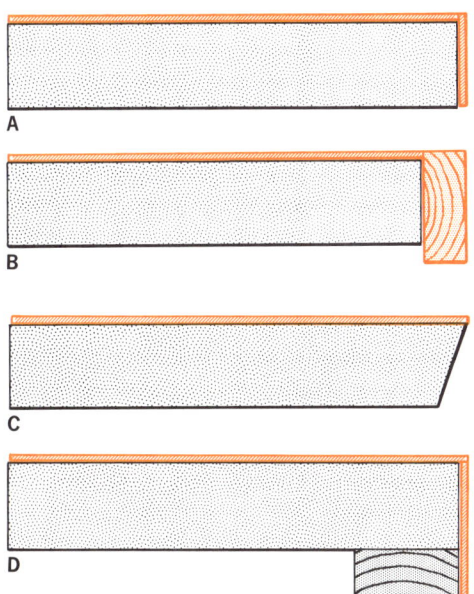

**44-11.** Types of edge treatment: A. Wood tape or veneer edge; B. Plain facing of solid wood; C. Bevel edge; D. Self edge.

**44-12a.** A handsome coffee table with a plastic laminate top.

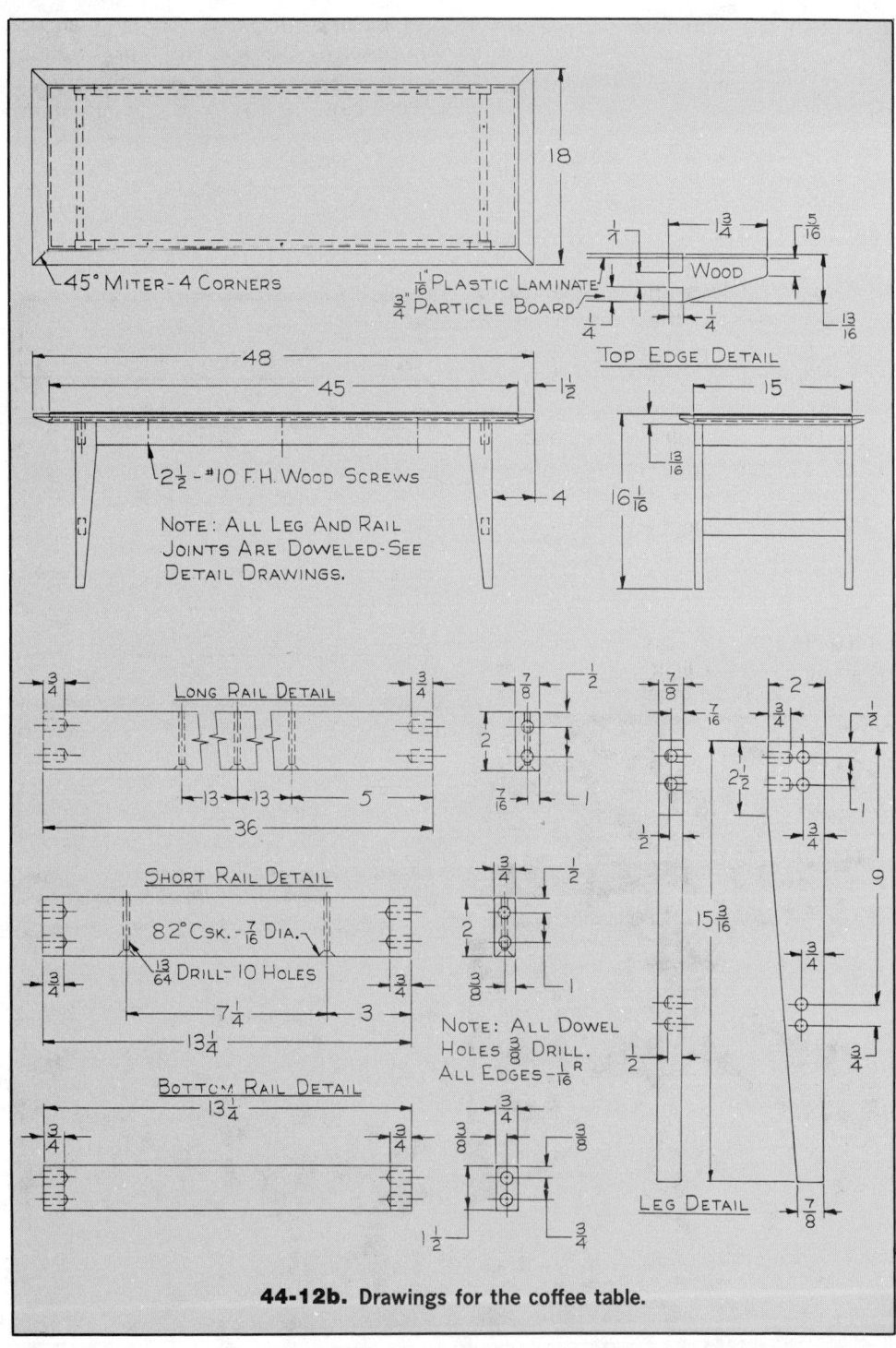

**44-12b.** Drawings for the coffee table.

| No. of Pieces | Part Name | Dimensions | Material |
|---|---|---|---|
| 1 | Top | $\frac{3}{4}$ x 15 x 45 inches (19 x 381 x 1143 mm) | Particle board |
| 1 | Top laminate | $\frac{1}{16}$ x 15$\frac{1}{4}$ x 45$\frac{1}{4}$ inches (1.5 x 387 x 1149 mm) | $\frac{1}{16}$ inch (1.5 mm) general purpose plastic laminate—woodgrain, plain, color, leather, or marble pattern; suede, satin, or sculptured finish |
| 2 | Top long edge | $\frac{3}{4}$ x 1$\frac{3}{4}$ x 48 inches (19 x 44.5 x 1219 mm) | Wood to complement or match laminate chosen |
| 2 | Top short edge | $\frac{3}{4}$ x 1$\frac{3}{4}$ x 18 inches (19 x 44.5 x 457 mm) | Wood to complement or match laminate chosen |
| 4 | Legs | $\frac{7}{8}$ x 2 x 15$\frac{3}{16}$ inches (22 x 51 x 386 mm) | Wood to complement or match laminate chosen |
| 2 | Long rails | $\frac{7}{8}$ x 2 x 36 inches (22 x 51 x 914 mm) | Wood to complement or match laminate chosen |
| 2 | Short top rails | $\frac{3}{4}$ x 2 x 13$\frac{1}{4}$ inches (19 x 51 x 337 mm) | Wood to complement or match laminate chosen |
| 2 | Short bottom rails | $\frac{3}{4}$ x 1$\frac{1}{2}$ x 13$\frac{1}{4}$ inches (19 x 38 x 337 mm) | Wood to complement or match laminate chosen |
| 8 | Dowel pins | $\frac{3}{8}$ inch (9.5 mm) dia. x 1$\frac{1}{2}$ inch (38 mm) lg. | |
| 16 | Dowel pins | $\frac{3}{8}$ inch (9.5 mm) dia. x 1$\frac{1}{4}$ inch (32 mm) lg. | |
| 12 | # 10 F. H. steel wood screws | 2$\frac{1}{2}$ inch (63.5 mm) | |
| | Contact cement Polyvinyl white glue | | |

**44-12c.** Bill of materials for the coffee table.

## CAN YOU ANSWER THESE QUESTIONS ON PLASTIC LAMINATES?

1. What is a plastic laminate?
2. Why is this material so popular for kitchen cabinet tops?
3. What is the best adhesive for gluing the material to the project?
4. How can you tell when the cement is ready for bonding?
5. Can you move the plastic laminate a little if you don't have it in the right place the first time? Explain why or why not.
6. Describe the method of trimming the edge of the plastic laminate after it is in place.

# MOSAIC TILES

**Mosaic tiles are** excellent for adding color and interest to cutting boards, hot pads, tops of tables, and similar projects. Figure 45-1. Three types of tiles can be used, namely, glass, ceramic, or vinyl plastic. Ceramic tile is best for small projects. The tiles can be applied over any kind of wood.

## TOOLS AND MATERIALS

Tiles of solid glass, ceramics, or plastic can be purchased in a wide range of colors. The common size is $\frac{3}{16}$ inch (5 mm) thick and $\frac{3}{4}$ inch (19 mm) square. Tiles can also be purchased $\frac{3}{16}$ inch (5 mm) thick and $\frac{3}{8}$ inch (9.5 mm) square. They come either loose or fastened to a sheet of paper. The latter must be separated by soaking the sheets in warm water for 15 minutes. Then allow the tiles to dry thoroughly before using.

A *cutter* is needed to cut tiles into smaller or irregular-shaped pieces. Figure 45-2. The cutter has curved edges that help prevent the tile from shattering.

A *palette knife*—a flexible artist's tool with a narrow, thin blade—is used to spread adhesive on small areas and to apply it to the individual tiles.

The most common adhesive used is *white resin glue*. It dries in a colorless state and is easy to apply from a squeeze bottle.

*Grout* is a cement paste that fills the spaces between the tiles. *Spackling cement,* available at paint or wallpaper stores, can also be used.

*Silicon polish* is applied to the finished tile surface to make it waterproof and to seal all joints. It also adds a protective luster to the tile surface.

## PROCEDURE FOR APPLYING TILE

Design and build the project. A commercial kit can be purchased if desired. When making a rectangular opening or form into which the tiles fit, remember tile size. Each tile is about $\frac{3}{4}$ inch (19 mm) square. About $\frac{1}{16}$ to $\frac{1}{8}$ inch (1.5

**45-1.** Mosaic tiles are excellent for adding beauty and utility to the top of a wood table.

to 3 mm) between the tiles should be allowed for the grout.

The mosaic design can be a geometric pattern made from full-size tiles. You can also make a design of irregular shapes and cut tiles to fill in the spaces. If the design is geometric and the tiles full size, lay the tiles on the project and arrange them to suit your own taste.

### Cutting Tiles

Mark the tile where it needs to be cut. Holding it in your fingers, place the entire curved surface of the blade directly over the line. Then squeeze the handles quickly. This will give a precise, full-length cut. If a circle or curve is needed, make several tiny cuts until you have the curved shape you want.

### Attaching Tiles

After you have worked out the design, start on the outside edge and work toward the center. Figure 45-3. On a round design, start by forming an outer rim. Remember that the tiles should be about $\frac{1}{16}$ to $\frac{1}{8}$ inch (1.5 to 3 mm) apart. Use white resin glue. Place a little on the back of each tile with a palette knife and attach to the surface. Press the tiles firmly in position and allow them to dry for 24 hours.

Mix the grout or spackling cement with cold water (usually half and half) until it is a thick, creamy solution. Then, with a rubber scraper or your hands, rub the grout over a small area at a time, going both lengthwise and crosswise, until the paste is firmly forced into all of the cracks. Figure 45-4. Carefully wipe the extra grout from the surface without digging in between the tiles. Use a damp cloth for this. Wait about 15 minutes or until a dusty film appears. Then wipe the surface with a dry cloth.

Allow the grout to dry overnight. If it is not flush with the tiles, you can apply a second coat as necessary. After the grout is completely dry, apply a silicon polish to make the tiles shiny.

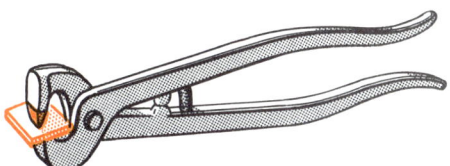

**45-2.** A cutter is used to divide the tile into smaller pieces. If the cutter blades are carbide-tipped and curved, the tile can be cut by holding it in the fingers, placing the entire cutting surface on the tile exactly where it should be broken. Then a quick squeeze on the handle cuts the material.

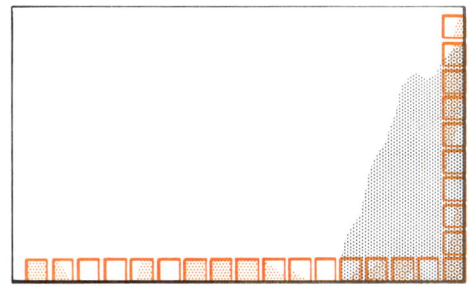

**45-3.** Spread the glue on the work and then start to arrange the outside edge. Set adjacent edges first to establish the spacing of the tiles.

**45-4.** Rub the grout between the tiles.

## CAN YOU ANSWER THESE QUESTIONS ABOUT MOSAIC TILES?

1. Name several materials used for tiles.
2. What tool is needed to cut the tiles?
3. What is the best adhesive to use for attaching tile to a wood surface?

4. Tell what grout is used for and describe the way it is used.
5. How much space should be allowed between tiles for the grout?

# Section VIII UNIT 46.

# ACRYLIC PLASTICS

**Plastics are man-made** in contrast to such natural materials as wood and metal. At some stage in their manufacture, all plastics are liquids. Therefore, they can be formed into different shapes, mostly through the application of heat and pressure. Plastics are difficult to define in simple terms because there are so many. Starting from many raw materials, a large number of different plastics are created. As the basic materials, industry uses such common substances as coal, petroleum, natural gas, air, water, sand, and salt. From these are derived the carbon, oxygen, hydrogen, nitrogen, and other elements which combine chemically to produce plastics.

Today more and more plastics are used in combination with other materials. This is especially true in the field of woodworking. Many plastics are used in both the furniture and building industries. Not too many years ago all furniture was made of wood, but today there is hardly a piece of furniture that does not contain some plastic. Highly decorative furniture such as French Provincial and Italian Provincial at one time had many hand-carved parts. Figure 46-1. Today rigid urethane or polystyrene foam is used extensively for decorative doors, picture frames, carved legs, and in any other place where highly decorative and functional shapes are needed. Figure 46-2. It is difficult even for an expert to tell which parts are real wood and which are plastic.

Plastics are used not only to make the actual parts but also as adhesives for holding the parts together. Plastics are found in almost all finishing materials including paint, lacquer, varnish, stain, and filler.

The widespread use of plastics in furniture, homes, and buildings is due to the many advantages of plastic materials: (a) light in weight; (b) good electrical insulation; (c) good forming qualities; and (d) attractive designs possible.

All plastics are of two types, *thermoplastic* (which soften each time heated) and *thermosetting* (which cannot be reshaped). The use of many plastics requires extensive equipment. However, acrylic plastics, which are thermoplastic, can be worked with standard woodworking tools and machines.

## WORKING WITH ACRYLICS

Acrylic plastics are tough, resilient materials noted for their durability and for their transparency. They are produced in the form of colorless, transparent sheet; transparent and translucent colored sheets; and sheets with patterns in a wide variety of thicknesses and sizes. Figure 46-3. Acrylic plastics are often called by their trade names, including Plexiglas, Lucite, and Acrylite.

Working with acrylic plastic can be fascinating because it can be cut by hand or with standard power tools. It can also be drilled, heated to form into interesting

shapes, and cemented with solvent to produce strong, transparent joints. Figure 46-4. In addition, acrylic plastic has the following qualities:

● Its crystal clarity, lustrous appearance, and light-transmitting capabilities make it a thoroughly modern material that will blend with any decor.

● It is much tougher than glass. Acrylics resist breakage and shattering, making them safer for homes. Figure 46-5.

● Unlike other plastics, neither time, outdoor exposure, nor artificial light causes any noticeable discoloration or loss of strength.

● Acrylics are not affected by many chemicals, including mineral acids, strong alkalis, kerosene, and white gasoline. However, many window cleaners,

**46-1.** This handsome coffee table is made of hardwood solids and veneers with decorative rails of molded styrene. It is far less expensive to make the rails of plastic than to hand carve them.

**46-2a.** Molded, rigid urethane or polystyrene is produced in a rubber mold when liquid plastic is poured into it. The result is a piece like this that looks like hand-carved woodwork.

**46-2b.** This clock frame is made of molded, rigid urethane foam.

leaded or ethyl gasolines, and such solvents as concentrated alcohol, benzene, acetone, lacquer thinner, and carbon tetrachloride should not be used on this plastic.

● Acrylics soften and can be formed when heated to temperatures ranging from 290 to 340 degrees F (143 to 171 degrees Celsius). Figure 46-6. In storage or service, acrylics should not be exposed to temperatures exceeding 180 to 200 degrees F (82 to 93 degrees Celsius).

● Acrylic plastic is slow burning and should be treated like an ordinary combustible material—wood, for example. Both materials will ignite and burn if placed in an open flame or in direct contact with any other source of ignition.

● Acrylics are easy to work with and extremely versatile.

**46-3.** Coffee tables made with a top sheet of clear acrylic. The legs are also acrylic plastic bent to shape. The top will not crack as it might if it were made of glass.

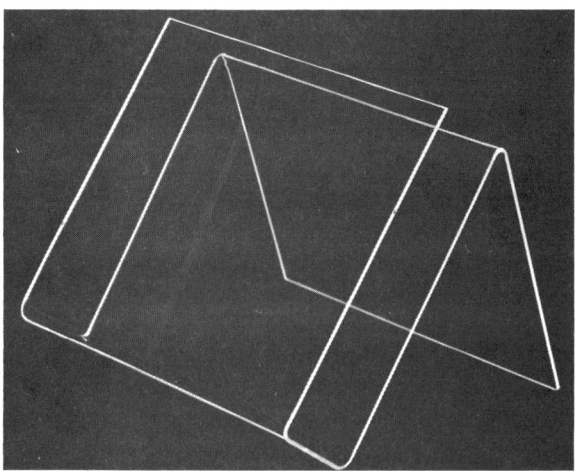

**46-4a.** This cookbook holder is made of a single sheet of acrylic bent to shape. Acrylic plastics should not be used like pieces of wood. Instead they should be used where appropriate, when bent pieces like this are needed, for example.

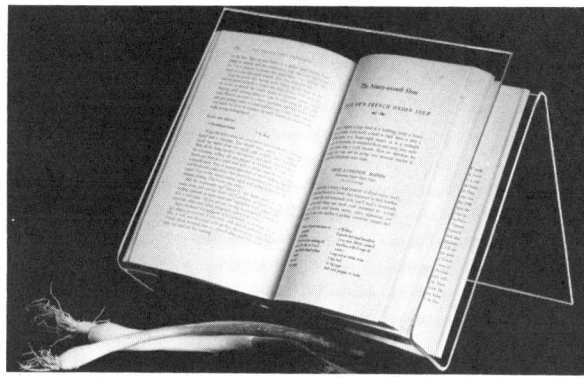

**46-4b.** The cookbook holder in use. The main advantage, of course, is that the crystal-clear acrylic permits one to read with no difficulty.

● Acrylics are compatible with the wood and metals normally used in the shop. It is a simple job to assemble acrylics with these materials.

## BASIC FABRICATING METHODS

### Scribing and Breaking

The scribing and breaking technique can be used on plastic up to ⅛ inch (3 mm) thick. A small manual scribing tool will score plastic adequately with four or five passes of the blade along a straight edge. Figure 46-7. The scribed line should be positioned face up over a ¾-inch (19 mm) wood dowel which runs the length of the intended break. Figure 46-8. To break, hold the sheet with one hand, and apply downward pressure on the short side of the line with the other. The hands should be kept adjacent to one another and successively repositioned about 2 inches (51 mm) in back of the break as it progresses along the

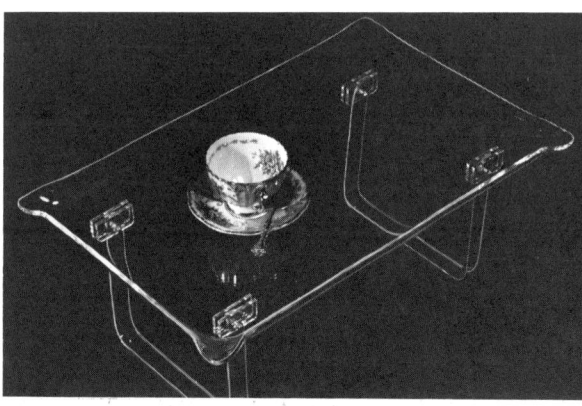

**46-5.** A coffee table made of colored acrylic plastic. Since it is unbreakable, it is a good material for use with dishes.

**46-6.** Bent plastic picture frames are attractive and easy to make.

**46-7.** Scoring plastic with a scribing tool before breaking.

scribed line. The minimum cut-off width is about 1½ inches (38 mm).

## Cutting with Saber, Band, and Jig Saws

Curved shapes are easily cut with any one of these saws. Saber and reciprocating jig saw blades should have at least 14 teeth per inch. Straight cuts can be made with a saber or hand jig saw by guiding the tool along a straight edge. Figure 46-9. Band saws should have at least 10 teeth per inch. Hold plastics down firmly when cutting. Do not force feed. Figure 46-10.

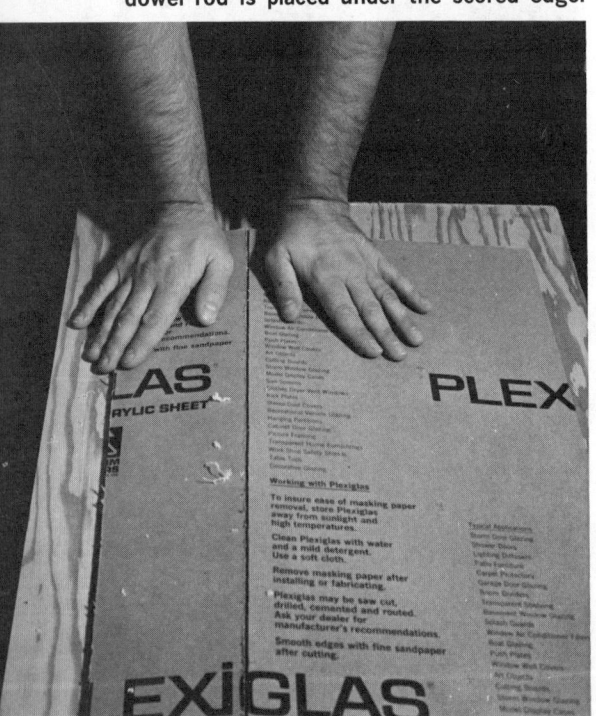

**46-8.** Breaking the plastic. Note that a dowel rod is placed under the scored edge.

**46-9.** Using a portable jig saw to cut plastic. Notice the strip of wood used as a guide. Never remove the masking paper during sawing operations. The paper protects the surface against chipping and marring, and helps to keep the saw blade cool.

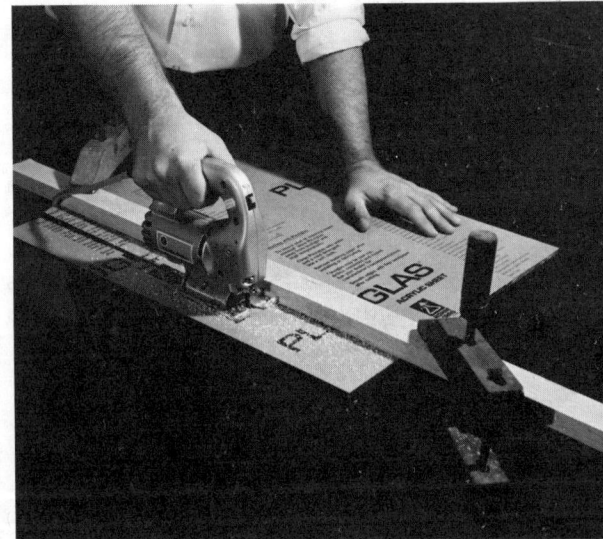

Four chairs of bent hardboard, designed and constructed completely by students. The wood is actually bent hardboard. Because hardboard has structural strength, it can be used to support upholstered furniture. The students even designed the forms for bending the hardboard. In some designs two thicknesses were needed for added strength.

This kitchen recreation room has many plastic items. One is the lighted end table. The shelves are plastic pieces, 18 x 24 x ¼ inch, supported at each end by ¾-inch grooves cut in the wood uprights. A light is mounted in the base with the fluorescent unit covered by white plastic. The 3-D tic-tac-toe game is made with ⅛-inch plastic of different colors. Strips of white pressure-sensitive tape were used to form the squares.

336B

In this room there are many items made of acrylic plastic. Most obvious is the transparent table before the davenport. This has a plastic base, 20 x 40 inches, formed at a 30-degree angle by strip heating. The top is an equilateral triangle with rounded corners. The cube table in red and white is made of six pieces of plastic.

These attractive, small products are made of acrylic plastics. Some of these you could design and build from flat sheet stock. Others require forms for heating and bending.

**336D**

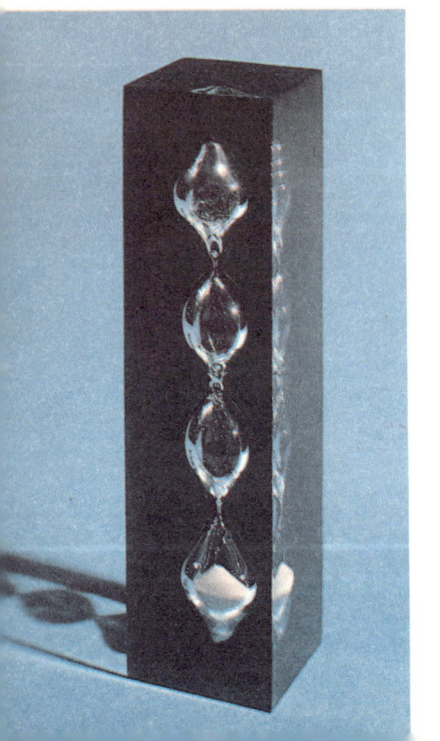

## Cutting with Circular Saws

Use a crosscut blade which is recommended for finish cuts on such materials as plywood, veneers, and laminates. The blade should have at least 6 teeth per inch. All the teeth should be the same shape, height, and point-to-point distance. Set the blade height just a little above the thickness of the sheet to prevent chipping. Hold the plastic down firmly when cutting. Do not force feed. Figure 46-11.

## Drilling

Standard twist drills commonly used for metals can be used to drill plastics if reasonable care is exercised. Figure 46-12. Use a plastics drill if one is available. Back the plastic with wood. Clamp or hold the plastic and wood firmly and maintain very slow speed and minimum pressure. CAUTION: *If too much speed is used, acrylic plastics tend to climb the drill. With too much pressure, chipping occurs on the back side of the hole.*

## Edge Finishing

Sawed edges and other tool marks should be removed by scraping the edges smooth with a sharp knife or by sanding with medium grit (60-80) paper. Figure 46-13. This insures maximum breakage resistance of the plastic part. To further improve the appearance of the surface or edge, follow the initial finishing with wet-or-dry, 150 grit, abrasive paper. For a transparent edge, follow this step with grits to 400 and buff with a clean muslin wheel dressed with a good grade of fine grit buffing compound. Finish with a clean, soft, cotton-flannel wheel.

## Cementing

Cementing with a solvent methylene chloride "MDC," ethylene dichloride

**46-10.** Using a band saw to cut irregular-shaped parts. The best saw blade for plastics is the skip-tooth type used in sawing soft metals.

**46-11.** Cutting acrylics on a circular saw. The blade should be about 3/32 to 1/8 inch (2 to 3 mm) thick. The height of the blade above the table should be just a little greater than the thickness of the plastic to prevent chipping. NOTE: Be sure to use a guard. In this illustration the guard has been removed for a clearer view of the cutting procedure.

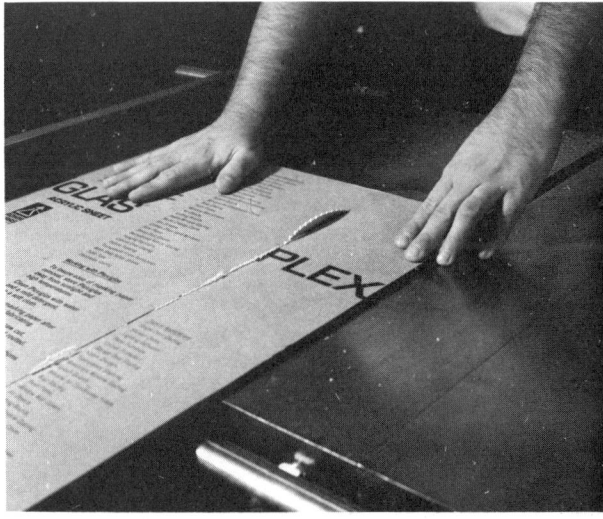

**46-12.** Drilling a hole in acrylic plastic. A lubricant of mild soap can be used. Never stop the drilling before the hole has been completed, since the softened material will freeze on the drill bed. Apply very light pressure as the drill is about to come through the other side.

**46-13.** For hand sanding, use garnet paper or wet-or-dry aluminum oxide paper. Dust the edge with very fine grit abrasive.

**46-14.** Before cementing, make sure the pieces fit accurately without forcing. The surfaces must be clean but not polished. Fewer air bubbles form if the surface is given a light sanding with 8-0 wet-or-dry garnet paper.

"EDC," or 1-1-2 trichloroethane is an easy method for joining two pieces of acrylic plastic. Sand surfaces to be cemented but do not polish. Figure 46-14. Remove protective masking paper. Apply solvent to the joint with a syringe, an oil can with a very fine spout, an eye dropper, or a small paint brush. Let the joint dry thoroughly. CAUTION: *Solvents may be toxic if inhaled for extended periods of time or if swallowed; many are also flammable.* Use in a well-ventilated area; keep away from flames and small children.

**Strip Heat Forming**

Acrylic plastics may be formed along a straight line by using a strip heater. This is an electric heater made from a nichrome-wire, resistance coil. Such heaters can be purchased or built from components at low-to-medium cost. Figure 46-15.

## EXPLODED VIEW OF STRIP HEATER

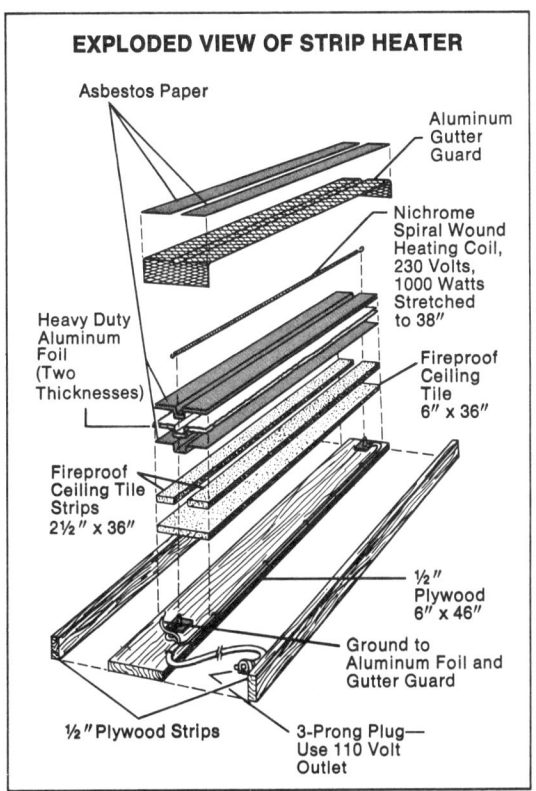

Asbestos Paper

Aluminum Gutter Guard

Nichrome Spiral Wound Heating Coil, 230 Volts, 1000 Watts Stretched to 38″

Heavy Duty Aluminum Foil (Two Thicknesses)

Fireproof Ceiling Tile 6″ x 36″

Fireproof Ceiling Tile Strips 2½″ x 36″

½″ Plywood 6″ x 46″

Ground to Aluminum Foil and Gutter Guard

½″ Plywood Strips

3-Prong Plug—Use 110 Volt Outlet

**46-15.** Plans for making a strip heater for bending acrylic plastics. A commercial unit can also be purchased to do this work.

**46-16.** Applying decorative plastic laminate to colored acrylic plastic.

Remove the protective masking paper. Place the plastic on the supporting frame with the area to be formed directly above the heating element. Do not let the plastic touch the heating element. Acrylic plastics should not be heated to temperatures higher than 340 degrees (171 degrees Celsius). Surface overheating will cause scorching and bubbling. If this occurs, increase the distance between the heating element and the plastic.

Allow the plastic to heat thoroughly (until it softens in the area to be formed). Bend gently to the desired angle and hold firmly until cool. NOTE: Bending

material before it is thoroughly heated results in stress crazing (small internal fractures) along the bend. Practice on scrap material first. Any plastic thicker than $\frac{1}{4}$ inch (6.5 mm) should not be strip formed.

*For safety, do not leave the strip heater unattended.* Work in a well-ventilated area. Have a general-purpose, ABC-rated (dry powder), fire extinguisher nearby. Do not heat plastic with an open flame or in kitchen ovens. Such ovens are not equipped with adequate temperature controls and safety devices for this type of work.

### DECORATING ACRYLIC PLASTIC SHEET

#### Painting Acrylic Plastics

Lacquers, enamels, and oil-based paints can be used to decorate plastics when no outdoor exposure is anticipated. If outdoor use is a factor, acrylic-based lacquers provide the best adhesion. Water-based or latex paints have relatively poor adhesion and difficult spreading characteristics when used on plastics. Spray painting provides the most uniform distribution of a coating. Brush coating tends to produce a fine pattern of brush hair strokes on the finished product. Allow a longer drying time than when painting porous surfaces such as wood.

### Applying Materials to Plastic

Decorative effects can be obtained by applying paper, cloth, foil, and other materials which have pressure-sensitive, adhesive backings. Figure 46-16. These are used to create artistic and decorative effects in partitions, doors, and window glazing. Paper, cloth, and foil without pressure-sensitive, adhesive backings can be applied with either spray-on adhesives applied to both surfaces or by spraying clear lacquer on the plastic.

## CAN YOU ANSWER THESE QUESTIONS ON ACRYLIC PLASTICS?

1. Why are plastics difficult to define?
2. Name some of the materials that are used in producing plastics.
3. Where are plastics used in the woodworking industry?
4. What decorative types of furniture use plastics that look hand carved?
5. Name the two basic types of plastics.
6. What are acrylic plastics?
7. List some of the qualities of acrylic plastics.
8. What tools can be used for cutting acrylic plastics?
9. How can you form acrylic plastic?
10. Describe some ways of finishing acrylic plastics.

# SECTION IX

## Finishing Projects

**What you must know and be able to do in Units 47–55:**

47. The basic steps in wood finishing; how to use and care for brushes; where finishing materials come from and how to use them; how to refinish.
48. The stains which are applied to beautify or to imitate: what they are and how to apply them to get the best results.
49. Using wood fillers on open- and closed-grain woods.
50. How to apply shellac; what shellac is; what makes it good for finishing.
51. The special considerations for applying varnish; method of application; steps in producing a varnish finish.
52. Penetrating and wipe-on finishes: what they are and how to apply them.
53. How a clear or colored lacquer finish differs from other finishes; how to apply lacquer.
54. How enamel differs from paint in its composition and application; painting a surface: mixing and applying paint.
55. Antiquing a surface to give it a special look: materials and tools needed and techniques to follow.

*A good start deserves a good "finish"! If you apply a good finish, your work will carry the mark of the fine craftsman. Don't ruin your project by applying the wrong finish or by putting on the right finish carelessly. Also remember that, although it is convenient to have a separate finishing room, you don't need one to do a good job. You do, however, need to do your part in taking care of the finishing area and supplies. Never, for example, use the shellac brush and then let it dry out or open a can of varnish and not reseal it properly.*

*Before you begin to apply the finish, visit a furniture store to look at fine furniture. Notice the rich finish which accounts greatly for its quality. You, too, will be proud of your work if you finish it well.*

# WOOD FINISHING AND FINISHING SUPPLIES

**Wood finishing** is one of the most important steps in the completion of attractive projects. Figure 47-1. Thanks to the chemist and "magic" of finishing materials, you have a wide selection of colors, and finishes that can be added to the things you make. Modern paint chemistry makes it possible to give wood furniture new color, new beauty, and new style. An important part of applying a good finish in woodworking is having the proper supplies in good condition.

## BASIC STEPS IN ACHIEVING A FINE FINISH

Although the materials may vary, all finishing is done in about the same way. There are several basic steps to follow. They are not all necessary, however, for the finishing of every piece of wood. Choose from the following only the steps needed for the type of finish you want:

1. *Bleaching.* Bleaching is done to lighten or to even out the color of unfinished wood. Very light, natural wood finishes are popular for contemporary furniture. For natural and darker finishes, bleaching, of course, is not necessary.

2. *Staining.* Staining is done to enhance the grain and to achieve the color you want.

3. *Sealing.* This is done to seal the stain to prevent bleeding (running of the stain). A wash coat (one part shellac to seven parts alcohol) is good for most stains. If lacquer is used, a lacquer sealer can be applied.

4. *Filling.* Filling is required for porous and semiporous woods. Lumber from some broad-leaf trees such as oak, mahogany, and walnut contain large cells and, therefore, are very porous. When the lumber is cut and planed, the cells are ruptured, leaving what amounts to tiny troughs running lengthwise. These must be filled in order to obtain a smooth

**47-1.** Selecting materials for finishing.

finish. Some woods such as birch, maple, and gum have smaller cells and these require a thinner filler or no filler at all. Nonporous woods such as pine, cedar, and redwood do not require a paste filler.

5. *The second sealing.* A sealer should again be applied over a filler. It can be a commercial lacquer sealer or a wash coat of shellac.

6. *Applying the standard finish.* A shellac, varnish, lacquer, or synthetic finish is applied after sealing. Usually two or more coats are needed. Always sand the surface with 5/0 (180) sandpaper after each coat is dry. The final coat may be gloss or satin—a duller gloss.

7. *Rubbing, buffing, and waxing.* To get a hand-rubbed finish, the normal gloss is removed and reduced by using an abrasive material. The surface to be rubbed should have at least three or four coats of the final finish in order to withstand the rubbing. The common method of rubbing is to use a felt pad and pumice. Several layers of felt should be tacked to a piece of wood. Then mix the pumice in water to a paste consistency. Wet the surface. Dab the pad in water, then in pumice paste, and rub the surface with the grain. Use long strokes with moderate pressure.

For an even finer polished surface, rub with a felt pad or cloth, using powdered rottenstone and water or rottenstone and rubbing oil. Figure 47-2.

Another method of rubbing the surface is to use wet-or-dry sandpaper. Lubricate the surface with soapy water. Then rub with the grain, using long strokes. Use very fine wet-or-dry sandpaper, grades 360 to 380. Figure 47-3.

**47-3.** Rubbing a surface using soapy water and wet-or-dry abrasive paper.

**47-2.** Rubbing a surface using a cloth and rottenstone.

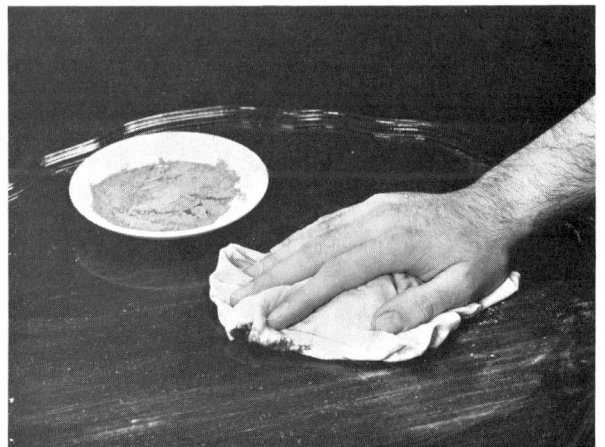

When uniformly dull, polish with a clean, soft felt pad or cloth.

A simpler method of getting a rubbed surface is to rub with 4/0 steel wool until the surface is uniformly dull. Figure 47-4. The final step is to apply a good coat of paste wax and rub vigorously with a soft cloth. Figure 47-5.

In order to get a good finish, you will need to choose a brush carefully. Figure 47-6.

● Natural bristle brushes are made with hog hair. This type of brush was originally recommended for applying oil base paints, varnishes, lacquers, and other finishes, because natural fibers resist most strong solvents.

● Synthetic bristle brushes are made from synthetic fiber, usually nylon. Today's nylon brushes are recommended for both latex (water soluble) and oil-base paints. This is because the fiber absorbs

less water than natural bristles do, while also resisting most strong paint and lacquer solvents. In addition, nylon bristles are easier to clean than natural bristles.

● Brush quality determines painting ease, plus the quality of the finished job. A good brush holds more paint, controls dripping and spattering, plus applies paint more smoothly to minimize brush marks. To assure that you are buying a quality brush, check the following factors:

● Flagged bristles have split ends which help load the brush with more paint, while assisting the paint to flow on more smoothly. Cheaper brushes will have less flagging or none at all. Figure 47-7.

● Tapered bristles also help paint flow and provide smooth paint release. Check to see that the base of each bristle is thicker than the tip. This helps give the brush tip a fine painting edge for more even and accurate work.

**47-4.** Rubbing a surface using a steel wool pad.

**47-5.** Applying a coat of paste wax.

● Fullness is important, too. As you press the bristles against your hand, they should feel full and springy. If the divider in the brush setting is too large, the bristles will feel skimpy, and there will be a large hollow space in the center of the brush.

● Bristle length should vary. As you run your hand over the bristles, some shorter ones should pop up first, indicating a variety of bristle lengths for better paint loading and smoother release.

● A strong setting is important for bristle retention and maximum brush life. Bristles should be firmly bonded into the setting with epoxy glue, and nails should only be used to hold the ferrule to the handle.

● Size and shape of a brush are also important. Choice of brush width is determined by the amount of open or flat area to be painted. Figure 47-8 may be used as a guide for choosing the right size but should not be considered a limiting factor when selecting a brush.

**Good Use of Brushes**

The following are some general suggestions for using brushes:

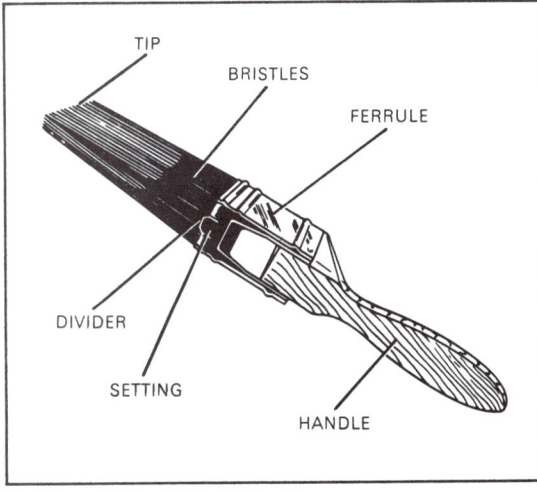

**47-6.** Parts of a brush.

**47-7.** Two types of bristles.

**47-8.** A guide to selecting the proper brush size for a job.

| Size | Application |
| --- | --- |
| 1 to 1½ inches (25 to 38 mm) | Touch-ups and little jobs, such as toys, tools, furniture legs, and hard-to-reach corners. |
| 2 to 3 inches (51 to 76 mm) | Trim work, such as sashes, frames, molding, or other flat surfaces. An angular-cut brush helps do clean, neat, sash or narrow trim work and makes edge cutting easier. |
| 3½ to 4 inches (89 to 101 mm) | For large flat surfaces, such as floors, walls, or ceilings. |
| 4½ to 6 inches (114 to 152 mm) | Large flat areas, particularly masonry surfaces, barns, or white-washing board fences. |

• Revolve a new brush rapidly by the handle to dislodge loose bristles. Remember that all new brushes have them. Figure 47-9.

• Dip the brush into the finishing material about one-third the bristle length. Tap the excess against the side of the can. Figure 47-10. Never scrape against the rim of the can.

• When using a brush, always hold it at a slight angle to the work surface.

• Never paint with the side of the brush.

• Never use a wide brush to paint small round surfaces such as dowel rods. Your brush will "fishtail."

• Never let the brush stand on its bristle end. Its own weight bends and curls the bristle. Figure 47-11. This would make painting difficult.

• When not in use, brushes should be put into a solvent suited to the material used on the brush. The proper solvents for finishing materials are shown in Figure 47-12.

**Cleaning Brushes**

It pays to take care of brushes immediately after they have been used. The same solvents used to thin down finishes are generally recommended for cleaning brushes. There are also special brush and roller cleaners that can be used. Figure 47-13. Work the cleaner thoroughly into the heel of the brush and, with your fingers, open the hairs to clean out the waste material. Wipe the brush dry. If the brush is to be stored longer than just overnight, wash it in good commercial cleaning solvent mixed in water or a good grade of detergent. Figure

**47-10.** Tapping a brush on the side of a can. Never rub the bristles on the edge of the can. A larger mouthed container is better. Why?

**47-9.** Twirling a brush to get rid of the loose bristles.

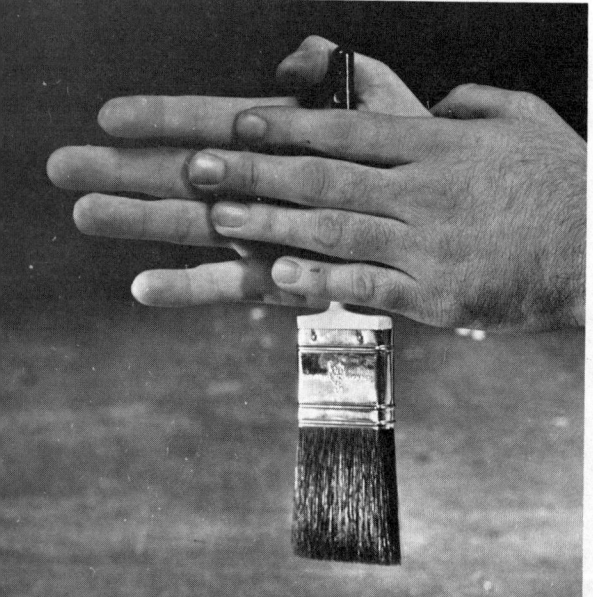

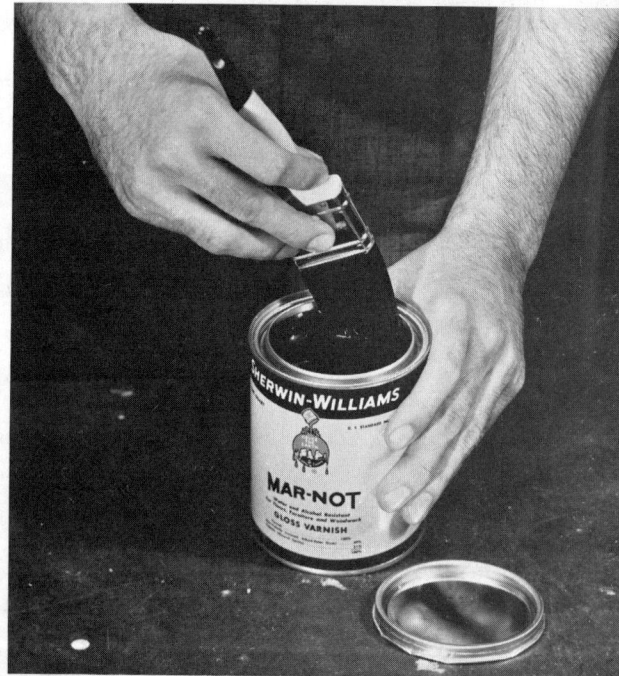

47-14. Wash the brush thoroughly. Comb the bristles with a metal comb. Rinse well, shake out the excess water, and allow to dry. Then wrap the brush in heavy wax paper.

## FINISHING SUPPLIES

*Turpentine* is made from the resin drippings of pine trees. These drippings are distilled by boiling in large copper vats and then running the solution through a condensing coil to a collection barrel. Turpentine rises to the surface and is drained off.

*Linseed oil* is made from flaxseed. The oil is obtained by compressing the seed under high pressure to squeeze out the oil. The oil is used either in its raw state or is boiled to improve its drying qualities

as a paint ingredient. Linseed oil is used by itself to finish certain types of furniture. The oil is applied with a rag and then rubbed into the surface. Several

| Solvent | Finishing Material |
|---|---|
| Turpentine | Oil stain<br>Filler for varnish and shellac finish<br>Varnish<br>Enamel |
| Turpentine and linseed oil | Paint |
| Alcohol | Shellac |
| Lacquer thinner | Filler for lacquer finish<br>Lacquer |

**47-11.** One method of suspending brushes to make sure that the bristles don't become bent.

**47-12.** The proper solvents to be used with certain finishing materials.

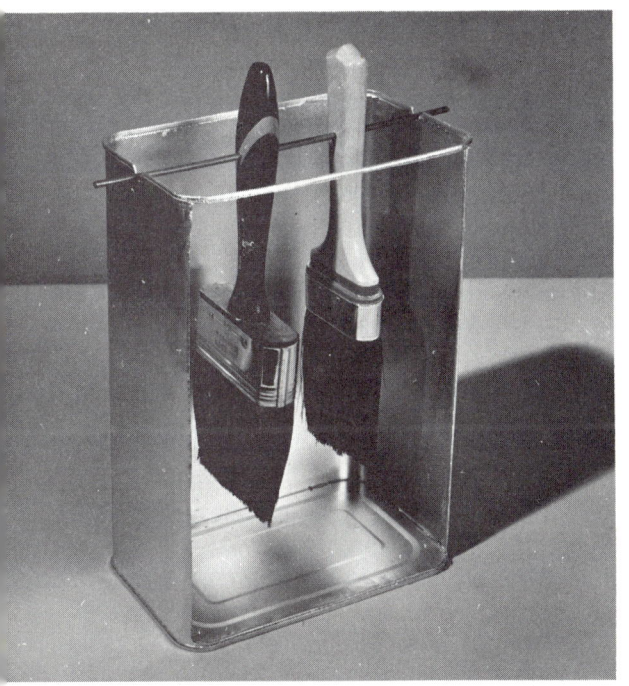

**47-13.** Using a commercial brush cleaner.

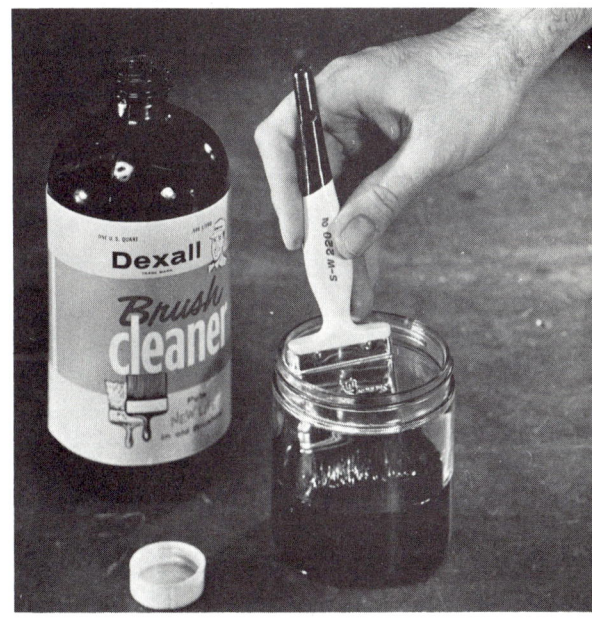

coats are applied in this manner. After the oil is dry, a paste wax is applied and rubbed to a high polish.

The best *alcohol* for mixing shellac is made from wood drippings or chemicals, if available. The government has estab-

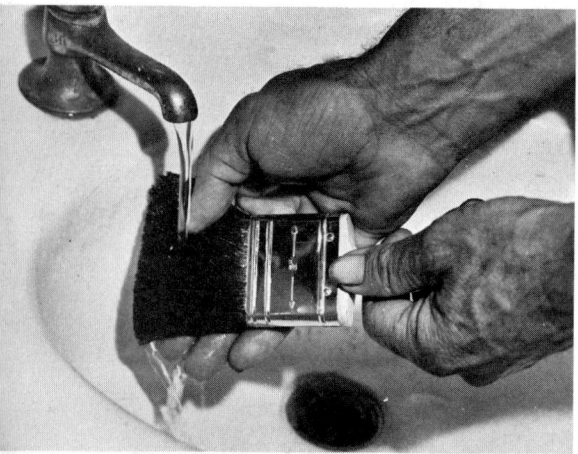

**47-14.** Rinsing a brush. First use a commercial cleaning solvent or a good grade of detergent.

**47-15.** Wiping the surface of the project with a tack rag before applying a finish.

lished a standard alcohol mix that is called Formula Special No. 1 denatured alcohol, which contains ethyl alcohol and wood alcohol.

*Benzene,* used as a solvent and a cleaning fluid, is made from coal tar.

*Mineral spirits* is a pure distillation of petroleum that will do everything that turpentine will do. It can be used as a thinner or solvent.

*Waxes* can be either liquid or paste. Both are made from a base of beeswax, paraffin, carnauba wax, and turpentine. Wax provides a good water-resistant surface that can be renewed often.

*Steel wool* is made of thin metal shavings. It comes in pads or rolls and can be purchased in grades from 000, very fine, to 3, coarse.

*Pumice* is a white-colored powder made from lava. It is available in several grades. The most common for wood finishing are FF and FFF. It is combined with water or oil to rub down the finish.

*Rottenstone* is a reddish brown or grayish black iron oxide vehicle that comes from shale. It is much finer than pumice. It is used with water or oil to produce a smoother finish after the surface has been rubbed with pumice.

*Rubbing oil* should be either petroleum or paraffin oil. If oil refined from petroleum is used, be sure it is a thin grade.

*Abrasive papers* needed are garnet or aluminum oxide finishing papers in grades No. 4/0 (150) and No. 6/0 (220). No. 4/0 (150) is used for sanding after staining, after applying the first coat of shellac, and before applying the filler coat. No. 6/0 (220) is used for final smoothing after shellac coats or other finish. These grades may be used dry or with oil.

*Waterproof (wet-or-dry)* abrasive papers in grades from 240 to 400 grit are used with water for hand sanding between lacquer coats or for rubbing enamel or lacquer.

A *tack rag* is a piece of cheesecloth or cotton rag moistened with thinned varnish. It is used to pick up tiny particles of dust from the wood surface before applying any finish. Figure 47-15.

### REFINISHING

The first step in refinishing a project is to remove the old finish. A simple, inexpensive way to do this is to apply a paint and varnish remover. Flow on a liberal coat of remover on an area about 2 x 2 feet (610 x 610 mm) in size. Don't work too large an area at one time. Allow it to stand about 10 to 30 minutes until the old finish is soft. Figure 47-16.

When the old finish is well softened, remove most of it with a wide scraper or putty knife. Then apply a second coat of the remover and quickly clean up the surface, wiping away the remaining paint with water and a cloth. Figure 47-17. A little detergent added to the water will help. After the old finish has been removed, sand the surface with fine sandpaper until the old finish has been removed down to the bare wood. *Use steel wool for carvings* instead of sandpaper.

**47-16.** Removing the finish by using a commercial paint remover.

**47-17.** Wiping the surface with a damp rag.

## CAN YOU ANSWER THESE QUESTIONS ON WOOD FINISHING AND FINISHING SUPPLIES?

1. Explain how to achieve a fine finish.
2. What are the bristles for most finishing brushes made from?
3. What is linseed oil? How do raw and boiled linseed oil differ?
4. From what is the best alcohol made?
5. What are waxes made from?
6. What is pumice? Rottenstone? Which is finer?
7. Tell how to refinish a project.

# Section IX
## UNIT 48.

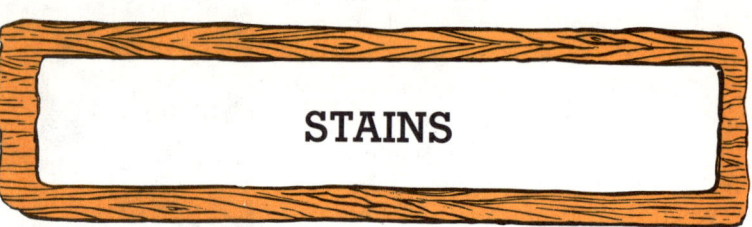

# STAINS

**Stain** is transparent (can be seen through). It is applied to wood to improve its appearance and add color, to bring out the grain, to preserve it, and sometimes to imitate the more expensive woods. Figure 48-1. There are many kinds of stains, but only oil and water stains are used commonly by the beginner.

Stains are usually applied with a brush, sponge, or rag. Then the excess is wiped off with a clean cheesecloth or a pad of cotton waste. It is easiest to use 1½- to 2-inch (38- to 51 mm) brush, especially when applying water stains. Before applying the stain, a small scrap piece of the same kind of wood as the project should be stained first. In this way you see how the stain will look on your project. If you are closely matching the color of another piece of furniture, the entire finishing process on the scrap piece has to be done to make sure you have the finish you want.

### OIL STAIN

Oil stain is coloring that has been mixed in an oil base. You can mix your own oil stain by adding such pigments (colors) as raw and burnt umber, raw and burnt sienna, ochre, orange, light green, turquoise, dark green, blue, red oxide, Venetian red, black drop, and Vandyke brown to linseed oil and turpentine. However, it is much simpler and easier to buy ready-made oil stains. They are available in all ranges of colors: walnut; oak in light, medium, and dark; various shades of mahogany; cherry; rosewood; and many others.

### WATER STAIN

A water stain is made by mixing aniline dye in hot water. The dye usually comes in powdered form and you can mix it yourself. The strength of the stain can be changed by increasing or decreasing the amount of dye.

Water stains also come in ready-mixed

form. Water stain has several advantages. It is cheaper than other stains, has a more even color, and is less likely to fade. However, it raises grain.

## APPLYING OIL STAIN

Choose the color stain you want and test it on a scrap piece. When you find the right color, mix up enough for the entire job. For example, it will take about 1 pint (0.47 litre) of stain to cover about 25 square feet (2.3 m²) of porous wood such as oak.

End grain of wood absorbs more stain than the surface grain and, therefore, looks darker. To prevent this, soak a rag in some linseed oil and rub the end grain before applying the stain. Now you are ready to apply the stain to the surface.

Pour out about one-third cup into a porcelain, glass, or enamel container. Use a good brush. A rag or sponge can be used also, although not as easily.

If possible, apply the stain with the wood held in a horizontal position, to avoid streaking caused by gravity flow. Always stain the lower surfaces first, beginning at the corner and working out. To stain a large, flat surface, dip about one-third of the brush into the liquid, wipe off the excess stain on the side of the jar, and begin at the center of the surface. Figure 48-2. With light strokes, work out toward the edges, brushing on the stain evenly. With each new brushful of stain, begin on the unfinished surface and stroke toward the stained surface. As you near the edges and ends of the wood, brush carefully to keep from spattering the stain. Apply the stain to one small area at a time, wiping off the excess with a clean, dry cloth. Figure 48-3.

One reason oil stains are less satisfactory is that they are slow to dry. Make sure that you cover and wipe off the total surface evenly. Allow the work to dry

**48-1.** A warm, tawny finish was obtained on this cracker bin by using the right color of stains as a base for the finish.

**48-2.** Applying stain. Dip the brush into the stain about one-third of the bristle length and brush on a uniform coat, following the wood grain.

from 12 to 24 hours before continuing with the finishing operation. Then apply a wash coat of shellac (6 parts of alcohol to 1 part shellac). When this is dry, re-sand lightly with 6/0 sandpaper.

## APPLYING WATER STAIN

Before applying water stain, sponge the surface of the wood lightly with water. Figure 48-4. After the surface is dry, sand with 2/0 sandpaper. Figure 48-5. This will help the stain flow on evenly and give a clear, transparent color. Apply the water stain in the same general way as the oil stain. Wipe off the excess with a cloth. Let it dry from 12 to 24 hours. Apply a wash coat of shellac. Then use a small piece of 6/0 sandpaper to sand the surface lightly, removing the high surfaces of the wood. Wipe clean of dust.

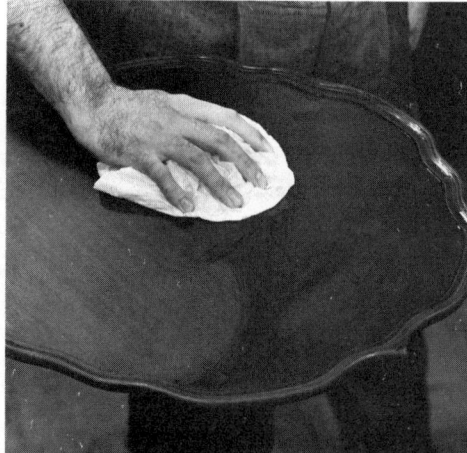

**48-3.** After the stain loses its wet appearance and looks flat, wipe lightly until the depth of color or desired effect is obtained. Use a clean, lint-free cloth formed into a pad and follow the grain of the wood. This will bring out the full beauty of the dark and light grain highlights.

**48-4.** Dampening the wood surface with a sponge before water staining. Do not saturate the surface.

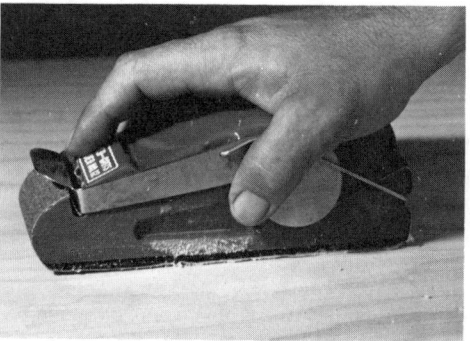

**48-5.** Sand the surface thoroughly with the grain before applying the water stain.

**48-6.** Select the stain color you want and then add tinting color to get the desired effect.

## USING SYNTHETIC SEALERS
## AS STAINS

There are many commercial synthetic sealers that can be used for both the stain and the final finish. These materials give a close-to-the-grain appearance and are partly penetrating and partly surface finishes. The sealers are usually available in clear and satin. The stain can be made by mixing a tube of tinting color (pigments) in the sealer. Figure 48-6. For example, ochre added to the sealer produces a pleasing, light walnut stain. The stain is brushed on and then wiped off with a cloth. Figures 48-7 and 48-8. Then, if necessary, a filler is added. Sand between coats and wipe the surface with a tack rag before applying the final coat. The same sealer without the coloring is used as the final finish. With this kind of material, avoid excessive brushing strokes. Flow it on the surface rather than brush it on. Figure 48-9.

48-7. Applying a stain made by adding color to a sealer.

48-8. Wiping off the stain until it is uniform in color.

**48-9.** Using sealer for the finish coat.

## CAN YOU ANSWER THESE QUESTIONS ON STAINS?

1. Name the two common types of stains.
2. What pigments are found in oil stain?
3. What is the advantage of buying commercially prepared oil stain?
4. How can the strength of water stain be varied?
5. What advantage has water stain? What disadvantage?
6. How can you judge the amount of oil stain needed?
7. Tell how stains are applied.
8. How can you prevent the end grain of wood from taking up too much stain?
9. Describe the brushing technique for staining.
10. What should be done to prepare the wood surface before water stain is applied?
11. Explain how to use a sealer finish as a stain.

# Section IX
## UNIT 49.

# APPLYING WOOD FILLER

**Fillers are used** to seal the pores of wood and to add beauty to the finish. Open-grained woods, such as oak, walnut, chestnut, hickory, pecan, and mahogany, need a medium or heavy paste filler. For closed-grained woods, like birch, fir, and pine, the best filler is a liquid type such as shellac. Figure 49-1.

*Paste filler* is made of ground silicon, linseed oil, turpentine, drier, and coloring. You can buy it canned in natural color or in colors to match wood stains. The paste usually is thinned a little with turpentine, but if applied under a lacquer finish, the filler must be thinned with a lacquer thinner. On bleach finishes, white lead or pure zinc paste is sometimes the filler. Either of these can be colored by adding burnt umber, raw sienna, or other pigment.

In preparing for use, add turpentine until the paste is like a thin cream. Remember, the filler should be thick for open-grained woods such as oak, elm, or chestnut, and it should be thinner for medium open-grained woods like cherry, red gum, soft maple, and redwood. If the filler is to be applied over a stained surface, a wash coat of shellac (1 part shellac to 6 or 7 parts of alcohol) should be applied on the stain. This prevents any bleeding of the finish. Then the surface should be sanded with No. 6/0 sandpaper before the filler is applied.

Apply paste filler with a stiff brush, thoroughly covering the surface. Brush first with the grain, then across it. Figure 49-2. Do not cover too large an area at one time, as the filler dries very rapidly. Rub in the paste filler with the palm of your hand, going over the entire surface

**49-1a.** The kind of filler needed will depend on the wood in the product. A paste filler is used on this pecan writing desk.

**49-1b.** A liquid filler is needed for this birch dough box magazine rack.

**49-2.** Applying a wood filler with a stiff brush. Brush both with and across the grain.

in a circular motion. Allow the filler to dry until the surface loses its shiny appearance. This will take up to 20 minutes. Then wipe across the grain with burlap or rough cloth to remove the excess filler. Figure 49-3.

After most of the filler has been removed, you can use a thin, clean cloth (cheesecloth or cotton) to go over the surface lightly *with the grain* to remove the remainder of the surface filler. Do not press too hard, though, or you will rub some of the filler out of the pores. If necessary, you can add another coat of filler in the same way as the first one. After the filler has dried from 6 to 8 hours, proceed with shellac, lacquer, or varnish finish.

### CAN YOU ANSWER THESE QUESTIONS ON APPLYING WOOD FILLER?

1. Name the two kinds of wood filler.
2. What kind is applied to open-grained woods?
3. Filler is thinned with what solvent? Can this solvent be used for all types of finishes?
4. What filler is chosen for modern bleached finishes?
5. How can you make a wash coat of shellac?
6. How long should a filler remain on the surface before it is wiped off?

**49-3.** Rub across the grain with burlap or coarse cloth to remove the excess filler. Then wipe lightly with the grain, using a fine cloth.

# SHELLAC FINISH

**Shellac** is a good finish for many projects because it is easy to apply, dries quickly, and produces a hard surface. It isn't a good choice, however, if the wood is to be exposed to moisture; shellac turns a cloudy color in dampness. Shellac is frequently used as a finish by itself. It is sometimes used as a sealer over a stain or filler coat before varnish is applied. It is also applied to knots before painting to seal in the pitch (resin in the wood). Figure 50-1.

The shellac itself is a resinous substance which is the product of the lac bug. Most of our supply comes from India and Siam, where these bugs feed on resinous material and deposit the lac on trees. This is removed twice yearly and heated, purified, and laid out in strips to dry. The lac is then ground and mixed in denatured alcohol. Standard shellac, called a 4-pound (1.8 kg) cut, is a mixture of 4 pounds (1.8 kg) to a gallon 3.78 litres) of alcohol.

Natural shellac is orange in color and provides a good, tough finish. However, on many of the light woods, this natural shellac gives the finish an unattractive, yellow-orange tint. Therefore it is used over dark woods or dark stains. Shellac is available in a bleached form called white shellac. This is more satisfactory for general use, especially for light wood finishes.

## APPLYING SHELLAC

The wood must first be clean and dry. The surface should be wiped clean with a lint-free cloth that has been dipped in alcohol. Pour a small amount of shellac into a glass or porcelain container and add an equal amount of alcohol to thin it.

It is far better to apply several thin coats than a few heavy coats. Thinned shellac sinks into the surface of the wood better, providing a smoother finish. Apply the shellac with a clean varnish brush about $1\frac{1}{2}$ to 3 inches (38 to 75 mm) wide. Dip about one-third of the brush length into the shellac and wipe off the sides of the brush on the container. Begin at the center of a flat surface or near the top of a vertical surface and work out toward the edges. Work quickly and evenly, taking light, long strokes. Do not brush over the same surface several times, as shellac dries very rapidly and becomes sticky.

**50-1.** Applying shellac over a wood knot. This seals the knot and helps prevent resin in the wood from leaking out and discoloring the paint or enamel.

A beginner tends to put shellac on too thick, producing a yellowish cast. On the edges of your project, be careful to keep the shellac from piling up and running. After the entire surface has been covered, soak the brush in pure alcohol. Allow the project to dry 2 to 4 hours.

After the surface is dry, go over it with steel wool or 5/0 sandpaper. *Rub with the grain of the wood.* Steel wool has the advantage of following the wood better and covering both high and low spots. If using sandpaper, do not use a sanding block but hold the paper in your fingers.

Before applying the second coat, wipe the surface with a clean rag to remove all dust and dirt. This coat is applied the same way as the first coat but may have only about 40 percent alcohol. After the second coat has been applied, go over the surface again with steel wool or sandpaper. Then apply a third coat with even less alcohol, perhaps 25 percent.

After the last coat, rub the surface lightly with fine sandpaper. To get a very even, smooth surface, mix some ground pumice in oil and rub down the surface with a felt pad. After this, a still smoother surface can be obtained by mixing rottenstone with oil and rubbing it in.

Clean the surface with a clean cloth dipped in benzine. Allow it to dry about one-half hour. Apply a good coat of wax to the surface and let it dry thoroughly. For a good polish, rub briskly with a soft cloth.

The shellac brush should be cleaned immediately with alcohol.

## CAN YOU ANSWER THESE QUESTIONS ON APPLYING SHELLAC?

1. What is the source of shellac? What countries supply it?
2. How is shellac made?
3. What is meant by a 4-pound cut?
4. Shellac is what color naturally?
5. What good rule should be followed in applying shellac?
6. Shellac is available bleached. Why?
7. Describe the special brushing technique for applying shellac.
8. What is the common error made by the beginner in applying shellac?
9. List the steps that must be followed in applying a shellac finish.

# Section IX

## UNIT 51.

# VARNISH FINISH

**Varnish is** an excellent finishing material which will produce a very fine, practical surface. Figure 51-1. However, it is difficult to get a good varnish finish anywhere but in a dust-free room. The objection to using varnish in the small shop is that it dries so slowly that the surface becomes marred with tiny dust particles.

Varnish is a liquid that can be spread on a surface in a thin film, giving the wood an even, transparent coating. It protects the surface of the wood and brightens the color of the stain. Varnishes are made by mixing gum resins with vegetable oils plus necessary thinners and driers. Old-style natural varnish took from 24 to 48 hours to dry. There-

fore, it had the disadvantage of giving dust more time to collect and mar the surface. Synthetic, quick-drying varnishes dry overnight and are dust-free in two hours after applying. For most work, select a quick-drying, high-gloss or satin-finish varnish. It is easier to apply and makes it easier to get a satisfactory finish.

For outside finishes subject to moisture, the best type of varnish is spar varnish. Spar varnish is also excellent for the tops of tables, cabinets, and other pieces that will have hard wear. Spar varnish is made by adding China wood oil to regular varnish, making it water repellent and heat resistant.

**51-1.** A varnish finish can be used successfully on a small accessory such as this wall-hung bookcase.

**51-2.** For a good varnish job, tap the side of the varnish brush against a wire stretched across the pail. Don't rub the varnish brush against the edge of the can.

**51-3.** Apply varnish generously and brush with the wood grain.

For the small shop, varnish should be purchased in small cans. Once a can has been opened, a scum forms on the surface. This is difficult to remove and interferes with a good finish. If necessary, the varnish can be strained through a silk or fine muslin cloth to remove the scum.

## APPLYING VARNISH

Find a dust-free place. If no finishing room is available, wait to do your varnishing until no woodworking machines or tools have been used for some time. Then sprinkle the floor with water to settle the dust. Also, do not varnish anything on cold and damp or hot and humid days. Make sure that the temperature is between 70 and 80 degrees F (21 and 27 degrees Celsius). Wipe the project completely with a tack rag to remove any dust particles.

Open a small can of quick-drying (synthetic-resin) varnish and pour some into a porcelain or glass container. For a first coat, add about 25 percent turpentine. Select a 2- to 3-inch (50 to 75 mm) brush with long bristles. Wipe the wood surface with a clean cloth dipped in benzine.

Dip the brush in the varnish to about one-third the length of the brush. Do not overload it. *Do not wipe the brush on the side of the can,* or the varnish will dry on the rim and on the inside. These dried particles fall into the varnish and mar the finish. Figure 51-2. Apply the varnish with long, easy strokes. Brush first with the grain and then across the grain. Figures 51-3 and 51-4. When the brush is "dry," brush out the varnish with the grain, using only the tip of the brush. You can do more brushing out with varnish than you can with shellac. Continue to work from the center toward the outside edges. As you near the edges, have very little varnish on the brush to keep it from running over the edges or from piling up along the arrises. Never put your brush down on a dusty surface.

After applying the first coat, soak the brush immediately in a can of turpentine. Also, cover the varnish left in the can to keep scum from forming. Allow the varnish coat to dry about 24 hours or until all tackiness has gone. After it is dry, rub the surface with the grain, using No. 6/0 sandpaper.

Make sure that the varnish is perfectly dry before applying another coat. Most of the trouble that comes when applying a varnish finish is from hurrying to apply the second and third coats. When applying the second coat, use the varnish just as it comes from the can. Brush the same way as for the first coat. Allow it to dry and rub down the surface with No. 6/0 sandpaper. If you want a dull, rubbed appearance, you can either apply a dull finish (satin) varnish as a third coat or rub down the regular varnish with pumice and oil or water and rottenstone and oil. Figure 51-5. You can also rub the surface with 3/0 steel wool to get a dull finish.

After the varnish has dried thoroughly, apply a good paste wax. Polish with a clean piece of cheesecloth.

## VARNISH STAINS

A simple finish for many projects is a varnish stain that will give the desired color and finish in one coat. Varnish stain finish is especially satisfactory for simple woodworking projects or when the time cannot be given to applying many coats of regular varnish. Varnish stains can be purchased in different colors. Apply the same as varnish; drying time varies between 2 and 8 hours.

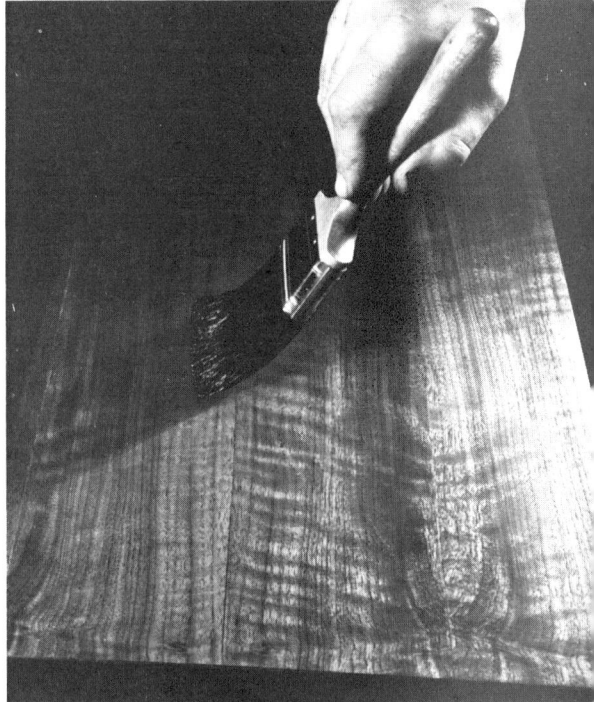

**51-4.** Brush across the grain to level out the varnish.

**51-5.** Rubbing down a varnished surface with pumice and oil or water, using a felt pad.

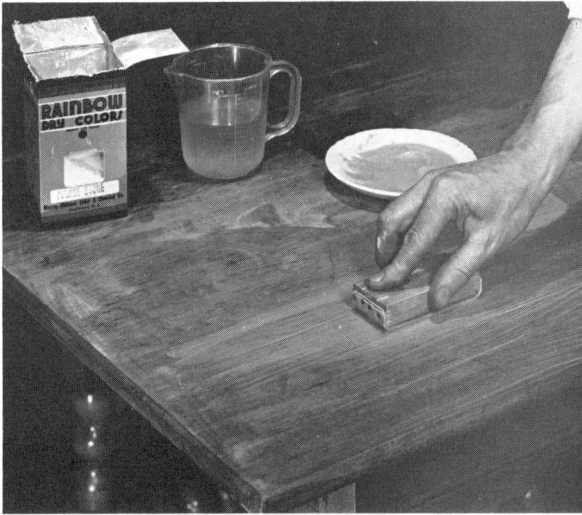

## CAN YOU ANSWER THESE QUESTIONS ON A VARNISH FINISH?

1. Why is it difficult to obtain a good varnished surface?
2. Tell from what and how varnishes are made.
3. When buying varnish, what considerations should be taken into account?
4. How and why is varnish strained?
5. What conditions must prevail to obtain a good varnish surface?
6. Describe the technique for applying varnish. How does it differ from the technique for applying shellac?
7. Should the first varnish coat be applied full strength?
8. List the steps to be followed in applying a varnish finish.
9. Name the most common mistake made in varnishing.
10. How can a dull finish be obtained?
11. What is a varnish stain? Why is it commonly used by beginners?

Section

IX

UNIT 52.

# APPLYING PENETRATING AND WIPE-ON FINISHES

**There are many** modern commercial finishes that can be used in the shop with a minimum of difficulty. Figure 52-1. These include finishes that sink into the wood. Figure 52-2. Most can be applied with a small cloth or pad, eliminating the need for spray equipment or brushes. These finishes also do away with the dust problem that is so bothersome when using varnish. Penetrating and wipe-on finishes are synthetic, chemical materials.

### SEALACELL

This is a three-step process involving three different materials to complete the finish. Each can be applied with a rag or cloth. The materials are as follows:

1. *Sealacell* is a moisture-repellent, penetrating wood sealer that is applied over the raw wood. (Ground-in-oil pigments can be mixed with the Sealacell to serve as a stain). Stain and filler can be applied in one step by mixing paste filler in the Sealacell and then adding ground-in-oil pigment to get the desired color. Apply very liberally with a cloth, because the depth of penetration depends upon the amount applied. Let dry overnight. Buff lightly with fine steel wool.

2. *Varno wax* is a blend of gums and waxes. To apply, make a small cloth pad about 1 x 2 inches (25.5 to 51 mm). Coat with wax and rub with a circular motion first and then wipe out with the grain. Buff lightly with 3/0 steel wool.

3. *Royal finish* is the final coat. It is applied in the same manner as the Varno wax. Two or more applications of Royal

finish increase the depth and luster. A soft, egg-shell finish can be obtained by buffing the finish with fine steel wool.

## MINWAX WOOD

Minwax is a penetrating wood seal and wax that is applied directly to raw wood. Two coats will complete the job. The natural beauty of the wood is preserved because this finish penetrates and seals, leaving the finish in the wood with very little on the surface. Minwax is available in natural, light oak, pine, dark walnut, colonial maple, and red mahogany. It dries rapidly. This makes it possible to apply more than one coat in a day. It is not necessary that this finish be rubbed after each coat. However, by rubbing with 4/0 steel wool, a very fine finish can be obtained.

## DEFT

Deft is a semigloss, clear, interior, wood finish. It is easy to use, requires no thinning, will not show brush marks, and will not darken. This material seals, primes, finishes the wood, and dries in 30 minutes. Three coats are recommended. The first coat seals the wood. The second coat adds depth. The third coat results in a mirror-smooth, fine furniture finish. The third coat can be sanded with 6/0 wet-or-dry sandpaper or rubbed mirror-smooth with pumice and rottenstone. All three coats can be applied in a few hours. Deft can also be applied from an aerosol spray can.

## PENETRATING FLOOR FINISH AND WAX

There are many commercial penetrating floor finishes for projects. Apply one coat with a rag. Allow to dry as specified on the container. Buff the surface with a pad of 3/0 steel wool. Apply a second coat and buff with 6/0 steel wool. Then apply a good coat of paste wax and wipe with a soft cloth. Figure 52-3.

**52-1.** This table was given a finish completed in a simple three-step process.

## OIL ("FRENCH" STYLE) FINISH

Woods like walnut, mahogany, and cherry can be finished by applying many coats of linseed oil mixed with turpentine. The common mixtures are either two-thirds boiled linseed oil and one-third

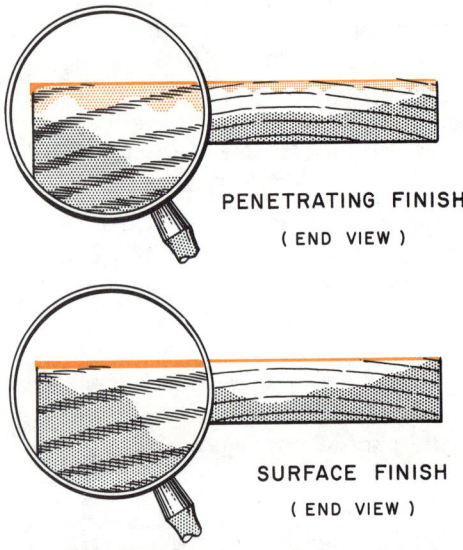

**PENETRATING FINISH**

( END VIEW )

**SURFACE FINISH**

( END VIEW )

**52-2.** Here you see the difference between a penetrating finish and a surface finish.

turpentine or one-half raw linseed oil and one-half turpentine heated quite hot. To apply the finish, soak a soft, lint-free cloth with the mixture and rub vigorously over the entire surface. Allow to dry for about 15 minutes and then wipe thoroughly with a clean cloth. Each coat must dry about 24 hours. Then rub the surface hard for about 15 minutes. Dry at least a week this time. Then apply a minimum of three additional coats in the same manner. This should be repeated over several weeks until a very lustrous finish appears. To prevent warping, oil the underside of the wood.

## DANISH OIL FINISH

Penetrating oil finishes like linseed oil have long been used to beautify and preserve gun stocks and other fine woods. To produce a Danish oil finish, penetrating resin-oil is needed. This finish actually improves the wood without hours of hand rubbing. Danish oil requires only a simple application, is long lasting, seldom needs replenishing, and never needs resanding. One of the big advantages is that a surface that has become

**52-3.** A penetrating floor finish is a simple finish for completing a project.

marred from hard usage is relatively simple to refinish. Figure 52-4.

Danish oil finish is applied as follows:

1. After sanding, apply a quick-dry, alcohol (or water-base), wood stain with a clean cloth or brush. Figures 52-5 and 52-6.

2. Let stand to dry for about 45 minutes.

3. Apply liberal amounts of the penetrating, resin-oil finish.

4. Allow the oil to soak into the wood for about 30 minutes or until penetration stops. Keep the surface uniformly wet with the finish.

5. Wipe the surface completely dry with a soft, absorbent cloth. Figure 52-7.

6. For more luster, let the surface dry for 4 hours.

7. Wet-sand lightly with a small amount of resin-oil finish.

8. Dry the wood thoroughly with a clean cloth.

9. Polish briskly with another cloth.

**52-5.** Sanding the surface.

**52-6a.** Applying the oil with a brush.

**52-4.** With a penetrating oil finish, a bench with spike marks can be repaired easily. Rub with light steel wool, followed by the application of an oil finish.

**52-6b.** Applying the oil with a rag.

**52-7.** Cleaning off the excess oil with a lint-free, dry, clean cloth.

### CAN YOU ANSWER THESE QUESTIONS ON APPLYING PENETRATING AND WIPE-ON FINISHES?

1. What does "penetrating" mean? How does it differ from a surface finish?
2. Describe the way to apply a Sealacell finish.
3. Tell how to apply an oil finish.
4. How many coats of Deft should be used?
5. On what woods is an oil finish often applied?
6. What is the oil in a Danish oil finish?

# LACQUER

**Lacquer** is a chemical composition of nitrocellulose, resins, and solvents. Lacquers have come into common use in both clear and colored forms for wood surfaces. Figure 53-1. They dry quickly and produce a hard finish. Most commercial lacquer finishes are applied by spraying, but the brush finish is usually done in most small shops. Figure 53-2. Because lacquer contains substances that are similar to paint and varnish remover, it cannot be applied directly over paint or varnish. Always use a lacquer thinner for thinning the materials and for cleaning the brushes.

## APPLYING A CLEAR BRUSH LACQUER FINISH

Apply the stain and filler coats the same as for shellac and varnish finishes. It is better to use a water stain than an oil stain in a lacquer finish, since this does not "bleed" so much. Apply a thin coat of shellac as a sealer before applying the lacquer.

Open a can of clear brushing lacquer and stir it well. Lacquer usually does not have to be thinned but, if it does, use a commercial lacquer thinner. Select a brush with soft bristles such as a camel's hair brush. Dip the brush about one-third of the way into the lacquer but do not wipe any off on the side of the container. Load the brush heavily. Flow on the lacquer with long, rapid strokes. Lap the sides of each stroke. Do not attempt to brush it in as you would paint or varnish.

Remember, lacquer dries very quickly and gives a smooth, tough surface. Allow the lacquer to dry about 2 hours. Then go over the surface lightly with No. 6/0 sandpaper.

Apply second and third coats in the same way. After the third coat is dry, the surface is rubbed with rottenstone and

**53-1.** Lacquer is the most commonly used finishing material for manufactured furniture like this end table.

oil and pumice stone and oil. Lacquer brushes should be cleaned with commercial lacquer thinner.

## APPLYING COLORED LACQUER FINISH

Sand the wood surface with No. 2/0 sandpaper. Then apply a thin coat of shellac to the wood as a base for the lacquer. Apply two or three coats of the colored lacquer the same as for clear lacquer. To finish the surface, rub it down with rottenstone and oil after the lacquer is dry.

## APPLYING LACQUER FROM AN AEROSOL CAN

For small projects and for repair work, one of the best methods of applying clear or colored lacquer is from a self-spraying (aerosol) can. The aerosol can contains about half lacquer (or paint) and half liquid gas.

In using a spray can, hold so the valve is about 12 to 15 inches (305 to 381 mm) from the surface. Figure 53-3. Move the can back and forth, keeping it an equal distance from the surface. If sags or runs develop, you are trying to cover too fast.

Remember that the hiding power of lacquers varies with the color. If you are spraying light-colored lacquer, apply a series of several light coats. Sand the surface lightly between coats.

## APPLYING A SPRAY LACQUER FINISH

Spraying is the most common method in industry of applying a lacquer finish. A spray booth should be available. Spraying can be done out of doors on a calm day; however, a mask must be worn. There are many kinds of spraying equipment. For simple work, a small spray gun

**53-2.** Spraying the final coat of lacquer on cabinets that are moving along a production line.

**53-3.** Applying lacquer from an aerosol can.

and compressor are all you will need. Figure 53-4.

## Spraying a project

1. First clean the surface with a tack rag.

2. Check the gun to make sure that it is clean.

3. Fill the spray container about half full of lacquer and one-fourth full of lacquer thinner.

4. Try the spray gun on a piece of scrap stock or wrapping paper. It should spray with a fine, even mist. Figure 53-5.

5. Spray on four or five coats of thin lacquer. Usually the first two coats are gloss or bright and the last two coats are made dull or semigloss by rubbing. When

**53-4.** This type of spraying unit is satisfactory for small projects.

**53-5.** Test the spraying action before applying the finish.

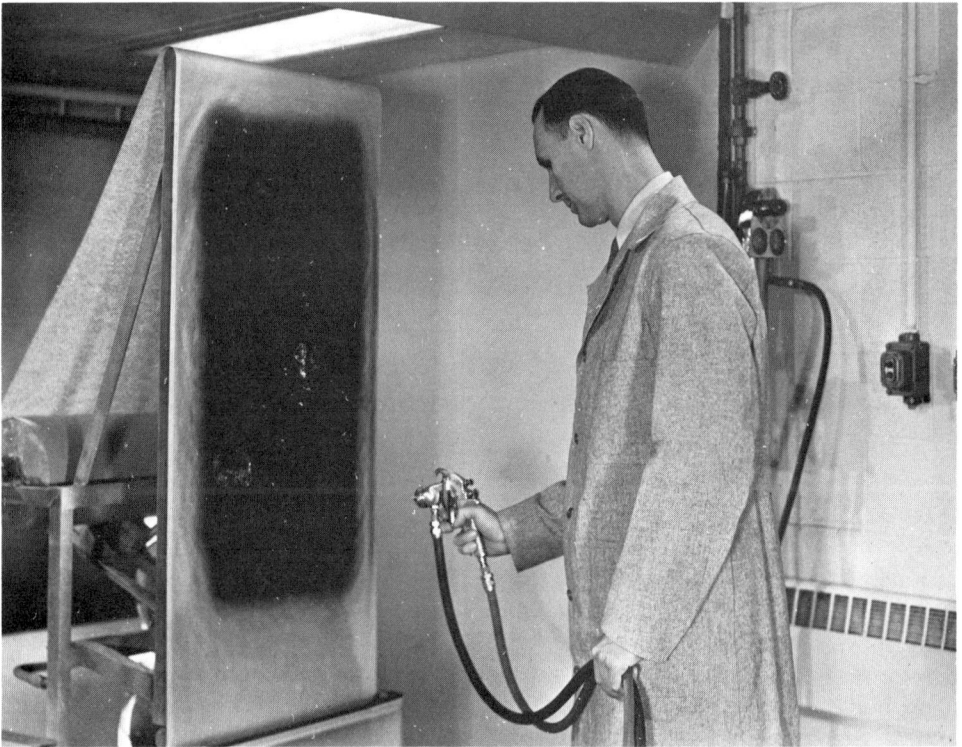

**53-6.** Spraying a cedar chest in a ventilated spray booth.

spraying, hold the gun about 6 to 8 inches (152 to 203 mm) from the work and move back and forth with straight, uniform strokes. Figure 53-6. Keep the gun perpendicular to the surface at all times. Start the stroke off the work and pull the trigger when the gun is just opposite the edge. Release the trigger at the other end.

6. After you have finished spraying, clean all the equipment with lacquer thinner.

## CAN YOU ANSWER THESE QUESTIONS ON LACQUER?

1. What is lacquer? Can it be applied over a painted or varnished surface?
2. How is lacquer most often applied commercially?
3. Describe the correct brushing technique for applying lacquer.
4. How many coats of lacquer are usually needed to obtain a good finish?
5. What is the principal advantage of a lacquer finish?
6. Describe the correct method of using spraying equipment.

Section

IX

UNIT 54.

# ENAMEL AND PAINT

**Enamel and paint** are protective and decorative coatings used on inexpensive wood. Both materials provide colorful finishes for furniture, cabinets, and accessories. Figure 54-1.

### ENAMELING

Enamel is composed largely of colored varnish. It differs from paint in that it contains varnish resins. Enamel is also only semiopaque (partly transparent). Therefore the primer coat must be opaque (can't be seen through) to be suitable. Enamels dry with either a high gloss or semigloss, depending on the amount of resins. Enamels are extremely satisfactory for small projects on which a colored finish is desired. Figure 54-2.

### Applying Enamel Finish

Sand the wood surface with No. 2/0 sandpaper. Cover all knots and sap streaks with a coat of thin shellac. Select a can of enamel paint undercoat and mix it thoroughly. Use a 2- or 3-inch (50 or 75 mm) brush and apply the undercoat the same as varnish. In applying enamel, flow the finish on with short, light strokes. Figure 54-3. Work in small areas about two feet (609 mm) wide. When the brush is as dry as possible, go back over the surface, stroking the same direction.

To paint knobs, first attach the knobs to a piece of cardboard and then paint with a small brush. Figure 54-4. To paint legs, first insert a large tack part way into the bottom of each table leg to raise the table slightly off the floor. Figure 54-5. Then apply the enamel from top to bottom with long, smooth brush strokes.

After the surface has thoroughly dried, sand lightly with No. 2/0 sandpaper. Then apply a second undercoat. Select quick-drying finish enamel of the desired color. Apply one or two coats the same way as the undercoat. If you want a dull finish, use satin varnish or allow the final gloss coat to dry for a day or two and then rub the surface with pumice stone and water.

**54-1a.** Paint or enamel can be used to complete something as simple as a house sign.

**54-1b.** Paint or enamel can also be used to finish a complete set of furniture.

## PAINTING

Painting is a good way to finish inexpensive pieces of furniture and cabinets. Paints are made from many materials, including white lead and zinc, linseed oil, turpentine, drier, and coloring. Many of the newer paints are made entirely from chemicals. The basic source of many paints is petroleum. Paints are

**54-2.** This decorator lamp was made from inexpensive wood and then finished by applying several coats of colored enamel.

**54-3.** Flow enamel on with even, horizontal strokes.

**54-4.** Paint knobs like this.

**54-5.** Note the correct technique for painting round tapered legs.

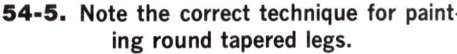
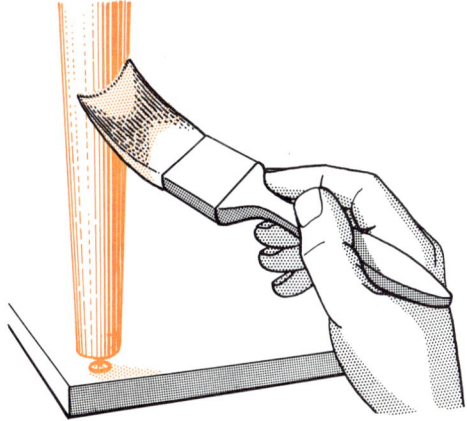

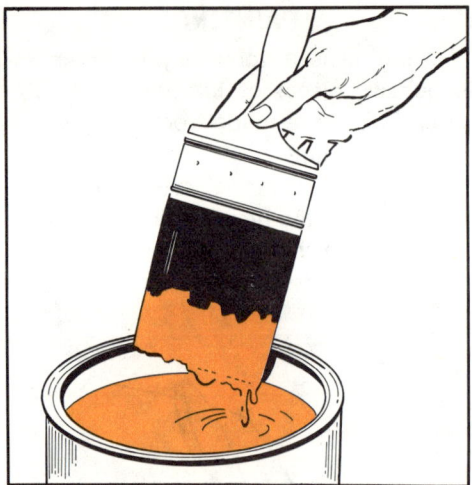

**54-6.** Dip the brush into the paint at least one-third the length of the bristles. When the brush is well filled, remove and tap lightly against the inside of the can lid.

**54-7.** Hold the brush comfortably near the base of the handle, exerting light pressure with your fingertips. Do not bear down, but exert enough pressure to make the bristles flex slightly toward the top as you begin the brush stroke.

available either as outside or inside types. In applying paint to a surface, usually three coats are given: primer, undercoat, and finishing.

### Applying a Paint Finish

Sand the wood surface with No. 1 or No. 0 sandpaper. Apply a light coat of shellac to wood that is porous or that contains knots and sap streaks. Open a can of the primer paint. Pour off the light liquid on the top into a second container. Thoroughly stir the primer and then gradually add the clear liquid until it is mixed. For the first coat, thin the paint

**54-8.** Masking tape protects the edge of the top surface from accidental brush marks and smears. This eliminates the time-consuming job of clean-up. The tape is readily stripped off afterwards, assuring a neater finish than by any other method.

with turpentine and/or linseed oil. Sometimes a small amount of yellow ochre is also added to the primer for better coverage. Use a good brush of the right size for the project and apply a thin coat of the primer.

To apply paint, put a small amount on the brush and brush it into the surface. Figure 54-6. Beginners usually apply paint too thick and do not brush it in thoroughly. Figure 54-7. Allow the paint to dry from 12 to 24 hours and then go over the surface with No. 1 sandpaper. Now apply the undercoat. This coat should be thinned somewhat with turpentine. Go over the surface thoroughly, covering all parts of the project. Apply the final coat just as it comes from the can, after a thorough mixing. Thoroughly brush the paint in, making sure that a smooth, even coat is applied. When painting two or more colors on the same project, it is a good idea to use masking tape for color separation. Figure 54-8.

## CAN YOU ANSWER THESE QUESTIONS ON ENAMEL AND PAINT?

1. In what ways does enamel differ from paint?
2. Why is a primer coat put on first?
3. Why is enamel a desirable finish for small projects?
4. What things should be done before the first coat of enamel is applied?
5. How does the brushing technique differ from that for applying paint?
6. How can you get a dull finish?
7. From what are paints made?
8. How many coats are usually applied to obtain a good surface?
9. Describe the proper method of mixing a primer paint.
10. Beginners usually encounter certain difficulties in learning to paint correctly. How can these difficulties be overcome?
11. What material can be added to the primer which will provide better coverage?
12. List the steps followed in painting a wood surface, beginning with the primer coat and continuing until the final coat is applied.

# ANTIQUING

**Antiquing,** sometimes called color glazing, is a refinishing method of developing a soft, mellow surface tone normally associated with age and many hours of hand rubbing. It is one of the simplest and most attractive wood finishes that can be applied. Figure 55-1. Because it is opaque, it can be used successfully on relatively inexpensive woods like pine and poplar.

Antiquing is done in two simple steps. First, a paint-like undercoat is applied to cover the entire project (including any old paint or varnish). This provides a base color for the second step—the application of the color glaze. Wood tones and other special effects are achieved by wiping or texturing the color glaze before it dries. The result is a soft-toned luster plus a tough finish. It has the beauty of old-world masterpieces. For added protection, a finish coat of varnish can be applied.

Antiquing can be used on chests, tables, picture frames, and almost all decorative items.

## PROCEDURE FOR ANTIQUING

The first step is to select an antiquing kit which contains the color base undercoat and the color glaze. These kits are available in light and dark tones and in wood-tone effects. Most of the light tones have an undercoat base of white with a glaze of blue, gold, olive, red, or pink to produce an antique-white finish. The deeper tones use a base color of gold, blue, olive, green, or red with a glaze of similar or contrasting color. For wood-tone effects, select an undercoat of cherry, fruitwood, walnut, butternut, or beechwood with a glaze to match. In addition to the antiquing kit, other materials and tools may be needed. Figure 55-2.

Prepare the project for antiquing by first removing all of the hardware, including knobs and pulls. If there are any imperfections in the surface, fill these with patching plaster or plastic wood.

**55-1a.** This small chairside chest has an antique white finish with gold inserts.

Figure 55-3. Then sand the surface lightly. Figure 55-4. Make sure that all oil, grease, or wax has been removed with paint thinner. Stir the undercoat thoroughly and apply to the clean surface. Apply a generous coat, working it well into the surface by brushing in all directions. Make the final smoothing brush strokes in the direction of the wood grain without cross-brushing. Figure 55-5. Allow the undercoat to dry overnight. On new or unfinished wood, two coats of undercoat may be needed. The first coat will be partly absorbed in the wood pores, sealing them. The second coat will remain on the surface to give a full, rich

color effect. Allow the second coat to dry overnight also.

Apply the color glaze with a brush, in a thin, even coat. Make sure all indentations, crevices, and other low places are covered since this is where the glaze will remain on the surface, giving the project its antique appearance. Let the glaze stand about 15 minutes. Figure 55-6. Wipe lightly with cheesecloth in the direction of the grain. The amount of glaze removed can vary. Wipe heavily in areas that you want highlighted, such as the center panels or the high points of carvings or other features. Figure 55-7. Allow the glaze to remain in the crevices and corners. If you are finishing a large piece of furniture, it is perhaps better to glaze only a section at a time. Do the wiping of that part before going on to the next.

**55-1b.** A picture frame with an antique finish is a suitable choice for this painting.

**55-1c.** The bottom of this drawer commode is finished in antique white and the top is wood-grain plastic laminate.

When using wood-tone glazes, apply the glaze to only one section at a time and then proceed to the wiping operations. Brush on a very light, thin coat of glaze, spreading it as far as it will go before dipping the brush again. As soon as the glaze is applied to one section, wipe it with cheesecloth in the direction of the wood grain. Remember that grain usually runs the long way on a project. After the glaze is completely dry, preserve the finish by applying a coat of varnish. Figure 55-8.

**55-2.** Some other tools and materials that may be needed for antiquing.

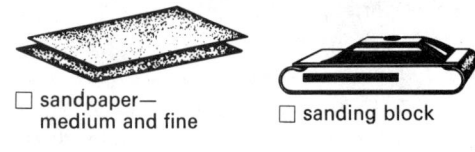

☐ sandpaper— medium and fine

☐ sanding block

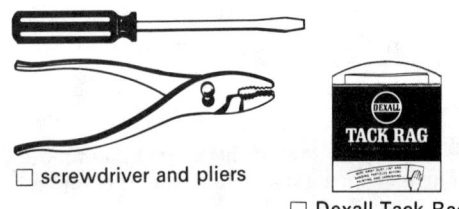

☐ screwdriver and pliers

☐ Dexall Tack Rag

☐ drop cloth or newspapers

☐ cheese cloth, texturing material

☐ Dexall Patching Paste

☐ masking tape

☐ wipe-up rags

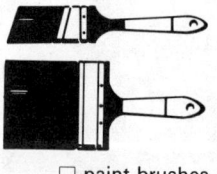

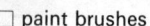

☐ paint brushes

**55-3.** To prepare the project for antiquing, remove all hardware. Also, if there are any cracks, gouges, or imperfections, fill them with plastic wood or patching paste.

**55-4.** Sand the entire surface lightly with the grain.

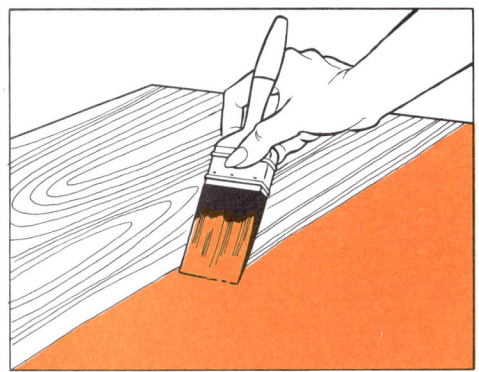

**55-5.** Apply the colored undercoat with a brush. Make sure that this is dry before applying the glaze.

**55-7.** Continue to wipe the glaze until you have achieved the antique effect desired. Highlights can be obtained by working the glaze into the corners with the cloth.

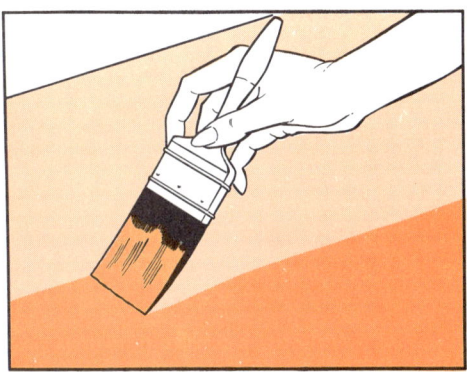

**55-6.** Apply the glaze with a brush. Before it dries, wipe the surface with cheesecloth to create the antique effect.

**55-8.** For a more durable finish, add a coat of clear varnish.

## CAN YOU ANSWER THESE QUESTIONS ON ANTIQUING?

1. Describe the process of antiquing.
2. Discuss the two basic steps in antiquing a product.
3. How are color combinations achieved?
4. Is it necessary to remove the old finish before applying an antique finish?
5. What is the best method of preserving an antique finish?

# SECTION X

## Tool Maintenance

**What you must know and be able to do in Unit 56:**

56. Single-edge cutting tools: all steps in securing a good, new cutting edge—removing the old edge, grinding the angle, whetting the edge, and testing for sharpness; special problems in sharpening a hand scraper, an auger bit, a drawknife, small knives, a handsaw, and turning tools; grinding a screwdriver.

In this book, only one unit is devoted to tool maintenance. However, this is a step ahead. In earlier woodworking experiences, your teacher may have kept tools sharp for the class. Here is an opportunity to learn how to put a bad edge in condition yourself by grinding to the correct angle and honing. The unit also includes sharpening an auger bit and maintaining a screwdriver blade.

# SHARPENING HAND TOOLS

**If one rule which** is more important than any other in woodworking could be chosen, it might be this: *Successful woodwork depends upon good cutting edges.*

For example, if you have used a plane that digs in, sticks, is hard to push, or leaves grooves in the work, you will understand why good cutting tools are so necessary. Time spent on tool sharpening is well rewarded in better and easier work.

Nothing is so important to good workmanship as well-conditioned tools. With tools that are correctly ground, woodworking can be interesting and pleasant. Dull, marred tools, on the other hand, cause accidents or bad temper and always contribute to poor workmanship.

## SHARPENING SINGLE-EDGED TOOLS

Several single-edged tools, such as plane irons, chisels, and spokeshave blades, are sharpened in the same general way. A description of sharpening a plane iron will show how to sharpen all of these tools.

A plane iron needs to be reground if it is badly nicked or untrue or if the bevel is rounded, too blunt, or too thin. Before regrinding the plane iron, decide what the shape of the cutting edge should be. For most general work the cutting edge should be straight, with the corners slightly rounded to keep them from digging into the wood. For rough planing, the entire edge should be slightly rounded, with the center of the cutting edge about $\frac{1}{32}$ inch (1 mm) higher than the corners.

### Removing the Old Edge

Leave the plane-iron cap fastened to the iron to act as a guide. Hold the plane iron at right angles to the grinding wheel. Move it back and forth to grind off the old cutting edge until all nicks are removed and the edge is square with the sides. (This last reshaping needs to be done only when the plane iron is in very poor condition.) Check the edge for squareness with a try square. Hold the handle against the side of the plane iron. After the edge is square, remove the cap.

### Grinding

The plane iron, chisel, and other single-edge tools usually are ground with a bevel that is 2 or $2\frac{1}{2}$ times longer than the thickness of the blade. Figure 56-1. The smaller angle, about 20 degrees, is used on softwoods and the more blunt angle, about 25 to 30 degrees, on hardwoods. Before grinding the bevel, the wheel should be checked to make sure that it is true and that the face is square. Also, the wheel must turn toward the cutting edge.

If a grinding attachment is available, use it to hold the plane iron. This will assure you that the correct bevel will be ground. Figure 56-2. If one is not available, hold the plane iron in both hands.

Figure 56-3. Carefully move the plane iron back and forth across the grinding wheel. Figure 56-4. Do not apply too much pressure, as this will overheat the edge. Frequently remove the blade and dip it in water to cool it and to prevent the temper from being drawn from the steel. If you are grinding freehand, move the tool slowly back to the wheel to get the "feel" of the angle. Be sure that you continue grinding at the same angle as

**56-3.** Grinding a plane-iron blade without the use of a guide. In using this method, the plane iron should be moved from right to left constantly and should be cooled frequently in water. It takes considerable skill to keep the bevel even when grinding in this manner.

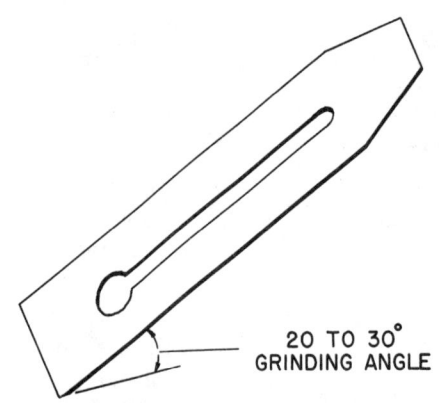

20 TO 30° GRINDING ANGLE

**56-1.** A plane-iron blade should be ground at an angle of 20 to 30 degrees. The length of the bevel should be about 2 to 2½ times the thickness of the blade.

**56-4.** Grinding a chisel. Notice especially that safety glasses are worn and that the eye shield is in place.

**56-2.** Grinding a plane-iron blade held in an attachment. This is the simplest method since, once the angle has been set, it is easy to keep the bevel even. However, care must be taken not to burn the cutting edge, especially when using a dry grinder, as shown here.

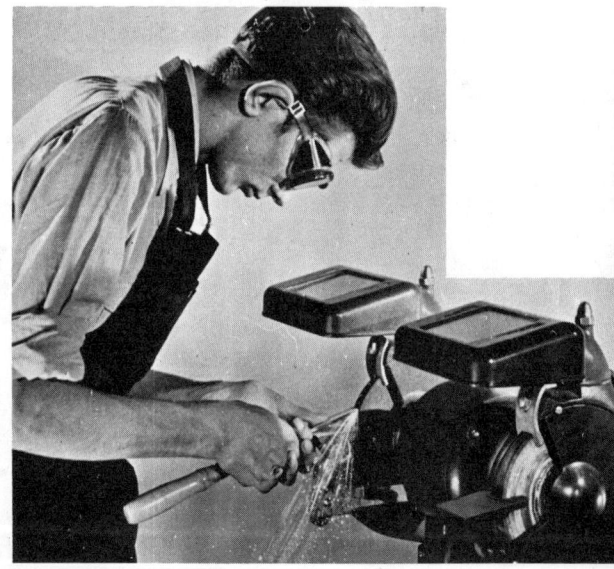

before. As the cutting edge is formed, a slight burr may appear. This will be removed later. As the final grinding is done, make sure that you have a single surface on the bevel and that the bevel is at the correct angle. This can be checked with a sliding T bevel or the protractor head of a combination set.

### Whetting or Honing the Edge

Select an oilstone with a flat, true surface. There are two classes of oilstone for this purpose. The natural stones, such as the Arkansas and Washita, are white in color; the artificial oilstones are made either of aluminum oxide, which is brownish in color, or silicon carbide, which is grayish in color. A combination artificial oilstone is best; one surface is coarse and the other surface is fine. Figure 56-5.

Wipe off the stone and then apply a mixture of half kerosene and half machine oil to the surface. Hold the plane iron on the oilstone with the bevel side down. Figure 56-6. First apply pressure on the heel of the bevel, then slowly raise the plane iron until the bevel is in contact with the oilstone surface. Figure 56-7.

The whetting angle should be between 30 and 35 degrees. Move the tool back and forth on the face of the oilstone or in a circular motion to form a figure 8. Figure 56-8. A wire or feather edge will form on the cutting edge. To remove this, turn the plane iron around with the side opposite the bevel flat against the oil-

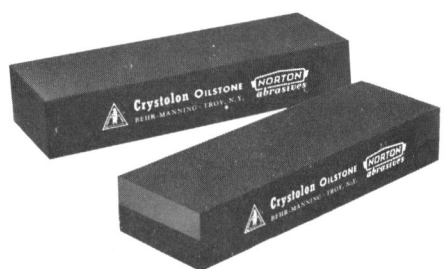

**56-5.** Fine and coarse oilstones.

**56-6.** A chisel-sharpening holder can be used to keep the tool at the correct angle. The holder can be adjusted to provide the correct bevel angle.

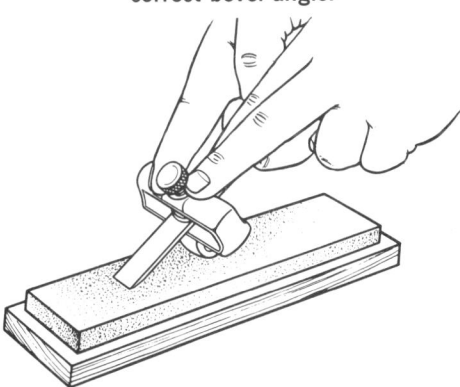

**56-7.** Whetting a plane iron. Hold the iron with the bevel side down at a slightly greater angle than that at which it is ground. Apply oil to the stone and move the plane iron back and forth or in a figure-8 movement.

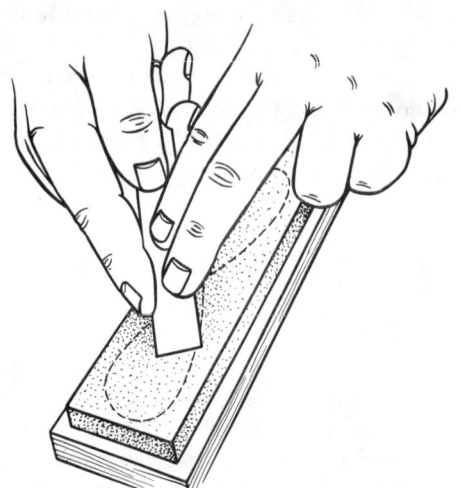

**56-8.** A figure-8 movement of the tool will distribute wear evenly on the stone.

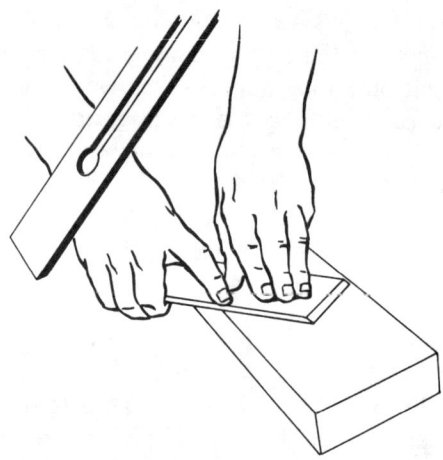

**56-9a.** Remove the burr from the cutting edge by holding the plane iron flat on the stone.

stone. Move it back and forth a few times. *Make sure that you hold the tool flat.* Figure 56-9. The slightest bevel on this side will prevent the plane-iron cap from fitting properly. Chips can then get between the cap and the iron.

If the wire edge is not completely removed, the cutting edge should be pushed across the corner of a piece of softwood. The finer side of the oilstone can be used to sharpen the plane iron to an even keener edge.

## Testing for Sharpness

One method is to hold the plane iron with the cutting edge down and allow the edge to rest lightly on the thumbnail. As the tool is moved, it tends to "bite" into the nail if it is sharp. It will slide across easily if it is dull. Another method is to look carefully at the edge. If it is sharp,

**56-9b.** An enlargement of the cutting edge before and after the burr has been removed.

**56-10.** Drawfiling the hand scraper. Use a fine file in this manner until the edge is square with the sides of the scraper. To prevent surplus vibration, lower the scraper in the vise.

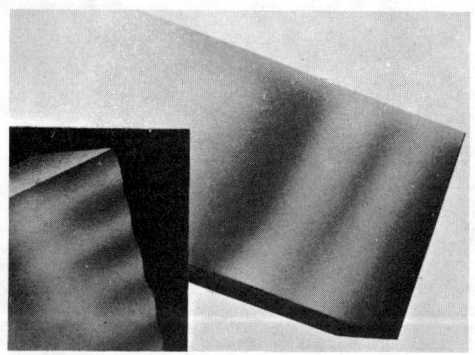

the edge cannot be seen. If it is dull, a thin, white line can be seen.

Be careful when assembling the plane iron and cap and when inserting them into the plane so as not to nick the cutting edge.

### SHARPENING A HAND SCRAPER

A hand scraper must be sharpened frequently. The good woodworker sharpens it every time he uses it. Place the tool in a vise with the cutting edge showing. To remove the old cutting edge, hold a file flat against the side of the scraper and take a few strokes. Then use a fine file to drawfile the edge until it is square with the sides of the scraper. Figure 56-10.

Whet the cutting edge by moving it back and forth across an oilstone. Hold the blade at right angles to the surface. Figure 56-11. Then hold the sides of the blade flat against the stone, again working it back and forth, to remove the wire edge. Figure 56-12.

Place the scraper flat on the bench with the cutting edge extending slightly over the edge of the bench. Hold a burn-

isher flat on the side of the scraper and take a few, firm strokes toward you to draw the edge. Figure 56-13.

Then hold the scraper on edge as shown in Figure 56-14. Use the burnishing tool held at an angle of about 85 degrees to turn the edge of the scraper.

**56-12.** Hold the scraper flat against the stone on both sides to remove any burr.

**56-13.** A burnisher.

**56-11.** Whetting the edge of the scraper. Hold the scraper at right angles to the stone and move it back and forth.

**56-14.** Use a burnisher to turn the edge of the scraper. Hold the scraper as shown.

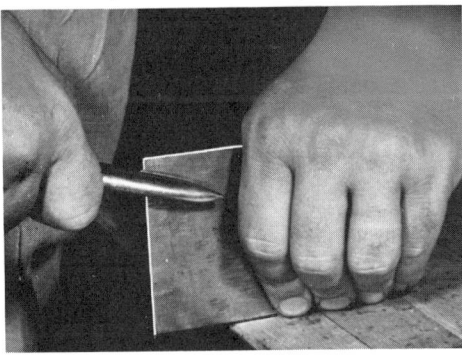

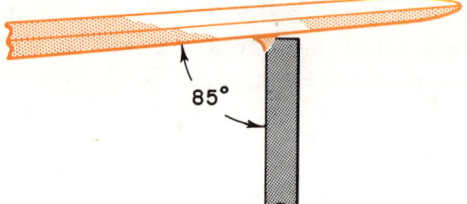

**56-15.** Hold the burnishing tool at an angle of about 85 degrees to the side of the scraper to turn the edge.

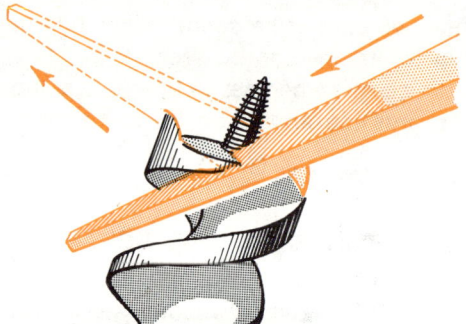

**56-16b.** Sharpening the lip of an auger bit, using a triangular-shaped file.

Figure 56-15. This is done by drawing the burnisher up with a firm, brisk stroke. The edge is sharp when it will catch your thumbnail as it is drawn across it.

## SHARPENING AN AUGER BIT

The auger bit must be kept sharp to obtain best results. Sharpening is done by filing the spur and the lip with a small half-round or three-cornered file. Figure 56-16. File the spur on the inside to keep the same general shape. Never file the outside. File the lip on the underside or the side toward the shank until it has a sharp cutting edge. Keep the bits in good

condition by cleaning off the pitch with solvent. Use steel wool to polish the surface. Sharpen a speed bit on the two cutting edges. Figure 56-17.

## SHARPENING A DRAWKNIFE AND SMALL KNIVES

The drawknife can be sharpened on the grinding wheel in the same general way as a plane iron. Hold the drawknife with one handle against the top of the bench and the other handle in your hand.

**56-16a.** Sharpening the spur. Hold the bit with the feed screw uppermost. Place the twist against the bench. File the inside of the spur only—never the outside.

**56-17.** Sharpen a speed bit with a small slipstone or dead-smooth file. Make sure that the original angles are maintained and that each side of the nose is sharpened equally. Do not file the sides of the blade or the boring diameter will be reduced.

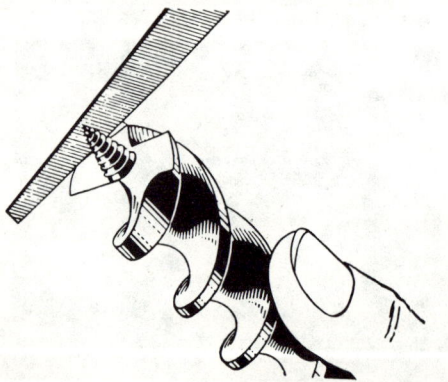

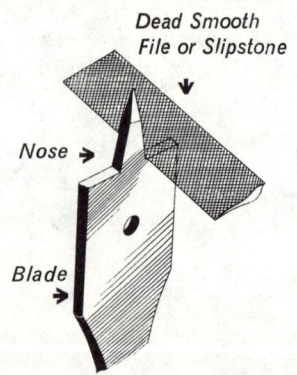

*Dead Smooth File or Slipstone*

*Nose*

*Blade*

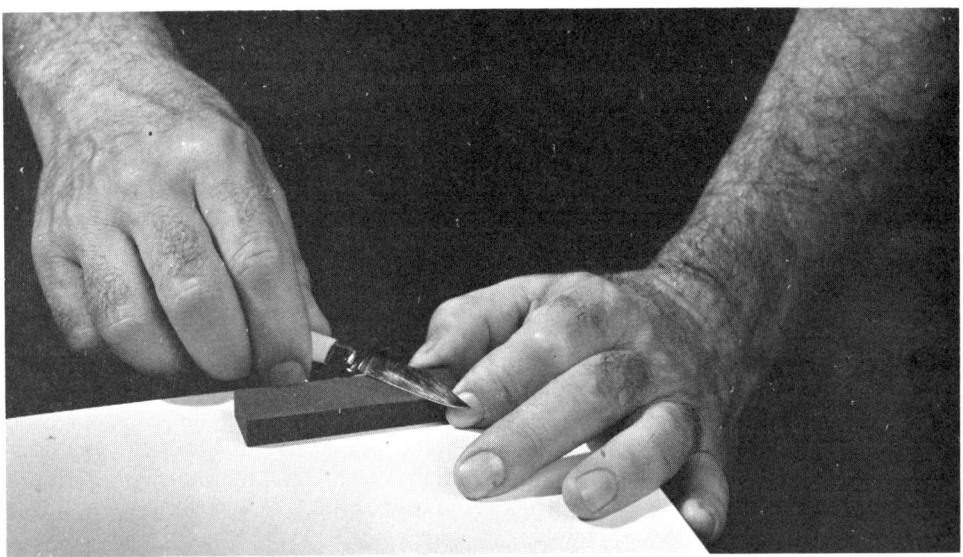

**56-18.** Place the blade against the stone at a 30-degree angle. Draw the blade against the stone in a diagonal direction, beginning at the heel and ending at the tip. Flip the blade and repeat. Continue rhythmically for several strokes, until the blade is sufficiently sharp.

Hold a small oilstone in the other hand and move it back and forth along the bevel to make a keen edge. A small knife is sharpened on an abrasive stone. Figure 56-18.

### GRINDING A SCREWDRIVER

The screwdriver is one of the most badly misused tools in the woodshop.

Figure 56-19. Very often it is not ground properly, with the result that a burr forms when screws are set. These burrs in screws are both dangerous and unsightly. The screwdriver should be ground with a slight taper on each side and the end flat, as shown in Figure 56-20.

**56-20.** Sharpening the tip of the screwdriver.

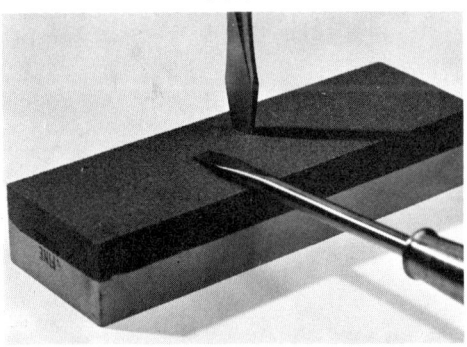

**56-19.** Good and bad tips: a damaged tip that needs regrinding; a worn tip that should be reground; and a correctly ground screwdriver.

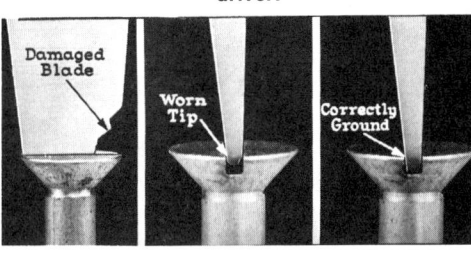

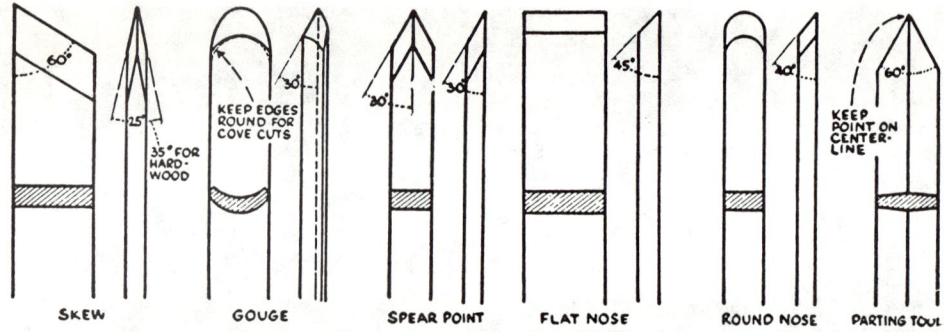

**56-21.** Grinding angles for wood-turning tools.

## SHARPENING A SAW

Sharpening and setting a handsaw takes much experience. It should not be attempted by anyone who does not perform the job frequently. All the teeth have to be filed until they are all the same height. Then they must be reshaped by filing. Finally the teeth have to be set by bending them alternately to left and right. In using a saw, therefore, one should appreciate how difficult resharpening is. The need for sharpening can be greatly cut down by proper use of the saw at all times.

## SHARPENING TURNING TOOLS

Proper grinding angles for wood-turning tools are shown in Figure 56-21. Sharpening is done the same as for a chisel.

### CAN YOU ANSWER THESE QUESTIONS ON SHARPENING HAND TOOLS?

1. Why is it important to keep the tools sharp?
2. What can be done to correct a badly nicked cutting edge?
3. At what angle should a plane iron be ground for softwood? For hardwood?
4. At what angle should a plane iron be whetted?
5. How is the edge of a hand scraper shaped? At what angle should the burnishing tool be held?
6. Tell how to test a plane iron for sharpness.
7. Describe the correct way to grind a screwdriver.
8. Are saws commonly sharpened by beginners in woodworking? Explain your answer.

# SECTION XI
## Machine Woodworking

**What you must know and be able to do in Units 57–67:**

57. The parts of a planer, or surfacer; safe use of the planer; how to square legs on the planer.

58. The main parts of a circular saw; safe use of the circular saw; how to perform these operations on the circular saw: ripping, crosscutting, mitering, beveling and chamfering, grooving, rabbeting, tenoning, using a dado head, cutting a taper.

59. The parts of a radial-arm saw; how to adjust and use the radial-arm saw safely; crosscutting and ripping operations on the radial-arm saw.

60. The parts of a band saw; how to install a blade; how to perform these operations on the band saw: cutting curves, resawing, ripping, crosscutting, mitering, tilt-table work.

61. The parts of a jig saw; how to install a blade; how to cut with a jig saw, including internal curves, tilt-table work, and marquetry.

62. Identification of three portable saws; how to do crosscutting, ripping, and pocket cutting on the portable power saw; how to do straight cutting and cutting of curves and internal openings on the portable jig saw.

63. The parts of a jointer; how to perform these operations safely on the jointer: face planing, jointing an edge, beveling, chamfering, rabbeting; use of the rotary jointer-surfacer.

64. Use of the drill press for drilling, boring, countersinking, mortising, shaping, routing, and sanding.

65. Use of the belt and disc sander, portable belt sander, and finishing sander.

**Continued on page 390**

66. The parts of a portable router; how to do freehand routing, shape an edge, make molding, do inlaying.

67. The parts of a wood lathe; turning stock safely; two basic methods of turning; using the lathe for rough turning, squaring off ends, cutting a shoulder, tapered surface, V's, and beads, turning concave and convex designs, turning on the faceplate, finishing, making duplicate parts with a duplicator attachment.

*Industry makes use of power equipment to process lumber from raw material to the finished product. With machines, much of the hard work of using hand tools is eliminated. Machines also do a much more accurate job than can be done by most woodworkers with hand tools. Machine tools, however, require skills that are entirely different.*

*Making wood products with power tools is an interesting and satisfying experience. The work progresses very rapidly and with less effort than hand tools require. Of course, it is very important to make sure that all power tools are in top working condition before attempting to use them. Also, it is important that you be safety conscious. Power tools can be dangerous, especially if used carelessly or by inexperienced persons. Make sure that you study the safety rules and regulations and learn the proper procedures before attempting to use any machine.*

## GENERAL SAFETY RULES

• Never use woodworking machinery until you have been given proper safety instruction. Always get your teacher's permission before using a machine.

• Keep all safety guards in proper position. There are few operations on the circular saw for which it is necessary to remove the guard. Make sure that you use special setups and extreme care for these operations.

• Always wear clothes properly. Roll up your sleeves, tuck in your tie, and put on a shop apron.

• Always remove rings, wristwatches, pins, and other jewelry before operating a machine.

• Plan your work before you start to use the machine.

• Never start or stop a machine for another student.

• Keep your fingers and hands away from moving parts of machines.

• Keep the floor around the machine clear of lumber scraps, waste pieces, and oil.

• Never force material into the machine faster than it will cut.

• Never stand in line with a revolving blade or wheel.

• Make sure that all clamps are securely fastened before turning on the power.

• Never remove or change a guard without getting your teacher's permission.

• Inspect wood carefully for nails, screws, and knots before machining.

• Keep the table of the machine and other work surfaces clear of excess materials and tools.

• Never feed stock into a machine until it has reached full speed.

• Never hurry when working on a machine.

• Always make sure that the machine has come to a dead stop before oiling, cleaning, or adjusting.

• Always clean sawdust and scraps of wood from the machine with a brush.

• Turn off the power immediately if the machine does not sound right.

• Never attempt cutting with a dull blade.

• Never stand around a machine that is operated by other students.

• Use hand tools and processes for very simple operations or for work on very small pieces of wood.

• For special setups make sure that all clamps are securely fastened. It is a good idea to have the instructor check the setup before doing the machining.

• Keep your mind on your work. Don't become distracted by other students in the class. Be careful not to bother other students who are operating a machine.

• If a machine is not operating properly, always report it to your instructor.

• Take your time when working with a machine. Most accidents happen by not following instructions or by trying to do things too fast.

• Never try to stop a machine after the power is off by forcing a piece of wood into the blade or knives.

• Always stay next to a machine until it has come to a dead stop.

• When you are through using a machine, always remove any special setups, clean off the waste stock and place it in the scrap box, and leave the machine in its normal operating condition with the power shut off.

# PLANER OR SURFACER

**The thickness planer,** or *surfacer,* is a simple machine to use. It is designed to do one job, namely, to surface boards to thickness. Figure 57-1. It will not straighten a board that is warped. The cutting head of the planer is mounted above the table so only the top of a board is surfaced. This machine is self-feeding. After stock has been fed into it, it will continue through the machine by itself. The size of the planer is indicated by the maximum width and thickness that can be surfaced. For example, if the capacity is 18 by 6 inches (457 x 152 mm), the largest pieces that can be surfaced are ones that are 18 inches (457 mm) wide and 6 inches (152 mm) thick.

## PARTS OF THE PLANER

Major parts include a motor, cutter head, in-feed and out-feed rolls, chip breaker, pressure bar, table, and feed control wheel. The machine operates as follows: As the stock is fed in, the upper corrugated *in-feed roll* grips the stock and moves it toward the cutter head. Figure 57-2. The *chip breaker* presses firmly on the top of the wood to prevent the grain from tearing out. The *rotating cutter head* surfaces the board much like a jointer. The *pressure bar,* back of the cutter head, holds the stock firmly against the table. The *out-feed roll* helps move the stock out the back of the machine.

**57-1a.** An 18-inch (457 mm) thickness planer, or surfacer.

CUTTING FEED SELECTOR HANDLE

SWITCH

TABLE

ELEVATING HAND WHEEL

**57-1b.** A 24-inch (610 mm) planer that will handle stock up to 9 inches (229 mm) thick.

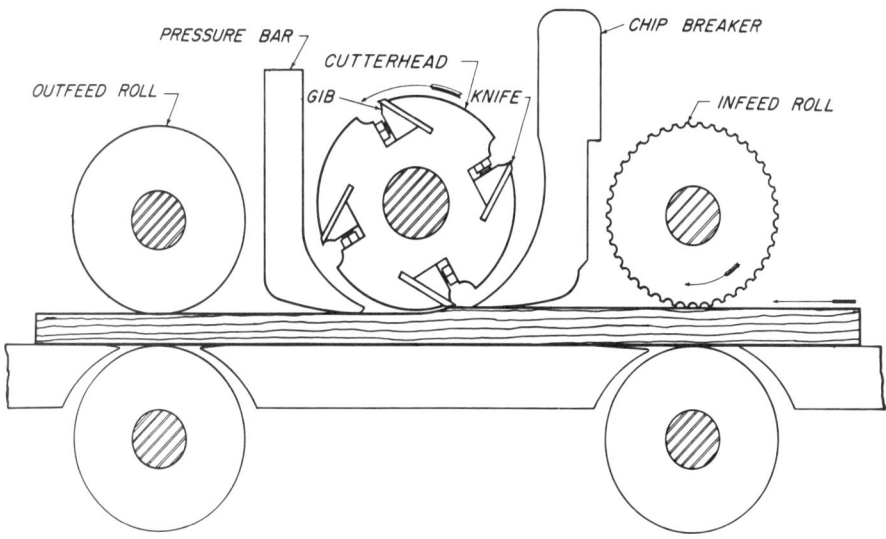

**57-2.** Cross section of a planer head.

On small machines the controls are relatively simple: (a) a switch to turn on the machine; (b) a hand wheel which elevates or lowers the table; (c) the pointer on the table that indicates thickness of the stock after it has been fed through the machine; (d) a feed control lever which operates the feed control; and (e) a control that regulates the rate of feed from slow to fast (some machines do not have this feature). Figure 57-3.

## SAFETY

• Check the board to be sure it is free of nails, loose knots, and other imperfections.

• Always stand to one side when planing, never directly behind the board.

• Never attempt to plane more than one thickness at a time. If several boards of different thicknesses are to be surfaced, always plane the thick one first until it is about the same thickness as the others.

• Never look into the planer as the board is passing through. Loose chips

may be thrown back with great force, causing an eye injury.

• Plane a warped board only when one surface has been trued on a jointer.

**57-3.** The variable speed cutting feed makes it possible to select any feed range from 15 to 36 feet (4.6 to 11 m) per minute.

**57-4.** Feeding the stock through the planer.

**57-5a.** These student-built chairs make use of square legs.

**57-5b.** This student-built coffee table also has square legs.

● Make sure that the board is at least 2 inches (51 mm) longer than the distance between the feed rolls. For a small planer, this usually means a board should be at least 14 inches (355 mm) long.

● When thin stock is to be planed, always place it on a thicker piece that has larger dimensions of width and length.

● Keep your hands away from the board after it starts through the planer.

● If a board sticks, turn off the switch. Wait for the cutterhead to stop. Then lower the table.

## USING THE PLANER

1. Measure the thickness of the board at its thickest point.

2. Adjust the machine for the correct thickness, about $\frac{1}{16}$ to $\frac{1}{8}$ inch (1.5 to 3 mm) less than the measurement obtained in Step 1. Never try to remove more than $\frac{1}{8}$ inch (3 mm) in thickness for rough work and $\frac{1}{16}$ inch (1.5 mm) for finished work.

3. Turn on the power and pull in the feed control.

4. Place the working face of the stock on the table so that the stock will feed with the grain. Figure 57-4.

5. Start the stock into the surfacer. As soon as it takes hold, remove your hands. If it should get started at a slight angle, a quick shove may straighten it.

6. After at least half the board has passed through the machine, walk around to the back and hold the end up as it goes the rest of the way through. On long stock it is a good idea to ask a helper to guide the board as it comes off the table.

7. Check the stock and then reset for thickness if another cut is to be made. The last cut should remove not more than $\frac{1}{32}$ to $\frac{1}{16}$ inch (1 to 1.5 mm) of material.

## SQUARING LEGS

The planer is used to square stock to be used for legs. Figure 57-5.

Begin the squaring operation by cutting the stock to rough size. Joint one face and then one edge 90 degrees to the jointed face (This face and edge are shown as sides A and B, Figure 57-6.) Mark these surfaces for identification. Place the stock with jointed surface on the planer table and the jointed edge to the right. Set the planer for the necessary cut. Figure 57-6, side C. Make the cut. When the stock is taken from the outfeed table, care should be taken not to alter the position of the pieces. Place the stock on the infeed table in the same position as for the first cut. Turn each piece one-quarter turn clockwise. Don't change the thickness setting. Feed the stock through the planer for the second cut. Figure 57-6, side D. Measure the stock and, if necessary, repeat the two cuts on sides A and B. It may also be necessary to make additional cuts on sides C and D, continuing until the stock is the correct size. Plan your cuts so an equal amount of material is removed from all sides.

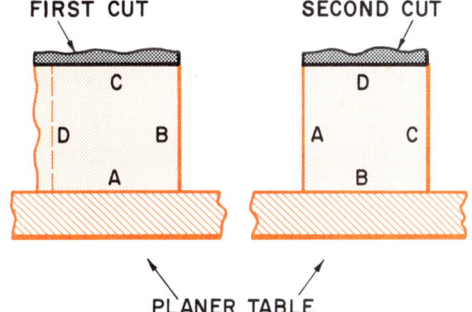

**57-6.** Squaring stock on the planer.

FIRST CUT    SECOND CUT

PLANER TABLE

## CAN YOU ANSWER THESE QUESTIONS ON THE PLANER OR SURFACER?

1. What is the purpose of a planer?
2. List eight safety rules to follow when using the planer.
3. What is the maximum amount of stock that should be removed at one cut?
4. Tell what to do if the board sticks in the planer.

## Section XI UNIT 58.

# CIRCULAR SAW

**The circular** saw is used more than any other machine tool in the woodshop. It consists of a *frame,* an *arbor* to hold the saw blade, the *saw blade,* a *table,* a *ripping fence,* and a *crosscutting* or *mitering gage.* In addition, the machine should be equipped with a *guard* and *splitter* to protect the operator from injury. Figure 58-1. The size of the circular saw is indicated by the largest diameter of saw blade that can be used on the machine. The most common sizes for small shops are the 8- and 10-inch (203 and 254 mm) *tilt arbor saws.*

The two adjusting levers used the most are the raising wheel and the tilting wheel. The *raising wheel* is usually located under the front of the table. It is used to raise and lower the saw blade. The *tilt wheel* is usually on the left side. It is used to tilt the arbor to the right or left. There are three common types of saw blades: the ripsaw, the crosscut, and the combination. Figure 58-2. In the small shop in which many different operations must be done, one after another, it is a good idea to keep a combination saw blade in the machine. Then it can be used for ripping, crosscutting, beveling, rabbeting, and many other operations. Figure 58-3.

### SAFETY

The circular saw is one of the most dangerous tools in the woodshop, especially in the hands of the beginner. Therefore it is suggested that the following safety practices be followed when using a circular saw:

● Make sure that the saw has a guard and splitter. The splitter holds the stock open after it has been cut so that it won't tend to bend or kick back. Figure 58-4.

● Always stand to one side of the saw blade, never directly in back of it. If a piece does kick back, it won't strike you. Figure 58-5.

● Make sure that the saw blade is sharpened properly. A dull saw is frequently the cause of kickback.

● Always set the saw so that it is about $\frac{1}{8}$ inch (3 mm) higher than the thickness of the stock to be cut. Figure 58-6 (Page 400).

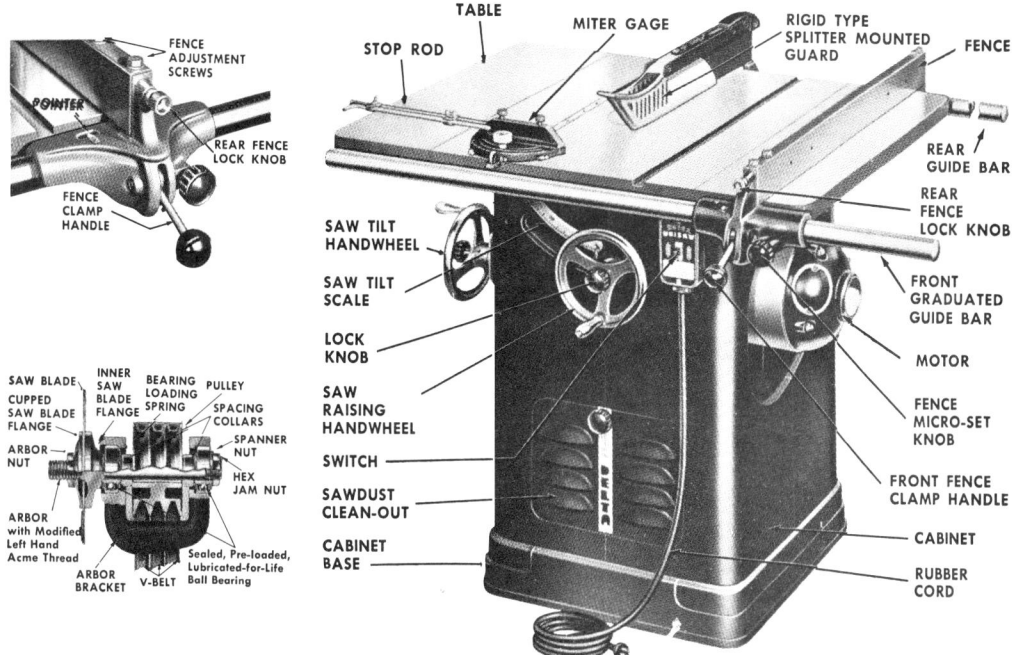

**58-1.** A 10-inch (254 mm), floor-type, circular saw of the kind most suited to school shops. Study the names of the parts. You should become familiar with them.

• Never reach over the saw with your hand.

• When ripping stock to narrow widths, always use a push stick to complete the ripping. Do not ever place your hand between the saw and the ripping fence.

• Never saw freehand on a circular saw. Always use the guide intended for this purpose.

• Pay attention to business when using the circular saw. One small lapse in your attention could cost you a finger or hand.

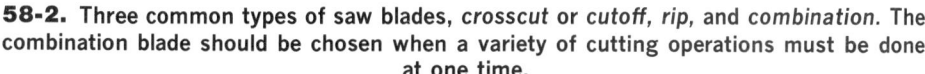

**58-2.** Three common types of saw blades, *crosscut* or *cutoff*, *rip*, and *combination*. The combination blade should be chosen when a variety of cutting operations must be done at one time.

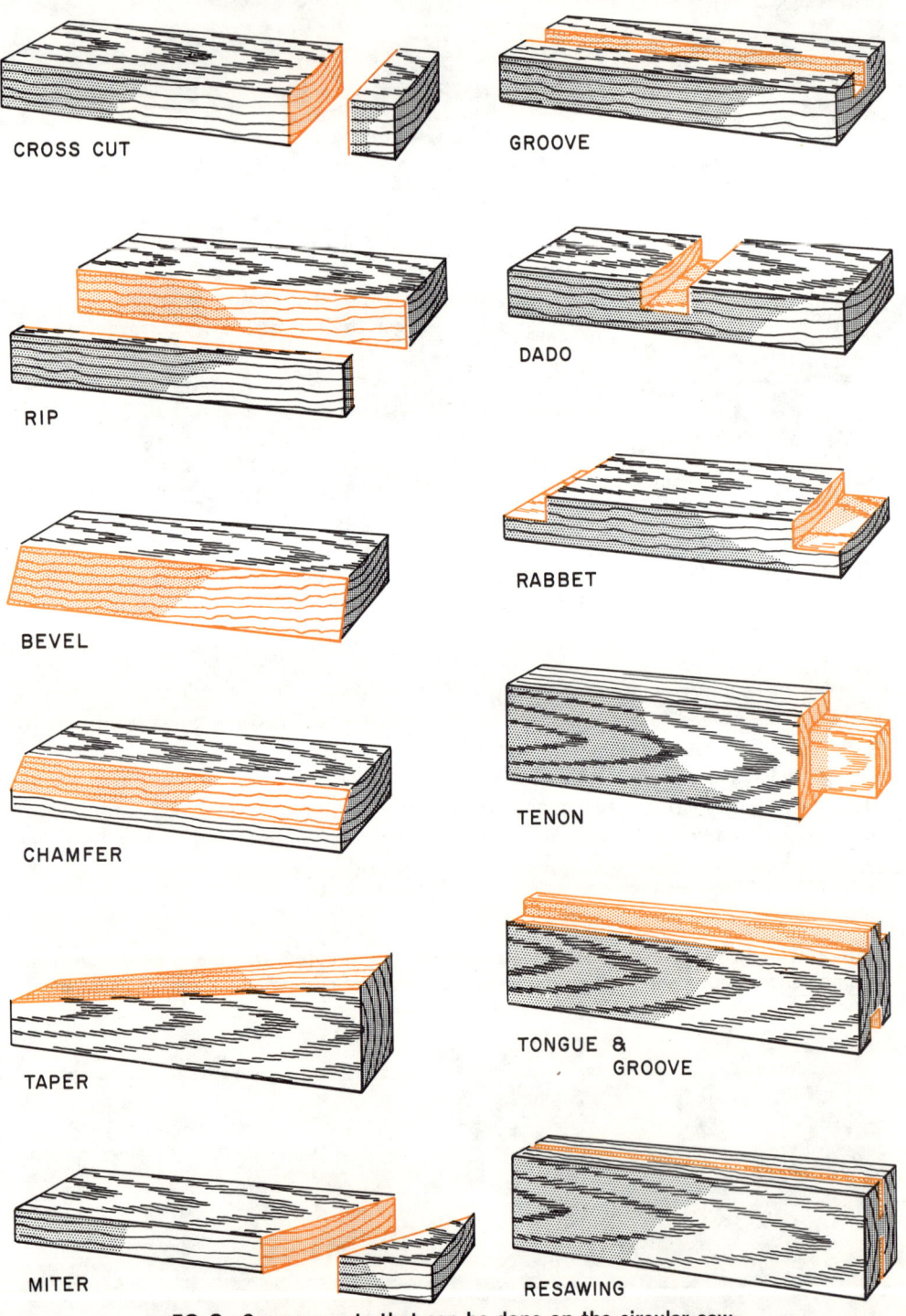

CROSS CUT

GROOVE

RIP

DADO

BEVEL

RABBET

CHAMFER

TENON

TAPER

TONGUE &
GROOVE

MITER

RESAWING

**58-3.** Common cuts that can be done on the circular saw.

**58-4a.** A standard basket-type saw guard with splitter and anti-kickback device.

**58-4b.** The guard should be used for sawing operations whenever possible. With this double-basket guard, many more operations can be done than with a standard guard, including such cuts as rabbeting and dadoing. The *splitter* directly behind the saw blade is slightly thicker than the blade. It keeps the saw kerf open as the cutting is done.

**58-5a.** This operator is following good safety practices in using the circular saw.

**58-5b.** Do you see what's wrong in this picture? The student should be wearing safety glasses.

## CHANGING A BLADE

Snap out the throat plate around the saw. Obtain a wrench that will fit the arbor nut. On most circular saws, the arbor has a left-hand thread and must be turned clockwise to loosen. Figure 58-7. However, some manufacturers use a right-hand thread on the arbor. If so, you must turn it counterclockwise to remove. Always check the thread before loosening. If the nut doesn't come off easily, force a piece of scrap wood against the blade to keep the arbor from turning. Remove the nut, the collar, and the blade. Now mark the arbor with a slight file cut or prick-punch mark. Always turn the arbor so the mark is "up" before putting on a new blade. Place the trademark on the blade at the top, in line with the mark on the arbor. Replace the collar and nut.

## RIPPING

Before you rip stock to width on the circular saw, make sure that one edge of the stock is true. If it is not, plane one edge. Then, with the power off, adjust the saw blade to a height of ⅛ inch (3 mm) more than the thickness of the stock. Adjust the ripping fence to the correct

width by holding a rule or try square against the fence and measuring the distance to the saw blade. On many machines, the width for ripping is found directly on a scale mounted on the front edge of the saw table. Lock the ripping

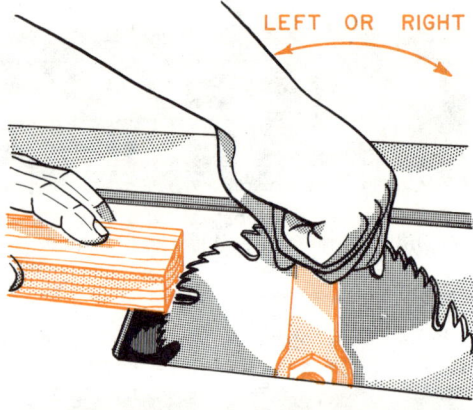

**58-7.** Removing a blade. Hold a piece of wood against the blade to keep it from turning. Then turn the nut with a wrench of the proper size. On most saws the arbor has a left-hand thread and must be turned clockwise to loosen it. However, some arbors have a right-hand thread. If so, you must turn it counterclockwise to remove it.

**58-8.** Ripping stock to width. *The guard has been raised to show the operation.*

**58-6.** Adjust the saw to extend ⅛ inch (3 mm) above the stock. (Guard removed for clarity.)

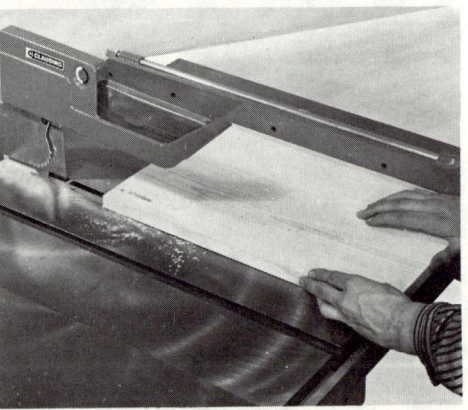

fence so it is tight. Turn on the power. Place the stock on the table. Stand to one side, not directly in back of the saw blade. To start the cut, apply forward pressure with one hand as you hold the stock with the other. Do not apply too much forward pressure on a small saw, as this will make the saw burn or stop altogether. Continue to feed the work into the saw easily. Figure 58-8.

If the stock is hardwood and quite thick, it may be necessary to begin with the saw set at less than the total thickness and run it through several times rather than trying to cut through the thickness in one operation.

When you are cutting to narrow widths, hold the push stick in your right hand. As the rear edge of the stock clears the table, apply forward pressure with the push stick until the cut is completed. Figure 58-9. Another method of sawing thin stock is shown in Figure 58-10.

## CROSSCUTTING

The mitering or crosscutting gage fits into either groove of the table but is most often placed in the left groove. Some operators attach a squared piece of stock the same width as the miter gage to its face. This provides better support for the work. To make a square cut, set the gage at a 90-degree angle. This can be checked by holding a try square against the gage and the saw blade. Carefully mark the location of the cut, making the mark very clear on the front edge or face of the stock. Set the blade to the correct height. Hold the stock firmly against the gage and slide both the work and gage along the table to complete the cut. Figure 58-11. If you must cut several pieces to the same length, one of the following methods can be followed:

● Set the stop rod that is attached to the miter gage to the correct length. Figure 58-12.

● Clamp a small block of wood to the ripping fence just in front of the saw blade. The fence with block attached acts as a length guide. Figure 58-13. Never use the ripping fence as a length guide

**58-9.** Cutting stock to narrow width. A push stick is used to apply the forward pressure. Never run your hand between the revolving blade and the fence if narrow widths are being ripped. *The guard has been left out in order to show the operation.*

**58-10.** Another method of ripping narrow stock. Note that you saw halfway through and then remove the material. Turn the stock around to complete the cut.

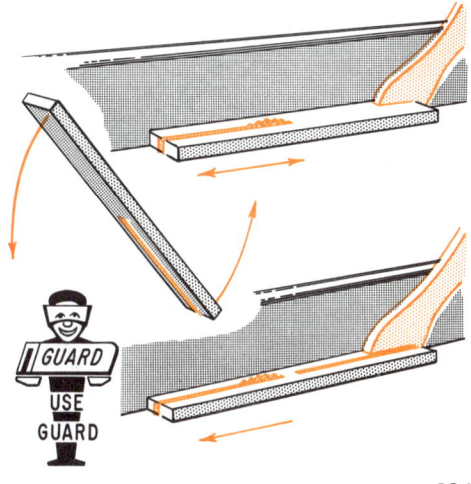

**58-11.** Crosscutting. The miter gage is set at a right angle to the blade. An even forward pressure should be applied to the stock and gage.

**58-12.** Using a stop rod.

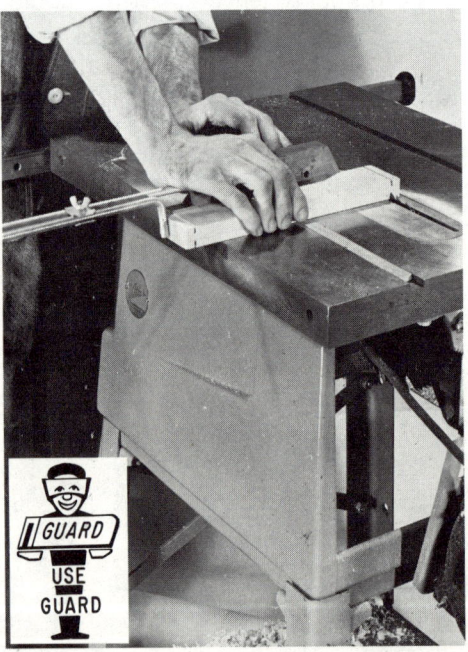

only. If you do, the piece will become lodged between the revolving saw and the ripping fence and may kick back with terrific force.

● Fasten a wood extension to the miter gage. Then clamp a stop block to it to control the length of cut. Figure 58-14.

## MITERING

To make a miter cut, adjust the miter gage to the correct angle and proceed as in crosscutting. Make sure that you hold the stock firmly against the miter gage, as it tends to creep toward the revolving saw as the cut is made. Figure 58-15. To make a compound miter cut, the gage

**58-13.** Cutting stock to length with a block attached to the ripping fence. This is one of the simplest methods of cutting many pieces of stock to the same length. Note that as the stock is cut off there is plenty of clearance between the saw blade and the fence. In this way there is never a danger of kickback. *The guard has been removed to show the operation.*

must be set to the correct angle and the blade tilted. Figure 58-16.

### BEVELING AND CHAMFERING

To cut a bevel or chamfer when you are either ripping or crosscutting, you must tilt the saw blade to the correct angle for the cut. The gage, which shows the angle of tilt of the saw blade, is found on the front of the saw just below the table. After the adjustment is made, check the angle by holding a sliding T bevel against the table top and saw blade. After you have the correct angle, you can proceed as for ripping or crosscutting. Figure 58-17.

### GROOVING

Cutting a groove on the circular saw will simplify the making of a spline joint. Figure 58-18. Lay out the groove on the edge of the stock. Set the circular saw

**58-14.** An auxiliary wood fence has been fastened to the miter gage. Then a stop block is clamped to this fence.

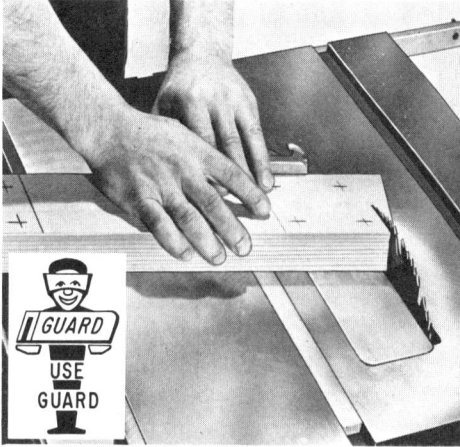

**58-15.** Making a miter cut. Adjust the miter gage to the correct angle. Hold the stock firmly against the gage as the cut is made. *The guard has been removed to show the operation.*

**58-16.** Making a compound miter cut. The miter gage is set at an angle and the blade is tilted. The stop rod on the miter gage is used to control the length of cut.

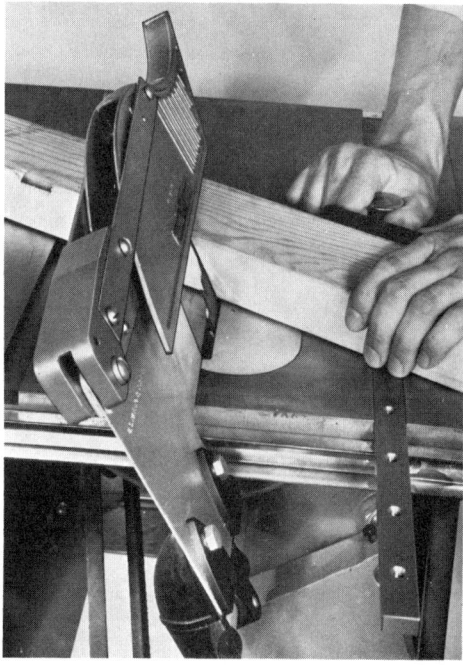

to a height equal to the depth of the groove. Adjust the ripping fence to allow the cut to be made just inside the layout line. Hold one surface of the stock firmly against the fence and make a cut. Reverse the stock and make a second cut. If necessary, you can make several cuts in the waste stock of the groove. Clean out the groove with a sharp chisel. A groove can also be cut with a dado head.

## RABBETING

A rabbet can easily be cut on the end or edge of stock with a circular saw. Lay out the rabbet joint. (See the unit on making a rabbet joint.) Set the saw blade to a height equal to the depth of the rabbet. If the rabbet is to be cut at the end of the board, hold the stock against a miter gage and make the shoulder cut. Figure 58-19. Then set the saw blade to a height equal to the width of the rabbet. Set the ripping fence to a position that will permit the saw kerf to be just inside the layout line. Hold the stock on end with the surface opposite the rabbet firmly against the ripping fence. Make the second cut.

**58-17.** Be particularly careful where you place your hands when cutting stock at an angle with the arbor tilted (either to the right or left). The danger zone is much wider than you think. *The guard has been removed to show the operation.*

An edge rabbet is cut in the same way except that the ripping fence is used for making both cuts.

## TENONING

Making mortise-and-tenon joints is quite simple when the tenon is cut on the circular saw. Lay out the tenon. (SEE THE UNIT ON MAKING A MORTISE-AND-TENON JOINT.) Set the saw blade to a height equal to the thickness of stock to be removed from one side of the tenon. Hold the stock against the miter gage and make the *shoulder* cuts. After this is done, set the saw blade to a height equal to the length of the tenon. Now select a homemade or commercial tenoning jig. Figure 58-20. The simplest method of cutting the cheek is to clamp the stock to the tenoning jig and position the jig and fence so as to cut out the cheek on the side away from the jig. Figure 58-21. Then turn the stock around and cut the other cheek without changing the location of the fence.

## USING A DADO HEAD

A dado head (Figures 58-22 and 58-23) can be purchased that will cut grooves or dadoes from $\frac{1}{8}$ to 2 inches (3 to 51 mm) in width and which is equally adapted to cutting with or across the grain. One dado blade will cut a groove $\frac{1}{8}$ inch (3 mm) thick, and two will make

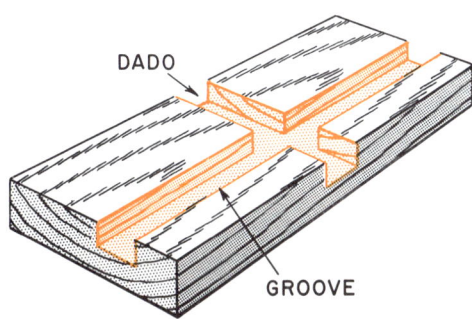

**58-18.** Here you see the difference between a groove and a dado.

**58-19.** Making the first cut of a rabbet.

**58-20a.** If the shoulder cut is made free-hand, use a homemade circular-saw guard to protect your hands while cutting the tenon.

**58-20b.** A commercial tenoning jig is an excellent accessory for cutting tenons and grooves. This one will take stock up to 2¾ inches (70 mm) thick and any width within the capacity of the saw.

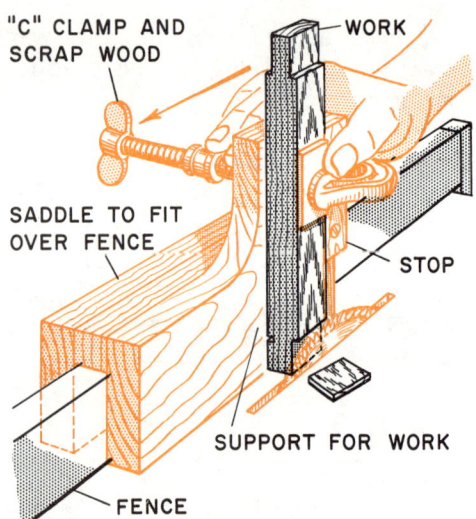

"C" CLAMP AND SCRAP WOOD

WORK

SADDLE TO FIT OVER FENCE

STOP

SUPPORT FOR WORK

FENCE

**58-21.** Making the cheek cut with a hand-made tenoning jig.

**58-22.** A dado head attached to the saw arbor in preparation for use. The plate that must be used over the head has a wider opening than that used with the regular saw blade.

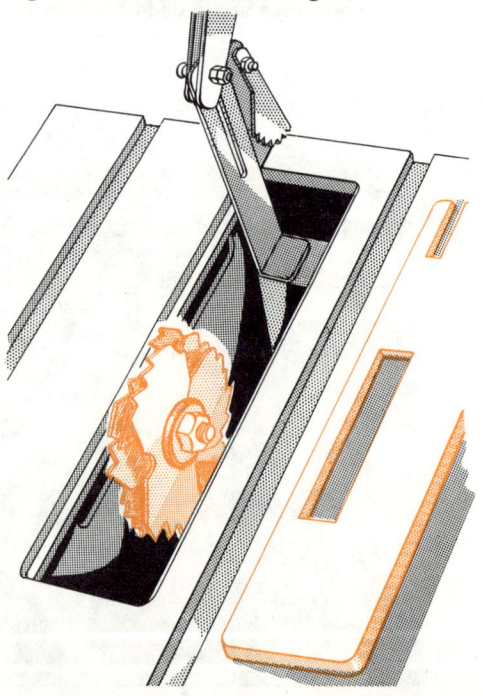

a cut ¼ inch (6.5 mm) thick. Cutters of different widths can be put between these two dado cutters to cut a groove of any width. This attachment is especially useful for cutting grooves, tenons, dadoes, and lap joints. Figures 58-24 and 58-25.

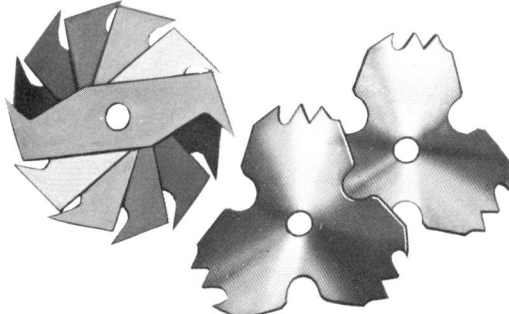

**58-23.** A typical dado head has two outside blades that are ⅛ inch (3 mm) thick. It also has four chipper blades: one that is ¹⁄₁₆ inch (1.5 mm) thick; two that are ⅛ inch (3 mm) thick; and one that is ¼ inch (6.5 mm) thick. With this assortment you can cut grooves from ⅛ to ¹³⁄₁₆ inch (3 to 20.5 mm) in intervals of ¹⁄₁₆ inch (1.5 mm).

**58-24.** Cutting a groove with a dado head. Note how simple it is to cut a groove of any width and depth with this attachment. When the groove is cut across grain, it is called a dado, which is a common type of joint construction.

**58-25.** Cutting a series of dadoes.

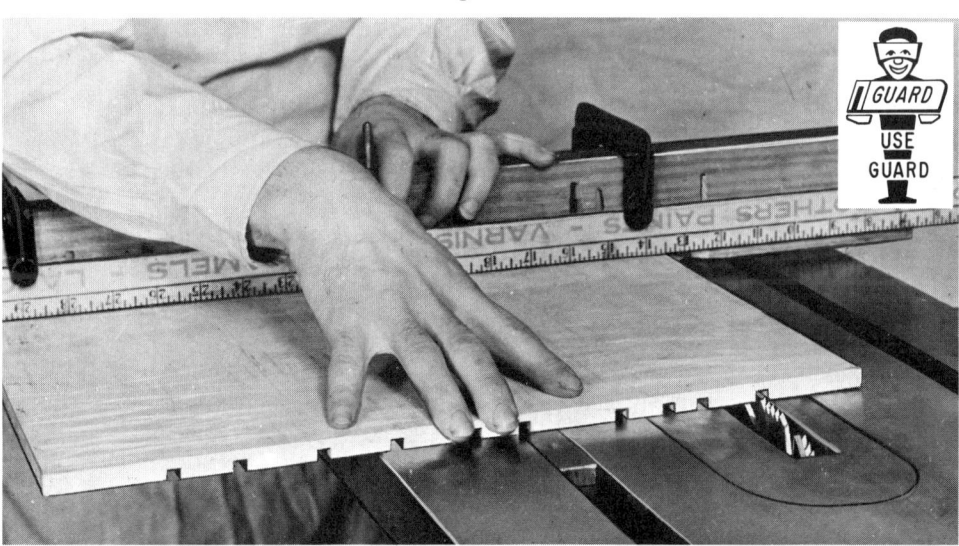

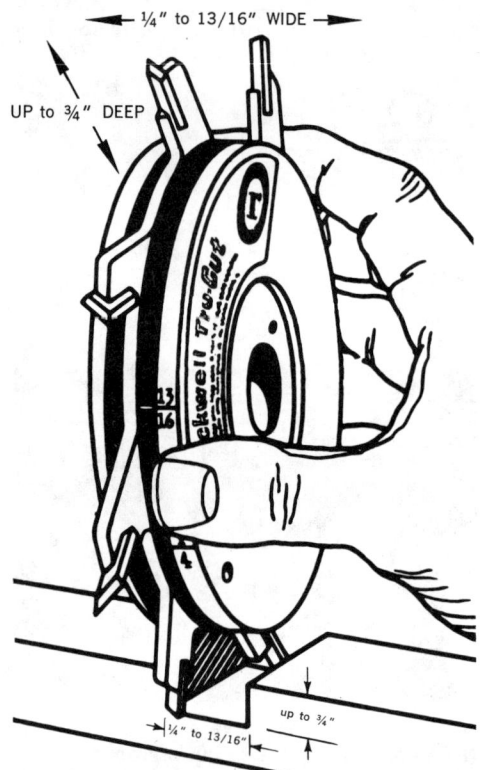

←— ¼″ to 13/16″ WIDE —→

UP to ¾″ DEEP

¼″ to 13/16″     up to ¾″

**58-26a.** A 6-inch (152 mm) adjustable dado cutter.

**58-26b.** A few of the cuts that can be made.

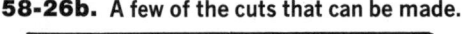

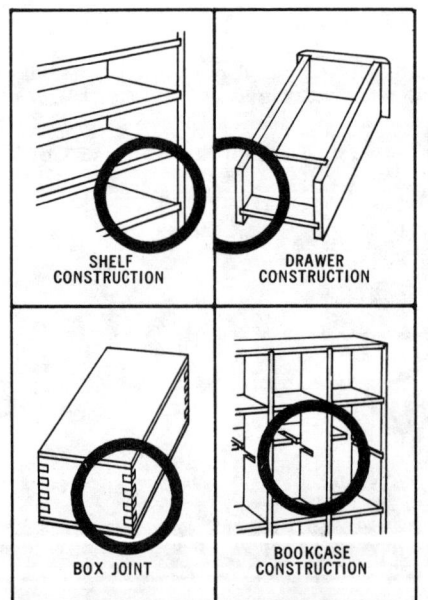

SHELF CONSTRUCTION

DRAWER CONSTRUCTION

BOX JOINT

BOOKCASE CONSTRUCTION

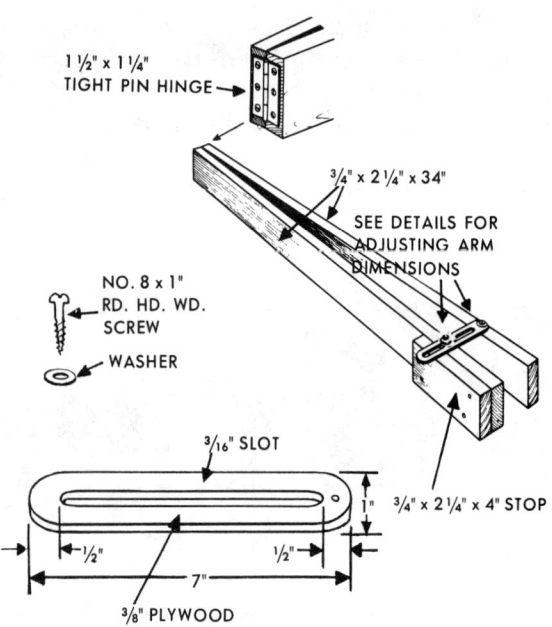

1 ½″ x 1 ¼″ TIGHT PIN HINGE

¾″ x 2 ¼″ x 34″

SEE DETAILS FOR ADJUSTING ARM DIMENSIONS

NO. 8 x 1″ RD. HD. WD. SCREW

WASHER

3/16″ SLOT

¾″ x 2 ¼″ x 4″ STOP

1″

½″     ½″

7″

3/8″ PLYWOOD

**58-27a.** A simple adjustable taper jig. Detail drawings are at top and lower left.

**58-27b.** Using an adjustable taper jig. *Note: The guard has been removed to show the action.*

GUARD USE GUARD

## Using An Adjustable Dado Head

An adjustable dado head gives a good, clean cut and is easy to use. Figure 58-26. The width can be set by loosening the arbor nut and rotating the center section of the head until the width mark on this part is opposite the correct dimension. This adjustable dado head will make cuts from $\frac{1}{4}$ to $\frac{13}{16}$ inch (6.5 to 20.5 mm) wide and up to $\frac{3}{4}$ inch (19 mm) deep. It can be used for making all kinds of cuts in the construction of furniture and cabinets.

## CUTTING A TAPER

The best way to cut a taper is to use some type of adjustable taper jig. Mark a line to indicate the taper to be cut. Then adjust the jig until the line of the taper cut is parallel to the fence. Figure 58-27.

## CAN YOU ANSWER THESE QUESTIONS ON THE CIRCULAR SAW?

1. Sketch a circular saw and name the parts.
2. Name the two types of circular saws.
3. What are the three types of saw blades? Which is best for use in the average shop?
4. List the safety precautions to observe when using a circular saw.
5. At what height should the saw blade be set for ripping?
6. Tell how to make a cut on hardwood that is quite thick.
7. At what times should a push stick be used?
8. Name the gage employed for doing crosscutting.
9. How can a compound miter cut be made?
10. Relate the three methods of cutting several pieces to the same length.
11. What is the difficulty frequently encountered when making a miter cut?
12. Point out the difference between a bevel and a chamfer.
13. How can a groove be cut?
14. Tell how to make the cheek cut in tenoning.
15. What is a dado head? What is it used for?
16. What is the difference between a dado blade and cutter?
17. Tell how to cut a taper.

# RADIAL-ARM SAW

**The radial-arm** saw is an ideal machine for many kinds of cutting operations. It is an upside-down saw on which you can see all the mechanisms for adjusting and cutting. For this reason, some people consider this saw more dangerous. The truth, however, is that if handled correctly it is as safe as the circular saw. For all crosscutting operations, including straight cutting and cutting a miter, bevel, dado, or rabbet, the stock is held firmly on the table in a stationary position and the saw is moved to do the cutting. For all ripping operations, the saw is locked in a fixed position and the stock moved into the revolving blade just as in using a circular saw. There are several designs for the radial-arm saw. On one type the saw unit moves back and forth under the overarm. Figure 59-1. Another type has an extra track under the overarm on which the saw moves. Figure 59-2. The size of the machine is determined by the size of the blades. The common size for the school shop is 9- to 10-inch (229 to 254 mm).

## ADJUSTMENTS

The *overarm* or *track* can rotate in a complete circle. The *yoke* that holds the motor can be turned in a 360-degree circle, and the blade can be tilted to the right or left 90 degrees. The three principal adjustments can be made as follows:

● The *depth of cut* is made by turning the elevator crank that is located either directly above the column or on the front of the machine.

● The *angle of cut* is adjusted by turning the overarm or track to the correct angle. There is a *locking lever* at the column or the outer end of the overarm for making this adjustment.

● *Bevel cuts* are made by tilting the motor to the right or left.

## SAFETY

● Get personal instruction on the use of this machine before operating it.

● Make sure a sharp blade of the correct kind is installed. The same blades are used on the radial-arm saw as on the circular saw.

**59-1.** On this radial-arm saw, the saw moves back and forth under the overarm.

● Mount the blade on the arbor so that the cutting edges turn toward you.

● Make sure the guard is always in place.

● See to it that all clamps are tight before starting the motor.

● Hold the stock firmly against the table for doing all kinds of crosscutting operations.

● Keep your hands away from the danger area—the path of the blade.

● Don't try to stop the blade after turning off the machine by holding a stick or similar item against it.

● Make all adjustments *with the motor at a dead stop.*

## CROSSCUTTING OPERATIONS

To make a straight crosscut, make sure that the arm or track is at right angles to the guide fence. Adjust the depth of cut so that the teeth of the blade

**59-2.** On this radial-arm saw, the saw moves back and forth under a track that is attached to the overarm.

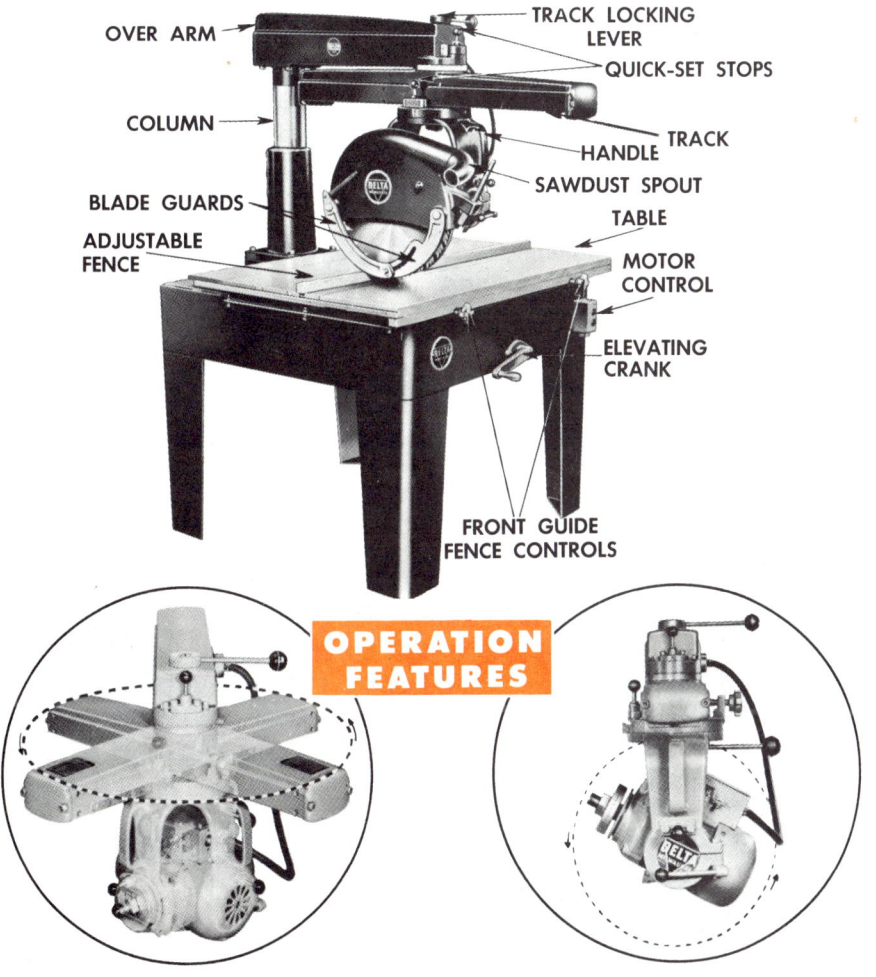

OVER ARM

TRACK LOCKING LEVER

QUICK-SET STOPS

COLUMN

TRACK

HANDLE

SAWDUST SPOUT

BLADE GUARDS

TABLE

ADJUSTABLE FENCE

MOTOR CONTROL

ELEVATING CRANK

FRONT GUIDE FENCE CONTROLS

OPERATION FEATURES

are about $\frac{1}{16}$ inch (1.5 mm) below the surface of the wood table. Set the anti-kickback device about $\frac{1}{8}$ inch (3 mm) above the work surface. This will act as a safety device to keep your fingers away from the rotating blade. Hold the stock firmly on the table with the cutoff line in line with the saw blade. Start the machine and allow it to come to full speed. Now pull the motor slowly so that the blade cuts into the stock. Figure 59-3. This will take very little effort, since the cutting action tends to feed the blade into the stock. After the cut is made, return the saw to its place behind the guide fence and turn off the machine. To make a miter cut, simply adjust the arm or track to the angle you want and do the cutting as you would for straight crosscutting. Figure 59-4. To cut a bevel, adjust the track or arm for straight cross-cutting and then tilt the saw to the desired angle. Figure 59-5. The angle is 45 degrees for most bevel or end miter cuts.

**59-3.** To do straight cutting, pull the saw smoothly through the stock.

A compound miter is made by adjusting the arm or track to the correct angle and then tilting the saw. Figure 59-6. A rabbet or dado can easily be cut by installing a dado head on the arbor and using it as you would a saw blade.

### RIPPING OPERATIONS

Set the track or overarm at right angles to the guide fence. Turn the saw so that the blade is parallel to the guide fence. Then move the saw in or out until the correct distance between the guide

**59-4.** The arm adjusted to make a miter cut.

**59-5.** Making a bevel cut.

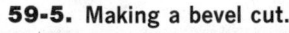

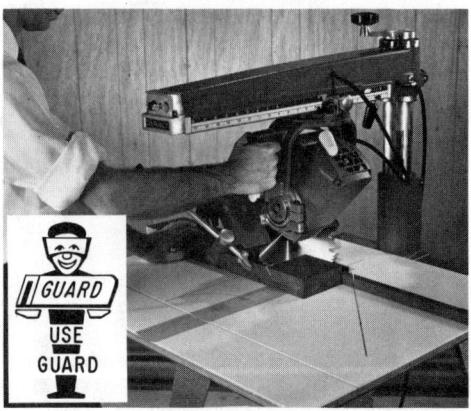

**59-6.** Making a compound miter or hopper cut.

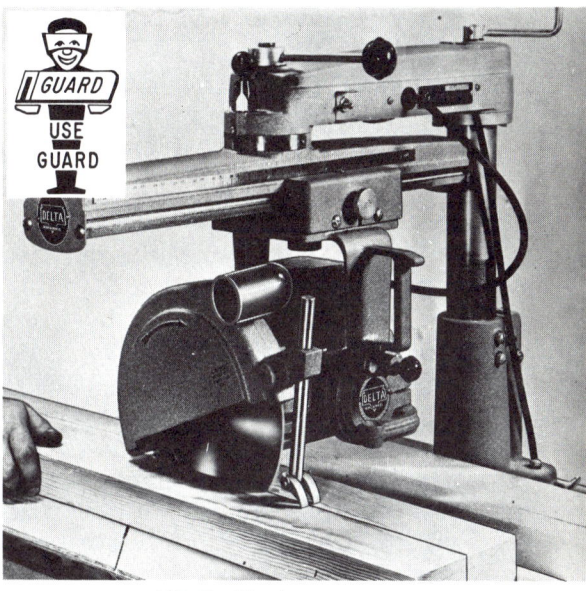

**59-7.** Ripping.

fence and blade is obtained. Lock it in position. Set the depth of cut. Adjust the guard so that it is close to the work. Set the anti-kickback device so that the fingers rest firmly on the wood surface and hold it against the table. Check to make sure that the saw is rotating up and toward you. Turn on the power and move the stock slowly into the blade. Figure 59-7.

## CAN YOU ANSWER THESE QUESTIONS ON THE RADIAL-ARM SAW?

1. How does the radial-arm saw differ from the circular saw?
2. What advantage does the radial-arm saw have over the circular saw?
3. Describe the three principal adjustments that are made on a radial-arm saw.
4. List five safety precautions to follow when using this saw.
5. Tell how to adjust the saw for straight crosscutting.
6. Describe two other types of crosscutting operations.
7. Tell how to adjust the saw for ripping.

# THE BAND SAW

**A band saw** has two wheels mounted on a *frame*, a *table*, *guides*, a *saw blade*, and *guards*. Figure 60-1. In addition, a *ripping fence* and *miter gage* are sometimes used. The table can be tilted to different angles. The size of the band saw is indicated by the diameter of the wheels. The saw is used mostly for cutting curves, circles, and irregular designs. Figure 60-2. It can also be used for straight crosscutting, ripping, and resawing. Figure 60-3.

## INSTALLING A BLADE

To install a saw blade, remove the guards over the wheel, loosen the top wheel, and remove the throat plate. Grasping the blade in both hands, slip it through the slot in the table and then over the wheels. Figure 60-4. Then tighten the upper wheel to apply tension

**60-1b.** A small, 14-inch (356 mm) band saw that can be mounted on a table or bench. It has all the features of a large machine, such as a tilting table, ball-bearing guides, and an adjustable upper wheel. It differs only in that it has a smaller capacity.

**60-1a.** A 20-inch (508 mm) band saw.

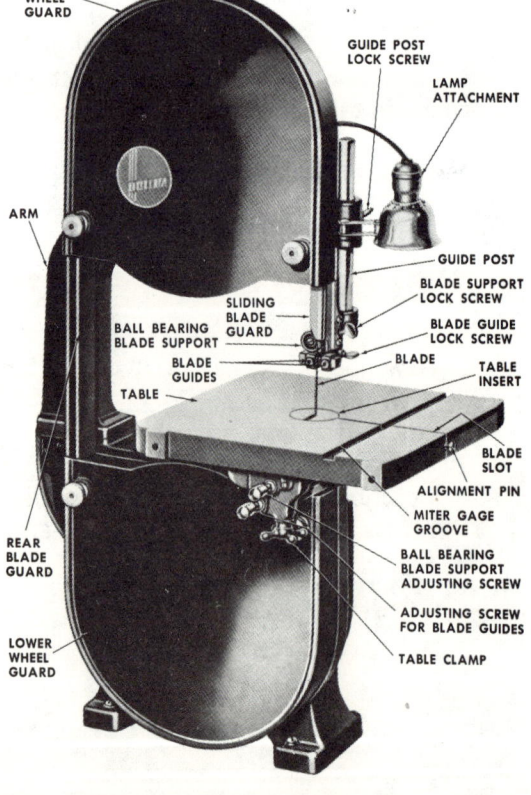

UPPER WHEEL GUARD

GUIDE POST LOCK SCREW

LAMP ATTACHMENT

ARM

GUIDE POST

BLADE SUPPORT LOCK SCREW

SLIDING BLADE GUARD

BLADE GUIDE LOCK SCREW

BALL BEARING BLADE SUPPORT

BLADE GUIDES

BLADE

TABLE INSERT

TABLE

BLADE SLOT

ALIGNMENT PIN

REAR BLADE GUARD

MITER GAGE GROOVE

BALL BEARING BLADE SUPPORT ADJUSTING SCREW

ADJUSTING SCREW FOR BLADE GUIDES

LOWER WHEEL GUARD

TABLE CLAMP

to the blade. This wheel can be tilted to move the blade forward or backward. Replace the little throat plate around the blade and look to see if the blade is running in the guide properly. Turn the wheels over by hand once or twice to check the operation of the blade.

## CUTTING WITH A BAND SAW

Adjust the upper saw guide just to clear the stock. Figure 60-5. Stand slightly to the left and in front of the table. Guide the stock with one hand and apply forward pressure with the other. Do

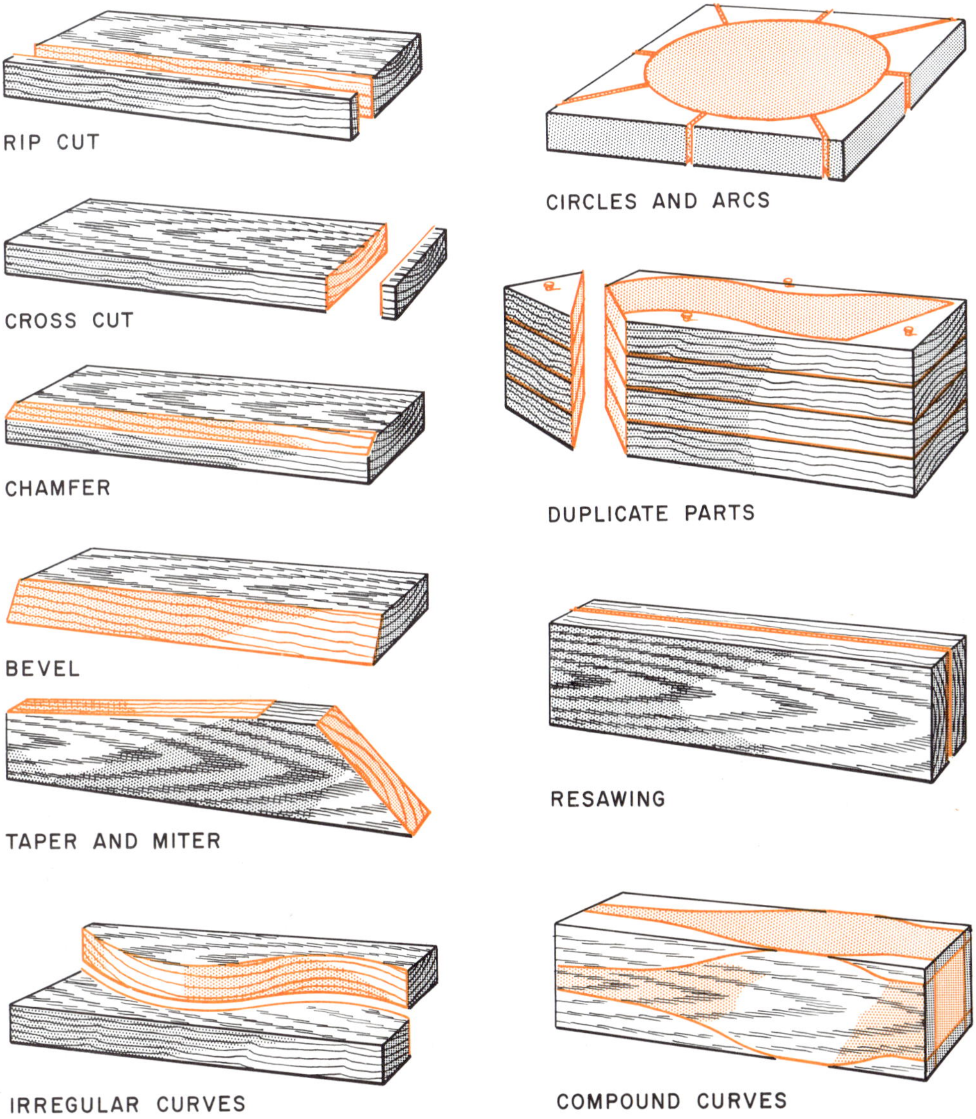

**60-2.** Common cuts that can be made on the band saw.

RIP CUT

CROSS CUT

CHAMFER

BEVEL

TAPER AND MITER

IRREGULAR CURVES

CIRCLES AND ARCS

DUPLICATE PARTS

RESAWING

COMPOUND CURVES

**60-3.** The legs of this table can be cut on the band saw.

**60-4.** Installing a band-saw blade. The guards have been removed and the upper wheel released to permit the new blade to be slipped over the two wheels. There are adjustments on the reverse side of the upper wheel for tension and for tilting the wheel back and forth. This will, of course, move the blade.

not force the work into the saw. Follow these general suggestions:

● *Watch the feed direction.* Before making the cut, think through the path that it must make. Some pieces will swing in such a way as to hit the upper arm if the plan is not correct. Figure 60-6.

● *Make short cuts before long cuts.* It is much easier to backtrack out of a short cut than a long one. Figure 60-7.

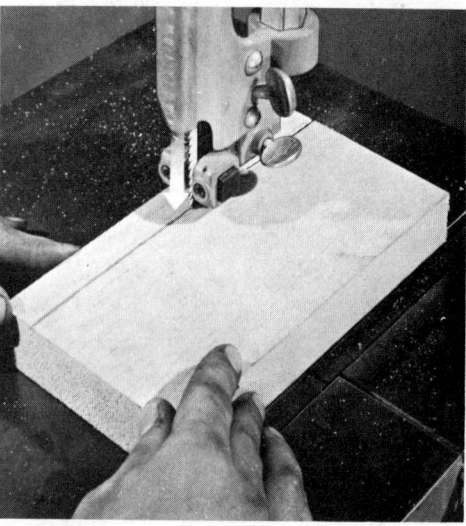

**60-5a.** The band saw with the guide properly adjusted. The stock, which just clears the guide, is held with the thumb and forefinger of both hands.

**60-5b.** Make two straight cuts on an outside sharp corner. A continuous cut will round the corners and may break the blade.

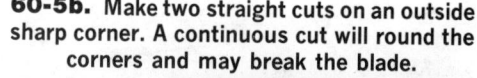

Second Cut

First Cut

● *Make use of turning holes.* Depending on the design, a round or square hole can first be cut in the waste stock before band-sawing. Figure 60-8.

● *Break up complicated curves.* Look at each job to see if a combination cut can be completed by making several simpler cuts. Figure 60-9.

● *Rough cut complex curves.* Make a simple cut through the waste stock to follow as much of the line as possible. Then cut to the layout line. Figure 60-10.

● *Backtrack out of corners.* Narrow grooves are cut out by "nibbling" at the closed end. On large rectangular openings, cut to one corner and then back-

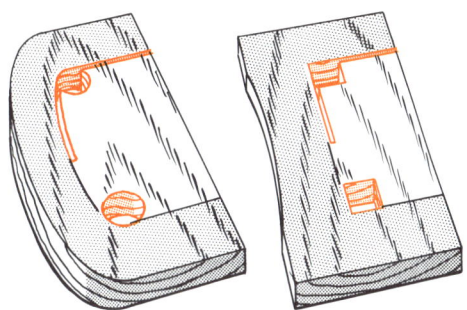

AN AUGER AND MORTISING CHISEL USED TO MAKE TURNING HOLES

**60-8.** Use the auger bit and mortising chisel to cut starting holes shown.

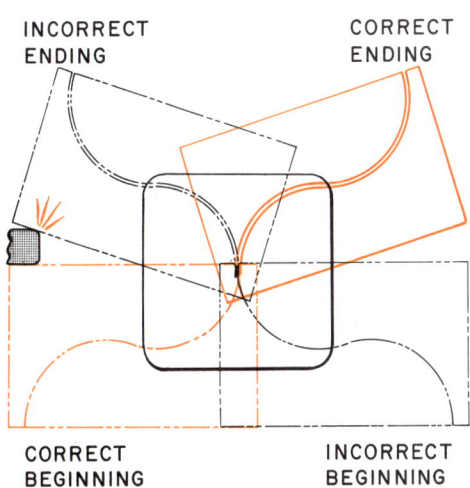

INCORRECT ENDING  CORRECT ENDING

CORRECT BEGINNING  INCORRECT BEGINNING

**60-6.** Checking the feed direction so that the work does not hit the saw arm.

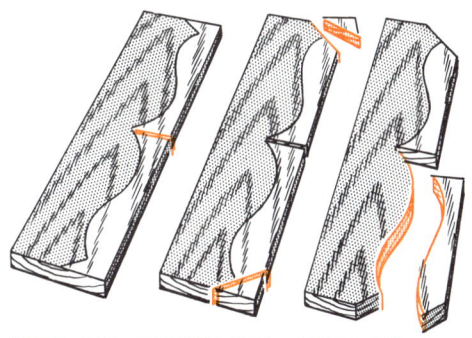

FIRST CUT  SECOND CUT  THIRD CUT

**60-9.** The correct sequence in cutting a combination curve.

**60-7.** Make short cuts before long cuts.

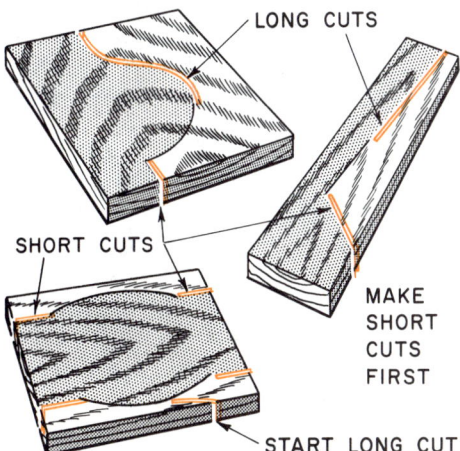

LONG CUTS

SHORT CUTS

MAKE SHORT CUTS FIRST

START LONG CUT

**60-10.** Rough-cut for a curve.

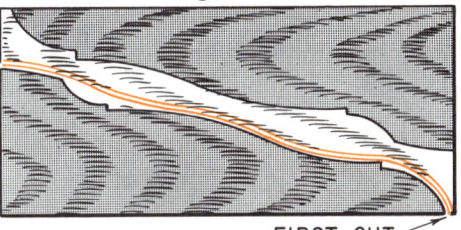

FIRST CUT

**417**

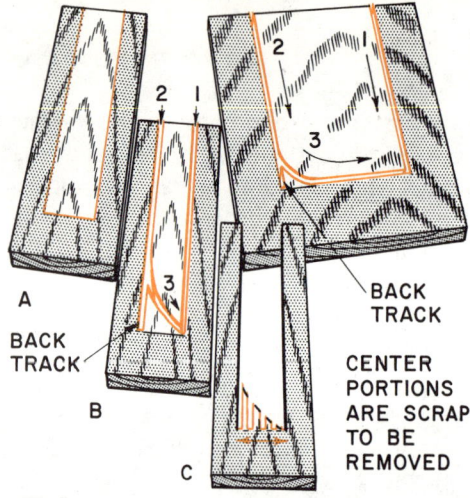

**60-11.** Sequence in cutting rectangular openings.

A

BACK TRACK

B

C

BACK TRACK

BACK TRACK

CENTER PORTIONS ARE SCRAP TO BE REMOVED

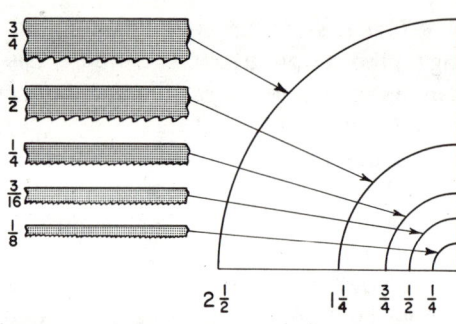

**60-12.** This chart shows how to select the right blade. For example, a ½-inch (12.5 mm) blade cannot cut a circle smaller than 2½ inches (63.5 mm) in diameter. (Remember, radius is half of diameter.)

track slightly before cutting to another corner. Figure 60-11.

## CUTTING CURVES

Select a band-saw blade for cutting curves, following this general rule: A ⅛-inch (3 mm) blade will cut down to about a ½-inch (12.5 mm) circle, and a ⅜-inch (9.5 mm) blade will cut down to about a 2-inch (51 mm) circle. Figure 60-12. The width of blade depends on the thickness and kind of wood to be cut and also on the sharpness of the curve.

In cutting curves, apply even, forward pressure. Carefully guide the work with your left hand to keep the cut just outside the layout line. Figure 60-13. If you are cutting sharp curves, you should make many relief cuts from the outside edge to within less than the thickness of the blade from the layout line. Figure 60-14. Then, as you cut along the layout line,

**60-13.** Cutting a curve on a band saw. The stock is carefully guided along the layout line.

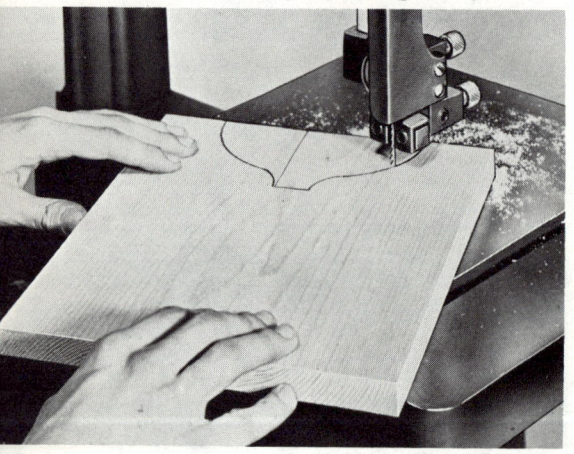

**60-14.** Cutting a sharp curve. When the blade on the band saw is a little too wide, a "closer" cut can be made with the aid of relief cuts.

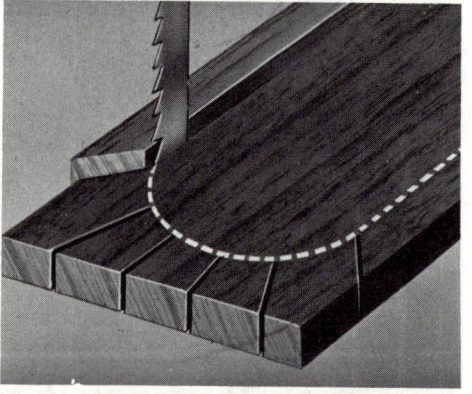

418

**60-15.** Cutting a circle freehand on the band saw.

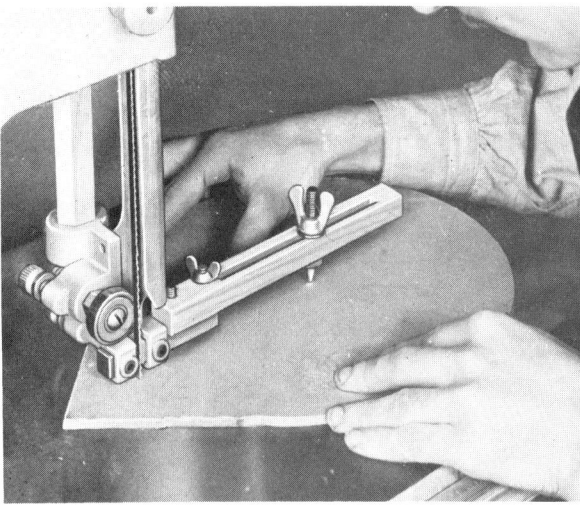

**60-16.** Using an extension guide bar type of circle jig for cutting a true circle.

the waste stock will fall away freely. Circles can be cut freehand or with a circle jig. Figures 60-15 and 60-16.

### RESAWING

When stock is much thicker than needed, it is resawed. This can be done on the band saw. The widest possible blade should be selected and a fence or pivot block attached to the table. A layout line across the end and edge of the board is helpful. Hold the stock against the fence or block and slowly feed the work against the blade. Figure 60-17.

**60-17.** Resawing stock. A pivot block is fastened to the table with a C clamp to control the thickness of the cut. A band saw is better for resawing than a circular saw because less stock is wasted with the thinner blade and because the exposed blade is longer. Notice the tension nut for tightening the upper wheel and the adjustment for tilting the wheel.

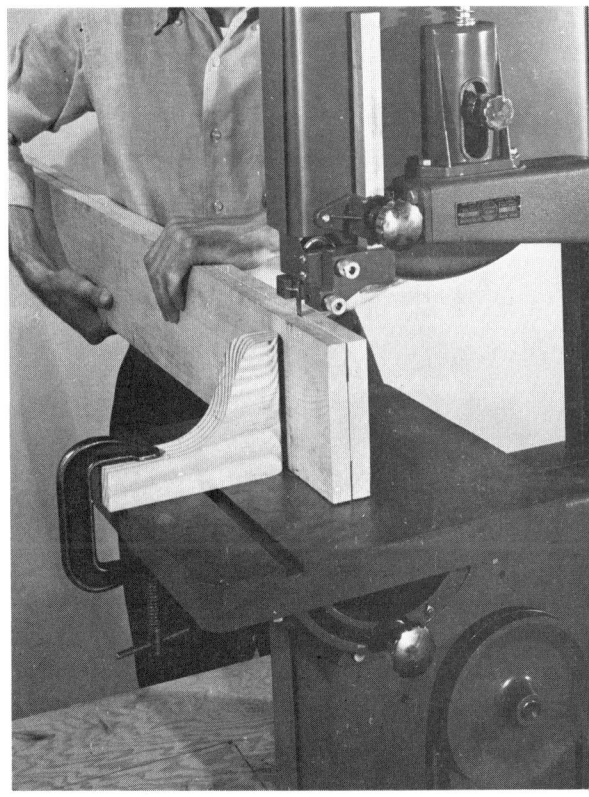

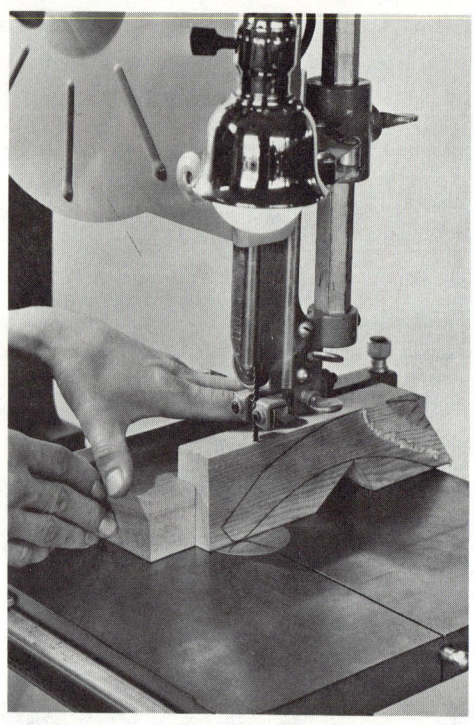

## RIPPING

If a circular saw is not available, stock can be ripped to width by fastening a fence or pivot block to the table and proceeding in the same way as with a circular saw. Figure 60-18.

## CROSSCUTTING AND MITERING

The table of the band saw has a groove into which a miter gage will fit. Stock can be held against this miter gage to do accurate crosscutting or miter cutting on a band saw.

## TILT-TABLE WORK

The table can be tilted to do many jobs such as beveling and chamfering on curves and irregular designs.

**60-18.** Ripping stock to width, using the fence and a very simple wood jig.

## CAN YOU ANSWER THESE QUESTIONS ON THE BAND SAW?

1. Name the parts of the band saw.
2. How is the size of the band saw determined?
3. Describe the method followed for installing a saw blade.
4. Where should you stand when cutting with a band saw?
5. How can a sharp curve be cut?
6. There is a rule for selecting a band-saw blade for cutting curves. What is it?
7. What is resawing?
8. What is the advantage of resawing on a band saw over resawing on a circular saw?
9. How can ripping be done on the band saw?

## Section XI

## UNIT 61.

# JIG, OR SCROLL, SAW

**The jig, or scroll, saw** is a mechanically operated cutting tool. Figure 61-1. The saw moves up and down to do the same type of cutting that can be done by hand with a coping or compass saw. It will cut curves or irregular designs both externally and internally. Figure 61-2. It differs from other curve-cutting machines because it can make cuts inside a pattern without cutting through the stock.

### PARTS OF THE JIG SAW

The saw consists of a *frame* with *overarm* and *base*, a *driving mechanism* to convert rotating action into up-and-down action, *table*, *guide*, and *saw blade*. A tension sleeve is mounted in the end of the overarm, through which a plunger moves.

The size of a jig saw is indicated by the distance between the blade and the overarm measured horizontally. The speed of the jig saw can be adjusted by shifting a belt to various positions or by turning the variable speed control handle.

There are three types of blades. *Power jig-saw blades* are used for many kinds of cutting on wood. The *saber blade* is fastened only in the lower chuck. *Jeweler's piercing blades* are used to cut thin metal, and the saber blade is for heavier stock. Figure 61-3.

### INSTALLING A JIG-SAW BLADE

Select the correct type and thickness of blade. All are usually about 5 inches (127 mm) long. Remove the table insert.

Tilt the table so that you can see the lower chuck. Place the lower end of the blade in the lower chuck with the teeth pointing down. Tighten the set screw or thumbscrew, making sure that the blade is held securely in the chuck. Figure 61-4. Remember, the lower chuck does the driving. If external cutting is to be done,

**61-1a.** A jig, or scroll, saw with the names of the major parts.

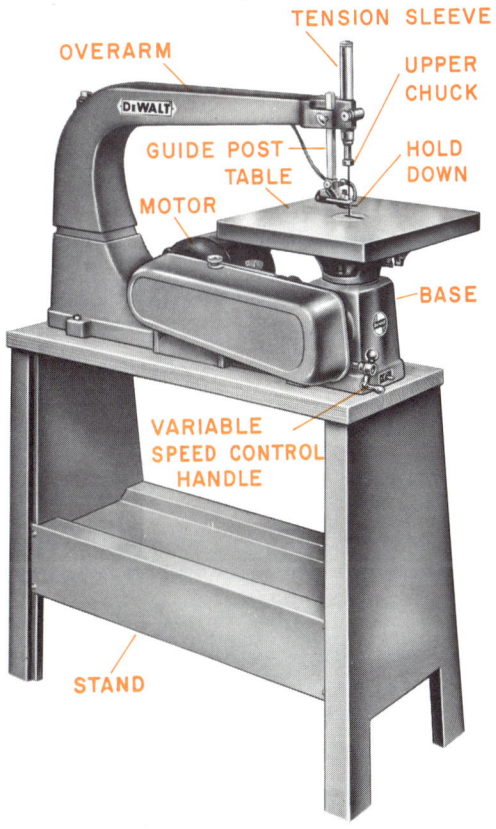

OVERARM

TENSION SLEEVE

UPPER CHUCK

GUIDE POST

TABLE

MOTOR

HOLD DOWN

BASE

VARIABLE SPEED CONTROL HANDLE

STAND

421

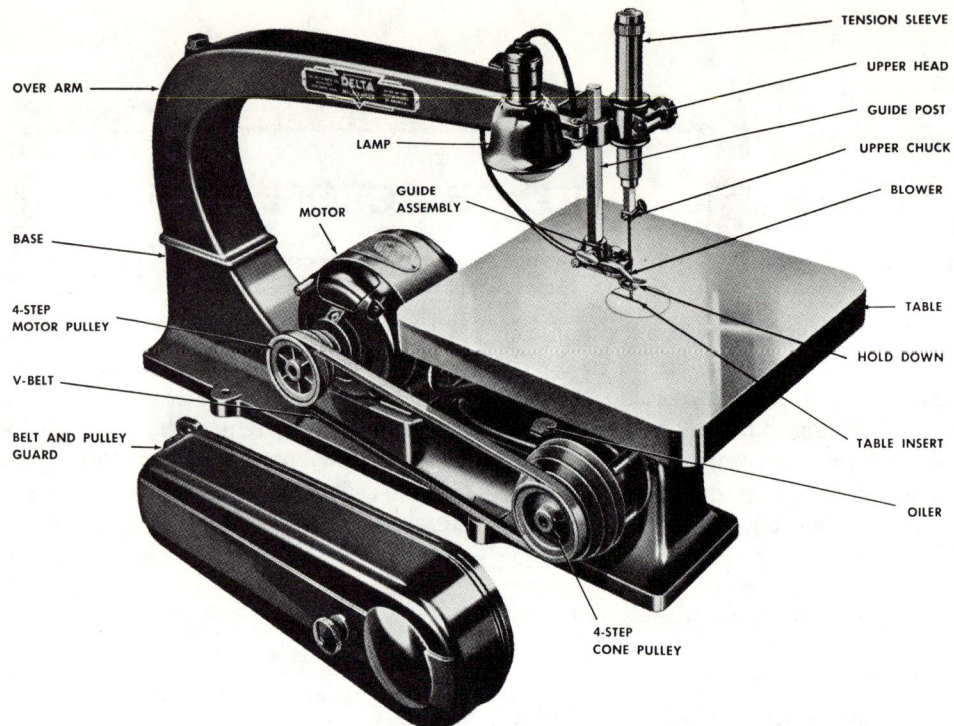

**61-1b.** A 24-inch (610 mm) jig, or scroll, saw with a 4-step cone pulley.

OVER ARM

TENSION SLEEVE

UPPER HEAD

GUIDE POST

LAMP

UPPER CHUCK

GUIDE ASSEMBLY

BLOWER

MOTOR

BASE

4-STEP MOTOR PULLEY

V-BELT

BELT AND PULLEY GUARD

TABLE

HOLD DOWN

TABLE INSERT

OILER

4-STEP CONE PULLEY

**61-2.** Common cuts that can be made on the jig saw.

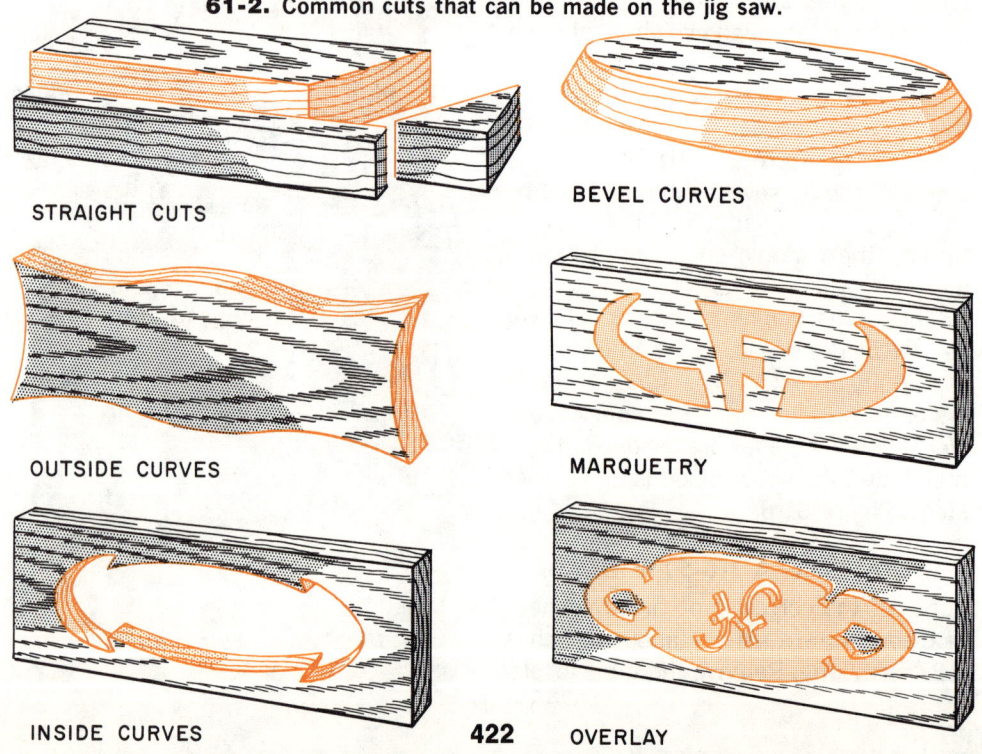

STRAIGHT CUTS

BEVEL CURVES

OUTSIDE CURVES

MARQUETRY

INSIDE CURVES

OVERLAY

422

fasten the blade in the upper chuck. Figure 61-5. This upper chuck controls the tension. Pull down on the upper chuck and attach the other end of the blade in this chuck. If necessary, move the tension sleeve up and down. Replace the table insert. If a saber blade is used for internal cutting, it is held only in the lower jaw. Figure 61-6. Now adjust the guide post until the hold down will apply light pressure on the workpiece. Figure 61-7. Adjust the roller guide to touch the

**61-3.** Blade selection chart.

| Material Cut | Thick In. | Width In. | Teeth Per Inch | Blade Full Size |
|---|---|---|---|---|
| Wood Veneer Plus Plastics Celluloid Hard Rubber Bakelite Ivory Extremely Thin Materials | .008 | .035 | 20 | |
| Plastics Celluloid Hard Rubber Bakelite Ivory Wood | .019 .019 .020 .020 | .050 .055 .070 .110 | 15 12 7 7 | |
| Wall Board Pressed Wood Wood Lead Bone Felt Paper Copper Ivory Aluminum | .020 | .110 | 15 | |
| Hard and Soft Wood | .020 .028 .028 | .110 .187 .250 | 10 10 7 | |
| Pearl Pewter Mica Pressed Wood Sea Shells Jewelry Metals Hard Leather | .016 .016 .020 .020 | .054 .054 .070 .085 | 30 20 15 12 | |

**61-4a.** The blade is clamped firmly in the lower jaw, using a hexagon wrench or a thumbscrew to tighten the jaws. Note that the table is tilted so that you can see what you are doing. Don't clamp too tight as you may shear the threads or break off the thumb control. The lower chuck does the driving while the upper chuck controls blade tension.

**61-4b.** Using a thumbscrew to tighten the jaws.

**61-5.** Install the blade with the teeth pointed down. Slant the blade toward the work to clear the stock on the upstroke. If it slants away, the teeth will catch and lift the stock.

**61-6.** Fastening a saber blade in the lower chuck. Notice that the chuck has been turned a quarter turn and the blade fastened in the V jaws. An extra support bracket has been fastened in place.

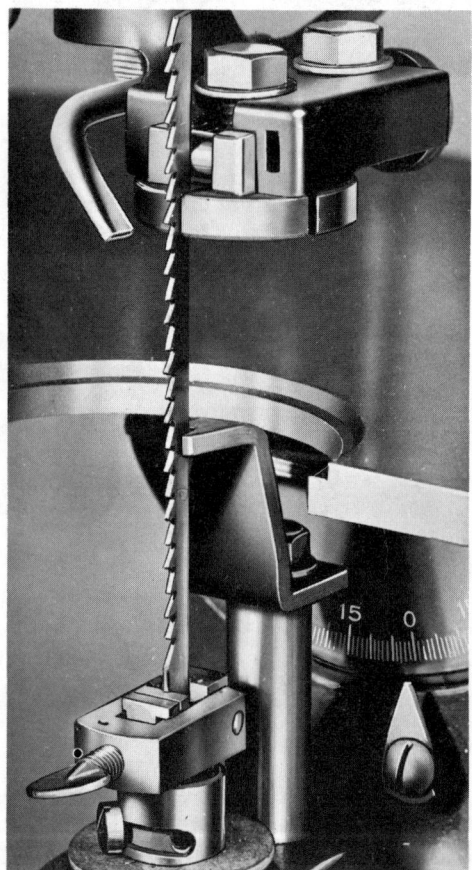

back of the blade lightly. Tighten it in position. Use the hand wheel without power to turn the machine to make sure that the blade moves freely. Now recheck with the power on. If the speed appears to be too fast, readjust the variable speed hand control. If the machine does not have one, turn off the power, remove the belt guide, and move the belt for a lower speed.

## CUTTING WITH A JIG SAW

Cutting with the jig saw requires the same care and attention as cutting with

**61-7.** Proper method of fastening a jeweler's blade in the upper and lower chucks of a jig saw.

a coping saw. Adjust the guide so that the small spring tension holds the stock firmly against the table. Figure 61-8. Hold the workpiece with thumb and forefinger of both hands. Apply even, forward pressure. Figure 61-9. Do not force the stock into the work. Turn the stock slowly when

cutting a curve. If it is turned too sharply it will break the blade. If rather complicated cuts must be made, plan the cutting carefully before you proceed. Figure 61-10.

### Cutting Internal Curves and Designs

Drill a relief hole in the center of the waste stock. Figure 61-11. If a jeweler's blade is to be used, remove the throat plate. After the blade is fastened in the lower chuck, put the stock over the blade.

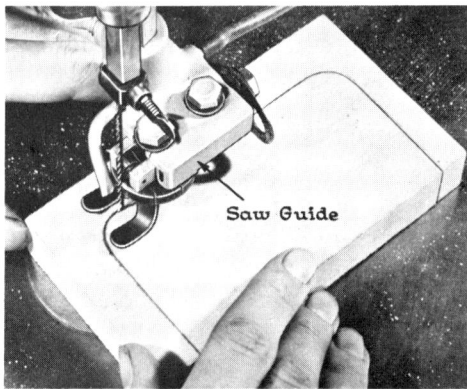

**61-8.** The saw guide properly adjusted. The small spring tension in the bottom of the saw guide holds the stock firmly against the table of the saw.

**61-9.** Guiding the work with the fingers as forward pressure is applied with the thumbs.

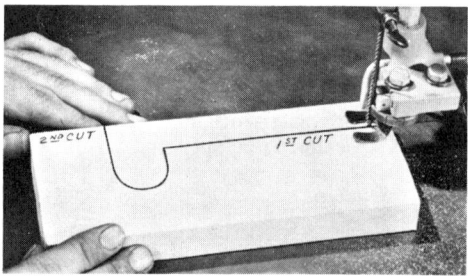

**61-10a.** Proper method of making complicated cuts on the jig saw. In cutting out this design, a straight cut is made first. Then the stock is backed off the saw and a curved cut is made until it joins the straight cut. This eliminates the necessity of trying to cut a sharp corner.

**61-10b.** Break up combination curves. A continuous *line* should not always mean a continuous *cut*. Most *complex* curves can be broken into *simple* curves for easier cutting.

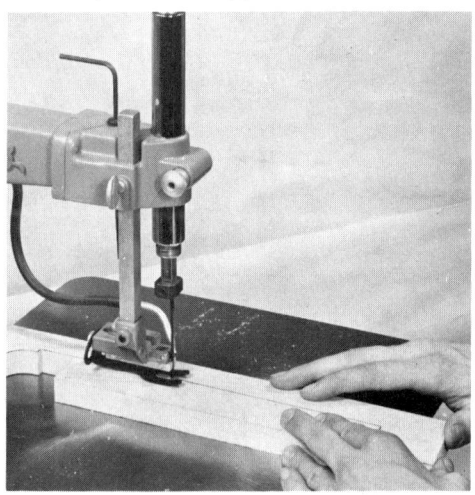

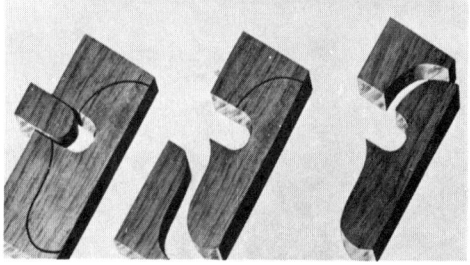

Fasten the other end of the blade to the plunger chuck, and then replace the throat plate. Adjust the guide to correct height. Then make a circular cut from the relief hole to the layout line. Figure 61-12.

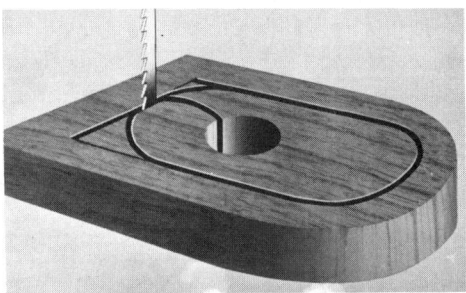

**61-11.** Making an internal cut on the jig saw. The relief hole has been drilled in the center of the waste stock and the cut is made to the layout line.

**61-12.** Doing internal cutting on the jig saw.

## Tilt-Table Work

The table of the jig saw can be tilted to cut a bevel on a straight, circular, or irregular design.

### Making an Inlay or Simple Marquetry

Inlaying (or marquetry) is a way of forming a design by using two or more different kinds of wood. To make a simple inlay, first fasten two pieces of wood together in a pad and nail them together with small brads at each corner. Drill a small hole at an inside corner of the design to start the blade. Now tilt the table of the saw 1 or 2 degrees. Make all necessary cuts with the work always on the same side of the blade. Figure 61-13. Take the pad apart and assemble the design. When pieces with a beveled edge are fitted together, there will be no space caused by a saw kerf. Figure 61-14.

**61-13.** The pad of material has been nailed together in the corner as the design is cut out.

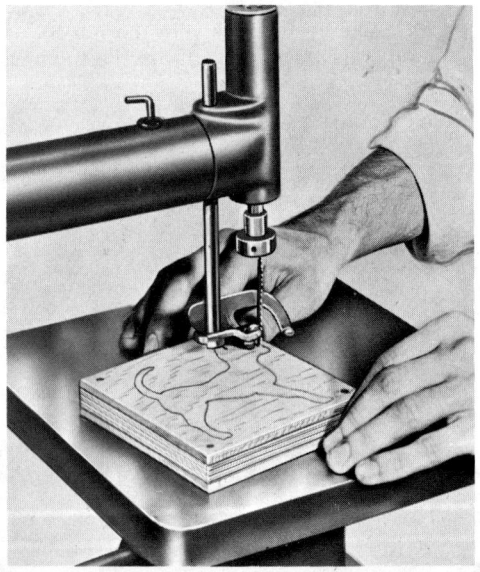

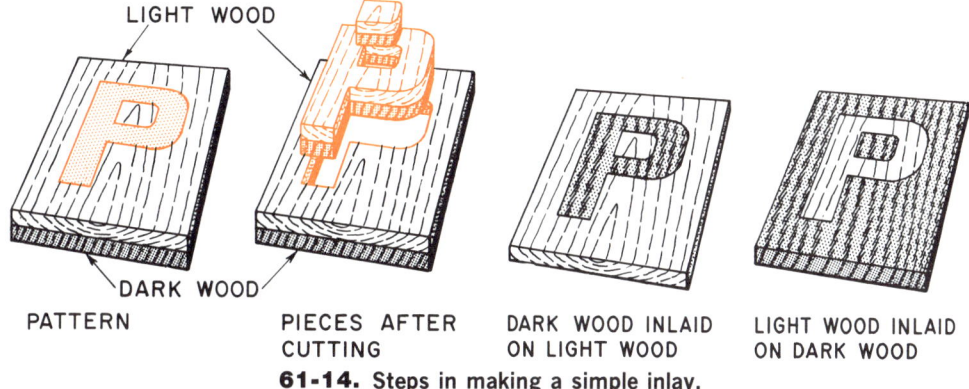

LIGHT WOOD

DARK WOOD

PATTERN

PIECES AFTER
CUTTING

DARK WOOD INLAID
ON LIGHT WOOD

LIGHT WOOD INLAID
ON DARK WOOD

**61-14.** Steps in making a simple inlay.

## CAN YOU ANSWER THESE QUESTIONS ON THE JIG, OR SCROLL, SAW?

1. Sketch a jig saw and locate its parts.
2. How is the size of the jig saw indicated?
3. Name the three types of blades.
4. What is the most common cause of blade breakage?
5. How can internal cutting be done?
6. Explain how to make an inlay.

# Section
# XI
# UNIT 62.

# PORTABLE SAWS

**Portable electric saws** are versatile tools that can cut materials ranging from thin plastics to thick lumber. With the correct change of blades, they can also be used for cutting metal, cement, and ceramics. The *portable power* (cutoff) saw is designed primarily for straight cutting of heavy lumber and plywood. It is used by the carpenter for pre-sizing lumber or for trimming off uneven ends of boards that are already nailed in place.

Figure 62-1. In this way, the cutoff saw eliminates much measuring and fitting. The *portable jig* (saber or bayonet) saw is the best choice for making curved and internal cuts. Some of these saws are designed to cut right up to a vertical wall. This is especially convenient when cutting openings for electrical outlets. Figure 62-2. The *reciprocating* saw is an all-purpose saw that operates with a back-and-forth movement. Figure 62-3.

## THE PORTABLE POWER SAW

The portable power saw consists of a *motor*, *handle*, *base plate* or *shoe*, a *fixed* and a *movable guard*, a *blade*, and a *switch*. The saw is rated principally by the

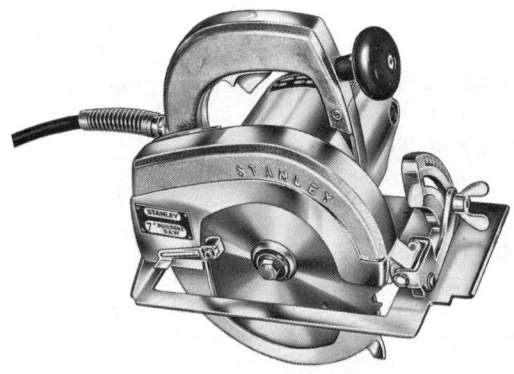

**62-1a.** A portable power saw.

**62-1b.** The portable power (cutoff) saw is popular with carpenters, since wood can be cut after it is fastened in place.

size of the blade, which determines the maximum depth of cut. A good size for most work is a 6- or 8-inch (152 or 203 mm) blade size with at least a $\frac{3}{4}$ horsepower motor. Before connecting your saw, make sure that it is grounded to protect you from possible shock. If an extension cord must be used, make sure that it is 12 gage or larger—up to 100 feet—and 10 gage or larger—up to 150 feet. Unlike the regular circular saw, the portable saw cuts with the thrust upward. Figure 62-4. Because of this, the good side of plywood and other materials should be placed face down for doing the cutting. Figure 62-5.

### Crosscutting and Ripping

Place the work to be cut over two or more sawhorses with a scrap piece of wood under each horse. Adjust the saw to a depth so that it will be slightly more than the thickness of the stock as shown in Figure 62-5. Rest the front of the base plate on the work and in line with the

**62-2.** This type of portable jig saw will cut right up to a vertical wall.

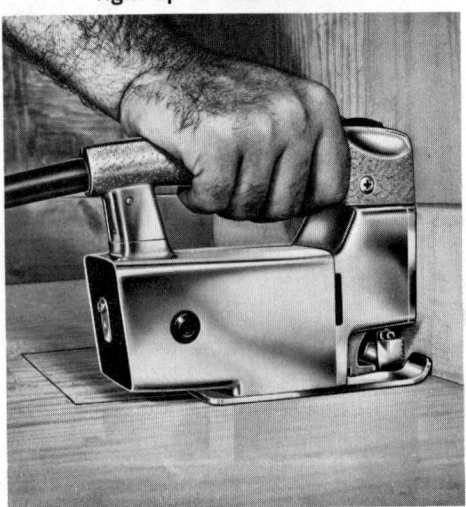

layout line. A combination blade is usually installed so that both crosscutting and ripping can be done. Hold the tool firmly against the work. Squeeze the switch and allow the blade to come to full speed before starting the cut. There is a line or guide edge on the front of the base plate which is exactly in line with the saw blade. Use this as a guide. Move the saw slowly along the line. Don't stand directly in line with the saw blade. If the blade binds, it may kick the saw back out of the cut. If this happens, turn off the switch immediately.

Ripping can be done freehand, but it is better to use some kind of guide. A guide can be attached to the saw, which makes ripping simpler. Figure 62-6.

**62-5.** The saw should be used with the good face of plywood and other materials down.

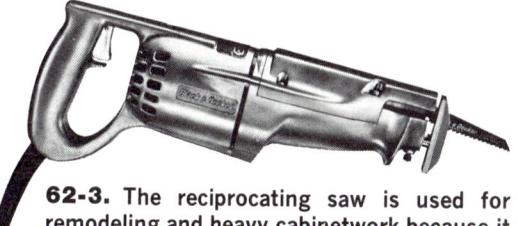

**62-3.** The reciprocating saw is used for remodeling and heavy cabinetwork because it can cut wood, plastics, metal, and other materials.

**62-4.** The cutting action of the portable power saw is exactly opposite that of the regular circular saw.

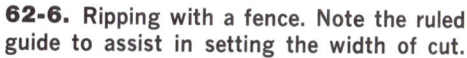

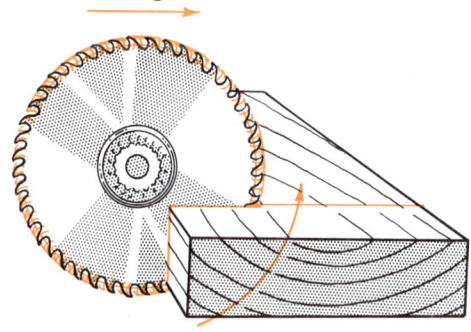

**62-6.** Ripping with a fence. Note the ruled guide to assist in setting the width of cut.

When making a long cut that is beyond your arms' reach, either walk with the saw or stop the saw and pull it back a few inches; then take a new position and resume the cutting. If a rip guide is not available, a board can be clamped over the work so that the base plate will ride against it.

For more accurate crosscutting, a simple T board can be held against the edge of the stock and used as a guide for the saw. Bevels can be cut by adjusting the base plate to the correct angle. A miter can be cut freehand or by using a miter gage. Figure 62-7.

### Pocket Cutting

To make a pocket cut, swing the guard out of the way. Figure 62-8. Then place the front edge of the base plate on the work. Start the saw and slowly lower the blade into the stock. When the cut is made, clean out the corners of the saw.

**62-7.** Making a compound miter cut with the saw.

**62-8.** Starting a pocket cut.

### PORTABLE JIG, OR SABER, SAW

The portable jig (saber or bayonet) saw is used for straight or irregular cutting. Figure 62-9. It will do the same kind of work as the floor-type jig saw. The machine consists of a *motor*, a *switch*, a *blade*, and a *base plate* or *shoe*. On some machines the base plate or shoe can be adjusted for making bevel cuts. The saw blades are designed to do many different kinds of cutting. Figure 62-10.

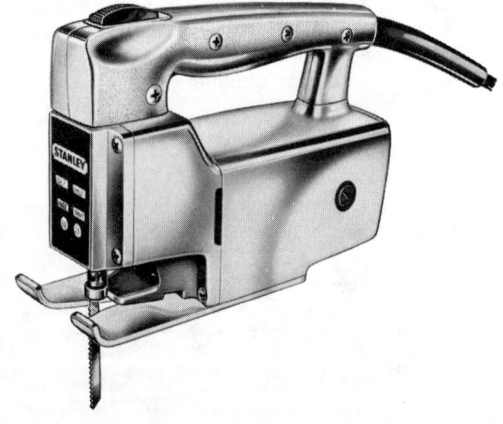

**62-9a.** A portable jig (saber) saw is a handy tool for a great variety of work.

Select a blade that will have at least two teeth in contact with the work at all times.

To install the blade, loosen the set screws or clamp and slip the blade in the slot. In using this saw, *always turn on the power* before bringing it in contact with the wood. Another most important thing to remember is that the base shoe must be held firmly against the material. If not, it will vibrate and break the blade.

### Straight Cutting

Straight cutting can be done freehand. However, it is always best to use a guide. Some machines come equipped with a rip guide that makes the job much simpler. Figure 62-11. If a standard guide is not available, clamp a piece of extra material over the stock as a guide. For crosscutting, a simple T board is best.

### Cutting Curves

Regular and irregular curves can both be cut. Remember that the smallest radius to be sawed should be at least three times the width of the blade. Fasten the work firmly to a bench, allow the saw to come to full speed, and then carefully guide it along the layout line. Figure 62-12. Circles can be cut by using the rip guide as a jig. Figure 62-13.

### Cutting Internal Openings

The simplest method of cutting openings is to drill a clearance hole in the scrap stock. However, the cut can be made without first drilling the hole. This is called *plunge cutting*. Mark the opening to be cut. Then hold the tool at an angle with the shoe resting on the surface. Turn on the power. Slowly lower the saw blade into the work until the blade cuts through the material. Then cut the opening. Figure 62-14.

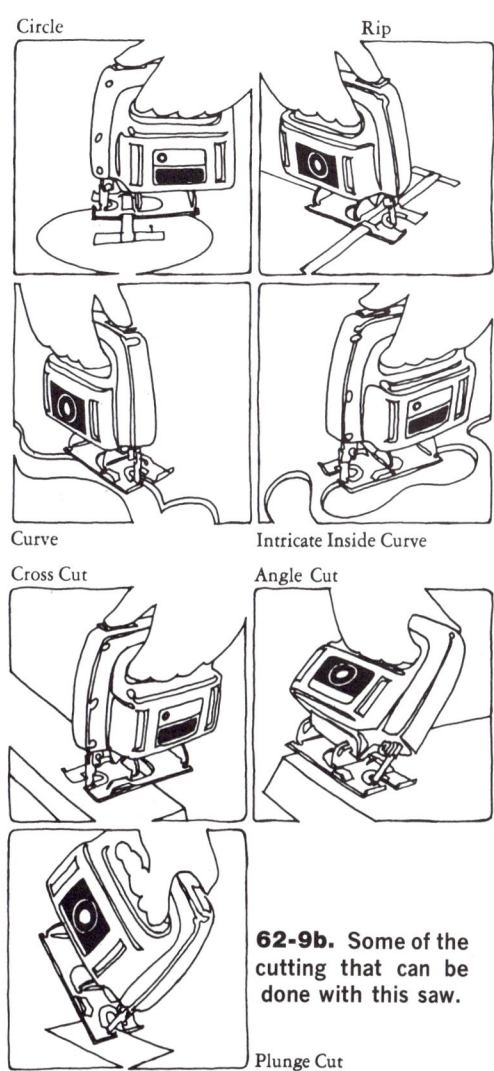

**62-9b.** Some of the cutting that can be done with this saw.

**62-10.** Chart for selecting the correct blade for a portable jig saw.

| | |
|---|---|
| Heavy cuts 2 x 4 inches (51 x 102 mm) at 45° | 6 teeth per inch |
| General cutting | 7, 10 |
| Smooth cuts | 12 |
| Plywood | 12 |
| Hardboard | 12 |
| Cardboard | Knife |
| Leather | Knife |

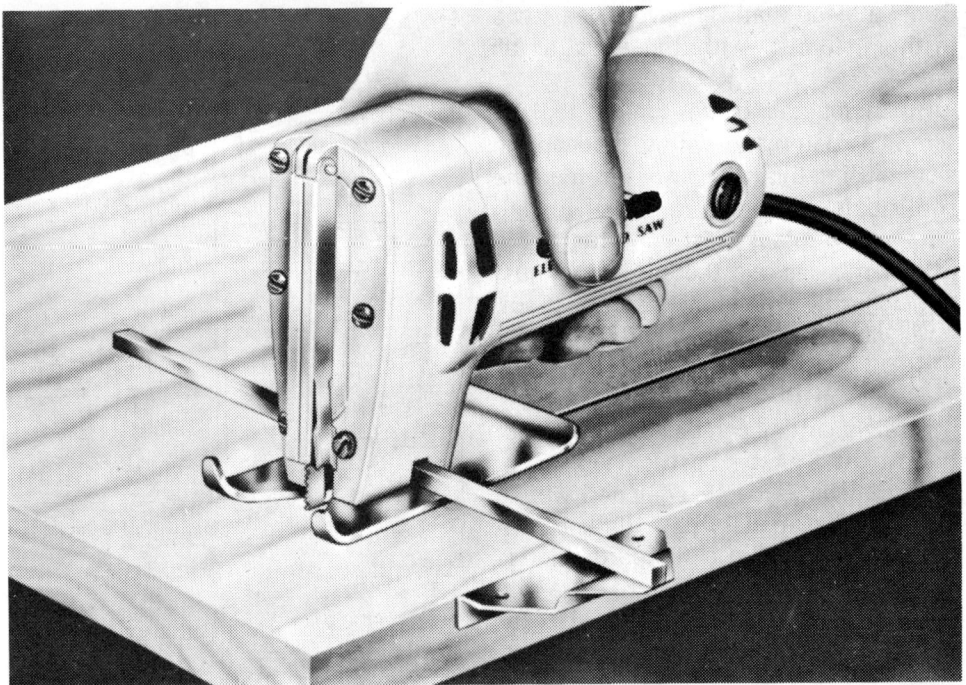

**62-11.** Using a fence for ripping.

**62-12.** Cutting a curve. Note that the work has been firmly clamped to the top of the bench.

**62-13.** Using the ripping guide to cut a true circle.

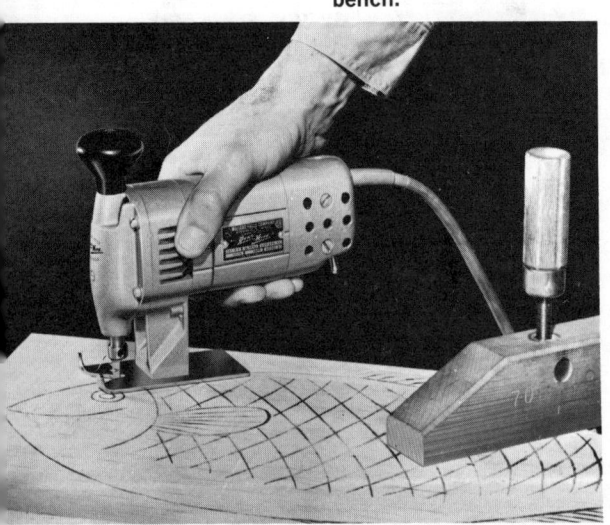

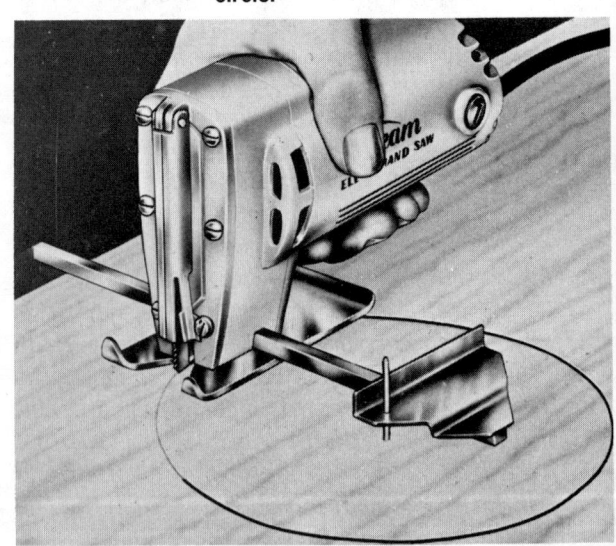

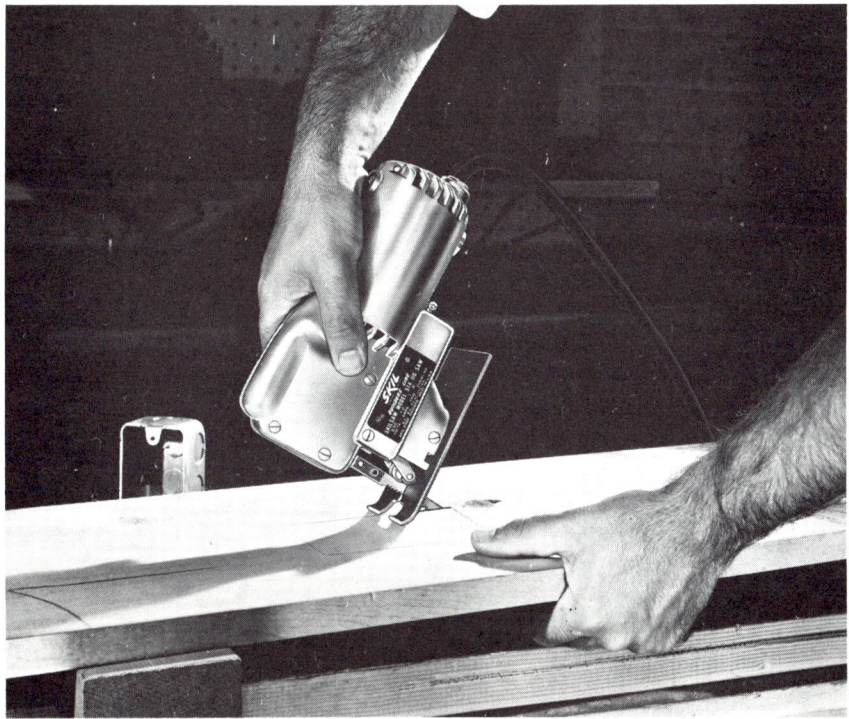

**62-14.** Starting an internal cut. Whenever possible it is better practice to drill a small hole in the waste stock.

## CAN YOU ANSWER THESE QUESTIONS ON PORTABLE SAWS?

1. Name the three kinds of portable saws.
2. Why should plywood be cut with the good face down when using portable saws?
3. What is pocket cutting?
4. Describe the methods of guiding portable saws for ripping.
5. Tell what plunge cutting is and how to do it.

# Section XI
## UNIT 63.

# JOINTER

The jointer is used for surfacing or face planing, jointing an edge or end, beveling, chamfering, tapering, and rabbeting. Figure 63-1. It consists of a *base*, two *tables* (the front, or infeed, table and the rear, or outfeed, table), a *cutterhead*, a *fence*, and a *guard*. Figure 63-2.

The circular cutterhead usually holds three knives firmly mounted with wedges and set screws. The size of the jointer is determined by the length of these knives. The most common size for the small shop is the 6- or 8-inch (152 or 203 mm) machine.

**63-1a.** A jointer is used for getting out stock, squaring up stock, and making joints like those used on this two-drawer commode.

**63-1b.** Common processes that can be done on the jointer.

FACE PLANING

EDGE & END PLANING

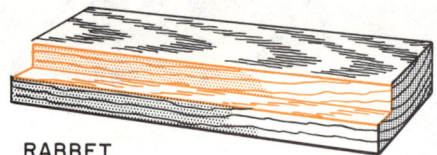

RABBET

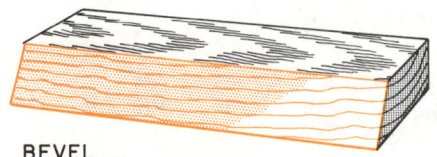

BEVEL

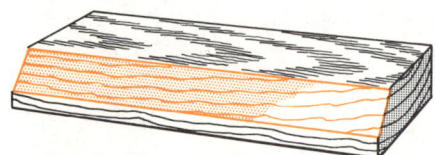

CHAMFER

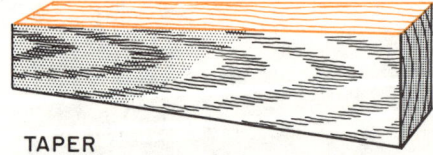

TAPER

The infeed and outfeed tables are mounted on sliding ways so that they may be raised and lowered to make adjustments. The outfeed table supports the work after it has been cut and therefore should be the same height as the cutting knives at their highest point. Figure 63-3. The infeed table supports the work before it is cut. Therefore the height of this table determines the thickness of the cut to be taken. Once the outfeed table has been adjusted to proper height, it can be locked in position and does not need to be changed. Figure 63-4. Only the infeed table should be moved up or down to change the thickness of the cut. The fence of a jointer is usually set at right angles to the table, but it can be adjusted to any angle when you want to plane a bevel or chamfer.

## SAFETY

The jointer is not dangerous if used correctly. It can be a hazard, however, if the following rules are not observed:

- Always make sure that the guard is over the cutterhead.
- Use a push block when surfacing thin stock. Figure 63-5.
- Feed the stock with the grain. Figure 63-6.
- Keep your hands clear of the danger zone. Figure 63-7.
- Never attempt to surface stock that is less than 10 inches (254 mm) in length.
- Stand to the left of the jointer, never directly in back of it.
- Do not attempt to take too heavy a cut.

## FACE PLANING OR SURFACING

Face planing, or surfacing, means planing the surfaces of stock true. Only stock that is less in width than the blades

**63-2.** A jointer with fence and guard. The parts include a base, the cutterhead, the infeed (or front) table, and the outfeed (or rear) table. This is a 6-inch (152 mm) jointer.

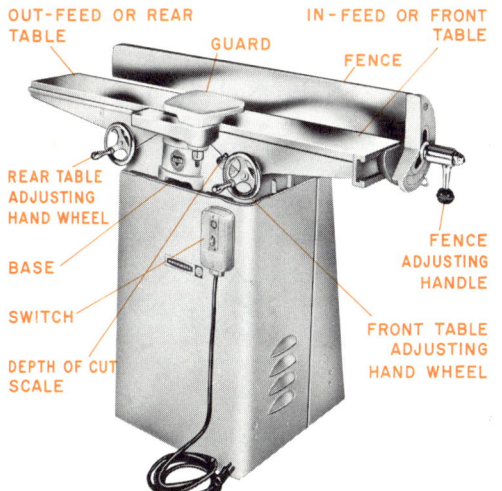

**63-3.** Using a straightedge to check the position of the outfeed table so that it is level with the knives.

of the jointer should be face planed. *Generally speaking, the jointer is not used for face planing.* If it is used, set the infeed table to take a very thin cut. Hold the stock firmly against the table. With one hand, push the stock with a push block as the other hand holds the front of the stock down. Slowly push the board through the cutters. As in hand planing, most pressure should be applied to the front of the board as the cutting is started. Then equal pressure is applied to both front and back as the board passes across the cutter. Finally, more

**63-4.** The jointer must be adjusted so the outfeed table is at exactly the same height as the cutterhead knife at its highest point.

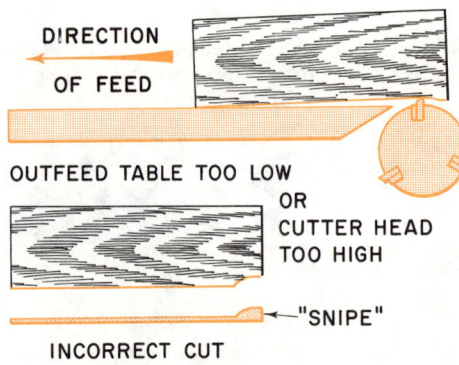

DIRECTION
OF FEED

OUTFEED TABLE AT CORRECT
HEIGHT

CORRECT CUT

DIRECTION
OF FEED

OUTFEED TABLE TOO LOW
OR
CUTTER HEAD
TOO HIGH

← "SNIPE"

INCORRECT CUT

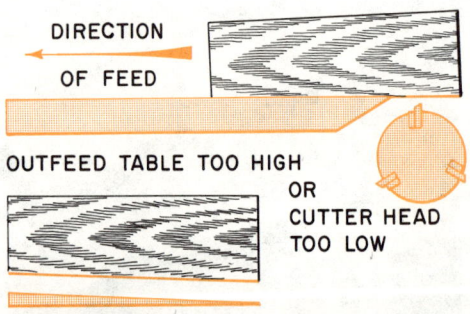

DIRECTION
OF FEED

OUTFEED TABLE TOO HIGH
OR
CUTTER HEAD
TOO LOW

INCORRECT CUT

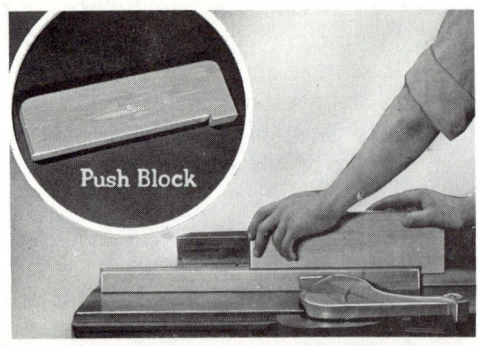

Push Block

**63-5.** Using a push block. Never attempt to surface thin stock or to joint the edge of narrow pieces without using a push block to keep your fingers away from the revolving cutter.

**63-6.** The correct way to feed stock into a jointer. Stock is fed into a jointer opposite the grain direction, with the result that the cutting action is the same as when using a hand plane with the grain.

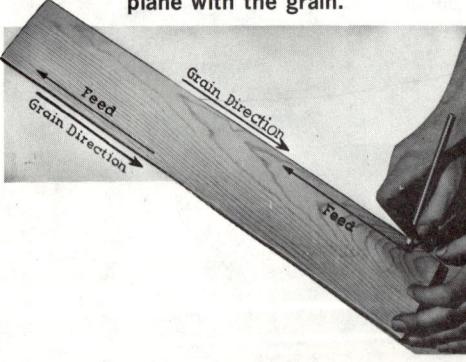

pressure is applied to the rear of the board as the major portion of it has passed the outfeed table. Figure 63-8.

## JOINTING AN EDGE

The most common use of the jointer is to square an edge true with the face surface. To do this, make sure that the fence is at right angles to the table. Check this with a try square. Hold the stock on the infeed table with the face

surface against the fence. Use one hand to guide the stock and the other hand to apply forward pressure. Figure 63-9. Do not push the stock through the jointer too fast, as this will cause little ripples to be formed by the revolving cutter.

## BEVELING AND CHAMFERING

To cut a bevel or chamfer on an edge with a jointer, set the fence at the proper angle to the table. The fence may be

**63-7.** The *danger zone* of a jointer is the area directly over the revolving cutter. This is the area you must guard against.

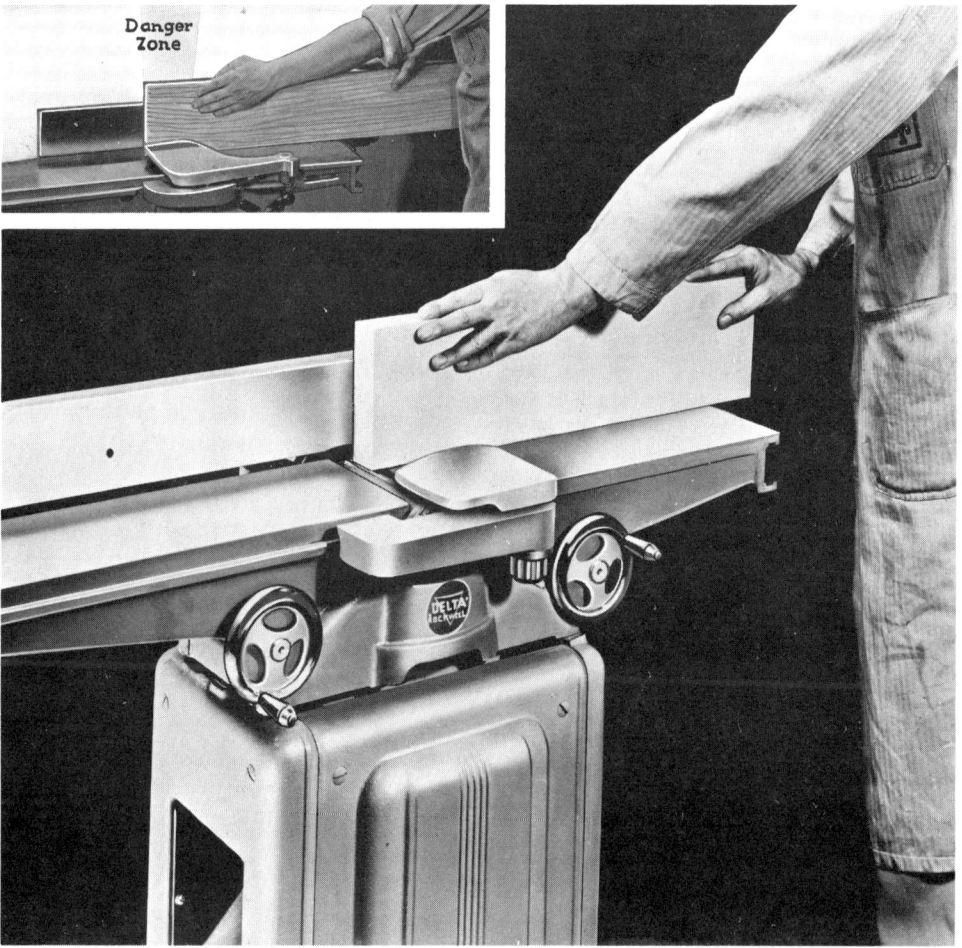

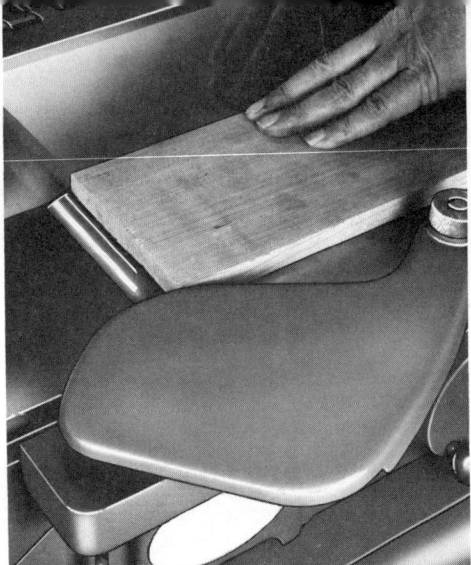

**63-8.** Surfacing or face planing. A push block should be used after the surfacing has started.

GUARD
USE
GUARD

**63-10.** Cutting a bevel or chamfer. The fence of the jointer can be tilted for the operation.

tilted in or out. Figure 63-10. Check this angle with a sliding T bevel; then proceed as in jointing an edge.

## RABBETING

A rabbet can be cut with the grain by first adjusting the fence to an amount equal to the width of the rabbet. Then the infeed table is adjusted to an amount equal to the depth of the rabbet. If the rabbet is quite deep, it may be necessary to cut it in two passes. CAUTION: The guard must be removed for this process, so be especially careful. Figure 63-11.

## ROTARY JOINTER-SURFACER

This machine, which is sold under the trade name *Uniplane*, will perform many

**63-9.** Jointing an edge. The stock is held firmly against the infeed table at the beginning of the cut; then even pressure is applied. Finally, pressure is applied on the outfeed table.

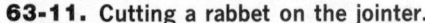

**63-11.** Cutting a rabbet on the jointer.

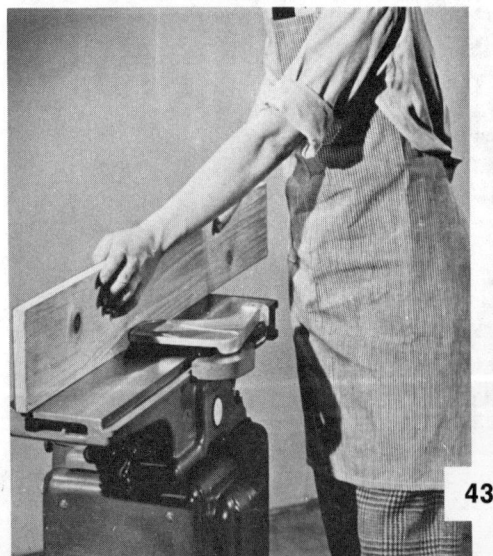

**63-12.** Using a rotary jointer-surfacer to surface small pieces. This *could not be* done on a jointer.

operations not easily done on the conventional jointer. It will safely and accurately plane, joint, bevel, chamfer, trim, and taper. Figure 63-12. This machine can surface stock up to 6 inches (152 mm) wide and can plane pieces as small as $\frac{1}{8}$ inch (3 mm) square. Figure 63-13.

The cutterhead contains eight cutters. Mounted alternately are four scoring cutters and four shearing cutters. The cutterhead operates at 4000 r.p.m.

**63-13.** Thin stock up to 6 inches (152 mm) wide can be planed smoothly.

**63-14.** Trimming end grain for a compound miter.

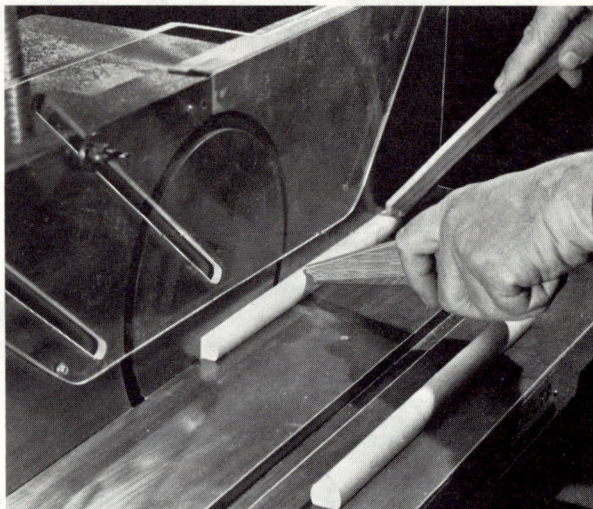

**63-15.** Cutting a flat side on round stock. Note the use of the push stick—to keep your fingers at a safe distance from the cutters. Note also the plastic guard that can be lowered to cover most of the cutterhead.

The depth-of-cut control is located on the front of the machine and is calibrated in sixty-fourths of an inch, with even finer settings possible to five-thousandths of an inch.

By loosening the two table-locking handles, one in the front and one in the rear, the table can be positioned at 90 degrees to the cutterhead or at any angle up to 45 degrees. The table has a slot in which a miter gage can be used to support the stock for trimming narrow pieces or for cutting miters or compound angles. Figure 63-14.

With a rotary jointer-surfacer you can work on much smaller pieces of stock than with a jointer. This machine will also do a good job on end grain. Keep in mind, however, that the safety precautions used for the conventional jointer must be followed. Figure 63-15.

## CAN YOU ANSWER THESE QUESTIONS ON THE JOINTER?

1. Name the parts of a jointer.
2. How can you tell what size it is?
3. Name the two common sizes of jointers used in school shops.
4. How is the depth of cut controlled?
5. List the safety precautions to be observed in operating the jointer.
6. Is the jointer commonly used for face-planing? Explain.
7. How can the fence of the jointer be checked for squareness?
8. What causes ripples to be formed on a board when it is run through the jointer?
9. How can you check the fence for cutting a bevel or chamfer?
10. What are some of the advantages of a jointer-surfacer?

# Section XI
## UNIT 64.

# DRILL PRESS

The **drill press,** although used less than the circular saw, is one of the most valuable tools to have in a small shop. Figure 64-1. It can be used not only for drilling, boring, and countersinking but also for such common operations as shaping, routing, carving, sanding, and mortising. Figure 64-2. Because of this and because the drill press is fairly inexpensive, it should be one of the first additions to a small shop. To do all types of work, the drill press should have variable-speed pulleys for varying spindle speed from a low speed of 450 to 500 r.p.m. for such work as drilling and mortising to a high speed of 5,000 r.p.m. for shaping and routing. Figure 64-3.

**64-1.** A bench-type drill press showing the major parts. Size is indicated by the largest diameter of stock through which a hole can be drilled.

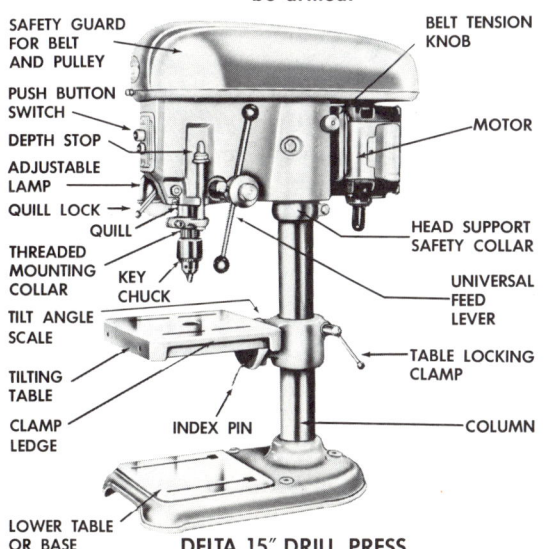

SAFETY GUARD FOR BELT AND PULLEY

PUSH BUTTON SWITCH

DEPTH STOP

ADJUSTABLE LAMP

QUILL LOCK

QUILL

THREADED MOUNTING COLLAR

KEY CHUCK

TILT ANGLE SCALE

TILTING TABLE

CLAMP LEDGE

INDEX PIN

LOWER TABLE OR BASE

BELT TENSION KNOB

MOTOR

HEAD SUPPORT SAFETY COLLAR

UNIVERSAL FEED LEVER

TABLE LOCKING CLAMP

COLUMN

**DELTA 15″ DRILL PRESS**

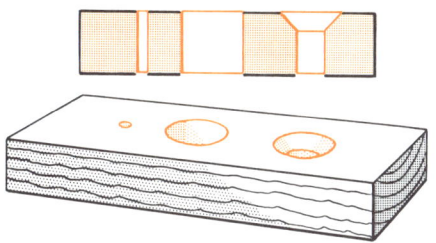

DRILLING, BORING, & COUNTERSINKING

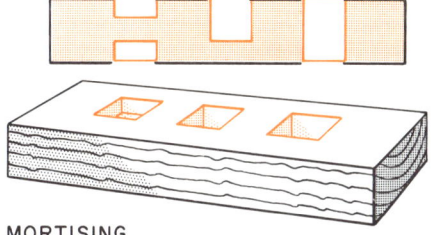

MORTISING

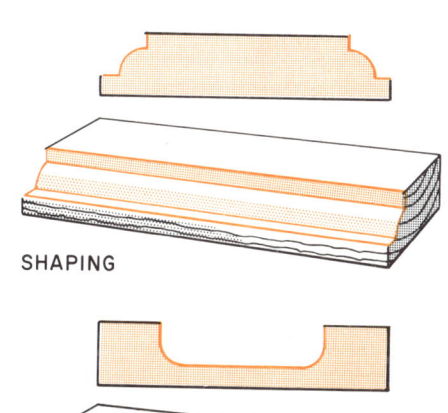

SHAPING

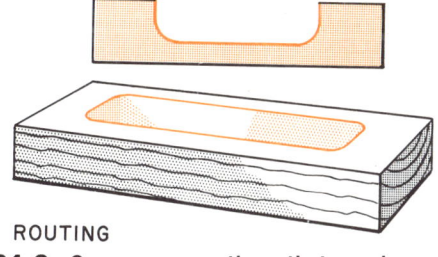

ROUTING

**64-2.** Common operations that can be performed on the drill press.

441

## DRILLING, BORING, AND COUNTERSINKING

Drill presses are usually equipped with a Jacob's chuck to hold drills, auger bits, and other cutting tools. To drill or bore holes, locate and punch the center of the hole. Select a drill or auger bit of the correct size and fasten it in the chuck. An auger bit must have a straight shank and brad point. There are several kinds of boring tools that can be used. Figure 64-4. Adjust the spindle speed to a slower speed for large drills and auger bits and a faster speed for small ones. Adjust the table to correct height. Make sure that the hole in the table is directly under the drill, or place a piece of scrap stock on the table under the piece to be drilled or

**64-3.** Drill press with variable speed pulleys. The range of speed is from 450 r.p.m. to 5,000 r.p.m. The speed is changed by moving the dial lever while the drill press is running. Never try to change the speed when the machine is off. This is the ideal machine for doing a wide variety of drill-press operations.

**64-4a.** *Speed (spade) power bits* come in diameters from ⅜ to 1 inch (9.5 to 25 mm).

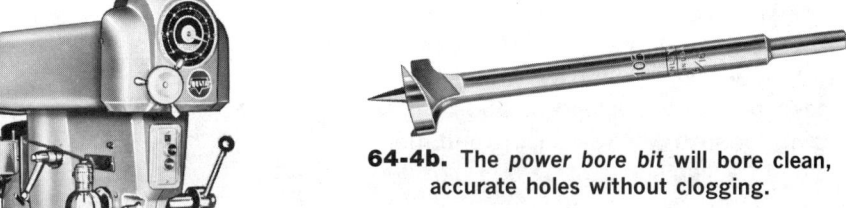

**64-4b.** The *power bore bit* will bore clean, accurate holes without clogging.

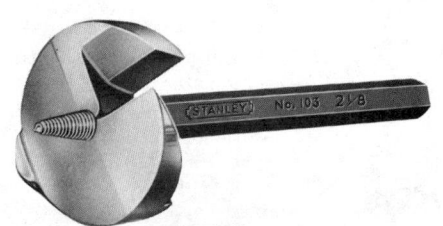

**64-4c.** *Lock set bits* are large-diameter bits that come in sizes of 1¾, 2, and 2⅛ inches (64.5, 51, and 54 mm).

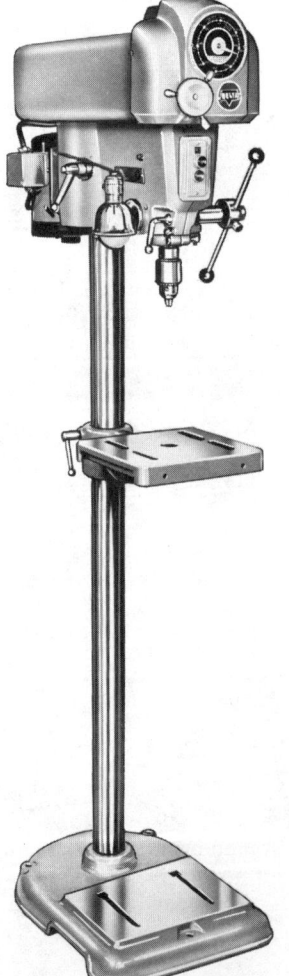

**64-4d.** A *hole saw* will bore a hole of a fixed diameter. It can cut large holes in thin stock such as wood, plywood, or plastic laminate. There are various styles. Some are fixed while others are adjustable to different hole sizes.

bored. Hold the piece securely and apply even pressure as you feed the drill slowly into the wood. Figures 64-5, 64-6, and 64-7. Never force a drill or auger bit into the wood. Drilling or boring holes in round stock can be done by holding the work in a V block. Figure 64-8. Countersinking is necessary when installing flathead screws. Figure 64-9.

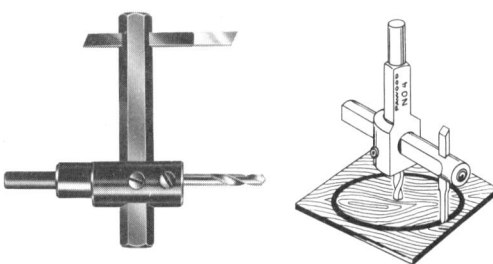

**64-4e.** A *fly cutter* can be used with an electric hand drill or drill press to cut large holes. It is adjustable from 1 to 4 inches (25.4 to 102 mm) in diameter. It has a self-starting drill bit. The center must be well into the stock before the cutter comes in contact with the surface. When using this tool, it is very important that the workpiece be clamped securely to the bench or table.

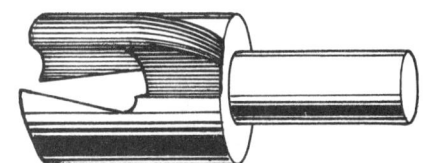

**64-4f.** A *plug cutter* cuts round plugs that are slightly beveled. These plugs are used to cover screw heads.

**64-4g.** A *countersink bit* is used to cut a tapered hole for installing flathead screws.

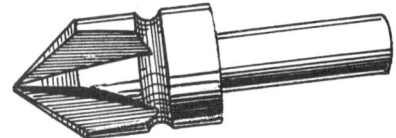

## MORTISING

If much furniture construction is done, a mortising attachment should be available. This greatly simplifies cutting a mortise-and-tenon joint. A mortising attachment consists of a hollow, square, mortising chisel in which an auger bit revolves. The chisel itself is ground to a sharp point at each corner. These points enter the wood just after the revolving bit and cut the square opening after the bit has removed most of the stock. On most mortising attachments, the chisel is fas-

**64-5.** Drilling wood with a twist drill. Make sure that the stock is held firmly against the table of the drill press while the drilling is done.

tened to the quill of the drill press and a straight-shank auger bit fastened in the chuck. Of course, the chisel should be the same width as the width of the mortise to be cut. A fence should be attached to the table to guide the stock. Figure 64-10.

### SHAPING

For shaping, it is necessary to have a spindle speed of 5,000 r.p.m. This speed can be attained by using the variable-speed pulley or a high-speed motor. It is also necessary to have a special adapter that will hold the shaper cutter. Figure 64-11. This adapter can be attached to the spindle of the drill press. Then an inexpensive set of shaper cutters will enable you to construct setups that will cut a variety of shapes. Never use a shaper cutter in a chuck. Select the shaper cutter for the particular shape you want to make. Figure 64-12.

The depth of the cut can be controlled by placing a collar of the correct diameter just above or below the cutter or by using a fence. Fasten the cutter and collar to the special adapter. Raise the table to the correct position and lock it in place. Make a trial cut in a piece of scrap stock of the same thickness as the finished piece. In using a shaper attachment, force the wood into the cutter very slowly. Sometimes it is a good idea to cut the design to partial depth and then go over it again. If the design is cut on three or four edges, finish the ends first and then the sides. If the trial cut is satisfactory, cut the edge. Figure 64-13.

### ROUTING

A routing tool is fastened in a special router attachment. The spindle speed must be about 5,000 r.p.m. Various types

**64-7.** Using a power Foerstner bit with the work securely clamped to the table.

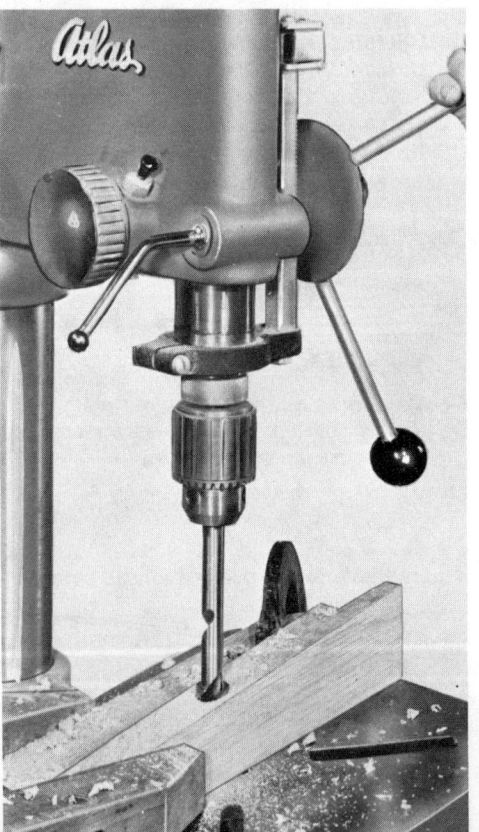

**64-6.** Boring a hole with an auger bit. Stock is clamped to the bed with a C clamp. The auger bit must have a straight shank in order to be used in a three-jaw chuck.

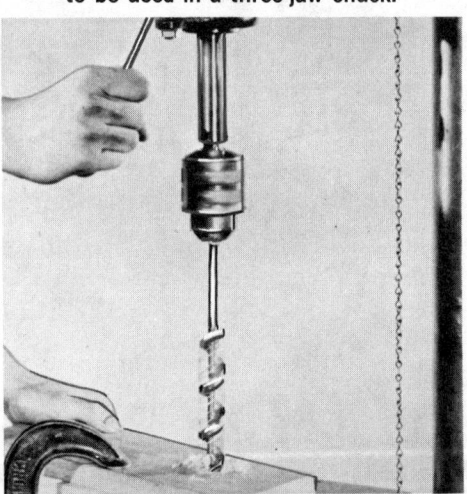

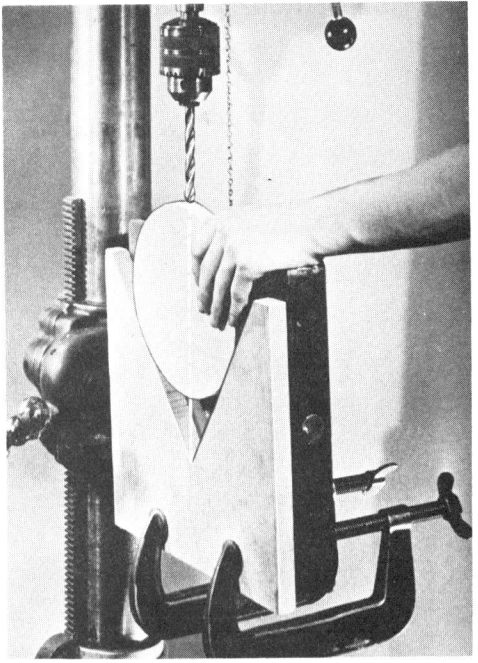

**64-8.** Drilling holes in a cylindrical piece of stock, using a V block. The table has been turned at a 90-degree angle to its original position and a V block clamped to the table with two C clamps.

**64-9.** Countersinking holes on the drill press.

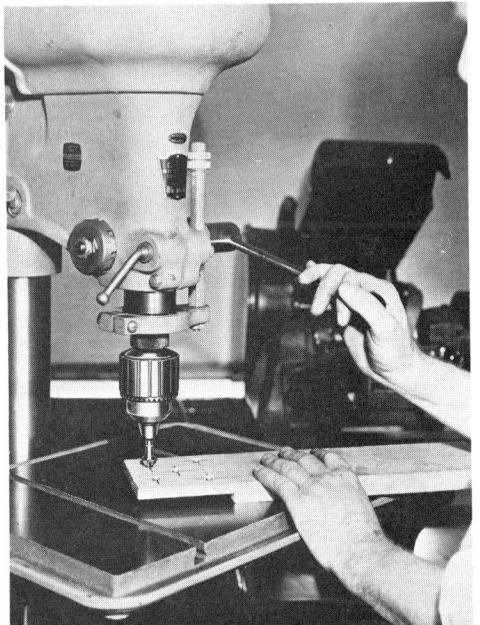

**64-10.** Using a mortising attachment. The part for holding the chisel is locked to the quill of the drill press, and the auger bit is fastened in the chuck. A fence is locked to the table, and clamps are attached to hold the stock in place.

**64-11.** An adapter for holding shaper cutters. This one is fastened to the spindle of the drill press so that side pressure can be exerted on the shaper cutters. Never attempt to hold shaper or router cutters in a drill-press chuck unless you are sure that the chuck is a part of the spindle assembly as a unit.

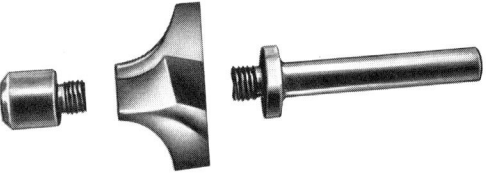

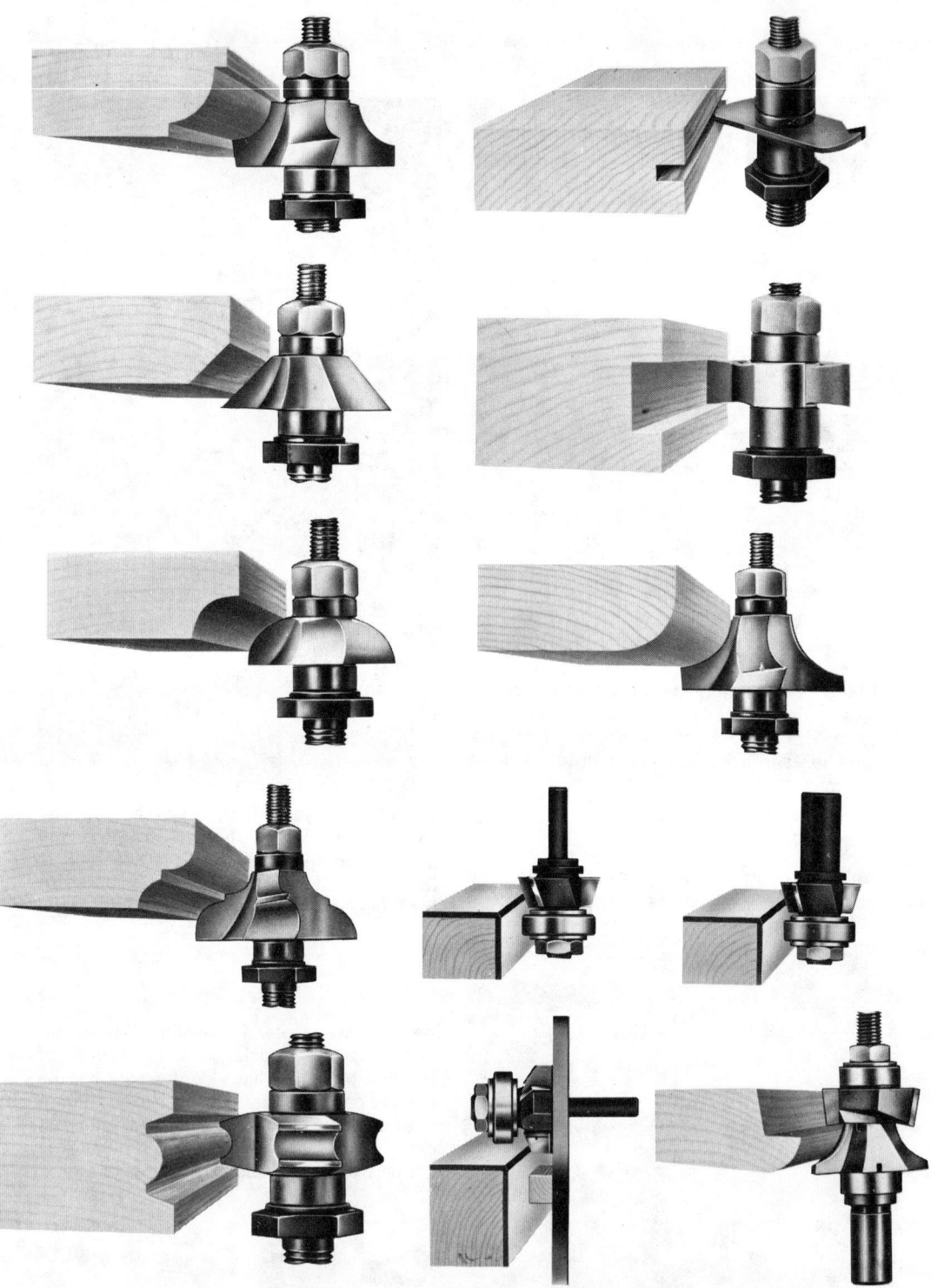

**64-12.** Shaper cutters. Various shapes are needed to make the designs in shaper operations.

**64-13.** Using the drill press as a shaper. When doing shaping operations, a high spindle speed is required.

**64-14.** Doing router work on a drill press. Router cutters are fastened in a special adapter. Make sure that the stock is held firmly against the table and a fence when doing the routing. Notice the guides that have been clamped to the machine to hold the stock in place.

of routing such as grooves, slots, and irregular openings can be done on the drill press. Figure 64-14.

## SANDING

Sanding drums are available in several sizes that can be used on the drill press to do edge sanding. Manufacturers supply sanding sleeves in grits and sizes to fit the drums. Figure 64-15.

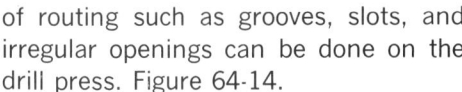

**64-15.** Sanding can be done using a sanding drum.

## CAN YOU ANSWER THESE QUESTIONS ON THE DRILL PRESS?

1. Drilling is not the only operation performed on the drill press. Name several others.
2. About what speed is necessary for shaping and routing?
3. What kind of auger bits can be fastened in the drill press?
4. Name the parts of a mortising attachment and describe how it is used.
5. What two machines are most commonly used for making mortise-and-tenon joints?
6. How do you control the depth of cut for shaping?

Section
XI
UNIT 65.

# SANDERS

**With the correct** power sander you can save much tedious work yet give the project a smooth finish. All sanders make use of an abrasive paper or cloth in the form of a sheet, disc, or belt.

### BELT AND DISC SANDER

The combination bench or floor belt and disc sander is used when the workpiece can be brought to the sander. Figure 65-1. It is especially good for sanding individual parts.

The *belt sander* consists of two drums over which an endless abrasive belt moves. Figure 65-2. One drum has two adjustments on it, one for belt tension and the other for centering the belt on the drums. The machine also comes equipped with a table against which the work can be held. The sanding unit can be adjusted to a vertical or horizontal position for sanding. Figure 65-3. Before using the machine, make sure that the belt is not too tight and that the guards are in place. When sanding work, hold it

square with the abrasive belt. CAUTION: Never attempt to hold a very small piece in your hand since the belt will tend to

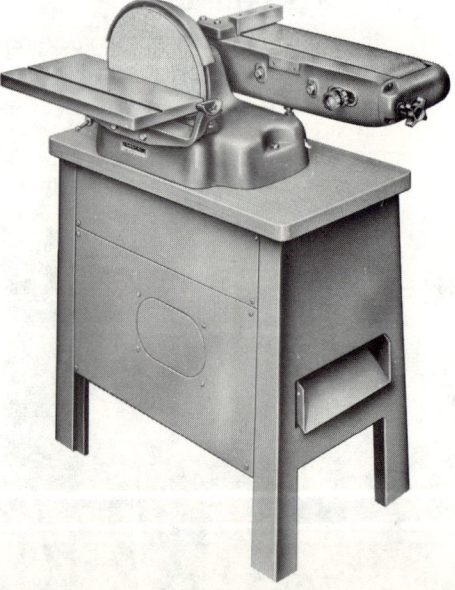

**65-1.** A combination disc and belt sander. While these can be separate machines, the combined sander works very well.

pull it out of your fingers. Always use a push block when sanding thin pieces.

The *disc sander* is really a motor with a flat disc on one end. An abrasive cloth is cemented to the disc. It has rather violent action, so is good for fast, rough work. When using, always work on the side that revolves into the table. Remember that the outside of the disc cuts faster than the inside.

This machine is very good for sanding the edges of irregular-shaped pieces. Figure 65-4.

## PORTABLE BELT SANDER

A portable belt sander operates in a manner similar to the floor machine ex-

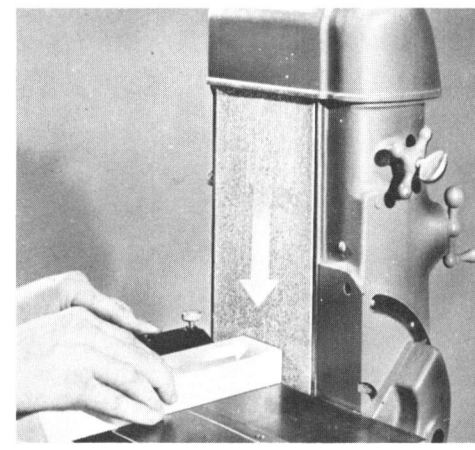

**65-3a.** Using the belt sander in a vertical position. Note how the abrasive belt moves toward the work, tending to hold it to the table.

**65-2.** This 6-inch (153 mm), floor-type, belt sander can be adjusted to a vertical or horizontal position.

**65-3b.** Using a belt sander in a horizontal position to sand the face of a workpiece.

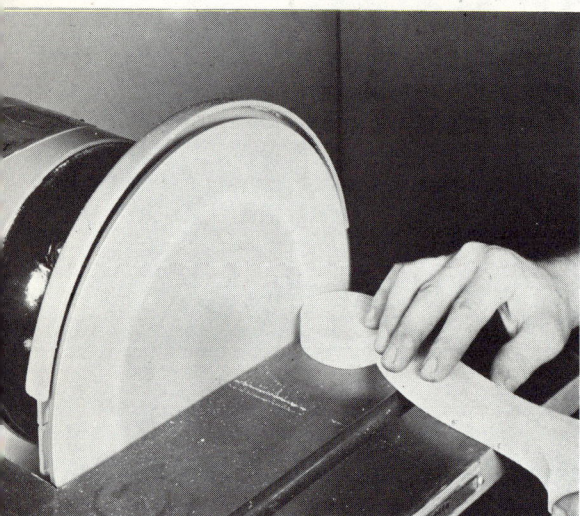

**65-4.** Sanding the edge of an irregular-shaped piece on a disc sander.

**65-5.** Portable belt sander. This machine will sand large surfaces such as a table top.

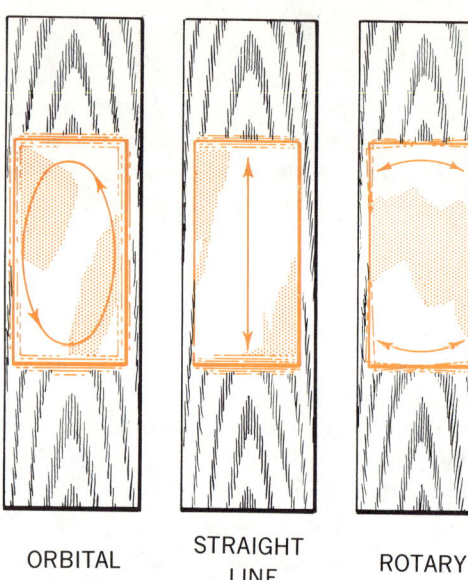

ORBITAL ACTION

STRAIGHT LINE ACTION

ROTARY ACTION

**65-6.** Sanding action of finishing sanders. On some machines two types of action can be obtained by moving a switch.

**65-7.** Using the finishing, or pad, sander. This is the best machine to use after the project is assembled.

cept that the revolving belt is placed over the work instead of the work against the belt. As this machine is used, the belt tends to carry it away from the operator. Therefore always grip the sander firmly with both hands. Figure 65-5. Then move it evenly in a straight line with the wood grain. Never apply pressure to this machine since it will cut very rapidly. Move the machine evenly in a straight line with the grain. Also be careful that you do not round the edges. Remember never to turn on the motor while the machine is resting on the wood to be sanded.

## FINISHING SANDER

There are several kinds of finishing sanders, all of which operate on one of three basic principles: rotary, orbital, or straight-line action. Figure 65-6. Straight-line action leaves the least amount of cross-grain scratches. Finishing sanders are used primarily for fine sanding after the project is completed. Figure 65-7.

## CAN YOU ANSWER THESE QUESTIONS ON SANDERS?

1. Name four sanders commonly found in the shop.
2. What determines the quality of smoothness or roughness of the wood surface after sanding?
3. What is the best sander to use for a light finishing sanding after the project is assembled?
4. Describe the way to use a portable belt sander.

Section
XI

UNIT 66.

# PORTABLE ROUTER

The portable router can do many cutting and shaping jobs. Figure 66-1. It consists of a powerful motor mounted in an adjustable base. There is a collet chuck at the end of the motor shaft that can hold many different kinds of cutting tools. Some of the common router bits and cutters are shown in Figure 66-2. To install the cutter bit, loosen the nut on the chuck and slip the bit in place. Then tighten the nut or nuts. Figure 66-3. To adjust for depth of cut, the base is raised or lowered. In some routers the base screws onto the motor housing. In others it slides up and down. The bit revolves clockwise. Therefore when cutting straight edges, move the router from left to right. When making circular cuts, move the router in a counterclockwise direction. Figure 66-4 (Page 454). Common uses are:

● *Freehand routing.* Routing is called freehand when the operator does the routing without guides. Figure 66-5 (Page 454). A good example of this would be routing out a name plate or numbers of an address. Sometimes the letters or numbers are formed by the cutter bit. In

**66-1a.** A portable router. This model is open on one side and has a light under the motor, to make it easy to see the working section.

other cases, the background around the letters and numbers is routed so the numbers stand out.

● *Shaping an edge or making a molding.* By using a bit with a pilot on the end, the edge of a table top or molding for a picture frame can be made. Figure 66-6. The pilot edge can be shaped without a guide. Select the right bit shape and fasten it in the chuck. Move the base up and down until the bit is out the correct distance. Select a piece of scrap wood of the same thickness as the finished article. Try the bit on the scrap stock.

● *Routing with a guide.* For making such cuts as a groove or a dado, a guide is attached. Figure 66-7. The width of the cut is determined by the bit. Of course,

**66-1b.** Common cuts made with a router.

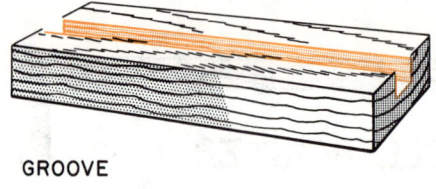

GROOVE

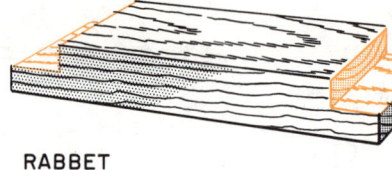

RABBET

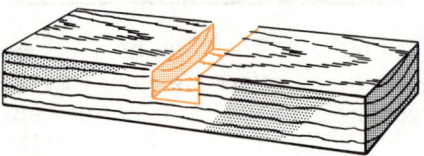

DADO

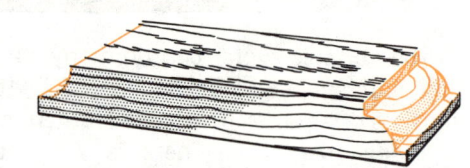

EDGE ROUTING, ROUND OVER, BEAD, COVE, ETC

FREE HAND ROUTING

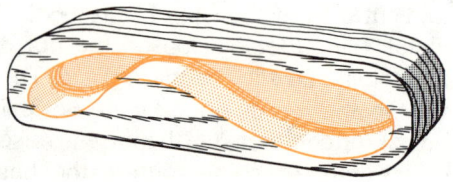

INTERNAL ROUTING

**66-2a.** Some standard sizes and shapes of router bits.

**66-2b.** A few of the common router bits: A. Straight bit; B. Rounding-over bit; C. Beading bit; D. Cove bit; E. Rabbeting bit; F. V-grooving bit.

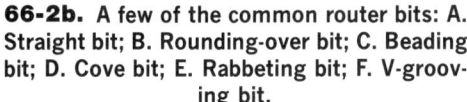

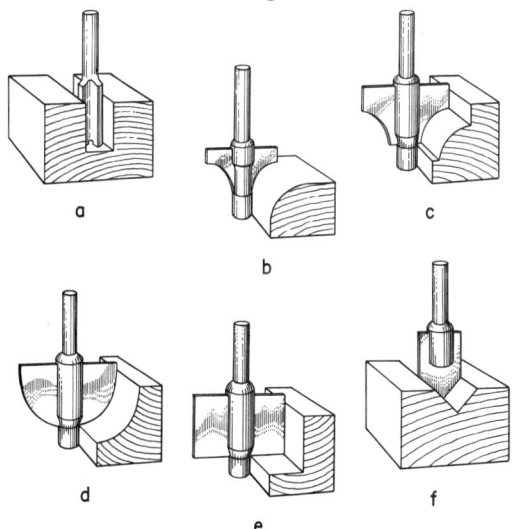

a

b

c

d

e

f

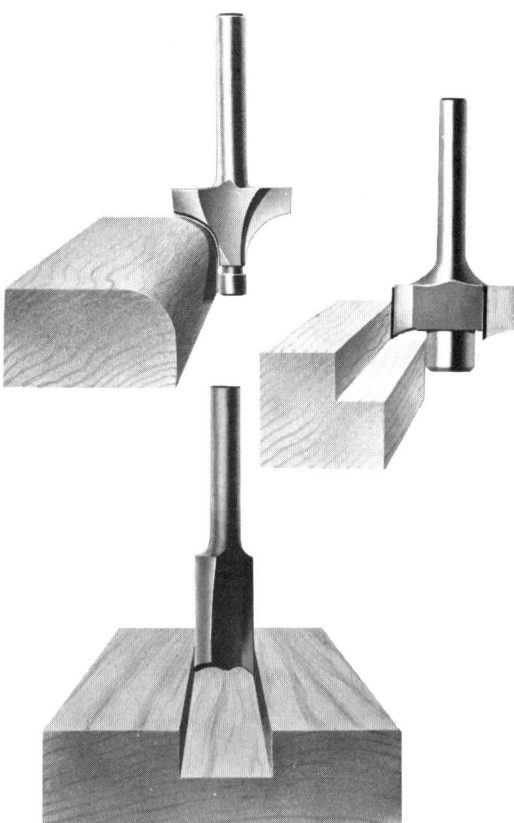

**66-2c.** The three most common router bits in use. Can you name them?

**66-3.** Select the proper bit and insert it all the way into the collet chuck. With the safety switch in a locked position, the shaft is held firmly. The chuck can be tightened readily, using only one wrench.

a wide cut can be made with a narrow bit by making two or more passes. The depth of cut can be changed by adjusting the base to the motor housing.

## INLAYING

An interesting surface decoration for wood is the addition of a strip or block of inlay for contrast. To add this strip, first cut a groove the desired distance from the edge, using a left-hand spiral bit. Use a gage of some sort to guide the router. Set the bit for the correct depth, which should be equal to the thickness of the inlaying material. Carefully cut a groove around the edge of the material. Figure 66-8. The corners will be rounded and must be trimmed out with a chisel. The groove must be cut the exact width of the inlay strip. Then cut the strip of inlay material with a miter corner. Fit each piece in to check the final design.

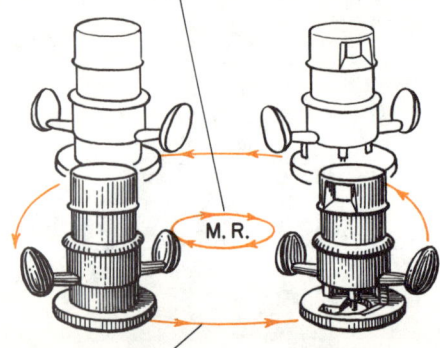

DIRECTION OF MOTOR ROTATION (M.R.)

M. R.

DIRECTION OF FEED

**66-4.** Use the correct direction of feed in cutting with a router.

**66-6.** The pilot on the end of the cutter controls the amount of cut. It rides on the edge and does no cutting.

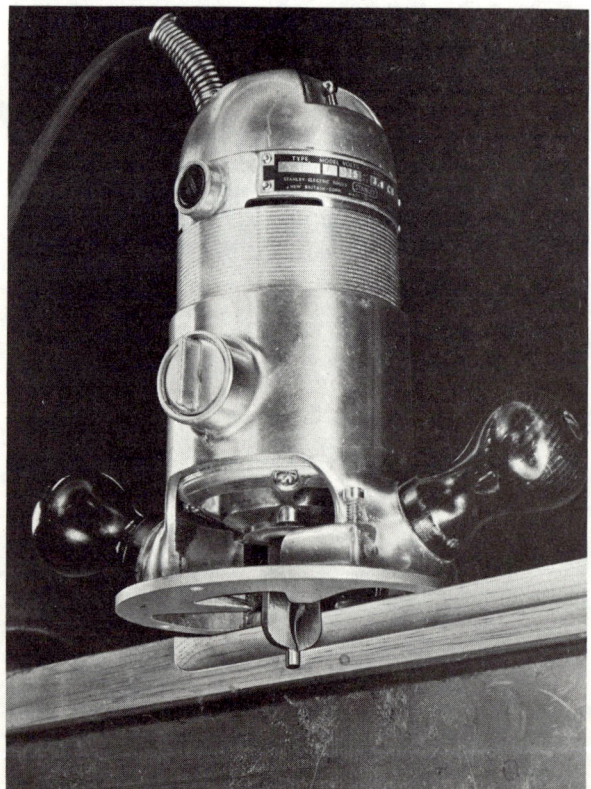

**66-5.** Freehand routing. The router is moved and controlled by the operator.

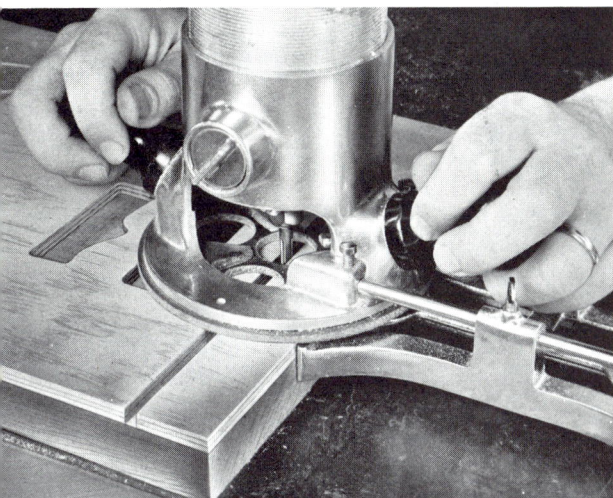

**66-7.** Using a guide attachment for cutting a dado.

**66-8a.** Using a router equipped with a small diameter bit (equal to the width of the inlay) and a guide to cut the groove.

Then apply glue to the back of the inlay and fasten it in the groove. Place a piece of wood over the inlay and clamp it until the glue is dry.

Interesting block inlays can be purchased for mounting in the tops of tables and other projects. Place the piece of inlay material over the location and trace the outline with a sharp pencil. Then mark it with a sharp knife. Set a bit to the correct depth and rout out the area in which the block inlay is to be placed. The sharp corners must be cleaned out with a knife. Then glue the inlay in place.

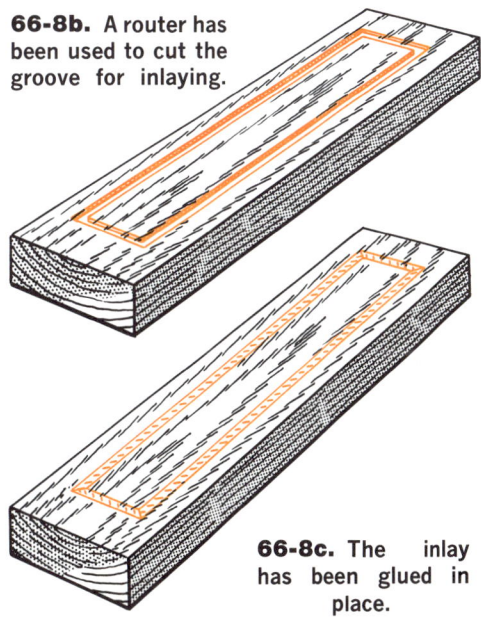

**66-8b.** A router has been used to cut the groove for inlaying.

## OTHER ROUTER CUTS

Many other kinds of router cuts can be made using various guides and attachments. The procedure differs slightly with each model. Therefore it is a good idea to check the manufacturer's instruction manual for details. Figures 66-9 and 66-10.

**66-8c.** The inlay has been glued in place.

**455**

**66-9.** Using a circle guide to cut a circular design.

**66-10.** Making a dovetail joint, using a dovetail attachment. The dovetail joint is the best one to use for drawer construction.

## CAN YOU ANSWER THESE QUESTIONS ON THE ROUTER?

1. Name the major parts of the router.
2. What is freehand routing?
3. Is a guide necessary in shaping an edge?
4. Name some of the common router bits.
5. Name some other cuts that can be done with a router.

# WOOD LATHE

**The wood lathe** performs many basic operations that cannot be done by hand. It has important industrial uses. You will find a variety of uses for it in making turned parts for your projects. Figure 67-1. The machine consists of a *bed*, the *headstock assembly* that is permanently fastened to the bed, a *tailstock* that slides along and can be locked in any position on the bed, and a *tool rest*. Figure 67-2. The *headstock spindle* has a hollow-ground *taper* into which is fastened the *spur*, or *live center*. The outside of the spindle is threaded to receive the faceplate. The speed of the lathe is controlled by changing the belts to the various positions. Figure 67-3 (Page 460). The tailstock is also taper-ground and a dead or cup center is inserted in the spindle.

The common cutting tools include a *1-inch (25 mm) gouge*, a *½-inch (13 mm)*

**67-1b.** This column floor lamp is another example of fine wood turning.

**67-1a.** Parts of this cherry tier table were expertly turned on a wood lathe.

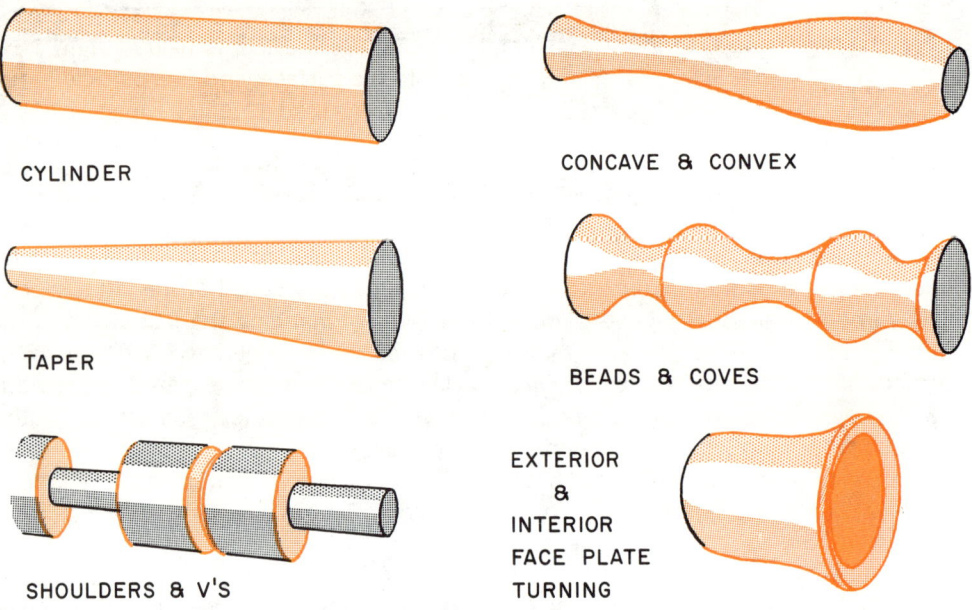

CYLINDER

CONCAVE & CONVEX

TAPER

BEADS & COVES

SHOULDERS & V'S

EXTERIOR
&
INTERIOR
FACE PLATE
TURNING

**67-1c.** Common cuts that can be made on the wood lathe.

**67-2a.** A wood lathe showing the major parts. Lathe size is designated by the largest diameter the lathe will turn and by bed length.

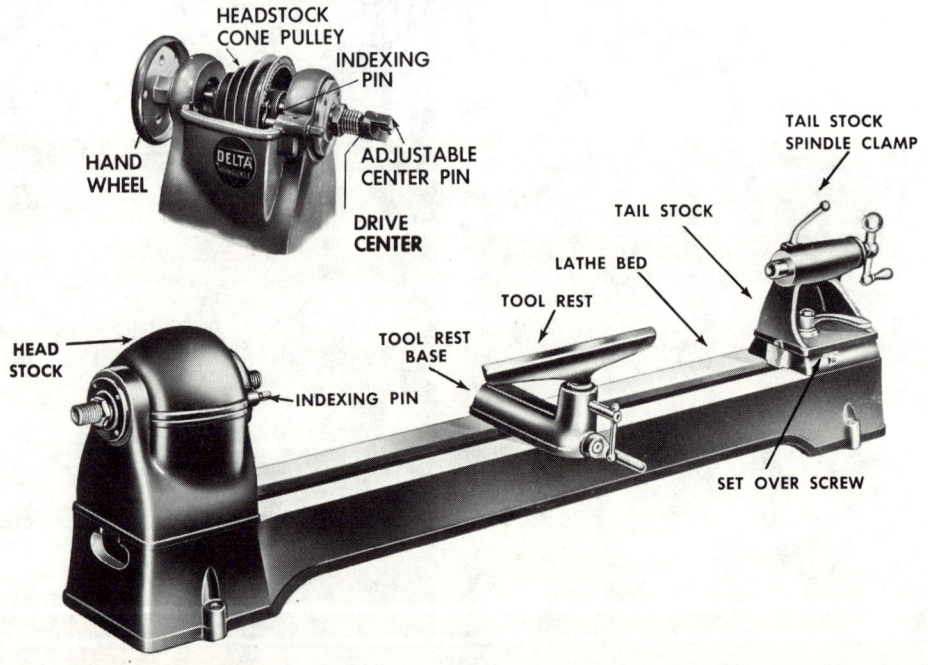

HEADSTOCK
CONE PULLEY

INDEXING
PIN

HAND
WHEEL

ADJUSTABLE
CENTER PIN

DRIVE
**CENTER**

TAIL STOCK
SPINDLE CLAMP

TAIL STOCK

LATHE BED

TOOL REST

HEAD
STOCK

TOOL REST
BASE

INDEXING PIN

SET OVER SCREW

gouge, a *1-inch (25 mm) skew*, a ½-*inch* (13 mm) *skew*, a *roundnose*, a *spear*, and a *parting tool*. Figure 67-4. In addition, the operator must have a good *bench rule*, a pair of inside and outside *calipers*, a *pencil*, *dividers*, and *hermaphrodite caliper*. Figure 67-5.

## METHODS OF TURNING

There are two basic methods of turning wood, namely cutting and scraping. In *cutting*, the tool is held so that the cutting edge actually digs into the revolving stock to peel off the shaving. Figure 67-6. This is a faster method, but it requires much skill. It produces a smooth surface that requires very little sanding. In *scraping*, the tool is held at right angles to the surface, and fine particles are worn away instead of shavings. Figure 67-7. Scraping is easier to do and is accurate, but the surface is rougher and requires more sanding. All faceplate turning is done by the scraping method.

## SAFETY RULES

● Obtain permission to use the wood lathe.

● Make sure that the setup has been checked by your instructor before turning on the machine.

**67-2b.** Parts of a gap-bed lathe.

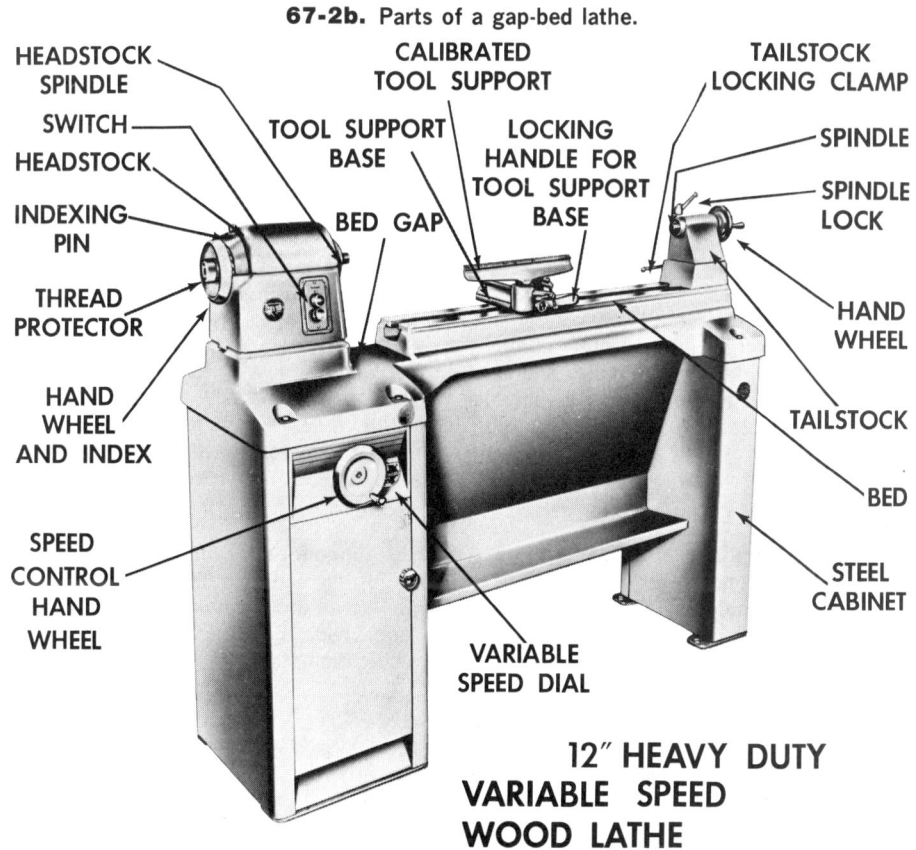

HEADSTOCK SPINDLE
SWITCH
HEADSTOCK
INDEXING PIN
THREAD PROTECTOR
HAND WHEEL AND INDEX
SPEED CONTROL HAND WHEEL
TOOL SUPPORT BASE
BED GAP
CALIBRATED TOOL SUPPORT
LOCKING HANDLE FOR TOOL SUPPORT BASE
VARIABLE SPEED DIAL
TAILSTOCK LOCKING CLAMP
SPINDLE
SPINDLE LOCK
HAND WHEEL
TAILSTOCK
BED
STEEL CABINET

## 12″ HEAVY DUTY VARIABLE SPEED WOOD LATHE

• Always examine the stock before you start turning to make sure it is not split and is free of nails.

• Apply beeswax to the tailstock center point when turning stock between centers (spindle turning). This will prevent burning the wood.

**67-3.** The headstock assembly, illustrating the threaded headstock spindle. The inner end has a right-hand thread and the outer end has a left-hand thread. Note the V pulley and also the indexing mechanism. The assembly is used for dividing faceplate work and for doing such jobs as fluting and reeding.

• When stock is mounted between centers, be sure the tailstock is locked securely.

• When using the faceplate for turning, be sure the work is solidly mounted.

• Keep the tool slide and rest locked securely.

• Never adjust the tool rest while the lathe is running.

• Hold wood-turning chisels firmly to prevent them from "hogging" into the wood or flying out of your hand.

• Remove the tool rest before sanding or polishing operations.

• Keep the tools sharp.

• Wear goggles or a face shield for all turning.

## PREPARING STOCK TO BE TURNED

Choose a piece of wood with a rectangular measurement larger than the diameter to be turned. It should be about 1 inch (25.5 mm) longer than the finished piece will be. Mark a line across the corners of each end to locate the center of the stock. Figure 67-8. Place the live center over the stock and tap it with a wooden mallet to force the spur into the wood. Figure 67-9.

With hardwood, it may be necessary to make two saw kerfs across the corners so that the wood will hold. If the stock

**67-4.** The common turning tools include: A. A large gouge for roughing cuts and a smaller gouge for small concave cuts; B. A large skew for smoothing and a smaller skew for squaring ends, cutting shoulders, V grooves, and beads; C. A roundnose for cutting out concave curves; D. A spearpoint for finishing V grooves and beads; E. A parting tool for cutting off and for cutting to specific diameters.

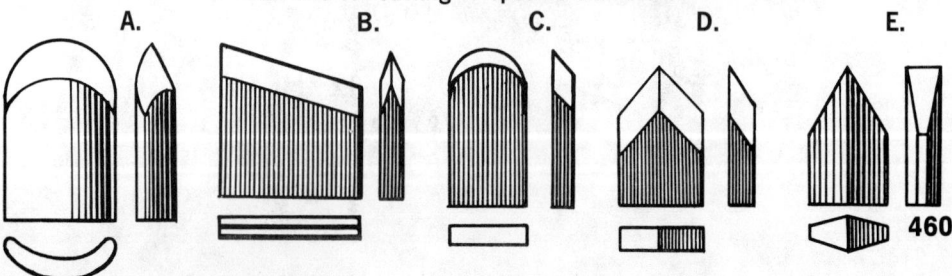

A.  B.  C.  D.  E.

is over 3 inches (76 mm) thick, the corners should be trimmed off to form an octagon shape before inserting the wood in the lathe.

Hold the wood against the live center and bring the tailstock to within about $1\frac{1}{2}$ inches (38 mm) of the end of the stock. Lock the tailstock to the bed and then turn up the tailstock handle, forcing the cup center into the wood about $\frac{1}{32}$ inch (1 mm). Back off the cup center and rub a little oil or wax on the end of the stock to lubricate it. Then tighten up the tailstock handle and lock it in position. Adjust the tool rest to clear the stock by about $\frac{1}{8}$ inch (3 mm) and about $\frac{1}{8}$ inch (3 mm) above center. If the stock is

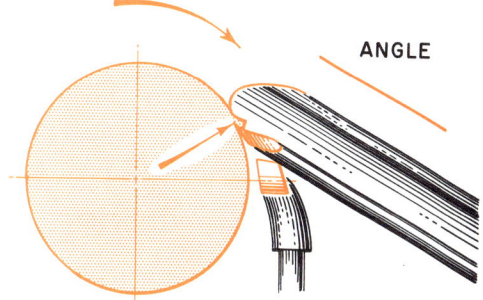

**67-6.** How the chisel cuts away the chips, using a *cutting* action.

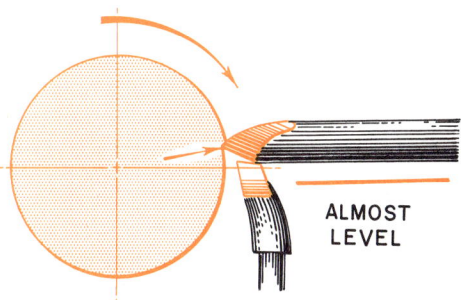
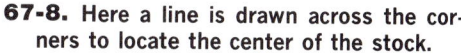

**67-7.** Action of the chisel scraping fine particles instead of shavings.

**67-5.** Tools needed for measuring.

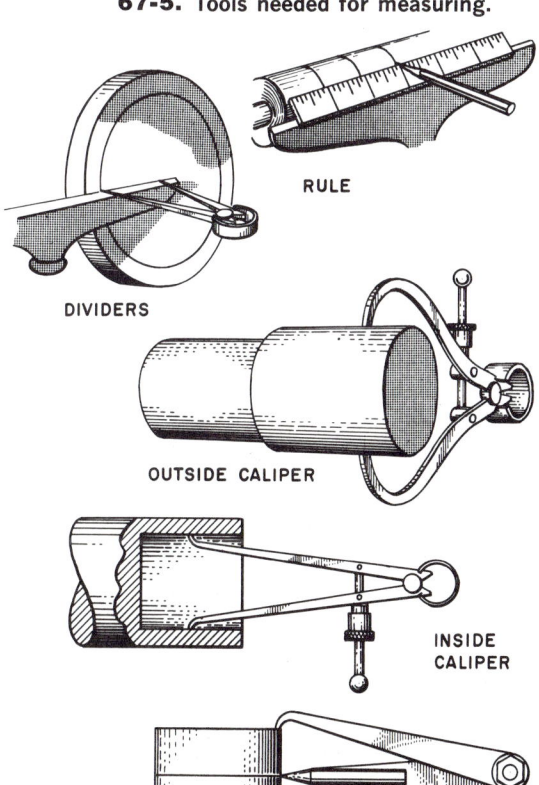

DIVIDERS

RULE

OUTSIDE CALIPER

INSIDE CALIPER

HERMAPHRODITE CALIPER

**67-8.** Here a line is drawn across the corners to locate the center of the stock.

rather large in diameter, adjust the lathe to its lowest speed; if medium diameter, to medium speed; if small diameter, to the highest speed.

Rotate the stock by hand to see if it has enough clearance.

## ROUGH TURNING WITH A GOUGE

The blade of a large gouge can be held in two ways. It can be grasped close to the cutting point with the hand underneath and the thumb over it. The forefinger then serves as a stop against the tool rest as shown in Figure 67-10. Another way is to place your hand over the tool with the wrist bent at an angle to form the stop, as shown in Figure 67-11.

Grasp the handle of the gouge in the other hand, tilting it down and away from the direction in which the cut is to be made. Be sure to hold the tool tightly against the tool rest. Begin about one-third of the way in from the tailstock. Twist the gouge to the right so that a

shearing cut will be taken. Then move the cutting edge toward the dead center. Make certain that you grasp the tool firmly during this operation, since the revolving corners tend to throw the tool out of your hand. After each cut, begin about 2 inches (51 mm) closer to the live center.

To finish the rough turning, tip the cutting edge to the left and work toward the live center. Turn off the lathe and check the diameter of the stock with an outside caliper. Continue to use the large gouge to rough turn until the stock is about $\frac{1}{8}$ inch (3 mm) over finished size.

**67-9b.** One method of setting a spur, or live center, is to drive it into the wood with a mallet.

**67-9a.** On hardwoods it is a good idea to cut a saw kerf across the corners. This can also be done on softwood, but it isn't necessary.

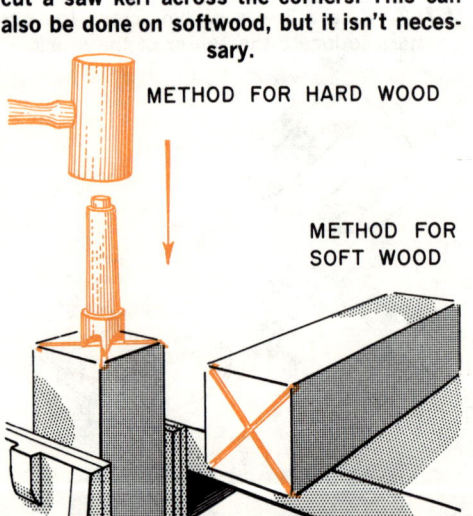

METHOD FOR HARD WOOD

METHOD FOR SOFT WOOD

The beginner can hold the point of the gouge at right angles to the work to produce a scraping action. The tool rest position is less important than it is in cutting. When scraping with the gouge, it is important to remove the tool occasionally so that it doesn't become overheated.

### FINISH TURNING WITH A SKEW

The skew is more difficult to handle. The cutting edge is tapered. The uppermost point is called the toe and the lower point the heel. Grasp the tool, holding it firmly against the tool rest with the cutting edge well above and beyond the work. Then slowly draw the skew back, turning it at a slight angle until the center of the cutting edge comes in contact with the wood. Figure 67-12. Lift the handle slightly and force the cutting edge into the wood. Work from the center toward the live and dead centers, taking a shearing cut. CAUTION: Never attempt to start at the ends of the stock to do the cutting. Make sure that the toe does not catch in the revolving stock, since this could easily throw the tool out of your hands. A little

practice will tell you when you are getting a good cut. If the skew is properly sharpened, the surface will be so smooth and true that it needs no sanding.

To scrape stock to finish the sides, use a square-nosed tool or a large skew. Adjust the lathe for high speed. Hold the cutting edge parallel to the cylinder and force it into the stock until the scraping begins. Figure 67-13. Then move it from one side to the other. Always start the scraping some distance in from the ends to prevent the tool from catching and splitting the wood.

On long cylinders or tapers, work can be smoothed down accurately with a small block plane. The plane is held at an angle of approximately 45 degrees with the axis of the work. Figure 67-14. Make sure that the tool is adjusted for a very light cut so that there will be a clean, continuous shaving and a smooth surface. The plane can be supported on the tool rest.

### SQUARING OFF THE ENDS

When the stock is turned to the correct diameter, use a pencil and rule to lay out

**67-10.** The first method of holding a gouge. The thumb is placed over the tool and the other fingers under it; the forefinger is used as a guide against the rest.

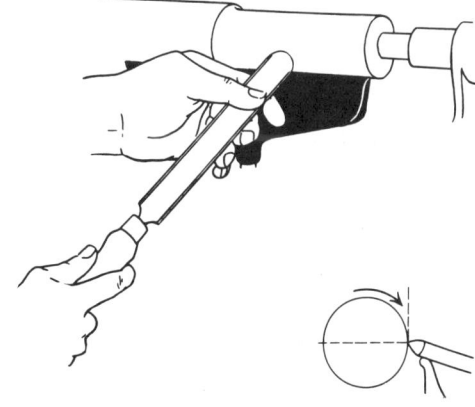

the length needed. Force a parting tool into the revolving wood about $\frac{1}{8}$ inch (3 mm) from the measured length. Figure 67-15. Make the groove slightly wider than the width of the tool so that the cutting edge will not burn as it is forced into the wood. Reduce the stock at this point to a diameter of about $\frac{3}{8}$ inch (9.5 mm).

Use a small skew to finish off the end. Hold it with the toe edge against the tool rest. Turn the handle until the bevel or ground edge of the tool is parallel with the surface to be cut. Figure 67-16. Use the toe of the tool to do the cutting and remove about $\frac{1}{32}$ inch (1 mm) with each cut. As the cut becomes deeper, it will be necessary to provide clearance for the tool. This can be done by turning the handle away from the cuts being made and then making some tapered cuts to form a half V.

## CUTTING A SHOULDER

The procedure for cutting a shoulder is similar to that for squaring off the end. First use a parting tool to cut a groove, cutting down the diameter at this point to slightly more than the smaller size. Then, with a small gouge, remove most of the stock from the smaller diameter. Cut the vertical part of the shoulder, using the toe of the skew. Cut the horizontal part of the shoulder with the heel

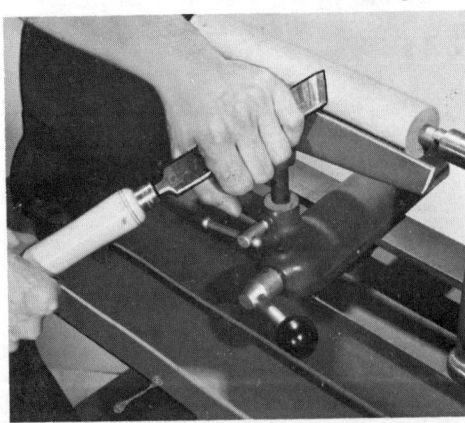

**67-11.** The second method of holding a gouge. Here the hand is placed over the tool—with the wrist bent—and against the tool rest.

**67-12.** Using the skew as a cutting tool.

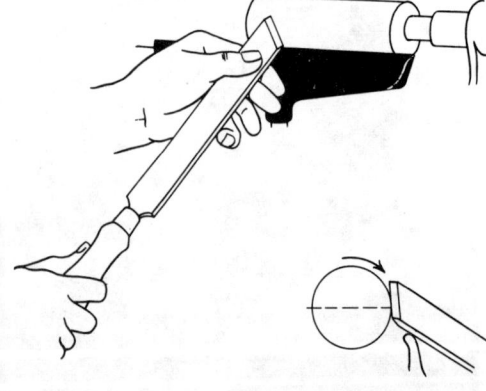

of the skew in a manner similar to finish turning. Figure 67-17. It is also possible to form a shoulder or square an end by the scraping method. Figure 67-18.

### CUTTING A TAPERED SURFACE

Turn the stock to the largest diameter. Then use a parting tool to mark the smallest diameter. Make several grooves each of lesser depth as guides for the turning. Rough out the taper with a gouge. Then finish turn the taper with a skew, using the heel to do most of the cutting. Figure 67-19.

### CUTTING V'S

Use a small skew to do the cutting. Force the heel into the stock a small amount and then work in at an angle, as shown in Figure 67-20, to cut one side

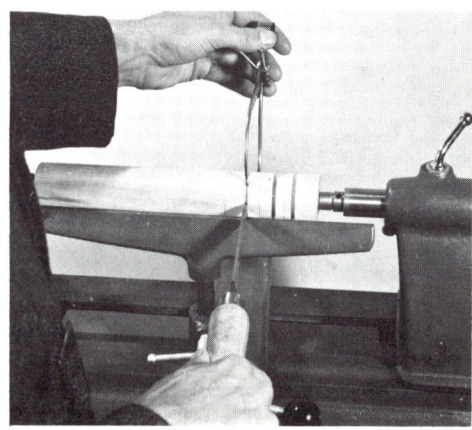

**67-15a.** Using a parting tool. It is held with the narrow edge against the rest and is forced into the wood. At the same time, the diameter is checked with an outside caliper. In using the caliper on revolving stock, be careful not to apply any pressure, as this will cause it to spring over the stock.

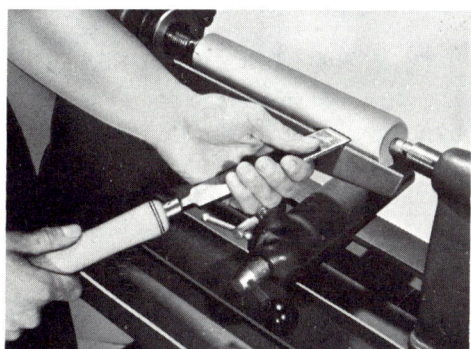

**67-13.** Using the skew as a scraping tool. This is the simplest method of using turning tools, but is satisfactory only for making a straight cut.

**67-15b.** The parting tool has two purposes—the cutting of diameter grooves and the cutting of stock, particularly in faceplate turning. It is a scraping tool and should be held as shown—tool upright with narrow edge on the tool rest. The tool is slowly pushed into the work with the point slightly above center. As the tool advances into the work, the handle should be raised slightly until the desired diameter is obtained.

**67-14.** Using the block plane to smooth a cylinder.

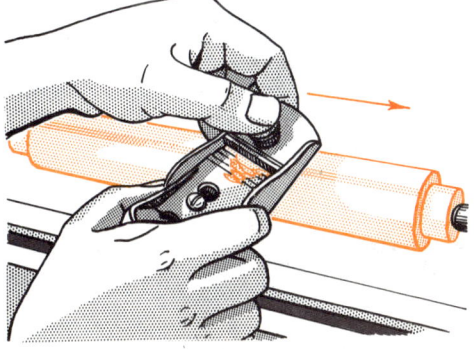

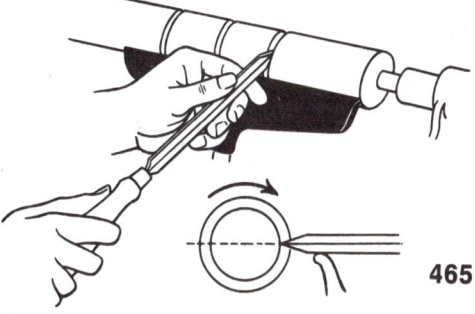

**67-16.** Using a small skew to square off the end of the stock. The toe of the skew is doing the cutting, with the bevel, or ground edge, parallel to the end of the stock. This is accomplished by tipping the handle to the right.

**67-17.** Using the skew to make a horizontal cut of a shoulder. The heel of the skew is doing most of the cutting.

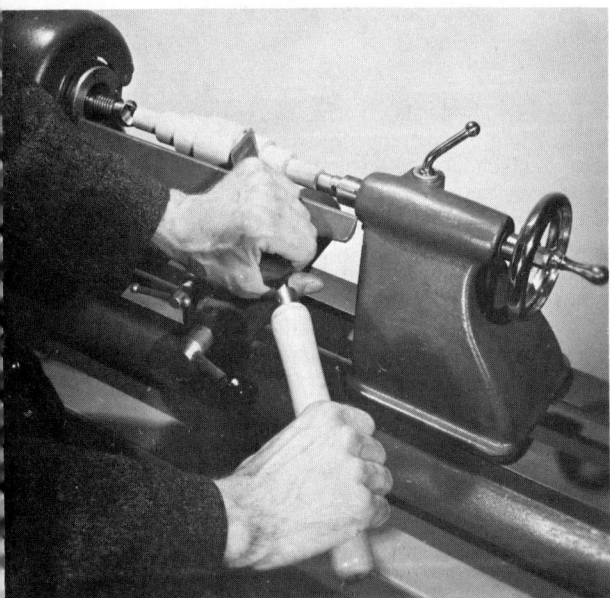

of the V. Continue to correct depth and then turn the skew in the opposite direction to finish the V on the other side.

## CUTTING BEADS

Cutting accurate beads is rather difficult. With the toe of a small skew, mark the point at which the beads are to join. Continue to cut a V shape in the stock with the toe of the skew. Now turn the skew around and use the heel to cut the bead. Hold the tool high on the stock to start the bead. Then slowly draw the handle back, at the same time turning the cutting edge to form the arc. Figure 67-21. Repeat in the opposite way to form the other half of the bead.

## TURNING CONCAVE SURFACES

Concave surfaces can be turned either by scraping with a roundnosed tool or by cutting with a small gouge. The simplest way is to force a roundnosed tool into the wood and work the handle back and forth

**67-18.** Forming a shoulder by the scraping method.

to form the concave surface. If a small gouge is used, tip it on edge and begin the concave cut by rolling the gouge as pressure is applied. Continue to take shearing cuts, first from one side and then the other, until the concave surface is formed. Figure 67-22.

**TURNING CONVEX DESIGNS**

Most turned pieces are a combination of straight turning, beads, V's, and long

**67-19.** Using the skew to cut a taper.

**67-20.** Cutting V's with the heel of the skew. The tool is forced into the stock at the angle of the V.

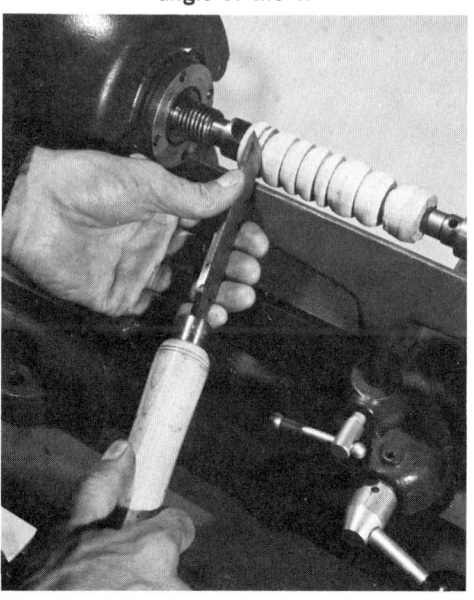

**67-21a.** Cutting beads. Here again the skew is used. The cut is started with the tool held fairly high, and as the bead is formed, the tool is drawn back and turned at the same time.

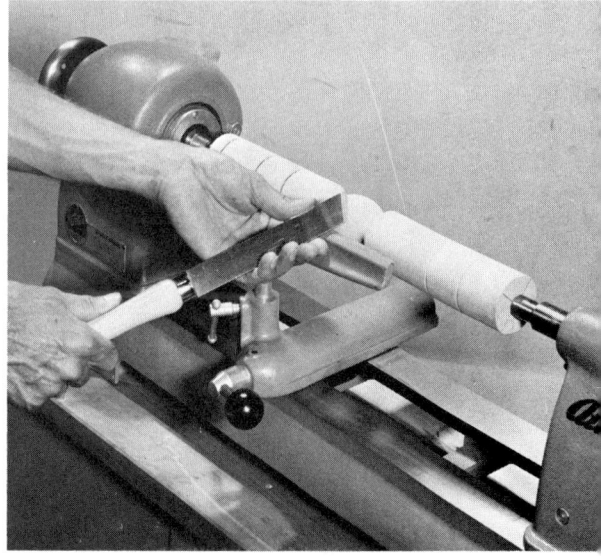

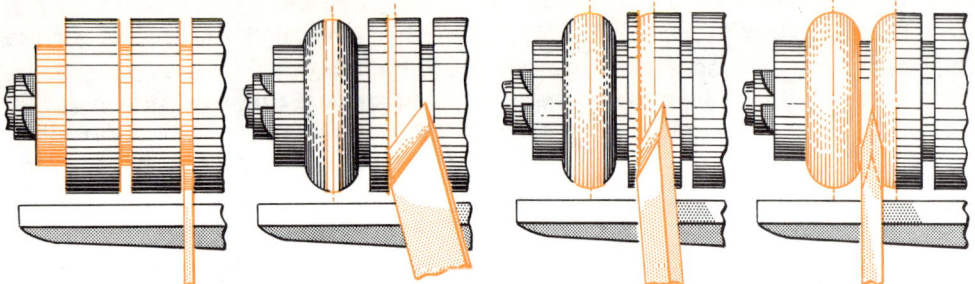

**67-21b.** Correct steps in cutting beads.

concave or convex surfaces. For convex work, the usual procedure is to turn the piece to the largest diameter to be finished and then, with a parting tool, mark points along the stock where extra material is to be removed. In many cases the parting tool is used at several points to show where stock is to be removed and to what depth. Then the gouge, skew, and roundnosed tool are used to form the design. If necessary, a file and sandpaper may be used to smooth the surface. Figure 67-23.

## DUPLICATOR ATTACHMENT

There are many types of duplicator attachments that can be used to make duplicate parts with relative ease. Figure 67-24. The templet, or pattern, to use for other parts can be either the original turning done by hand or a flat templet that has been cut on the jig saw. For example, if it is necessary to turn a duplicator in repair work, one good part can be used as the pattern to make the replacement part. Figure 67-25.

**67-22.** Using a small gouge to turn a concave surface. The tool should be rolled to form the curve.

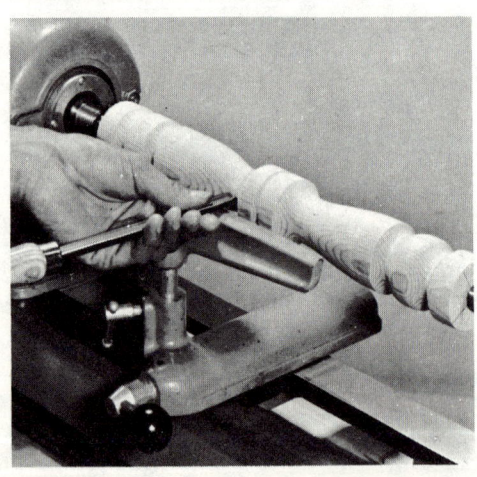

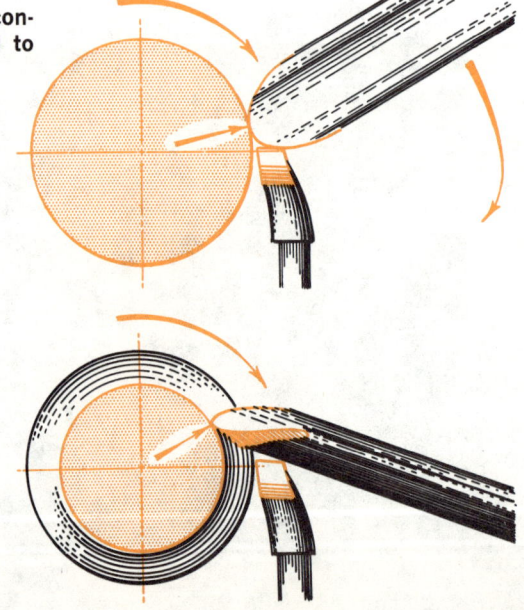

## TURNING ON THE FACEPLATE

To turn many small articles such as bowls, the stock is fastened to a faceplate, and then all of the cutting is done by the scraping method. Figures 67-26 and 67-27. Two common types of faceplates are the *screw center* for small work and the *standard faceplate* with screw holes for larger work. Figure 67-28. The cutting tools most commonly used for faceplate turning include the *roundnose, spear,* and *gouge.*

To make a small bowl, first cut out stock of correct thickness on a band or scroll saw to a circle slightly larger than the project itself. See Unit 23 for treatment of wood to prevent splits, checks, or warping. If the back of the stock will be damaged greatly by screws, protect it with a piece of scrap stock. Cut a piece of scrap stock at least an inch (25.5 mm) in thickness and about the same size as the base of the bowl. Glue the two pieces together with a piece of wrapping paper between them so that they will separate easily later. Figure 67-29.

Fasten the material to the faceplate with about ¾-inch (19 mm) screws. Make sure that they are not so long that they will mar the bottom of your bowl. Remove the live center and fasten the faceplate on the headstock spindle. Adjust the rest parallel to the outside of the round stock about ¼ inch (6 mm) away. Set the lathe to a slow speed and dress the outside edge of the stock. Figure 67-30. Once the circle is trued, the speed can be increased.

Now make a cardboard templet that will match the interior and exterior shape of the bowl. Turn the tool rest parallel to the face of the bowl and begin to shape

**67-23.** Smoothing the surface with abrasive paper.

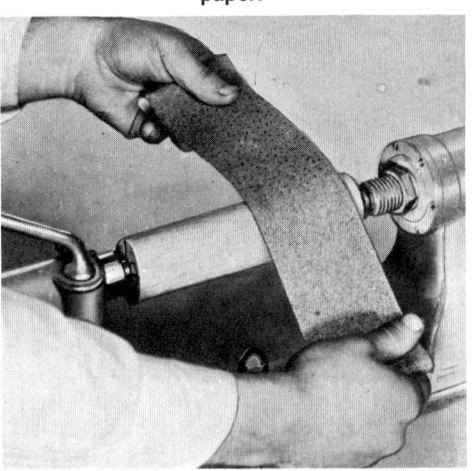

**67-24.** The best way to make duplicate parts for a product such as this corner stand is with a lathe duplicator. Using this device will give you an understanding of how industry produces parts for a short-run production.

the inside. Figure 67-31. Use a gouge or a roundnose tool and always work from the outside edge nearest you to the center. Figures 67-32 and 67-33. Never try to cut across the entire diameter, since once you pass the center, the tool will move up and away from a tool holder.

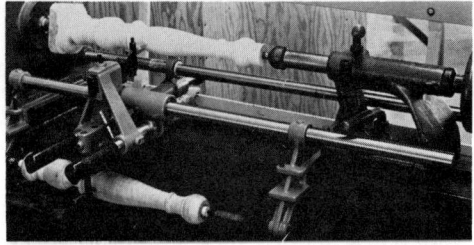

**67-25c.** Making an identical wood turning from a round pattern. A follower stylus touches the pattern, and as it moves in and out, the cutting tool follows the same path.

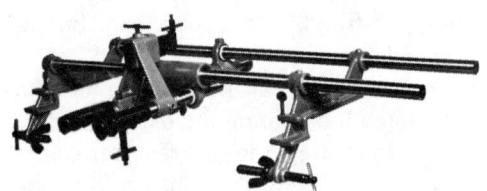

**67-25a.** Lathe duplicator attachment.

**67-25b.** A flat pattern, or templet, can also be used as the guide.

**67-26.** These salad bowls can be turned on a faceplate.

**67-27a.** Drawing for the nut bowl.

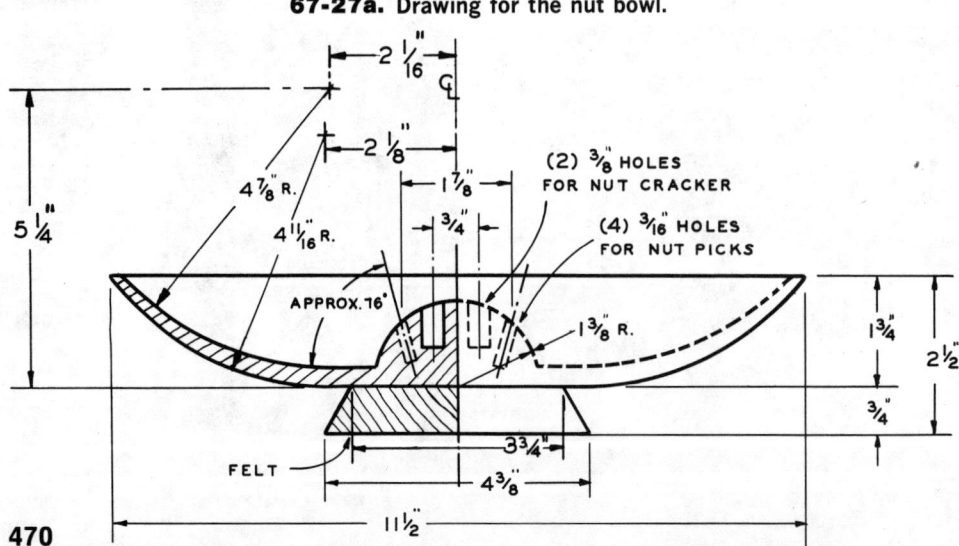

**67-27b.** Nut bowl to be turned on a face-plate.

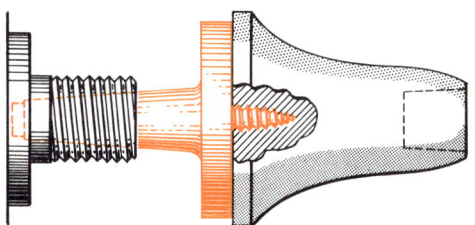

**67-28a.** Screw center for holding small work.

| No. of Pieces | Part Name | Thickness | Width | Length |
|---|---|---|---|---|
| 1 | Bowl | $1\frac{3}{4}''$ | $11\frac{3}{4}''$ | $11\frac{3}{4}''$ |
| 1 | Base | $\frac{3}{4}''$ | $4\frac{3}{8}''$ | $4\frac{3}{8}''$ |
| 1 | Felt | | $4\frac{3}{8}''$ dia. | |

STOCK: Oak, Pine, Maple, Cherry or Walnut
Important: All dimensions listed below are FINISHED size.

**67-27c.** Bill of materials for the nut bowl.

**67-27d.** Procedure for the nut bowl.

1. Cut out exact square, $11\frac{3}{4}$ x $11\frac{3}{4}$ x $1\frac{3}{4}$ inches, and draw diagonal lines to locate exact center. Then draw $11\frac{3}{4}$-inch diameter circle on back. Band saw the circle.
2. Cut out exact square, $4\frac{3}{8}$ x $4\frac{3}{8}$ x $\frac{3}{4}$ inches, and then draw diagonal lines and $4\frac{3}{8}$-inch diameter circle. Band saw the circle.
3. Glue above discs together, using diagonal lines to get them centered perfectly.
4. Mount securely on $3\frac{1}{2}$-inch faceplate.
5. Prepare templets for inside and outside contour of bowl.
6. Turn base and outside contour of bowl to match outside templet.
7. Turn inside contour of bowl to match inside templet.
8. Drill two $\frac{3}{8}$-inch holes $\frac{3}{4}$ inch deep for nut cracker.
9. Set drill press table to 76-degree angle and drill four $\frac{3}{16}$-inch holes, $\frac{3}{4}$ inch deep, for nut picks.
10. Apply desired finish.
11. Cement felt to base.

**67-28b.** Fastening stock to the headstock spindle. The work has been fastened to the faceplate with short wood screws. The faceplate is attached to the headstock spindle.

**67-29.** How a piece may be glued to waste stock to do the turning.

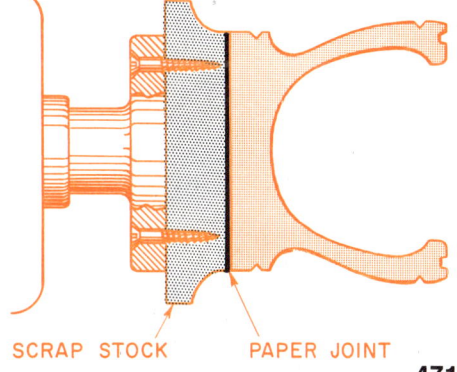

SCRAP STOCK        PAPER JOINT

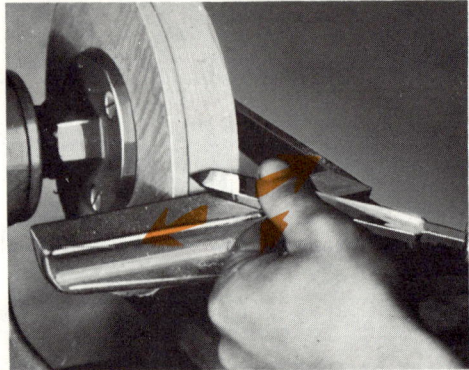

**67-30.** Truing the outside of stock fastened to the faceplate.

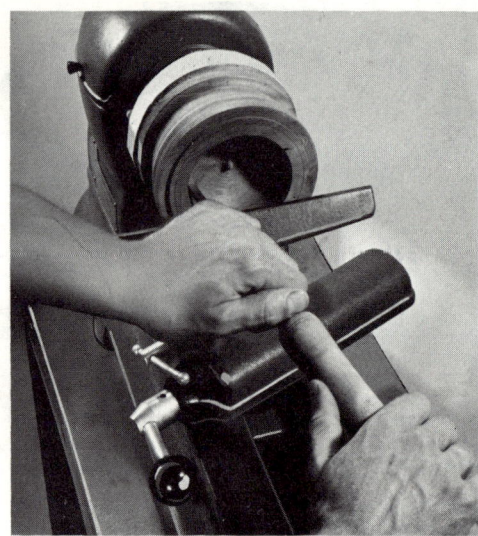

**67-33.** Turning a trinket box with a small gouge doing the internal work. The box has been glued to a piece of scrap stock and that piece then fastened to the faceplate with short screws.

**67-31.** Using a roundnosed tool to shape stock on the faceplate.

**67-34.** Using a parting tool to cut off the project after it has been turned.

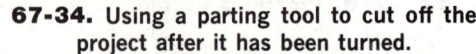

**67-32.** Keep the cutting tool on the side nearest you. Never try to cut across the entire diameter.

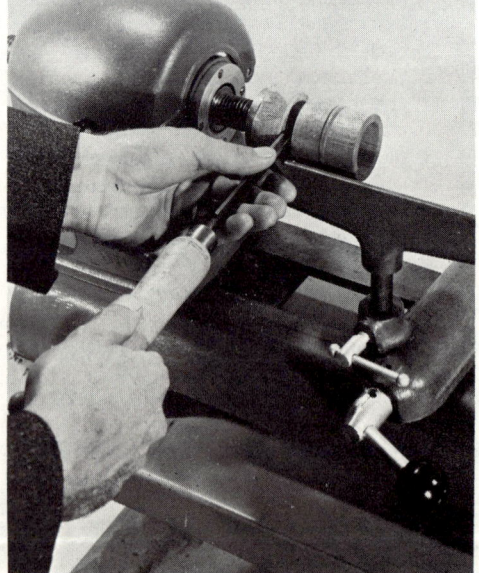

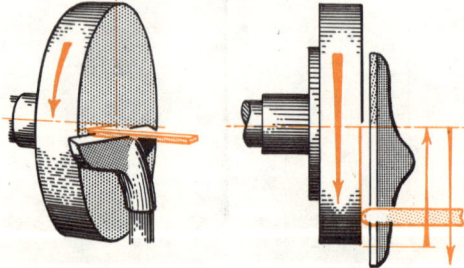

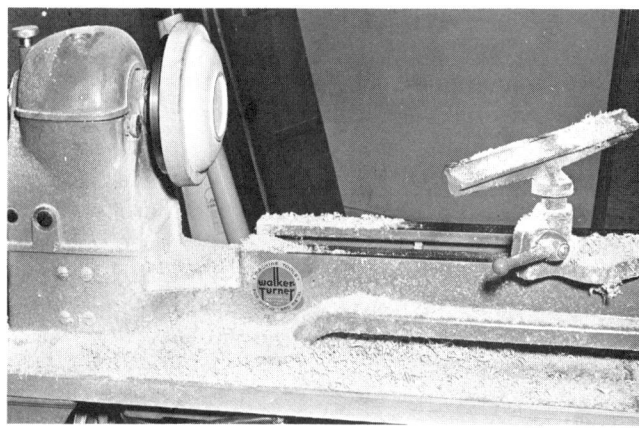

**67-35a.** This shows a bowl that has been fastened in a wood chuck to turn the back.

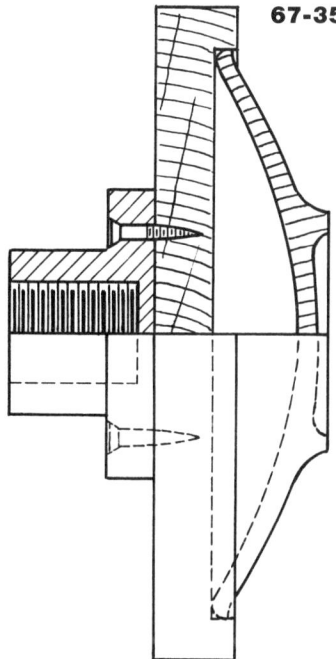

**67-35b.** A recessed wood chuck for turning the bottom of a dish.

**67-35c.** Turning a shallow tray with the piece held in a wood chuck. Whenever it is necessary to turn both the front and back of a piece, make a chuck to hold the stock for turning the second side.

After the inside is shaped, sand it with 2/0 or 1/0 sandpaper. Now move the tool rest around and shape the exterior of the bowl. Then sand this surface. Apply a finish to the bowl.

After turning is complete, the scrap stock can be cut or split away from the finished product with a sharp chisel. Figure 67-34. To do turning in which the base must be formed, a recessed wood chuck is used to hold the stock while it is turned. Figure 67-35.

## FINISHING ON THE LATHE

There are several ways to apply a finish as the piece revolves in the lathe. A simple method is to apply paste wax to a folded cloth and hold it on the revolving stock. You should repeat this application about a dozen times.

To apply a French-type oil polish, fold a piece of fine cotton or linen cloth into a pad. Apply about one teaspoon of white shellac to the pad and then add several drops of linseed or mineral oil. Hold the pad over the spinning work, moving it back and forth. As the pad gets dry, apply more shellac and oil to keep it moist until you get a mirrorlike finish. You can also wax the surface after it is dry.

Still another method of finishing a bowl is to apply several coats of clear lacquer before the bowl is removed from the faceplate. Then return the piece to the lathe. Apply a little rubbing oil and rottenstone to the cloth, then polish.

## CAN YOU ANSWER THESE QUESTIONS ON THE WOOD LATHE?

1. Describe a wood lathe and name its parts.
2. What are the tools needed for wood turning?
3. Describe the two methods of turning.
4. What are the two methods of fastening a live center to the stock?
5. What is the largest size stock that can be turned from a square without first trimming the corners?
6. Cup centers need what lubricants?
7. What is the relation between the diameter of the stock and the speed of the lathe?
8. What tool is selected for rough turning?
9. A gouge can be held in two ways. What are they?
10. How can the cutting action of a gouge be controlled?
11. What makes the skew a difficult tool to use?
12. What is the major danger involved in using the skew?
13. Tell how you can square off the ends of stock in the lathe.
14. What tools are used for cutting a shoulder?
15. When a tapered surface is to be produced, what part of the skew should do most of the cutting?
16. Cutting V's is done with what tool?
17. What kinds of work are turned on a faceplate?
18. Is it good practice to use a file and sandpaper on the lathe? Explain.

# SECTION XII

# Major Industrial Areas

**What you must know and be able to do in
Units 68–71:**

68. The basic tools and materials used in upholstering; how to make a pad seat.

69. How products are mass-produced; major resources necessary for mass production; how to mass-produce a product; how manufacturing differs from construction.

70. The importance of building construction; why wood is a most important building material; the steps that must be taken before construction can begin; how a house is constructed; how you can gain construction experiences without actually building a house.

71. The two kinds of patterns and how to use them; how to make a simple pattern; how to make a sand casting; the use of a core in casting; how to make a model.

*The two major American industries are manufacturing and construction. It is often difficult to distinguish between these two areas since many items that were once constructed on site are now manufactured and then assembled on site. Upholstery is an important part of the furniture manufacturing industry. Patternmaking and model making are important to the metal industries. You will read about all four of these industrial areas in this section.*

# Section XII

## UNIT 68.

# SIMPLE UPHOLSTERY

Although upholstery can be complicated, there are several simple procedures that the beginner can follow. Figure 68-1. Of the four basic types of upholstery work, the first three are done by older methods. (1) The simplest is a *pad seat* (made without springs) that fits into or on the completed chair. Dining-room chairs may have pad seats. Figure 68-2. (2) The next type is the *tight spring seat* found mostly in living-room chairs. A webbing foundation supports the springs. Figure 68-3. (3) Next is the *overstuffed seat and back* used in large chairs and sofas. In this type there are springs in both the seat and back. Figure 68-4. (4) The last type is the most modern: *sinuous springs with foam rubber or rubberized hair.*

**68-1.** This student-made chair has a single piece of leather for the seat.

## MATERIALS

Some upholstery materials must be ordered from a special supply house. Others can be found in hardware and department stores. Before starting a project, it is a good idea to see if needed materials are easy to find in your community.

*Upholstery tacks* are flathead tacks used for holding materials in place. The larger sizes (12 or 14 ounce, about ¾ inch, 19 mm, long) are needed for tacking webbing; the smaller sizes (6 or 8 ounce, about ½ inch, 12.5 mm, long) are used for fastening the coverings. The *gimp tack* is a small roundhead used wherever the head is meant to show.

*Webbing* is made from jute fiber; it is used as the foundation. The 3½-inch (85 mm) width is usually specified.

*Burlap* is used as a covering over webbing, springs, and stuffing. An 8- to 10-ounce (per square foot) weight in 40-inch (1016 mm) widths is best.

*Stuffing* means a variety of materials used for filling. Among the most common are *curled animal hair; Spanish moss,* a plant fiber; *tow,* made from the stalks of flax plants; and *shredded foam rubber.*

*Rubberized hair* is a light, elastic material made from curled hair and rubber. It comes in pads of standard thickness from ¾ to 2½ inches (19 to 64 mm).

*Foam rubber* (padding) is made from liquid latex. *Slab stock* comes in thicknesses of ½, ¾, 1 inch (12.5, 19,

25.5 mm), etc. It is possible to buy *cored utility stock* that has molded cylindrical openings in it. You can also buy fully *molded cushions* in many different sizes and shapes. Figure 68-5. *Rubber cement* is used to fasten tacking tape to foam rubber.

*Tacking tape* is a muslin cloth tape used to fasten the foam rubber to the base.

*Cotton* comes in batts that are 27 inches (686 mm) wide and about ½ inch (12.5 mm) thick. It is purchased in a roll to use over stuffing. *Muslin* of the unbleached type is 36 to 40 inches (914 to 1016 mm) wide. *Fancy furniture nails* come in a wide variety of head styles for places where the nails will show.

*Final covers* can be of fabric, plastic material, or leather.

Other materials include *coil springs* and *sewing twine,* for more extensive work.

### COMMON TOOLS

● An *upholsterer's hammer* is needed for extensive work in upholstery. One head should be magnetized for holding tacks. For simple jobs, a small *claw hammer* is satisfactory. Figure 68-6 (Page 480).

**68-2.** The pad seat is the simplest form of upholstery. The base can be plywood, hardboard, or a frame covered with webbing.

**68-3a.** This cutaway shows the construction of a tight spring seat. Note that the base is webbing to which the springs are tied. Over these is a piece of burlap. Over this is a fibrous padding or foam rubber. Finally, the cover is applied.

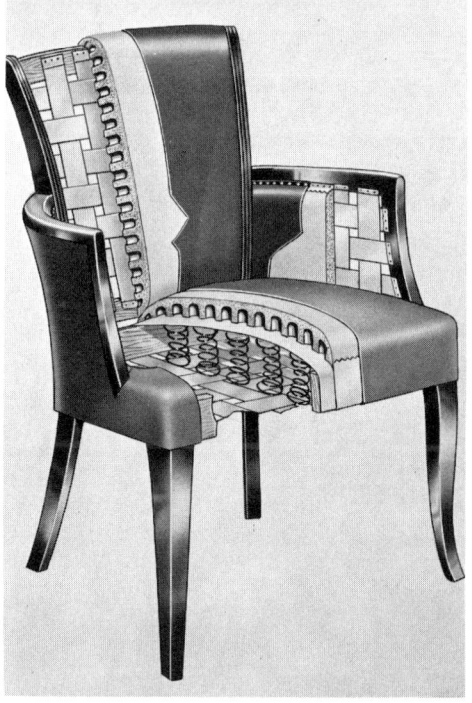

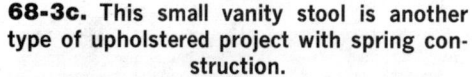

**68-3b.** This lounge chair with ottoman has a tight spring seat.

**68-3c.** This small vanity stool is another type of upholstered project with spring construction.

● *The spring-driven stapler or tacker* is an ideal machine for stapling on burlap, muslin, or the finished cover. Figure 68-7.

● A *webbing stretcher* (about 6 inches, 152.5 mm, long) is needed for stretching the webbing before tacking it down. Figure 68-8.

● *Trimmer's shears* are used for cutting foam rubber, rubberized hair, and fabrics.

● A *stuffing regulator* is a 10-inch (254 mm) metal pin with one sharp and one blunt end. It is used to even out irregularities under temporary coverings. An *ice pick* makes a good substitute.

**68-4.** This sofa and chair set is an example of frame construction with springs in both seat and back. The loose cushion can contain either fibrous padding or foam rubber.

## MAKING A PAD SEAT

Some of the more common ways of making a pad seat are described here.

### Making a Pad Seat with a Solid Base and Foam Rubber. Figure 68-9.

1. Cut a piece of ¼- to ½-inch (6.5 to 12.5 mm) fir plywood to the required shape for the base.

2. Drill several small holes distributed over the wood for air venting.

3. Select a piece of foam rubber about 1 inch (25.5 mm) thick.

4. Decide on the kind of edging you want on the seat.

**68-5.** This cutaway of a pad seat illustrates some of the basic materials used in upholstery.

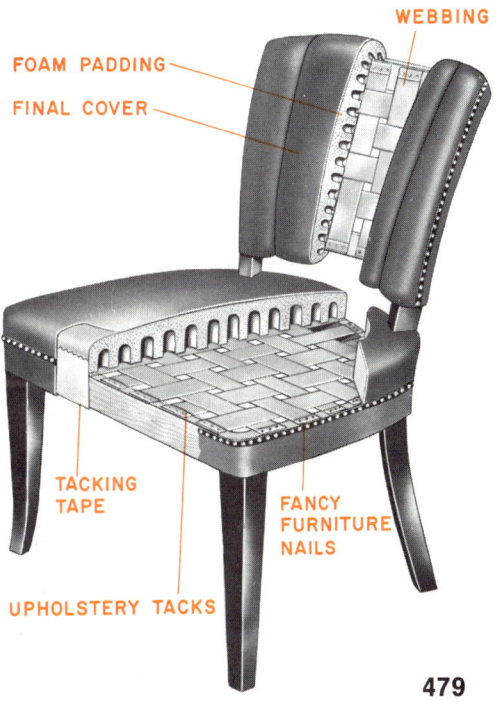

WEBBING

FOAM PADDING

FINAL COVER

TACKING TAPE

FANCY FURNITURE NAILS

UPHOLSTERY TACKS

● *For a cushioned edge.* Cut the foam rubber to shape with shears, allowing about ¼ inch (6.5 mm) extra all around, plus an extra ½ inch (12.5 mm) on the cushion edge or edges. Apply rubber cement to about half the width of the tacking tape and 1 inch (25.5 mm) along the upper edge of the foam rubber. Figure

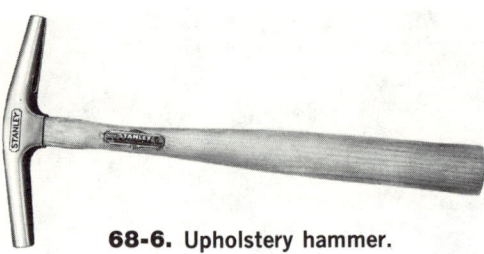

**68-6.** Upholstery hammer.

**68-7.** A spring-driven stapler is much quicker than tacks and a hammer. Heavy-duty shears are needed to cut the material. When cutting foam rubber, it helps to dip the shears in water to "lubricate" them. Do not use too much water. The foam rubber can also be cut on a band saw with a ¼-inch (6.5 mm) blade.

68-10. Cement the tape to the smooth top of the stock about 1 inch (25.5 mm) from the edge. Tuck the bottom edge of the cushion under so that its thickness is held flat against the base. Figure 68-11. Keep the tape taut to avoid wrinkling. Tack the tape on the underside with upholstery tacks.

● *For a feathered edge.* Cut the stock about ¼ inch (6.5 mm) oversize all around. Cement the tacking tape to the smooth top side about 1 inch (25.5 mm) from the edge. Bevel the lower edge as shown in Figure 68-12. Draw the tape down so that the beveled edge is held flat against the base; tack it in place.

● *For a square edge.* Cut the rubber, allowing the usual ¼-inch (6.5 mm) addition all around. Cement the tape flat against the edge of the material and tack the overhang to the base. Figure 68-13.

5. Cover the foam rubber with a final cover.

### Making a Slip Pad Seat with Webbed Base and Upholstery Cotton

1. Make an open frame of four pieces of ¾-inch (19 mm) stock that will fit into the main frame of the chair or bench. The corner can be made with dowel joints, end-lap joints, or open mortise-and-tenon joints. See Section VII. Round the upper edge so it won't cut the upholstery fabric.

**68-8.** Webbing stretcher.

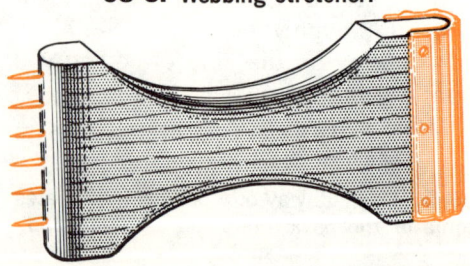

2. Apply the webbing. Fold the end of the webbing under about $1\frac{1}{4}$ inches (32 mm) and tack about $\frac{1}{2}$ inch (12.5 mm) from the outside of the frame. Figure 68-14. The tacks are staggered to keep the wood from splintering. Stretch the webbing tightly over the frame as shown in Figure 68-15 (Page 484), and tack it on the other side of the frame. Cut the webbing about $1\frac{1}{4}$ inches (32 mm) beyond the frame, fold over, and tack down again. Place the next piece of webbing about $1\frac{1}{2}$ to 2 inches (38 to 51 mm) away. Space the webbing so the piece will cover the opening. Then weave the other pieces through in the other direction. Figure 68-16 (Page 484).

**68-9a.** This contemporary chair has a pad seat and back.

3. Tack a piece of burlap over the webbing, making sure that it is not drawn tightly. If tacked too tightly, the cloth will tear when in use.

4. Cut a piece of upholstery cotton about 2 inches (51 mm) smaller in all directions than the frame. Center this over the burlap.

**68-9b.** Bill of materials for the chair.

| Important: All dimensions listed below are FINISHED size. | | | | | |
|---|---|---|---|---|---|
| No. of Pieces | Part Name | Thick-ness | Width | Length | Mate-rial |
| 2 | Back Posts | 1″ | 3″ | 30″ | White Oak |
| 2 | Front Legs | $1\frac{3}{4}$″ dia. | | $16\frac{1}{8}$″ | White Oak |
| 2 | Side Rails | $\frac{3}{4}$″ | $1\frac{5}{8}$″ | 14″ | White Oak |
| 2 | Back Rungs | $\frac{3}{4}$″ dia. | | $12\frac{3}{4}$″ | White Oak |
| 2 | Side Rungs | $\frac{3}{4}$″ dia. | | $16\frac{3}{4}$″ | White Oak |
| 1 | Front Rung | $\frac{3}{4}$″ dia. | | $13\frac{3}{4}$″ | White Oak |
| 2 | Cross Rails | 1″ | $1\frac{3}{4}$″ | $12\frac{3}{4}$″ | Hard-wood |
| 1 | Seat | $\frac{1}{2}$″ | $15\frac{1}{2}$″ | $17\frac{1}{2}$″ | Fir Ply-wood |
| 1 | Back | $\frac{1}{2}$″ | 8″ | 16″ | Fir Ply-wood |
| 8 | Dowels | $\frac{3}{8}$″ dia. | | $1\frac{1}{2}$″ | Hard-wood |
| 6 | No. 10 x $1\frac{1}{2}$″ F. H. Wood Screws | | | | |
| 2 | No. 12 x $1\frac{1}{2}$″ Oval Head Nickle Plated Wood Screws | | | | |
| 2 | No. 12 x 2″ Oval Head Nickle Plated Wood Screws | | | | |
| | Foam Rubber Padding | | | | |
| | Upholstery Material | | | | |
| | $\frac{5}{8}$″ Carpet Tacks | | | | |

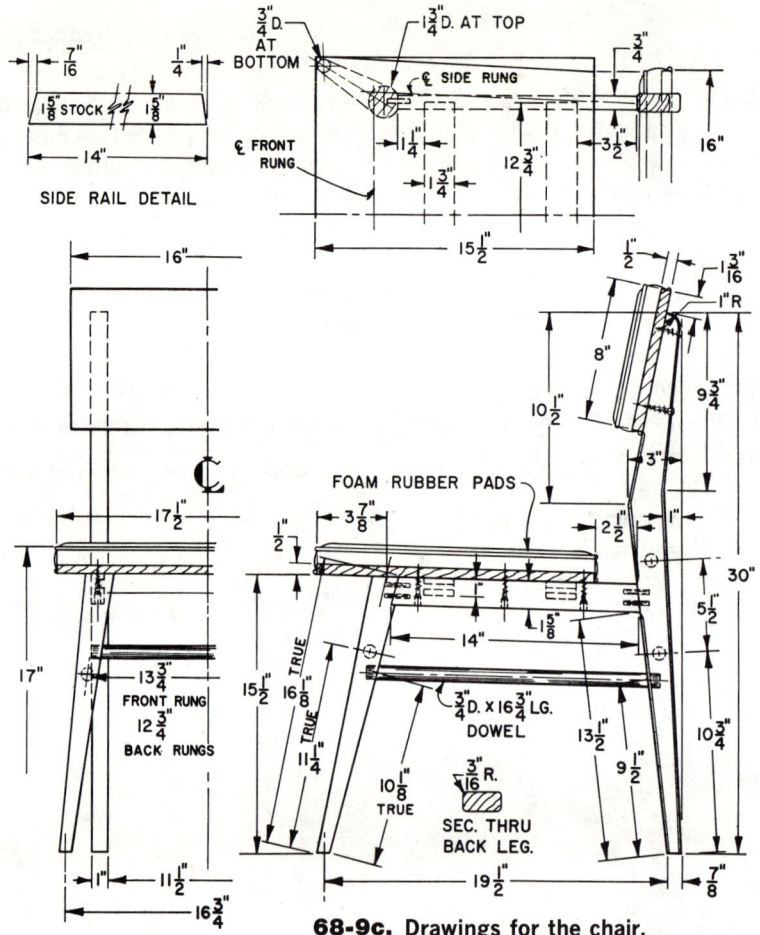

**SIDE RAIL DETAIL**

FOAM RUBBER PADS

SEC. THRU BACK LEG.

**68-9c.** Drawings for the chair.

APPLY RUBBER CEMENT 1" WIDE

TACKING TAPE

5. Cut another piece of cotton about ½ inch (12.5 mm) larger in all directions than the frame. Center this over the first piece.

6. Apply the final covering. Cut a piece that is about 2 inches (51 mm) larger in all directions than the frame. Place the cover material with the good side down on the bench. Lay the seat face down and start tacking at the center of each side.

**68-10.** Apply rubber cement along the upper edge of the foam rubber and then fasten the tacking tape in place.

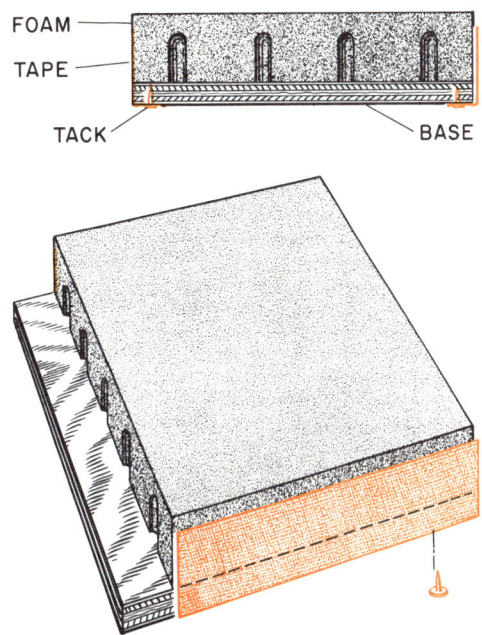

FOAM

TAPE

TACK

BASE

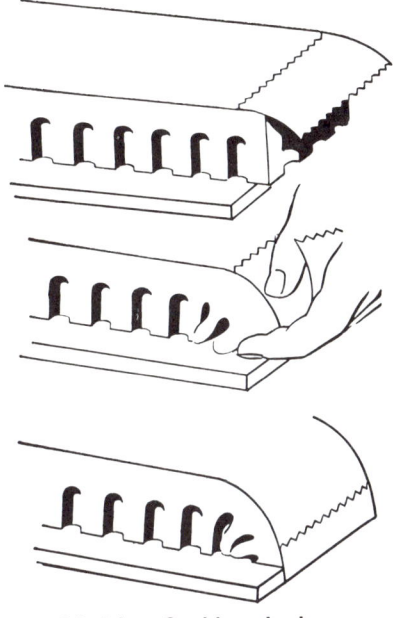

**68-11a.** Cushioned edge.

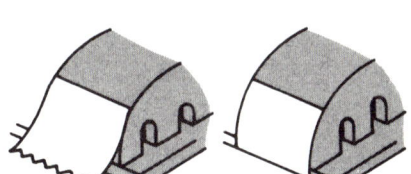

**68-11b.** The adhesive band sticks fast to foam. Staple, stitch, or tack it down for a finished job.

**68-13.** Square edge. Note that the tacking tape has been glued to the edge of the foam rubber and then tacked to the base. Note also the holes in the foam rubber for air ventilation.

**68-14.** Turn the loose end of the webbing under and tack in place.

**68-12.** Feathered edge.

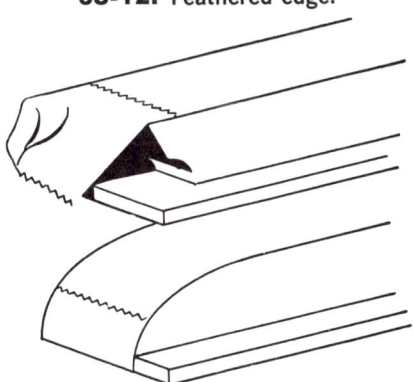

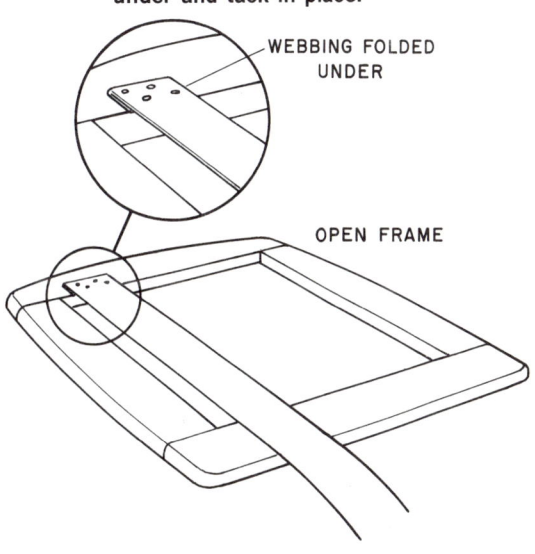

WEBBING FOLDED UNDER

OPEN FRAME

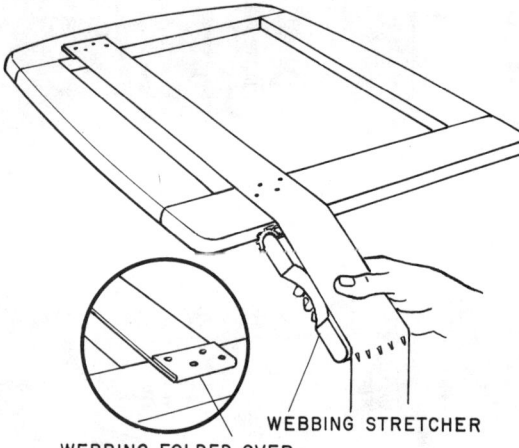

**68-15.** Stretch the webbing and tack to the other side.

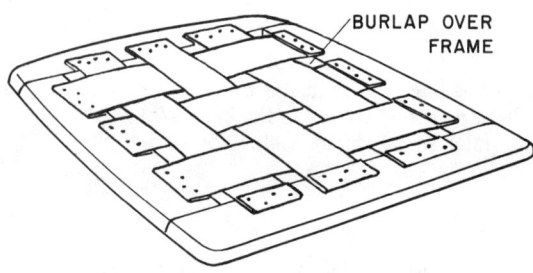

**68-16.** Webbing completed. Burlap must be fastened over the webbing.

Figure 68-17. Work toward the corners. Tack the corners as shown in Figure 68-18.

## Making a Slip Pad Seat With a Webbed Base and Stuffing

1. Make an open frame and cover with webbing and burlap.

2. Place stuffing of hair or moss over the burlap. Make sure the material is well separated and free of foreign matter such as sticks. Distribute handfuls of the stuffing over the base, working it together with your fingers. Cover to a depth of about 2 inches (51 mm). (A rubberized hair pad 1 inch, 25.5 mm, thick, cut to size, can be used instead of the stuffing.)

3. Cut a piece of burlap or muslin about 2 inches (51 mm) larger in all directions than the frame. Lay the cloth over the stuffing and hold it in place as you turn the entire unit over.

4. Start tacking at the center of each side and work toward the corners. Drive the tacks only a little way into the wood so you can remove them if necessary to tighten the cover. Check to see that the stuffing is distributed evenly. If not, poke a *regulator* through the cloth to move some of the stuffing around.

5. Place a layer of cotton over the cloth and then apply final cover material.

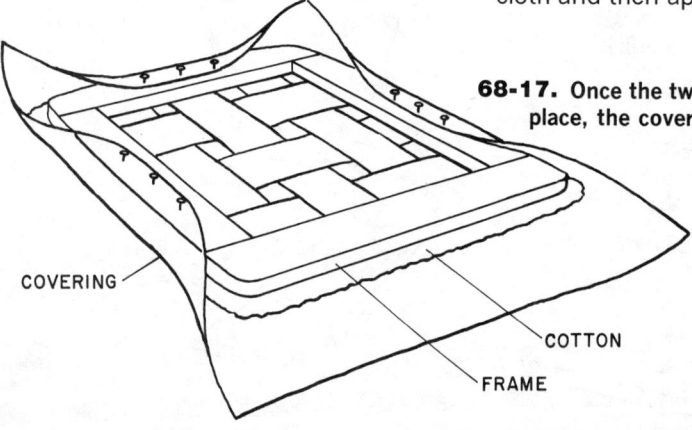

**68-17.** Once the two layers of cotton are in place, the cover can be tacked on.

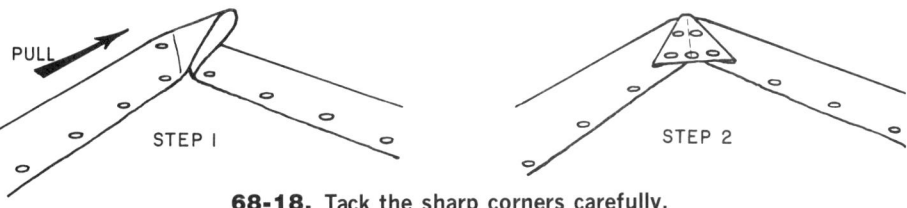

PULL

STEP I

STEP 2

**68-18.** Tack the sharp corners carefully.

**68-19.** A chair frame with a foundation of sinuous springs.

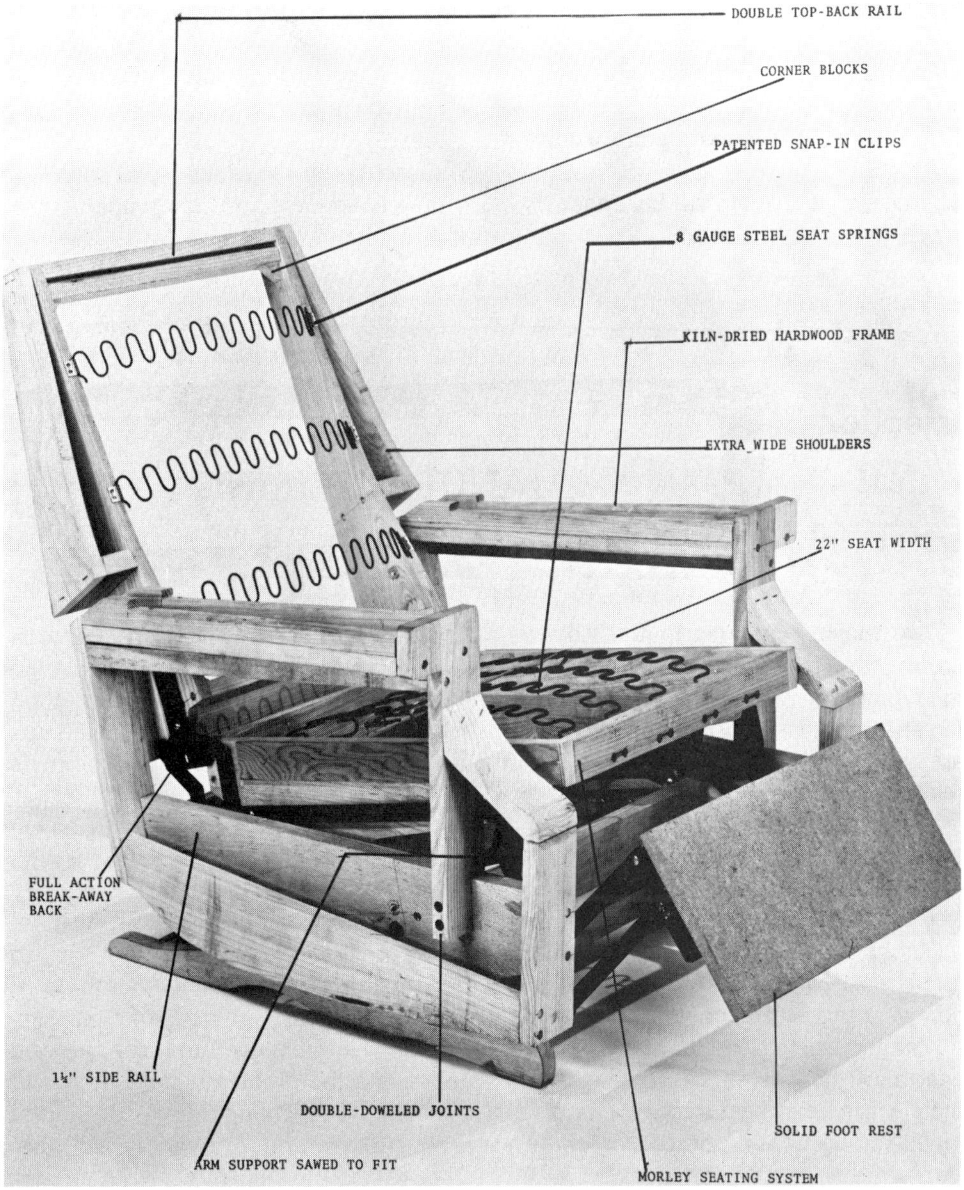

DOUBLE TOP-BACK RAIL

CORNER BLOCKS

PATENTED SNAP-IN CLIPS

8 GAUGE STEEL SEAT SPRINGS

KILN-DRIED HARDWOOD FRAME

EXTRA WIDE SHOULDERS

22" SEAT WIDTH

FULL ACTION
BREAK-AWAY
BACK

1¼" SIDE RAIL

DOUBLE-DOWELED JOINTS

SOLID FOOT REST

ARM SUPPORT SAWED TO FIT

MORLEY SEATING SYSTEM

## Making a Spring Seat With Sinuous Springs and Foam Rubber

An excellent upholstered spring seat or back can be made with sinuous springs. These springs are known by such trade names as No-Sag, Sagless, and Zigzag. Figure 68-19. Complete directions for ordering and installing these springs are available from the manufacturer, along with complete kits.*

---

*For instructions on how to upholster with these materials, see ADVANCED WOODWORK AND FURNITURE MAKING, by Feirer and Hutchings, Chas. A. Bennett Co., Inc., 1972.

## CAN YOU ANSWER THESE QUESTIONS ON SIMPLE UPHOLSTERY?

1. Name the three traditional methods of upholstery.
2. What kinds of materials are used for stuffing?
3. From what is foam rubber made?

4. What are the three kinds of edges that can be used on a foam-rubber pad seat?
5. Describe how to make a pad seat with a webbed base and cotton upholstery.

# Section XII
# UNIT 69.

# MANUFACTURING

**Two major industries** in this country are *manufacturing* and *construction*. In *manufacturing*, products are made in factories, but in *construction*, products are built at the site. In years past it was relatively easy to distinguish between manufactured and constructed wood products. Until recently, furniture, cabinets, sporting goods, and similar items were manufactured in plants, and office buildings, homes, churches, and apartments were constructed on the site. Now, however, this clear and easy distinction no longer exists. Today, many homes, apartment houses, office buildings, and motels are manufactured in plants as modules, sectional homes, or mobile homes. Figure 69-1. Each part of the total building is designed to a size that can be transported to the site by truck and then assembled. Manufactured (sometimes called industrialized) housing is complete inside and out, including plumbing, wiring, painting, and flooring, so that very little work remains to be done on the site.

The American manufacturing industry uses the concept of mass production, which makes it possible for factories to turn out products in great numbers at relatively low costs. A study of mass production will enable you to recognize and appreciate the problems encountered in large industrial plants such as those that produce furniture. You will have an opportunity to learn about many of the problems that face an industry which must produce goods at a profit.

Have you ever wondered why Americans have the highest standard of living in the world? Has it ever occurred to you that the many products that make life easier are the result of mass production? We have more goods and services because we have learned to produce many things at prices that people can afford, products such as automobiles, furniture, houses, radios, and TV sets. Figure 69-2. Today most people consider these things necessities rather than luxuries. However, without the aid of production machinery and know-how, profitable manu-

facture of these products would be impossible. Why? Well, that's the fascinating story of modern mass production and of the men and women who make it possible. It isn't based on luck, and it didn't happen overnight.

If you have visited a furniture museum, you have seen products made by

**69-2a.** Because of mass-production techniques, products like these tables can be manufactured efficiently and sold to the public at reasonable cost.

**69-1.** Fourteen families can utilize the apartments (12 x 56 feet or 3.66 x 17.1 m) in this modular (manufactured) high-rise. This is a scale model of the apartment project.

**69-2b.** Before furniture can be manufactured, lumber and other materials must be brought into the factory's reception center.

old-time craftspeople. These products were scarce. Good design and properly constructed furniture were available to only a few, usually the wealthy. Perhaps the first projects you built were made in the same manner as the early furniture, by the hand crafted or custom method. In the past, production specialization evolved slowly among artisans and their apprentices. Up to the time of the American Revolution, it took days to make a single musket, for example. The gunsmith had to hand fashion each piece separately and then carefully fit the pieces together to make one gun. The completed weapon fired accurately, but as the parts become worn or broken, there were no replacements. The gun was useless unless the gunsmith could make another part that matched.

Then a very farsighted man came up with an idea that dramatically improved production. Eli Whitney, better known for the invention of the cotton gin, developed many of the principles of mass production, including:

- Simplification of the product.
- Standardization of each part.
- Use of specialized machines.
- Organization of workers.

Whitney, by making practical use of the fact that things equal to the same things are equal to each other, helped

**488**      **69-2c.** Lumber must be cut to size in preparation for making parts.

pioneer the idea of mass production in America. Whitney reasoned that since individual parts of muskets are generally alike, they could be made exactly alike and, in fact, interchangeable by using machines specially designed to make each one. The muskets could then be put together by people of limited skill. The firearms would be less costly, of better quality, and could be produced in quantity. Around 1800, under a government contract, Whitney tooled up and built 10,000 muskets in a fraction of the time formerly required. This was a first step, the beginning of modern mass production.

Henry Ford was the first manufacturer to make a science of mass production by using these four main principles:

● Interchangeability of parts (developed by Eli Whitney).

● Automatic conveyance of parts to and from the work, the first assembly line (first put into use by Oliver Evans in his grain elevators).

● Division of labor (originated by Elihu Root, who aided in the development of the "Colt revolver").

**69-2e.** Lumber cores and veneers are stacked ready for the veneer press.

● Elimination of individual wasted motion (principle developed by Frederick W. Taylor, the original efficiency expert).

This new system of making things has since become the foundation of American business and industry. Today mass production feeds, clothes, and houses us, enables us to have good furniture and appliances, and gives us the opportunity to move easily from place to place.

**69-2d.** Lumber for a specific part is placed together.

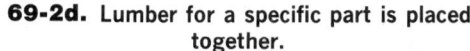

**69-2f.** Processing includes cutting to make the parts.

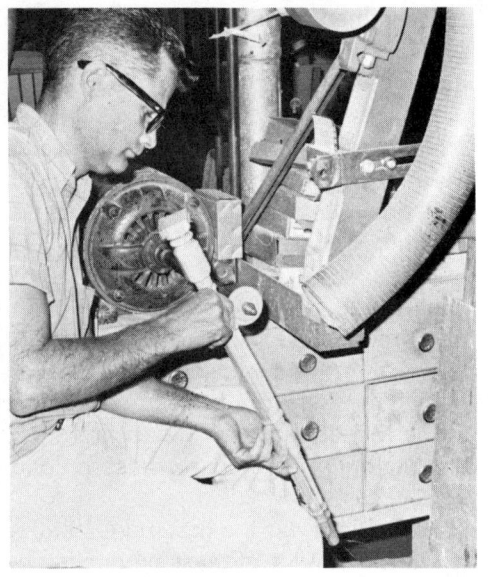

**69-2g.** Parts must be routed.

**69-2h.** Parts must be sanded.

**69-2i.** Once the parts are ready, they are assembled.

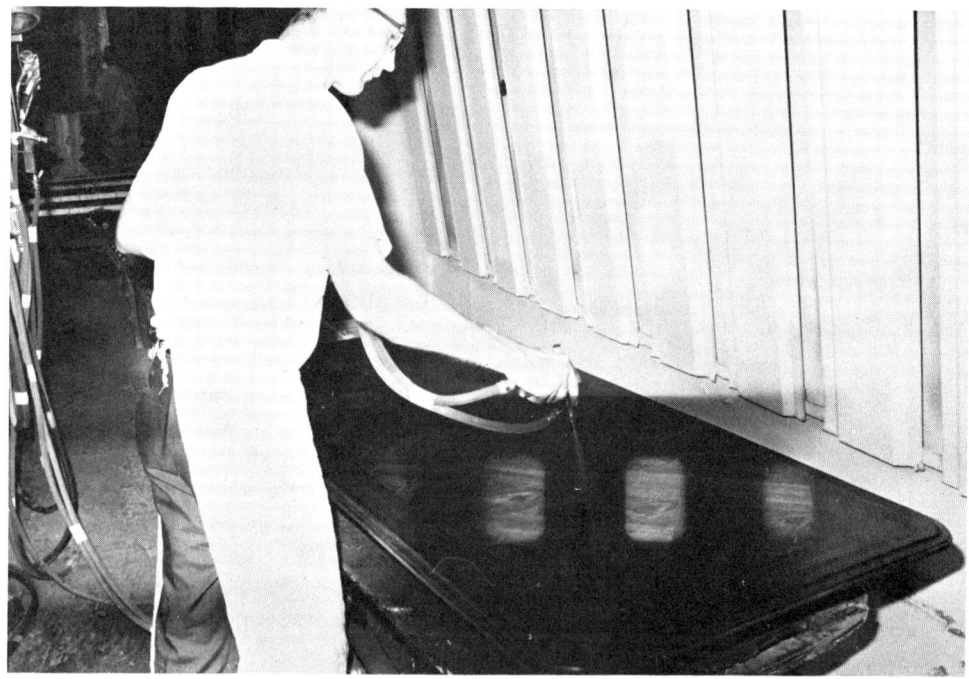

**69-2j.** A spray finish is applied.

**69-2k.** Each article is packaged for delivery to the customer.

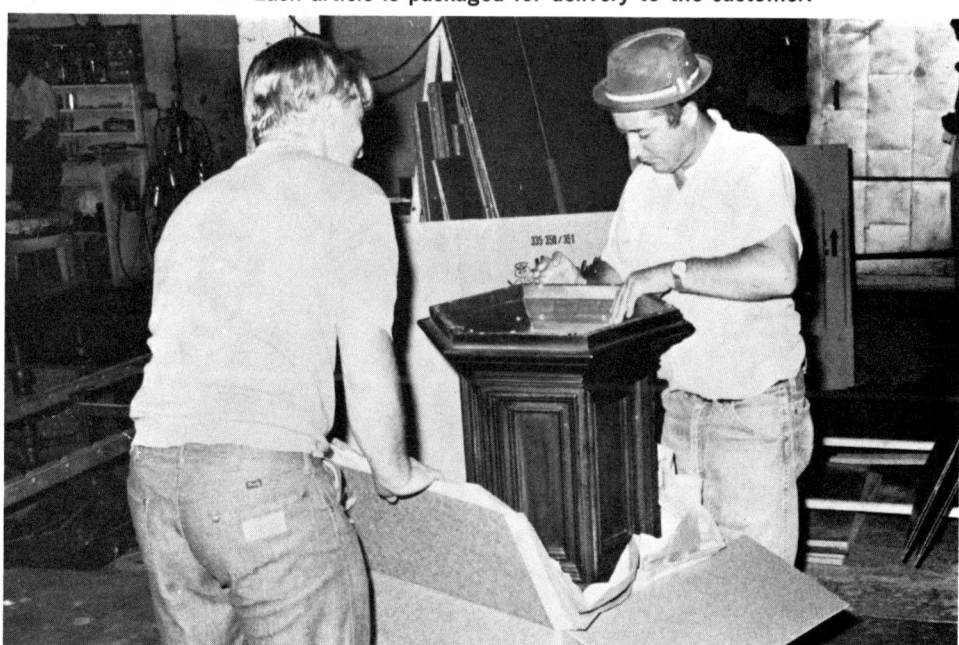

**69-3a.** The members of this student-managed manufacturing company have decided to produce a memo pad holder.

In order to mass-produce goods, three basic resources are needed:

- *Material resources,* including wood, plastics, metal, ceramics, and other materials that go into the products.

- *Capital resources,* including the factory and the machines and the tools with which men work.

- *Human resources,* which include the people themselves and their skills and abilities.

To get an idea of the way mass production functions in industry, it would be interesting for you to help plan and develop a mass-production project. There are three basic ways the mass-production project can be handled:

- Your class may review product designs and select one to produce. With this method, just enough of the product is

**69-3b.** A member of the board of directors signs up for stock in the company. In this company, stock at $1.00 a share is limited to one share per investor.

**69-3c.** Production of the memo pad holders begins.

manufactured so that each member of the class can take one home. No effort is made to sell the product.

• An alternative is to develop a product that can be given to a worthy organization, such as the Boy Scouts, Cub Scouts, or Red Cross. Often a toy or game can be produced in enough quantity to satisfy the needs of a local organization.

• For a more complete experience, your class could manufacture an item for sale. You will need to establish a company, sell stock, elect a board of directors, do market research, produce a product, sell it, and handle all the details of business. Figure 69-3. Some commercial items that are mass-produced for sale as gift items are shown in Figure 69-4.

**69-3d.** Assembling the memo pad holder.

**69-3e.** Packaging the product.

**69-3f.** Selling the product is an essential part of the company operation. Here a salesman shows the memo pad to a prospective purchaser.

**69-3g.** Helping with the accounting procedures. The company must keep a complete set of accounts and pay income tax on all the business expenses, just as a regular business does.

There are many steps that you and your class must take in order to mass-produce a project to sell. Some of these operations must be done even if you choose not to sell the product. These steps, which are described on the following pages, are also done in industry. Figure 69-5.

## RESEARCH AND DEVELOPMENT

Before a product can be manufactured for sale, a company must determine what the customer needs, wants, and will buy. Customers' attitudes lead to the development of many new products. Electric lawnmowers and carving knives, new types of cameras, and hundreds of other new products have been designed and developed to meet consumer demands. Industry must know the buying motives, tastes, and habits of the people they serve. Producers spend several hundreds of thousands of hours and millions of dollars annually to find out what the public wants and what to manufacture.

Before deciding on what to produce for sale, you need some idea of how much time can be spent on this experience. If only a few weeks are available, then a small product such as the server tray shown in Figure 69-6 might be

**69-4.** These attractive clock-storage boxes are typical of gift items produced by industry.

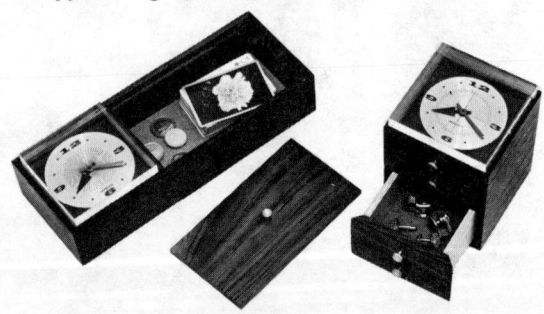

# MANUFACTURING A MASS PRODUCT

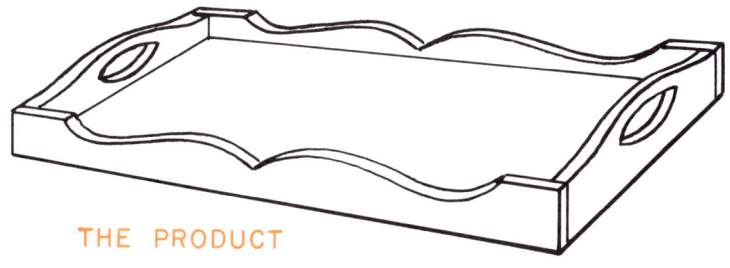

THE PRODUCT

## RESEARCH AND DEVELOPMENT

ORGANIZING

PLANNING

DESIGNING

DRAWING

PROTOTYPE
   BUILDING

## PRODUCTION PLANNING

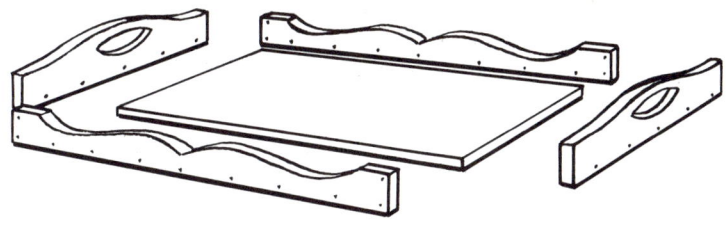

JIGS

FIXTURES

DIES

TEMPLATES

## PRODUCTION CONTROL

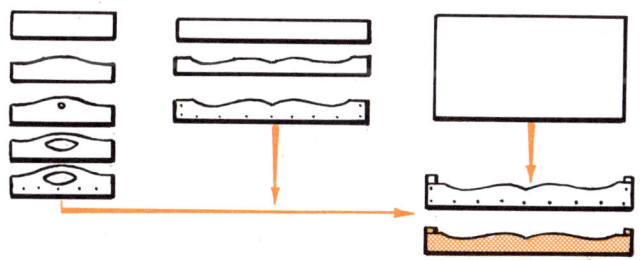

PRODUCTION CHARTS

FLOW CHARTS

**69-5.** Steps in a manufacturing operation, from planning through selling.
(Continued on page 496)

**69-5.** Continued

# QUALITY CONTROL

MATERIALS

PARTS

PRODUCTS

# PERSONNEL MANAGEMENT

HIRING

TRAINING

ASSIGNING

SUPERVISING

# MANUFACTURING

CUTTING

FORMING

FINISHING

ASSEMBLING

# MARKETING AND DISTRIBUTION

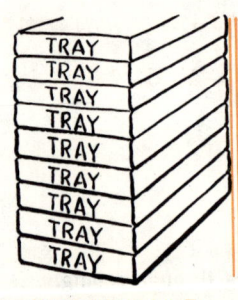

ADVERTISING

SELLING

DISTRIBUTING

SERVICING

WHOLESALE          RETAIL

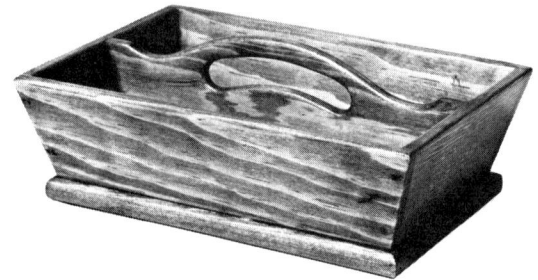

**69-6a.** A server tray that could be mass-produced.

the idea into a model. To do this, the idea must first be put on paper in the form of a drawing and then one or two of the prototypes, or pilot models, built. These pilot models must be accurately made so that all necessary jigs, fixtures, templets, and other items can be developed from the model. The models will also aid in deciding how to produce the product on an assembly line. All possible modifications and improvements should be made in the pilot model before production begins. To save time, your class may want to select a product already drawn, complete with a list of materials and procedure sheet. Figure 69-8.

chosen. With more time, a larger and more complicated project such as a planter spoon rack can be manufactured. Figure 69-7.

Once a product has been selected for manufacture, it is necessary to develop

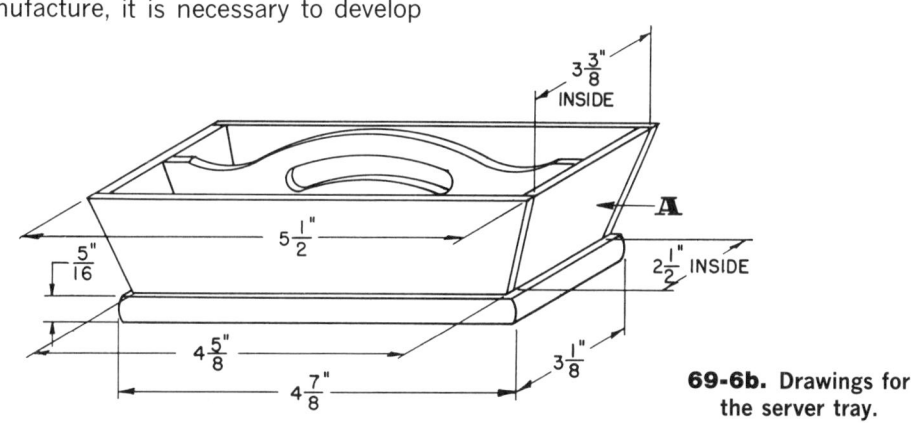

**69-6b.** Drawings for the server tray.

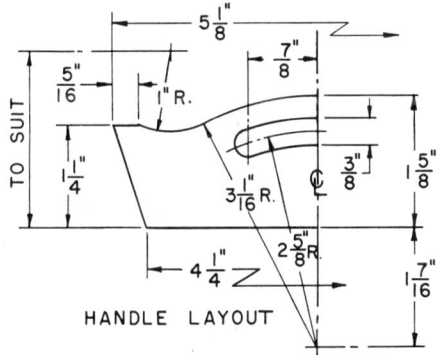

HANDLE LAYOUT

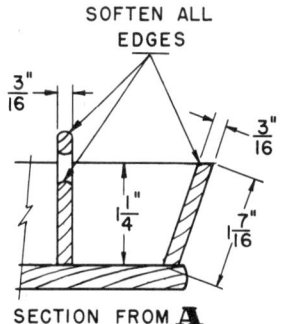

SOFTEN ALL EDGES

SECTION FROM **A**

## PRODUCTION PLANNING

Many things must be done to get ready for production. The pilot model must be analyzed to determine the operations and processes necessary for production. You must also know what standard and special equipment is needed. It will also be necessary to make jigs, fixtures, dies, and templets, A *jig* is a device made especially for holding work and guiding the cutting tool. A *fixture* is a device made to hold work. Its purpose is to make it easier for the operator to locate the work accurately, support it properly, and hold it securely. Figure 69-9 (Page 503). A *die* is a tool for cutting or shaping parts. Dies are not commonly used in woodworking plants except for plastic or metal parts. Figure 69-10 (Page 503). A *templet* is a metal, wood, or cardboard pattern used to draw the outline of a part, locate the holes, and lay out the pieces. Figure 69-11 (Page 503). These production devices have become an important part of every industry that makes products by mass-production methods.

| STOCK: Pine<br>Important: All dimensions listed below are FINISHED size. | | | | |
|---|---|---|---|---|
| No. of Pieces | Part Name | Thick-ness | Width | Length |
| 1 | Base | $5/16''$ | $3\frac{1}{8}''$ | $4\frac{7}{8}''$ |
| 2 | Sides | $3/16''$ | $1\frac{7}{16}''$ | $5\frac{1}{2}''$ |
| 2 | Ends | $3/16''$ | $1\frac{7}{16}''$ | $3\frac{3}{8}''$ |
| 1 | Handle | $3/16''$ | $1\frac{5}{8}''$ | $5\frac{1}{8}''$ |

**69-6c.** Bill of materials for the server tray.

**69-6d.** Procedure for the server tray.

1. Cut all pieces to size on circular saw.
2. Round edges of base on wood shaper or with file and sandpaper.
3. By measurement, lay out angles on side, end, and center pieces. Set circular saw miter gage to proper angle and cut ends of sides and end pieces.
4. Set saw arbor to 15-degree angle and cut angle on top and bottom edges of side and end pieces so that bottom edges will fit flush on base and top edges will be level.
5. Set saw arbor to 5-degree angle and cut angle on ends of side pieces to fit squarely against side pieces.
6. Lay out handle. Drill $3/8$-inch hole at each end of finger grip and cut out on jig saw.
7. Smooth all pieces with sandpaper.
8. Assemble with glue and wire brads. Drill nail holes slightly smaller than brads to prevent splitting the wood. It may be necessary to shorten length of handle slightly to fit in ends of tray.
9. Set brads. Fill holes.
10. Thoroughly soften all edges and finish sand entire project.
11. Apply antique pine finish.

**69-7a.** This planter spoon rack would be a much more complicated production problem than the server tray. Its manufacture would also involve producing a metal box.

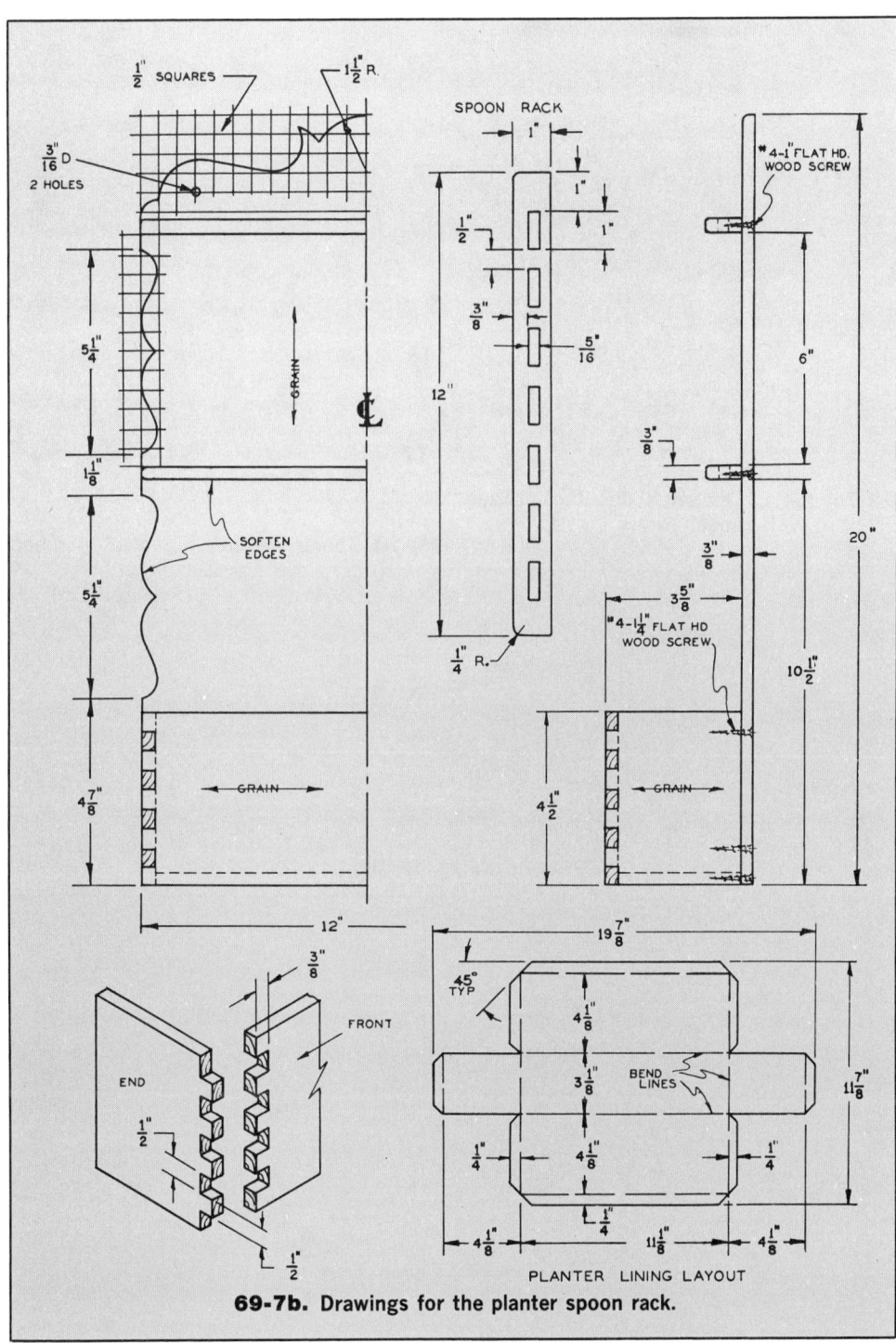

**69-7b.** Drawings for the planter spoon rack.

| STOCK: Pine | | | | |
|---|---|---|---|---|
| **Important: All dimensions listed below are FINISHED size.** | | | | |

| No. of Pieces | Part Name | Thick-ness | Width | Length |
|---|---|---|---|---|
| 1 | Back | $3/8''$ | $12''$ | $20''$ |
| 1 | Front | $3/8''$ | $4\frac{1}{2}''$ | $12''$ |
| 2 | Ends | $3/8''$ | $4\frac{1}{2}''$ | $3\frac{5}{8}''$ |
| 1 | Bottom | $3/8''$ | $3\frac{1}{4}''$ | $11\frac{1}{4}''$ |
| 2 | Spoon Racks | $3/8''$ | $1''$ | $12''$ |
| 10 | No. 4 x $1\frac{1}{4}''$ F. H. Wood Screws | | | |
| 8 | No. 4 x $1''$ F. H. Wood Screws | | | |
| 1 | Planter Lining No. 26 ga. (Galv. sheet steel or copper.) | | $11\frac{7}{8}''$ | $19\frac{7}{8}''$ |
| 10 | No. 18 x $1\frac{1}{4}''$ Wire Brads | | | |

**69-7c.** Bill of materials for the planter spoon rack.

1. Cut out all pieces to size on circular saw.
2. Lay out irregular design on back and cut out on jig saw.
3. Lay out holes in spoon racks. Drill $\frac{1}{4}$-inch holes in waste areas and cut out on jig saw.
4. Lay out corner joints on planter side and ends and cut out on circular saw.
5. Thoroughly soften edges of back and spoon racks. Smooth all pieces with sandpaper.
6. Glue up front and two end pieces of planter.
7. Fit, glue, and nail bottom to front and sides. Set nails.
8. Lay out, drill, and countersink screw shank holes. Drill anchor holes. Drill mounting holes in back.
9. Attach spoon racks and planter box to back with No. 4 F. H. wood screws.
10. Fill nail holes and finish sand entire project.
11. Apply antique pine finish.
12. Lay out, bend, and solder planter lining. Paint dark green if galvanized sheet steel is used.

**69-7d.** Procedure for the planter spoon rack.

**69-8a.** A tray that could be manufactured.

**69-8b.** Drawings for the tray.

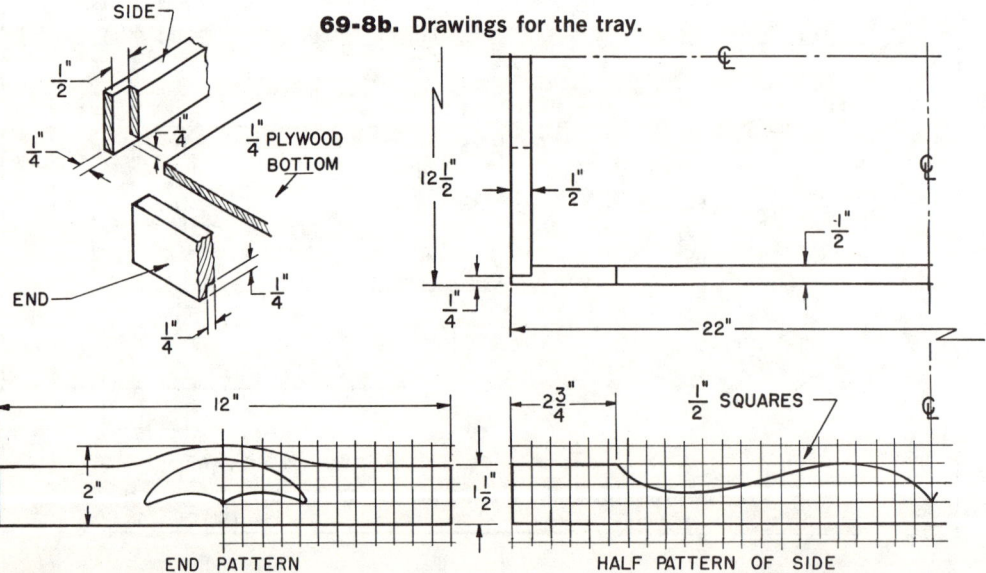

END PATTERN

HALF PATTERN OF SIDE

| No. of Pieces | Part Name | Thick-ness | Width | Length | Material |
|---|---|---|---|---|---|
| 2 | Sides | $\frac{1}{2}''$ | $1\frac{1}{2}''$ | 22'' | Maple or Birch |
| 2 | Ends | $\frac{1}{2}''$ | 2'' | 12'' | Maple or Birch |
| 1 | Bottom | $\frac{1}{4}''$ | 12'' | $21\frac{1}{2}''$ | Birch Plywood |
| 16 | No. 18 x $\frac{3}{4}''$ Wire Brads | | | | |

Important: All dimensions listed below are FINISHED size.

**69-8c.** Bill of materials for the tray.

**69-8d.** Procedure for the tray.

1. Cut sides and ends to size on circular saw.
2. Cut rabbet joints on bottom edge of side and end pieces on jointer or circular saw.
3. Cut end rabbet joints on ends of side pieces on circular saw.
4. Lay out irregular design on sides and ends, and cut out on band saw or jig saw.
5. Drill $\frac{1}{4}$-inch hole in hand grip in ends and cut out on jig saw.
6. Smooth pieces with sandpaper.
7. Assemble sides and ends with glue and wire brads, drilling nail holes slightly smaller than brads to prevent splitting the wood.
8. Cut bottom for snug fit. Sand and fasten into place with glue and wire brads.
9. Set brads, fill holes, and finish sand entire project.
10. Apply natural finish.

**69-8e.** Flow chart for the tray.

ENDS   CIR SAW   CIR SAW   CIR SAW   DRILL PRESS   JIG SAW   BAND SAW

SIZE CUTS — BOTTOM RABBET — END RABBET — HAND GRIP HOLES — HAND GRIP HOLES — SHAPE CUTS — HAND SAND — INSP

JIG 1   JIG 2

SIDES   CIR SAW   CIR SAW   BAND SAW

SIZE CUTS — BOTTOM RABBET — SHAPE CUTS — HAND SAND — INSP

JIG 3

FIXTURE — SUB ASSEM

BOTTOM   CIR SAW

SIZE CUTS — HAND SAND — INSP — ASSEM

FINISH

INSP

CODE

STORAGE   PROCESS   JIG FIXTURE DIE   INSPECTION

ALL STOCK S2S BEFORE PROCESSING.

TO PACKAGING AND SHIPPING

| Station | Activity | Equipment | Student Distribution |
|---|---|---|---|
| Foreman | Supervision of production | Flow charts and plans | 1 |
| 1 | Cut sides to width and length | Circular saw and jig | 2 |
| 2 | Cut ends to width and length | Circular saw and jig | 2 |
| 3 | Cut bottom to width and length | Circular saw and jig | 2 |
| 4 | Cut rabbet on bottom edges of sides and ends | Circular saw with dado head | 2 |
| 5 | Cut end rabbet joints on ends of side pieces | Circular saw with dado head | 2 |
| 6 | Drill holes in ends for hand grips | Drill press and drill with jig | 2 |
| 7 | Cut irregular shape of hand grips | Jig saw and jig | 2 |
| 8 | Cut irregular ends on sides and ends | Band saw and jig | 2 |
| 9 | Sand sides, ends, and bottom | Sandpaper and belt sander | 3 |
| 10 | Assemble sides and ends with glue and brads | Glue, brads, hammer, nailset, and fixture | 2 |
| 11 | Fasten base to sides and ends | Glue, brads, hammer, nailset, and fixture | |
| 12 | Finish sand complete product | Sandpaper | 3 |
| 13 | Apply wipe-on finish | Wipe-on finish and rags | 2 |

**69-8f.** Production chart for the tray.

**69-8g.** An analysis of needed materials, equipment, fixtures, and jigs.

| MATERIALS* |
|---|

1 piece $\frac{1}{2}$ x $1\frac{1}{2}$ x $44\frac{1}{4}$ inches (12.5 x 38 x 1124 mm) for the sides
1 piece $\frac{1}{2}$ x 2 x $24\frac{1}{4}$ inches (12.5 x 51 x 616 mm) for the ends
1 piece $\frac{1}{4}$ x 12 x $21\frac{1}{2}$ inches (6.5 x 305 x 546 mm) for the bottom
16 No. 18 x $\frac{3}{4}$ inch (19 mm) wire brads
2 ounces of wipe-on finish
$\frac{1}{4}$ ounce of white glue

| EQUIPMENT | FIXTURES AND JIGS |
|---|---|
| Circular saw<br>Dado head<br>Drill press<br>Drills<br>Band saw<br>Jig saw<br>Belt sander<br>Claw hammers<br>Nail set<br>Sandpaper | Jig for cutting sides and ends to length<br>Jig for cutting bottom to width and length<br>Jig for drilling hand grips<br>Jig for cutting hand grips<br>Jig for cutting irregular edges on sides and ends<br>Fixture for assembling the product |

*Extra lumber length has been added to allow for cutting.

## PRODUCTION CONTROL

Production control deals with the problems of setting up a production line so that there is a smooth flow of materials through the plant. Figure 69-12. Materials such as lumber, plywood, finishing materials, fasteners, and other materials must be ordered in adequate amounts. Figure 69-13. There must be places to store the material; keep an inventory; handle the job assignments; make the plant layout; prepare production charts, flow charts, and schedules; and to do

**69-10.** This model maker is putting the finishing touches on a wood die model that will be used in producing a metal part.

**69-9.** Using a fixture on a router.

**69-11.** A templet maker at work. This templet is an accurate pattern that can be placed on stock to trace the outline.

**69-12.** These men are making an accurate-scale, wood model for a new production line in a metal manufacturing plant.

**69-13.** Raw materials in the form of wood and wood products are necessary for any production. Note that the worker is checking a bill of materials as he removes the board from the storage rack.

many other things that will insure a smooth flow of the parts through the plant and provide for efficient production. Figure 69-14.

## QUALITY CONTROL

All items manufactured must meet certain standards of perfection. Quality control involves inspecting and testing the raw material that comes into the plant, checking the parts as they are produced, and inspecting and testing the finished product. Figure 69-15. In mass production the aim is to make a high percentage of acceptable parts and also to make sure that there are few rejects among the finished product. In industry, many types of *gages* are used to check each part as it is made and to inspect the final product. Much of quality control can be done by individually inspecting

**69-14.** Checking a production schedule chart. This chart shows when materials that have been ordered should arrive so that they can fit into the production schedule.

each part as it is made and by checking the assembly of the product, including its finish.

### PERSONNEL MANAGEMENT

Personnel management is concerned with the use of people in mass production. Figure 69-16. To produce a product, it is necessary to select, train, and supervise the workers. Figure 69-17. Your class may want to organize committees and spend some time in preparing and training the workers.

### MANUFACTURING

Once all the previous steps have been completed, your group is now ready to do the actual manufacturing of the product. This will mean using the raw materials to cut, form, fasten, and finish each part to make the completed product. Figures 69-18 and 69-19. The final worth of

**69-15.** Accuracy is important in manufacturing any product. Each part sub-assembly and assembly must be checked carefully.

**69-16a.** A group discussion of personnel problems in a manufacturing plant.

**69-16b.** This group of students is acquiring industrial skills as well as the ability to get along with one another in an organized manufacturing enterprise.

this experience is found in whether each part meets the standards established and whether the final product passes inspection.

## MARKETING AND DISTRIBUTION

Marketing and distribution include accounting procedures plus advertising, selling, distributing, and servicing the product. The finished goods must be moved from the plant to the people who use them. This is the business phase of mass production. If a market survey has been made, perhaps all of the products have been sold even before production is undertaken. However, it may still be necessary to package the products and deliver them to the buyers, collect the money, and keep the necessary records and receipts.

## MASS-PRODUCTION CHECK LIST

The following check list can be used in mass-producing any product:

● Select personnel. Determine who will be responsible for each phase: engineering, production, business.

● Discuss responsibilities of all personnel.

**69-17.** Workers must know their jobs. Therefore in-service factory training is given before production begins.

**69-18.** Rough cutting a wood part on a band saw.

- Select the product.
- Develop the working drawings.
- Make a bill of materials. Compute stock requirements for one product and then multiply by the number of items to be produced.
- Construct the pilot, or prototype, models, one assembled and one "loose" so that it can be taken apart.
- Disassemble the model and make the necessary jigs, fixtures, and templets.
- Test and time the production procedures at each stage of manufacture.
- Organize a flow chart for production.
- Establish the work stations and assign workers.
- Train workers.
- Conduct a test run for problems.
- Make necessary adjustments or changes in the production line.
- Prepare rough stock.
- Stock each work station with necessary tools and materials.
- Begin production.
- Inspect each part and all subassemblies.
- Assemble the parts of the product.
- Apply the finish to the product.

**69-19.** Finishing book cabinets that have been mass-produced.

- Make final inspection.
- Package the product.
- Distribute the product.
- Disassemble the assembly line.
- Clean up the work stations and store jigs, fixtures, templets, and other special items.
- Evaluate the product.

## CAN YOU ANSWER THESE QUESTIONS ON MASS PRODUCTION?

1. List some of the main principles of mass production.
2. Who was the first manufacturer to make a science of mass production and what four principles did he utilize?
3. Name the three basic resources needed for mass production.
4. Discuss the general ways a class can be organized for mass production.
5. Describe jigs, fixtures, and dies.

**Section**
**XII**
**UNIT 70.**

# CONSTRUCTION

**Bridges, roads,** office buildings, shopping centers, airports, and many other structures are built on site as part of the *construction* industry. Some years ago, all residential homes were part of the construction industry, but now many homes are built in factories as part of the manufacturing industry.

There are three basic types of manufactured housing:

• The *mobile home,* a transportable structure, which exceeds either 8 body feet (2.4 m) in width or 32 body feet (9.75 m) in length, is built on a chassis, and is designed to be used as a dwelling with or without a permanent foundation when connected to the required utilities. Figure 70-1.

• The *modular unit,* a factory-fabricated, transportable, building unit designed to be used by itself or to be incorporated with similar units at a building site into a modular structure. It may be used for residential, commercial, educational, or industrial purposes.

• The *sectional home,* a dwelling made of two or more modular units, factory-fabricated, and transported to the

**70-1a.** Building mobile homes on the production line.

**70-1b.** Mobile home living can be pleasant and attractive.

Nine out of ten homes in the United States are wood frame construction. These homes are often enclosed with wood siding, wood shingles, brick veneer, or stucco. Figure 70-3. Wood frame houses are relatively simple to construct, extremely sturdy, easy to maintain and repair, and relatively inexpensive. Figure 70-4.

## PREPARING TO BUILD

There are several steps that must precede the actual building of the home itself.

### Locating a Lot

It is important to find a suitable lot on which to build, since the lot can affect both the size and design of the house. The shape and contour of the lot will determine, to a large degree, the design of the home itself. In purchasing a lot, the cost should not exceed 14 percent of the total building budget.

home site where they are put on a foundation and joined to make a single house. Figure 70-2.

Except for mobile homes, which are built of lighter materials, a factory-built home is as expensive (or more so) as a house built on site.

**70-2.** Sectional home built in two parts. These homes are complete in every detail, including heating, plumbing, and wiring, and are moved to the site and assembled.

509

## Developing or Selecting Plans

Complete sets of house plans are available from many sources. Many companies specialize in good stock plans. These are available from home planning services, lumber yards, and lumber suppliers. To get a good idea of what the

**70-3a.** Wood and plywood are the main renewable building materials used in home construction. This home is being constructed on site in constrast to the manufactured home shown in Figure 70-2.

**70-3b.** Plywood is widely used in building construction because it comes in large sheets that are easy to handle and fast to assemble. The uses for plywood are many, as shown here: 1. Adds strength and rigidity as roof decking; 2. Creates a smooth, clean, easy-to-paint surface on gable ends and soffits; 3. Provides a firm, smooth base for flooring as subfloors and underlayment; 4. Has the warmth of real wood when used for interior walls; 5. Gives a smooth, flat, durable base for tile, cork, and decorative walls; 6. Can be used for built-ins; 7. As sheathing, makes walls warm, strong, and rigid; 8. Can be used in fences, windbreaks, and patio screens; 9. Useful for exteriors; 10. When used for concrete forms, it can be re-used for sheathing.

**70-4.** This relatively simple house plan could be used either for a second home or as a basic house.

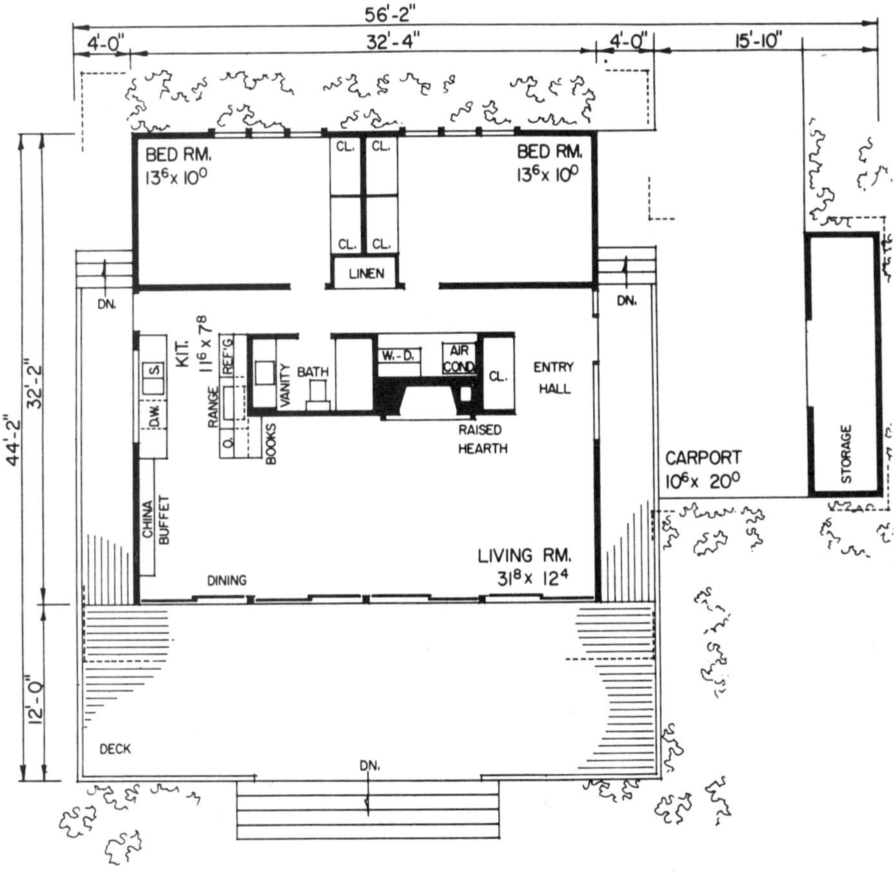

56'-2"

4'-0"  32'-4"  4'-0"  15'-10"

BED RM. 13⁶ x 10⁰

BED RM. 13⁶ x 10⁰

CL. CL.

CL. CL.

LINEN

DN.

DN.

44'-2"  32'-2"

KIT. 11⁶ x 7⁸

S

DW.

RANGE

O.

REF'G.

BOOKS

VANITY

BATH

W.-D.

AIR COND.

CL.

ENTRY HALL

RAISED HEARTH

CHINA BUFFET

DINING

LIVING RM. 31⁸ x 12⁴

CARPORT 10⁶ x 20⁰

STORAGE

12'-0"

DECK

DN.

house will cost, find out the average cost per square foot for building a home in your community. This average cost will vary with the design and detail of the house. A house with extra bathrooms, many built-ins, special windows, extra doors, and elaborate exterior features will cost a great deal more per square foot than a simple house. If an architect designs a home, his fee usually ranges from 5 to 10 percent of the total cost. By adding the costs of the lot, architect's service, basic home, carpeting, furnishings, and landscaping, you can get a good idea of the total cost of housing. As a rule, this total cost should not exceed two and one-half times the annual income of the family.

### Finding a Contractor

When the plans are all complete and the lot has been purchased, several contractors should be asked to bid on the cost of construction. The contractor should be carefully chosen. He in turn will hire subcontractors for doing electrical work, plumbing and heating installation, masonry, painting, and other jobs.

### Financing

When you know what the total cost of the building project will be, it is wise to go to a bank or savings and loan company concerning the mortgage. Here you can get help in determining what size down payment you must make and what size mortgage can be obtained. These people will also figure what your total monthly payments will be, including principal, interest, taxes, insurance, and any other fees.

### Getting the Necessary Permits

You or the builder must get the necessary building permits so that building can

get started. This should be done before you sign for a mortgage and for a building contract.

### Surveying and Excavation

A surveyor must set up a time to mark the lot lines and the building lines. Stakes are placed at the corners of the lot and also at the corners of the house to show where the house will be located. If it is not a flat lot, stakes must also be placed to indicate lot contours. At this point a bulldozer is usually brought in to excavate the ground for the basement and foundation. For a plan without a basement, only a trench may be dug for the foundation. There are three common ways of providing a foundation for a house. Homes without basements are built on a concrete slab or with a crawl space under the house, both of which require a trench to be dug for the footings that go below the frost line. For homes with a partial or full basement, mechanical equipment is brought in to excavate the basement. The actual foundation footings are usually dug by hand.

### BUILDING THE BASEMENT

*Footings* are the poured concrete bases on which the basement walls or the house is built. These must be deep enough to support the entire load of the house and at least 6 to 8 inches (152.5 to 203 mm) wider than the walls. Footings must rest on solid earth. Sometimes wood forms are used for the foundations. In other cases they are poured directly into the trench.

After the footings are cured, the foundation walls are built of either poured concrete or cement blocks. For a poured concrete basement, foundation forms of wood and metal are erected. The cement is brought in by truck and the basement walls poured. If cement block is used, the mason will build the walls block by block. The number of basement windows installed should be adequate to keep the basement fairly light and bright.

After the walls have been completed, drain tile is placed around the outside of the foundation walls to insure a dry basement. The exterior of the walls should also be waterproofed. *The earth is not replaced around the basement walls until the building has been erected* so that there is plenty of weight to keep the basement walls from caving in. A cement foundation must also be poured for the I-beam post used to hold up the floor. The top of the basement walls should be at least 6 to 8 inches (152.5 to 203 mm) above ground when the landscaping is finished.

At this stage of building, pipes for sewer, water, and gas are laid in the basement area where a meter and shut-off valves are installed for the water and gas. Temporary electric service is brought into the area for the builder's use.

## BUILDING THE HOME

Most on-site builders have at least part of the home prefabricated in a manufacturing plant. It is common practice, for

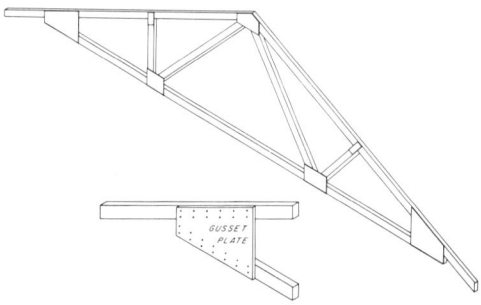

**70-5.** Roof trusses are commonly used even in homes that are built on site.

example, to buy lightweight, trussed rafters ready for installing. Figure 70-5. Some builders also buy prefabricated wall sections. Many other items may also be manufactured—prehung doors, kitchen cabinets, closet interiors, and many other items. As mentioned earlier, the entire house can be prefabricated in a manufacturing plant and brought to the site with all parts cut and ready for assembly. With this method, it takes only five or six days to rough in the house.

## FLOOR FRAMING

Lumber for framing the house is delivered and stacked on site. A metal beam (a horizontal, load-supporting member) spans the distance between the foundation walls and the bearing post. This beam is laid in pockets in the basement wall and fastened to the wood or metal-bearing posts spaced about 7 feet (2.13 m) apart across the basement. Holes are drilled in a sill plate to go with the anchor bolts and the foundation wall.

In some parts of the country it is important to place a metal termite shield over the foundation wall before putting the sill plate in place. Sills are set back far enough from the face of the foundation to allow for sheathing, siding, or brick veneer. When installing the sill plate, mortar is first spread on the foundation wall. Then the termite shield is placed and the sill fitted over the anchor bolts. Nuts are fastened to the anchor bolts to hold the sill firmly in place.

The most common method of framing a house is the western, or platform, frame in which the first floor is built on top of the foundation wall as though it were a platform. Figure 70-6. The outer ends of the floor joists rest on sills, and the inner ends rest on a beam. The floor joists are installed 16 inches (406 mm)

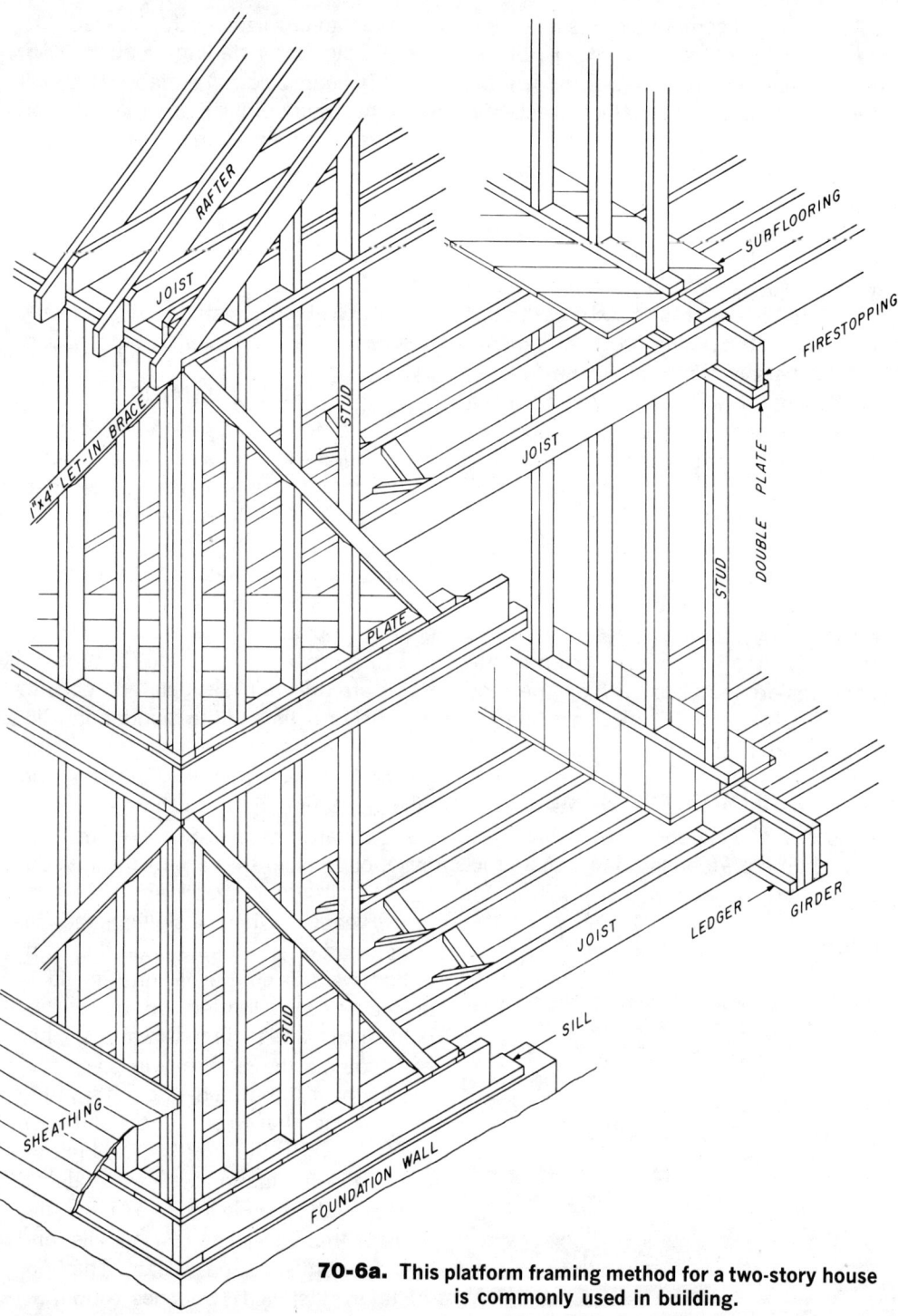

**70-6a.** This platform framing method for a two-story house is commonly used in building.

on center. Double joists are used for all partitions. A double header is placed around the basement stairwell and around an opening for the fireplace. These joists carry the weight of the floor and must be stiff enough not to bend or vibrate. *Bridging* is placed between the floor joists to stiffen the floor and distribute the load. Whenever regular joists must be cut to provide an opening for a stairwell or fireplace opening, extra joists called headers must be installed at right angles to the regular joists.

The next major step is to add the sub-flooring. A common practice is to use plywood, since this makes for a solid subfloor and is quickly installed.

## WALL FRAMING INCLUDING PARTITIONS AND STAIRS

Exterior wall framing which includes the sole plate, studs, headers, top plates and fire stops, is made of 2 x 4's (50 x 100 mm). Interior walls are similar but do not include fire stops. These walls are assembled on the subfloor and then

**70-6b.** Parts of a one-story house that has a slightly tapered flat roof.

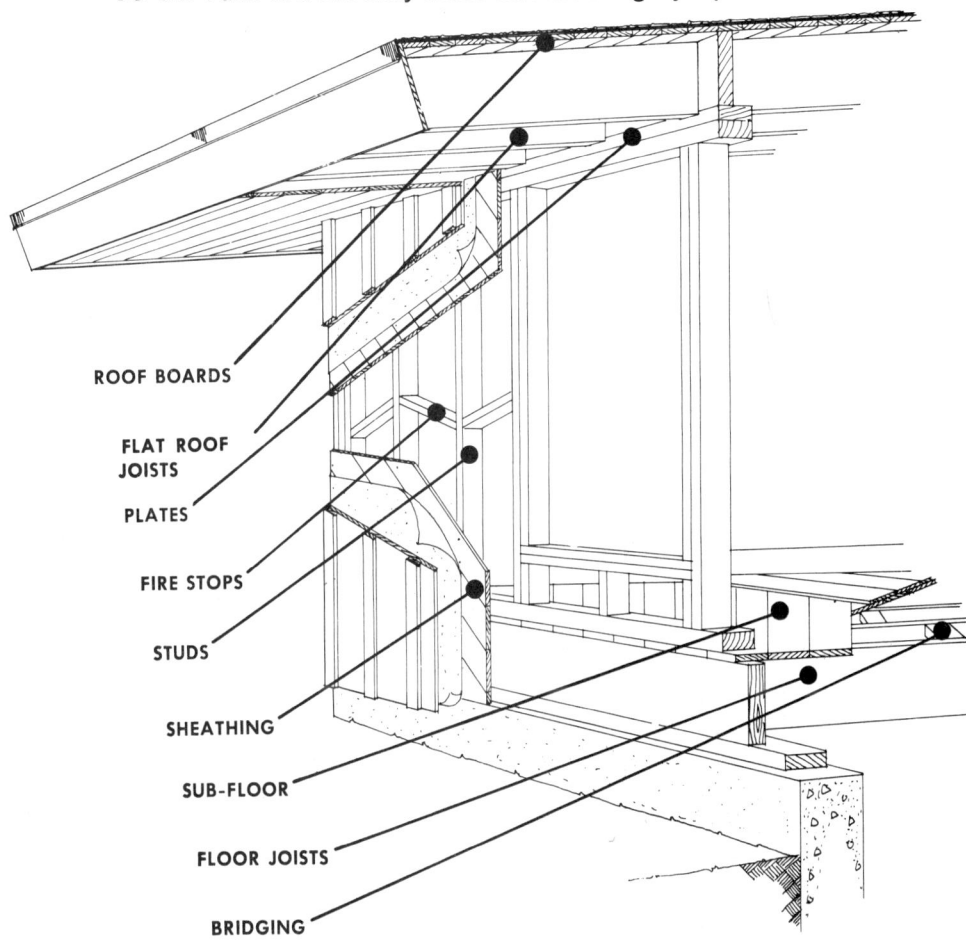

ROOF BOARDS

FLAT ROOF JOISTS

PLATES

FIRE STOPS

STUDS

SHEATHING

SUB-FLOOR

FLOOR JOISTS

BRIDGING

raised in place and nailed to the subfloor. These serve as a base for the exterior and interior wall covering; they also support the upper floors, ceiling, and roof. The openings for doors and windows must be adequately framed. To guard against plaster cracks at least a double 2 x 4 should be placed over small window openings and a double 2 x 6, 2 x 8, or 2 x 10 over the wider ones.

Partitions are built for the rooms and closets according to the floor plan. The corners are reinforced by using multiple studs. Sometimes the walls are reinforced by installing let-in braces or fire stops.

Immediately after the walls are up and in place, sheathing is added to the exterior. This is usually fiberboard, gypsum board, or plywood. Openings for windows and doors are cut in the sheathing after it has been installed.

## CEILING AND ROOF FRAMING

Ceiling joists are installed direct, as ties between the exterior wall and interior partitions. They can also serve as a basis for flooring in the attic. These ceiling joists carry no floor load except as might be used for light storage in an attic. They are usually spaced 16 inches (406 mm) on center. Roofs are built by installing rafters nailed to the top plate and to the ridge board. They may also be built with a trussed rafter roof.

## COMPLETING THE EXTERIOR

The roof is covered with plywood similar to that used for the rough floor. The edge of the roof is completed using two boards, one called the fascia and the other the soffit. After the sheathing has been added, a cover of the building paper is tacked in place. At this point masons build the chimney, fireplace, and brick exterior. Exterior windows and doors are installed before the exterior brickwork is completed. The roof is finished by installing flashing (metal used for waterproofing) and shingles, usually asphalt. The siding for the exterior walls may be of various kinds.

## INSTALLING UTILITIES

As the carpenters and sheet-metal men are working on the exterior of the house, work is also progressing on the inside. After the basement floor has been poured, sheet-metal men install the furnace and duct work for heating and air-conditioning. Wires are strung and rough wiring installed in the walls, with locations marked for outlets and switches. Plumbing is also installed and large pieces of equipment, such as the hot water heater, water softener, and bathtub, are put in place.

## COMPLETING THE INSIDE
## OF THE HOUSE

Blanket insulation is now nailed or stapled in place between the walls. The inside walls are covered with gypsum board or panel, if it is dry-wall construction, or rock lathe and plaster for wet-wall construction. Blanket or loose insulation can then be installed in the attic. Rough door openings are cased in and the doors hung. The finished flooring is installed, the stairways completed, and all of the trim added around doors and windows. Kitchen cabinets and other built-ins are constructed by the carpenter or brought in ready-made and fastened in place. Tile men complete the ceramic tile installation, and specialists install flooring material in the kitchen, bathroom, and utility room. Countertops are added and electrical fixtures, plumbing fixtures, and similar accessories are installed. All necessary interior and exterior painting and finishing is done. The home is then landscaped. Figure 70-7.

## MODEL CONSTRUCTION

If you don't have an opportunity to build an actual part of a home, one of the best ways to learn construction is to build part or all of a scale-model house. Figure 70-8. This can give you many experiences that will be worthwhile should you ever decide to enroll in a carpentry course or do some of your own carpentry work. Building a scale model also gives you a chance to see house plans in three dimensions and to learn about good construction techniques. Model building will help you get acquainted with the total construction industry. If you are building a model by yourself, you may want to construct only a portion of the home. However, as a team project, the complete house might be built. Here are some suggestions:

• *Scale.* The ideal scale for model building is $1\frac{1}{2}$ inches equal one foot, which means that the building will be $\frac{1}{8}$ full size. With this scale, a 2 x 4 would

be $\frac{1}{4}$ x $\frac{1}{2}$ inch; a 2 x 6 would be $\frac{1}{4}$ x $\frac{3}{4}$ inch; and a 2 x 10 would measure $\frac{1}{4}$ x $1\frac{1}{2}$ inches. Note that these are all the nominal (name sizes) of the lumber, not the actual sizes. In building the house you can then refer to these as 2 x 4's, 2 x 6's, etc., as you would in building a full-size house.

• *Materials.* The *lumber* used can be scraps of basswood, redwood, yellow poplar, or pine. Often, waste lumber can be obtained from lumber yards. Stock can be cut to size in quantity on a table saw, jointer, or planer. *Panel stock* for the interior and exterior of the house can be made from very thin hardboard; cardboard can also be used. One-sixteenth and $\frac{1}{32}$-inch veneers are also ideal. *Nails* should be in proportion to the scale size. For example, for framing use 19- or 20-gage wire nails. For spiking, use $\frac{5}{8}$-inch, No. 19, or $\frac{3}{4}$-inch, No. 18, gage nails. One-half-inch nails can also be used for nailing the shingles.

• *Tools.* The same basic tools used for other woodworking can be used in model construction. The important ones to have are a good, small hand-made miter box,

**70-7a.** Building this playhouse/winter-storage structure would provide a great deal of experience in building construction. The framing, however, is somewhat different from the framing in a full-size house.

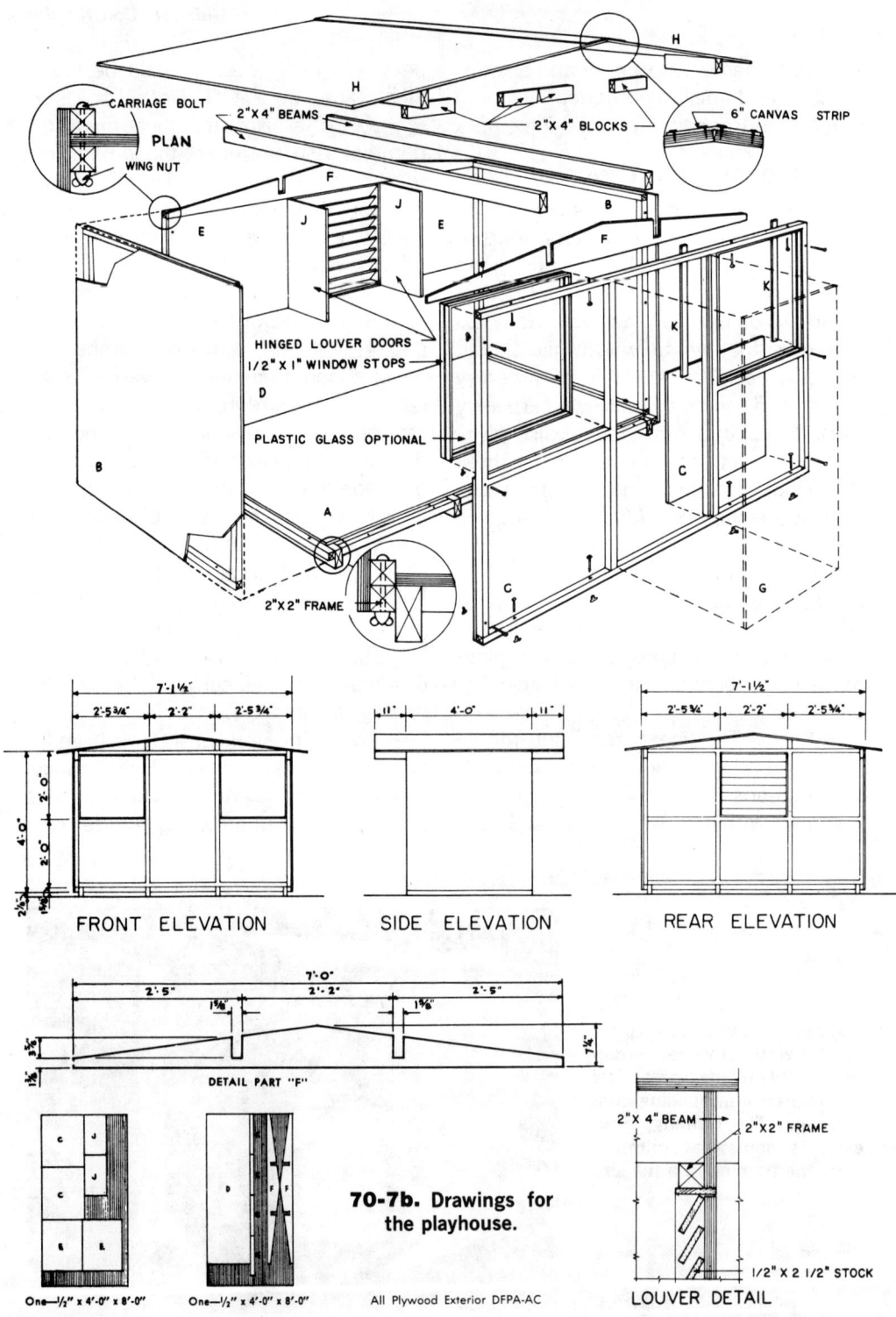

CARRIAGE BOLT

PLAN

WING NUT

2"X 4" BEAMS

2"X 4" BLOCKS

6" CANVAS STRIP

H

H

F

J    J

E    E

B

F

D

E

HINGED LOUVER DOORS

1/2" X 1" WINDOW STOPS

K

K

PLASTIC GLASS OPTIONAL

B

A

C

C

G

2"X 2" FRAME

7'-1½"

2'-5¾"    2'-2"    2'-5¾"

2'-0"

4'-0"

2'-0"

FRONT ELEVATION

11"    4'-0"    11"

SIDE ELEVATION

7'-1½"

2'-5¾"    2'-2"    2'-5¾"

REAR ELEVATION

7'-0"

2'-5"    2'-2"    2'-5"

1⅝"    1⅝"

3⅝"    7⅝"

DETAIL PART "F"

C    J

C    J

L    L

One—½" x 4'-0" x 8'-0"

D    F    F

One—½" x 4'-0" x 8'-0"

All Plywood Exterior DFPA-AC

**70-7b.** Drawings for the playhouse.

2"X 4" BEAM

2"X 2" FRAME

1/2" X 2 1/2" STOCK

LOUVER DETAIL

**518**

| Code | No. Req'd. | Size | Part Identification |
|------|-----------|------|---------------------|
| A | 1 | $\frac{3}{4}$'' x 3'-7$\frac{1}{2}$'' x 6'-9'' | Floor |
| B | 2 | $\frac{1}{2}$'' x 4'-0'' x 4'-0'' | Side |
| C | 2 | 2'-0'' x 2'-5'' | Front Panel |
| D | 1 | 2'-0'' x 7'-0'' | Rear Panel |
| E | 2 | 1-10$\frac{3}{8}$'' x 2'-5'' | Rear Panel |
| F | 2 | 7$\frac{1}{4}$'' x 7'-0'' | Beam Support |
| G | 1 | $\frac{3}{4}$'' x 2'-1$\frac{7}{8}$'' x 3'-7'' | Door |
| H | 2 | $\frac{3}{4}$'' x 4'-0'' x 6'-0'' | Roof |
| J | 2 | 1'-10$\frac{3}{8}$'' x 1'-1'' | Louver Door |
| K | 4 | 1$\frac{5}{8}$'' x 1'-10$\frac{3}{8}$'' | Casing |
|   | 32 Lin. Ft. | 2'' x 4'' Stock | Base and Beams |
|   | 122 Lin. Ft. | 2'' x 2'' Stock | Framing |
|   | 50 Lin. Ft. | $\frac{1}{2}$'' x 1'' Stock | Stops |
|   | 30 Lin. Ft. | $\frac{1}{2}$'' x 2$\frac{1}{2}$'' Stock | Louvers |
|   | 4 Ea. & 2 Ea. | For $\frac{1}{2}$'' x $\frac{3}{4}$'' Doors | Hinges |
|   | 40 Ea. | $\frac{1}{4}$'' Stove | Wing Nuts and Bolts |
|   | 2 Pcs. | 2'-1$\frac{1}{4}$'' x 1'-10$\frac{3}{8}$'' | Clear Plastic Sheets* |
|   | 1 Pc. | 6'' x 6'-0'' | Canvas Strip |

MISCELLANEOUS: 8d common and 6d finishing nails (Galvanized)
No cutting diagram needed for parts "A," "B," "H," "G."

\* Optional
Use EXT-DFPA● A-C plywood only.

**70-7c.** Bill of materials for the playhouse.

five-ounce tack hammer, long-nose pliers, back saw or dovetail saw, small block plane, architect's scale, and bench tool.

● *House plans.* Any standard set of house plans can be used for model building. It is best to select a one-story ranch home, since this will simplify construction problems.

● *Other materials.* A wide variety of other materials can be used to build a model. For example, a piece of plywood or particle board can form the lot layout, and the foundation can be made from a rigid foam plastic to which a mixture of portland cement and water has been applied. All layouts should be made using the architect's scale. The cutting, fitting, and nailing should be done in the same manner as for a small take-home project.

Perhaps only part of the interior and exterior wall needs to be covered with thin veneer and hardboard. The same is true for the roof. Shingles can be made from sandpaper or from thin wedges of cedar blocks. All materials for building model homes, even windows and doors, are available commercially from many com-

**70-8.** Building a scale model is one good method of learning about home construction.

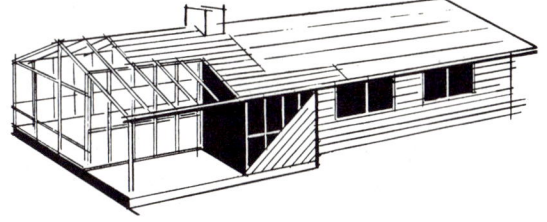

panies. For landscaping materials, flocking can be used for grass and wire and foam rubber for trees and shrubbery.

## BUILDING OUTDOOR FURNITURE

Carpentry differs from making small projects because in heavy construction, large-dimension framing stock and large nails are used and somewhat less accurate cutting is done. Some carpentry experiences can be obtained by building outdoor furniture, since you will be handling materials much the same as for building a home. Figure 70-9.

**70-9a.** This outdoor coffee table is built with heavy materials like those used in carpentry.

| No. of Pieces | Part Name | Thickness | Width | Length |
|---|---|---|---|---|
| | **STOCK: Redwood or Pine** | | | |
| | **Important: All dimensions listed below are FINISHED size.** | | | |
| 2 | Top | 1¼″ | 5½″ | 34″ |
| 2 | Top | 1¼″ | 5½″ | 32″ |
| 2 | Top | 1¼″ | 5½″ | 25″ |
| 2 | Cleats for Top | ¾″ | 3″ | 29½″ |
| 2 | Legs | 1¼″ | 2⅝″ | 20½″ |
| 2 | Legs | 1¼″ | 2⅝″ | 26⅞″ |
| 4 | Wheel (Exterior Ply) | ½″ | 7″ | 7″ |
| 2 | Wheel (Exterior Ply) | ¼″ | 7″ | 7″ |
| 1 | Axle (Hardwood Dowel) | 1½″ | | 25″ |
| 1 | Rung (Hardwood Dowel) | 1½″ | | 20″ |
| 28 | 1½″-10 Flathead Wood Screws | | | |
| 8 | 2½″-10 Flathead Wood Screws | | | |
| 4 | 1″ I. D. Plain Washers | | | |
| 2 | Pins (No. 16 or No. 20) Penny Nails | | | |
| 2 | Wedges (Hardwood) | | | |

**70-9b.** Bill of materials for the coffee table.

**70-9c.** Procedure for the coffee table.

1. Cut the pieces for the top ¼ inch longer than the finished length.
2. Cut the cleats for the top.
3. Fasten the top pieces to the cleats, allowing 3/16-inch spacing between the top pieces.
4. Lay out the circle for the top, and then take the top apart.
5. Cut the individual top pieces on a band saw and sand on a disc sander.
6. Assemble the top pieces and cleats with waterproof glue and screws.
7. Cut the legs to length, cut angles at the ends, and chamfer the outer edges as shown in the drawing.
8. Lay out the leg joint and cut with a circular saw.
9. Bore the holes in the legs for the axle and the rung.
10. Cut the axle to length, turn ends down to 1-inch diameter on lathe, and drill holes for the pins.
11. Cut the leg rung to length, turn the ends, and make cuts for wedges. Make the wedges from hardwood.
12. Assemble the legs with wedges and glue.
13. Assemble the top and the legs with glue and screws.
14. Cut 7 ¼-inch wood squares for making up wheels. Laminate pieces so that center ply grain is at 90-degree angle to grain of outer plies. Use waterproof glue. Cut wheels to size on band saw and sand with disc sander or turn on lathe. Bore 1-inch holes through center.
15. Cut the steel pins to length (16 or 20 penny nails).
16. Sand all surfaces, and apply desired finish.
17. Mount the wheels.

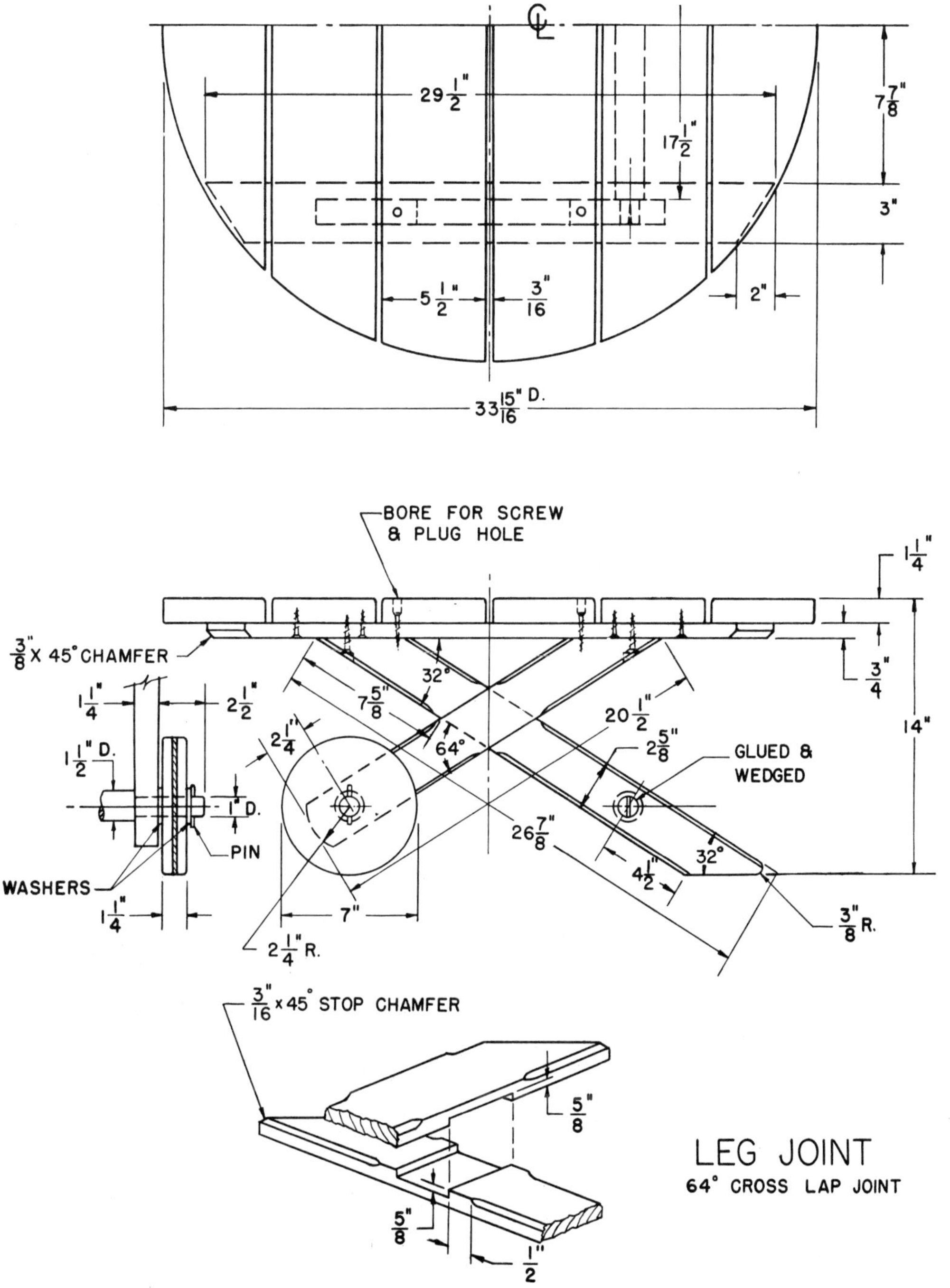

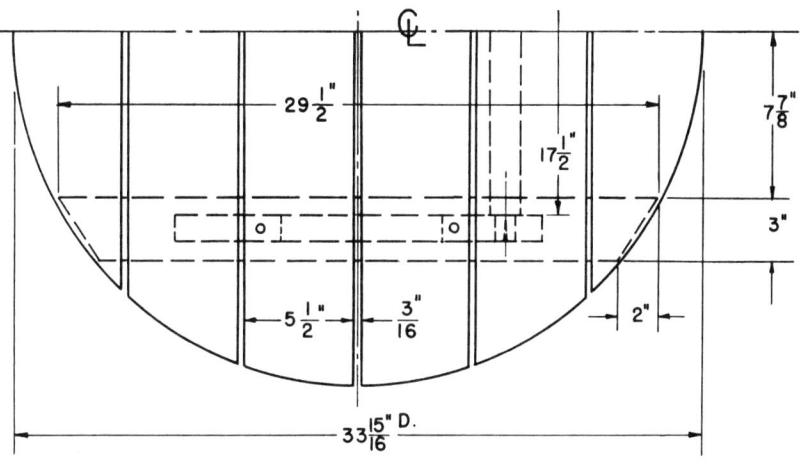

BORE FOR SCREW
& PLUG HOLE

$\frac{3}{8}$" X 45° CHAMFER

$1\frac{1}{4}$"

$2\frac{1}{2}$"

$1\frac{1}{2}$" D.

$2\frac{1}{4}$"

32°

$7\frac{5}{8}$"

$20\frac{1}{2}$"

$2\frac{5}{8}$"

64°

GLUED &
WEDGED

1" D.

PIN

WASHERS

$26\frac{7}{8}$"

$4\frac{1}{2}$"

32°

$\frac{3}{8}$" R.

$1\frac{1}{4}$"

$1\frac{1}{4}$"

7"

$2\frac{1}{4}$" R.

$\frac{3}{16}$" x 45° STOP CHAMFER

$\frac{5}{8}$"

$\frac{5}{8}$"

$\frac{1}{2}$"

LEG JOINT
64° CROSS LAP JOINT

$1\frac{1}{4}$"

$\frac{3}{4}$"

14"

**70-9d.** Drawings for the coffee table.

## CAN YOU ANSWER THESE QUESTIONS ON CONSTRUCTION?

1. How does a mobile home differ from other kinds of house construction?
2. Approximately what percentage of homes in the United States have wood-frame construction?
3. What is the most common method of framing a home?
4. Tell how to build a scale model.
5. What is the value of building outdoor furniture?

**Section XII**

**UNIT 71.**

# PATTERNMAKING AND MODEL MAKING

**Patternmaking** and model making are two areas of woodwork that demand very precise workmanship. Figure 71-1.

### PATTERNS

A pattern is a duplicate of something that will be cast of metal or plastic. Many parts of the machines that you use every day start as patterns made of wood. Figure 71-2.

In order to understand how a pattern is used, think in terms of three stages—pattern to mold to casting. A *pattern* is used to make a mold. The pattern forms an impression in a substance that will hold the shape of the pattern. This is the same principle you may have used when pushing an object into modeling clay and removing it to see the result. The hollow portion formed is the *mold cavity*. The term "mold," however, can be used to refer to just the cavity or to the cavity along with the surrounding substance. Two halves of a mold are placed together, with the hollow portion enclosed and an opening extending to the outside. The mold can then be used to make a *casting* by pouring molten metal into this open-

ing. Metal that is molten has been heated enough to become liquid. The quality of the casting is dependent on the design and quality of the wood pattern. This is why patternmaking is a very precise art.

There are two types of patterns—simple and split. A *simple*, or *solid*, *pattern* has only one piece. It has no loose

**71-1a. The patternmaker must be a skilled worker, since all measurements must be very precise. This pattern will be used to cast a metal part.**

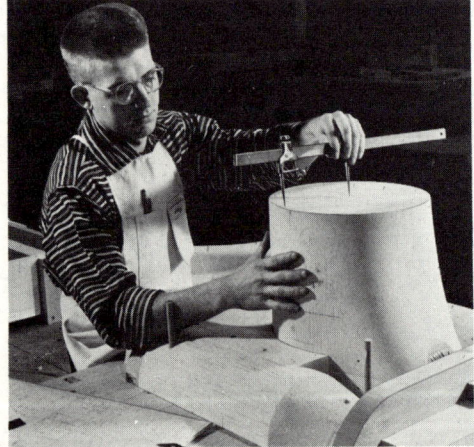

parts and is not divided, or split, in any way. Simple patterns with at least one flat side are usually made in one piece. Several pieces of wood may be used in constructing the pattern, but all are permanently fastened together before the mold is made. Figure 71-3.

A *split pattern* is made of two or more parts. Most round or irregular-shaped patterns are split to make casting easier. The pattern is divided for use in both halves of the mold. Figure 71-4.

Split patterns are made with dowel pins and holes so that the two parts will line up properly when the mold is made. The dowels are permanently fastened in one side of the pattern. Matching holes are drilled in the other half of the pattern. The length of each dowel should be twice its widest diameter. The half that is ex-

posed should be tapered somewhat so that it is about half diameter at the base.

## Patternmaking Principles

Before you make a pattern, it will help you to know something about the materials and techniques used.

The same types of tools and machines are used in making patterns as are used in other woodworking activities.

The best woods for patterns are white pine, mahogany, and cherry. Most patterns are made from white pine because it is somewhat less expensive, fairly easy to work, and very stable. Mahogany is excellent but is more expensive. The

**71-2.** Many machine parts used in the lab, such as the table and base of this drill press, are made from castings.

**71-1b.** This model maker is fitting parts of a new jet aircraft together.

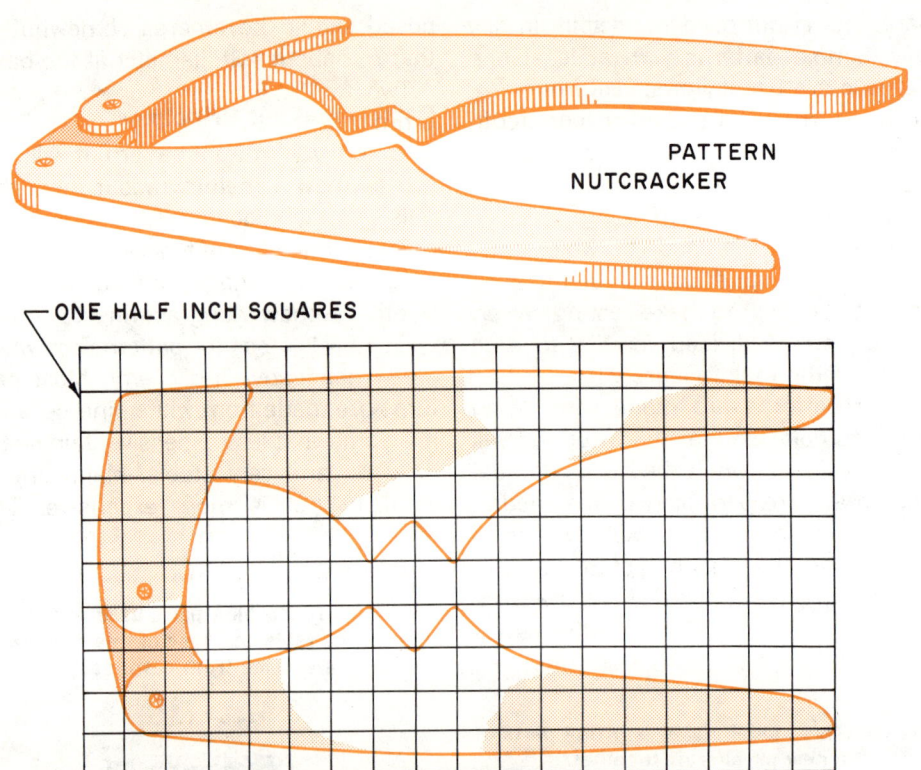

PATTERN
NUTCRACKER

ONE HALF INCH SQUARES

**71-3.** This nutcracker can be made from several one-piece patterns. Each part is molded separately as a single piece. Once all parts have been cast, they can be assembled to make the nutcracker.

**71-4.** A split pattern for a paperweight anvil. Note the dowels used on this split pattern.

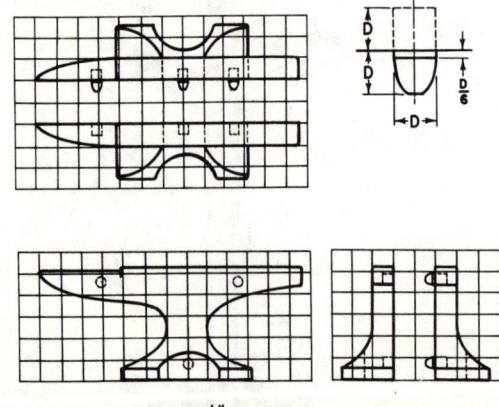

$\frac{1}{4}"$ SQUARES

wood must be kiln dried and free of any knots or other imperfections. For some simple (one-piece) patterns exterior waterproof plywood can be used.

A pattern in use tends to absorb moisture from the damp sand used to form the mold cavity. To reduce this problem, the pattern is covered with a shellac finish. The finish for patterns is described in Unit 45. If wood parts must be glued up to make the pattern, always use a waterproof glue. See Unit 13. Liquid hide glue can be used for simple patterns.

Metal always contracts (gets smaller) as it cools after it is poured to make a casting. Therefore on most patterns a shrinkage allowance is specified, depending on the kind of material. These allowances are as follows: *cast iron*—$\frac{3}{32}$ to $\frac{1}{8}$ inch (2.5 to 3 mm) per foot; *brass*—$\frac{3}{16}$ inch (5 mm) per foot; *bronze*—$\frac{5}{32}$ inch (4 mm) per foot; and *aluminum*—$\frac{1}{8}$ to $\frac{5}{32}$ inch (3 to 4 mm) per foot.

To simplify making a pattern, a shrink rule is used. This is a scale on which each inch (mm) is slightly longer than the standard inch (mm). There is a different shrink rule for each kind of metal. For example, if the pattern is cast of brass, a shrink rule that is about $\frac{3}{16}$ inch (5 mm) longer per foot (305 mm) is used. It must be remembered that shrinkage allowances are only approximate, since the exact amount depends on the size and kind of casting. For this reason, shrink rules are not used in making small patterns or in model making.

If a pattern is to be machined or finished in any other way, some additional material must be allowed. On small cast-ings, about $\frac{1}{8}$ inch (3 mm) is allowed for machining operations.

Two terms you should know in patternmaking are draft and fillet. *Draft* is a slight taper on the vertical sides of a pattern. This makes it easier to draw the pattern out of the mold. The general rule is to taper each side $\frac{1}{8}$ inch (3 mm) for each foot (305 mm) of surface to be drawn. Figure 71-5. The draft slopes away from the pattern face. On one-piece patterns an adequate draft can be obtained by adjusting saw cuts to an angle of 2 to 3 degrees.

A *fillet* is a concave piece of material used to round off the sharp inside corners of patterns. Fillets are usually wax, wood, or leather. The fillet lessens the danger of breakage, by rounding sharp corners in the mold cavity. Figure 71-6. It also helps prevent cracks and corner shrinkage.

**71-6.** Installing a leather fillet on a pattern with a fillet tool. This is done to round sharp corners which could break off the sand mold when the part is removed from the mold.

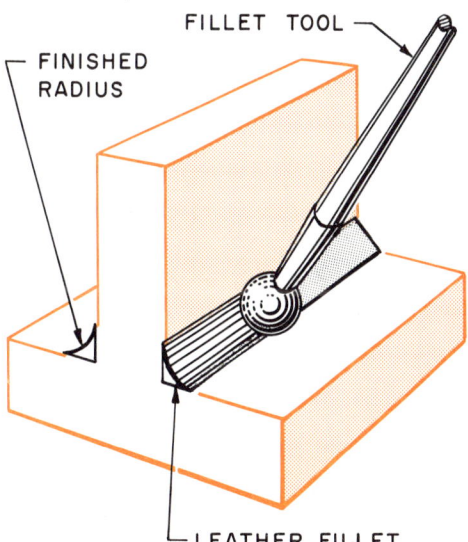

FILLET TOOL

FINISHED RADIUS

LEATHER FILLET

**71-5.** Note the direction the draft has been cut to make the pattern easier to draw (pull) from the mold.

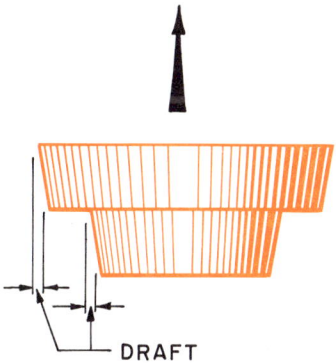

DIRECTION FOR DRAWING FROM SAND.

DRAFT

**71-7.** Common commercial patterns available for casting.

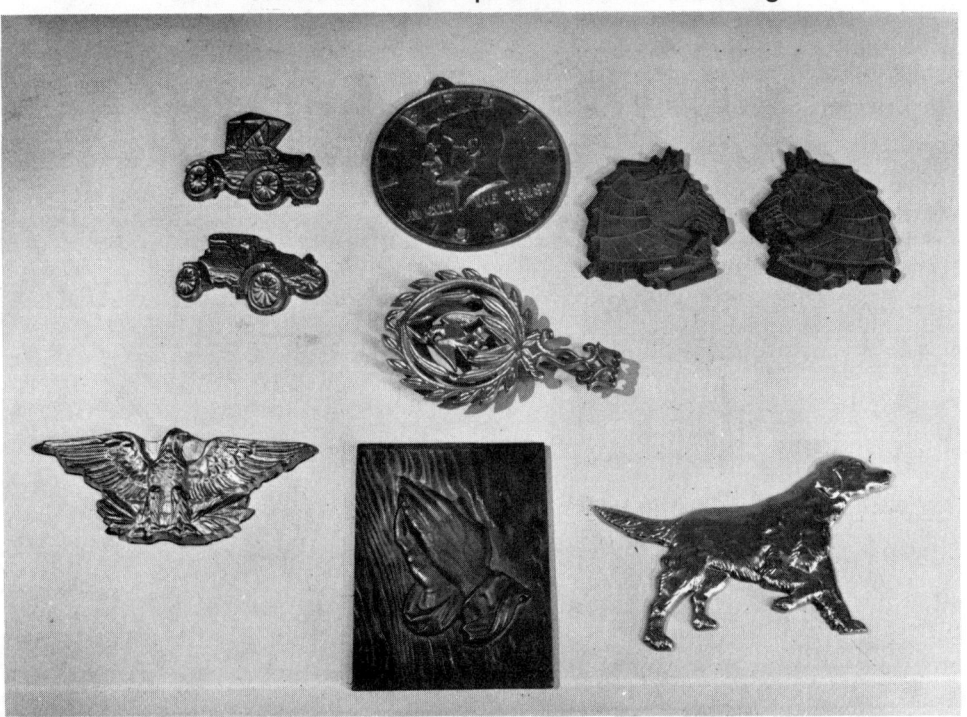

You may be interested in securing ready-made patterns. *Pattern letters* and *numbers* are of white metal and are available in many sizes and designs. They are used in simple one-piece patterns to make nameplates and house numbers. *Commercial patterns,* usually of metal, are available for making all kinds of decorative items. Figure 71-7.

### Making a Simple Pattern

A simple one-piece pattern, such as the penholder shown in Figure 71-8, is made as follows:

1. Obtain a suitable material, such as a piece of soft white pine about 5 x 7 inches (127 x 178 mm).

2. Square up the stock.

3. Plane or cut a slight draft toward the top side on the edges and ends.

4. Sand all surfaces thoroughly.

5. Apply two or three coats of orange shellac to all wood surfaces.

6. The pattern is now ready for casting.

### CASTING

In the early part of this unit, you read a little about how a pattern is used to make a mold into which molten metal is poured to make a casting. Now that you have learned how to make a pattern, you are ready to learn more about using that pattern to make a casting.

In sand casting (the simplest method of casting), a pattern is first made of wood, metal, plastic, or wax, with wood the most common choice. Figure 71-9. As you know, the pattern must be made slightly larger than the finished casting will be. (Remember that metal shrinks as it cools. Also, some areas of the cast part may need machining.) The pattern is placed on a molding board and a *drag* placed around it. A *drag* is one-half of an open box called a *flask*. Note that Figure 71-9 shows a one-piece pattern in use. Specially prepared sand or synthetic material is then rammed (pressed) around the pattern. This is called *ramming-up.* The mold is also vented to allow gases to escape by inserting a long needle into the sand close to but not touching the pattern. Another board, called a bottom board, is placed over the drag. The entire

**71-8.** A penholder that can be made with a simple pattern.

**71-9a.** To make a casting the pattern is first placed on the molding board with the draft side up.

**71-9b.** The drag side of the mold is rammed with sand and then inverted.

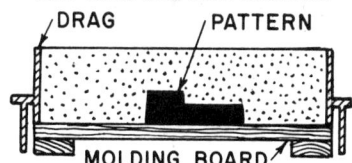

unit is then turned over, with the molding board on top and the bottom board on the bottom. The molding board is removed and fine parting sand is sprinkled over the surface. The cope (the other half of the flask) is placed over the drag. The parting sand in between prevents the two parts of the mold from sticking. A *sprue* (tapered pin) is placed about 2 or 3 inches (51 to 76 mm) away from the pattern. This provides the opening through which the molten metal is poured. Sometimes a *riser* (a straight pin) is placed between the sprue pin and the pattern. The riser can also be placed on the opposite side of the pattern from the sprue. The riser opening holds a column of additional metal which will feed the casting as it shrinks and hardens.

Sand is then packed in the cope until it is full and rammed firm. The sprue and riser pins are removed from the sand, leaving holes through the top half of the sand. A long metal needle is used to pierce holes in the sand to let out gas that may be trapped in the mold. The cope is then carefully lifted off and placed to one side. Next the pattern is carefully removed. A *gate* (channel) is cut from the mold cavity, where the pattern was, to the sprue and riser holes. This provides a track for the molten metal to

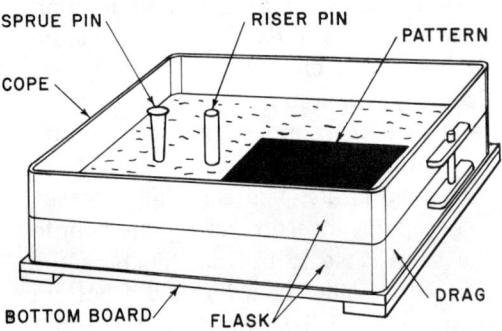

**71-9c.** The cope side is placed over the drag and the sprue and riser pins installed.

**71-9d.** After the cope has been rammed with sand, it is placed to one side and the pattern and pins are removed.

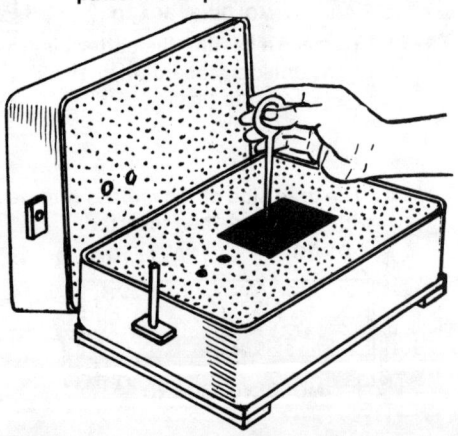

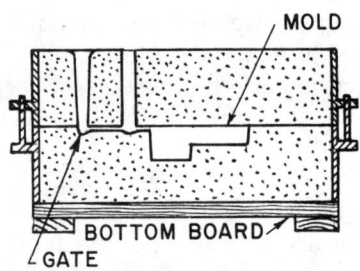

**71-9e.** The mold is closed.

**71-9f.** Molten metal is poured into the sprue hole to make the casting.

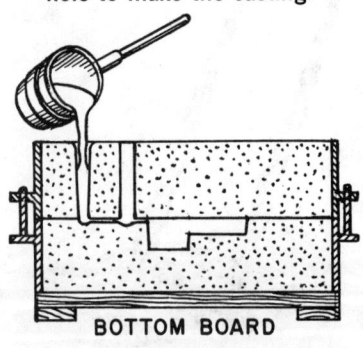

follow. The cope is then replaced. Molten metal is poured into the sprue hole to fill up the mold. After the metal has cooled, the sand is broken up in order to remove the casting. Some metal will have hardened outside the actual casting. These unusable parts—metal from the gate, sprue, and riser holes—are cut off. The casting is then ready for finishing.

If a split pattern is used, only half of the pattern is packed in the drag. When the drag is turned over, the other pattern half is placed on the drag. Dowel pins are inserted in the holes so the pattern pieces fit together correctly. Then the sand can be packed in the cope around the second half of the pattern.

Castings can be made from steel, aluminum, brass, bronze, copper, magnesium, and many other metals and alloys. Castings may range in size from a few ounces to several tons.

## MODELS

Whenever a design for a new product, such as a space shuttle, is to be pro-

**71-10.** This wood model of a space shuttle has been covered with fiber glass. It can be used for display purposes or for wind tunnel tests.

duced, the model maker must first build a scale *model.* The model is often cast in plastic or metal for wind tunnel tests. Usually models are irregular in design and vary in shape along their length. Figure 71-10. Full-size mock-ups of vehicles are also made of wood to check the design before production begins. Figure 71-11.

### Making a Model

1. Obtain a scale drawing with cross sections shown in full size. These sections, which are like slices of the object, are detail drawings showing the shape of the model at different positions along its length.

**71-11.** Sometimes a full-scale mock-up of wood is made. This section of the DC-10, 3-engine plane was built of wood so that all design elements could be checked out carefully.

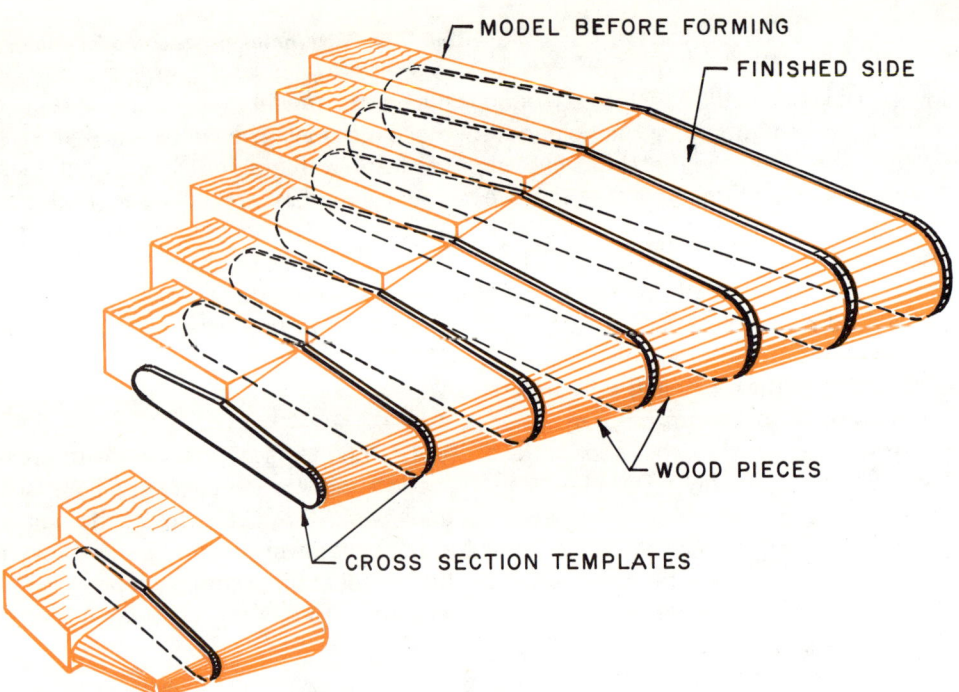

**MODEL BEFORE FORMING**

**FINISHED SIDE**

**WOOD PIECES**

**CROSS SECTION TEMPLATES**

**71-12.** Note how the cross section templets have been glued in place to serve as guides in shaping the model. The blocks of wood have been formed on the right side of the model and are ready to be formed on the left.

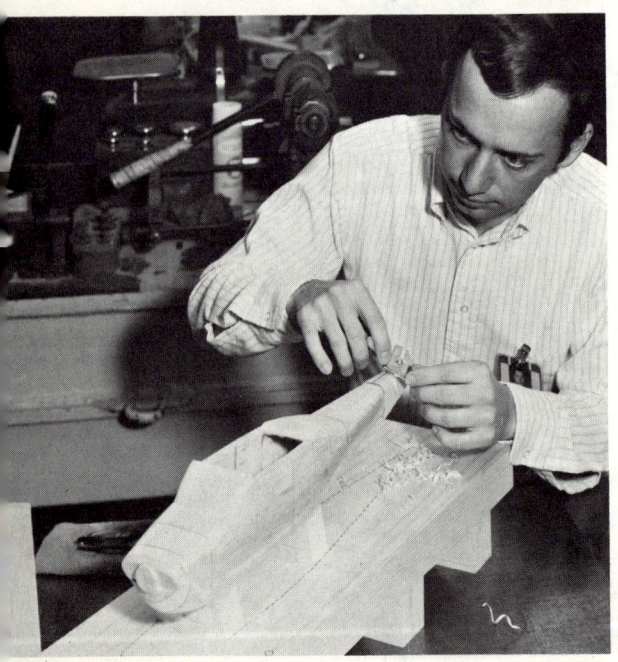

2. Make a copy of the scale drawing that can be cut up.

3. Cut out the paper cross sections, leaving them somewhat oversize and glue them to thin $\frac{1}{16}$-inch (1.5 mm) plywood or hardboard. These will be your templets (patterns).

4. Cut the templets to the correct shape. It is a good idea to leave a small straight section of the same length at the bottom of each section. This will help in aligning the templets along a center line.

5. Draw a center line on a piece of plywood or heavy wood that will be used as the work surface.

**71-13.** This technician is working down the aft (back) section of a wood model, using a small spokeshave. Note the darker lines which act as a guide.

530

**71-14.** On this model, the fuselage has been worked down to the plywood. Now the wing is attached.

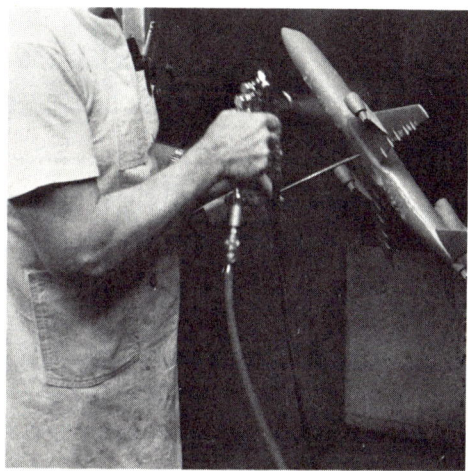

**71-15.** The completed model is usually sprayed with a metallic paint or covered with fiber glass.

6. Place the section templets at right angles to the center line at the correct locations. Check the dimensions between each division.

7. Cut mahogany blocks of the correct size to fit between the sections. The grain of the wood should run with the longitudinal axis of the model. Make the blocks slightly oversize for working them down to size. Figure 71-12.

8. Glue the parts together with white polyvinyl glue.

9. Now work the wood down, using the section divisions as a built-in templet. Figure 71-13. Both the roughing and finishing can be done with great savings in time. Figure 71-14.

10. Apply the finish. Figure 71-15. The wood model can then be used as a master for casting metal or plastic models.

## CAN YOU ANSWER THESE QUESTIONS ON PATTERN-MAKING AND MODEL MAKING?

1. Why does pattern making demand very precise workmanship?
2. What are the best woods for making patterns?
3. What is shrinkage? What causes it?
4. Describe draft. Why is it needed?
5. What is fillet?
6. Name several basic casting methods.
7. Name the two parts of a flask.
8. Describe how to build a model.

# SECTION XIII

# Materials in Woodworking

**What you must know and be able to do in Units 72–77:**

72. Two important problems related to wood that face our country: the relationship of trees to air, water, and noise pollution; how the lumber and paper industry deals with pollution.

73. How wood is classified as hard and soft; the structure of woods; how a tree grows; the parts of a tree; methods of cutting logs; how moisture affects logs; identifying the figure in wood.

74. What happens to timber from the time it is cut until it is turned into graded lumber ready for shipment; the meaning of reforestation and tree farming as related to forest conservation.

75. Major products of our American forests: saw logs; veneers and plywood; hardboard and particle board; paper; chemical products; by-products.

76. Identification of many hardwoods and softwoods: their qualities and uses.

77. The importance of research and experimentation; how to perform several wood experiments that provide information on wood and its uses.

*We all admire a rich wood finish. To appreciate quality, however, we must go back to the sources of our fine woods. We must recognize the talents and methods that men have and use as they work with woods. The subjects in this section are really as much a part of valuable woodworking experience as is the making of a product in the shop.*

# TREES AND OUR ENVIRONMENT

**Three major problems** facing our society are providing enough housing and energy and reducing pollution. Trees play a key role in all of these. Wood and wood products are important for home building and for saving energy. That is, a well-built home will be well insulated, so it will not waste heating energy. Also, forests collect and regulate the flow of water needed for home and industrial use. They prevent soil erosion which would waste the land and pollute rivers. Trees provide us with oxygen. Figure 72-1. Without trees we might have a standard and style of living similar to that of people who live in deserts.

Each American uses an average of 65 cubic feet of wood a year. This is 50 percent more than the citizens of timber-rich Russia and three and one-half times as much as the English. American foresters must grow the equivalent of a block of wood 48 feet wide, 48 feet thick, and 1,000 miles long each year to meet our need for forest products. The demand for forest products will double during the next thirty years.

## HOUSING AND FURNISHINGS

Three-quarters of all homes erected in the United States have wood frames. These modern homes with heating and air conditioning provide us with our most important environment. Larger homes are built today than in the recent past. During a recent ten-year period the average living space in a home increased 30 percent. Many homes are built on a mass basis. Factory fabrication of houses and house components is increasing in importance. Factories produce mobile homes, modular units, and completely manufactured homes.

Wood is also the basic material for most furniture. Modern wood technology has been applied to the furniture industry to improve both quality and quantity of items produced. The use of plywood, veneers, particle board, and hardboard has improved appearance. New adhesives and techniques for overlaying attractive veneers have made furniture stronger. Many other materials have been combined with wood, including paper, metal, leather, ceramics, and plastics, to make much more attractive and serviceable furniture. Furniture is basically made of wood, however, because it conducts heat slowly and is pleasantly warm to the touch.

## TREES AND AIR POLLUTION

Our atmosphere is primarily a mixture of invisible, odorless, tasteless gases, mainly oxygen, nitrogen, and carbon dioxide. Air is polluted, that is, robbed of its life-sustaining qualities and made unfit for breathing, in two basic ways: by the addition of foreign substances and by changes in the proportional makeup that diminish the supply of oxygen. *All known forms of combustion consume oxygen and release carbon dioxide.* This includes our power plants, home heating systems, automobile engines, and open fires. The proportion of carbon dioxide in the atmosphere has been increasing substantially in recent years. Trees reverse this process by consuming carbon dioxide and releasing the oxygen that men and animals need. Figure 72-2. Every ton of living wood consumes 1.47 tons of carbon dioxide and releases 1.07 tons of oxygen. Trees serve as filters to clean the air of impurities. They also slow air currents and wind, causing dust particles and other solid pollutants to settle out of the air.

Too much air pollution can cause trees to die. The major air pollutants are sulphur dioxide, which is the result of burning thousands of tons of coal; ozone, which is a photochemical product caused by automobile exhaust gases; and ethylene, a gas from the burning of certain kinds of treated gasolines. These pollutants kill many types of plant life, including trees. White pine is particularly sensitive to these air pollutants. Spotted needles, yellow needles, or needles with dead tips are the most common signs of pollution damage.

## TREES AND WATER POLLUTION

Soil, trees, and water, the three greatest renewable natural resources, depend on each other for their existence. If there were no trees, the uncontrollable runoff of rain or melted snow would wash away valuable top soil and cause serious flooding downstream. Silt carried off by runoffs also creates downstream problems. By reducing rapid surface runoff and water absorption in the ground, trees give water a better chance to become clean before entering streams, rivers, and lakes. Trees, by holding soil in place, are an extremely effective barrier against erosion. Although trees will not help clear up a polluted lake or stream, they do prevent additional pollution. Soil and timber conservation practices make it possible for the land to absorb and store water, not only preventing erosion, siltation, and floods but also insuring steady and adequate water flows during drier periods.

## TREES AND NOISE POLLUTION

During the past thirty years the noise level in the average urban community has increased over eight times. Noise is a cause of frustration which is associated with difficulty in concentration, disturbance of rest and sleep, and aggravation of certain mental disorders. Proper placement of trees and shrubs can reduce noise level up to 50 percent. It is important to have a good growth of shrubs and trees in every residential neighborhood

**72-1.** Without trees and the sea to produce enough oxygen, we might have to wear life support equipment such as the astronauts use.

as well as along highways, not only for beauty but also for noise control.

## POLLUTION IN THE LUMBER AND PAPER INDUSTRY

Modern technology not only gives us the good things of life but also causes many of our pollution problems. In order to use trees for wood and pulp for paper making, it is necessary to process the materials. This requires industrial complexes. In years past, the saw mill with its wigwam-shaped burner caused a good deal of smoke and air pollution. These have been largely replaced through modern technology. Paper and pulp mills, however, have been a major cause of pollution in rivers. Much of the wood chips that result from processing lumber are used for other purposes. Some go into particle-board manufacture. Others

are sent to pulp manufacturing plants to be made into paper. Unfortunately, in the process of making pulp for paper, a great many pollutants, particularly hydrochloric acid, have been dumped into the rivers. Many conscientious people are working to add treatment facilities for removing solid pollutants and chemicals from water before it is returned to streams.

Obviously, trees are vital in our environment, and yet using trees for lumber and paper products has helped cause air and water pollution to increase dramatically in recent years. Now industries have become conscious of their responsibility to society and are beginning to clean the water and air that they use. Pollution control systems are now installed as a fundamental part of all new plants. Many older plants are adding mechanical,

**72-2.** The trees and the ocean absorb the carbon dioxide from burning fossil fuels and return a good supply of important oxygen to the air we breathe. Four tons of oxygen per year are produced by one acre of growing forest, enough for 18 people a year. About 40 percent of the earth's oxygen is produced by growing forests and other green land plants. Photosynthesis by ocean plant life produces most of the remaining supply. Trees consume only solar energy and convert carbon dioxide, moisture, and solar energy into wood fiber at the rate of four tons per acre annually.

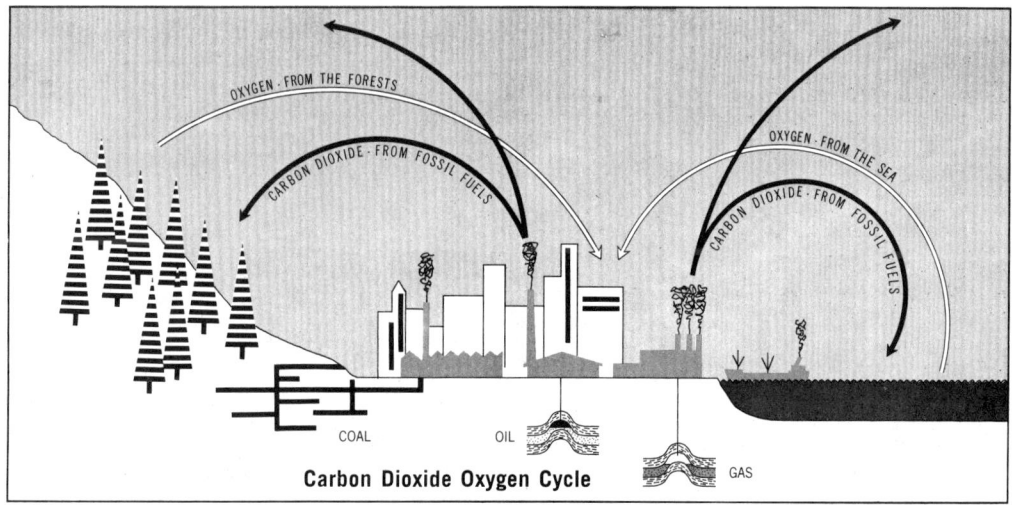

Carbon Dioxide Oxygen Cycle

chemical, electrical, and other devices to remove pollutants, to reduce them, or to change them into less harmful forms.

## WOOD AND ENERGY

Because of its dominant position in American home-building, wood makes a substantial contribution to energy conservation. Expanding the use and thickness of insulation in homes and increasing the use of wood-frame construction in other types of buildings can result in even greater energy savings. The following facts make a persuasive case for the use of wood and wood fiber for construction (Figure 72-3):

- Wood is the only renewable industrial raw material.
- Trees are being regenerated in an endless cycle—so long as there is soil, moisture, and the heat and light of the sun to promote growth.
- Trees, while growing, consume only solar energy.
- Trees convert carbon dioxide, moisture, and solar energy into wood fiber at the average rate of four tons per acre annually.

- Conversion of wood from the raw to the finished state, regardless of its form, consumes very little energy. Thus, much less fuel is consumed than for production of any comparable industrial building material.

- Use of wood wherever practical would substantially extend the supply of resources such as bauxite, iron ore, coal, petroleum and natural gas, which cannot be replaced. Sound forest management, as a national policy, can guarantee adequate supplies of timber to meet all foreseeable timber requirements.

- Among the major raw material resources, only wood is biodegradable. That is, it will break down into harmless, non-polluting substances. It contributes little to pollution problems at the source, during manufacture, in use, or after disposal. Many substances require much energy for recycling or other disposal. Wood does not.

- Wood insulates six times better than brick, 15 times better than concrete and 1,770 times better than aluminum.

**72-3.** A well-built home can help conserve energy.

1. What are the two major problems facing the United States that involve trees?
2. How much wood must be grown each year to satisfy our need for wood products?
3. How can trees help prevent water pollution?
4. What are the major causes of pollution in paper manufacture?
5. How can the increased use of wood help conserve our energy supply?

Section
XIII
UNIT 73.

# TREES AND LUMBER

**Almost everyone** knows what an oak, maple, or birch tree looks like, but only a few people can identify all kinds. A tree is a woody plant growing at least 20 feet (6.1 m) tall, with a single self-supporting stem or trunk. Wood makes up the bulk of the tree stem. You see wood every day in many different forms, including paper, plastics, and chemicals, as well as the familiar forms of solid wood and plywood.

Since woods are the raw material of woodworking, it is a good idea to learn about their classification, structure, parts, and identification.

## HARD AND SOFT WOODS

There are several ways to classify woods as hard or soft. One of the most common is to divide all trees into two classes: those that shed their leaves annually and those which produce cones. Those which shed their leaves—including oak, walnut, maple, ash, basswood, birch, cherry, and gumwood—are called

*hardwoods*. These trees have broad leaves. Figure 73-1. Those that produce cones (conifers)—including fir, pine, cedar, spruce, and redwood—are called *softwoods*. These trees have needles or scalelike leaves. Figure 73-2. In this method of classification, however, many of the so-called softwoods are harder than some of the hardwoods.

For purposes of use, woods are classified according to their *actual hardness* or *ability to resist wear*. In this method, which is most practical for the woodworker to follow, we have the following classifications:

| HARD | MEDIUM HARD | SOFT |
|---|---|---|
| Ash | Fir, Douglas | Basswood |
| Beech | Gum | Pine, |
| Birch | Mahogany, true | Ponderosa |
| Cherry | Mahogany, | Pine, Sugar |
| Maple | Philippine | Poplar |
| Oak, red | Walnut | Redwood |
| Oak, white | | Willow |

**73-1a.** A stand of mixed hardwood, including white ash.

**73-1b.** Twigs and leaves of white ash.

| OPEN GRAIN | CLOSED GRAIN |
|---|---|
| Ash | Basswood |
| Mahogany, true | Beech |
| Mahogany, | Birch |
| Philippine | Cherry |
| Oak, red | Gum |
| Oak, white | Maple |
| Walnut | Poplar |
| Willow | Fir, Douglas |
| | Pine, Ponderosa |
| | Pine, Sugar |
| | Redwood |

Another important method of classification is based on whether the wood has open or closed grain.* The wood finisher, especially, is concerned with this distinction because the open-grained woods offer greater opportunity for finishes and contrasting filler colors.

## STRUCTURE OF WOODS

Wood is so commonplace that we often take it for granted. A solid chunk of wood, however, is an intricate arrangement of strong, though tiny, cells when seen under a microscope. If you trim the surface of a piece of wood with a sharp knife and look at it under a 10x hand lens, you can see this cellular network. Figure 73-3.

The majority of wood cells are long and thin with tapered ends, rather like hollow toothpicks. Saying that they are long, however, means only that they are much longer than they are wide. For example, cells from white pine wood are about 4 millimetres long, which is about twice as long as this capital I. The long dimension of wood cells is nearly parallel to the long direction of the tree stem. Whether you see the large or small dimension of the cell depends on how the wood is cut.

*Open grain woods have larger pores than closed grain woods.

**73-1c.** A map showing where white ash grows.

The map shows the range of WHITE ASH, *Fraxinus americana*, with a scale bar marked MILES, 100, 0, 200.

**73-2a.** Trees like these big Douglas firs grow very slowly and may deteriorate and die when they become old. In commercial forests big trees are "clear cut" in blocks, leaving others standing to grow and reseed logged-off tracts.

**73-2b.** Douglas fir branch with cones.

539

Cells, which are about as fine as human hairs, are lined with still finer, spiral-wound strands of *cellulose.* The cells themselves are held together with a substance called *lignin.*

The arrangement of cells in a piece of *softwood* is shown in Figure 73-4a. There are three faces of wood—the cross sectional, radial, and tangential. The cross sectional face is the surface you see if you cut across a tree stem or look down at a tree stump.

When you look at the *hardwood* block, Figure 73-4b, you can see both similarities to, and differences from, the softwood. There are the same three faces and the general structure is similar, with the long dimension of most of the cells parallel to the length of the tree. How-ever, you find a greater variety of cells in hardwood than in softwood, and the cells are not arranged in the orderly radial rows found in the softwood.

## HOW A TREE GROWS

The cells provide the passageways into the tree for water and other growth-giving materials from the earth. During the spring and early summer when there is much moisture, the tree grows rapidly. Springwood, or early wood, is formed at this time. In the summer and fall, the tree develops more slowly. Summerwood, or late wood, forms during this time. When you look at a cross section of a tree, you can see the dark summerwood rings, called annual growth rings. Figure 73-5. Some idea of the age of the tree can be obtained by counting these rings.

## PARTS OF A TREE

Figure 73-6 shows the cross section of a tree trunk. Beginning at the center is a porous material called the *pith.* This sometimes becomes rotten, leaving a hollow center in the tree. Around the pith is the mature wood, the *heartwood.* This is generally darker in color because of the presence of resin and other materials during the many years of growth. Beyond the heartwood is the newer growth of *sapwood,* which is usually lighter in color. Between the sapwood and the inner bark is a pitchlike material called *cambium* in which the cell formation takes place to form more sapwood. Radiating out from the pith center of the tree are ray cells or *medullary rays.* These cell-like structures form passageways for food in feeding the tree for growth and development. The *outer bark* (protecting the tree) is the dead, corky covering that varies in thickness with the kind of tree. The *inner bark* (bast or phloem) carries the food made

**73-2c.** A map showing where Douglas firs grow.

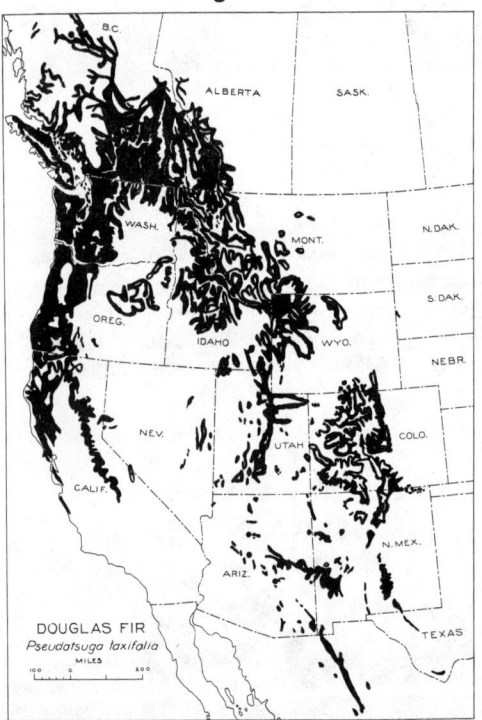

**73-2d.** Life span of a Douglas fir. Within its first 8 or 9 years, a fir may be harvested for a Christmas tree. At 30 years the lower limbs have begun to prune themselves as nearby trees shut off sunlight. When 50 to 60 years old, a tree may have reached a height of 100 feet (30.5 m) or more. It could be used as pulp for paper making or for a utility pole.

in the leaves down to the branches, trunk, and roots.

## METHODS OF CUTTING LOGS

Boards are cut from logs in two major ways. The cheapest and most economical is called *plain sawed* (when it is a hardwood tree) or *flat grained* (when it is a softwood tree). The log is squared and sawed lengthwise from one side to the other. *Quarter sawed* (for hardwood) or *edge grained* (for softwood) is a more expensive method of cutting. This shows

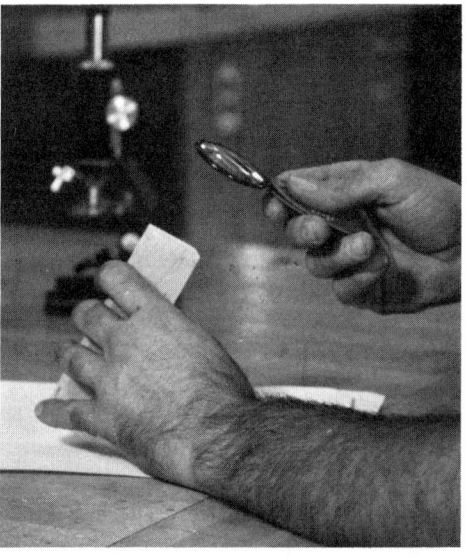

**73-3.** Studying the structure of wood with a hand lens.

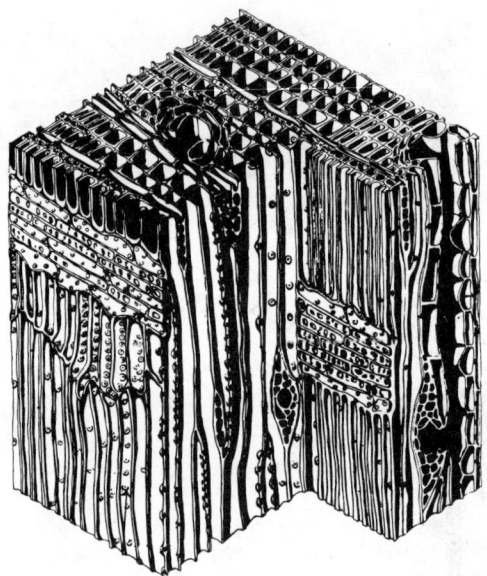

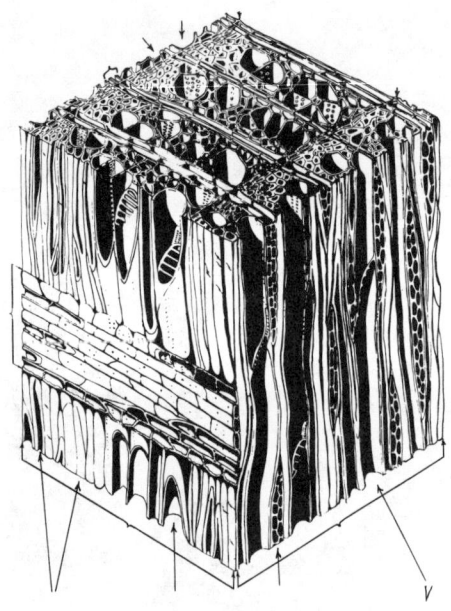

**73-4a.** An enlarged view of softwood, showing the tube structure. Here you can see why it is easier to cut with the grain than across it. The three faces of wood are also shown: (1) cross sectional; (2) radial; (3) tangential.

**73-4b.** Notice the different wood structure in hardwood. Can you see why it would be more difficult to cut and shape than softwood?

a better grain pattern, especially in oak and other hardwood. In quarter sawed lumber, the wood is cut parallel to the medullary rays, as shown in Figure 73-7. Wood is quarter sawed also to prevent warpage and to provide a better wearing surface.

## MOISTURE CONTENT AND SEASONING

When a tree is cut down, it may contain between 30 and 300 percent moisture. Before the wood can be used, a large part of this moisture must be re-

**73-5.** Section of a log showing the annual rings.

moved. This is done by air and/or kiln drying. See Unit 74.

Moisture in green wood exists both inside the cells and in the cell walls. In drying, the free water inside the cell cavities is removed first. When all of this is gone, it is said to be at the *fiber-saturation point,* and the wood will still contain about 23 to 30 percent moisture. When the water in the cell walls begins to evaporate, the wood shrinks in size. When wood is dried to 15 percent moisture, it will have attained about half its total shrinkage. As you read in an early unit, lumber for house framing construction dried to 19 percent, or less, moisture is called *dry* lumber and that above 19 percent is called *green* lumber. Lumber for furniture construction, however, should have only about 6 to 10 percent moisture content. If wood has too much moisture when the project is built, the wood will continue to dry out in the shop and at home, causing warpage and cracked joints. Remember, wood will continue to dry out or take on moisture until the moisture in the wood equals the moisture in the air.

## SHRINKAGE AND SWELLING

Wood shrinks as it dries and swells as it absorbs moisture. The way shrinkage affects lumber cut from different sections of a log is shown in Figure 73-8. Most of the difficulties of shrinkage and swelling can be avoided by making sure the wood has been dried to the correct moisture content. Wood shrinks or swells very little lengthwise. Most of the change in size is across the grain. However, flat-grained or plain-sawed lumber will change almost twice as much in width as quarter-sawed or edge-grained stock. Can you see why?

## FIGURE IN WOOD

A figure in wood is the pattern formed by the coloring matter, by the annular rings and the medullary rays, and by cross grain, wavy grain, knots, and other irregularities. As already mentioned, there is generally a difference in color between the darker heartwood and the

**73-7.** Two common methods of cutting lumber: A. Plain-sawed lumber (flat-grained); B. Quarter-sawed lumber (edge-grained).

**73-6.** Cross section of a tree trunk showing: a. Cambium; b. Phloem; c. Bark; d. Sapwood; e. Heartwood; f. Pith; g. Medullary ray.

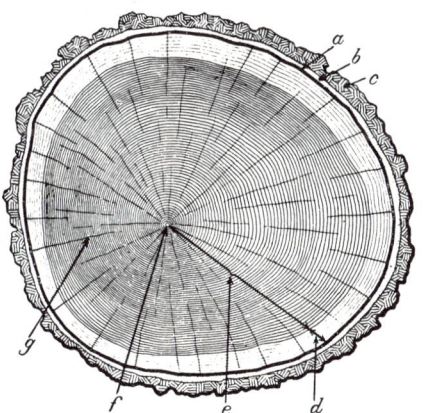

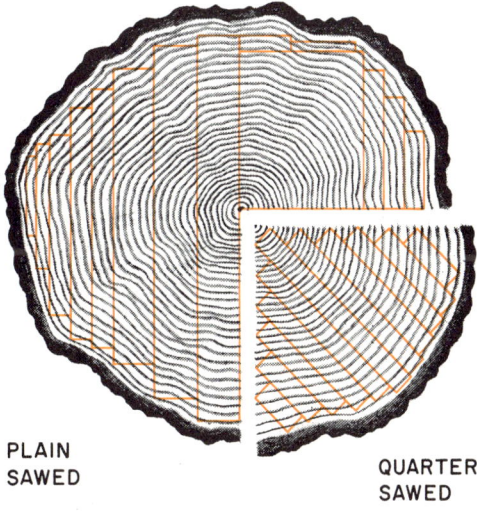

PLAIN SAWED

QUARTER SAWED

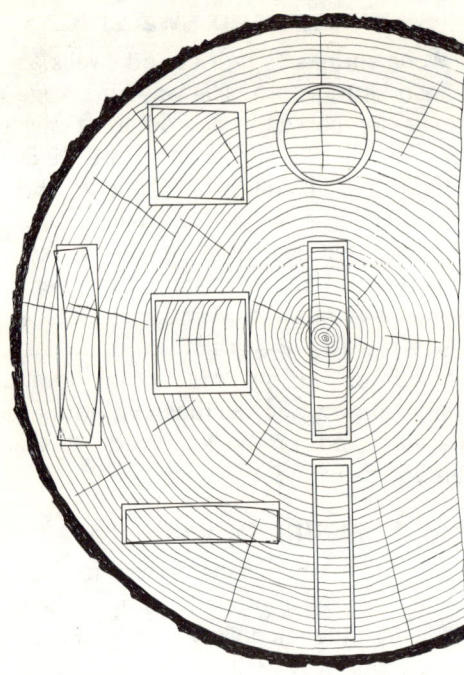

lighter sapwood. Some woods, such as walnut and gumwood, contain darker streaks that give the wood a distinctive figure. All woods have some figure, but often it is so difficult to see that the wood is considered uninteresting. The woods that have a distinct figure are considered superior for fine furniture. You'll find that no two pieces of wood have the same figure. This difference adds interest and beauty to a well-constructed piece of furniture.

**73-8.** Here you see how lumber will warp when cut from different parts of the log.

## CAN YOU ANSWER THESE QUESTIONS ON TREES AND LUMBER?

1. Name the substance that holds the tubes or cells of a tree together.
2. At what time does most of the growth take place in trees?
3. How can you determine the age of a tree?
4. What are the three ways to classify wood?
5. For *use*, which of the following woods are classified as hardwoods: oak, maple, white pine, fir, poplar, ash, hickory?
6. What is the advantage of quarter sawed lumber?
7. What is "fiber-saturation point"?
8. What forms the figure in wood?

# LUMBERING

**Lumbering** has always been one of the most fascinating and romantic of occupations. It has been glorified in song and story in our history. However, although some lumbering practices have not changed in the last hundred years, most lumbering has become mechanized and modernized into a highly efficient process. The actual methods of lumbering vary with geographic location and the size of the company. Generally speaking, however, the procedure includes cutting the trees, taking them to the mill, cutting the logs into lumber, and seasoning the lumber.

## CUTTING TREES

The first step is to locate and lay out the site for the logging camp. After this, the necessary roads and camps are built to provide working and living facilities for the men. The mature trees are marked for cutting. The first step in cutting the trees is to cut a notch in the side of the tree. This side faces the direction the tree will fall. Figure 74-1. Then, with a hand crosscut saw or a power saw, the tree is cut from the opposite side of the notch. Figure 74-2. As the cut is made, a wedge is driven into the saw kerf to force the tree to fall in the proper direction. After the tree is felled, the small branches are trimmed off. The logs are then dragged or pushed to a loading site where they are stacked. Figure 74-3.

In logging on steep slopes, an unusual method is used to move the logs from the cutting site to the landing station in the valley below. A helium-filled balloon controlled by a series of ropes picks up the log and brings it down the hill where it can be loaded on a truck. Figure 74-4. The balloon can be used over any kind of terrain, across valleys, swamps, steep slopes, standing timber, rivers, and other obstructions. This system eliminates the

**74-1.** Putting in the undercut. The logger uses a power saw to put the undercut (the lower cut of the notch) in a big pine. The notch determines the direction the tree will fall.

**74-2.** The modern method of felling timber. A wedge is driven into the saw kerf to direct the fall toward the undercut.

**74-3.** A rubber-tired skidder moves logs to the loading area on a tree farm. The skidder is one of many new pieces of equipment designed to harvest timber more efficiently.

cost and waste of road construction for logging. It also enables the logger to be selective in harvesting only the older timber on a slope, leaving the young trees undisturbed to grow under improved conditions.

## TRANSPORTING THE LOGS TO THE MILL

In years past, logs were moved to the nearest river or stream and allowed to collect there during the winter. In the spring, as the water rose, the logs were floated down the river to the mill. This still continues in some places, but it is not nearly so common. Today most logs are loaded by crane onto trucks or railroad flatcars and taken directly to the mill. Figure 74-5. At the mill they are placed in a millpond to keep them from drying out before cutting. Figure 74-6.

## LUMBER MANUFACTURE

From the millpond, the logs are taken to the mill on a bull chain. Figure 74-7. As they rise to the mill, they are sprayed with water to clean off the dirt. The bark is then removed. Figure 74-8. Inside the mill each log is loaded on a carriage which holds it as it is cut. Here the head sawyer takes over. He is one of the most important men in the mill since he knows lumber grades. He knows how to get the largest amount of high-quality lumber from each log. Figure 74-9. He does it by controlling the movement of the headrig (the carriage and the headsaw), where logs are cut into boards or timber. Small mills usually use a circular saw as a headsaw. In large mills, however, the headsaw is a band saw. As the carriage moves forward, the log is carried straight into the saw's sharp teeth. When the saw has passed through the log from one end to the other, the carriage shoots back and the position of the log is shifted for a second cut.

After the log is cut to size, it is carried by conveyors to other saws that cut it into standard sizes. Figure 74-10 (Pp. 550, 551). All soft lumber is cut into standard dimensions in thickness, width, and length. Hardwoods are cut in standard thickness only, since they are much more expensive then softwoods, and too much waste would result otherwise. In addition, the very nature of hardwood use does not require standard lengths.

**74-4.** This diagram shows the balloon system in three operating positions on a typical removal operation. 1. Balloon has been pulled up the hill by the haulback line and its own lift. When over its destination, the balloon is pulled to the ground by tightening the haulback line. Loggers secure chokers around the logs. 2. Balloon gains height as haulback is slackened. Mainline is pulled in, drawing balloon toward the landing. 3. Balloon deposits "turn" of logs at the landing as mainline is again tightened.

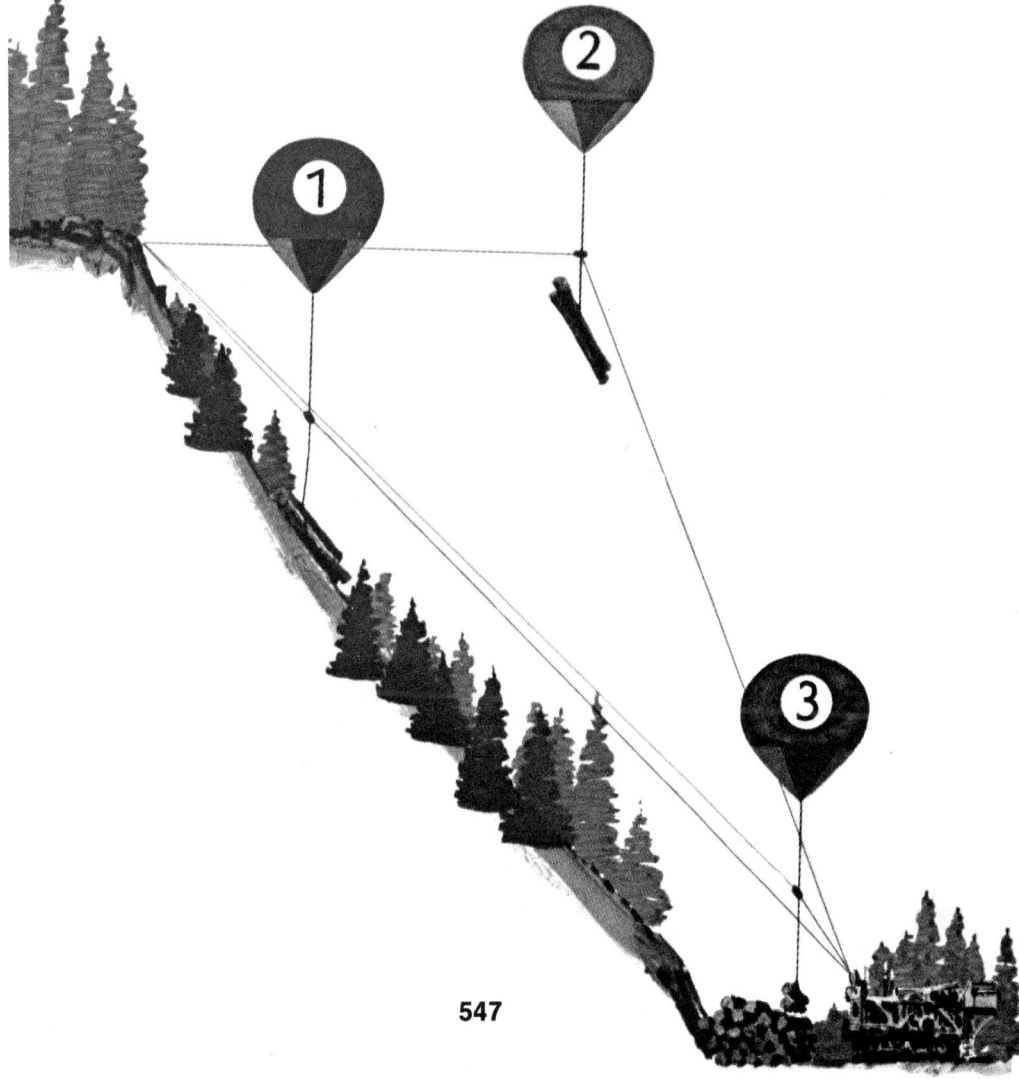

**74-5.** A huge heel-boom loader swings giant logs onto a truck on a tree farm in western Washington. Trucks transport the logs down mountain roadways for manufacture into hundreds of useful wood products.

**74-6.** Unloading logs from truck into a mill-pond. Logs are stored in water because it helps protect the wood from insect damage and decreases fire hazards.

**74-8.** Bark is blasted from logs by jets of water under 1,500 pounds of pressure at a lumber mill. Removing bark from logs is a conservation measure. It permits recovery of slabs and edgings for conversion to chips for pulp and other wood products.

**74-7.** Bull chain lifts log into mill.

Farther along the production line, an edger saws the boards into different widths, and trimmer saws cut the boards to proper lengths.

## SEASONING THE LUMBER

The "green" chain, which is a conveyor belt or chain, moves the boards into a sorting shed. Here the lumber is sorted and graded as to its size and quality. (The "green" refers to the sap moisture of the freshly cut lumber, not its color.) Then it is stacked in piles with small blocks between each piece to permit air to circulate around the wood.

Wood that comes from the mill contains a great deal of moisture. It is necessary to dry it out or season it before it is fit for use. There are two common methods of doing this. In the first, called *air drying,* the stacks of lumber are left out in the open in sheds where the wood can dry naturally over a period of several months. Much of our soft lumber is air dried. The second and more efficient way of controlling the moisture content of lumber is to dry the lumber artificially in a controlled moisture-temperature room called a kiln. Here woods are allowed to dry for several months. Then they are placed in a building usually made of cement brick or hollow tile. The stacks are first sprayed with steam. Then the steam is turned off and the building closed.

**74-9.** The head sawyer is a key man in the production of quality wood products. He saws each log into huge rough slices that are then transported through the mill for further cutting and shaping. He must know how to cut each log to get the greatest value from it.

**74-10a.** Edger saw squares edges of boards.

**74-10b.** Green chain moves boards for grading and sorting.

**74-10c.** Trimmer saw cuts boards into various lengths.

**74-10d.** Lumber is stacked for storage and drying and is frequently kiln dried before it is finished and shipped.

Warm air is circulated through the lumber. This continues over a period of two to eight days until the moisture content of the lumber is down to 6 to 10 percent. This lumber is called kiln dried. Kiln-dried lumber is the only satisfactory kind to use for furniture making and for all better construction.

## PLANING

Large sawmills usually have a planing mill section in which the rough lumber is finished by passing the boards through a set of rotating knives which give it a smooth surface. Boards are also made into flooring, siding, moldings, and other kinds of building "trim." There are also

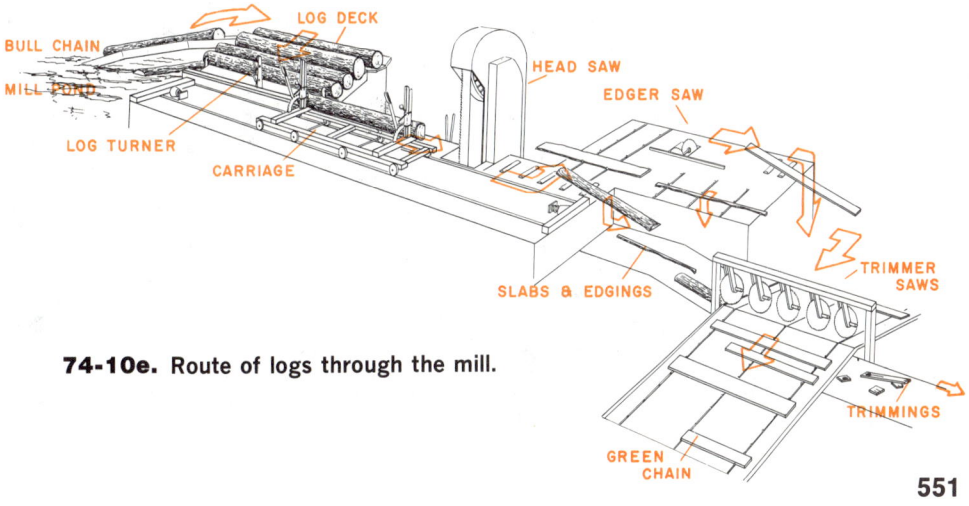

**74-10e.** Route of logs through the mill.

BULL CHAIN

MILL POND

LOG DECK

LOG TURNER

CARRIAGE

HEAD SAW

EDGER SAW

SLABS & EDGINGS

TRIMMER SAWS

TRIMMINGS

GREEN CHAIN

separate planing mills which buy rough lumber from small mills and sell the finished product, called "surface lumber." Finished lumber is again graded before it is shipped.

## FOREST CONSERVATION

Early settlers cleared forest land for farming and harvested the timber from the abundant forest reserve to provide for their needs. However, no reforestation (replanting of trees) was done and eventually people became alarmed with the dwindling timber supply. In recent years the practice of forestry management by professionally trained foresters has begun in this country. Today forest products companies do not cut and move along as they did years ago. They now grow trees as a crop. This is an economic benefit to the community. Timber is harvested on a systematic basis and new trees are planted to replace them. Figure 74-11. Presently the annual growth of timber exceeds the annual removal by about 8 percent. Our country has over 800 million acres of forest land, but only about 500 million acres are commercially

**74-11.** Timber suppliers select trees to be cut.

**74-12.** Machines have revolutionized logging and forestry in much the same way that factory and farm work have been revolutionized by automatic equipment. For example, this device is a hydraulic shear that can snip trees up to 18 inches (457 mm) in diameter like corn stalks. It is used to thin the forest. Thinning gives timber room to grow and provides a partial harvest of trees that would otherwise be lost through nature's own, but slower, survival process.

harvestable. Much of the timber grows on government-owned forest lands in our 154 national forests.

Another interesting development in forest conservation is tree farming. The American tree farm system, promoted by the forest industries, includes many thousands of certified tree farms totaling many millions of acres. With tree farming, timber is treated as a crop to be grown just like corn or wheat and is harvested and regrown to produce the maximum yield year after year. Good tree farming requires thinning, fire prevention, and fire control. Figure 74-12. Tree farmers also provide adequate protection for the trees against insects and diseases that could spoil the crop. There are more than 60 million acres in our tree farm program.

## Reforestation Methods

Wood is the one great natural resource that can be renewed by replanting. Since the United States is still growing about 8 percent more wood a year than it consumes, present demands are being met. However, this will not be enough in the years ahead. There is need to grow more trees faster with the same amount of land.

Many large lumber producers are using unusual techniques to replant the areas that have been cut. Even though the forest products industries own only 13 percent of the commercial forest land, they provide materials for more than one-third of the wood products used in the United States. The reason for this is that the timber companies practice intensive forest management. Like expert gardeners, they obtain superior crops and grow more timber than is harvested.

Two techniques widely used for planting trees are (1) with helicopters and (2) with special guns held in the hand. On rough terrain, hopper-equipped helicopters seed thousands of acres of land with new trees each year. Figure 74-13. A faster and more successful method of

**74-13.** Hopper-equipped helicopters like this one in Oregon have seeded 22,300 acres of one company's land in the West and South plus an experimental tract in Maine. This represents the first such aerial seeding in Maine's history. Another 13,700 acres not suited for aerial seeding were hand planted with young trees. These same timberlands were visited by more than 380,000 vacationers in the past year for hiking, hunting, fishing, picnicking, camping, and swimming. On a 50-year cycle, up to two percent of the forest ripens each year for the annual harvest.

growing trees is with an improved seed tree program and a planting gun. The seeds are first nursery planted in cone-shaped containers filled with a mixture of fertilizer and peat moss. After about six or eight months in the nursery, the healthy seedlings, called *plugs,* are shot into the ground with the special gun. Figure 74-14. With this technique one man can hand plant about 3½ times (about 1,500 seedlings in a day) the number of trees he could with the old method of hand planting.

**74-14.** The plugs are carefully removed from their containers and planted by a gun device recently perfected by forest researchers. Then, sun, rain, fertilizer, and the superior seedlings combine to produce faster growing, healthier trees with more usable wood fiber.

## CAN YOU ANSWER THESE QUESTIONS ON LUMBERING AND THE FOREST INDUSTRY?

1. Name the many ways in which lumbering has become mechanized.
2. What is the first step in cutting trees?
3. Why is a notch cut in the tree on the side toward which it is to fall?
4. Are most logs moved to the mill by floating them downstream?
5. Why are logs kept in a millpond for a time?
6. Describe the sawing of logs into planks, timbers, and boards.
7. Why is soft lumber cut into standard dimensions?
8. What are the two common methods of drying lumber? Which kind is better for furniture wood?
9. Explain the planing operation.
10. Are we using more wood than we are growing? Explain.

# PRODUCTS OF OUR AMERICAN FORESTS

**Our forests** are a storehouse of wealth for our use. Figure 75-1. Woods and lumbers and their by-products are such an important part of our life that we cannot list here all of their uses. Figure 75-2. There are thousands of specific uses for wood and wood products: from the lowly toothpick to the thousands of telephone and telegraph poles; from the woods used in novelties and trinkets to the woods used in home and industrial construction; and from the by-products that make paper to those used for making rayon, plastics, and other chemical materials.

America still has about 75 percent as much forest land as it had when Columbus landed. Figure 75-3 (Page 558). The total area is about 758 million acres. Of that total, about a third is set aside in parks, wilderness areas, watersheds, or is not suitable for growing commercial timber. This third of the American forest equals the total size of Norway, Sweden, Denmark, Austria, Switzerland, Holland, Belgium, and Israel.

The remaining 510 million acres is the commercial forest. This is the land that produces raw material for thousands of wood products.

Many people think that the commercial forest is owned by only a few large timber companies. However, this is not true. The biggest single owner of the commercial forest is the government, both state and federal. About 28 percent of the commercial forest land is publicly held. Private individuals, about four million persons, own almost 60 percent of the forest. The forest products industry comes in third, with control of about 12 percent of the commercial forest.

The need for wood is increasing rapidly. Contrary to what is commonly thought, namely, that wood is decreasing in use and is being replaced by metal, plastics, and other materials, nothing could be further from the truth. In the early 1980's the number of new dwellings will be more than $2\frac{1}{2}$ million a year, or 50 percent above the year 1970. Figure 75-4 (Page 558). Mobile home production will continue to increase in a similar fashion. A survey by the U.S. Forest Service indicates that by the year 2000 the demand for saw logs will be roughly double and the demand for veneer logs and pulp wood nearly triple. The total demand for industrial wood products will increase about $2\frac{1}{3}$ times. This includes such products as furniture, housing, and other wood items except fuel wood from our domestic source.

Today about 20 percent of the total lumber used in America comes from Canada and other parts of the world. At the same time, the United States exports an amount about equal to 11 percent of the total wood consumption in the United States. This means that our imports of lumber exceed the exports by about 9 percent. In order to meet the ever increasing demands for lumber, it is necessary for the United States to grow more

**555**

# Forest Regions of the United States

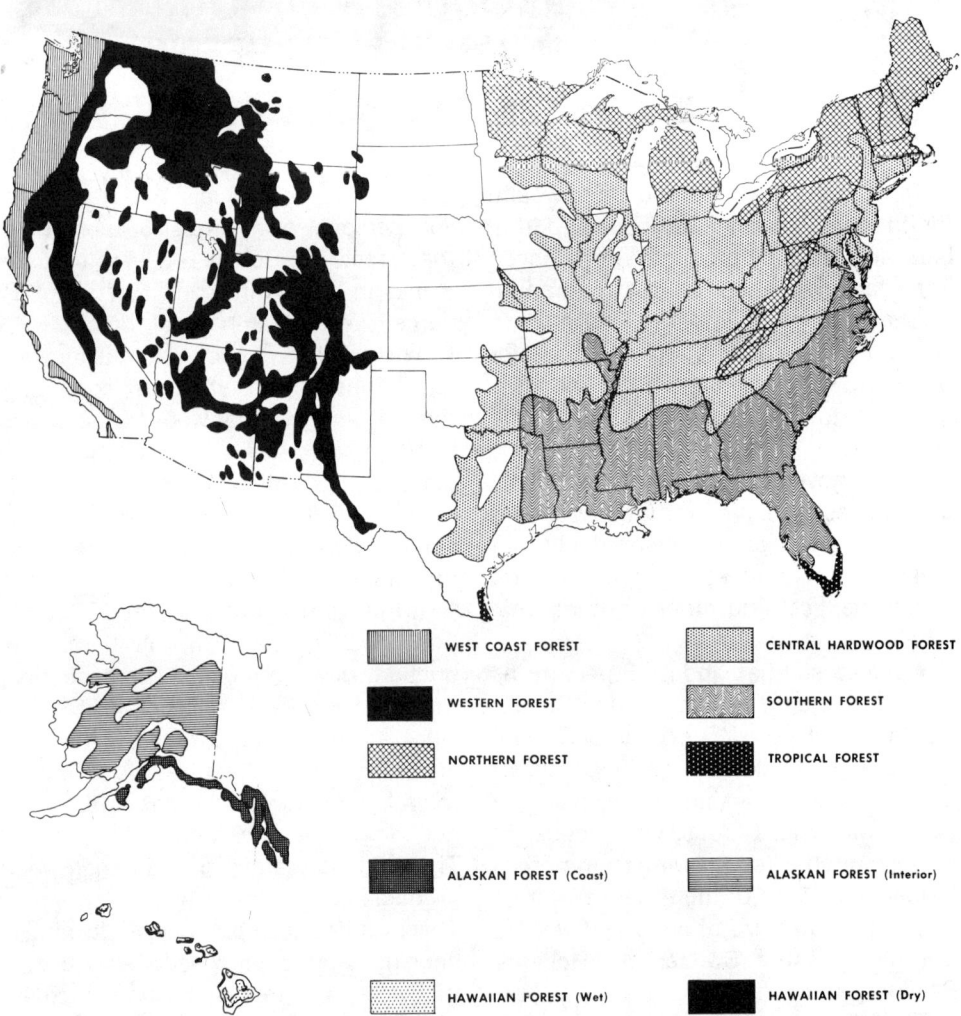

WEST COAST FOREST

WESTERN FOREST

NORTHERN FOREST

CENTRAL HARDWOOD FOREST

SOUTHERN FOREST

TROPICAL FOREST

ALASKAN FOREST (Coast)

ALASKAN FOREST (Interior)

HAWAIIAN FOREST (Wet)

HAWAIIAN FOREST (Dry)

**75-1.** This map shows areas of renewable natural wealth. The West Coast or Pacific forests are primarily Douglas fir. However, they also have western red cedar, spruce, and hemlock. The western forests include much of our softwood timber, primarily pine, although there are some hardwoods. The northern forests have such trees as hemlock, red spruce, white pine, and several kinds of hardwoods. The central hardwood forests include oak, cherry, birch, and many other kinds of hardwoods. In the southern forests are such softwoods as pine and cypress and many kinds of hardwoods. The tropical forests have ebony and palm trees. The coast regions of Alaska have primarily western hemlock and spruce, and the interior forests are heavy with white spruce and white birch. The Hawaiian forests include many softwoods and some unusual types such as monkey pod and koa.

**75-2.** All of these materials are forest products. They include glue-laminated beam, hardwood plywood, hardboard, paper, chemicals, rayon, and just plain lumber. It is hard to believe that so many different items are products of American forests.

| State | Total Area (1,000 Acres) | Forestland (1,000 Acres) | Percent |
|---|---|---|---|
| Alabama | 32,678 | 21,770 | 67 |
| Alaska | 365,481 | 119,051 | 33 |
| Arizona | 72,901 | 19,902 | 27 |
| Arkansas | 33,324 | 18,278 | 55 |
| California | 100,091 | 42,408 | 42 |
| Colorado | 66,510 | 22,583 | 34 |
| Connecticut | 3,117 | 2,186 | 70 |
| Delaware | 1,269 | 391 | 31 |
| Florida | 35,179 | 17,933 | 51 |
| Georgia | 37,295 | 27,399 | 73 |
| Hawaii | 4,118 | 2,118 | 51 |
| Idaho | 53,476 | 21,815 | 41 |
| Illinois | 35,761 | 3,790 | 11 |
| Indiana | 23,161 | 3,909 | 17 |
| Iowa | 35,868 | 2,455 | 7 |
| Kansas | 52,516 | 1,344 | 3 |
| Kentucky | 25,505 | 11,968 | 47 |
| Louisiana | 28,868 | 15,381 | 53 |
| Maine | 19,791 | 17,749 | 90 |
| Maryland | 6,370 | 2,960 | 46 |
| Massachusetts | 5,013 | 3,520 | 70 |
| Michigan | 36,492 | 19,273 | 53 |
| Minnesota | 50,745 | 18,984 | 37 |
| Mississippi | 30,291 | 16,913 | 56 |
| Missouri | 44,189 | 14,919 | 34 |
| Montana | 93,271 | 22,048 | 24 |
| Nebraska | 48,974 | 1,045 | 2 |
| Nevada | 70,746 | 12,036 | 17 |
| New Hampshire | 5,781 | 5,132 | 89 |
| New Jersey | 4,821 | 2,463 | 51 |
| New Mexico | 77,766 | 18,187 | 23 |
| New York | 30,636 | 17,378 | 57 |
| North Carolina | 31,367 | 20,614 | 66 |
| North Dakota | 44,339 | 422 | 1 |
| Ohio | 26,251 | 6,498 | 25 |
| Oklahoma | 44,150 | 9,340 | 21 |
| Oregon | 61,574 | 30,404 | 49 |
| Pennsylvania | 28,816 | 17,832 | 62 |
| Rhode Island | 671 | 433 | 65 |
| South Carolina | 19,366 | 12,494 | 65 |
| South Dakota | 48,606 | 1,734 | 4 |
| Tennessee | 26,474 | 13,907 | 53 |
| Texas | 168,301 | 24,092 | 14 |
| Utah | 52,697 | 14,865 | 28 |
| Vermont | 5,935 | 4,391 | 74 |
| Virginia | 25,496 | 16,389 | 64 |
| Washington | 42,665 | 23,098 | 54 |
| West Virginia | 15,414 | 12,172 | 79 |
| Wisconsin | 34,859 | 14,945 | 43 |
| Wyoming | 62,343 | 9,777 | 16 |

**75-3.** Forests cover a great part of our country. This chart shows total forest land acreage by states. What percent of your state is in forest land?

timber on both government and private lands. We also need to improve the utilization of lumber, veneer, and plywood.

## SAW LOGS

Although the forest products industry covers a wide area, most of its operations are in the rich timber-growing regions of the West and South. Approximately 10,000 lumber mills, 150 plywood mills, and 16,000 logging operators employ about 574,000 people throughout the nation. With related operations, the industry ranks as the fifth largest employer of manufacturing labor in the United States. Figure 75-5.

The forest products industry annually processes some 40 billion board feet of softwood sawtimber. This is roughly four-fifths of all wood fiber harvested each year in the United States, with the balance consumed largely by the pulp, paper, and hardwood industries. Large amounts of residue from the softwood lumber and plywood industry are also utilized in pulp, particle board, and hardboard manufacturing.

Most hardwoods go into industrial lumber which is used primarily for furniture making and vehicle construction, such as boats and trucks, for machinery and equipment, and for such manufac-

**75-4.** The average home requires about 13,000 board feet of lumber in some form. This large home would require at least twice that amount.

tured products as amusement devices, athletic equipment, and children's toys.

## VENEERS AND PLYWOOD

*Veneer* is a very thin sheet of wood that is sawed, peeled, or sliced from a log. In addition to all-wood veneers, manufactured veneers in wood patterns are available. These manufactured veneers are made of wood fibers and a chemical bond in thicknesses up to $\frac{1}{32}$ inch (1 mm). They can be so realistically printed with a grain and color that it is difficult, if not impossible, to tell them from the real wood veneer. Figure 75-6. These manufactured wood veneers are not to be confused with plastic laminates which are a solid material with the grain, color, and feel of real wood. Plastic lami-

nates are widely used in making lumber-core plywood for furniture.

*Plywood* consists of an odd number of layers of veneer and/or wood joined together by an adhesive. The grain of each layer or ply is approximately at right angles to the grain of the adjacent ply or plies. The exterior face of the plywood may be either softwood or hardwood. One surface is called the *face veneer* (the better side) and the other surface is called the *back veneer*. The innermost ply is called the *core*. All other plies between the core and face plies are called *crossbands*. Plywood is usually made with 3, 5, 7, or 9 plies, with 3 or 5 the most common. The common thicknesses are from $\frac{1}{4}$ to 1 inch (6.5 to 25.5 mm) in panel dimensions of 4 x 8 feet (1.22 x 2.44 m). Three common types of plywood construction are:

• *Lumber Core.* The core consists of strips of lumber bonded together. Figure 75-6.

• *Veneer Core.* The core is made of thick wood veneer. Most construction and industrial plywoods are this type. Figure 75-7.

**75-5.** This lumber will be used to make baskets. The tree being measured is at least 125 years old.

**75-6.** The veneer used to make this lumber-core plywood is manufactured from individual wood fibers covered with a resin coating and then placed in a hot press to produce the veneer.

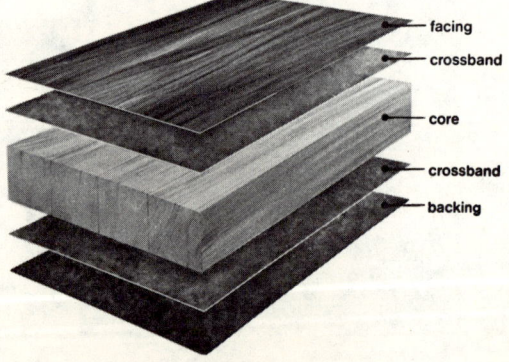

— facing
— crossband
— core
— crossband
— backing

• *Particle-Board Core.* The core is made of particle board which is a wood composition material. This kind of plywood is commonly used for the tops of tables and cabinets. Figure 75-8.

Plywood is held together with either moisture-resistant glue or moisture proof glue. The former is used on interior plywoods; the latter is for exterior use. Plywood provides great strength and, at the same time, surprising lightness. In addition to the soft and hard plywoods, there are many specialty types. Included are those with special or decorative surfaces. Figure 75-9. The face of plywood may have a striated (lined) surface to give it a combed look. Another may have a brushed face to accent the grain, another a sand-blasted surface. Plywoods are also available in many special grades for special purposes.

## Manufacture of Construction and Industrial Plywood

Before the manufacture of the plywood can begin, logs must be separated and stacked by wood species at the mill. Figure 75-10. They may also be sorted by length and grade quality.

A log stacker places logs on a barker deck. Figure 75-11. The logs then travel on a huge chain conveyor to the debarker machine. In the debarker, bark and other debris are removed by self-centering, revolving knives. Figure 75-12.

At some point the logs must be cut into peeler block lengths of 8 feet 4 inches (2.54 m). (A *peeler block* is a log suitable for cutting into veneer. The veneer will be cut, "peeled," with a lathe in one continuous piece from the rotating log.) Some mills cut logs into peeler

**75-7.** Plywood construction. A piece of 1-inch (25.5 mm), 7-ply plywood is cut away to show grain direction. Pound for pound, plywood is stronger than steel.

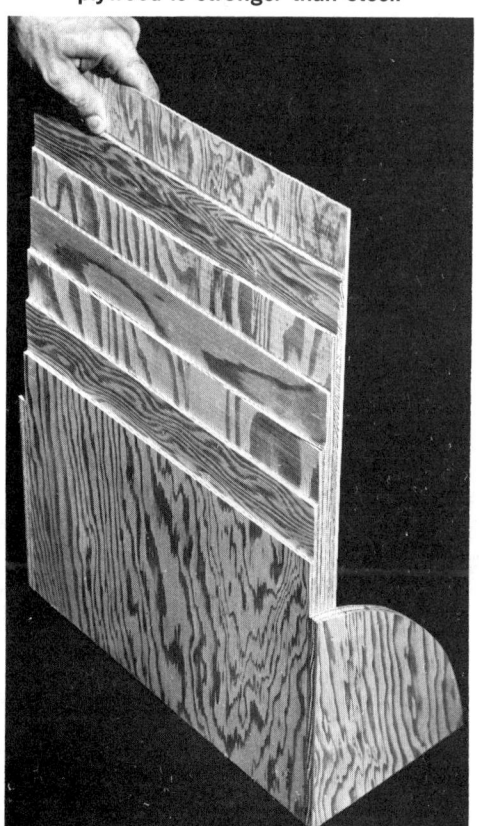

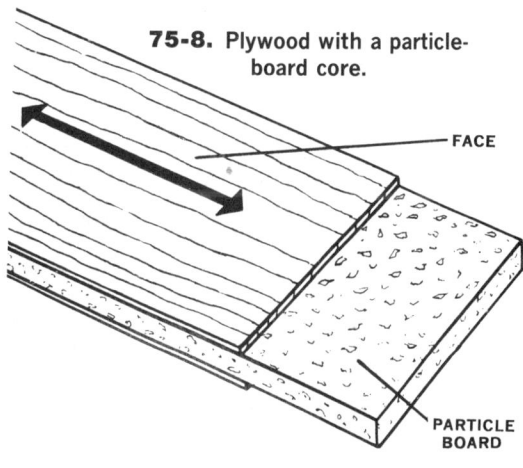

**75-8.** Plywood with a particle-board core.

FACE

PARTICLE BOARD

**75-9.** The plywood paneling in this room is textured and factory finished.

562          **75-10.** Logs are stacked at the mill.

**75-11.** A log stacker places logs on a barker deck.

blocks before removing the bark and some after.

After the logs have been debarked and cut into peeler blocks, they are sometimes steamed in large vats. This softens hard knots and produces a smoother veneer.

The peeler blocks next travel to a lathe spotter and charger. The spotter elevates

**75-12.** Bark is removed from the logs.

and levels each block to the charger. The charger then moves the block forward to lathe chucks which will hold the block against the lathe knife. Figure 75-13.

**75-13.** Here the charger moves the blocks to the lathe.

**563**

Lathe chucks revolve the block against a long knife which peels a continuous, thin ribbon of veneer at up to 600 lineal feet (182.9 m) per minute. Softwood veneer is usually peeled in thicknesses ranging from $\frac{1}{10}$ to $\frac{1}{4}$ inch (2.54 to 6.3 mm). Figure 75-14.

Mills may have three clippers. Veneer moves from storage trays to the clippers, which cut the veneer into usable widths, up to 54 inches (1372 mm), and clip out sections with defects. Figure 75-15.

Clipped veneer then moves by lift truck to the dryers.

Dryers have several long drying lines and may be 100 feet (30.48 m) or longer. In 5 to 20 minutes, the veneer is dried to about 5 percent moisture content at temperatures from 350 to 500 degrees F (176 to 260 degrees C). Figure 75-16.

After drying and patching the holes, veneer sheets move to the gluing department. Core veneer (plies) goes through the glue spreader and is sandwiched at

**75-14.** Rotary cutting of veneer.

right angles between large sheets of face and back veneer. Figure 75-17. The veneer sandwiches travel through the pre-press and then on to the hot press where they are pressed together and bonded under high heat and pressure to become plywood panels. Figure 75-18.

Rough plywood panels are then sawn into sheets, 4 x 8 feet (1.22 x 2.44 m)— or larger—sanded (construction-grade plywood requires no sanding), graded, and stamped. Finished panels will move by railroad car or truck to building supply wholesalers and distributors. Figure 75-19.

## HARDBOARD AND PARTICLE BOARD

All wood products consist basically of wood fiber. Wood fibers contain cellulose and lignin. Cellulose gives wood its strength. Lignin cements the wood fibers together and makes wood solid. Fibers in wood are fairly uniform in size, shape,

**75-15.** Mills have clippers (upper right) to cut the veneer into usable widths.

**75-16.** Drying the veneer.

**75-17.** Applying adhesive to the veneer.

**75-18.** Inspecting a plywood panel.

**75-19.** Finished panels are ready to be sent to wholesalers and distributors.    **567**

and properties. In lumber and plywood the fibers remain in the same position they had in the growing tree. This is not true of hardboard.

*Hardboard* is manufactured from wood which has been reduced to the individual basic wood fibers. Logs are cut into small wood chips which are reduced to fibers by steam or mechanical processes. These fibers are refined and then compressed under heat and pressure in giant presses to produce sturdy panels. Lignin holds the fibers together. Hardboard is closely related to other members of the wood products family. Figure 75-20.

*Particle board,* another man-made panel material, is made by combining wood particles with resin binders and then hot pressing them together in panels. Particle board is different from hardboard because wood particles which are not broken down into fibers are used to make particle board. Raw material is first classified by size and large particles are broken down mechanically, usually with a hammer mill. The small particles are then dried and mixed with a resin binder, formed into a mat, and pressed into a panel. Sanding may follow. Figure 75-21. The properties of particle board can be changed by using different sizes and kinds of wood particles and different binders. Particle board is made in many sizes and thicknesses and is widely used as core for plywood and plastic laminates.

## PAPER

Americans use a lot of paper. Each of us averages between 560 and 575 pounds (255 and 260 kg) every year. There are countless uses for paper. A government list shows 12,000 kinds of

**75-20.** Manufacture of hardboard: 1. Logs are moved from storage yards to huge chippers which reduce the wood to clean, uniformly sized chips; 2. The chips are reduced to individual wood fibers by either the steam or mechanical defibering processes; 3. Fibers are put through certain mechanical processes according to the method of manufacture, and small amounts of chemicals may be added to improve the properties of the board; 4. The fibers are interlocked into a continuous mat and compressed by heavy rollers; 5. Lengths of mat, or "wetlap," are fed into multiple presses where heat and pressure produce the thin, hard, dry, board sheets; 6. Leaving the press, moisture is added to the board in a humidifier so that the board will not be too dry; 7. The board is trimmed to standard dimensions, wrapped, and readied for shipment.

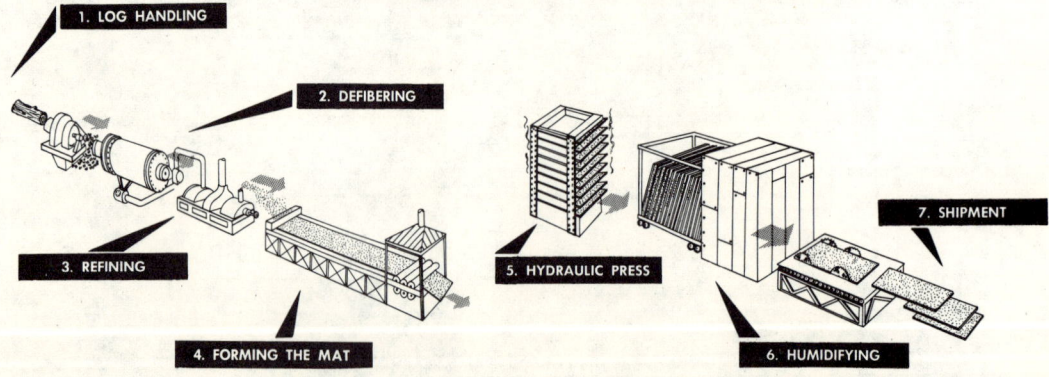

1. LOG HANDLING
2. DEFIBERING
3. REFINING
4. FORMING THE MAT
5. HYDRAULIC PRESS
6. HUMIDIFYING
7. SHIPMENT

paper, with 1,000,000 uses for them. Although we are surrounded by paper, few people know much about where it comes from. Almost all paper is made from wood. There are three fiber sources: new wood, recycled paper, and residue from the manufacture of other wood products.

Much attention has been paid recently to the re-use of paper through recycling. This method has been promoted as one good way to conserve trees and help solve the nation's waste disposal problems. Figure 75-22. Recycling isn't a new idea. The paper industry gets more than 20 percent of its raw material from wastepaper. Some paper mills get all of their fiber from recycling.

Another important source of raw material for making paper is the residue from the manufacture of other wood

products such as lumber and plywood. This amounts to over 19 million cords, more than one-quarter of all the wood used to manufacture pulp. This compares with a total of 15 million cords of wood from all sources used to make paper in 1945.

## WOOD CHEMISTRY

While the commercial uses of wood involving chemistry are not of direct concern to the woodworker, it is important to have an appreciation of woods in this respect. Figure 75-23. A recent development in the use of pulpwood flour and sawdust is the making of cellulose products such as rayon cloth, plastics, dyes, paints, explosives, linoleum, turpentine, and resins. Wood is also a source of sugar, alcohol, and feed for cattle. With many new chemical developments, wood provides the raw material for thousands of commercial products.

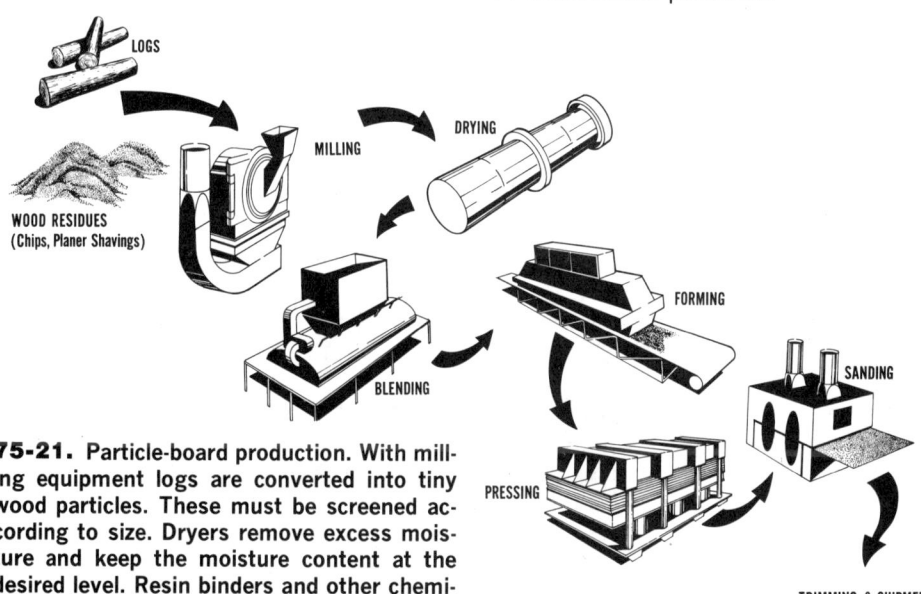

**75-21.** Particle-board production. With milling equipment logs are converted into tiny wood particles. These must be screened according to size. Dryers remove excess moisture and keep the moisture content at the desired level. Resin binders and other chemicals are sprayed onto the wood particles in a blending operation. Mats are formed and pressed. Sanding, trimming, and shipment complete the process.

## MISCELLANEOUS USES

In addition to all of the previously discussed uses, many of the by-products of wood that once were considered waste materials are now valuable. Sawdust, for example, is used for insulation, for packing, and other commercial uses. Bark is made into flavorings, drugs, and chemicals. Roots are made into oils and tea and are used for smoking pipes and trinkets.

**75-22.** These old telephone directories are loaded for the recycling journey to a paper mill.

**75-23.** Some of the materials we get from trees.

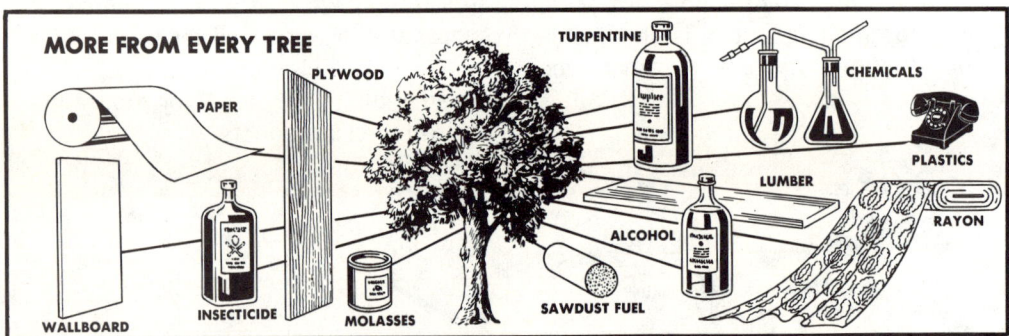

## CAN YOU ANSWER THESE QUESTIONS ON PRODUCTS OF OUR AMERICAN FORESTS?

1. How many acres of forestland does America have?
2. List the three groups that own our commercial forests and tell what percent each group owns.
3. Approximately how many people are employed in lumber and plywood mills plus logging operations?
4. List the common numbers of plies in plywood.
5. Describe the difference between veneer core and lumber core plywood.
6. Describe the steps in the manufacture of plywood.
7. What is hardboard and how is it manufactured?
8. Describe what particle board is made from.
9. About how much paper does the average American use?

# Section XIII

## UNIT 76.

# WOODS: KINDS, QUALITIES, AND USES

**Here is a brief** description of some of the woods in common use. Selection of the wood for each project should be made with care. Each kind of wood has its own peculiar color, working qualities, and properties. Figure 76-1. If you become particularly interested in one furniture wood, you can find many books and government bulletins devoted entirely to that one kind. There are also national associations which will supply all information concerning a particular wood. Some of these associations are: American Walnut Manufacturer's Association, Mahogany Association, Western Pine Association, and National Oak Flooring Manufacturer's Association.

The Forest Products Laboratory at Madison, Wisconsin, will send upon request technical and scientific information about wood and wood products.

## HARDWOODS
### (Broad-leafed Species)

### Ash, White

The three most common types of ash are white, green, and black. White ash is very popular for furniture construction; it is used widely for sports equipment such as skis, baseball bats, and toboggans. Figure 76-2. It is well suited to these things because of its strength and hardness but particularly because it holds its shape well after it has been formed.

### Basswood, American

Softest of commercial hardwoods, basswood is white with a few black streaks. Figure 76-3. It is fuzzy because of its long fibers, is fairly strong for bending, is nonwarping, and has little or no grain marking. Basswood is the best wood for drawing boards, small moldings, burned designs, and thin lumber for jigsaw work. It is not durable for outside uses. It makes a very strong glue joint and is easy to plane or sand. However, it does not scrape well because of its long fibers and yielding surface. It is usually painted but may be stained to imitate other woods.

### Beech, American

Beech is one of the very best of the utility hardwoods. The wood is white or slightly reddish. Figure 76-4. It has no figure to make it ornamental and it is rarely used for the exterior of furniture, other than chairs. It is sometimes chosen as a substitute for more expensive birch or hard maple. Beech is high in strength and very durable. It is commonly used for medium-priced chairs.

### Birch, Yellow and Curly

Birch is a hardwood of fine texture and close grain, coming primarily from the north-central states and Canada. Figure 76-5. Yellow birch is the most common. Curly birch is found only in occasional trees, the result of rare grain development. It has a delicate, wavy figure and is sought after for fine furniture and panels. Birch is difficult to work and must be finished by scraping. The heartwood is red in color and the sapwood is white.

**571**

**76-1. Common woods and their characteristics.**

| Species | Comparative Weights[1] | Color[2] | Hand Tool Working | Nail Ability[3] | Relative Density | General Strength[4] | Resistance to Decay[5] | Wood Finishing[6] |
|---|---|---|---|---|---|---|---|---|
| **Hardwoods[7]** | | | | | | | | |
| ASH, tough white | Heavy | Off-White | Hard | Poor | Hard | Good | Low | Medium |
| ASH, soft white | Medium | Off-White | Medium | Medium | Medium | Low | Low | Medium |
| BALSAWOOD | Light | Cream White | Easy | Good | Soft | Low | Low | Poor |
| BASSWOOD | Light | Cream White | Easy | Good | Soft | Low | Low | Medium |
| BEECH | Heavy | Light Brown | Hard | Poor | Hard | Good | Low | Easy |
| BIRCH | Heavy | Light Brown | Hard | Poor | Hard | Good | Low | Easy |
| BUTTERNUT | Light | Light Brown | Easy | Good | Soft | Low | Medium | Medium |
| CHERRY, black | Medium | Med. Red-Brown | Hard | Poor | Hard | Good | Medium | Easy |
| CHESTNUT | Light | Light Brown | Medium | Medium | Medium | Medium | High | Poor |
| COTTONWOOD | Light | Grayish White | Medium | Good | Soft | Low | Low | Poor |
| ELM, soft, Northern | Medium | Cream Tan | Hard | Good | Medium | Medium | Medium | Medium |
| GUM, sap | Medium | Tannish White | Medium | Medium | Medium | Medium | Medium | Medium |
| HICKORY, true | Heavy | Reddish Tan | Hard | Poor | Hard | Good | Low | Medium |
| MAHOGANY, African | Medium | Reddish-Brown | Easy | Good | Medium | Medium | High | Medium |
| MAHOGANY, Honduras | Medium | Golden Brown | Easy | Good | Medium | Medium | High | Medium |
| MAHOGANY, Philippine | Medium | Medium Red | Easy | Good | Medium | Medium | High | Medium |
| MAPLE, hard | Heavy | Reddish Cream | Hard | Poor | Hard | Good | Low | Easy |
| MAPLE, soft | Medium | Reddish Brown | Hard | Poor | Hard | Good | Low | Easy |
| OAK, red (average) | Heavy | Flesh Brown | Hard | Medium | Hard | Good | Low | Medium |
| OAK, white (average) | Heavy | Grayish Brown | Hard | Medium | Hard | Good | High | Medium |
| POPLAR, yellow | Medium | Lt. to Dk. Yellow | Easy | Good | Soft | Low | Low | Easy |
| WALNUT, black | Heavy | Dark Brown | Medium | Medium | Hard | Good | High | Medium |
| WILLOW, black | Light | Medium Brown | Easy | Good | Soft | Low | Low | Medium |
| **SOFTWOODS[8]** | | | | | | | | |
| CEDAR, Tennessee Red | Medium | Red | Medium | Poor | Medium | Medium | High | Easy |
| CYPRESS | Medium | Yellow to Reddish Brown | Medium | Good | Soft | Medium | High | Poor |
| FIR, Douglas | Medium | Orange-Brown | Hard | Medium | Soft | Medium | Medium | Medium |
| PINE, ponderosa | Light | Orange to Reddish Brown | Easy | Good | Soft | Low | Low | Medium |
| PINE, sugar | Light | Creamy Brown | Easy | Good | Soft | Low | Medium | Poor |
| REDWOOD | Light | Deep Red-Brown | Easy | Good | Soft | Medium | High | Poor |

[1] Kiln-dried weight.
[2] Heartwood. Sap is whitish.
[3] Comparative splitting tendencies.
[4] Combined bending and compressive strength.
[5] No wood will decay unless exposed to moisture.
[6] Ease of finishing with clear or "natural" finishes.
[7] Leaf-bearing tree.
[8] Cone-and-needle-bearing trees.

Resistance to decay estimate refers to heartwood only.

Therefore a single board may be either red or white, or red with white edges. It is a good wood for table tops, doors, rails, and any furniture parts that require extra strength. Birch will take practically any color of stain and is one of the finest woods for enamel finishes. It is sometimes finished to resemble mahogany, walnut, or maple.

### Cherry, Black

Black cherry is found in most parts of the United States. Figure 76-6. It is not abundant enough to be a common furniture wood, even though it is very desirable for that purpose. The heartwood is reddish brown and the sapwood is white.

Cherry resembles unfinished mahogany. It is a very durable wood, does not dent easily, and warps very little. There are many heirlooms of genuine cherry, indicating that it was more common many years ago. Cherry darkens with age. It is best finished with shellac or lacquer. Because of this it has a natural suitability to contemporary as well as period furniture.

### Sweetgum or Red Gum

Gumwood is a native of river deltas throughout the South. Figure 76-7. Because of its tendency to warp in seasoning, gumwood was not commonly used for many years. Only recently has it be-

In each illustration the top view shows the end surface; the middle view shows quarter-sawed surface; and the bottom view shows the plain-sawed surface.

**76-2.** White ash.  **76-3.** American basswood.  **76-4.** American beech.  **76-5.** Yellow birch.

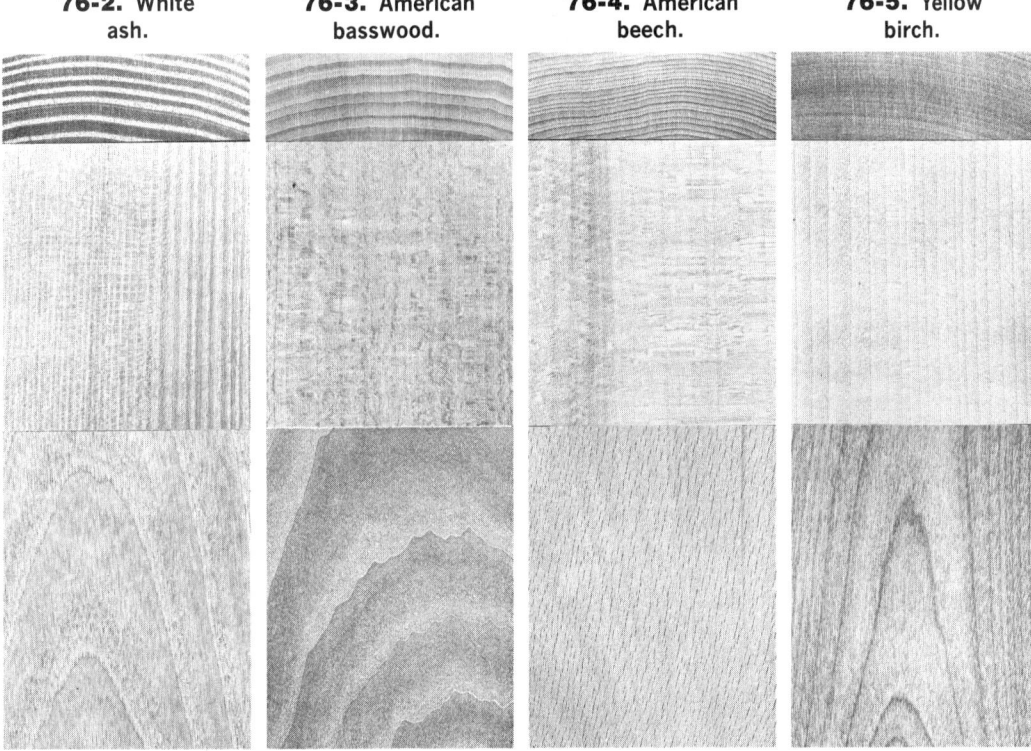

come popular. Previously, when used at all, it was finished to imitate some other wood. Now it is recognized as a wood of great beauty with a wide range of usefulness. The heartwood, called red gum, ranges from light to deep reddish brown. The sapwood is light colored and is referred to as sap gum. Although gumwood is considered a hardwood by its producers, it is really a medium hardwood, not so hard as maple and harder than many pines.

Fine furniture and trim are made from gumwood. It is one of our most decorative woods. One of its unusual features is that no two long boards produce the same figure in the wood. The wood is closed-grained and has a very fine tex-

ture. Gumwood is plain sawed, quarter sawed, or veneered. Selected gumwood finishes very well in the natural color, but best results come when it is given a light brown stain. Light streaks often appear next to the dark. When this happens, it is good practice to give the light wood a thin preparatory coat, wipe it off, and then treat the entire surface.

Water stains should always be chosen for gumwood even though these raise the grain. A light sanding is required before the finishing can be completed. The beauty of gumwood is better preserved by a dull treatment than by a gloss or polished finish. Dull lacquer, dull varnish, or hand-rubbed varnish produce the best effect on either interior trim or furniture. Because of its coarse grain, gumwood is excellent for enameled finishes.

## Mahogany, True or Genuine

The two kinds of genuine mahogany most commonly used for furniture are the Honduras and the African. Figure 76-8. True mahogany is considered the ideal cabinet wood. The heartwood of mahogany varies in color from pale to a deep reddish brown, becoming darker on exposure to light. It is tough, strong, easy to work, and polishes well. Mahogany is prized for its distinctive, fine grain figure, uniform texture, and natural color. It can be finished either dark for traditional furniture or bleached or natural for contemporary designs.

## Mahogany, Philippine

Philippine mahogany is the name given to a group of woods known as lauans that come from the Philippine Islands. Figure 76-9. Although they resemble genuine mahogany, these woods are coarser in texture and general appearance. They are usually classified as

**In each illustration the top view shows the end surface; the middle view shows quarter-sawed surface; and the bottom view shows the plain-sawed surface.**

**76-6.** Black cherry.          **76-7.** Sweetgum.

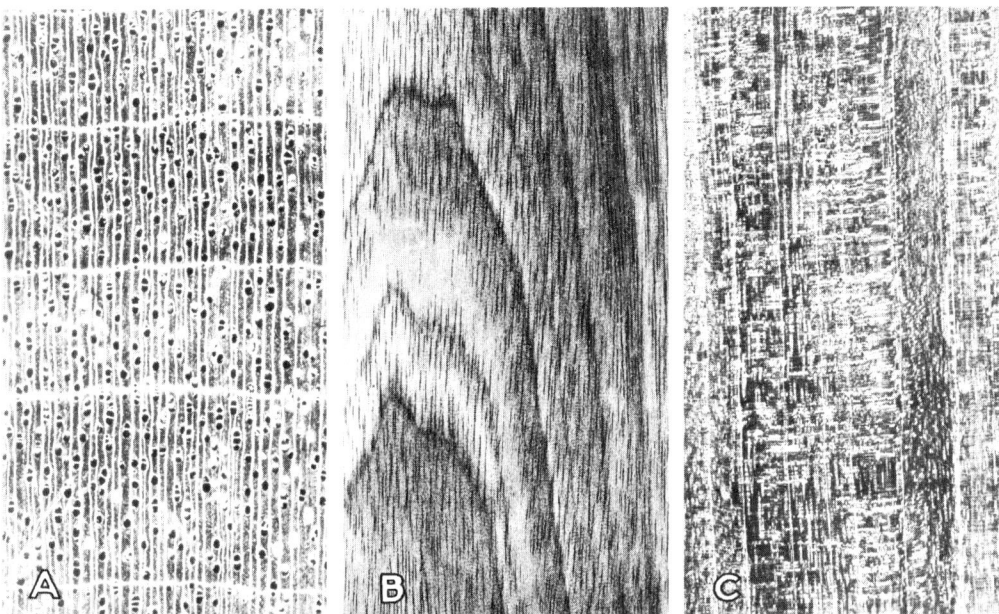

**76-8.** True or genuine mahogany: A. End surface (magnified 7½ diameters); B. Plain-sawed surface (natural size); C. Quarter-sawed surface (natural size).

**76-9.** Philippine mahogany: A. End surface (magnified 7½ diameters); B. Plain-sawed surface; C. Quarter-sawed surface.

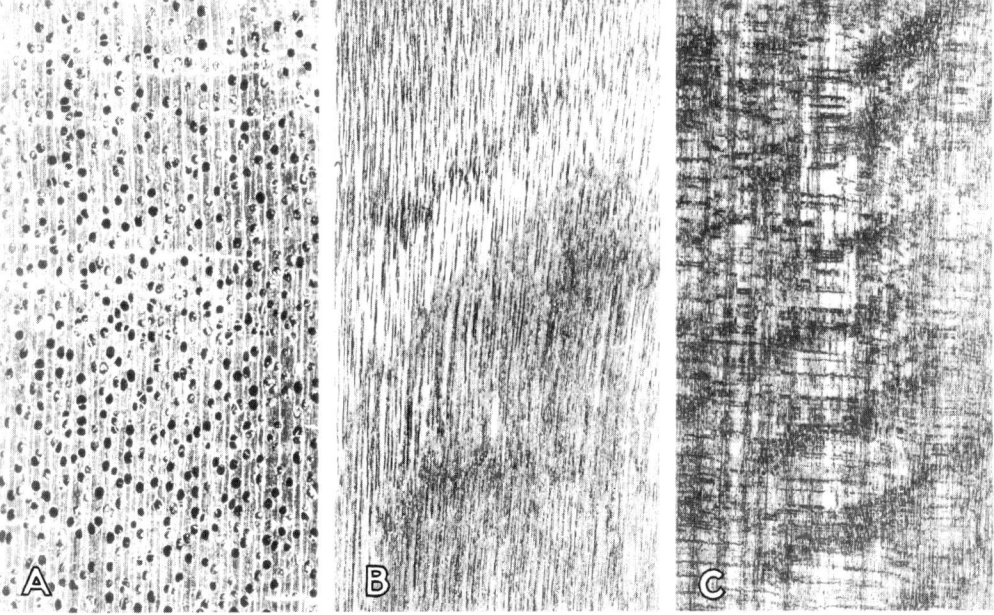

light red or dark red Philippine mahoganies. The dark red looks most like true mahogany. This wood is free from knots, checking, and shrinking. It is very easy to work with hand tools. Many different finishes can be used. It is an excellent, inexpensive wood to use for furniture, cabinetwork, trim, and boats.

### Maple, Sugar

Maple is a hard, tough, strong wood that wears very well and has good resistance to shock. Figure 76-10. The grain is usually straight and fine in texture. The heartwood is light reddish brown and the sapwood is white. Because of its wear-resisting qualities, maple is ideal for fine flooring. It is used extensively for both Colonial and contemporary furniture. A

white, clear grade of maple, which comes from the sapwood, is especially light. It is the white wood which can be made into furniture and fine floors on which natural finish is to be used. The brown heartwood makes a good base for a brown, mahogany, or dark stain. Curly maple is the result of twisted growth and the manner in which the lumber is sawed. Bird's-eye maple is cut from sugar-maple trees and the texture is probably the result of thwarted bud growth.

### Oak, Red

There are nearly 300 kinds of oak in the United States, but from the woodworker's standpoint there are only two main kinds, namely, red and white oak. Red oak is one of the most widely distributed trees in the United States. Figure 76-11. Because of its slightly reddish tinge and its coarseness in grain, it is used very successfully to get certain decorative effects. Red oak is used largely for furniture, flooring, interior finish, and construction. It is hard, heavy, and strong. Red oak is quite difficult to work.

### Oak, White

White oak is preferred for furniture and other items that are to be given a natural finish. Figure 76-12. It is usually free of the reddish tinge. White oak is one of the most valuable trees in the United States. It has better color, finer texture, and more prominent figure than the red oak. White oak has always been one of the most popular cabinet woods. Now and then one or more other woods come in vogue for a few years, but there is always a sure demand for oak. White oak is fairly difficult to work. The finished product, however, is beautiful and durable.

**76-10.** Sugar maple.    **76-11.** Red oak.

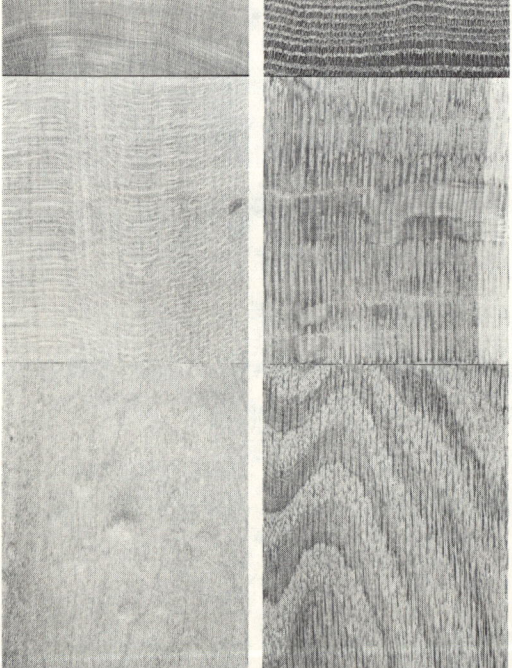

## Poplar, Yellow

Poplar is a durable, soft, medium-strong hardwood. Figure 76-13. It is one of the largest native trees supplying lumber. The sapwood, which is frequently several inches thick, is white and the heartwood is yellowish brown with a green tinge. The wood is moderately light in weight, straight-grained, uniform in texture, and easy to nail because it does not split readily. It is easy to glue, stays in place well, holds paint and enamels well, is easily worked, and finishes smoothly. Because of all these qualities, it is excellent for inexpensive furniture which is painted and enameled. It is a good wood for beginners.

## Walnut, Black

Walnut, a medium hardwood, is one of the most beautiful native woods. Figure 76-14. It is found in the eastern half of the United States. The heartwood is brown and the sapwood is nearly white. Walnut is a strong, durable, and stiff wood. It is used chiefly for cabinetwork, furniture, veneers, and gunstocks. The veneer is cut from the best grade of walnut and is made into panel stock and plywood. Walnut is excellent for cabinetwork because it works well, glues up very satisfactorily, and takes a good finish. Walnut is usually finished natural. It is open-grained and requires a filler. Usually the filler is very dark, but at times a lighter filler is applied for contrast. The wood can be finished with a high-gloss varnish and rubbed to a high polish. Hand-rubbed oil finishes are also very popular.

## Willow, Black

Willow is a hardwood that is extremely light and soft textured. It is easy to work, glue, and finish. Figure 76-15. It is fre-quently used as a substitute for walnut. Willow is pale reddish brown in color. It is commonly used in furniture and for veneer cores. There is a wide color range in willow. Since it is easy to work with hand and machine tools and much less expensive than walnut, it is a good wood to use for beginning projects.

## Elm, American

Elm grows throughout the eastern United States. It is moderately heavy and hard. The wood has large shrinkage and care must be taken to prevent warping. It has excellent bending qualities which makes it desirable in many kinds of furniture work, particularly for the bent parts of chairs. The heartwood is brown

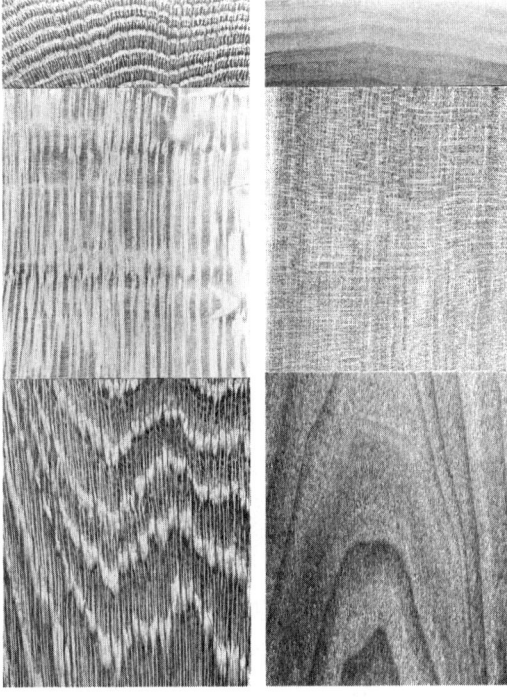

**76-12.** White oak.　**76-13.** Yellow poplar.

to dark brown, sometimes containing shades of red.

## SOFTWOODS
## (Cone-Bearing Species)

### Aromatic Red Cedar

Cedar is a light, soft, fine-grained, pleasantly aromatic wood that is easily worked. The sapwood is white and the heartwood is reddish purple. The wood is in great demand for use in cedar chests and clothes closet linings. Because of its resistance to moisture, it is also used for canoes and fence posts. Red cedar is normally left unfinished, although varnish may be used to avoid undesirable gray undertones.

In each illustration the top view shows the end surface; the middle view shows the quarter-sawed surface; and the bottom view shows the plain-sawed surface.

**76-14.** Black walnut.     **76-15.** Black willow.

### Douglas Fir

Douglas fir is used very extensively for lumber and plywood manufacture. Figure 76-16. The wood is moderately hard, heavy, and very stiff. It has a pronounced grain pattern, especially when made into plywood. The largest known fir tree in the world exists in Oregon. It measures more than 48 feet (14.6 m) in circumference. The first limb is 104 feet (31.7 m) up. The tree, 200 feet, 6 inches (61.1 m) tall, is believed to be at least 1,000 years old. It contains enough lumber for 10 two-bedroom frame houses.

### Pine, Ponderosa

Ponderosa pine is used primarily for building lumber and to a lesser degree for post poles and veneers. Figure 76-17. The wood from this tree varies considerably in its properties. It is moderately light in weight, soft, and low in resistance. It is an excellent wood for home construction.

### Pine, Sugar

Sugar pine is used almost entirely for lumber for building boxes, foundry patterns, and mill work. Figure 76-18. The wood is light in color, soft, smooth, straight-grained, and easily worked. The wood has very small shrinkage and seasons very readily. An oil stain or shellac finish can be used very easily on sugar pine.

### Redwood

Redwood is a widely used wood for home construction, fences, and outdoor furniture. Figure 76-19. It is light in weight, moderately hard, and strong. Redwood is very resistant to decay. This wood shrinks very little, is quite easy to season, and holds its shape well after seasoning.

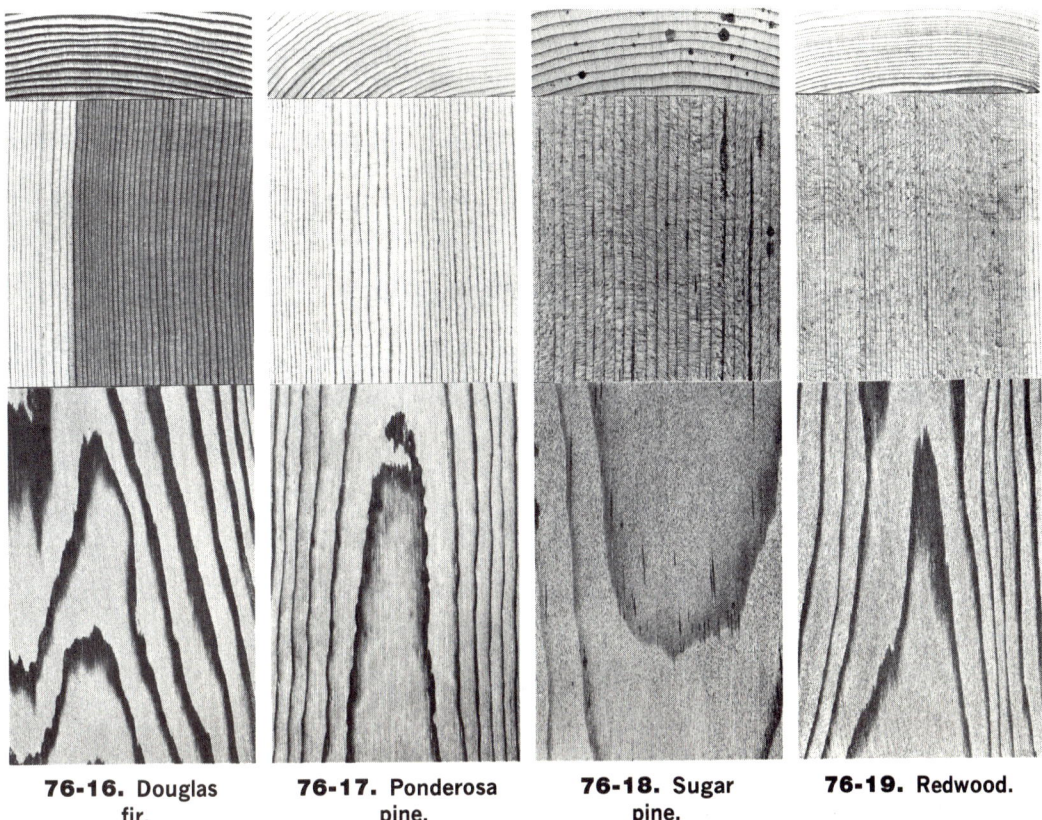

**76-16.** Douglas fir.　　**76-17.** Ponderosa pine.　　**76-18.** Sugar pine.　　**76-19.** Redwood.

In each illustration the top view shows the end surface; the middle view shows quarter-sawed surface; and the bottom view shows the plain-sawed surface.

## CAN YOU ANSWER THESE QUESTIONS ON WOODS: KINDS, QUALITIES, AND USES?

1. Where can you obtain information of a technical and scientific nature about wood and wood products?
2. Name the three common types of ash. What are among the chief uses of ash?
3. Why is willow a good choice for beginning projects?
4. What is the color range of birch? Why is birch chosen for making bed rails?
5. For what kind of wood is willow used as a substitute?
6. Cherry resembles what other kind of wood?
7. Is cherry as common today as it was many years ago? Why or why not?
8. Has gumwood increased or decreased in popularity in recent years? Why?
9. What kind of stain should be put on gumwood?
10. What are the characteristics of true mahogany that make it a desirable furniture wood?

**579**

11. Would you consider true mahogany a rather common wood? What are the chief sources of this wood?

12. Why is maple considered a very desirable material for flooring?

13. What style of furniture is usually made from maple?

14. How many kinds of oak are there? Why is oak consistently popular as a cabinet wood?

15. Name the two large classifications of oak. Why is oak quarter sawed?

16. Is sugar pine usually finished by staining? Explain in detail.

17. Yellow poplar is a very good selection for beginning woodworking projects. What are the reasons for this?

18. Give the color range for yellow poplar.

19. Name the chief uses for walnut. Why is walnut so often chosen for gunstocks and other articles that must be formed?

20. Describe the grain of walnut.

21. Is Douglas fir used for furniture? What are its uses?

22. Describe the characteristics of redwood. Compare with ponderosa pine.

## Section XIII

### UNIT 77.

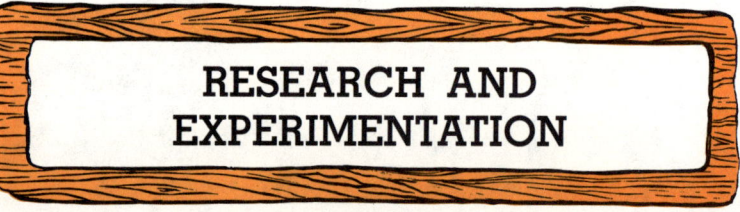

# RESEARCH AND EXPERIMENTATION

**Millions of dollars** a year are spent on research and experimentation to obtain greater dividends from wood and wood products. The United States government operates the Forest Products Laboratory in Madison, Wisconsin, for research and experimentation. Large associations, such as the American Plywood Association, the Western Wood Products Association, and many others do research and expermimetation to find new and better ways to use wood. All large corporations that deal in wood and wood products have extensive research departments. Figure 77-1. You can learn a great deal about wood and its uses by doing some elementary research and experimentation yourself. Several wood experiments are included in this unit. Others can be obtained by writing to the Forest Products Laboratory. These will help you find the answers to such questions as:

● What is the best wood species or man-made wood product to use for the product you want to produce?

● How can you keep wood from changing in size due to moisture?

● What is the best design for a wood product to make it structurally sound?

● What is the best method of joining wood parts together to make products?

### SPECIFIC GRAVITY

The specific gravity of wood is the ratio of the weight of a wood to the weight of an equal volume of water at a standard temperature. For example, the specific gravity of ash is .50, meaning it weighs

**77-1.** Large companies have research facilities for finding new and better ways to use wood. Unlike oil, iron ore, or bauxite, wood is a renewable material that can be used for food, clothing, shelter, fuel, and other needs.

half as much as an equal volume of water. This figure is determined by expressing the ratio and dividing to get the specific gravity. If the weight of the ash were 10 pounds and the weight of an equal volume of water were 20 pounds, the ratio would be 10:20, or $\frac{10}{20}$. When the bottom number is divided into the top, the resulting answer is the specific gravity, or .50. Specific gravity is not followed by any units (like pounds) because it is purely a mathematical expression.

Will ash float in water? If your answer is yes, you are correct. Any wood whose specific gravity is lower than 1.0 will float because these woods weigh less than equal volumes of water. Any wood whose specific gravity is greater than 1.0 will sink because the wood weighs more than an equal volume of water. For example, a wood with a specific gravity of 1.5 has one and a half times the weight of an equal volume of water. Thus, it sinks.

Specific gravity tells you something about the density of wood. *Density* is quantity per unit volume. For example, two blocks of wood, A and B, are the same size. A, however, has more wood substance and less air space inside than B. A is therefore more dense. Because A is more dense, it is also heavier, stronger, and harder. Which would be more likely to sink, A or B? A because it has less air space inside. Which will have the higher specific gravity? A, the more dense wood, will because woods that sink have specific gravities over 1.0 and woods that float have specific gravities under 1.0. This means that, in general, the higher the specific gravity, the more dense and therefore heavy, strong, and hard the wood will be. Knowing this, you can use specific gravity to help you pick the best wood for a job.

You can measure the specific gravity of wood with a simple procedure. Cut pieces of wood that measure 1 x 1 x 10 inches (25.5 x 25.5 x 254 mm). Mark ten equal divisions along the length of each piece. Place each piece of wood end down in a tube of water. Each will sink to a depth in proportion to its specific gravity. For example, if the water line is

**77-2.** A tall glass cylinder is needed for the specific gravity test. The block must float almost upright, showing the water mark at about right angles to the length of the piece.

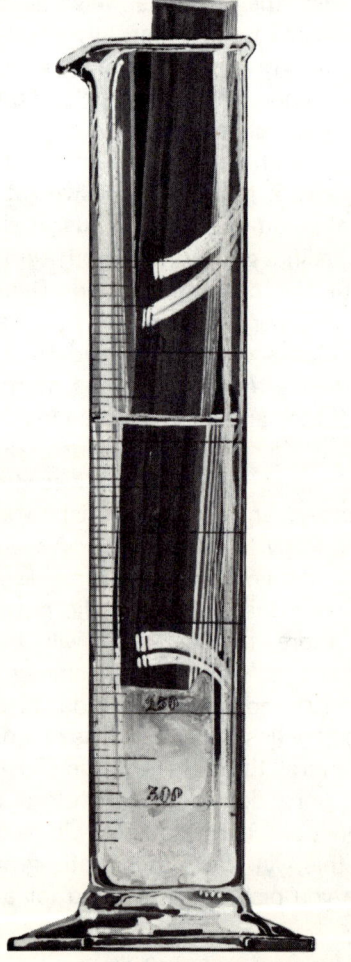

between the fourth and fifth marking line from the bottom of the wood, the specific gravity is between 0.4 and 0.5. Figure 77-2.

## WOOD POROSITY

As you can see in Figure 73-4a & b, wood is made of pores that have open spaces. Some woods are less porous than others, meaning moisture moves through them more slowly. Heartwood and sapwood of some species differ in porosity. This is also true in some woods that are similar in appearance. For example, a piece of red oak heartwood has open pores, but white oak heartwood has a filmlike deposit which plugs the pores.

To test for porosity, cut blocks of wood measuring about 2 x 2 x ½ inch (51 x 51 x 12.5 mm). These should be three different kinds of wood. For some pieces have the wood grain running parallel to the ½-inch (12.5 mm) dimension. On other pieces have the grain at right angles to the ½-inch (12.5 mm) dimension. Figure 77-3. Now place some alcohol, a wetting agent such as detergent, and some colored dye in a shallow pan. Carefully place the pieces of wood in the liquid with the ½-inch (12.5 mm) dimension at right angles to the bottom of the pan. The liquid should not cover the wood. In a short time the liquid will penetrate the wood and the dye will appear on the top side if the wood is porous enough. You can judge the porosity of the different pieces of wood by observing how long it takes the liquid to rise through the wood.

Which piece of wood in Figure 77-3 do you think will show the dye faster? You will discover that moisture travels more easily along the grain, that is, along the cells rather than across them. Therefore the lower piece of wood will show the dye faster than the upper one.

## BENDING STRENGTH OF WOOD

Cut several pieces of hardwood and softwood measuring $\frac{1}{2}$ x $\frac{1}{2}$ x 45 inches (12.5 x 12.5 x 1143 mm). Also obtain a piece of metal wire or rod 45 inches (1143 mm) in length and equal in weight to one of the hardwood pieces. Now support the wood pieces at points about $2\frac{1}{2}$ inches (63.5 mm) from each end. This can be done by clamping two pieces of angle iron to a bench with the ends extending out from the bench. Place the hardwood piece across the two pieces of angle iron. At the center of the wood sample, loop a heavy metal hook that will hold a bucket. Figure 77-4. Pour sand into the bucket and continue to measure the amount of bending deflection as the bucket weight increases. Continue until the wood breaks. Now load the steel wire or rod in the same way and determine the load it will take before it bends. This will show the relative strength of the hardwood piece. Try this with the other wood pieces and compare results.

## CHECKING MOISTURE CONTENT FOR EXPANSION

Cut several species of wood, 2 x 2 x 1 inch (51 x 51 x 25.5 mm), as shown in Figure 77-5. Dry these woods in an oven at 105 degrees Celsius (220 degrees F.) until they are completely dry. Then make a fixture that will hold a dial indicator and the pieces of wood. Figure 77-6. Place the wood against the dial indicator set at 0. Add drops of water to the end grain and determine how much each species expands as water is absorbed.

## INSULATING PROPERTY OF WOOD

Get a piece of $\frac{1}{4}$-inch (6 mm) dowel rod and a steel rod 12 inches (305 mm) long. Place one end of each in boiling water for a few minutes. Now touch the opposite end of each of the two materials. You can easily feel the difference in heat conductivity. Try this with other materials.

## USE OF GLUE IN LAMINATED CONSTRUCTION

Cut nine pieces of softwood, $\frac{1}{4}$ x 1 x 18 inches (6 x 25.5 x 457 mm). Glue three pieces together and allow the glue to set. Nail three other strips together, one on top of the other. Do nothing to the other three pieces. Make two V supports and place a cardboard backdrop on a bench. Place the loose strips together over the supports and add a heavy weight to determine how far the beam will bend. Mark this point on the cardboard. Then place the three pieces that have been nailed together over the

**77-3.** Two types of pieces required for the liquid penetration test. The upper block has the grain at right angles to the short dimensions, and the lower block has the grain parallel to it.

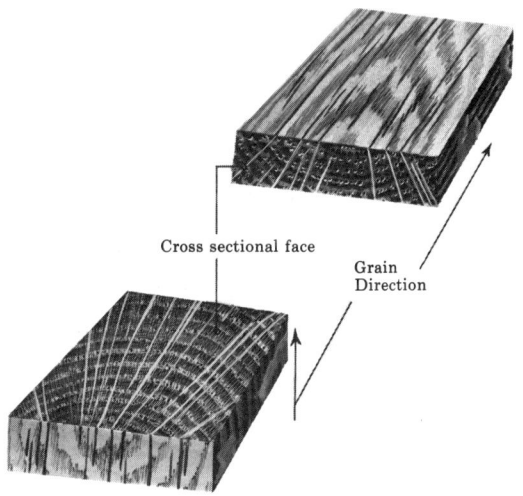

Cross sectional face

Grain Direction

supports and check the amount of bend with the same weight. Mark this point on the cardboard. Figure 77-7. Finally, do the same with the pieces that have been glued together. By looking at the marks on the cardboard, you can compare strengths. Of the three techniques used, which would be best for heavy construction?

## MAKING PAPER

You can make a sample piece of paper. You need a block of softwood; a knife; some bleach; a small, large-mouth, heat-resistant jar; and some fine wire screen. Cut the block of softwood along the grain into toothpick-size pieces. Place the pieces in a jar. Add bleach and put into an oven at 50 degrees Celsius (112 degrees F.) for about 24 hours. Remove the jar from the oven and stir the mix. When maceration (the wood becomes soft and separated into basic chemical materials) is complete, allow the fibers to settle. Pour off the bleach and wash with water three times. Fill the jar one-quarter

**77-4.** This is a simple setup for checking the strength of wood pieces. You'll find that the strength is related to moisture content and direction of cut as well as the kind of wood.

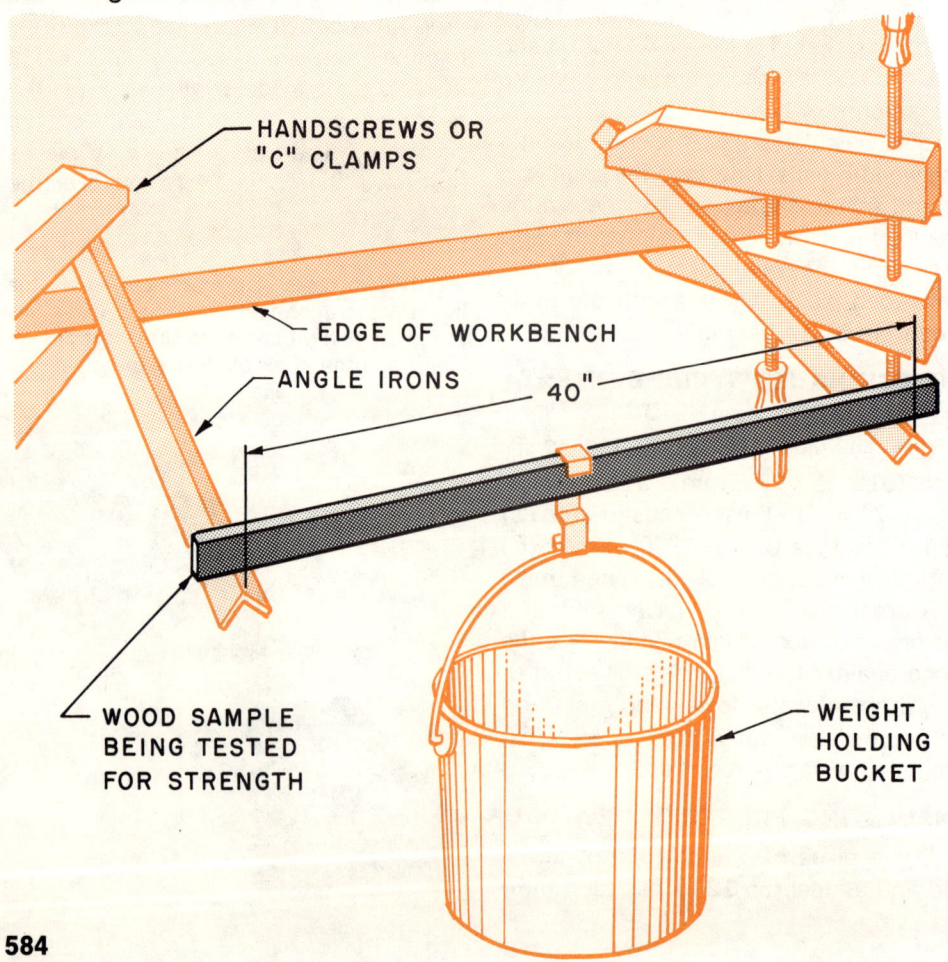

HANDSCREWS OR "C" CLAMPS

EDGE OF WORKBENCH

ANGLE IRONS

40"

WOOD SAMPLE BEING TESTED FOR STRENGTH

WEIGHT HOLDING BUCKET

full of water and fit the screen over the jar mouth. Shake the mixture thoroughly so that the fibers are in suspension and then turn the jar over in the sink. The water will run through the screen, allowing the fibers to remain on the screen. When the water has been drained off, remove the screen and fibers from the jar and dry them in an oven or over a radiator. When dry, the fiber sheet can be lifted off the screen as a sheet of paper.

In paper manufacturing, wood must be reduced into individual cells by chemically separating the cells or grinding them apart. The fibers are then mixed with water and chemicals. These are spread on a moving screen where the water is removed. The wet sheet is passed over warm rolls to complete the drying. Then the paper is run through a series of polished rolls to make the finished sheet.

## CHEMICAL RESISTANCE OF WOOD

Many woods will resist mild or dilute chemicals. Some chemicals will destroy

**77-5.** When checking moisture content for expansion, the blocks of wood must be cut so that the growth rings are as shown here.

Cross sectional face

Cross sectional face

Tangential Face

CORRECT

INCORRECT

**77-6.** This fixture with a dial indicator in place will show how much the wood expands as moisture is added.

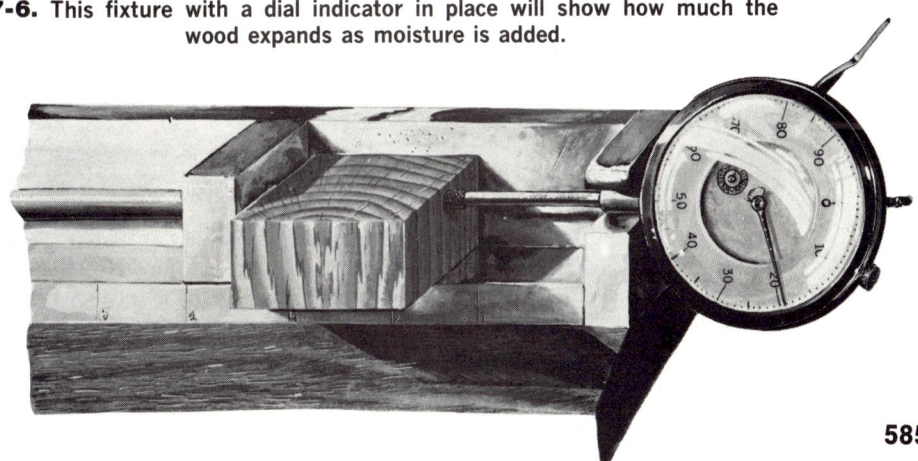

metal containers very rapidly, yet they have no effect on wood. Therefore in large industrial plants, wood tanks instead of metal are often used for mixing certain products. Any solution of common salt is very corrosive to metal but has little effect on wood. Cut a piece of ¼-inch (6 mm) dowel rod and ¼-inch (6 mm) metal, about 10 inches (254 mm) long. Place the ends of each in a solution of dilute hydrochloric or sulfuric acid. Leave the test pieces in for several hours. Remove them and note the effect of the acid on the wood and on the metal.

### SHOCK ABSORPTION OF WOOD

Shock absorption, or resilience, is the ability of wood to absorb shock without permanent change in size. A floor is said to be resilient when it absorbs shock. Select several pieces of wood, about ½ x 4 x 10 inches (12.5 x 102 x 254 mm) of different species. Lay them on a flat surface. Now drop a hard, rubber ball from a height of approximately 2 feet (0.61 m) and allow it to bounce off each piece. Measure the height of the bounce

for each of the test pieces and rank them according to their resilience. The more resilient the wood, the shorter the distance the ball bounces. The ability to resist shock is one of the reasons why baseball bats are made of wood.

### THE EASE OF WORKING WOOD

Drill a pilot hole $\frac{1}{16}$ inch (1.5 mm) in diameter through several different species of wood. Now install a No. 5 flathead brass screw in each hole. Which woods are more difficult to work? Compare a softwood with a hardwood. Try to install a brass screw in oak *without* a pilot hole. What happens?

### WOOD JOINTS

Which is stronger? A chair with the corners assembled with a mortise-and-tenon joint or one with a dowel joint? A great deal depends on the quality of workmanship, the kind of glue used, and several other factors. You can do several experiments by making samples of joints and testing them. Clamp one arm of the joint in a vise and then

**77-7.** Use at least a 500-gram weight on the glued beam. Marks on the cardboard show the limit of bending.

add weight to the other arm until it breaks. You can vary the test with different kinds of joints, glue, and wood species.

## PARTICLE BOARD AND HARDBOARD

As you know, two widely used man-made materials are particle board and hardboard. It is possible to experiment to produce a kind of man-made lumber using waste materials found in the lab and adhesive. Use shavings from a jointer or planer and sawdust as the base material, and mix with a urea resin glue. Generally about three parts of glue to eighteen parts of shavings and sawdust should be used. The glue is mixed two parts of glue to one part of water. Use a large five-gallon mixing can. Combine the shavings and sawdust first and then add the liquid glue, making sure that all are thoroughly mixed. Now cut a piece of $\frac{3}{4}$-inch (19 mm) plywood the same as the inside diameter of the five-gallon can. Place this cover over the mixture in the can and tighten down in a press. An arbor press or a book-binding press may be used. Allow the pressure to remain for at least 72 hours. Then remove the material from the press and allow it to cure for four or five days. It will be necessary to cut the metal can away from the material. Experiments such as turning the material on a lathe, installing screws or nails, and many others can be performed on your man-made lumber.

## CAN YOU ANSWER THESE QUESTIONS ON RESEARCH AND EXPERIMENTATION?

1. List some of the reasons for doing research.
2. Describe how to check the specific gravity of wood.
3. Which is more porous—red oak heartwood or white oak heartwood? Why?
4. Weight for weight which is stronger, wood or metal?
5. Is wood a better conductor of heat than metal?
6. Explain a simple method for making paper.
7. Does wood resist chemical action better than metal?
8. Explain how to make a material similar to hardboard and particle board.

# Index

# Index